NEW YORK

A Guide to
the Metropolis

WALKING TOURS
OF ARCHITECTURE
AND HISTORY

Second Edition

by GERARD R. WOLFE

McGRAW-HILL, INC.

New York   San Francisco   Washington, D.C.   Auckland   Bogotá
Caracas   Lisbon   London   Madrid   Mexico City   Milan
Montreal   New Delhi   San Juan   Singapore
Sydney   Tokyo   Toronto

Library of Congress Cataloging-in-Publication Data

Wolfe, Gerard R., date.
    New York, a guide to the metropolis / Gerard R. Wolfe.—2nd ed.
       p.   cm.
    Includes index.
    ISBN 0-07-071397-9
      1. Architecture—New York (N.Y.)—Guidebooks. 2. New York (N.Y.)—
Buildings, structures, etc.—Guidebooks. 3. New York (N.Y.)—
Guidebooks. I. Title.
NA735.N5W64   1994
720′.9747′1—dc20   93-6119
                                                         CIP

2 3 4 5 6 7 8 9 0 DOC/DOC 9 9 8 7 6 5 4

ISBN 0-07-071397-9

The sponsoring editor for this book was Joel E. Stein, the editing supervisor was Stephen M. Smith, and the production supervisor was Suzanne W. Babeuf. It was set in Times Roman by McGraw-Hill's Professional Book Group composition unit.

Designed by Philip Grushkin; maps by Henry Siwek.

Printed and bound by R. R. Donnelley & Sons Company.

This book is printed on acid-free paper.

Publication history:
    First New York University Press edition, 1975
    First McGraw-Hill paperback edition, 1983
    New, revised McGraw-Hill paperback edition, 1988
    Second McGraw-Hill paperback edition, 1994

To my students, colleagues, and friends,
whose insatiable curiosity about
New York's fascinating cityscape and history
was the inspiration for this work.

Contents

Note: The following are the landmark symbols used in this guide:

    Designated Landmark by the New York City Landmarks
Preservation Commission

    Listed on the National Register of Historic Places

Foreword

My goal in preparing this guide is to help you learn to look at buildings with a discerning and appreciative eye. New York City is a treasure house of architecture, with virtually every style—original or revival—represented in its varied repertory of public buildings, residences, and commercial structures.

With the passage of the Landmarks Preservation Law in 1965, the city succeeded in stemming the relentless destruction of its heritage, although not before the tragic loss of such gems as Pennsylvania Station, the Produce Exchange, the Singer Tower, and the Jerome Mansion. Enough does remain, however, to provide miles of exciting discoveries, not only of our rich past, but also of the new and innovative building designs that have broken with the dull tradition of the glass box and are now offering bright punctuation to the changing skyline.

In selecting the walking tours it was necessary to choose the most important areas, both architecturally and historically, and to keep the number to twenty— the maximum if the book were still to be portable. Unfortunately, some interesting neighborhoods had to be omitted, which perhaps in a forthcoming supplement can be included. The tours begin in lower Manhattan and are arranged to correspond with the northward growth of the city, ending uptown with the Upper East Side and Upper West Side. The five tours of Brooklyn follow the same chronological route, from Brooklyn Heights, the first suburb, to Fort Greene and Clinton Hill. The tour of Flushing, in Queens, includes several examples of surviving Dutch Colonial architecture, since not one building in Manhattan erected when the Dutch built New Amsterdam survived the Great Fire of 1835.

The tours vary in length from two to five hours, and some, such as the Lower East Side, Brooklyn Heights, or Manhattan's Financial District, may be divided into two itineraries. The tours are all marked on accompanying maps, with travel directions included. Buildings or districts that have been designated as New York City landmarks by the Landmarks Preservation Commission are identified with a small black disk; those which are National Historic Landmarks, that is, listed on the National Register of Historic Places, are indicated with a star. Following the practice of the Landmarks Commission, no individual buildings within a historic district are identified separately, since technically all buildings within a designated district are landmarks. A glossary of common architectural terms will be found at the end of Chapter 7. In some tours whose points of interest are at some distance from each other, key numbers have been used in the text and on the corresponding map.

For the first-time visitor to New York, the New York Convention and Visitors Bureau (located at No. 2 Columbus Circle) can provide free literature on the city's major tourist attractions that are not within the purview of this book. The Landmarks Commission has published the useful reference *Guide to New York City Landmarks*, which can be purchased at Citybooks, 61 Chambers Street; the New York Bound Bookshop, 50 Rockefeller Plaza; Urban Center Books, 457 Madison Avenue; and other bookshops throughout the city.

This guide is designed not only for the out-of-towner, but for the usually blasé New Yorker as well, who rarely, if ever, looks at buildings above the first floor. I learned to my surprise that my students, who were so enthusiastic about my New York University course, "The Many Faces of Gotham," were mostly native Gothamites themselves who were perpetually astonished at the beauty of the buildings they had passed every day without so much as an upward glance. I therefore earnestly hope that you will be encouraged to explore New York on foot and derive pleasure and satisfaction from the discovery of our great architectural heritage...and at the same time become an outspoken and vigorous advocate of its preservation.

In this second, completely revised McGraw-Hill edition, many changes were made to include the most recent and important additions to the cityscape, as well as deletions of buildings that were lost. New in this edition are a complete tour of Battery Park City, including the World Financial Center; a tour of Roosevelt Island; a look at the newly restored Bryant Park; an in-depth tour of Times Square; an expanded tour of Battery Park; all the latest landmark and national register designations; and a much larger walking tour of the SoHo Cast-Iron District, including all the new museums that have opened on lower Broadway.

Enjoy exploring the city through these walking tours, and by following the itineraries you will relive its exciting 365-year history and see vivid reminders of the millions of people who lived and worked here, as well as the splendid architectural heritage of the greatest city in the world.

GERARD R. WOLFE
October 1993

Acknowledgments

In putting together a book of this scope, one must rely on the knowledge, advice, and suggestions of many people and organizations. By the time the first New York University Press edition was ready for the printer in 1975, I had amassed a list of individuals who had been particularly helpful, and I feel it only proper to include them again. In addition, there are a number of others who made significant contributions to the revised and updated McGraw-Hill editions, and they are listed separately below.

For help in the preparation of the first edition, I owe a special debt of gratitude to the New York City Landmarks Preservation Commission, which in the interest of having the public better informed about the architectural and historic importance of New York buildings, granted me permission to quote occasionally from its landmark designation reports. Among the members of the professional staff of the Commission who read the original manuscript and made many helpful suggestions, Dr. Ellen Kramer and the late Alan Burnham deserve special recognition.

Much valuable assistance came from the staffs of the Long Island Historical Society (now the Brooklyn Historical Society), the South Street Seaport Museum, the Queens Historical Society, the New-York Historical Society, the Museum of the City of New York, the Colonial Dames of America, the Brooklyn Heights Association, and the Friends of Cast-Iron Architecture.

Among the individuals who gave of themselves to provide background information, old newspaper clippings and letters, and personal reminiscences were the late Joseph Roberto, architect emeritus of New York University; Bob Gesslein, Long Island University; John Virgil, Wurlitzer Music Company; Dr. George Litch Knight, Lafayette Avenue Presbyterian Church; Rev. David L. Slater, Cadman Memorial Church; Capt. Joseph Zito, New York City Police Department (retired); Harry Kirschbaum, architect; Alex Parker, One Times Square; Judith Ann Yavarkovsky, Metropolitan Life Insurance Company; Gruzen & Partners; Barbara Bruer; and my father, Samuel Wolfe, whose inexhaustible recollections of life on the Lower East Side were priceless.

For the contribution of old photographs and prints, I am indebted to Ernest Pawel, New York Life Insurance Company; William H. Hand, Brooklyn Union Gas Company; Henry J. DiRocco, Office of the Borough President of Queens;

Susan C. Holahan, Consolidated Edison Company of New York; Eleanor C. Waters, Seamen's Bank for Savings; Dorothy C. Gates, Home Insurance Company; Margaret Knowles, Community Service Society of New York; David G. Oates, *Flushing Tribune*; The Library of the Metropolitan Life Insurance Company; The American Telephone & Telegraph Company; the South Street Seaport Museum; the Equitable Life Assurance Society of the United States; the Singer Company; the Fred F. French Investing Company; the Firefighting Museum of the Home Insurance Company; the Port Authority of New York & New Jersey; the United Nations Photo Service; and the late Margaret I. Carman, Bowne House Historical Society.

I acknowledge with thanks the permission of Warner Brothers Music, Hollywood, to reproduce Al Dubin's lyrics to "Forty-Second Street"; and also that of Fleet Press Corporation, New York, to use a quote from Robert Baral's "Turn West on 23rd," copyright 1965.

Two friends who were especially helpful throughout, lending support, counsel, and encouragement, were Dr. Toby B. Bieber and the late Professor Mendor T. Brunetti, great teacher and close colleague.

In 1982, when the first McGraw-Hill edition was in preparation, I received invaluable assistance from Hugh A. Dunne, New York City Transit Authority and the Electric Railroaders' Association; Christopher Gray, Office for Metropolitan History; Fox & Fowle, architects; Capt. Wolf Spille, Sirius Ships' Brokers, Inc.; Leo Katz, New York Telephone Company; Pratt Institute Public Information Office; Kent Barwick, president, Municipal Art Society and former chairman, New York City Landmarks Preservation Commission; and Edwin Friedman, Andrew S. Dolkart, and Luella Adams, then with the Landmarks Commission.

For help received for the new, revised McGraw-Hill edition of 1988, I owe a debt of gratitude to Gene A. Norman, then chairman of the Landmarks Preservation Commission, and to director of research Marjorie Pearson. Thanks, too, are due to Emery Roth & Sons, architects; the late Paul E. Gay, chairman and president, James N. Wells, Inc.; Suzanne C. Stirn, assistant director, Abigail Adams Smith Museum; Ruth Tetamore and Val Ginter; and Mosette Broderick, whose expertise on McKim, Mead & White was most helpful. And a special note of appreciation goes to Richard McDermott, publisher of the *New York Chronicle,* for his critical reading and advice; the late Israel Ginsberg, formerly of the *East Side News,* for his many suggestions and lively anecdotes; and Barbara Cohen, who let me prowl through the storehouse of out-of-print New York material in her New York Bound Bookshop.

Many people provided invaluable assistance in bringing to fruition this second (1994) McGraw-Hill edition. To ensure the accuracy and up-to-the-minute completeness of the book, a number of friends and colleagues—all devotees of New York City architecture and history—volunteered to re-read the text, re-walk the tours (often in below-freezing winter weather), and make corrections and suggestions as a backup to my own research and revisions. I owe a heartfelt debt of gratitude to Val Ginter, Joyce Mendelsohn, Brian G. Andersson , Barbara

Gautier, Eliot Niles, Anthony Bowman, Gemma Fastiggi, Joyce Gold, Richard McDermott (founder, publisher, and editor of the *New York Chronicle*) and Jack Taylor, president of The Drive to Protect the Ladies' Mile District.

A few really special people, however, deserve more thanks than I ever could give. For their tireless trekking, meticulous research, and undefatigable dedication to "getting it right," I shall always be indebted to Justin Ferate, Joan Bielefeld, Robert Search, and Sheila Heitner.

Many members of my walking-tour group in New York, who, to my embarrassment, call themselves the "Wolfe-Walkers," have kept me constantly inundated with pertinent newspaper and magazine clippings to help build my data bank on the Big Apple. For those stacks of most useful material, I am greatly indebted to Ann Anielewski, Ruth Tetamore, Ruth Smith, Mimi Olanoff, Barbara Bruer, Shirley Frank, Mimi Rothberg, Ida Schwartz, and Richard Hull.

Other New Yorkers or New York organizations who gave of their time and provided valuable information, maps, or photographs are Leslie Gottlieb of the Roosevelt Island Operating Corporation, Matthew G. Monahan of the Battery Park City Authority, Joan Olshansky of the Landmarks Preservation Commission, Jonathan Kuhn of the New York City Parks and Recreation Department, Barbara Hayward of the New York City Fire Museum, and Ann Bridges Bradley.

I am very grateful for the enthusiastic support of Joel Stein, senior editor at McGraw-Hill, and a devoted fan of the Great Metropolis, for bringing this prodigious project to fruition. I would also be remiss if I did not add a word of praise for my copy editor, Bernice Margulies, a very knowledgeable New Yorker, whose many suggestions and ideas helped enliven the text.

Finally, to those who have used previous editions of the book and walked the tours, and who have taken the trouble to write to me about their experiences and pleasure of discovery, as well as to offer suggestions and comments, I am sincerely grateful.

G.R.W.

NEW YORK
A Guide to the Metropolis

1. Lower Broadway, Battery Park City, and the Battery

[Subways: Broadway–Seventh Avenue Nos. 1, 9 to Cortlandt Street–World Trade Center; Lexington Ave. Nos. 2, 3 to Fulton Street; Eighth Avenue A, C to Broadway–Nassau Street; Broadway Line N, R to City Hall; Nassau Street Line M, J, Z to Fulton Street. Buses: M1 (weekdays only), M6 to Fulton Street]

The walking tour begins at Fulton Street and Broadway.

St. Paul's Chapel is the oldest church in Manhattan (and its oldest public building as well). With its back to Broadway, it faces a peaceful churchyard, oblivious to the noise and clamor of the tumultuous thoroughfare. A branch of Trinity Church downtown, St. Paul's was completed in 1766, the tower and steeple in 1796. Architect Thomas McBean was undoubtedly influenced by London's St. Martin's-in-the-Fields when he designed this stately landmark. It is built of locally quarried Manhattan schist, and the tower (designed by James Crommelin Lawrence) is of brownstone. The church is an almost perfect example of the Georgian style, reflecting the tradition of the Colonial period. Much of the interior decoration of this National Historic Landmark was done by Pierre L'Enfant, the French-born architect who later became a Major of Engineers in the Continental Army, and who helped lay the plans of the city of Washington, D.C. His main work in the church is the altar, with its railing and sculptured "Glory" above it. Other splendid artifacts are the hand-carved and

Note: Since most of the points of interest on this tour are situated quite close to each other, the customary system of numbering each stop in the text and on the map will not be used; rather, the description and location of each point of interest will be a separate entry, indicating in boldface type. As usual the route is shown on the map.

3

Broadway, 1850, at the foot of City Hall Park, looking south. Barnum's Museum, left, was destroyed by fire in 1865. The Astor House, the city's finest hotel at the time, is to the right, with the portico of St. Paul's Chapel adjoining. Trinity Church's spire dominates the thoroughfare. (The J. Clarence Davies Collection, Museum of the City of New York)

gold-leafed pulpit, 14 original Waterford cut-glass chandeliers, and the beautifully crafted organ case. The graceful columns are hollow and contain solid oak tree trunks which add support to the roof. The pew where George Washington regularly worshiped is in the north aisle, with the original seal of the United States on the wall behind. It was originally the canopied pew of the royal governor of the Province of New York. The pew of first governor of the state, George Clinton, is in the south aisle. Among other distinguished worshipers were Prince William of Orange (later King William IV), Lords Cornwallis and Howe, Maj. John André, the Marquis de Lafayette, and presidents Grover Cleveland and Benjamin Harrison.

The quiet churchyard with its numerous 18th-century headstones of prominent early New York families is well worth a visit.

The former American Telephone & Telegraph Building, just south of St. Paul's, was built in 1917 from plans by Welles Bosworth. No other building in the city can boast so many columns; in fact, in its eight Ionic tiers stacked on a Doric base, it has more columns than the Parthenon. A gilt statue that once graced the tower (*The Spirit of Communication,* by Evelyn Beatrice Longman), was removed and for a time was mounted in the lobby of AT&T's former cor-

porate headquarters at 550 Madison Avenue. "Golden Boy," as the 10-ton statue is frequently called, now resides at the AT&T campus in Somerset County,
New Jersey. A weekday visit to the marble colonnaded lobby reveals a sculpture of Alexander Graham Bell, and two lovely brass floor medallions, as well
as a large marble and bronze sculpture, *Service to the Nation* by Chester Beach.

No. 192 Broadway, across the street, is an undistinguished survivor from the
1880s, somehow bypassed by the land developers. Interesting are the so-called
Queen Anne cast-iron bay windows. A few feet around the corner was the **site of
the John Street Theater,** from 1767 to 1798. During the British occupation of
New York in the Revolutionary War, General Howe's army officers frequently
would take part in the cast and production of plays. Later, Royall Tyler's play,
The Contrast, opened as the first comedy work by a native author ever produced
in America. George Washington was an often-seen theatergoer here.

No. 175 Broadway, the Germania Building, an even older survivor, is a
typical commercial building, erected in 1865 in Italian Renaissance style. This
was the style so often copied by the cast-iron architects and later recopied in
stone. That this 1865 building remains at all is a minor miracle.

Cross Broadway to the northeast corner of Maiden Lane.

Set in the sidewalk is a large glass clock. Dating from around 1925, it is
said to have replaced an earlier model installed by the same firm of William
Barthman just before the turn of the century. The timepiece is adjusted from the
basement, and the protective glass, which had to be changed every few months

*Busy Broadway in the mid-1880s, lined
with horse-drawn traffic. All the
buildings on the right side, to the corner
of Cortlandt Street, are still standing;
but only one, the narrow, white
Germania Building, erected in 1865, has
not undergone a "face-lift." (American
Telephone & Telegraph Company)*

because of the constant scuffing from millions of pedestrians' shoes, now has been supplanted by a type of quartz glass which lasts up to nine months. While the history of the earlier clock cannot be documented, a legend persists that in 1911 a runaway horse smashed into the store window, splintering the showcase and scattering a quarter-of-a-million dollars in jewelry across Broadway. Yet the street clock below the pavement survived undamaged.

Turn right (west) at Cortlandt Street.

Until the arrival of the World Trade Center, Cortlandt Street was the center of the amateur radio hobbyist. Rows of stores selling electronic gadgets, used parts, and an endless variety of radio hardware lined both Cortlandt Street and neighboring Church Street.

The East River Savings Bank, at the northeast corner of Cortlandt and Church streets, is an almost perfect example of the Art Deco style of the 1930s. This was the approximate **site of a large windmill** built ca. 1686 that appears in many old prints of the early city. New York became an important flour-milling center, and two flour barrels and a pair of crossed windmill arms are a part of the city's Great Seal.

The World Trade Center, created by the Port Authority of New York and New Jersey, was planned as a center of world commerce, and took more than ten years to complete. Consisting of two 110-story towers rising 1,350 feet, four low-rise Plaza Buildings, and the Vista International Hotel, on a 16-acre site, it is the world's largest commercial complex. In 4 WTC are the Commodity Exchange, New York Mercantile Exchange, Coffee, Sugar, & Cocoa Exchange, and Cotton Exchange. In

The twin Hudson Terminal buildings were razed to make way for the 110-story World Trade Center. Underneath was the terminal of the Hudson & Manhattan "Tubes," now called the PATH, and presently located about 100 yards west, beneath the twin Trade Center towers. (Port Authority of New York & New Jersey)

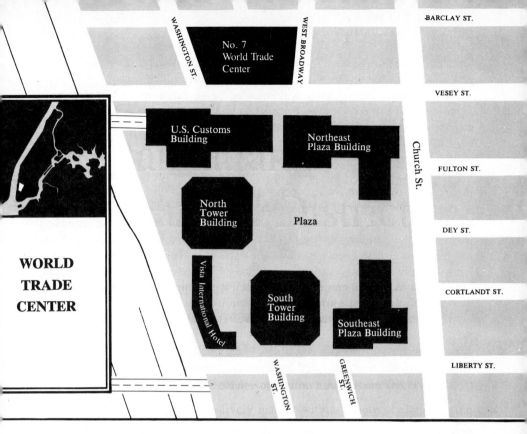

the lower concourse is the World Trade Center terminal of the PATH (Port Authority Trans Hudson) subway to New Jersey.

The design of the towers involved some revolutionary concepts in skyscraper technology. The conventional skyscraper is built as a skeleton of structural steel supports, with the outer walls as the "skin." In the World Trade Center Towers, the exterior walls bear the load and consist of closely spaced vertical columns, tied together by massive horizontal spandrel beams that girdle the tower at every floor. The only interior columns are in the core, which contains the elevators. Thus there is a maximum open, column-free floor space, but large "picture windows" had to be sacrificed. Because of their near-record height, the towers had to be erected from within. Four kangaroo cranes, nestled in the elevator shafts, lifted the tons of steel up the sides of the building; and when the walls rose to the height of the cranes, they were jacked up to a new position to begin again. When the top was finally reached, each crane was dismantled and lowered by a neighboring crane. The last one hoisted up a guy derrick that disassembled the remaining kangaroo crane, lowered its parts to the ground, and was in turn dismantled and brought down by freight elevator. A neat trick and a spectacular show for the thousands of lunchtime "sidewalk superintendents."

To provide efficient access to the upper floors of the towers, the elevator system is divided into three zones, each with its own lobby. Above the

Concourse are "skylobbies" on the 44th and 78th floors. There are 23 express and 72 local elevators plus 4 large freight elevators in each tower.

The five-acre central plaza is dominated by an enormous bronze revolving globe by the German sculptor, Fritz Koenig, set on a fountain. More than 1.2 million cubic yards of earth and rock were removed from the excavation and used for landfill for the nearby Battery Park City project. The architects of this mammoth center were Minoru Yamasaki and Emery Roth & Sons.

The World Trade Center was the site of the most destructive terrorist bombing in American history, when on February 26, 1993, a powerful explosive was detonated in a van parked in the underground garage beneath 2 WTC. The midday blast killed six and injured more than 1,000, and caused severe structural damage to the buildings as well as considerable damage to the adjacent Vista International Hotel. The World Trade Center was forced to close for several weeks, disrupting the operations of hundreds of business firms and dislocating the daily lives of more than 50,000 people employed there—all at a cost to the city's economy of well over a billion dollars.

After exploring the Plaza and its modern sculpture, and a brief walk through the Concourse level below, proceed to 2 WTC and take the elevator to the 107th-floor **Observation Deck** (open 9:30 A.M.–9:30 P.M. daily), and enjoy a spectacular view. And if you're in the mood for a splurge, return to the World Trade Center at sunset for a drink or meal at **Windows on the World,** atop 1 WTC.

Follow the signs to 6 WTC, plaza level, and peek into the cylindrical glass passageway to 7 WTC. This 47-story, polished and flame-roughened red granite veneer structure acts as a striking backdrop to Alexander Calder's 25-foot-high bright red stabile, *Three Red Wings.* (Calder originally planned it to be 150 feet high, but was forced to compromise.)

Re-enter 6 WTC and follow the signs leading to the World Financial Center escalator. Then walk through the glass-enclosed North Bridge which spans West Street.

BATTERY PARK CITY

The **World Financial Center**, one of Manhattan's truly great architectural achievements, was designed by the firm of Cesar Pelli & Associates and developed by Olympia & York. The project, which occupies the center of Battery Park City, took six years to construct, and was completed in 1987. The WFC consists of four 34- to 51-story towers clad in sagami granite and reflective glass, each topped by a different geometrically shaped copper dome. Two nine-story octagonal gatehouses flank the project's entrance. It is an eight-million square foot mixed-use complex and is the business and commercial hub of Battery Park City. Constructed on 13.5 acres of landfill along the Hudson River, the buildings rise from a granite-sheathed base, and at each setback the proportion of glass to stone increases, until the walls at the top are entirely of glass. The WFC houses in its four towers the world headquarters of American

Aerial view of Battery Park City on Manhattan's lower-west-side Hudson River waterfront. In the center are the four major buildings of the World Financial Center (each with a distinctive dome), and to the right, the residential section. The twin towers of the World Trade Center dominate the attractive skyline. (Battery Park City Authority)

Express, Merrill Lynch & Co., Dow Jones & Co., and Oppenheimer & Co., plus other major firms, restaurants, and upscale retail establishments. The area just to the north of the World Financial Center some day will house the North Residential Neighborhood. Just beyond is the newly constructed Stuyvesant High School, a public secondary school for gifted youngsters, which moved here from its original location on East 15th Street. A bridge across West Street provides safe access to Chambers Street.

The North Bridge leads directly into the centerpiece of the WFC, the astonishing **Winter Garden.** Rising 120 feet, this modern-day Crystal Palace of vaulted glass and steel has become one of the most popular attractions in the city. (Stop at the Information Desk and pick up a map and schedule of public arts and events.) A broad, hourglass-shaped grand staircase cascades onto a marble floor graced with a grove of sixteen 45-foot tall *Washington robusta* palm trees from California's Mojave Desert—the hardiest of the species, but helped by grow-lights. The Winter Garden is open daily from 7 A.M. to 1 A.M., as are the other WFC public spaces.

Follow the main passageway to the right between WFC 3 and WFC 4 to the **Courtyard,** a three-story, glass-roofed European-style piazza, surrounded by balconies and punctuated with columns that rise 45 feet from the patterned floor. Five brass canopies give a gazebo-like effect, creating an intimate atmosphere for the several international restaurants.

Return to the Winter Garden and exit out onto the **Plaza,** a 3.5-acre park on the river that features outdoor dining, lush landscaping, a pair of 80-foot reflecting pools, the North Cove Yacht Harbor, and a long esplanade that offers dramatic views of the Hudson, the Statue of Liberty, Ellis Island, and the New Jersey shoreline. And don't miss the ornamental fence with the quotes from Walt Whitman ("City of the World...") and Frank O'Hara ("One need never leave the confines of New York...") inscribed in brass letters. Just to the north of the Cove is the passenger ferry to Hoboken.

Walk south and re-enter at WFC 2, walk through the first of the two octagonal gatehouse rotundas. (This is one of Cesar Pelli's finest spaces, with its dome decorated with stencil patterns.) Then walk through the second rotunda, and at WFC 1 take the escalator down to Liberty Street, turn toward the river, and enter the residential section of Battery Park City.

Battery Park City is the first really successful attempt to create a coherent and formal, yet intimate, community within the city, while at the same time relating it architecturally to New York's historic skyline. "A triumph of urban design," says Paul Goldberger, architecture critic of *The New York Times*. "It is just right, nothing shrill, cheap, or slick." Walking along the newly created streets of the complex, one is reminded of other desirable areas—Tudor City, Gramercy Park, Riverside Drive—all part of the innovative master plan by the firm of Cooper, Eckstut Associates under the aegis of the Battery Park City Authority, a state agency of the Urban Development Corporation. Some have even called the new urban scene "an instant past."

Following the map, walk to the river past Gateway Plaza (Jack Brown & Irving E. Gershon, 1982–83), a grouping of six apartment houses and the first to be completed. This complex is the least successful element in the development. Its 1,712 units have been called a modern dinosaur and compared with Lefrak City. Walk south to the next corner.

Little **Albany Street Park** is dominated by the huge environmental sculpture *Upper Room,* by sculptor Ned Smyth. Made of cast concrete, glass, stone, and mosaic, with its Renaissance arcade and atrium, it is supposed to "summarize" Egypt's dynasties and the Roman Empire. The sculptor used texture and color to integrate into the complex art that harmonizes with the neighboring post-modern architecture.

Continue south to **Hudson Tower** (Davis, Brody & Assocs., 1986), with its bay windows and cantilevered corner windows. The American Institute of Architects calls it "a happy building." Note the contrasting low-rise structures to the east, designed to resemble a row of 19th-century townhouses. Return to the esplanade and continue one block further south to Rector Place.

Fronting on lush **Rector Park,** a two-part one-acre open landscaped area, are seven apartment houses. The design by Innocenti & Webel with Vollmer Assocs. is reminiscent of Gramercy Park. While all the buildings are different, they harmonize well in their diversity. The most understated and appropriately detailed of the group is **Parc Place,** 225 Rector Street (Gruzen & Partners, 1987), which is more effective in holding to the original design concept than are Soundings, Battery Pointe, or River Rose. Turn right (south) on South End Avenue.

Passing the arcaded shops look back (north) to appreciate how the distant entrance to No. 2 World Financial Center is framed in the curve of South End Avenue. Turn right at The Regatta (Gruzen Sampton Steinglass, 1989), an upscale condominium apartment, to the esplanade and the sculpture, *Living Room* (Richard Artschwager, 1988) made of granite, cast iron, and redwood, plus plantings, resulting in six pieces of park furniture of various materials. The esplanade benches are replicas of those used at the New York World's Fair of 1939–40, and the light poles are "B" pole fixtures and copies of turn-of-the-century Bishop's Crook lampposts.

Turn left to South Cove, with its unusual *Lookout, Bridge, and Circular Jetty* (Mary Miss, sculptor; Stanton Eckstut, architect; Susan Child, landscaping; 1987). It is described by Paul Goldberger as "a fantasy structure evoking the Statue of Liberty, and a gentle comment on the nature of the urban waterfront." The result is a park, a piece of sculpture, and a structure, "a reminder of the serious intent that has characterized every aspect of Battery Park City." On the far south side of the Cove is the proposed site of the Museum of Jewish Heritage.

Walk back up South End Avenue to Liberty Street and turn right; cross West Street and continue east to No. 1 Liberty Plaza, just before the corner of Broadway.

1 Liberty Plaza (Skidmore, Owings & Merrill, 1974) was designed to show the vertical faces of its steel structure. The 53-story tower occupies the site of the late lamented Singer (Sewing Machine Company) Tower as well as the ornate City Investing Building. When the Singer Tower was completed in 1908, it was the tallest building in the world, until it was eclipsed by the Metropolitan Life Tower 18 months later. Architect Ernest Flagg's liberal use of metal and glass, incorporated into a graceful shaft in Renaissance Eclectic style, produced one of the most beautiful buildings ever to grace the New York skyline. Its replacement, built in 1974, adds nothing exciting to the cityscape and only heightens the feeling of loss. (The *AIA Guide* calls the building "a gloomy, cadaverous hulk.") The plaza area was built in accordance with the new zoning regulations, which impose a ratio of open space to a building's verticality. Relax in the cheerful plaza and take a seat on the bench next to the lifelike **bronze sculpture,** *Double Check,* by J. Seward Johnson, Jr. The figure originally was cast with a memorandum in its hand from the firm of Merrill Lynch, whose offices were then in front of the sculpture at No. 1 Liberty Plaza; after the company moved to the World Financial Center, the memo mysteriously disappeared. See what the sculptor placed in the attaché case, the contents of which are often augmented by articles dropped in by passers-by. In mid-plaza, note the puzzling street sign for the nonexistent "Temple Street."

Cross Broadway and continue east on Liberty Street.

The former Chamber of Commerce of the State of New York, now the International Commercial Bank of China (65 Liberty Street) is an attractive example of the French Beaux Arts style. Designed in 1901 by James Barnes Baker, it was built for the State Chamber of Commerce, which was founded at

New York's skyline lost one of its great landmarks when U.S. Steel demolished the Singer Tower in 1968 to erect No. 1 Liberty Plaza on the site. The Tower was the crowning achievement of architect Ernest Flagg, and was completed in 1908. For a brief time it was the world's tallest building. The Singer Tower was the tallest building ever demolished.

Fraunces Tavern in 1768. The solid Ionic columns seem to frame empty spaces. Originally there were three large sculpture groups, which did not survive New York's air pollution (and pigeons) and suffered so much decay that they were removed some years ago. The impressive white marble edifice was dedicated by President Theodore Roosevelt in an elaborate ceremony witnessed by former President Grover Cleveland and several foreign ambassadors. In 1973, the Chamber of Commerce merged with the Commerce and Industry Association, and seven years later the organization moved to other quarters.

The **Liberty Tower** (55 Liberty Street) is a good example of the neo-Gothic style applied to commercial skyscrapers. It was designed by Henry Ives Cobb in 1909, and from 1919 served as the headquarters of the Sinclair Oil Company. The building, with its white terra-cotta walls, is now a cooperative apartment house. Step back a few yards down narrow Liberty Place, and observe the fantasy of Gothic reflections in the glassy façade of the Marine Midland Building. The building was erected on the site of the Manhattan home of poet William Cullen Bryant.

Return to the plaza in front of 140 Broadway.

The **Marine Midland Building,** designed by Skidmore, Owings & Merrill in 1967, is one of the first New York skyscrapers to have its own plaza. The use of matte black spandrels between rows of glass gives an unexpected effect of sleekness, in sharp contrast to the ornamented façades of nearby buildings. The dark, smooth appearance is further offset by the orange, cube-shaped stabile in the plaza, by sculptor Isamu Noguchi. Before the Marine Midland Bank erected its tower, the site was occupied by the Guaranty Trust Company Building—a very impressive classic structure, designed by York & Sawyer in 1912, which received the American Institute of Architects Medal for Distinguished Architecture two years after its completion.

Continue south on Broadway.

   The U.S. Realty Building (115 Broadway) and its neighbor to the south, **The Trinity Building** (111 Broadway), are a delightful pair of early 20th-century skyscrapers. Both were designed in the year 1906 by architect Francis H. Kimball, in a modified Gothic style. There is an intimate quality about these narrow twins lacking in most modern buildings. Despite their height, they seem almost like charming residences. Look up at the catwalk connecting the two like a prop for a silent thriller movie. Diminutive Thames Street was originally an 18th-century carriageway leading to the DeLancey stables. Stephen DeLancey's home would later become Fraunces Tavern.

   The Equitable Building (120 Broadway), designed by Ernest R. Graham in 1915, replaced an earlier Equitable Life Building that was destroyed by fire in 1912. Using every square inch of space, this blockbuster of a building rises 41 stories without setback for a total of 1,200,000 square feet of floor space on a site slightly under an acre! The result is a floor area of about 30 times the plot's. Present zoning laws allow less than 12. Upon completion of the building there arose such a tremendous clamor against the enormous building density that in 1916 new zoning laws were introduced, establishing the setback requirements that have been progressively tightened through the years.

   The Bank of Tokyo (100 Broadway) was formerly the American Surety Building, and was built in 1895 from plans by Bruce Price. The eight allegorical figures were sculpted by J. Massey Rhind.

   Trinity Church, designed by Richard Upjohn in 1846, is the third church on the site. Its location at the head of Wall Street makes it one of the best-known landmark churches in the city. The original church was established in 1697 by Royal Charter of King William III of England, but it remained for Queen Anne to grant the land in 1705. The first church was destroyed by the Great Fire of 1776, and the second was demolished because of structural failure. Artistically, the most striking feature of Trinity Church is the three sets of huge bronze doors, designed by Richard Morris Hunt. They were a gift of William Waldorf Astor, and are patterned after the famous Ghiberti bronze doors of the Baptistery in Florence. The sculpture work for the main entrance doors was executed by Karl Bitter, the south doors by Charles H. Niehaus, and the north doors by J. Massey Rhind. The splendid stained-glass chancel window was designed by Upjohn himself. The building exterior is of brownstone. It was cleaned recently, and the church, once blackened by pollution and soot, is now a rosy pink (but for how long?). The 280-foot spire was for years a prominent New York landmark until it was dwarfed by the surrounding skyscrapers. The "ring" of ten bells in the steeple is played before services, and adds a quieting note to the commotion of the neighborhood. The side wall buttresses, while inserting a touch of Gothic glamour, are false, as the ceiling vaults are made of plaster and are hung for decoration only. The interior, however, is somber and majestic. To the left of the sanctuary is the lovely All Saints Chapel, built in 1913, as well as an interesting little museum of early New York history. (Hours: Mon.–Fri. 9:00 A.M. to 11:45 A.M. and 1:00 P.M. to 3:45 P.M., Sat. 10:00 A.M. to 3:45 P.M., Sun. 1:00 P.M. to 3:45 P.M.; free.) Short tours of Trinity Church are given daily at 2:00 P.M. by one of the vergers.

★ Surrounding the church is the **burial ground,** shaded by trees of many species. In the north section is the ornate Gothic-style Martyrs' Monument, a memorial to Continental soldiers who, during the American Revolution, died while imprisoned in a sugar house on Liberty (then Crown) Street. The various monuments read like a page from American history: Alexander Hamilton, Robert Fulton (whose steamboat *Clermont* set sail from the foot of Cortlandt Street), Captain James Lawrence (who, as commander of the ship *Chesapeake* in the War of 1812, immortalized himself with his dying command, "Don't Give Up the Ship!"), Albert Gallatin (twice Secretary of the Treasury under Thomas Jefferson, and a founder of New York University), Francis Lewis (signer of the Declaration of Independence), and William Bradford (early

The classic Guaranty Trust Company Building, built in 1912, was awarded the AIA Medal for Distinguished Architecture. In its place at 140 Broadway stands the Marine Midland Building. (Morgan Guaranty Trust Company)

champion of freedom of the press, and editor of New York's first newspaper, the *New York Gazette*). In 1987 the Church constructed an ornate cast-iron footbridge across Trinity Place connecting the second floor of the parish building with the church complex. The churchyard is a favorite lunch-hour retreat in warm weather for office workers in the surrounding financial district; and the Church presents noontime concerts every Monday and Thursday.

The Bank of New York Building (formerly the Irving Trust Company Building) at 1 Wall Street is a massive limestone pile of Art Deco. An interesting touch by architects Voorhees, Gmelin & Walker in this 1932 building are the fluted walls and chamfered corners. An addition to the building was built in 1965. The attractive lobby is decorated with a polychrome mosaic design that gives a startling flamelike appearance. When seen from the street at night it literally glows in patterns of bright red and orange.

Wall Street is named for the original palisade fence or wall, built in 1653 on orders from Dutch Governor Peter Stuyvesant. Although generally believed to have been erected as a defense against hostile Indians, it was intended as a bulwark against an invasion by British colonists from New England. The wall stood from river to river for about 50 years. [For a tour of the Wall Street area and neighboring streets, see Manhattan's Financial District walking tour.]

No. 71 Broadway, the **Empire Building** (Renwick, Aspinwall and Tucker, 1894) at the southwest corner of Rector Street, was the headquarters of the United States Steel Corporation (now USX), until their recent move uptown.

The former American Express Company Building (65 Broadway) was the New York headquarters of the worldwide firm that began as a one-man operation in 1839, when William F. Harnden made four trips by train to Boston every week to deliver parcels and make collections. In 1850 he merged with two other express companies, operating a fleet of delivery wagons. Under the leadership of president Henry Wells and secretary William G. Fargo, the American Express Company's new subsidiary, Wells Fargo, helped open the West. The novel "Traveler's Cheque" was introduced in 1891, but by 1918 express services were abandoned altogether. With its merger in 1981 with Shearson Loeb Rhoades, the company expanded its financial operations, which are now conducted at its new corporate headquarters at the American Express Tower in the World Financial Center at Battery Park City. Travel services, however, are still conducted in this building, designed in 1917 by Renwick, Aspinwall and Tucker.

No. 55 Broadway, called **One Exchange Plaza,** at the corner of Exchange Alley, is in striking contrast to its neighbors. Designed in 1982 by Fox & Fowle, it is a 31-story office tower with buff-colored horizontal brick spandrels and clear glass bands, with radial corners. In the rear, facing Trinity Place, is a second-level shopping way, required by the City Planning Commission to provide appropriate pedestrian space and a continuous link with the street. Its neighbor down the street at No. 45, **The Broadway Atrium,** completed in 1983, is another Fox & Fowle–designed building, of the same height and color scheme, but set back, and with serrated corners in a sawtooth pattern. It, too, has a second-level shopping way on Trinity Place.

No. 50 Broadway marks the **site of New York's first skyscraper.** The Tower Building, designed by Bradford L. Gilbert, was an 11-story steel-skeleton building, completed in 1889. Gilbert had to occupy the topmost floor himself to dispel fears of New Yorkers that such a "tall" structure might collapse.

No. 39 Broadway has a plaque indicating the site of the Alexander McComb Mansion—George Washington's second presidential residence, occupied from February 23 to August 30, 1790.

No. 26 Broadway, the **former Standard Oil Building,** was the corporate headquarters of John D. Rockefeller's Standard Oil. Later, the company became SOCONY (*Standard Oil CO. of N.Y.*) when the government "trust busters" took action; then Socony-Mobil; and with a final simplification to Mobil Oil, the firm moved into new headquarters on East 42nd Street. The curved façade conforms to the principle of the "street wall"—so vital in good urban planning. The firm of Carrère & Hastings (which designed the New York Public Library at Fifth Avenue and 42nd Street, among other fine buildings) with Shreve, Lamb & Blake planned this imposing building in 1922 with the skyline in mind. Although the lower section of the building conforms to the path of Broadway, the upper tower coincides with the geometry of the Manhattan street grid. Atop the tower an appropriately symbolic oil-burning lantern (actually the chimney) crowns the massive structure. The building is best viewed from a distance. Before the rash of post-World War II boxlike skyscrapers obscured it from view, the Standard Oil Building formed an integral part of the lovely New York skyline, and was clearly visible from the harbor.

At No. 24, the side entrance of the Standard Oil Building, is the diminutive **Museum of American Financial History.** On display are artifacts and historical documents that relate to the story of the stock exchanges and various Wall Street brokerage houses. Founded by John E. Herzog in 1988, it opened here four years later. It portrays many aspects of the nation's financial history, including an array of beautifully engraved stock certificates, and a stock ticker. It probably is the smallest museum in New York. (Weekdays, 11:30 A.M. to 2:30 P.M., free.)

Across Bowling Green, the immense **Cunard Building** (25 Broadway) is a harmonious counterpart to the Standard Oil Building. Constructed in 1921 from plans by Benjamin Wistar Morris, when a transatlantic crossing by luxurious ocean liner was "the only way to travel," it is one of the finest office buildings in the world. The Cunard Line arrived in New York with the maiden voyage of Samuel Cunard's *Britannia* on July 4, 1840, and remained in the forefront in ocean travel until fairly recently. Merging with the White Star Line in the 1920s, it became the largest passenger ship company in the world. (The names of Cunard ships always ended in *-ia: Mauretania, Lusitania,* etc., White Star's in *-ic: Britannic, Titanic,* etc. Later exceptions were the great "Queens" including the *QE2.*) The building's ornate Renaissance façade is quite handsome with its three arched entranceways and second-story colonnade, but the charm of the impressive structure is in its vestibule and Great Hall—certainly one of the most beautiful interior spaces anywhere. Passing through one of the central bronze doors, the visitor enters the high vaulted vestibule whose ornament was created by artist Ezra Winter. Beyond high wrought-iron gates (by Samuel Yellin) is the *pièce de résistance,* the Great Hall. Now housing a post office branch, the octagonally shaped chamber measures 185 feet long by 74 feet wide, and the central section is surmounted by a dome 65 feet above the floor. Study the magnificent murals and pendentives covered in fresco. The walls and floor are covered with travertine with considerable detail, and the artistic maps of the world were executed by Barry Faulkner. The aesthetic climax of the great room is its groined, vaulted ceiling ornamented with arabesques and a multitude of design motifs. Ezra Winter and most of the artists who combined their talents here were winners of the Rome Prize. The four supporting pendentives created by Winter represent the ships of Christopher Columbus, John Cabot, Sir Francis Drake, and Leif Ericson. In the heyday of steamship travel, the rooms were called the Freight Distribution Hall and the Bill of Lading Hall. Thomas Hastings (of the firm of Carrère & Hastings) was a consultant to architect Morris, and is said to have suggested the plan of the Great Hall based on Raphael's Villa Madama in Rome. The Cunard Building is unquestionably one of the finest examples of the American Renaissance and, in the words of Henry Hope Reed, author of *The Golden City* and curator of Central Park, "Great art is to be found not in a glorified warehouse called a museum, but in such buildings as 25 Broadway."

Bowling Green was New York City's first park. It lay just beyond the original fort, and was merely an open space leading into *De Heere Wegh* (The Main Street, or Broadway). It served as a cattle market and also as a parade ground. In 1733 it was rented privately for "one peppercorn per year for the recreation and delight of the inhabitants of this city." An iron fence ornamented with crowns was erected in 1771 to protect the little park and its newly erected statue of King George III. A symbol of British tyranny, the gilt-lead statue was pulled down by patriots after General Washington ordered the Declaration of Independence read publicly on July 9, 1776. The crowns that topped the fence posts also were destroyed. Curiously, parts of the original statue still exist, and pieces later turned up near the town of Wilton, Connecticut, where the pieces had been taken to be melted into musket balls. The **park** and **fence** have been restored recently as part of a major renovation of Bowling Green, which also included a pedestrian mall and a reconstructed subway station beneath.

Dominating Bowling Green is an enormous bronze **statue of a charging bull.** The work of sculptor Arturo DiModica, it was cast by Domenico Ranieri and placed here in 1992. Strangely, the statue of the larger-than-life six-foot bull was installed without the required permission of the Parks Department, which is less than "bullish" about its being here. Whether it stays or not is uncertain, but what *is* certain is that the cost of removal is prohibitive. Meanwhile, it has become a favored photo spot for tourists who enjoy posing in front of it.

No. 11 Broadway, on the west side of Bowling Green, is an amusing hodgepodge of styles. Framing the entrances are "Egyptian" pylons, while above the third story the building takes on the bold look of the Chicago School of Architecture, with its glazed brick piers and articulated spandrels. It was

The Produce Exchange on Bowling Green was completed in 1884 and was replaced in 1957 by No. 2 Broadway. One of George B. Post's most notable works, the enormous red brick structure had a true iron skeleton and a main hall measuring 220 by 144 feet. At the right foreground is the statue of Abraham de Peyster which has been moved to Hanover Square. (Museum of the City of New York)

designed in 1898 by W. G. Audsley. Adjacent **No. 9 Broadway,** the Bowling Green Offices, is a continuation of the "west wall."

No. 1 Broadway, the United States Lines–Panama Pacific Lines Building, also hearkens to the days of sea power, when our country had at least some semblance of a respectable merchant marine. Built in 1921 from plans by Walter B. Chambers, the enormous structure is more famous for what used to be there. This was almost the southern tip of Manhattan Island and the site of the original Dutch fort that stood just a few yards to the south. During the late 18th century the Kennedy House was headquarters for Generals Washington and Lee. No. 1 Broadway was first called the Washington Building after its predecessor on the site with the same name, demolished in 1919.

No. 2 Broadway (to the left of the Custom House), built in 1959 by Emery Roth & Sons, marks the site of one of our most tragic building losses, the Produce Exchange. Designed in 1881 by noted architect George B. Post and completed three years later, it was a true iron skeleton building, faced with dark red brick, and several years ahead of its time. The façade was adorned with terra-cotta motifs of the various products traded within. The second-floor Main Hall was an astonishing 220 feet by 144 feet, with a huge latticework skylight 60 feet above the floor. As Nathan Silver sadly comments in *Lost New York,* "The Produce Exchange, one of the best buildings in New York, was replaced after 1957 by one of the worst."

The former United States Custom House is considered the finest example of the French Beaux Arts style in the city. It will be the new home of the **George Gustave Heye Center of the National Museum of the American Indian,** at the Alexander Hamilton U.S. Custom House, under the aegis of the Smithsonian Institution. After a brief preview in 1992, it officially opened in 1994. The Museum has vacated its former building on Audubon Terrace uptown, and will house one of the most important collections of Native American art and artifacts. The building, designed by Cass Gilbert and completed in 1907, is one of the city's architectural treasures.

Spend a few minutes examining the superb façade and the exceptional collection of sculpture:

Contrasting with the dark gray granite of the building are four monumental white limestone sculpture groups by Daniel Chester French. Left to right, they represent the continents of Asia, America, Europe, and Africa. Above the cornice are statues symbolizing the 12 great mercantile nations of history: Greece, Rome, Phoenicia, Genoa, Venice, Spain, Holland, Portugal, Denmark, Germany, England, and France. The heroic cartouche atop the upper balustrade is by sculptor Karl Bitter. Ranged around the Custom House are 44 Corinthian columns.

The **interior's** second-floor rotunda has a splendid display of Reginald Marsh murals depicting early events on the site, and various seafaring themes. The Custom House is now located at the World Trade Center; however the Government retains the 5th and 6th floors for the U.S. Bankruptcy Court.

The original nearby fortification called Fort Amsterdam was constructed in 1623 with the arrival of the first settlers. Then a more substantial fort was built in 1626, going through eight name changes until, as Fort George, it was demolished in 1787. Government House, intended as the presidential residence, replaced the fort three years later, but with the removal of the nation's capital to Philadelphia, it became the Governor's Mansion. It later became a boarding house, then the Custom House, and after a fire, was razed in 1815. Subse-quently, town houses lined the site, but by midcentury they were taken over as shipping offices and known as "Steamship Row," as the area became devoted entirely to commerce. (Detailed and colorful dioramas of the early Dutch fort and surrounding settlement are displayed at the Museum of the City of New York.)

Enter Battery Park at the main entrance, directly to the right of the Custom House, across State Street.

Battery Park is named for the battery of cannon that, between 1683 and 1688, were mounted along what is now the sidewalk opposite the Custom House, extending to just below the present Battery Place. From then until 1807

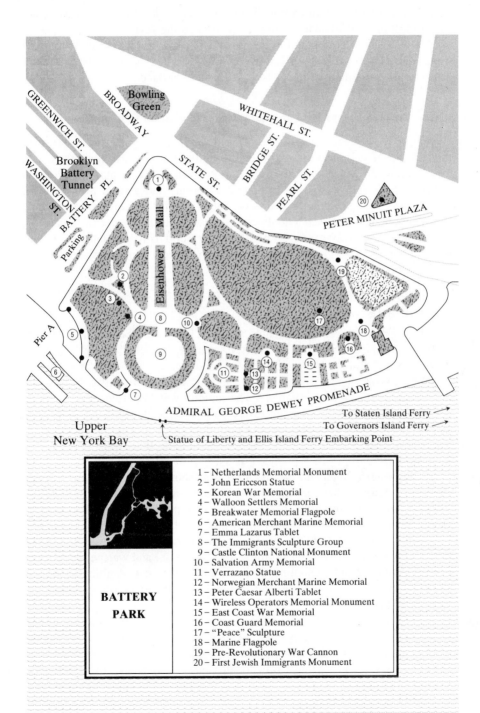

BATTERY PARK

1 – Netherlands Memorial Monument
2 – John Ericcson Statue
3 – Korean War Memorial
4 – Walloon Settlers Memorial
5 – Breakwater Memorial Flagpole
6 – American Merchant Marine Memorial
7 – Emma Lazarus Tablet
8 – The Immigrants Sculpture Group
9 – Castle Clinton National Monument
10 – Salvation Army Memorial
11 – Verrazano Statue
12 – Norwegian Merchant Marine Memorial
13 – Peter Caesar Alberti Tablet
14 – Wireless Operators Memorial Monument
15 – East Coast War Memorial
16 – Coast Guard Memorial
17 – "Peace" Sculpture
18 – Marine Flagpole
19 – Pre-Revolutionary War Cannon
20 – First Jewish Immigrants Monument

the area was fortified with additional batteries of artillery pieces. Most of the Park is built on landfill added periodically through the years.

The tall flagpole and sculptured pedestal is the **Netherlands Memorial Monument,** inscribed in both English and 17th-century Dutch, giving a brief history of the settlement of the Colony of New Netherland.

Bear to the right at the first path to the Statue of John Ericcson.

John Ericcson was the Swedish-born mechanical engineer who designed and built the first ironclad warship, the *Monitor*—the famous "cheesebox on a raft," which, on March 9, 1862, at Hampton Roads, Virginia, engaged the Confederate frigate *Merrimac* (renamed *Virginia*) and altered the course of naval history. The *Monitor*'s deck stood only 18 inches out of the water, while its revolving turret carried two 11-inch guns. Note the model in Ericcson's hand. The statue was executed by Jonathan Scott Hartley in 1893. It was replaced ten years later by the sculptor, who produced a better version.

Follow the numbers on the map of Battery Park for a tour of the Park and its monuments.

Bear to the right before reaching Castle Clinton, to see the black granite obelisk that marks the **Korean War Memorial.** Installed in 1991, it has a rather unusual design with the outline of a soldier cut through the stone and highlighted with metal. Around the base are the flags of the allied nations that participated in the conflict, 1950–53. The sculptor was MacAdams.

Walk to the right to the edge of the park and then toward the waterfront, passing the **Breakwater Memorial Flagpole,** which recalls the construction and landfill that created the park. Notice the dolphin that wraps itself around the base.

At the water's edge, and located 40 feet offshore, is the striking **American Merchant Marine Memorial.** The sculpture group depicts four merchant mariners and their sinking ship—three still standing on the vessel as it slides under the waves, and a fourth in the water reaching up for assistance. The sculpture, by Marisol, (1991) is based on a photograph taken during World War II by a U-boat officer whose ship torpedoed the vessel and watched it go down with all hands without attempting to rescue any of the crew. Adding to the emotional impact of the sculpture, the figure in the water is almost completely engulfed at high tide.

To the right is **Pier A,** built in 1886. It was built for the city's Department of Docks and Harbor Police (George Sears Greene, Jr., engineer). The last survivor of the early Hudson River piers, until recently it was a fireboat station. The clock on the 70-foot tower was donated in 1919 by Daniel Reed, a founder of the United States Steel Corporation, as a memorial to the 116,000 servicemen who died while serving in World War I. The clock peals the time on ships' bells. The city is planning to make Pier A a visitors' center, with restaurants, shops, and an information bureau.

Walk left along the promenade to just before Castle Clinton. A few feet inside the park is the **Emma Lazarus tablet,** honoring the poet who in 1883 penned her immortal sonnet "The New Colossus" to help raise funds for the construction of the pedestal and the mounting of the Statue of Liberty. Her oft-quoted lines, "Give me your tired, your poor,/ Your huddled masses yearning to breathe free..." are emblazoned on the base of the statue she helped secure.

Go around to the front of Castle Clinton, but before entering, examine the impressive statue of **The Immigrants** (Luis Sanguino, 1981), which represents many of the immigrant groups that have come to these shores.

Castle Clinton National Monument. In 1807 it appeared that another war with England was imminent, and several fortifications were hastily erected to protect the unguarded harbor. Among them was Castle Williams on nearby Governors Island, and the West Battery (now Castle Clinton) on a small rocky islet connected to the tip of Manhattan by a 200-foot causeway. (The intervening land was not filled in until the mid-19th century.) Constructed from plans by John McComb, Jr., in a circular shape with red sandstone walls over eight feet thick, the battery's 28 guns never fired a shot in anger. Renamed in 1815 in honor of DeWitt Clinton, former mayor and later governor, the fort remained in the hands of the military until 1821, when Commanding General Winfield Scott moved the garrison to Governors Island. Two years later Castle Clinton was ceded to the City of New York.

In June 1824 the city leased it as a place of public entertainment, and redecorated with a garden, shrubbery, a fountain, and a promenade above, it opened as **Castle Garden.** Among the variety of public events presented, including concerts, fireworks displays, and balloon ascensions, was Samuel F. B. Morse's demonstration in 1842 of his electric telegraph. Then, on September 11, 1850, P. T. Barnum, in the musical event of the century, presented Jenny Lind, the "Swedish Nightingale," in her American concert debut. At the close of the sell-out performance at which more than 6,000 had paid the exorbitant fee of at least three dollars a seat, the audience broke into a "tempest of cheers."

In 1855 Castle Garden became the immigrant landing station, and for the next 34 years witnessed the arrival of over 8 million new Americans. With the closing of the Garden in 1890, the nearby Barge Office (now demolished) handled the growing tide of immigrants until the new immigration depot was opened two years later on Ellis Island.

The Garden was then remodeled by the architectural firm of McKim, Mead & White to serve as the **New York Aquarium,** opening on December 10, 1896, to a crowd of 30,000. In 1941 the Aquarium was closed, moving to new and spacious quarters at Coney Island, and the building was slated for demolition to make way for access roads to the new Brooklyn-Battery tunnel. However, public hue and cry saved it, and in 1946 Congress authorized the establishment of Castle Clinton as a national monument under the administration of the National Park Service of the Department of the Interior. It has been carefully restored as a fort, and provides a dramatic, if somewhat fanciful, link with the past.

Castle Clinton has a small museum, and in the center is the ticket office for the Ellis Island–Statue of Liberty boat. Check the schedules, as the last depar-

The Lusitania arrived on her maiden voyage to New York on September 13, 1907. Crowds jammed the waterfront between the Aquarium (formerly Castle Garden) and Pier A as the liner steamed up the Hudson, eight years before her ill-fated rendezvous with a U-boat off the English coast. (New-York Historical Society)

ture for both islands is around 3:00 P.M. A visit to both is an absolute *must*...but on another day. There is also a small bookshop. The monument is open daily, 8:30 A.M. to 5:00 P.M.

On exiting Castle Clinton, turn right, past the Statue of Evangeline Booth, general of the Salvation Army, and along the path to the statue of Verrazano.

Giovanni da Verrazano was the first to sight these shores. Arriving in the small caravel *La Dauphine* in 1524, the Florentine merchant sailing for Francis I of France claimed the new land for the king, naming it *Terre d'Angoulême*. The French, however, did not follow up the claim, and Verrazano himself fell victim to cannibals on a voyage to the Caribbean four years later. The statue is the work of Ettore Ximenes, and was completed in 1909.

The same year, Esteban Gómez, a Portuguese mariner sailing under the Spanish flag, entered the harbor and named the mouth of the river Río San Antonio. It was not until 1609, however, that Henry Hudson, in his *Half-Moon*, actually sailed up the river that bears his name and brought back to Holland extensive reports on this "Great River of the Mountains." Four years later Adriaen Block, a Dutch trader, landed at the tip of Manhattan Island with a small group of men. When their ship *Tiger* caught fire and burned to the water, they were forced to spend the winter. The following spring they built a new

An almost deserted view of Broadway, looking north from Cortlandt Street in the mid-1880s. Midday crowds often gathered in front of the tall Western Union Building to watch a ball descend from the top of the pole precisely at noon. George B. Post's flamboyant Renaissance structure, built in 1873–75—and considered one of New York's first skyscrapers—was demolished when the City Investing Building was erected. After the Blizzard of 1888 the maze of telegraph wires was removed and buried beneath the street. (New-York Historical Society)

During the deep excavation for the World Trade Center, the two tubes of the PATH subway lines were exposed, and passers-by could hear the eerie roar of the trains in what at first glance seemed to be enormous sewer pipes. The eastbound tube is in the foreground, the westbound is just visible, passing to the right rear of the early framework of the WTC's North Tower. (Port Authority of New York & New Jersey)

The statue of stern-faced Abraham de Peyster, son of a leading Dutch burgher and mayor of New York from 1691 to 1695, was formerly situated in Bowling Green. After the renovation of the late 1970s, de Peyster was "banished" to Hanover Square. Except for the Bowling Green Offices at left, not one building survives from the time this photo was taken about 1900. (Museum of the City of New York)

A lithograph of Wall Street looking east from Trinity Church in 1834. In the distance is the cupola of the Merchants' Exchange, destroyed the following year in the Great Fire of 1835. (The J. Clarence Davies Collection, Museum of the City of New York)

Looking west on Fulton Street across Broadway in 1892, horsecars have been replaced by electric trolleys, but Dobbin still reigns. In the background are the Sixth and Ninth Avenue els. (American Telephone & Telegraph Company)

The former Equitable Building on Broadway, between Cedar and Pine streets. The Second Empire–style structure, built in 1872, was destroyed in a spectacular fire which burned for three days in January 1912. A replacement, completed in 1916, caused objections due to its sheer bulk, leading to a drastic revision in the building code. (King's Views of New York, 1909)

Firefighters work in vain to save the Equitable Building. The conflagration had begun in the basement Café Savarin and quickly engulfed the entire structure. (Museum of the City of New York)

Equitable founder Henry B. Hyde seems to be contemplating the destruction of the lobby. Only slightly damaged, the statue by J. Q. A. Ward now graces the lobby of the Equitable Center, 787 Seventh Avenue, uptown. (Equitable Life Assurance Society of the United States)

A mid-1880s advertisement for loft space in the headquarters of a predecessor of the New York Telephone Company (then located on the north side of Cortlandt Street between Broadway and Church Street). The Romanesque Revival–style building was one of several newly opened exchanges. (American Telephone & Telegraph Company)

Castle Garden in 1870 when it served as the State Emigrant Landing Depot. Millions of immigrants passed through its portals between 1855 and 1890, when a new center was opened on Ellis Island. (New-York Historical Society)

In this lithograph by Nathaniel Currier, "Swedish Nightingale" Jenny Lind makes her American debut on September 11, 1850, as P. T. Barnum inaugurates Castle Garden as the city's leading showplace. The structure has now been restored to its original appearance as Castle Clinton National Monument. (New-York Historical Society)

A Sunday promenade along the Battery in an 1830 engraving, depicting Castle Clinton to the right, and Castle Williams on Governors Island across the busy harbor to the left. (New-York Historical Society)

The City Hall area from atop the American Telephone & Telegraph Company Building, ca. 1917. In front of the lofty Woolworth Tower (the tallest skyscraper in the world at the time) is the Second Empire–style "Mullett" Post Office which virtually obscures City Hall from view. To the left rear are the "Tweed" Court House and twin wings of the Emigrant Industrial Savings Bank. To the right, the massive Municipal Building faces the diminutive Probate Court Building. Farther to the right are the twin cupolas of the Park Row Building, just beyond the narrow St. Paul Building in the right foreground. (American Telephone & Telegraph Company)

ship which they called the *Onrust* (Restless), and returned to Holland. One can only admire these stalwart men who with their bare hands were able to fashion a seaworthy vessel from the trees of the forest and sail it thousands of miles safely across the rough Atlantic.

Nieuw Amsterdam as a permanent settlement was established in 1625, and one year later, Peter Minuit made his famous purchase from the Indians. In 1664 the Colony was captured by the English and named for the Duke of York. For a few months in 1673 the Dutch regained control, but they lost it again to Britain.

Several yards further east and closer to the Promenade is the Norwegian Merchant Marine Memorial, consisting of a plaque and boulder. It honors the merchant mariners of Norway who served on ships of many nations during World War II.

A short distance to the east, and a bit further into the park, is the **Wireless Operators Memorial Monument,** dedicated to those radiomen who went down with their ship. A new name is added with each tragedy, and some are quite recent. Note the name of Jack Phillips, the wireless operator of the *Titanic*, which struck an iceberg on her maiden voyage to America and sank on the night of April 14–15, 1912, with a loss of 1,517 out of 2,000 passengers.

Walk out on the **Admiral George Dewey Promenade,** at the water's edge. Considered the finest view in the city, the broad panorama includes (from left to right) Brooklyn Heights, Governors Island, distant Staten Island, the Statue of Liberty on Liberty Island, Ellis Island with its former immigration depot, and the New Jersey harborfront. And in the bay is the constant parade of ships of all types, which bring the harbor to life. Turning around, the view of the lower Manhattan skyline, now somewhat obscured by modern, and rather uninterest- ing, additions, is awesome. The finest view, of course, is from the Staten Island Ferry or from the Statue of Liberty excursion boat.

Facing the Promenade is the **East Coast War Memorial** (William Gehron and Gilbert Seltzer, 1960), which honors the 4,596 seamen, soldiers, and air- men lost in the American coastal waters of the North Atlantic during World War II. All the names are carved into the eight granite pylons. In the center is an immense sculpture of an American Eagle by sculptor Albino Manca, unveiled in 1963 by President Kennedy.

Continuing to the east, the dramatic **Coast Guard Memorial** stands facing the bay. It depicts two men supporting a wounded comrade. The eight-foot bronze sculpture group was erected after World War II through one-dollar con- tributions from every Coast Guard member to help defray the $25,000 cost. There was some controversy at the time as to whether the work met the Municipal Art Commission's artistic standards, but under pressure from then Parks Commissioner Robert Moses, it was approved. Sculptor Norman M. Thomas was himself a Coast Guardsman and served in the war.

Look to the left, in the center of the large open field, called the Eisenhower Mall, is the impressionistic Cor-Ten steel sculpture, *Peace,* by Charles (Chuck) Ginnever (1970). Its title is represented by a peace symbol.

Follow the Promenade eastward to the end, and walk north on the park side of State Street.

A **new Whitehall ferry terminal,** to replace the one which burned in 1992, is scheduled to be completed in 1998. In a design competition for the new Staten Island ferry terminal, the winning entry was submitted by Philadelphia architects Robert Venturi and Denise Scott Brown, in association with the Manhattan firm of Anderson/Schwartz Architects. The plan calls for a barrel-vaulted structure of green-tinted glass, and in deference to the past, the south wall (facing the harbor) will have a full-scale painted rendering of the adjacent 1907 Battery Maritime Building. The waiting room will boast a 125-foot ceiling with panoramic views of the bay, a SONY Jumbotron television sign, and possibly direct connections to the Battery Maritime Building and Battery Park. An unusual addition will be a typical Venturi touch—a 120-foot-high clock, the largest in the world—dominating the south side (twice the size of the Colgate clock on the Hoboken waterfront). Ferry commuters doubtless will be delighted to learn that they are late again as the ferry arrives in the morning mist.

To the left of the Staten Island Ferry Terminal is the **Battery Maritime Building,** originally Municipal Ferry Piers (Walker & Morris, 1907), the last surviving ferry building on the East River. It was the terminal for ferries to Brooklyn until 1938, and now serves the Governors Island Ferry.

At approximately the site of the Governors Island Ferry slip was the point of embarkation in Dutch Colonial times for ships sailing to the mother country or to other distant points. The little wharf was soon called **Schreijers Hoek** (Weepers' Hook), since the perils of a long sea voyage threatened the safe return of loved ones. The name was taken from the *Schreijerstoren* (Weepers' Tower) on the Amstel River in Amsterdam, where relatives bade a tearful farewell to those departing on distant journeys.

Just inside the park fence is the **Oyster Pasty Mount Cannon,** a relic from English Colonial days which was uncovered during building excavations. The Oyster Pasty was a derisive name given to the battery mounted near a pile of oyster shells.

Cross Peter Minuit Plaza.

The flagpole in the mini-park is New York City's tribute to the first group of Jews to arrive at these shores in 1654—23 men, women, and children, refugees from the Inquisition in Brazil. Attempting to return to Holland, their ship was taken by a Spanish pirate who in turn was captured by a French privateer. Pledging their possessions to the French captain, they were brought to Nieuw Amsterdam, where Peter Stuyvesant gave them a less-than-cordial welcome, but permitted them to stay. The townspeople paid off the captain, allowing the refugees to discharge their debt and keep the clothes on their backs. Practicing their religion privately, the small group of Sephardic Jews was later able to rent a room for services in a windmill, and ultimately built the first synagogue in America in 1730 on Mill Street (now South William Street), about one-quarter mile north.

Peter Minuit Plaza is named for one of the first Dutch governors, who purchased the Island of "Manhattes" in 1626 from the Reckagawawanc Indians (who didn't really own it anyway, as the concept of private land ownership was foreign to them), for an amount of trinkets valued at 60 guilders, or about $24.

At 7 State Street the former **James Watson House** is now the **Shrine of the Blessed Elizabeth Ann Seton,** the first American-born saint. Mother Seton (1774–1821) was the founder of the American Sisters of Charity, the first order of nuns in the United States. She is also credited with the establishment of the American Catholic parochial school system. Mother Seton was elevated to sainthood in September 1975. The house is a lone survivor of a magnificent row of elegant Federal mansions that lined State Street. Note the freestanding slender Ionic columns and the Georgian details. The building is completely original, and was built in the early 1800s, probably by John McComb, the architect of City Hall. What a splendid sight the long colonnade must have presented to approaching ships. The church of Our Lady of the Rosary, adjoining the shrine, occupies the site of a former residence of Mother Seton.

No. 17 State Street (Emery Roth & Sons, 1987) is a striking, if somewhat jarring, addition to the lower Manhattan skyline. In the shape of a quarter cylinder, its 44 stories of silver reflecting glass and anodized aluminum loom high over Battery Park. The building's curved contour was determined by its plot, which coincidentally follows closely the original 17th-century shoreline. It is another *tour de force* by developer Mel Kaufman, although less zany than his 127 John Street or his Disney-like setting for 77 Water Street. [*See* both in Chapter 2.] The site, until 1985, was occupied by the romantically designed and much cherished Seamen's Church Institute; and in 1819 it was the birthplace of author Herman Melville. Enter the shiny, hi-tech lobby where glass-enclosed elevator shafts disappear skyward—the first time this system has been employed. Compare the bold design of this building with that of its bland, box-like neighbor to the north, No. 1 Battery Park Plaza. Both were designed by the same architectural firm, but the latter was built 16 years earlier.

In the courtyard behind 17 State Street is **New York Unearthed,** a unique little museum dedicated to New York City's archaeological heritage; there, remains of the past tell the story of the city's history. The museum has two levels (one below ground), on one of which there is an interesting "time-line" depicting what was unearthed under the city's streets every few decades, eventually displaying artifacts excavated from the Dutch Colonial period. One can watch a conservator at work and even enter a darkened "elevator" and descend on an imaginary trip below Wall Street to experience an archaeological "dig." The museum, a program of the South Street Seaport Museum, was financed in part by the developers of 17 State Street, to compensate for their not having conducted the required archaeological study before excavations were begun on their building. (Open Mon.–Sat. 12:00 noon to 6:00 P.M.; free.)

Walk one short block down Pearl Street to Whitehall Street.

No. 33 Whitehall Street, to the left, is another new behemoth, the 30-story **Broad Financial Center** (Fox & Fowle, 1986), its dark-blue reflecting façade described as "a two-sided butt-glazed curtain wall." The postmodern indented walls give welcome relief from the architectural doldrums of the 1950s and '60s that is so evident in the dull array of skyscrapers that mushroomed along the waterfront and obscured the picturesque New York City skyline. The lofty blue and gray granite lobby is stark and overwhelming, dominated by four tall stone pylons mounted on polished black granite spheres supporting gilt metal globes; and on the bare stone wall, a clock of enormous proportions.

Much less interesting is its neighbor to the south, **No. 39 Whitehall Street,** a huge unimaginative cube sheathed in dark-green reflecting glass. The building, in a new skin, is the 1880s U.S. Army Building, remembered for its Induction Center and the anti-draft demonstrations of the Vietnam War era.

Return to State Street and turn right along Battery Park.

The little subway entrance building on the park side is one of the last remaining kiosks of the city's first subway system, and is known as the **Battery Park Control House.** The name derives from the original concept that once passengers had entered the building they were under the control of the transit company. The structure was built in 1904–05 in French Beaux Arts style from plans by Heins & LaFarge, the first architects of the Cathedral Church of St. John the Divine.

End of tour. Walk up State Street to the Bowling Green station of the Lexington Avenue subway. Take any northbound train two stops to Fulton Street for connections to other subways.

BROADWAY

ANN ST.

Start

FULTON ST.

DUTCH ST.

WILLIAM ST.

JOHN ST.

GOLD ST.

RIDERS AL.

FULTON ST.

BEEKMAN ST.

WATER ST.

FONT ST.

CLIFF ST.

PEARL ST.

PLATT ST.

Schermerhorn Row

LIBERTY ST.

NASSAU ST.

FLETCHER ST.

MAIDEN LANE

CEDAR ST.

Federal Hall

PINE ST.

DE PEYSTER ST.

FRONT ST.

SOUTH ST.

South

WALL ST.

EXCHANGE PL.

HANOVER ST.

WATER ST.

GOUVERNEUR LA.

SOUTH STREET VIADUCT (F.D.R. DRIVE)

NEW ST.

BROAD ST.

HANOVER SQ.

BEAVER ST.

OLD SLIP

OLD SLIP

East River

MILL LA.

S. WILLIAM ST.

STONE ST.

CUYLERS AL.

MARKETFIELD ST.

COENTIES AL.

COENTIES SLIP

Downtown Heliport

STONE ST.

WHITEHALL ST.

BRIDGE ST.

PEARL ST.

MANHATTAN'S FINANCIAL DISTRICT

2. Manhattan's Financial District

[Broadway–Seventh Avenue line to Fulton Street; A and C lines to Broadway–Nassau Street; M, J, Z lines to Fulton Street; Lexington Avenue Express to Fulton Street; M6, M15, M101, M102 buses to Broadway and Fulton Street]

The walking tour begins at the corner of Fulton and Nassau streets.

The Nassau Street Mall is a lively market with a variety of shops. In the years prior to World War II, Nassau Street was synonymous with philately, as most New York stamp dealers were located here. On the northwest corner is the startling, multicolor, cast-iron **Bennett Building,** erected in 1872 from plans by Arthur D. Gilman. Originally six stories high, it was raised to ten in 1888. Especially attractive is the texture of the façade with its recessed windows and curved glass corner windows. The building is named for the James Gordon Bennett family that published the sensationalist New York *Herald* whose building stood behind it.

Walk east on Fulton Street, past William Street—once known as "Insurance Row," where so many large insurance companies had their offices—to Gold Street.

Turn right on Gold Street.

A few yards down Gold Street, on the right side and almost hidden among its neighbors, is a surprising relic of the beginning of the mechanical age—the **Excelsior Power Company** building. Completed in 1888 from plans by William G. Grinnell, it was one of the city's first power houses. The whine of the huge dynamos has long been silenced, and the sturdy Romanesque Revival Industrial-style building has been converted into a co-op. Excelsior Power built the plant just six years after Thomas Edison inaugurated the world's first electrical generating station, a few blocks away at 225 Pearl Street.

Looking east on Fulton Street toward the Fulton Ferry Terminal about 1900. The Fulton Fish Market building, to the left, is long since gone, but the gabled-roof block across the street, known as Schermerhorn Row, survives from the first decade of the 19th century, and is a designated landmark—the focus of the South Street Seaport Area. (South Street Seaport Museum)

Walk up the little cobblestoned lane, called **Ryder's Alley,** which makes an abrupt left turn, returning to Fulton Street. The street is named for Robert Ryder, an English surveyor during the Colonial Period.

The Southbridge Towers housing project was completed in 1972. The plans originally called for enormous high-rise apartment houses, but the city fathers felt that such height would overwhelm the adjacent South Street Seaport area. The modified plan by Gruzen & Partners is a pleasant blending with the surroundings, with considerable "breathing space."

At the corner of Water and Fulton streets is New York's "fun skyscraper," known only by its official address, **127 John Street.** Walk around the building and into the lobby. According to the owners, it is designed "to create an atmosphere of pleasure, humor, and excitement for people." See for yourself, as you relax for a moment on the north-side sun deck; then enter through the main entrance's neon-lit "vacuum cleaner pipe" and step into either a red or blue elevator. Set your watch by the world's largest digital clock mounted on the east wall. Note, too, the iron "bicycle rack" sculpture and *Telephone Booth* by Albert Wilson; and from a distance, the gaily painted adornments up to the roof's water tank. The clock was built as an extension of the wall to hide an old building whose owner would not sell to complete the land parcel. The imaginative building, with all its novel amenities, was designed by Emery Roth & Sons in 1972, and the amusing and creative sidewalk and ground-floor adornments are the work of developer Mel Kaufman, who also planned the pedestrian areas of 17 State Street and also 77 Water Street (to be seen later). The lobby and plaza were designed by Rudolph de Harak. The site was occupied in the mid-19th century by the famous United States Hotel.

The Titanic Memorial Tower marks the entrance to the South Street Seaport. This memorial to the 1,517 victims of the *Titanic* who perished when the "unsinkable" liner struck an iceberg and sank on the night of April 14–15, 1912, was erected by public subscription in 1913 and stood atop the old Seamen's Church Institute Building on South Street until 1967. The time ball at the top of the lighthouse would drop down the pole to signal the hour of twelve noon to the ships in the harbor, its mechanism activated by telegraph signal from the National Observatory in Washington, D.C.

The South Street Seaport Historic District is a 19th-century waterfront area that survives almost intact. The entire seaport area was redeveloped by the Rouse Company, whose restorations of Boston's Quincy Market and Baltimore's Harborplace have been highly acclaimed.

Begin your visit at the **Museum Visitors' Center** at 12 Fulton Street, where you can pick up the free *Map & Guide* to all points of interest. You may explore the streets, markets, shops, and piers on your own, but to visit the historic ships and some exhibits, as well as boat tours, there is an extra fee. Admission fees are: $6.00 adults, $5.00 seniors or students, $4.00 children, under 6 free. Hours:

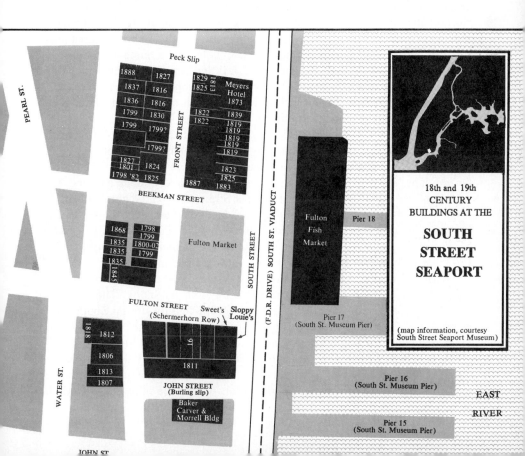

18th and 19th CENTURY BUILDINGS AT THE

SOUTH STREET SEAPORT

(map information, courtesy South Street Seaport Museum)

daily 10 A.M. to 4 P.M., phone (212) 669-9400. There are also harbor cruises aboard the excursion boat *DeWitt Clinton,* the sidewheeler *Andrew Fletcher,* and the schooner *Pioneer.*

The following is a suggested itinerary: On leaving the Visitors' Center, stop at nearby **Bowne & Co., Stationers,** a re-creation of a 19th-century printing establishment and a working commercial enterprise. Then browse in the adjacent **Book & Chart Store** with its fine collection of nautical literature and memorabilia. To the left is the **Museum Gallery and Museum Library.** The Museum features changing exhibitions on maritime New York.

Return to Fulton Street and turn left. In this same Museum Block is **Cannon's Walk,** a narrow court between the 19th- and 20th-century buildings, opened to the public in 1983, with a variety of shops. As you emerge on Front Street, turn right, back to Fulton Street.

The corner building of the same block is called the **New "Bogardus" Building.** It is a re-creation based on New York's first cast-iron building, the Edgar Laing Store of 1848. [*See* photo of the original on page 177.] To the left, across Front Street, is the huge **Fulton Market Building,** erected in 1983 on the site of three earlier markets, the first built in 1822. The present Market with its several floors of shops and restaurants recalls the time when the old market featured butchers, fishmongers, vegetable dealers, and dairymen.

Across Fulton Street is **Schermerhorn Row,** the heart of the Seaport. Built in 1811–12, this row of peaked-roof buildings, lovingly restored as the centerpiece of the Seaport project, is the only surviving block of Georgian-Federal–style and Greek Revival commercial structures in the city. When the area prospered in the Great Age of Sail, these structures housed a number of industries serving the sea, with ships' chandleries, sail and rope lofts, and naval-store warehouses. The Row is named for its original developer, Peter Schermerhorn.

Return to Front Street and turn right. Just north of Beekman Street is the brand-new **Seamens' Church Institute**.

At the northeast corner of Beekman Street (**No. 142,** or 211 Front Street) is an unusual building. It was designed by George B. Post (later architect of the Stock Exchange) and served the fish market area since 1885. Note the starfish tie-rod caps, the cockleshell cornice, and terra-cotta keystones adorned with fish. Continue north on Front Street to Peck Slip, where on the north side of the street is a **Con Edison substation** disguised behind a fantastic trompe l'oeil by Richard Haas of a Greek Revival arcade through which the Brooklyn Bridge can be "seen." The adjacent building to the right is the **Jasper Ward Store,** built in 1807, ten years before Peck Slip's waterfront was filled in.

Turn right, and at the corner of South Street is the old Victorian-style **Meyer's Hotel,** built in 1873 from plans by John B. Snook. The building, recently restored, represents a lustier era of 19th-century life on South Street when it was the great "street of ships." Walk south on South Street to Fulton Street and under the South Street Viaduct to the **South Street Seaport Piers.**

In the center of the main pier is the **Pilothouse,** originally the pilothouse of the steam tugboat *New York Central No. 31,* built in 1923. The tug moved barges loaded with railroad cars in New York harbor. Among the ships anchored at the

The Andrew Fletcher, *a replica of a 19th-century paddlewheel excursion steamboat, sails regularly from the South Street Seaport on tours of New York Harbor. (Photo by author)*

piers are the lightship *Ambrose,* the fishing schooner *Lettie G. Howard,* the wooden tugboat *W.O. Decker,* the schooner *Pioneer,* the full-rigged ship *Wavertree,* and the pièce de résistance of the Seaport, the 321-foot four-masted bark **Peking,** one of the largest sailing ships ever built. To the left is the multi-million-dollar **Pier 17 Pavilion,** erected in 1985. Standing on the site of the fish market's old piers, it contains a variety of retail establishments and restaurants, and offers an absolutely super riverside panorama! (Go up to the third floor and out onto the deck!)

From this excellent vantage point one can appreciate the majesty and architectural brilliance of the **Brooklyn Bridge,** considered by many to be the most beautiful ever built. [*See* page 432 of the Brooklyn Heights chapter for a description.]

Return to South Street, corner of Fulton Street. At No. 2 Fulton Street, in Schermerhorn Row, is the oldest seafood restaurant in the city, **Sweet's,** which still retains much of its 19th-century atmosphere. It was here that illegal slave traders, called "blackbirders," met during the last century to conduct their nefarious deals. Around the corner on South Street is a more modest yet colorful seafood establishment called *Sloppy Louie's.*

Walk south one block to John Street, originally called Burling Slip. To the right, at No. 171 John Street (1850), is the **former counting house of Abiel Abbot Low,** New York's first China Trade merchant. The building now serves as the Norway Galleries of the Museum. Its iron front was cast by Daniel Badger's Architectural Iron Works, and the façade is faced with brownstone.

During the "Great Age of Sail" of the mid-to-late 19th century, South Street was lined with the tall masts of graceful sailing ships from all over the world. Here, near Burling Slip, are a four- and three-master, loading cargo for far-distant ports. (South Street Seaport Museum)

Cross John Street (Burling Slip) to the south side.

Burling Slip, like so many former "slips" along the East River waterfront, is a reminder of the 18th and 19th century when they were docking areas. Other slips were James, Pike, Catherine, Beekman, Old, and Coenties. No. 170 John Street is the **former Baker, Carver & Morell Building,** erected in 1840. Originally a ship's chandlery, this attractive Greek Revival–style building, designed by Ithiel Town and Alexander Jackson Davis, may be the last commercial survivor of its type. It is faced with granite, with massive piers separating the windows. Since 1982 it has been a condominium.

Turn left (south) on Front Street.

Walking south on Front Street, we pass a trio of new skyscrapers begun in the winter of 1981–82. **One Seaport Plaza,** according to its architects, Swanke Hayden Connell, is designed as a "contextual" 34-story office tower with two distinctly different façades "in context" with its surroundings. The Front Street side is planned to be "reminiscent of another architectural era, echoing the mood of the 19th-century seaport community," while the Water Street side, with its polished granite face and ribbon windows, "is designed to be totally modern and compatible with its neighboring high-rise buildings in an urban environment."

Young boys enjoying an illegal dip "in the raw" at the Fulton Fish Market pier at the foot of Beekman Street, ca. 1892, apparently oblivious to the photographer, the man dragging the basket of fish, and the law banning swimming in the East River. Among the myriad sailing ships' masts in the background are the twin pilot houses of a Fulton Ferryboat. (New-York Historical Society)

No. 175 Water Street, a 30-story office building designed by Fox & Fowle, is the headquarters of the National Westminster Bank Group. During the excavation for the foundation, workers made a fascinating and important discovery. Buried in the mud only six feet below ground level they uncovered the complete hull of a mid-18th-century British merchant ship! The developer halted work and summoned archaeologists who, working under the supervision of the Landmarks Commission, rushed to learn as much as possible about the vessel. The 85-foot-long wooden hull belonged to a ship that had been scuttled some time between 1746 and 1755 to be used as part of a harbor landfill project extending Manhattan Island. The unexpected find attracted tens of thousands of visitors who waited in line for hours in the bitter cold for a view of the derelict ship, before it would disappear forever into the concrete foundations of the emerging skyscraper. The unusually shaped building is an example of the post-modern approach to high-rise construction, a welcome relief from the ubiquitous "glass boxes" that dominated architectural thought beginning in the 1950s.

The Continental Tower, 180 Maiden Lane, between Front and South streets, designed by Swanke Hayden Connell in 1982, is an even more dramatic example of post-modernism. A 41-story hexagonally shaped building, its blue-green reflective skin contrasts sharply with its neighbors.

Look up Pine Street to the towering **former Cities Service Building** (Clinton & Russell, Holton & George, 1932). When completed it was the third tallest building in the world (after the Empire State and Chrysler), and boasted

Archaeologists scramble over the hull of a derelict mid-18th-century British merchant ship, unearthed unexpectedly during the excavation for a new office tower at 175 Water Street, near the South Street Seaport. The ship had been scuttled and used for landfill, and remained undiscovered until the site was cleared in the late winter of 1982. (Fox & Fowle, Architects)

Charming Hanover Square was not enhanced by the Third Avenue El roaring overhead along Pearl Street. At the time this photo was taken in the early 1880s India House was then the Cotton Exchange, and the lower level was rented to commercial tenants. (Museum of the City of New York)

Looking north on New Street the morning after the Great Blizzard of 1888. The storm wreaked such havoc with the overhead wires that the City thereafter required all utilities to run their wires underground. (Museum of the City of New York)

At the turn of the century the Consolidated Stock Exchange operated briefly as a rival to the "Big Board," dealing mostly in mining stocks. The huge Greek Revival–style building stood at the southeast corner of Broad and Wall streets. (King's Views of New York, 1909)

Looking west on Wall Street, ca. 1890, from South Street to Trinity Church, with the Third Avenue El passing overhead at Pearl Street. To the right of the church is the cupola of the Gillender Building, now the site of the Bankers Trust Company Building at the corner of Nassau Street. (Museum of the City of New York)

novel double-deck elevators (since discontinued). Now called the American International Building, its 67 stories soar to a slender Gothic-style spire, illuminated at night.

At Maiden Lane, turn right to Water Street and turn south (left).

Water Street once was the commercial hub of a thriving waterfront. The street was widened some years ago to provide a much needed traffic artery. In the process, however, many lovely old buildings were lost, and nothing now remains from the 19th century.

Maiden Lane, translated literally from the Dutch *Het Maagde Paatje,* was the site of a freshwater stream where young maidens in the 17th century did their laundry. Look up Maiden Lane to the fortresslike Federal Reserve Bank.

A refreshing change from the usual uninspired "glass box" is No. 88 Pine Street, now known as **Wall Street Plaza,** a breezy, light tower of white-painted metal and large windows. Designed by James I. Freed of I. M. Pei Associates and completed in 1971, the building occupies a pleasant plaza, and with its see-through quality is ideally suited for a site close to the river. Look for the *Queen Elizabeth* plaque and two-piece mirrored sculpture by Yu Yu Yang, just to the south.

On the southeast corner of Wall and Water streets was the **Merchants' Coffee House,** built in 1740. It was a popular gathering place for Revolutionary War plotters, and the area became known as Coffee House Slip.

The northwest corner was the site of the **Tontine Coffee House,** erected in 1792. It was here that the Stock Exchange had its beginnings, with transactions taking place on the street under a buttonwood (sycamore) tree and later within the Coffee House, the present site of No. 70 Wall Street. The building at the northwest corner (No. 82 Wall Street) commemorates the site in its name, Tontine House.

Turn right on Wall Street to Pearl Street.

Pearl Street was originally the shore of the East River in Dutch Colonial times and is named for the mother-of-pearl oyster shells that were scattered along the beach. **No. 100 Wall Street** on the north side, and **No. 111** on the south, were built on landfill added in 1801. The Third Avenue El once followed the winding course of narrow Pearl Street.

Wall Street is the site of the original protective wall, built by order of Governor Peter Stuyvesant in 1653, at the northern limits of the town of Nieuw Amsterdam. At the site of Wall and Pearl streets, a blockhouse commanded the eastern end of the wall, and a large water gate was built between the blockhouse and the wall itself. It was called *'t Water Poort* to distinguish it from *'t Landt Poort* at Broadway. The Dutch referred to the path along the wall as *de Cingel* (the Rampart). The wall was a fortified palisade fence, not, as is commonly believed, to keep out hostile Indians, but to prevent an invasion by the English from the New England colonies. The fortification gradually deteriorated (helped by colonists who "borrowed" planks for house repairs and firewood), and as the city grew northward, it was demolished around 1695. In 1709 the area became a slave market and later a grain market.

No. 74 Wall Street, at the northwest corner of Pearl Street, was built for the Seamen's Bank for Savings in 1926 from plans by Benjamin Wistar Morris, but at this writing remains unoccupied. The handsome building has an attractive façade of multicolored seamed-face granite blocks, and upon completion was cited by the Downtown League as "the finest building of the year." The tall structure with its artistic setbacks cannot be categorized as belonging to any particular style, but the huge entrance arch is Romanesque in character, while the graceful upper buttresses are vaguely Gothic. Stretching a point, it might be called a very early example of Art Deco. Attractive are the low-relief blocks around the arch, representing nautical themes. The Seamen's Bank for Savings was the city's second oldest, chartered in 1829. Its original charter restricted banking activities to seamen only, in the belief that too many sailors were losing their hard-earned wages, accumulated during long sea voyages, in waterfront saloons as soon as their ships returned to port. When the building was dedicated, the directors decided to change the street address from 76 to 74 Wall Street, as some "old salts" who had been longtime depositors suggested that the combination of numbers totaling 13 "was a thing to make good seamen wary." A plaque on the building marks the site of the home of Edward Livingston, Secretary of State in 1831, who may hold the record in number of public offices held: senator, mayor, congressman, and minister to France.

Across Wall Street is **Barclay's Bank Building,** No. 75 (Welton Becket Assocs., 1987). At the rear corner and facing the mini-park behind are archaeological window displays showing artifacts from Colonial days that were discovered at the site prior to excavation as part of an archaeological study undertaken by the developers to comply with New York City's environmental laws, and overseen by the Landmarks Preservation Commission. Among the finds were items from backyard privies, cisterns, and house and building foundations from the late 17th to late 19th centuries.

Turn back (east) and take the first right to Pearl Street as far as Beaver Street.

Beaver Street honors the little furry rodent on which so much of early commerce depended. Beaver pelts were shipped in such large quantities, and figured so vitally in the early colony's business life, that the animal was incorporated into the seal of Nieuw Amsterdam and later into the seal of the City of New York. The corner building at **82–92 Beaver Street,** remodeled as "One Wall Street Court," was formerly the New York Cocoa Exchange, and now houses a branch of Dean & DeLuca's specialty food shop.

Turn right on Pearl Street to Hanover Square.

Pearl Street marked the eastern edge of Manhattan during Colonial times, and although named for the mother-of-pearl oyster shells found in such abundance along the shore, it was more often called the Strand.

Hanover Square is an attractive oasis among the towering canyons of lower Manhattan. The intersection where Hanover, Pearl, Stone, and William streets meet Old Slip was originally a public common as far back as 1637, surrounded by elegant residences and situated very close to the river. At the site of nearby No. 119 Pearl Street, Captain (William) Kidd maintained a home. Captain Kidd was really not the pirate he was reputed to be. Although he was tried and hanged in England in 1701 for piracy, recent studies seem to indicate that he was an honorable sea captain who was the scapegoat of an unfair trial. Hanover Square, named for the royal house of England, is one of the few public places whose name was not changed during the Revolution, perhaps because George I was not disliked as much as his descendant, two Georges later. As the district became commercial, Hanover Square was the first "Printing House Square" of the city [*see* City Hall, "Old Newspaper Row," Foley Square, and "Five Points" Nos. 2, 3, 4]. It was here that New York's first newspaper, the *New York Gazette,* was published by William Bradford in 1725.

Dominating Hanover Square is the landmark **India House.** It was built in 1851–54 by Richard Carman, a carpenter, for the Hanover Bank. From 1870 to 1885 it housed the New York Cotton Exchange, and later W. R. Grace & Company. India House was organized as a private businessmen's club in 1914, and is dedicated to the furtherance of foreign trade. It contains a large collection of maritime artifacts and paintings in the charmingly reconstructed Marine Room. The lower floor of India House is occupied by *Harry's,* a restaurant popular with bankers and brokers. The brownstone exterior in Italianate style is reminiscent of a Tuscan villa.

Hanover Square was remodeled in 1978 and made into a pedestrian mall, and **the statue of Abraham de Peyster** (George E. Bissell, 1896) was moved here from Bowling Green. The carved legend in the base records the list of public offices held by de Peyster during his long career as a civil servant. (For some reason, de Peyster turns his back on the square, as he did at Bowling Green and Broadway.)

No. 7 Hanover Square, a 26-story office tower (Emery Roth & Sons, and Norman Jaffe, 1982), stands on the site of the old W. R. Grace & Company Building. Unable to find a tenant for its Florentine-style *palazzo* when the firm moved its headquarters uptown to 42nd Street in 1974, they demolished it, and the lot then lay "fallow" until later demand for office space brought a developer to the site. Had the need come a few years sooner, the lovely old predecessor might have had a new lease on life.

Walk east on Hanover Square to Water Street and turn left (north).

No. 77 Water Street, designed by Emery Roth & Sons in 1970, is another iconoclastic structure two years older than the same architect's 127 John Street building. Although the superstructure is not particularly engaging, the handling of the open lobby area and its "fantasies" is most pleasant, and is a credit to developer Mel Kaufman. Walk across the mini-stream's bridges, examine the metal sculptures, including *Rejected Skin,* by sculptors Rudolph de Harak and William Tarr (and indeed made from rejected parts of the building's aluminum siding). Visit Ye Olde Time Country Candy Store, and in little Bennett Park to the north, note the modern sculptures, *Helix* and *City Fountains*. One unique bit of sculpture is *not* visible, except to tenants of nearby taller buildings. Perched on the roof is an almost full-scale **model of a World War II biplane,** designed by Rudolph de Harak and executed by sculptor William Tarr in 1969. Alas, it is not open to the public. Walk around to the rear of the building and turn right to Old Slip.

The flashy building to the left (32 Old Slip) is one of the newer additions to the skyline. **Financial Square,** a 35-story structure designed by Edward Durrell Stone Associates and completed in 1987, displays alternating gray granite bands that open on a gradually widening gray reflecting-glass curtain wall. A fire house which once blocked Old Slip has been incorporated, garage-like, into the ground floor, leaving a pleasant open space for pedestrians as one of the required zoning amenities. Financial Square occupies the **site of the United States Assay Building,** built in 1930 and demolished in 1985.

In the center of Old Slip, where sailing ships once docked, is the **former First Precinct Police Station (100 Old Slip),** once called the "Old Slip Station." Built in the style of an Italian *palazzo,* it is a trim, solid Italian Renaissance–style structure of pleasing proportion, and was designed by Joseph Howland Hunt and Richard Howland Hunt in 1909. Now owned by the city, it is the new home of the Landmarks Commission.

Return to Hanover Square and turn left (south) into Pearl Street.

At the site of No. 81 Pearl Street, William Bradford (buried in Trinity Churchyard) installed **New York's first printing press** in 1693. Note the commemorative plaque.

On the southwest corner of Pearl Street and Coenties Alley once stood the **Stadt Huys,** the first City Hall. Built originally as the *Stadt Herberg,* or City Tavern, by Governor William Kieft in 1641, it was an imposing five-story stone structure—the tallest in town—overlooking the harbor. When Nieuw Amsterdam was granted its municipal charter 12 years later, New York's first hotel was converted into the *Stadt Huys,* and remained the seat of city government until 1699. Two years later a new City Hall was built on Wall Street (on the site of the present Federal Hall). Not long ago, when the buildings which occupied the site of Nos. 71 and 73 Pearl Street were removed, the *Stadt Huys*'s foundations were discovered underneath. A team of archaeologists studied and mapped the site before the plot was resurfaced. In addition to the foundation walls, the dig unearthed Delft and English pottery, fragments of Indian wampum, as well as clay pipes and wine bottles from Lovelace Tavern, built by Francis Lovelace, the second English governor of New York. The commercial building of the early 19th century which stood on the site of No. 71 was carefully dismantled, declared a landmark, and placed in storage pending re-erection at the South Street Seaport. The old *Stadt Huys* served a number of functions, including a jail and debtors' prison, a courthouse, and a public warehouse. In front of the building, at the river's edge, stood the gallows, a pillory and stocks, and even a ducking stool, in which violators of the strict Dutch Reformed moral codes were tied and plunged repeatedly into the cold water of the East River.

and scale is destroyed by the towering buildings that surround the block and overwhelm it.

Turn right at Broad Street to Pearl Street.

At the corner of Broad and Pearl streets is one of our most cherished landmarks, **Fraunces Tavern.** A handsome neo-Georgian building, it is a splendid recreation of the Stephen DeLancey house, built in 1719. Except for some Dutch brick in the west wall, nothing remains of the original structure. Nonetheless, it is an excellent example of a formal English house of the 18th century. James DeLancey, a descendant of the wealthy merchant, lost all his family holdings by choosing the wrong side in the American Revolution, and suffered confiscation of his property. (Delancey Street on the Lower East Side is today the only physical reminder of the family name and the large estate he once owned in that part of Manhattan.) In 1757 the building became a warehouse, and five years later was purchased by Samuel Fraunces who converted it into the *Queen's Head Tavern.* Fraunces, a West Indian of French ancestry, operated the tavern successfully for a number of years and subsequently came into the employ of George Washington as his chief steward. What is now the New York State Chamber of Commerce was founded here in 1768, and just before the outbreak of the Revolutionary War, the Committees of Correspondence—soon to become the Continental Congress—held their first meeting at the tavern. On November 24, 1783, Governor Clinton gave a gala dinner here to celebrate the British evacuation of the city, and that December 4th, Washington bade his famous farewell to his officers in the Long Room on the second floor. During the 19th century, the tavern gradually deteriorated, suffered several fires, and fell victim to a number of unauthentic reconstructions. In 1904 the Sons of the Revolution of New York State purchased the building and spent three years restoring it to its present elegance. The **Fraunces Tavern Museum** conducts a wide variety of interpretive programs for young and old (phone 425-1778). There is also a library, a gift shop, and a charming ground-floor restaurant. (Open Monday to Friday, 10 A.M. to 4 P.M., and Washington's Birthday and the Fourth of July. Admission: adults $2.50, children, seniors, and students $1.00.)

Take a moment for a brief lesson in Georgian-style architecture by crossing the street and admiring the details: the slate hipped roof crowned by a balustrade, the tall chimneys, shed-roof dormers, a cornice set over a row of modillions, red brick walls with stone trim, and an ornate doorway flanked by classic columns and crowned by a pediment. The style was inspired by the north-Italian Renaissance as applied by the architect Palladio to many of the great Venetian and Lombardian villas.

On January 24, 1975, a bomb was exploded in the adjacent Anglers' Club, causing several deaths and many injuries. Allegedly placed by a Puerto Rican extremist group, the blast virtually destroyed the club, but luckily caused only minor damage to Fraunces Tavern.

Look back down Broad Street toward the river. At the corner of Water Street is the unusual and controversial 50-story **One New York Plaza,** designed in 1969 by William Lascaze and Associates. Its novel façade with recessed picture-frame windows has been called derisively "the waffle iron." To its left, **No. 4 New York Plaza,** just seen close at hand, is another monolith that altered (but did not improve) the city skyline during the building boom of the 1960s and '70s. But even with its fortresslike proportions it is somewhat less overwhelming. Perhaps Manufacturers Hanover Trust was seeking an appropriate corporate symbol.

On the triangular plot across Broad Street, bounded by Pearl and Bridge streets (No. 100), is one of the offices of the **New York Clearing House,** erected in 1962. The institution oversees the daily clearing of billions of dollars of member banks' checks. To the rear is the blue-glass Broad Financial Center.

Continue north on Broad Street.

Broad Street in Dutch Colonial days was a wide canal, called the *Heere Graft* (Great Canal), which extended inland from the East River as far as the present Exchange Place, with a small side canal up Beaver Street. (The broad dimensions of the old canal account for the disproportionately wide size of Broad Street today.) By 1676, the canal became polluted and rather malodorous, and was filled in. In its place, *Brede Straet* survives in translation to the present. It is interesting to note that unlike other north-south streets, the numbers on Broad Street *decrease* in a northward direction.

No. 85 Broad Street (Skidmore, Owings & Merrill, 1982) rises 30 stories and occupies what was once several blocks of low-rise 19th-century commercial buildings. The rough-textured surface of the office tower is precast concrete exposed aggregate. In making way for this giant, it was necessary to close diminutive Stone Street at Coenties Alley. At its front and rear entrances are bronze plaques set into the sidewalk showing the early street pattern. As you reach South William Street, notice how the "street wall" of the 85 Broad Street building has been designed to conform to the curvature of the winding street.

No. 67 Broad Street, the **International Telephone & Telegraph Building,** was erected in 1930 from plans by Louis S. Weeks. When opened, the building housed ITT's world-wide communications headquarters, including a number of subsidiary cable and telegraph companies that comprised its vast network. Above the recessed corner entrance is a fine mosaic depicting the hemispheres linked by radio communication.

Directly across the street, a narrow trellised plaza leads to the rear of No. 2 Broadway, where a plaque marks the **site of the first Huguenot church in New York.** Return to Broad Street and continue to Marketfield Street.

Another plaque at the entrance to tiny Marketfield Street marks the site of "the lost thoroughfare, Petticoat Lane." The diminutive street takes its name from the *Marcktveldt,* or Market Place, that once existed along the old canal. A market was held every Friday morning at the cattle bridge, one of several that crossed the *Heere Graft.*

Between Marketfield and Beaver streets stands the solid, Classic Revival–style **American Bank Note Company Building.** Before the establishment of the government's Bureau of Engraving and Printing, many security printers such as the American Banknote Company printed our paper currency, bonds, and postage stamps. The company, which traces its origin to 1795, still produces paper currency for many foreign countries and is the largest printer of securities in the world.

Turn left on Beaver Street to New Street.

No. 18 Beaver Street is an ornate survivor of the "Elegant '80s"—probably a fancy restaurant of yesteryear, better known as a dining saloon.

Nowhere else in the city can the expression **"The Canyons of New York"** be more dramatically visualized than from this point looking north on New Street. (Return to Broad Street.)

Walking up Broad Street, observe the variety of early 20th-century office buildings: No. 50 (Willauer, Shape & Bready, 1911); No. 37; and No. 25, the **Broad-Exchange Building** (Clinton & Russell, 1901), which when completed was the largest office building in the world.

Exchange Place, named for a merchants' exchange located here during the Dutch Colonial period, is one of the city's narrowest streets. The surprising little hill leading to Broadway gives it the dubious distinction of being the steepest street in downtown Manhattan.

Across from the Broad-Exchange Building, on the northeast side of Broad Street and Exchange Place, stood the **Old Ferry House** from which boats to Long Island shore points departed down the "Great Canal." Passengers were sometimes forced to spend the night here waiting for fair winds to make the trip. Looking up Exchange Place with its massed skyscrapers, it is hard to imagine that the area during the mid-17th century was a sheep pasture.

Approaching the end of Broad Street is one of the most famous panoramas of the financial center (left to right): **The New York Stock Exchange** (southwest corner), the **Bankers Trust Company** with its stepped pyramid atop the tower (northwest corner), **Federal Hall National Memorial** (northeast corner), and the **Morgan Guaranty Trust Company** (southeast corner).

The New York Stock Exchange (8 Broad Street), synonymous with Wall Street, is the largest securities exchange in the world. The "Big Board" lists more than 3,500 different stocks and bonds owned by about 30 million share- and bondholders. Transactions are printed on a nationwide ticker network and activity is centered on the trading floor, two-thirds the size of a football field, where member firms' telephoned orders to buy and sell are handled by 22 horse-shoe-shaped trading posts on the main floor and in annexes. The often hectic scene, which seems almost incomprehensible to the casual visitor in the gallery, is explained on the daily tours given by the Exchange. The enormous Classic-style building was completed in 1903 by George B. Post, with a 22-story addition in 1923 by Trowbridge & Livingston. The sculpture in the pediment is by John Quincy Adams Ward and Paul W. Bartlett. The busy Stock Exchange is a far cry from the old Tontine Coffee House and buttonwood tree of 1792, when 24 brokers drew up the original trading agreement. A reminder of those days is the little buttonwood tree planted in front of the Exchange.

Until the opening of the American Stock Exchange on nearby Trinity Place, some stock transactions were conducted along the sidewalks of Broad Street, with brokers or their representatives waving frenetic hand signals signifying "buy" or "sell" orders to correspondents in adjacent buildings. This very active "Curb Exchange" is now housed in the much more modern "Amex."

Federal Hall National Memorial, built in 1842 as the U.S. Custom House, is considered the Parthenon of public buildings in the city and possibly its finest Greek Revival–style building. Its predecessor on the site was our second City Hall, which replaced the *Stadt Huys* in 1701. It was here that Peter Zenger, editor of the *New York Weekly Journal,* was tried in 1735 for "seditious libels" against the royal government, and particularly against Governor William Cosby. His acquittal for printing the truth was the first major victory in the battle for a free press. Thirty years later, the Stamp Act Congress met to draft a Declaration of Rights and Grievances in which the colonists strongly protested the imposition by England of the Stamp Act. After this first public protest by a colony against "taxation without representation" and a subsequent boycott of the hated stamps, the British government repealed the tax. On July 18, 1776, the Declaration of Independence was read here. During the Revolutionary War, the occupying British forces used the City Hall as their headquarters. After the war, The Second Continental Congress met here in 1785, and two years later passed the Northwest Ordinance (explained on the building plaque to the left). In 1789 the building was renovated under supervision of Maj. Pierre L'Enfant, and for a little over a year it served as the Capitol of the United States. Congress met here for the first time on March 4, 1789, and as its first official act, counted the electoral ballots for President George Washington's unanimous election. On April 30, Washington was inaugurated on the steps of the renamed Federal Hall. **The statue of Washington,** sculpted by J. Q. A. Ward in 1883, stands at about the same place where Washington took his oath of office. Congress also adopted the Bill of Rights here on September 25, 1789, and sent it out to the states for ratification.

Unfortunately, the building later fell into disuse and was sold in 1812 for scrap for the sum of $425. In 1862, after 20 years as the Custom House, the present building became a branch of the Independent Treasury System. Of the six subtreasuries established, New York's was the most important and, as the Subtreasury Building, served until 1920. One of the old thick-walled vaults may be seen inside. Federal Hall was designed by Ithiel Town and Alexander Jackson Davis, under surveillance of John Frazee and Samuel Thomson, and is built of Westchester marble. The rather incongruously shaped **interior rotunda** (a circular space in a rectangular building) forms part of an extensive museum which should not be missed. [Federal Hall is open weekdays only, from 9:00 A.M. to 5:00 P.M.; enter on Pine Street.] It is one of seven national sites within the City of New York administered by the National Park Service of the Department of the Interior.*

---

*Castle Clinton National Monument, in Battery Park; The Statue of Liberty National Monument and Ellis Island; General Grant National Memorial, in Riverside Park at 122nd Street; Theodore Roosevelt Birthplace National Historic Site, 28 East 20th Street; Hamilton Grange National Memorial, Convent Avenue between 141st and 142nd streets; and Federal Hall National Memorial, Wall Street, corner of Nassau Street.

In 1826 this charming Greek Revival structure was built by the government as the New York branch of the Bank of the United States. Later, it became the Assay Office, and upon demolition in 1915 its dignified façade was carefully dismantled and later re-erected in the American Wing of the Metropolitan Museum of Art. A subsequent Assay Office occupied the site briefly, and the building was acquired by the now-defunct Seamen's Bank for Savings. (The Seamen's Bank for Savings)

The Morgan Guaranty Trust Company Building, across from Federal Hall, was formerly the offices of J. P. Morgan & Company, America's most powerful private bank. The austere building, completed in 1914 from plans by Trowbridge & Livingston, was the assumed target of an anarchist's bomb. At about noon on September 16, 1920, a horse-drawn wagon parked in front of the bank exploded, killing 33 passers-by (and the horse), and injuring scores of others. The devastating blast occurred during the post-World War I period of anti-radical hysteria, and was said by some to be an act of violence against "one of the strongest bastions of capitalism." Another theory is that the wagon belonged to an explosives manufacturing company, and had been traveling on a prohibited street when the dynamite accidentally ignited. Numerous scars from the explosion are plainly visible on the bank's façade—and for some reason, the bank has never made an effort to patch them up.

Continue east on Wall Street.

No. 30 Wall Street, formerly the Seamen's Bank for Savings, has an interesting architectural history. Its predecessor on the site, a lovely Greek

Revival–style building designed by Martin E. Thompson, was built in 1826 as the New York branch of the Bank of the United States. After ten years the building was turned over to private banking interests, and in 1853 it was acquired by the Federal Government for the Assay Office. In 1915, the structure—by now the oldest federal edifice in the city—was demolished, but its charming Tuckahoe marble façade was carefully dismantled and stored away, to be re-erected in 1924 outside the American Wing of the Metropolitan Museum of Art. With the opening of the new American Wing in 1980, the lovely façade is now the centerpiece of the gallery. A new Assay Office was constructed on the 30 Wall Street site from plans by York & Sawyer, supervised by James A. Wetmore, and was completed in 1919, "designed to last a thousand years." However, it remained only until another Assay Office was constructed at Old Slip (demolished in 1986), where Wetmore's experience was again called on for the design.

In 1955 the handsome building was purchased by the Seamen's Bank for Savings, which found the five underground floors of bullion vaults in excellent condition and preserved them for the bank's archives. The 1919 Assay Office building was considered one of the best examples of Renaissance-style architecture. Because of its quality and beauty and the architectural harmony with adjoining Federal Hall, it was decided to preserve this historic landmark and retain its limestone façade while an eight-story addition was erected above it. Architects Halsey, McCormack & Helmer incorporated the superstructure most successfully, proving that a good building need not be demolished when more space is required. In the lobby, to the right of the main banking rooms, are the original marble cornerstones of the 1826 and 1919 buildings. The building is now owned by a Japanese firm.

Across the street, at No. 37, is the Renaissance Eclectic–style building designed by Francis H. Kimball in 1907 for the Trust Company of America. At the time of its completion, it was the tallest on Wall Street.

Diagonally across Wall Street is lofty **40 Wall Tower,** built in 1929 for the Bank of the Manhattan Company. Designed by architects H. Craig Severance and Yasuo Matsui, it was planned to be the tallest building in the world. At the same time, Severance's former partner, William Van Alen, was completing the Chrysler Building uptown—also touted to become the world's tallest. The developing rivalry led Severance to add two feet to his 40 Wall Tower when it was announced that the Chrysler Building had reached its maximum height of 925 feet. To everyone's surprise (and Severance's chagrin), Van Alen's workmen secretly assembled a towering stainless-steel spire *inside* the building, and raised the Chrysler Building to a record height of 1,046 feet—the uncontested winner. Within nine months, however, Severance enjoyed the last laugh, as the newly completed Empire State Building rose almost 40 feet higher! The Bank of the Manhattan Company (since merged with the Chase National Bank to become the sprawling Chase Manhattan Bank) began its career as the city's first water supply company, a quasi-public utility known as **The Manhattan Company.** Founded by Aaron Burr in 1799, and chartered by the State Legislature, the company was the target of severe criticism from Alexander Hamilton, for the terms of the charter permitted it to engage in rather disparate financial pursuits, including banking. Hamilton saw this as an opportunity for Burr to gain banking privileges for his political party. This was one of the first confrontations between the two men that ultimately led to their tragic duel in 1804. The Manhattan Company did provide water to the growing city by means of pine-wood pipes bringing water from a reservoir on Chambers Street; however, banking became its primary interest. When the Croton Water System was opened in 1842, the Bank of the Manhattan Company became a financial institution exclusively, ultimately merging with the Chase National Bank to become today's Chase Manhattan Bank. Nevertheless, its assets are still "liquid." [*See* page 67.]

An exciting newcomer on the block is the striking **60 Wall Street,** headquarters of J. P. Morgan & Company. The 47-story tower, designed by Kevin Roche, Dinkeloo & Assocs., and completed in 1989, replaced an earlier 60 Wall Tower designed by Clinton & Russell in 1932, which was built as an extension of the still-extant 70 Pine Street. (The owners at the time wanted the more prestigious Wall Street address.) The new building sports a huge block-through atrium with trees and shops, and is open to the public seven days a week, 7:00 A.M. to 10:00 P.M.—an amenity that offers a moment of respite and relaxation. Note how the imposing gray granite arcade relates to the multi-columned façade of Citibank's landmark building across Wall Street. The view is particularly impressive from inside the atrium.

The imposing Classic façade of the **Citibank Building** at No. 55 (the southeast corner of William Street) is a dominant landmark on Wall Street. The original ground floor was built in 1836–42, from plans by Isaiah Rogers, as the Merchants Exchange. An earlier Merchants Exchange was destroyed in the Great Fire of 1835. From 1862 to 1907 it served as the Custom House after moving from its former Federal Hall site. When the Custom House at Bowling Green was opened, the vacant building was remodeled for the National City Bank by the firm of McKim, Mead & White [Stanford White was murdered the year before; *see* Madison Square, 11], and a second tier was added, doubling the size of the building. Note that the lower colonnade is Ionic, the upper, Corinthian. In designating the building a landmark, the New York City Landmarks Preservation Commission called it "a remarkable example of how a notable building can be sympathetically extended." The successor, the First National City Bank, now Citibank, chartered in 1812 and an outgrowth of the First Bank of the United States, still occupies the impressive structure.

Turn right into William Street, to the corner of Exchange Place.

Named for William Beekman, who came from Holland with Peter Stuyvesant (not for King William of England, as is commonly believed), **William Street** forms another of the deep, winding canyons that give the neighborhood so much atmosphere. Beekman's descendants settled farther uptown in the area now known as Beekman Place [*see* East River Panoramas, 6].

The 20 Exchange Place Building (also known as No. 22 William Street and No. 65 Beaver Street) is a striking 57-story limestone Art Deco shaft on an irregularly shaped base, designed by Cross & Cross and completed in 1931. Formerly the City Bank Farmers Trust Company and later the First National City Trust Company, it is now one of the major buildings of Citibank. The history of coinage is vividly displayed on plaques above the ground-floor windows (even our old Buffalo Nickel is there!). A "Bridge of Sighs" connects with the No. 55 Wall Street Citibank building. Although the street pattern is helter-skelter, the tower of the tall building conforms to the north-south city grid.

The west side of William Street, between Exchange Place and Beaver Street, recalls the late 19th century. **The Lords Court Building** (27 William Street and 40 Exchange Place) is a functional Renaissance-style structure of 1898 with the usual ornamentation found on the first skyscrapers built with structural-steel skeletons. **No. 11–15** was built in 1894 from plans by R.H. Robertson for the Corn Exchange Bank. The bank, whose interests at the time were primarily in corn and other grains, coffee, and cotton, merged in 1954 with the Chemical Bank. The impressive limestone building, with its Romanesque arch-topped windows, is alas, slated for demolition, as the permit for its razing was issued before the Landmarks Commission could consider it for designation. Hopefully the building's elegant façade can be incorporated into its replacement.

The famous **Delmonico's Restaurant,** at 56 Beaver Street, was founded in 1827 by Peter and John Delmonico, recent immigrants from Italy. In 1836 they built Beaver Street House for their establishment, which remained until the present building, designed by James Lord, replaced it in 1890. Although the original Delmonico's is long since gone, the present restaurant carries on the name and tradition. The establishment was always fashionable, and in Moses King's 1893 *Handbook of New York City,* it is described as "a familiar name among the epicures of two continents for nearly three-quarters of a century...where it will cost you from $3 upward for a good dinner" (a high price in those days!). The building was converted to residential apartments under the J-51 program, and Delmonico's was restored in 19th-century style.

Across William Street (now called South William Street), in the building whose prominent cupola sits above an indented corner, was originally the banking firm of J. & W. Seligman & Company and later the house of Lehman Brothers. The Renaissance Revival–style edifice was designed by Francis H. Kimball and Julian C. Levi and completed in 1907. Both former banking tenants are still in business, and the present occupant is the Banca Commerciale Italiana—an appropriate neighbor for Delmonico's.

Continue down South William Street to Mill Lane.

South William Street was originally called Mill Street, and near this site in 1626, the Dutch West India Company had erected a large mill. Not only did it grind flour, but its large upper room served as a house of worship for the first settlers until their Reformed Church was completed within Fort Amsterdam (on the site of the former Custom House). The room later served the first Jewish immigrants, who had arrived in 1653 but were not permitted to hold services until several years later. Two millstones from the old mill are preserved in the

Spanish & Portuguese Synagogue at 8 West 70th Street [*see* West of Central Park, 1]. It was here, too, that on August 29, 1664, the Dutch formally signed the document of surrender of Nieuw Amsterdam to the English.

The view down Mill Lane to Stone Street (visited earlier in the tour) is in sharp contrast to the surrounding tall buildings, and with a little squinting it is not difficult to imagine oneself back in the early 19th century.

Farther down South William Street, at No. 26, is the **site of the first synagogue in America,** built in 1730. A descriptive commemorative plaque on the building was stolen recently.

Return to Beaver Street, and proceed to Hanover Street and turn left.

Note again the coin motifs on the 65 Beaver Street entrance of the 20 Exchange Place Building, this time Biblical coins, as well as the transportation motifs of the 1920s on the bronze doors. The corner of the building at the juncture of Beaver and Hanover streets is the **site of the Great Fire of 1835** [*see* map].

At nine o'clock in the evening on December 17, fire broke out in the store of Comstock & Adams at 25 Merchant Street (the street has since been demapped). The temperature had dropped to a near-record 17° and a howling gale was blowing. The fire, caused by a gas-pipe explosion, spread rapidly to adjoining buildings and within minutes the blaze raged out of control, fed by stores of dry goods

The Merchants' Exchange ablaze during the Great Fire of 1835, the worst conflagration in the city's history. A valiant attempt was made to rescue the statue of Alexander Hamilton (seen in this lithograph brightly lit by the flames) but the cupola, tilting dangerously, collapsed through the roof and shattered the sculpture. (New-York Historical Society)

and chemicals and driven by the wind. Fire companies fought desperately but ineffectively to stem the conflagration, hampered by frozen hydrants and hoses that became clogged almost instantly with ice. As the fire advanced in both east and west directions, whole blocks seemed to erupt spontaneously into flames. By the early morning hours the blaze had engulfed almost every block to the East River from Wall Street to Coenties Slip, and west nearly to Broad Street. Help was summoned from as far away as Philadelphia, and pump wagons were hastily put aboard freight cars of the newly built railroad and transported to New York. It is said that the flame-reddened sky was visible from as far away as Camden, New Jersey, and New Haven, Connecticut. By noon the following day, the fire had consumed all of Hanover Square, including the merchandise that had been saved from threatened buildings and stacked for protection in the square. Adding to the horror were mobs of looters who converged on the area and overwhelmed the small police force in their mad scramble to steal what had not been burned. A supply of gunpowder was obtained from the Navy Yard in Brooklyn and rowed across the East River to blast a firebreak and hopefully to contain the still-roaring inferno. Fortunately, the masonry walls of the line of buildings along Wall Street helped contain the flames, although the magnificent Merchants Exchange, one of the city's commercial and architectural showplaces, was itself completely destroyed. By late December 18, the fire burned itself out, leaving an area of 17

The corner of Broad and Wall streets in 1882. In the center, the former New York Stock Exchange Building dominates Broad Street, and to the left are the banking offices of Drexel, Morgan & Company (now the site of the Morgan Guaranty Trust Co.). (The J. Clarence Davies Collection, Museum of the City of New York)

blocks—about 20 acres—a smoldering field of ashes, with the incredible loss of 674 buildings from the very heart of the financial district! The disaster was compounded by the total destruction of many fire insurance companies, which left their insureds with no chance of compensation. The 1835 fire was the worst in our young nation's history and completely obliterated every remaining Dutch Colonial building in the city. That is why there is not a single structure left in Manhattan from the 17th century. As if this were not enough, another fire ten years later destroyed 345 buildings in the same general area.

Continue on Hanover Street to Wall Street.

The building on the right, **No. 63 Wall Street,** is also decorated with coin plaques—drachmas of Ancient Greece on large plaques above the fourth floor.

Turn left on Wall Street to the northeast corner of William Street.

The view to Trinity Church down Wall Street is one of the best known scenes of New York. [Trinity Church is described in the tour of Lower Broadway, Battery Park City, and the Battery; *see* pages 14 to 16.]

*Wall Street in 1864, seen from the Subtreasury Building. In the rear is the Merchants'
Exchange, rebuilt after the Great Fire of 1835 (now sporting another story as the Citibank
Building), and the only building in the view still standing. (Museum of the City of New York)*

*A classic view of Wall Street, Trinity Church and the Subtreasury Building (now Federal Hall),
as seen in a magic lantern slide photo taken about 1875. (The Picture Decorator, Inc., N.Y.C.)*

The oldest commercial bank in the country is the **Bank of New York,** founded by Alexander Hamilton in 1784. Several plaques describe its history, including the story of its predecessor on the site, the United States Branch Bank. The original cornerstone of the Bank of New York has been reset several times for each new building in its history. A low-relief bronze plaque above the subway entrance, commemorating the famous Wall, includes an early map, and was placed there in 1909 during the Hudson-Fulton Celebration. The building, long a landmark in the lower Manhattan skyline, was designed in 1927 by Benjamin Wistar Morris. It is a graceful structure with a Georgian-style cupola and lantern best seen at a distance.

Turn right (north) on William Street to Pine Street.

To the left soars the 800-foot aluminum and glass **Chase Manhattan Bank,** set on one of the largest plazas in the city. When completed in 1960 it was the trendsetter for the series of plazas to follow, conforming to the revised zoning regulations requiring more street-level space. The plaza is elevated at the William Street end due to the topography. Take a few minutes and climb the stairs to the plaza level. The sunken circular courtyard with its fountain is paved with granite blocks in an unusual undulating form. It was originally planned to have fish and even dolphins in the fountain, but the idea was quickly abandoned because of the dangers of pollution (by air and people). Sculptor Isamu Noguchi is responsible for the innovative design, and Skidmore, Owings & Merrill for the towering 800-foot aluminum and glass shaft. Stand beneath the edge of the lofty building and listen as the wind plays delicate tunes on the vertical metal strips. Dominating the plaza is Jean Dubuffet's enormous free-form black and white sculpture, *Group of Four Trees,* the subject of considerable comment since its installation in 1972. A weekday visit to the building's concourse reveals an atomic clock run by gamma rays from its cesium power supply; and to the left of the lobby a charming Japanese garden. There are guided tours of the building (telephone for schedule), which include many antiques and works of art in the executive offices, as well as paintings from president David Rockefeller's private collection. The building also houses the world's largest bank vault, five levels below ground. The vaults are reputed to hold over $40 billion in securities, and just a few scant millions in cash. The bank is the successor of the Bank of the Manhattan Company and the Chase National Bank. The latter was named for Salmon P. Chase, Secretary of the Treasury in Lincoln's administration, and founder of our national currency system and federal banking system. (There was no government-issued paper money prior to 1861.) Chase Manhattan occupies the first 35 of the 60 stories above ground.

Continue north on William Street to Liberty Street.

The Federal Reserve Bank of New York, occupying the entire block between Liberty Street and Maiden Lane, is *the* great bank for banks—one of 12 of our Federal Reserve System. A Florentine *palazzo* that would have warmed

Intersection of William Street and Maiden Lane, looking west, ca. 1760. The site is now occupied by The Home Insurance Company Building. In this E. P. Chrystie drawing, a beer barrel is being lowered from the third floor of Rutgers' Brew House. During the British occupation of New York it was a storehouse. (The Home Insurance Company)

the heart of Lorenzo de' Medici, it is actually based on the design of the Strozzi Palace of the Italian Renaissance. Completed in 1924 from plans by York & Sawyer, the Federal Reserve Bank is a dramatic and imposing structure with its massive walls of rusticated Ohio sandstone and Indiana limestone, fortresslike machicolations, and extensive wrought-iron ornamentation. The lovely triple lanterns and the window grilles in the great arched windows were executed by Samuel Yellin. An enormous subterranean vault five stories below street level and protected by 90-ton doors contains gold bullion stored for many foreign governments; when trade balances are settled, gold is moved from one nation's room to another, rarely leaving the building. The tremendous volume of check handling and coin operations can be seen on visitors' tours, which begin in the impressive entrance lobby on Liberty Street (telephone 720-6130 for reservations). All paper currency issued by the Government through the New York branch of the Federal Reserve Bank bears the letter *B* on the face of each note. Bank notes issued by the Federal Reserve Bank in Boston have an *A*, Philadelphia, *C*, etc., through San Francisco, *L*. The Federal Reserve System, our nation's central banking establishment, was organized in 1913. All national banks must belong to a regional branch and keep a specific cash reserve on deposit. It is said that the vaults here house more gold than does Fort Knox.

Louise Nevelson Plaza, the triangular plot where Liberty Street joins Maiden Lane, and once the site of the Germania Life Insurance Building, has been remodeled into an outdoor gallery of the sculptor's work. *Shadows and*

Flags, made of Cor-Ten steel (1978), dominates the little plaza known as Legion Memorial Square.

No. 90 Maiden Lane, just a few feet down the street, is a strange "survivor" among its tall neighbors. A handsome four-story cast-iron-front building, designed in 1872 by Charles Wright, it shows to good advantage how cast-iron construction—the forerunner of the steel curtain-wall skyscraper—permitted large windows, unlike its masonry contemporaries.

Back across William Street is the 44-story **Home Insurance Company Building** (Office of Alfred Easton Poor, 1966), set on a neat plaza. A plaque in the triangular plaza marks the **site of Thomas Jefferson's residence** while he lived in New York City serving as the nation's first Secretary of State. New York was the seat of the federal government when Jefferson took office on March 21, 1790.

No. 100 William Street, on the northeast corner of Platt Street, is the city's first building to take advantage of the special 1970 zoning resolution that encouraged builders to create a covered pedestrian space as an alternative to the open plaza—outdoor space that was often uninspired and of minimal utilitarian design and, of course, subject to the vagaries of the weather. This 21-story building, sheathed in green slate, was completed in 1972 from plans by Davis, Brody & Associates with Emery Roth & Sons. Taking advantage of provisions of the new law, the architects have designed an impressive 80-foot *galleria,* cutting diagonally through the ground floor of the building, providing an attractive arcade between William and John streets. The arcade is lined with shops, lit in part by angular windows and light troughs. The building received the Award for Excellence in Design for 1973 from the New York Society of Architects. Walk through the stainless-steel, black glass, and slate *galleria* (open weekdays only).

Continue to the corner of John Street.

About a hundred yards to the east, at the present corner of John and Gold streets, was a small hillock covered with bright yellow flowers, which the Dutch had called *De Gouwenberg,* or Golden Hill. On January 18, 1770, it was the site of the first bloodshed between the colonists and the British army. Tempers had been running high since the imposition of the hated tax on tea, and particularly over the event of the previous night when soldiers knocked down a Liberty Pole and deposited the remnants in front of a tavern that was the meeting place of the Sons of Liberty. That afternoon several thousand citizens massed in "The Fields" near Broadway to vow punishment to any soldiers caught armed in the streets. The British reacted with taunts and ridicule, and after a series of provocative acts on both sides, a running brawl broke out between the mob and 20 British soldiers. Both groups retired to nearby Golden Hill where they were met by a detachment of regulars who opened fire on the civilians, killing one and wounding several. The encounter, known as the **Battle of Golden Hill,** occurred two months before the Boston Massacre and five years before the first major hostilities at Bunker Hill.

Turn left on John Street.

   The John Street United Methodist Church, 44 John Street, built in 1841, is the third on the site. The first Methodist church in America was built on this site in 1768, and traces its roots to John Wesley, the founder of Methodism. Under the leadership of Philip Embury and Barbara Heck, the congregation, which had been meeting in a rigging loft on Horse and Cart Street (now William Street), established the meeting house. Since that time, the building has been rebuilt twice, in 1818 and 1841, and was restored in 1965. Spend a moment and enjoy the intimate quality of the Georgian-style interior, including the original Wesley Chapel. Built in late Georgian style, the church is somewhat austere, yet cozy and inviting. Many of the original artifacts from the 1768 chapel still remain, including candelabra, John Wesley's great clock, foot warmers, and Embury's hand-carved pulpit. Climb the staircase to the gallery for a good perspective of the interior. There is a little museum which is open Mon., Wed., Fri., 11:30 A.M.–3:00 P.M. (A voluntary contribution would be appreciated.) The small brownstone church is a delightful surprise in the bustling financial district.

   One Federal Reserve Plaza, officially 33 Maiden Lane, is a striking (some say outrageous) example of the post-modern style. The 26-story office tower with cavernous lobby was designed by Philip Johnson and John Burgee in 1985 to be contextual with the adjacent Federal Reserve Bank. Unusual are its *donjon* towers with crenellated roof parapets, creating a castle-like effect.

End of tour. The subway entrance is in the lobby. On weekends walk one block north on Nassau Street to Fulton Street, then left to Broadway.

Broadway Chambers

(A. T. Stewart's "Marble Palace") (Later Sun Bldg.) 15

clock

16

CHAMBERS ST.

ELK ST.

Hall of Records 19

CENTRE ST.

Municipal Bldg. 1

Police Pla 20

WARREN ST.

Tweed Court House 17

IRT 2

APPROACHES

TO Park Row

BROOKLYN BRIDGE

Home Life Bldg. 14

City Hall 18

Horace Greeley

Nathan Hale

MURRAY ST.

3 Pace Univ.

(Frankfort St.)

City Hall Park 13

4 Benjamin Franklin

Newspaper Row (c. 1895):

Staats-Zeitung

PARK PL.

SPRUCE ST.

World

(Mail St.)

Daily Recorder

Potter Bldg. 5

Am. Tract Soc. Bldg.

Sun

Woolworth Bldg. 12

Site of "Mullett" Post Office

Tribune

Evening Telegram

BROADWAY

BEEKMAN ST.

Evening Journal

BARCLAY ST.

PARK ROW

American

Transportation Bldg.

6

THEATER ALLEY

NASSAU ST.

Times

N.Y. County Lawyers Bldg. 11

Park Row Bldg. 7

Press

Evening Post Bldg.

Daily News

VESEY ST.

Globe & Commercial Advertis

ANN ST.

St. Paul's Chapel 9

Herald

Evening Post

Mail & Express

FULTON ST.

8

10

CITY HALL AREA
AND
"NEWSPAPER ROW"

3. City Hall, Old "Newspaper Row," Foley Square, and "Five Points"

[Lexington Avenue Line to Brooklyn Bridge station; Nassau Street J, M, Z lines to Chambers Street; M6, M15, M101, M102 buses to City Hall]

The tour begins at Centre and Chambers streets.

1. Classic in style and original in design, the imposing **Municipal Building** is our greatest civic skyscraper and the focus of the new Civic Center plan. In scale it is complementary to nearby City Hall as well as to the modern counterparts mushrooming about it. Built in 1914 from plans by McKim, Mead & White, it now houses only a fraction of the city offices which oversee the functioning of the metropolis. Particularly attractive is the row of freestanding columns, the extensive sculpture work, and the lofty colonnaded tower topped by Adolph A. Weinman's 25-foot high gilt statue of *Civic Fame.* Pause for a moment to examine the sculpture: on the north arch, *Progress*; on the north panel, *Civic Duty*; on the central arch, *Guidance* and *Executive Power*; on the south panel, *Civic Pride*; and on the south arch, *Prudence.* Between the windows on the second floor are symbols of the various city departments. Note the collection of plaques, among which is the "triple-X" emblem of the city of Amsterdam, Holland. A lavish subway entrance is incorporated into the south section, under a vaulted ceiling. Chambers Street, which originally passed through the building, is now closed to vehicular traffic and forms a part of a pedestrian mall leading to Police Plaza. (We will return later after a loop around City Hall Park.)

Cross Centre Street to City Hall Park.

2. Go down the subway stairs directly in front of the Greeley statue. At the foot of the staircase, mounted on the right-hand wall, are three enormous bronze plaques honoring those responsible for the construction of **"The First Municipal Rapid Transit Railroad of the City of New York."** The subway, a brainchild of financier August Belmont, took four years (and three mayors) to build (1900–04). The first station, City Hall, is no longer in service, although local No. 6 trains still rumble past it on a loop underneath City Hall Park. The original line followed the present Lexington Avenue route to Grand Central, swung west under 42nd Street to Times Square, then north on Broadway to 145th Street.

The **statue of Horace Greeley** in the park was executed in 1890 by John Quincy Adams Ward, and was moved here from its former site in front of the Tribune Building in 1916. Ward was the first American sculptor not trained abroad. His sculpture is typical of post–Civil War realism and captures the relaxed attitude, moon face, and odd beard of the *Tribune's* founder. The base is by Richard Morris Hunt. Horace Greeley (1811–1872) founded the New York *Tribune,* which he edited for 30 years. The newspaper was published in a building across Park Row designed by Richard Morris Hunt in 1873 (*see first photo in this chapter*). Greeley was an outspoken reformer and fighter for social justice. He attacked slavery, championed women's rights, promoted labor unions, fought railroad monopolies, promoted westward expansion ("Go West young man, go West!"), and waged an unsuccessful campaign for the presidency, losing to Grant in 1872.

In front of Horace Greeley is a **replica of one of the original subway entrance kiosks,** although this one is designed to provide elevator service to the subway station below (4, 5, and 6 lines). Note the bishop's crook lampposts around and in back of City Hall.

Continue south about 100 yards.

3. Across Park Row (Centre Street joins it at this point), where modern Pace University is situated, was the beginning of the so-called **"Newspaper Row"** from the 1840s till after the turn of the century. In the year 1893, for example, there were 19 daily newspapers printed in the City of New York plus a score of foreign-language papers. In the year 1993, there were only four, yet the population of the city has grown from a million and a half in 1893 to almost five times that number!

Where the Municipal Building's south section is now was the site of the building of the *New-Yorker Staats-Zeitung,* the largest German-language newspaper in the country (and still publishing). To the right of the intertwining ramps of the Brooklyn Bridge stood the 26-story gold-domed *New York World,* the tallest building in the world when completed in 1890. Designed by George B. Post, the "World Tower" was a dominant feature of the lower Manhattan skyline. After Joseph Pulitzer purchased the *World* seven years earlier, the newspaper soon became one of the most literate and influential in the city.

City Hall and its panorama of newspaper office buildings around 1910. Center to right, the domed World, *the diminutive* Sun, *and Richard Morris Hunt's Tribune Tower. The* Times *had moved uptown from the large building at the right. Between City Hall and the* World *is the Park Row terminal of the Second Avenue El, connected to a large iron train shed serving Brooklyn Bridge trains. Note the kiosk entrance to the now-abandoned City Hall subway station (although trains still roll by its darkened platform underneath). (New-York Historical Society)*

Immediately to its right, across narrow Frankfort Street, stood the **Sun Building.** The *Sun* really "shone" after its acquisition by Charles Anderson Dana, becoming the city's first penny newspaper, with a broad popular appeal. The paper lived out its remaining years in a building which will be discussed shortly.

Adjacent to the *Sun* stood the exuberant Victorian Gothic–style **Tribune Building.** The *Tribune* was acknowledged as New York's most important newspaper. When Greeley left the newspaper to help found the Republican party, he left the management to Whitelaw Reid, himself an active political leader (minister to France and unsuccessful candidate for vice-president in 1892). Reid was one of a line of distinguished journalists who began their careers on the *"Trib"*; others were Carl Schurz, William Dean Howells, Charles A. Dana, Henry James, Bayard Taylor, and Margaret Fuller, to name but a few. When the Tribune Tower was demolished, the city lost a great architectural treasure.

4. A bit farther we see little **Printing House Square** with Ernst Plassman's statue of Benjamin Franklin, presented in 1872. Behind Franklin, at the corner of Spruce Street, is the former **American Tract Society Building.** Designed in 1896 by R. H. Robertson, it is a massive Romanesque Revival–style edifice that no longer houses any religious publishing concern, and is known merely by its address, No. 150 Nassau Street.

A block east of Printing House Square, on William Street, were William Randolph Hearst's *New York American* (an outgrowth of the earlier *Morning Journal*) and the *New York Evening Journal.* His *Journal* represented the archetype of "yellow journalism," as its rabble rousing and drum beating were held in great part responsible for our entry into the Spanish-American War.

To the right, at the corner of Park Row (No. 41), is the **former New York Times Building,** now an integral part of the Pace campus. Designed in 1889 by George B. Post, and later remodeled by Robert Maynicke (1895), it housed the *Times* until its move to Longacre Square (now Times Square) in 1904. Note the plaque commemorating "Newspaper Row."

5. Abutting the former New York Times Building is the dazzlingly ornate **Potter Building** (38 Park Row), constructed in 1883. It was one of the first fireproof "skyscrapers," built with an iron framework encased in the then brand-new terra cotta building material, and was the first major building to sport an ornamental terra-cotta façade in both cast and pressed forms. The fireproof quality of terra cotta was appropriately chosen, as the predecessor on the site, the old New

The Park Theater, ca. 1820, on Park Row, facing City Hall. One of the nation's first legitimate theaters, it was built at the time of the American Revolution. (Consolidated Edison Company of New York)

York World Building, was destroyed a year before in one of the city's most spectacular blazes. For a time, the *Press* was published in the Potter Building. It is now a luxury residence.

To the right rear, at 5 Beekman Street, are the twin pyramidal towers of the curious **Temple Court Building.**

6. "Newspaper Row" continued with a line of five-story brick buildings that housed a number of popular dailies. The *New York Daily News,* at 25 Park Row, was a relatively small evening paper at the turn of the century, and pro-Democratic at that. Adjoining was the *Morning Advertiser,* and two doors farther, the *Mail and Express.* Cyrus Field purchased the *Evening Mail* and the *Evening Express* in 1880 and 1882, respectively, and made them a financially successful enterprise. He later housed them in an interesting, rococo, T-shaped building near the corner of Fulton Street. The *Recorder* was at No. 21 and nearby, the *Evening Telegram.* Near Ann Street was the *Globe and Commercial Advertiser,* at the time the oldest newspaper in New York, dating from 1797.

7. When completed in 1899, the lofty **Park Row Building,** at No. 15, was the tallest in the world, and its twin cupolas added interest and variety to the growing skyline. The skyscraper was designed by R. H. Robertson, and the four caryatids (including the 16 figures on the cupola) are attributed to J. Massey Rhind.

At the southeast corner of Park Row and Ann Street stood the white marble French Second Empire **Herald Building.** Founded in 1835 by James Gordon Bennett, it soon gained popularity for its frequent "scoops," as well as for printing news of the financial world. Although a penny newspaper, it made Bennett a fortune. His son, James Gordon Bennett, Jr., startled the "Fourth Estate" by moving the *Herald* uptown in 1894 to a magnificent McKim, Mead & White *palazzo* on what is now Herald Square. Although the Herald Building is now gone from the uptown square, the Bennett Clock still rings the hours while figures with hammers strike an enormous bell. The building on "Newspaper Row" was later replaced by the 25-story St. Paul Building, which in turn was razed for the present Western Electric Building.

8. Occupying the same relative position one block south was the **Evening Post Building.** Founded in 1801 by Alexander Hamilton, the *Evening Post* was possibly the most conservative of all New York dailies. Under the leadership of editor William Cullen Bryant, the paper spoke out for free trade. Bryant, by the way, staunchly opposed allowing women to enter the journalism field. Later, under Carl Schurz, the paper adopted a more liberal attitude, both politically and toward women. In 1906 it moved to new quarters on Vesey Street (to be seen shortly).

9. The oldest church in Manhattan (and the oldest building as well) is magnificent **St. Paul's Chapel.** Turning its back on Broadway, it faces a peaceful churchyard, oblivious to the noise and clamor of the crowded thoroughfare. St. Paul's, a chapel of Trinity Church downtown, was completed in 1766, the tower and steeple in 1796. Architect Thomas McBean undoubtedly was influenced by London's St. Martin's-in-the Fields when he designed this majestic landmark. It is built of locally quarried Manhattan schist, and the tower (by James Crommelin Lawrence) is of brownstone. The church is an almost perfect example of Georgian style, reflecting the elegant tradition of the Colonial period. Much of the interior decoration of this National Historic Landmark was done by Pierre L'Enfant, the French-born architect who later became a Major of Engineers in the Continental Army and helped lay out the City of Washington, D.C. One can still see the pew where Washington regularly worshipped. Among the list of distinguished worshippers were Prince William (later King William IV), Lords Cornwallis and Howe, Maj. John André, the Marquis de Lafayette, and Presidents Grover Cleveland and Benjamin Harrison. [*See* pages 3 and 4 for a description of the interior.]

The quiet churchyard is well worth a visit. Note the numerous 18th-century headstones with names of well-known families of early new York.

To the right of the churchyard on Vesey Street are two interesting landmark buildings. At No. 20 is the **Garrison Building,** formerly the home of the *Evening Post,* from 1907 to 1926. This is a rare example of Art Nouveau architecture. The bronze-finished cast-iron spandrels are decorated with the colophons of well-known 16th- and 17th-century printers, and the statues on the ninth floor represent "The Four Periods of Publicity"—the Spoken Word, the Written Word, the Printed Word, and the Newspaper, by Gutzon Borglum and Estelle Rumbold Kohn. The building was designed by Robert D. Kohn in 1906 (sculptor Estelle was his wife).

To its right, at No. 14, is the **New York County Lawyers Association Building**—"the Home of Law." Constructed in 1930 of Vermont marble and limestone, it was designed by Cass Gilbert in a neo-Federal style. Its auditorium is a reproduction of Independence Hall in Philadelphia. Vesey Street is named for William Vesey, first rector of Trinity Church.

10. Looking south from the churchyard, across Fulton Street, is the multicolumned **former American Telephone & Telegraph Building,** built in 1917 from plans by Welles Bosworth. It was formerly crowned with a gilt statue, *The Spirit of Communication,* by Evelyn Beatrice Longman; but the statue was removed and placed in the atrium of AT&T's former headquarters at 550 Madison Avenue. It has since been brought to AT&T's Somerset County, N.J. campus. A weekday visit to the spacious lobby reveals an interesting and educational display, including sculptor Chester Beach's marble and bronze statue, *Service to the Nation.* Interestingly, the ex-American "Tel & Tel" Building, with its eight tiers of colonnades, has more columns than the Parthenon—or any other building, for that matter.

11. Turn north on Broadway to No. 255. The **Transportation Building,** designed by York & Sawyer in 1915, occupies the site of one of New York's most celebrated hostelries, the Astor House, which catered to affluent visitors from 1836 to 1913.

12. Possibly the most beautiful commercial building in the world is the dramatic Gothic Revival–style **Woolworth Building,** 233 Broadway. When dedicated in 1913, the Rev. S. Parkes Cadman, a famous New York clergyman, in a burst of enthusiastic rhetoric, referred to it as a "Cathedral of Commerce"—and the sobriquet still stands. Many believe it to be architect Cass Gilbert's greatest triumph. Rising 729 feet (plus 1 inch!), the Woolworth Tower eclipsed the Metropolitan Life Tower to become the tallest building in the world for 17 years.

The Federal Building at the intersection of Broadway and Park Row became the city's main post office in 1875 An elaborate Second Empire pile designed by government architect A. B. Mullett, it obstructed the view of City Hall until its demolition just before World War II. (Museum of the City of New York)

The opening ceremony was climaxed when President Wilson pressed a button in Washington, illuminating 80,000 bulbs on the 60-story structure. Two years later, at the Panama-Pacific Exposition, it received a gold medal as the "most beautiful building in all the world erected to commerce." The observation deck on the 55th floor, which unfortunately is no longer open to the public, provided a breathtaking view, as visitors were whisked to the top at dizzying speed in the newest in high-speed electric elevators.

Frank Woolworth, the founder of the ubiquitous five-and-ten-cent-store chain, paid the $15,500,000 cost of the building in cash! Note the typical Gothic elements: gargoyles, flying buttresses, arches, spires, traceries, trefoils, etc., all seen to good advantage after an extensive face-lift of the entire building. The style is followed in the interior as well. The lobby presents one of the most striking interior spaces in the city, with its vaulted, mosaic ceiling that sparkles in a jewellike effect; the delicate bronzework; the walls of veined marble; an imposing grand staircase; lacy wrought-iron cornices covered with gold leaf; polished terrazzo floors; and the amusing little sculptured caricatures of Mr. Woolworth (counting his nickels and dimes), Cass Gilbert (holding a model of his pet project), Louis Horowitz, the builder, and others involved with the construction of the "Cathedral." The 25th-floor office of Frank Woolworth, who died in 1919, is preserved as a private museum, but is not generally open to the public. (Ask the guard for a free descriptive leaflet.)

13. Cross Broadway to City Hall Park. Called the Common in the 18th century, it was then at the northern edge of the city, a triangular plot formed by the confluence of the Bloomingdale Road (now Broadway) and the Boston Post Road (now Park Row and farther north, the Bowery). On the Common a prison was constructed, and nearby, a poor house, as well as a powder house and barracks as part of the city's defenses. A short distance to the west on the now demapped College Place was King's College (now Columbia University). As the city expanded northward, it became a popular public gathering place, and figured in a series of anti-British incidents for a ten-year period prior to the Revolution, in which patriots forcefully displayed their displeasure with the Crown by harassing the military post and erecting a series of Liberty Poles. After the Revolution, the city entered an era of prosperity and growth that required the construction of a new City Hall. In 1811 the present seat of town government was erected in what was the new City Hall Park. The park was enlarged to its present size in the late 1930s with the razing of the old Federal Building that occupied most of the southern corner of the triangle and housed a post office and court. The so-called "Mullett" (after the architect) Post Office was a massive granite pile of "wedding cake" built in 1878 in the French Second Empire style; its demolition provided light and space and a sweeping view of (and from) City Hall.

A bit farther north, beyond the private driveway leading to City Hall, is the splendid **statue of Nathan Hale,** by Frederick MacMonnies, erected in the Park in 1893. Hale, a young schoolteacher captured by the British for spying early in the Revolution, shows a disdainful look as he is about to be hanged. Legend has it that he said, "I only regret that I have but one life to lose for my country." Stanford White designed the pedestal. On the lawn beyond, the flagpole commemorates the raising of the five **Liberty Poles** by Colonial patriots. Those poles were anathema to the British, not only for their symbolism, but also because they were cut from the prohibited white pine, a tree reserved exclusively for the masts of His Majesty's navy. The name Sons of Liberty was first applied to those who demonstrated against the hated Stamp Act by freedom-sympathizer Lt. Col. Sir Isaac Barré, a Member of Parliament, who is remembered with a plaque on the far side of the lawn (beside City Hall) and also in the names of Barre, Vermont, and Wilkes-Barre, Pennsylvania. At the side of City Hall is a **"bishop's crook" lamppost.** Several more of these cast-iron relics have been rescued and placed around the building.

Located under Broadway, between Murray and Warren streets, was the **City's first subway.** In a short-lived experiment using compressed air for propulsion, Alfred Ely Beach constructed a 312-foot-long tube that was opened to the public in 1870. The subway was built in secret to prevent interference from corrupt "Boss" Tweed who had his own plans for mass transit. The passengers rode in a luxurious car, built to fit snugly against the tube's wall, and the "train" was propelled by air from a huge fan blowing through the tunnel. An elaborate waiting room was fully carpeted and furnished with paintings, a fountain, and even a grand piano. The entrance, waiting room, and ticket office were located at the southwest corner of Warren Street and Broadway. After his failure

The recently completed American Telephone & Telegraph Company Building dwarfs St. Paul's Chapel at Fulton Street and Broadway in this ca. 1919 view. Nestled in the T-shaped structure is the Victorian-style Evening Mail Building which was later demolished when AT&T extended its building to Fulton Street. To the extreme left is the St. Paul Building, now the site of the Western Electric Building. (The American Telephone & Telegraph Company)

The oldest German daily in the United States, the Staats-Zeitung, began publishing in this Victorian pile on Park Row and Centre Street in the 1870s. Statues of Gutenberg and Franklin by Ernst Plassman adorn the third floor. To the right is the City Hall terminal of the Second Avenue El. The site is now occupied by the Municipal Building. (Museum of the City of New York)

The buildings at Centre and Chambers streets represent a variety of styles. Note the pedestrian crossings, slightly elevated so rain could run off and vehicles would slow down, and also much easier on the feet than cobblestones. (Museum of the City of New York)

The Rhinelander Building at Duane and Rose streets was demolished in 1971. The marble entrance columns as well as the barred "Old Sugar House" window are now preserved on Police Plaza. (New York City Landmarks Preservation Commission)

Mulberry Street with its infamous "bend" between Park and Bayard streets in the early 1880s was, and remains, heavily Italian. Mulberry Bend Park (later Columbus Park) replaced the buildings on the left side of the street. (New-York Historical Society)

One of the few surviving photos (left) of the Beach Pneumatic Subway shows the approach to the Warren Street station in 1870. Below, the remains of the subway car found in a 1912 excavation. (New-York Historical Society)

to secure adequate financial backing to extend the line, Beach abandoned the pneumatic underground railway a year later. In 1912, workmen excavating for the BMT subway came upon the old tube with its single car and lavish station.

14. No. 255 is the elegant former headquarters of the **Home Life Insurance Company.** Designed in Eclectic style by Napoleon LeBrun and completed in 1894, its pyramided gable atop the building is best seen from a distance.

At the northwest corner of Chambers Street, No. 277, the **Broadway Chambers,** designed by Cass Gilbert and completed in 1900, is a good example of "tripartite" skyscraper construction, where the building façade is divided into three basic sections, similar to the components of a Classic column.

15. Situated at the northeast corner of Chambers Street and Broadway is the **former A. T. Stewart "Marble Palace"** [*see* Ladies' Mile, 1]. Designed by John B. Snook and Joseph Trench, with marble cutting by Ottavino Gori, it was completed in 1846, and promptly became a trendsetter in American architecture. As the first commercial Italianate building, its *palazzo* style was copied widely; and in this extravagant edifice, the tradition of the large retail emporium was firmly established. After Stewart moved his flourishing dry-goods business uptown in 1862, he retained the building as a warehouse. His later successor added two additional floors, and in 1884 the building was converted to commercial use. In 1917, the *Sun* moved in from across the Park, publishing here until its demise in 1952. The attractive **Sun Clock** on the corner of the building, bearing the motto "The Sun it Shines for All," has been preserved through the efforts of a local committee of businessmen and city employees who raised the funds to restore it, and it has become a kind of unofficial landmark. The *Sun*'s thermometer on the opposite corner, however, remains adamantly at 40°. In 1970, New

New York's first subway was the Beach Pneumatic Tube, built in 1869–70. It ran one block on Broadway from Warren Street to a point just south of Murray Street. In this rendering of the proposed car, the giant steam-operated fan which supplied the power through air pressure cannot be seen. (New-York Historical Society)

York City acquired the building, and plans are now underway to restore the exterior and rennovate the upper floors.

At No. 61, visit **Citybooks,** New York's municipal bookshop where you can purchase the *Green Book,* the official city directory, plus a selection of New York books, memorabilia, and souvenirs.

One block north of Chambers Street, between Reade and Duane Streets, is the new **Federal Office Building,** 290 Broadway (Hellmuth Obata Kassabaum, 1993). Excavation for the structure was preceded by the required archaeological investigation, and it was then that about 400 graves were unearthed dating to the mid-18th century. Historians had long known that a "Negros Burial Ground" existed in this area, which in the 1750s was outside the city limits. The lands that encompassed what is now City Hall Park, the few blocks above, and part of Foley Square, had been set aside as common grounds by the Dutch colonial government of Nieuw Amsterdam. The northern part of the Commons was used as a graveyard for as many as 20,000 slave and free blacks until the late 18th century, as well as a potter's field and a burial ground for American prisoners during the Revolutionary War. The discovery revealed the nation's earliest known African American cemetery, and because of the site's historic significance, the Landmarks Preservation Commission designated the **African Burial Ground and the Commons** as an historic district. The burial ground has the unique distinction of being the city's only underground landmark with no visible traces. Return to Chambers Street.

16. No. 51 Chambers Street is the **former Emigrant Industrial Savings Bank Building** (Raymond F. Almirall, 1908). Now owned by the city, its double towers, topped by spread eagles and globes, must have inspired confidence in the strength and security of the bank.

17. The Italianate "villa" back-to-back with City Hall, No. 52, is the famous (or infamous) Criminal Courts Building. Known familiarly as the **Tweed Courthouse,** it stands as a monument to graft and corruption. Completed in 1872, it took nine years to construct, and the city's treasury found itself between $8 million and $12.5 million poorer. Approximately three-quarters of that amount was diverted into the pockets of "Boss" William Marcy Tweed and his Ring. Nevertheless, the city did inherit an attractive architectural addition. Its future, however, was in question, as the Mayor's Civic Center Task Force reported that the much needed renovation would be "substantially more costly" than building a new City Hall Annex. But considerable opposition arose from within the administration and from the public at large, and the historic Tweed Courthouse was spared. Subsequent landmark designation assured its future. Visit the interior with its imposing central well, then walk to the rear to the *pièce de résistance* of the tour, City Hall.

18. The greatest architectural treasure in the city is palatial **City Hall,** built in 1811. The competition for its design was won by Frenchman Joseph F. Mangin and Scotsman John McComb, Jr., who combined their talents to produce a French Renaissance–Georgian-style building of consummate beauty. McComb remained the guiding hand throughout the period of construction, but Mangin seems to have slipped into obscurity.

Once faced with demolition as part of the projected Civic Center, the Criminal Courts Building on Chambers Street behind City Hall is a monument to civic corruption. Between $8 million and $12 million of taxpayers' money went into "Boss" Tweed's pocket. The building, now a designated landmark, serves as additional office space for City Hall. (Photo by author)

City Hall, 1826, from a colored aquatint by W. G. Hall, Mangin and McComb's French Renaissance and Georgian-style building, completed in 1811, is considered one of New York's greatest architectural treasures. (The J. Clarence Davies Collection, Museum of the City of New York)

City Hall has always been the nerve center and civic hub of the metropolis, the site of many public celebrations, and the traditional place of welcome for heroes. Noteworthy were the receptions given in honor of Lafayette, the opening of the Erie Canal, the state visits of a parade of royalty, the welcoming of Lindbergh in 1927, and, in more recent times, of the hometown winners of the baseball World Series. The rotunda of City Hall was also the laying-in-state site of a number of famous citizens: Maj. Gen. William J. Worth [*see* Madison Square, 18], Horace Greeley, John Howard Payne, President U. S. Grant, and Mayors Gaynor and Mitchell. Nothing, however, could equal the homage paid to Abraham Lincoln after his assassination, when his remains lay in the rotunda on April 24 and 25, 1865. In the following funeral procession, 60,000 New Yorkers joined in the mournful parade up Broadway.

The structure has undergone many renovations and repairs throughout its history. The first addition was an illuminated public clock—the first in the city—installed in the cupola in 1831. In the same year an ugly fire tower was erected on the roof, remaining for 34 years until the volunteer fire department was replaced by a paid staff. In 1858 City Hall suffered extensive damage in a roaring blaze resulting from a fireworks display on the roof during the Atlantic Cable Celebration. Following the fire, City Hall began to deteriorate, neglected through the years by many corrupt city administrations. Someone referred to those days as the "tobacco juice period," as the building became more and more decrepit and dismal. It was even suggested that City Hall be demolished in favor of a new, "more modern" municipal building.

In 1895 the Board of Aldermen declared that "...the present appearance and condition of the City Hall is an offence to the sight of the community and a menace to the health of those whose business necessitates their presence in the building." A minor renovation followed. During the next 20 years, additional restoration was conducted with outside philanthropic assistance. In 1917, fire struck again, this time from a workman's charcoal burner in the cupola. Major reconstruction was begun under the direction of Grosvenor Atterbury, who restored the copper dome to its original appearance. Little was done, however, to save the decaying exterior until 1954, when the Board of Estimate voted the necessary funds for a complete restoration of the building. The eroded Massachusetts marble façade was carefully cut away and replaced with Alabama veined limestone, the base with Missouri red granite. The north façade, which was originally faced with brownstone ("Who would see it, since nobody of importance in those days lived north of City Hall"), was also refaced with limestone.

The **interior,** too, was completely restored to what was believed to be its original elegance. City Hall is open to the public, weekdays, 10 A.M. to 4 P.M., except during special events. Among the most attractive features are the double curved staircase, the colonnaded rotunda, the Office of the President of the City Council, the City Council Chamber, the Board of Estimate Chamber, the Mayor's Reception Room, the Committee of the Whole Room, and the Governor's Room (now a museum) with its famous Trumbull portrait of Washington and the desk used by Washington at Federal Hall. Visitors should be prepared to pass through a security checkpoint.

The clock in the City Hall cupola has kept perfect time for many years, but the bells have been silent for a generation. Many may recall the old announcements on the municipal radio station, WNYC, giving the time "by the century-old bells of historic City Hall." The striking mechanism now has been repaired, thanks to the city's newly designated clockmaster, Marvin Schneider. He was appointed officially to the position after tending a number of old city clocks for 12 years, and once again the bells in the old City Hall clock ring out the hours.

In the sidewalk in front of City Hall is a tablet marking "the first shovelful of dirt" for **the construction of the New York City subway,** March 24, 1900. The first line (now the Lexington Avenue subway) was opened four years later. A loop of that line passes directly underneath, and is used by the No. 6 trains to turn around at the end of the line. It passes through the **abandoned City Hall station,** which is still intact with its original tile vaults and even chandeliers, but can be seen only by the motormen and conductors.

Return to Park Row, past the Horace Greeley statue, to the corner of Chambers Street.

 19. Directly across Chambers Street is the city's second most splendid Beaux Arts–style building (after the old Custom House at Bowling Green), the **Surrogate's Court, originally the Hall of Records,** No. 31. The sculpture groups at the entrance represent "New York in its Infancy" and "New York in Revolutionary Times," by Philip Martiny. The eight cornice figures are: David

The elaborate City Hall subway station, closed to the public for many years, now serves only as a turnaround for the No. 6 trains after their last stop at the Brooklyn Bridge station. In this photo, taken in 1979, the last surviving set of old IRT subway cars snakes around the station's sharp curve on a final trip before being consigned to the NYC Transit Museum in Brooklyn. Note the impressive arches with their Guastavino tile vaults. The decorative chandeliers must have added a homey touch when this first subway station was opened in 1904.

Pietersen de Vries, Caleb Heathcote, DeWitt Clinton, Abram S. Hewitt, Philip Hone, Peter Stuyvesant, Cadwallader D. Colden, and James Duane, all by the same sculptor. In the attic are ten allegorical figures by Henry Kirke Bush-Brown. The building dates from 1901 and was designed by architects John R. Thomas, and Horgan and Slattery. On a weekday, visit the colonnaded rotunda. This is also the location of the **Municipal Archives,** an excellent collection of city history and an important resource for researchers.

20. Cross Centre Street to the Municipal Building, and walk through to the pedestrian mall that was formerly Chambers Street into **Police Plaza.** As the first major accomplishment in the Civic Center plan, this enormous public space, together with its decorations and adjoining modern structures, is a tribute to the Office of Lower Manhattan Development, as well as to the architectural firm of Gruzen & Partners.

As you enter the Plaza, designed by landscape architect W. Paul Friedberg, turn right to the small **"prison window" monument** of the Rhinelander Sugar House, which commemorates the dismal Revolutionary War prison in which hundreds of American patriots died of starvation, neglect, and disease. When the Sugar House was demolished in 1892, a window from the prison was preserved and built into the Rhinelander Building, which occupied the site until it, too, was razed in 1968, to make way for the new Police Headquarters Building. The window was rescued again and mounted here in the Plaza.

In the center of the three-acre plaza—the city's largest public plaza—is the arresting **steel sculpture** by Bernard Rosenthal, *Five in One,* consisting of five 30-foot-high rolled steel discs painted bright red.

To the right are rows of newly planted honey-locust trees in front of the entrance to a five-tier **Municipal Parking Garage,** hidden beneath the Plaza.

Looking ahead, the dominant feature of Police Plaza is the red-brick-and-concrete **Police Headquarters Building.** Designed by Gruzen & Partners in 1972, this $58 million center for "New York's Finest" is a restrained and tasteful addition to the city skyscape. Enter (ask permission at the desk), and enjoy the broad lobby with Josef Twirbutt's 20-foot-square brick sculpture, and the vista of the Municipal Building and the panorama of City Hall Park skyscrapers seen through the plate glass entrance windows.

Leaving Police Headquarters, turn left and walk down the staircase to the Madison Street entrance and the "Grecian Ruin." This **group of five Ionic marble columns** is a nostalgic artifact of the old Rhinelander Building, which stood on the site from 1892. To the east is **Murry Bergtraum High School for Business Careers,** named for a late president of the Board of Education; and behind it, a New York Telephone Company skyscraper, whose unusual height was achieved by "borrowing" the air rights from the adjacent high school.

Return to Police Plaza.

To the right is the **Federal Court House Annex** and the 12-story **Federal Metropolitan Correctional Center** (Gruzen & Partners, 1973), the lines of its gray split-faced concrete façade blending well with neighboring buildings. Note that the support columns are of the same height as those of adjoining St.

Rhinelander's "Old Sugar House," at the corner of Rose and Duane streets, was erected in 1763 and during the Revolutionary War served as a prison during the British occupation of New York. It was demolished in 1892 to make way for an office building which kept the Rhinelander name. The building preserved a barred window of the "Old Sugar House" prison in its façade, and when the structure was razed in 1968 the window was removed and mounted on a special base adjacent to the Municipal Building, along with a commemorative plaque. (New-York Historical Society)

Andrew's Church and the Municipal Building. A special type of tinted shatter-proof glass with built-in alarm system has been installed in the prison section, replacing the traditional gloomy look of barred windows.

St. Andrew's Church was consecrated in 1939, replacing an earlier church, named Carroll Hall, built in 1842. Just before the Civil War when the City Hall area became the center of the printing and newspaper industry, the church received special dispensation to say a "Printer's Mass" at 2:30 A.M. for the night shift of newsmen and printers. It later became the first parish church to offer a noon mass for the growing number of businessmen in the area. The Latin phrase in the frieze means "Blessed are those who walk in the law of the Lord." The Plaza at this point is called St. Andrew's Plaza, although the church's address is 20 Cardinal Hayes Place.

Walk through to Centre Street and Foley Square.

A STROLL AROUND FOLEY SQUARE

Follow the route of the broken line on the Foley Square Area map, beginning (and ending) at St. Andrew's Plaza:

U.S. Court of International Trade, 1 Federal Plaza (Alfred Easton Poor, Kahn & Jacobs, Eggers & Higgins, 1966). The customs court is an attractive glassy box set above ground level. Walk under it and explore its broad passageways and ceramic tile murals. During hot summer days, the neighboring community finds it a place of respite.

Jacob K. Javits Federal Building, 26 Federal Plaza (same architectural firms as above). Built in two sections, in 1967 and 1976, the whole appears to overwhelm the Foley Square complex. The eastern wing, built first, resembles a gargantuan checkerboard.

Department of Health of the City of New York Building (1933). Note the names of great men of medicine emblazoned around the frieze of this dignified but otherwise undistinguished civic building.

Old New York Life Insurance Company Building, 346 Broadway (Griffith Thomas, 1870; remodeled and enlarged by McKim, Mead & White, 1896). Architect Thomas created a very imposing but appropriately sober headquarters for the company. Note the two clock towers, minus their cupolas, on this Renaissance Revival–style early skyscraper. The tower facing Broadway once sported a huge iron globe surmounted by an eagle. The company moved its headquarters to Madison Square in 1928, and the building is now temporarily used for government offices and the Clocktower Art Gallery. Cast-iron ornamentation on the Broadway side shows the New York Life Insurance monogram.

Family Court and Office of Probation (Haines, Lundberg & Waehler, 1975). A recent addition to Foley Square, this polished black granite behemoth

The original "Tombs" prison in an 1873 view. Built across Centre Street from the present "Tombs" site, this was the main city jail from 1838 to 1892. Compared to a pharaoh's tomb because of its columns, sun god motifs, and trapezoidal windows, this and the Croton Reservoir at Forty-Second Street were two examples of Egyptian-style architecture in the city. (Museum of the City of New York)

is overbearing and pretentious; and its angular façade is distracting rather than relieving.

Municipal and Civil Court Building (William Lascaze and Matthew Del Gaudio, 1960). This undistinguished building houses the Small Claims Court and the spillover from the Criminal Courts' calendar, as well as the courts of civil claims.

Engine Company 31, 87 Lafayette Street (Napoleon LeBrun & Sons, 1895). This French Renaissance "chateau," no longer in use as a firehouse, is a delightful gem of a building—a pleasant surprise in this neighborhood of towering monoliths. The building is now partially occupied by Downtown Community Television Center, which provides, among other services, free media services to the community. DCTV claims to offer the most heavily attended media arts classes in the country, providing an opportunity for poor students to study the television arts without cost.

New York City Criminal Courts Building and former Manhattan Detention Center for Men (1939). The dramatic zigguratlike towers represent the height of the 1930s "moderne" or Art Deco style. Known familiarly as the **"Tombs"** since it incorporates the Men's House of Detention, it was built opposite the site of the original "Tombs" prison (so called because of its Egyptian-

Dominating the lower Manhattan skyline at the turn of the century was the 26-story gold-domed "World Tower," the tallest building in the world when it was completed in 1890. Designed by George B. Post for Joseph Pulitzer's Evening World, *it was demolished in the early 1950s to make way for new approaches to the Brooklyn Bridge. (New-York Historical Society)*

The most notorious section of the city in the mid-19th century was the festering slum and den of criminals called Five Points. In this 1859 print from Valentine's Manual *we see the crossing of three of the five streets: Baxter, Park, and Worth streets. (Museum of the City of New York)*

style architecture) which stood across Centre Street. The Men's House of Detention was moved in 1974 to Riker's Island, but reopened a few years later to relieve crowding at the island prison. The "Tombs" was designed by Harvey Wiley Corbett.

In the area encompassed by Franklin, Worth, Centre, and Lafayette streets was a small pond known as the **Collect.** A source of fresh water during colonial days, it became polluted as the city grew around it, and was ultimately filled in at the beginning of the 19th century. John Fitch tested his prototype of a steamboat on the Collect in 1796. Aboard was Robert Fulton, who received all the accolades for the invention some years later.

Columbus Park, formerly Mulberry Bend Park, was created just before the turn of the century after the razing of many of the Five Points slums. Its name was changed in 1911.

State of New York Building (1928). Built on a wedge-shaped plot, this functional building is known by all as the location of the automobile License Bureau.

Five Points [*see* special map] was probably the worst festering slum in the history of this country. So named because of the intersection of three streets, it began as a district of cheap amusement at the beginning of the 19th century, but by 1840 it had become a foul, crime-ridden "rabbit warren" of the most depraved

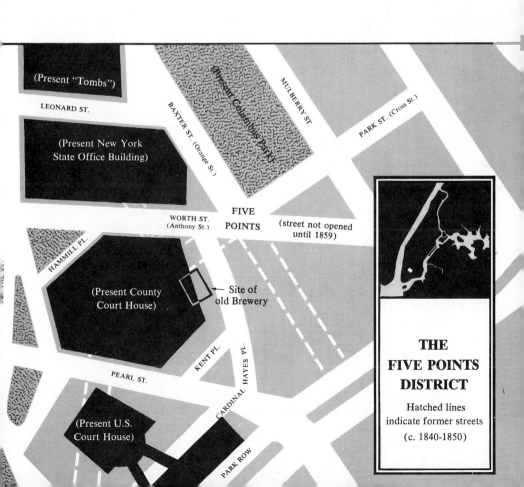

(Present "Tombs")

LEONARD ST.

BAXTER ST. (Orange St.)

(Present Columbus Park)

MULBERRY ST.

PARK ST. (Cross St.)

(Present New York
State Office Building)

FIVE

WORTH ST.
(Anthony St.)   POINTS   (street not opened
until 1859)

HAMMILL PL.

(Present County
Court House)   ← Site of
old Brewery

KENT PL.

CARDINAL HAYES PL.

PEARL ST.

(Present U.S.
Court House)

PARK ROW

**THE
FIVE POINTS
DISTRICT**

Hatched lines
indicate former streets
(c. 1840-1850)

The Old Brewery at Five Points was the City's most infamous slum. Known locally as the "Den of Thieves," it is shown in this pen and ink sketch, just before its purchase and demolition by the Ladies' Home Missionary Society for the Construction of the Five Points Mission. (Museum of the City of New York)

elements of the city. Centered about an old brewery, whose surrounding lane was known as Murderers' Alley, it housed over a thousand men, women, and children in filth, squalor, and crime. More than a murder a day occurred in the former brewery and its surrounding slums; the area was so dangerous that even the police shunned it. It was the hangout of such notorious gangs as the "Plug Uglies," "Shirt Tails," and "Dead Rabbits." By mid-century the brewery was finally demolished and many of the ramshackle Five Points houses were razed. With the completion of the Foley Square courthouse complex, not a trace remains of that infamous district.

● **New York County Court House** (1912). The New York State Supreme Court occupies this hexagon-shaped building with an enormous Corinthian portico. Architect Guy Lowell won the competition for the unique design of a building to occupy the irregularly shaped plot.

● **United States Court House** (1936). Designed by Cass Gilbert and Cass Gilbert, Jr., its gold pyramid set on a skyscraper shaft above a neo-Classic base is a familiar site on the city skyline. A pedestrian walkway has been created between the Court House and its brand-new Annex. Note the two connecting bridges in the rear. The old powerhouse was preserved, and can be seen nestled in the new addition.

At this writing, a new Federal Courthouse building is rising at Foley Square, at 140 Worth Street. Designed by Kohn Pederson Fox, the 27-story gray limestone and marble structure is scheduled for completion in 1994.

End of tour. Return to Foley Square, turn left (south) on Centre Street to the Municipal Building. Underneath and across the street are the Lexington Avenue line and the Nassau Street line.

GREENWICH
VILLAGE

(Shaded Area Indicates
Historic District)

4. Greenwich Village

[A, B, C, D, E, F, Q lines to West 4th Street–Washington Square]

Greenwich Village, a town within a city, has a unique character and personality of its own. Designated a **Historic District** of New York City, the Village dates back to an old Algonquin Indian settlement called Sapokanickan. When the Dutch arrived in 1626 they named it *Bossen Bouwerie* (Farm in the Woods) and developed it as a large tobacco plantation. After the British captured Nieuw Amsterdam in 1664, the plantation was purchased by naval squadron commander Sir Peter Warren, who then renamed it Greenwich. Gradually the settlement was transformed into a small town, and by the early 19th century, "Village" was added to the name. A series of smallpox and yellow fever epidemics in the lower city in the early 1800s drove thousands of city dwellers northward to the town of Greenwich, seeking the "healthful climate and quiet" of this distant suburb which somehow escaped these recurring plagues.

You may note that the streets of the Village do not conform to the orderly grid pattern of most of Manhattan, since the town of Greenwich had already been established with its own layout of streets before the city expanded northward. As the Village grew, its crazy-quilt pattern of streets spread from the banks of the Hudson River to what is now Broadway. Many of the winding streets were originally cow paths, or followed meandering brooks. One of these waterways, Minetta Brook, still causes problems far beneath today's busy streets, especially when foundations are dug for new buildings. The visitor may be flabbergasted to discover that West 4th Street, for example, runs west only briefly, then abruptly swings north to intersect West 10th, West 11th, and West 12 streets!

In the 19th century the Village began to attract writers and artists, and boasted such residents as O. Henry, Mark Twain, Edgar Allan Poe, Henry James, Stephen Crane, Winslow Homer, John La Farge, and Augustus St. Gaudens. Rents were low and the atmosphere was very attractive. After the turn of the century, Greenwich Village began to earn its reputation as the cradle of bohemia in

Engraving of the Jefferson Market Police Court on Sixth Avenue looking north from 9th Street, showing the first train of the Gilbert Elevated Railway (ultimately the Interborough Rapid Transit's Sixth Avenue El), on April 29, 1878. (Museum of the City of New York)

America. The rents are much higher now, and many of the *literati* have departed, but the Village still retains much of its charm in its narrow, winding streets, the houses of many architectural styles, the variety of curious shops, and an assortment of colorful Village "types." There are many boutiques, exotic food stores, coffee shops, fine restaurants serving food from many nations, art schools, and drama workshops, as well as the largest private university in the country.

   1. The tour begins at the corner of **Avenue of the Americas and West 8th Street,** facing Village Square, the hub of the Village. Most Villagers refer to Avenue of the Americas by its former (and more logical) name, Sixth Avenue. The sidewalk along the Avenue just south of 8th Street, once a gathering place for exponents of a wide variety of political and religious views, it now is lined with street vendors offering books and a wide variety of mostly junk. Walk quickly down 8th Street, once the bustling "main drag" of the Village; now it is a dismal and seedy thoroughfare lined with shoe stores and cheap boutiques, with many establishments now boarded-up, including the once highly popular Eighth Street Playhouse. The theater, which opened in 1928 as the Film Guild Cinema, was designed by architect Frederick Kiesler, and was billed as "the first 100% cinema." For old-time Villagers the scene is most depressing. (Hardly an auspicious way to begin a tour...but just wait!) Turn right at the first corner (Macdougal Street), and walk the short distance to the gates of Macdougal Alley.

   2. Macdougal Alley, with its picturesque and individually redesigned carriage houses, is a private dead-end street, of which there are several in the Village. The picturesque little houses were built as stables in the 1850s for the wealthy residents of 8th Street (then called Clinton Place) and Washington

Square. Some residents claim that the two gas lamps are the last remaining in the city maintained free by the Consolidated Edison Company, but "'taint so!"

At No. 1, now a restaurant, poet Edwin Arlington Robinson wrote his famous *Tristram,* winning himself his third Pulitzer Prize. Facing the alley across Macdougal Street is the massive brick façade of the Tenth Church of Christ Scientist, remodeled in 1967. Turn left on leaving the Alley and walk to the corner of Washington Square.

3. Washington Square originally was a marshland teeming with wildlife and a favorite hunting ground of the colonists. In 1797 it became a municipal Potter's Field. Recent excavations during the park's renovation revealed skeletons of some of the 10,000 early New Yorkers buried here. Equally grim was the field's popularity as a dueling ground and its use as a site of public executions. Directly across from you is the famous (or infamous) **Hanging Elm,** said to be the oldest tree in the city. It is one of 27 varieties in the park. The public hangings drew large crowds in a festive mood from the downtown districts. It is said that in 1824, on his triumphal return to America, the Marquis de Lafayette was the honored guest at the hanging of 20 highwaymen. Two years later, the park was officially designated as the Washington Military Parade Grounds, and at its dedication, two oxen, 200 hams, and a quarter-mile of barreled beer were consumed in the largest public picnic ever held here. In 1831, the grounds became the unofficial campus of the newly established University of the City of New York—now New York University, the nation's largest private institution of higher education.

As you turn left and walk along Washington Square North, note the group of imposing town houses, Nos. 26–21. These elegant homes were built in the 1830s for the social elite, as were the houses farther down the street across Fifth Avenue. Known as **"The Row,"** they represent the finest group of Greek Revival–style houses in America. Henry James's novel *Washington Square,* written in 1881, had its setting at No. 18—his grandmother's house. Unfortunately, the building was demolished along with neighboring houses in 1950 to make way for the huge apartment house at the corner. The five-story annex in a pseudo-Georgian style is a sad replacement, but represents a compromise, as the builders of the huge apartment house originally intended to erect it directly on the square. Detour around the corner of Fifth Avenue for a moment, to the right side of the entrance to No. 2 Fifth Avenue, where through the plate glass you can see a small domed fountain that is **Minetta Brook** bubbling up from its meanderings way below. A descriptive plaque is affixed to the wall.

4. The Washington Arch, designed by famed architect Stanford White, is one of the world's finest triumphal arches. Built of marble in 1891–92, it commemorates the centenary of George Washington's inauguration as first President. This arch replaced an earlier model constructed of wood in 1889, which spanned Fifth Avenue near the corner. The arch had proved so popular that the permanent stone monument was erected afterward by public subscription. The civilian statue of Washington was sculpted by Alexander Stirling Calder, the military statue, by Hermon Atkins MacNeil. The carved relief work on the arch was done by Frederick William MacMonnies, whose statue of

Nathan Hale can be seen in City Hall Park. At Christmastime, a tall fir tree is placed in front of the arch, illuminated with hundreds of colored bulbs. Neighbors gather to sing carols, often to the accompaniment of student musicians from N.Y.U., or even guitars. At night, the floodlighting on the arch can be seen from as far north as 42nd Street.

There is an interior staircase in the right section leading to the top, which figured in an unseemly escapade back in 1916, known as John Sloan's Revolution. Sloan, considered the father of the "Ashcan School" of painting, forced open the door to the stairs and led a group of slightly tipsy art students and fellow bohemians to the top of the arch on a cold January night. They built a fire in a large beanpot, spread out food, and lit an array of colorful Japanese lanterns—all to the consternation and indignation of the very staid and proper residents of "The Row." The boisterous group read poems, fired cap pistols, and noisily declared the independence of the state of "New Bohemia." The arrival of a detachment of unsympathetic constabulary brought a quick end to the abortive "rebellion."

On weekends and during the warmer weather, the fountain and mall areas are a mecca for roller skaters, instrumentalists, frisbee "pros," speechmakers, and exhibitionists of all kinds, as well as a gathering place for crowds of sightseers who come to watch them "do their thing." In June and September, the adjacent streets are host to the semiannual Greenwich Village Outdoor Art Show, where professional and amateur painters have the opportunity to "show and sell."

Fifth Avenue just north of Washington Square in 1889, showing the temporary wooden arch built for the centennial of Washington's inauguration. A horse-drawn omnibus waits for passengers as a street vendor dispenses goodies to well-dressed youngsters on this once fashionable avenue. (New-York Historical Society)

Stereograph view of the Washington Arch, taken as it neared completion in 1892. The arch, larger than any in antiquity, is considered one of architect Stanford White's major achievements. (New-York Historical Society)

Celebrating the completion of the Washington Arch, community and civic leaders gather for their picture on the roof of the arch. William Rhinelander Stewart, one of the driving forces behind its construction, with ceremonial mallet and top hat, poses thoughtfully while architect Stanford White, to his right, looks down. In the rear is N.Y.U.'s neo-Gothic building. (New-York Historical Society)

Nos. 4, 6, and 8 Fifth Avenue, corner of 8th Street—stately town houses designed by Henry J. Hardenbergh (the Plaza Hotel, the Dakota, etc.). The photo was taken in 1936 by Berenice Abbott for the Federal Art Project "Changing New York." All three buildings were razed in the early 1950s for an enormous apartment house, No. 2 Fifth Avenue. (Museum of the City of New York)

Cross Fifth Avenue and walk down Washington Square North to the lions in front of No. 6.

5. This magnificent **row of Greek Revival houses,** like their counterparts which you saw before, were built around 1831 for wealthy New York merchants. In later years, "The Row" was the residence of writer John Dos Passos, artists Rockwell Kent and Edward Hopper, and Mayor Stephen Allen. Although the houses are similar (except for No. 3), each has its own minor architectural differences. The stately entranceways, graced by marble columns and carved wooden colonnettes, are evidence of the graceful style of living of the original owners. Observe the brickwork—an alternating long and short brick in each row. This arrangement is called Flemish Bond, and was used on the more expensive early houses. Nos. 7–13 are mere façade, as all were gutted in 1939 to make way for an apartment house, carefully hidden behind. Sacrificed was the elaborate cornice, which still remains on the houses to the right, to make way for a fifth floor. How different, and how much more aesthetic a treatment than the architectural vandalism committed on the previous block! The cast-iron fence, in a remarkable state of preservation, helps unify the row of houses. Note the honeysuckle adornments, called anthemions, the intervening obelisks, the fret design along the base, and the lyres at intervals. These are all Greek motifs so popular during the Greek Revival period. As for the stone lions in front of No. 6, they are copies of bronzes cast in 1883 by sculptor Samuel Kitson, which were said to be from the former William K. Vanderbilt Mansion on Fifth Avenue.

Return to Fifth Avenue, turn right, and stop at the arcaded entranceway to the apartment house masked by the Greek Revival façade on the square. Peek into "Willy's Garden," named for the late gardener. Against the rear wall is a bronze statue of Cervantes, which was a gift to New York from the city of Madrid, and is a 19th-century replica of a monument in the Spanish capital's Plaza Mayor. It was originally intended for placement in Washington Square, but because of its fragility it was given to N.Y.U. A few steps up the Avenue is:

6. Charming **Washington Mews,** was formerly a row of stables—in fact it was called Stable Alley until the 20th century. These converted carriage houses are vaguely reminiscent of London's Chelsea district, and were the residences of such celebrities as Gertrude Vanderbilt Whitney (founder of the Whitney Museum), diplomat and writer Walter Lippmann, and former Official City Greeter Grover Whalen. Walk through the cobblestoned mews to University Place. No 1 is now the Irish House, and the last house on the right is the French House of New York University, remodeled in an authentic rural French architectural style. Across from it is the German House. Turn right to the northeast corner of Washington Square.

7. Diagonally across the street (southeast corner) is the **Main Building of New York University.** Built in 1894, it replaced a handsome Gothic Revival structure completed in 1837, six years after the founding of the University. Then

Stalled in the snow on University Place and 9th Street, the morning after the Great Blizzard of 1888, the horsecar's "motive power" is nowhere to be seen, in spite of the rush hour crowd aboard. In the rear is the Hotel Martin, an elegant French establishment with a famous basement restaurant. (Museum of the City of New York)

called the University of the City of New York, it had as one of its founders Albert Gallatin, Secretary of the Treasury under Thomas Jefferson, and boasted many creative teachers. Among them was a member of the art faculty who in his spare time changed the course of history by inventing the telegraph—Samuel F. B. Morse. Professor of Chemistry and Physiology John W. Draper made the first successful outdoor photographic portrait on the roof of his house adjoining the university building. Walt Whitman conducted classes in poetry, and Winslow Homer painted in a top-floor studio. Less academic perhaps was science professor Samuel Colt's invention of the "six-shooter." In later years, Thomas Wolfe gave courses in fiction writing.

The construction of the original building in 1834 led to a riot which lasted for several days. It seems that some of the founding fathers thought they could save money by using inmates from the nearby state prison. This aroused the anger of guild laborers who demonstrated so forcefully that the local National Guard unit had to be summoned to quell the violence. The university gave in and peace was restored, and the incident became known as the **Stone Cutters' Guild Riot,** the first demonstration by organized labor in New York City.

Note the plaque honoring Manhattan's first schoolteachers; then walk south along the Main Building to Washington Place. Turn east to the northwest corner

The great neo-Gothic tower of New York University was completed in 1837, facing Washington Square, and was designed to resemble King's College Chapel in Cambridge, England. It is the first important example of the Collegiate Gothic style in America. It was in this building that Samuel F. B. Morse perfected the electric telegraph, Walt Whitman conducted classes in poetry, Winslow Homer painted in a top floor studio, and Samuel Colt invented the six-shooter. N.Y.U. demolished it in 1894 to build its present Main Building. (New-York Historical Society)

of Washington Place and Greene Street. Novelist Henry James was born on Washington Place near the northeast corner in 1843.

8. This is the architecturally undistinguished Brown Building of N.Y.U. Built in 1900 for commercial use and known then as the Asch Building, it was advertised as a fireproof structure. Nevertheless, on March 25, 1911, fire *did* break out in piles of discarded cloth in the ninth-floor workroom of the **Triangle Shirtwaist Company.** Efforts to extinguish the blaze were unsuccessful, and within minutes the eighth, ninth, and tenth floors became a roaring inferno. Although the building was equipped with fire exits, the terrified workers discovered to their horror that the ninth-floor exit doors had been locked by supervisors. A single fire escape was wholly inadequate for the crush of panic-stricken employees from the three floors, and the firemen's hastily stretched nets proved useless in breaking the fall from the upper floors of the dozens of workers who leaped—often hand-in-hand, and with their hair and clothing ablaze—to their death on the pavement below. In less than an hour it was over. One hundred forty-six young people, most of them recent immigrants living on the Lower East Side, had perished—and the city was in a state of shock! As a result of the tragedy, improved fire-safety regulations were quickly adopted by the City Council, and the newly organized International Ladies' Garment Workers Union succeeded in having labor laws enacted to improve working conditions for the tens of thousands still working in similar sweatshops. A plaque commemorates the sad event, and the site has been designated a National Historic Landmark.

Return to Washington Square and enter the park. Walk past the imposing statue of Garibaldi (at this writing, minus his sword—a victim of vandals), the Italian patriot who made Staten Island his home for a number of years. The statue was sculpted by Giovanni Turini in 1888; it is said that Garibaldi will always draw his sword to protect a damsel in distress. Spend a few minutes walking around the mall and fountain area, and observe the variety of people (most of the more colorful types enjoy being looked at, anyway). You may be drawn into a folk-music session, a frisbee-tossing match, a political discussion, or a volleyball game; *but be discreet!*

Continue to the south side of the park, and notice the bocce court, a highly popular sport facility, particularly among the elderly Italian men of the neighborhood. Cross Washington Square South and turn left, past the **Generoso Pope Catholic Center of N.Y.U. and the Holy Trinity Chapel** with their modern stained glass, to the **Loeb Student Center** at the corner of LaGuardia Place.

The Student Center occupies the site of Mrs. Marie Branchard's Boarding House, demolished in 1948. Known as the "House of Genius," some of its most famous boarders were Metropolitan Opera coloratura soprano Adelina Patti; writers Theodore Dreiser, who penned his *An American Tragedy* in a tiny garret room in 1915; Stephen Crane, who began *The Red Badge of Courage* in an adjoining room; O. Henry; Frank Norris; Gelett Burgess ("I never saw a purple cow..."); Eugene O'Neill; and Maxwell Bodenheim. Mrs. Branchard outlived most of her celebrated tenants and died just after her 81st birthday in 1937.

Turn right (south) on LaGuardia Place and walk one block to West 3rd Street; cross to the east side.

Firemen pouring tons of water into the Asch Building at the corner of Washington Place and Greene Street on March 25, 1911, as the Triangle Shirtwaist Company burns in one of the worst disasters in the city's history. One hundred forty-six young garment workers lost their lives in this tragic fire which engulfed the upper three stories of the structure. The building still exists as the Brown Building of New York University. (Brown Brothers)

Burned out sewing machines are the only recognizable artifact in the charred debris of the 9th floor, the morning after the dread Triangle Fire. (Brown Brothers)

The attractive landscaped strip that extends to Bleecker Street, called LaGuardia Gardens, is a tribute to the efforts of the Friends of LaGuardia Place, a local civic group that solicited the funds to have the landscaping and lighting installed. The street, formerly called West Broadway, was widened in the 1870s. At the time, "Boss" Tweed planned an up-scale residential neighborhood, and even renamed what was then Laurens Street Fifth Avenue South, with the intention of slicing the thoroughfare through Washington Square. The plan failed, as did a similar project by Parks Commissioner Robert Moses in the late 1940s.

The centerpiece of the minipark is the imposing new **statue of Fiorello H. LaGuardia**, the feisty reform mayor of New York from 1934 to 1945. LaGuardia, who was born on nearby Sullivan Street, also represented this district when he served several terms as U.S. congressman. The six-and-a-half-foot dark bronze figure, by sculptor Neil Estern, was cast in 1993, and is set on two bluestone platforms above a granite base. In a typical LaGuardia striding stance, the statue portrays the impetuosity and vigor of the "Little Flower." [*See* also Estern's bust of John F. Kennedy in Grand Army Plaza, pages 469 and 470.]

Return to Washington Square South, turn left, and walk one block to the Judson Memorial Church.

9. Named for the first American Baptist missionary, Adinoram D. Judson, the **Judson Memorial Church and Tower** are fine examples of the Italian Renaissance style, designed by Stanford White and built in 1892 by his architectural firm of McKim, Mead & White. If the church is open, look inside at the splendid stained-glass work of artist John LaFarge, the painter who is credited with reviving the lost art of stained-glass making in this country. The tower now serves as a dormitory wing of the adjacent **Judson Residence Hall** of N.Y.U.

In the annex of the Judson dormitory was the **studio of artist John Sloan.** Other painters of "The Eight" who rebelled against the sugary style of the National Academy of Art, and who had studios on Washington Square, were Maurice Prendergast, Everett Shinn, Ernest Lawson, and William Glackens. The artists' own show, staged at the 69th Regiment Armory in 1913 together with others, became known as the "Armory Show," and is considered the birth of modern American art. Their realistic work was derided by critics who called it the "ashcan school."

During the time when the Square was the site for public executions, the hangman's house was located where the Catholic Center is now. The shack later became a gathering place for early bohemians, and was known as Bruno's Garret, after the somewhat eccentric owner. Bruno invited the public to visit (for a fee) and observe at first hand how the ostentatious tenants lived.

Walk west to Sullivan Street, and go around the corner to the entrance to the **Hagop Kevorkian Center for Near Eastern Studies** of N.Y.U. Designed by Philip Johnson and Richard Foster, the entrance hall contains a reconstruction of the interior of a 1797 house built in Damascus, Syria, for a merchant family, in whose possession it remained until the mid-1920s. The interior work was supervised by the late university architect Joseph Roberto.

Immediately to the left (east) of the Kevorkian Center (No. 51) is N.Y.U.'s **Skirball Department of Hebrew and Judaic Studies.**

Continue west along the Square to N.Y.U.'s neo-Georgian style **Vanderbilt Hall** (Eggers & Higgins, 1951), modeled after an English Inn of Court. Previously on the site was a rather pathetic structure known as "Papa Strunsky's," a rooming house for artists, most of whom could rarely afford the rent and who were subsidized by the beneficent Strunsky who never pressed them for payment. Among the threadbare boarders was the young writer Lincoln Steffens. The lease of the property was held by Columbia University, which was less charitable than Strunsky, and by the late 1940s they foreclosed. Knowing that N.Y.U. needed the space for its Law School, Columbia held out for a reported $1 million to close the deal so that Vanderbilt Hall could be erected.

Walk to the corner of Macdougal Street where a ca. 1890 apartment house has given itself No. 39 1/2 to keep its identity with Washington Square.

10. Macdougal Street and its adjacent blocks south of Washington Square are considered the "real Village" by the mobs of young people who throng here evenings and weekends. Before turning down Macdougal Street, make a short detour straight ahead along West 4th Street (the continuation of Washington Square South). John Barrymore, "The Great Profile," lived at No. 132; and at a former café at No. 148, Al Jolson and Grace Moore were discovered, while Norma Shearer worked as a hat-check girl. At No. 150, once "The Mad Hatter" Café, Hendrik Willem van Loon wrote his *Story of Mankind.* On the north side of the street is the Washington Square United Methodist Church, built in 1860.

As you stroll down Macdougal Street, note the Provincetown Playhouse, Eugene O'Neill's theater. Nos. 127–131 (best seen from across the street) are little Federal houses that were built for Aaron Burr in 1829 and are among the oldest in the city. Notice the typical dormer windows in the peaked roof, and the pineapples on the cast-iron newel posts on No. 129—traditional symbols of hospitality. Around the corner at 106 West 3rd street, Aaron Burr's ghost is reputedly still haunting the building. At 130 Macdougal Street, south of West 3rd Street, Louisa May Alcott wrote her classic *Little Women.* Take an optional side

A Fifth Avenue bus parked in Washington Square in 1936. These popular "double deckers" disappeared after World War II. In the rear is the Washington Arch and No. 1 Fifth Avenue. (Photograph by Berenice Abbott for the Federal Art Project "Changing New York," Museum of the City of New York)

trip one block farther to Bleecker Street and turn left. Try some of the exotic foods from around the world at the "hand held" food shops that line the street: souvlaki, tacos, sweet and hot sausage, empanadas, tandoori chicken, knishes, shish kebab, and Turkish coffee (but not all at once!).

11. Pause for a moment before turning the corner of Minetta Lane. The building on the southwest corner, No. 113 Macdougal Street, now the Minetta Tavern, was a speakeasy during Prohibition, and in the basement below, the *Reader's Digest* was born. Founded in 1922 by DeWitt Wallace, its first edition had a press run of only 5,000 copies. At narrow **Minetta Street** turn left. During the Prohibition Era, these narrow alleys were lined with speakeasies. Later these night spots became legitimate cabarets offering drink and amateur theatrical productions. Now, with stricter city licensing, few genuine cabarets remain, and the small theater groups have moved into their own "Off-Off" Broadway playhouses. Both streets follow the winding path of old Minetta Brook; and it is said that on a very quiet night, the gurgling waters can be heard below ground. However, there are very few quiet nights in this neighborhood. You will emerge at Sixth Avenue—rather, Avenue of the Americas—on Father Demo Square. Cross the avenue, turn half right, and you will be at the corner of Bleecker and Carmine streets.

12. The Roman Catholic **Church of Our Lady of Pompeii** (1926) is the parish church of the large Italian community in this part of the Village. Mother Francis Xavier Cabrini, the first American saint, often prayed here. Walk along Bleecker Street and savor the aroma of the many Italian food specialty shops, and buy a fresh-baked bread at Zito's at No. 259 Bleecker Street. Turn west on Leroy Street and notice the variety of architectural styles, ranging from Federal-style houses to "Old Law" tenements. Cross Seventh Avenue (carefully!).

13. As you round the bend on Leroy Street, the atmosphere suddenly changes. You are now on **St. Luke's Place,** with its charming row of Italianate brownstone town houses of the 1850s. The gingko trees, which line both sides of the street, are particularly resistant to air pollution. The twin lanterns on the stairway of No. 6 mark the former residence of Mayor James J. Walker—the popular "Jimmy" Walker of Prohibition days. Rampant corruption in municipal government forced his resignation, but he remained a beloved and colorful figure until his death in 1946. Until Gracie Mansion was made the official residence of all New York City mayors, a pair of lanterns customarily adorned the entrance to "his honor's" home. Across the street in James J. Walker Park, there is an interesting monument near the entrance, which honors two firemen from the Eagle Fire Company who lost their lives in a building collapse in 1834. The memorial is the lone surviving artifact from the former Trinity Parish cemetery which occupied this site before the park was built. Turn right at Hudson Street one block to Morton Street.

14. Had you stood on this spot 300 years ago, you would have been on the bank of the Hudson River. The land to the west was filled in gradually, until today the river is three blocks away. The tall building halfway down the block to the right is the former Federal House of Detention, now the New York State Manhattan Mental Development Center. Walk north one block to Barrow Street and make a brief detour west. On both sides of the street are typical early 19th-century houses. No. 97 was remodeled later in the century with the addition of ornate neo-Grec details on all the lintels.

To the northwest, on Washington Street, is the enormous red brick **former U.S. Federal Building.** Completed in 1899 as the Customs Appraisers' Warehouse, it took seven years to build, and its style is the fortresslike Romanesque Revival. It once housed records from the National Archives and had a branch of the U.S. Post Office. The architect of this massive masonry building with its great brick arches is unknown; however, the designer of the lower two floors was Willoughby J. Edbrooke. It has since been recycled by a private developer as a luxury apartment house. Return to Hudson Street and turn left (north) one-half block to St. Luke's Chapel.

15. "St. Luke-in-the-Fields," as it was called when the cornerstone was laid in 1821, stood at the river's edge and overlooked small farms, wandering streams, and shady country lanes. In those days most visitors came from the lower city by boat, as the trip by carriage was very arduous, and the canal that bisected most of Manhattan island (site of present Canal Street) could be crossed in only two places. The first warden of St. Luke's was Clement Clarke Moore, who immortalized himself not with his dedicated church duties, but with the poem *A Visit from St. Nicholas* ("'Twas the Night before Christmas..."). The church, a branch of the downtown Trinity Parish, has always been dedicated to education, and today boasts an excellent elementary school, visible behind the church. A tragic fire in 1981 virtually destroyed the landmark church, but a generous outpouring of public support helped St. Luke's rise, phoenix-like, from its ashes.

16. Adjoining the church are **Nos. 487–491 Hudson Street.** Observe how these restored Federal houses form a harmonious unit with the brick church. Built in 1825, they are the property of St. Luke's. Bret Harte, journalist, teacher, "gold rusher," and author of *Tales of Roaring Camp* and *The Outcasts of Poker Flat,* lived at No. 487 and maintained a steady feud with his contemporary Mark Twain, also a Villager.

Continue to Christopher Street, turn right, then right again into Bedford Street.

17. As you rounded the corner, you probably noticed the **Lucille Lortel Theater** on Christopher Street, one of the oldest off-Broadway playhouses, formerly called the Theater de Lys. Kurt Weill's *Three Penny Opera* had its New York premiere here and ran for nine years, with Weill's wife Lotte Lenya in a starring role.

You now are entering the most charming section of the so-called West Village. Homeowners take special pride in restoring and preserving their attractive houses. There are more original Federal-style houses in this neighborhood than anywhere else in the city. Note the **row of houses at Nos. 115–111** and **109–107,** the latter only two bays wide. Stop just before the next corner, which is Grove Street, and stay on the right side of Bedford Street.

18. The wooden house on your left, **No. 100 Bedford Street,** was originally the workshop of sash maker William Hyde, who lived in the corner house. The sash maker's trade has now been assumed by the glazier and carpenter. In the early 19th century, window making was an important craft. The workshop is now a private residence. **No. 102,** which you just passed, is best seen from a distance. It is no accident that it resembles a fairy-tale house. Although the building dates from 1835, it was remodeled extensively in 1926 by Clifford Reed Daily and financed by Otto H. Kahn, who sought to convert the decaying house into "an inspiring home for creative artists." When the city's Building Department approved the radical plans, **"Twin Peaks"** was born.

At the corner, **No. 17 Grove Street,** which dates from 1822, is the most complete wooden frame house in Greenwich Village. Turn right on Grove Street to No. 4.

19. The row of **Nos. 4–10** (1825–34) presents one of the most authentic groups of classic Federal-style houses in America. Unfortunately, No. 6's dormers have been "modernized" and the shutters have been removed. Note the charming oasis that is **Grove Court**—a secluded, shady mews. Now converted into triplexes, the row of old houses was built as laborers' quarters in 1854, and Grove Court was known by the not-so-charming name of Mixed Ale Alley. Return to Bedford Street and turn right, stopping opposite No. 86.

20. Can you guess what **No. 86 Bedford Street** is (or was)? There are no visible signs of identification, but to Village *cognoscenti* it is Chumley's Restaurant. It was a notorious speakeasy during the Prohibition days, and patrons had to identify themselves at the little glass window in the door before being admitted. It was also a favored hangout for writers, and faded dust jackets of long-forgotten titles line the walls inside. The restaurant's popularity is so widespread in the Village, that former owner Lee Chumley never felt the need for a sign. During Prohibition, when the premises were raided by the police, patrons could beat a hasty retreat out a back exit in the rear of the restaurant, opposite the bar. This passageway, which leads through the courtyard of the adjacent building to Barrow Street, is still there. See for yourself around the corner!

Turn right on Barrow Street to No. 70.

21. No. 70 Barrow Street, when built in 1852, was Empire Hose Company No. 1. In those days each neighborhood had its own volunteer fire brigade. Look carefully and you will see where the old carriageway was bricked in.

Across the street is a rather large double house with mansard roofs, **Nos. 39 and 41 Commerce Street.** Both halves were built in 1831 for Peter Huyler, a milkman. "The Twins," as they are called, were built in Federal style with Second Empire roofs superimposed, and share a common garden. Walk ahead into Commerce Street, around the bend to the little theater.

22. A group of local playwrights seeking a stage for their own works converted an old brewery malt house into the **Cherry Lane Theater** (Commerce Street was then called Cherry Lane). Among some premieres were Samuel Beckett's *Waiting for Godot* and *Endgame,* as well as plays by Ionesco and Edward Albee.

23. At the corner of Bedford Street is the **Isaacs-Hendricks House,** built in 1799. Like the two wooden houses seen earlier, it is typical of the architecture of old Greenwich, and is the oldest surviving house in the Village, although a questionable restoration in the mid-1980s created a rather mysterious side wall on

A row of pristine Greek Revival–style town houses, Nos. 3 through 6 Sheridan Square, was lost forever when an apartment was erected on the site in the early 1950s. The photo by Wurts Bros. was taken in 1915. A saddle and harness shop is barely visible at right. (Consolidated Edison Company of New York)

Commerce Street. Its entrance is in the rear, behind the fence. Around the corner at **No. 75 1/2 Bedford Street** is the narrowest house in the city, measuring only 9 1/2 feet wide! The first floor was formerly a carriage entrance, with living quarters above. A cobbler had his shop here, and later it was a candy factory. Between 1923 and 1924, poet Edna St. Vincent Millay lived here. Like the Isaacs-Hendricks House, this diminutive structure had its entrance facing the rear. Note the plaque on No. 70. Turn right on Commerce Street to No. 17.

24. Two years before killing Alexander Hamilton in that fateful duel in 1802, Aaron Burr lived briefly at **the site of No. 17. Nos. 16–18** across the street were built in 1830, as was No. 17. At **No. 11,** the plaque informs us that Washington Irving was a resident, where he was supposed to have penned his *Legend of Sleepy Hollow.* Continue to Seventh Avenue, turn right briefly to an abandoned gas station, which has been recycled as a residence, and has the distinction of being **the smallest building in Manhattan.** Cross Seventh Avenue and walk north to Barrow Street.

25. At the corner of Barrow Street and Seventh Avenue is **Greenwich House,** No. 27. Originally a settlement house, it has expanded its services to the community with recreational facilities, arts and crafts studios, concerts, antique shows, and cultural programs for senior citizens. Proceed along Barrow Street. **No. 15** was once a stable. Note the horse heads indicating that it was a public livery stable; it is now a restaurant. No. 17, a restaurant called One if by Land, Two if by Sea, is believed to have been a stable built on the site of Aaron Burr's carriage house.

26. At **Sheridan Square,** turn right briefly on West 4th Street to Numbers 175–185, charming houses dating from the 1830s. West 4th Street has many interesting little shops, and, except for the storefronts, most of the buildings remain unchanged. Return to Sheridan Square, bearing to the right, and make a sharp right turn into Grove Street, just before reaching Seventh Avenue.

27. Sheridan Square is shaped like a huge butterfly, with two distinct "wings." So many streets converge at this point that visitors often become confused (Villagers, too, for that matter). Because of heavy traffic at this intersection, the corner has been called "The Mousetrap." Pass through the second "wing" of the butterfly by walking along Grove Street, opposite the little park with the equestrian statue of Civil War Cavalry General Philip Henry Sheridan (Joseph Pollia, 1936). Actually, this half of Sheridan Square is called **Christopher Park,** but nobody ever calls it that. The Ellsworth Flagpole honors a 24-year-old colonel, the first of his rank to be killed in the Civil War. The Square figures in another aspect of the Civil War—the Draft Riots. In 1863, mobs of bloodthirsty rioters, in the worst civil insurrection in the city's history, gathered in the Square and attacked a number of freed slaves. They would certainly have hanged them from nearby lampposts, had not the residents of **No. 92 Grove Street** risked their lives to save them. The house has since been extensively remodeled, and is now called the Burges Chamber Studio. Its design won a prize from the American Institute of Architects.

A recent addition to the little park is the sculpture group by George Segal, in bronze with white patina, entitled *Gay Liberation* (1992). It is in a spot directly across Christopher Street from a former tavern called the Stonewall Inn. It was here in June 1969 that a large group of gays had a confrontation with the police, and for the first time fought back for what they considered their right to assemble peaceably. The event is commemorated every June by a large "Gay Pride" parade in the Village.

28. Grove Street now becomes Waverly Place, and as you stand before **the Northern Dispensary,** you are at the corner of Waverly Place and Waverly Place! Since the street divides at this point to meet Grove Street and also to swing northward, it has given rise to the saying that the Dispensary "has two sides on one street, and one street on two sides." Built in 1831 in Greek Revival style by Henry Bayard, carpenter, and John C. Tucker, stonemason, and surprisingly unchanged in appearance, the Northern Dispensary still functions as a public clinic. According to its records, Edgar Allen Poe was treated here (free) for a head cold in 1837.

Continue in the same direction, and turn left into narrow Gay Street.

29. Gay Street was the center of a small black neighborhood in the latter half of the 19th century. In the 1920s the street was lined with speakeasies. **No. 14** was the site of Ruth McKenny's play *My Sister Eileen.* Later it was filmed here on location. Walk ahead to Christopher Street, and spend a few minutes window shopping in the curious shops to the left. Then turn right to Greenwich Avenue, and turn left and walk to the corner of West 10th Street.

30. The garden across the street marks the **site of the former New York City Women's House of Detention.** The massive orange brick Art Deco structure was demolished in 1973–74 after considerable community pressure, and the inmates were moved to Riker's Island. Cross Greenwich Avenue to the Peacock Caffè, 24 Greenwich Avenue, and enjoy a cup of capuccino and an Italian pastry. Turn east on West 10th Street to the entrance gates of Patchin Place. Illuminating the rear of this charming cul-de-sac is a cast-iron **bishop's crook lamppost,** of the type that first provided electric street lighting in the city in the 1890s.

31. The houses on quaint **Patchin Place** were built in the mid-19th century to house workers of the then-posh Brevoort Hotel on Fifth Avenue. The narrow street later became the residence of such famous authors as poet laureate John Masefield, Theodore Dreiser, e. e. cummings (at No. 4), as well as Harry Kemp (the "Hobo Poet"), and William Brinckley, who wrote *Don't Go Near the Water.* Enjoy the peaceful atmosphere of this unusual cul-de-sac, away from the noise and clamor of nearby thoroughfares. Turn left, walk to Avenue of the Americas (we'll get to the "castle" across the street shortly), and turn left again. Watch carefully, or you'll miss the iron gates marking the entrance to Milligan Place.

32. Milligan Place is named for the original landowner, Samuel Milligan, who settled here in 1799. His daughter married the surveyor of his property, Aaron Patchin. Perhaps part of the dowry was the small street named for him. Many native Villagers are unaware of this tiny, secluded mews. Walk ahead to West 11th Street, turn right and cross the avenue. Fifty feet down the street is a small cemetery.

33. The Second Cemetery of the Spanish & Portuguese Synagogue was one of three burial grounds of this first Jewish congregation in New York. The first cemetery, near Chatham Square, and the third, on West 21st Street, kept pace with the northward growth of the Jewish community from the 17th through the 19th centuries. The peculiar triangular shape of the cemetery resulted from the opening of West 11th Street through to Sixth Avenue in the mid-19th century, cutting off a substantial piece of the graveyard. As a result, it is the smallest cemetery in Manhattan. Return to Avenue of the Americas, turn left, and stop at the "castle."

34. The Jefferson Market Library, the Village's most magnificent Victorian Gothic structure, was built in 1874–77 as a courthouse, with an adjoining jail, firehouse, and market. Designed by architects Frederick Clarke Withers and Calvert Vaux, it was listed among the ten most beautiful buildings in America at the time. (Vaux, by the way, worked with Frederick Law Olmsted on the design for Central Park.) Note the striking effect of the red brick and white stone, the Gothic motifs, stained-glass windows, and dramatic clock tower. The tower replaces an earlier wooden fire lookout, one of many throughout the city, long before the advent of the electric fire-alarm system. In 1967 the building was saved from the wrecker's ball at the eleventh hour by a dedicated committee of neighborhood residents, who not only saved it but convinced the city to restore it and make it a branch of the New York Public Library. Architect Giorgio Cavaglieri designed and supervised the restoration. The clock, known affectionately as "Old Jeff," was repaired and illumination for the dials installed. During the Christmas season the belfry is festooned with gaily colored lights. Read the plaques at the base of the tower and visit the library. Take the elevator to the third floor and walk down the intriguing spiral staircase to the dungeonlike basement, which houses the reference room. As you leave the building, cross the avenue and explore **Balducci's,** the Village's major gourmet landmark, which began as a produce pushcart when founder Luigi Balducci immigrated from Italy in 1916; then walk south one block to West 8th Street, where the tour began.

End of tour. The entrance to the West 4th Street–Washington Square subway station is a half-block down Avenue of the Americas toward Waverly Place.

E. 12TH ST.

E. 11TH ST.

28

4TH AVE.

27

E. 10TH ST.

3RD AVE.

STUYVESANT ST.

2ND AVE.

WANAMAKER PL.

E. 9TH ST.

26

E. 8TH ST.

ST. MARKS PL.

25

16

17

ASTOR PL.

18

15

21   22   23

BROADWAY

19   20

E. 7TH ST.

24

14

E. 6TH ST.

COOPER
SQUARE

TARAS
SHEVCHENKO
PL.

E. 5TH ST.

13

12

11   9   10

E. 4TH ST.

8

7   6

LAFAYETTE ST.

GREAT JONES ST.

E. 3RD ST.

JONES AL.

BOWERY

4   5

E. 2ND ST.

SHINBONE AL.

3

2

BOND ST.

BLEECKER ST.

E. 1ST ST.

CROSBY ST.

MULBERRY ST.

MOTT ST.

ELIZABETH ST.

THE
LAFAYETTE
HISTORIC
GROUP

and

THE EAST
VILLAGE

start

HOUSTON ST.

1

JERSEY ST.

5. The Lafayette Historic Group and the East Village

[Lexington Avenue line No. 6 to Bleecker Street; B, D, F, Q lines to Broadway-Lafayette station; Lexington Avenue–Third Avenue M101, M102 buses to Houston Street; Broadway M6 bus or Fifth Avenue M5 bus to Houston Street]

With the end of the American Revolution, New York City, which had stagnated under years of British occupation, came alive again, regaining its position as an important port and commercial center. A burgeoning population began to push the city's frontiers northward, swallowing up the once-remote and peaceful farms of mid-Manhattan and crisscrossing them with a latticework of newly opened streets.

In 1811, the City Commissioners drew up their famous plan, laying out a gridwork street pattern for the entire island, numbering all east-west streets and north-south avenues, commencing roughly at the point of departure of this tour. By the end of the 19th century the last farms disappeared from Manhattan, yielding to the ever increasing needs for *lebensraum*.

By the 1830s this neighborhood became the "gold coast" of the city, boasting the most lavish residences—including that of the nation's wealthiest citizen, John Jacob Astor. Within 20 years the area gave way to commerce and public entertainment, and by the 1880s and 1890s it became a center for the printing trades. Light industry followed with factories, loft buildings, and warehouses.

Surprisingly, so many vestiges remain from each period of development that within the half-square-mile area can be found such diverse "artifacts" as opulent Greek Revival residences, Italian Renaissance cultural institutions, Romanesque

Revival industrial structures, cast-iron commercial "palaces," plus a number of historic and architecturally unique buildings—most in an excellent state of preservation.

The tour begins at Houston and Lafayette streets. [For background information on Houston Street, see SoHo Cast-Iron District, page 194.]

1. On the southeast corner stands the **Puck Building** (295–309 Lafayette Street). Built in 1885, with an addition in 1892, it is a fine example of the industrial Romanesque Revival style so popular in the last two decades of the 19th century. Architect Albert Wagner designed it for the publishers of the humor magazine *Puck*, whose Shakespearean character proclaimed "What Fools These Mortals Be!" across the magazine's cover. The publication lasted more than a "Midsummer's Night," entertaining New Yorkers for some 30 years, until it was absorbed by the now-defunct *New York Journal-American*, which kept only the old magazine's logo. Puck, however, lives on in two larger-than-life statues perched on a third-floor ledge at the northeast corner of the building and above the elegant marble-columned entranceway, which opens on Lafayette Street. The gilt cherubic figures are by Bohemian immigrant Carl Buberl.

Walk west on Houston Street to Crosby Street. Turn north (right), and stop about three-quarters of the way to Bleecker Street.

2. The startlingly ornate building directly ahead (65 Bleecker Street), almost hidden in the shadows of the dark narrow streets, is the **Bayard-Condict Building,** New York City's only building designed by Louis H. Sullivan. The guiding spirit of the "Chicago School," Sullivan was the teacher (and employer) of Frank Lloyd Wright. Ignore the altered ground floor and study the ornamented façade of this 12-story steel-frame structure, which is clad entirely in white terra cotta, noting the vertical clarity and romantic detail leading up to an astonishing cornice above six supporting angels. It is said that Sullivan objected strenuously to the figures, but placed them there at the insistence of Silas Alden Condict, the original owner. Architectural historian Carl W. Condit, commenting on the location of the Bayard Building, was heard to say, "Who would expect an aesthetic experience on Bleecker Street?" The building was erected 1897–99.

To the right, on the southeast corner, are the decaying remains of a once-proud Federal-style residence, with dormers in both the front and rear of its typical peaked roof. It was a Roosevelt property and owned by FDR's great-great-grandfather.

Turn east (right) to Lafayette Street, then left past Jones Alley, turning left into Bond Street.

3. In the 1830s Bond Street was one of the city's most fashionable. Lined with Greek Revival–style houses, it was a secluded, peaceful street whose most celebrated resident, Albert Gallatin, lived at No. 1. As Secretary of the Treasury

The last horsecar in the City of New York on the Bleecker Street Line, on its farewell trip on Bleecker Street, between Mercer Street and Broadway, July 26, 1917. Horse car service began in 1832. Although electrification was begun before the turn of the century, New York held on tenaciously to a number of its "horse power" lines long after most other cities had electrified theirs. (Museum of the City of New York)

under Thomas Jefferson and later minister to France, he helped reshape the financial structure of the country, and was a founder of the nearby University of the City of New York, later to be called N.Y.U. A few badly misshapen Federal-style houses survive on the north side of the street. Curiously, Jones Alley makes a right turn in the middle of the block, and goes north for about a block; its lower segment was once called "Shinbone Alley."

On the site of Gallatin's residence is one of the best preserved cast-iron buildings in the city. Built in French Second Empire style, it was designed by Stephen D. Hatch in 1879 for the firm of **Robbins & Appleton,** watchmakers. Shortly thereafter, the publishing house of D. Appleton & Company (no relation) moved into No. 1–3–5 Bond Street. The six-story office building, with floor upon floor of large recessed plate glass windows separated by graceful columns and surmounted at each level by a simple cornice, is topped by an enormous mansard roof with three ornate pavilions. The light and airy interior must have provided a relatively pleasant place to work. Adjacent No. 7–9, also in cast iron, has been joined to it as part of a new condominium.

At the northeast corner of Bond Street and Broadway is the very handsome red brick **former Brooks Brothers Store** (670 Broadway). Best viewed from across Broadway, this engaging 1873 Victorian pile, planned by George E. Harney, clearly shows the influence of English designer Charles Eastlake in its many decorative motifs. Find the date of construction in the ornaments on the

Broadway, looking north from the old Broadway Central Hotel toward Great Jones Street, ca. 1895. Elegantly clad ladies and gentlemen walk by hansom cabs waiting at the curb, while horse-drawn traffic and Broadway cable cars clatter by. (Consolidated Edison Company of New York)

four pilasters. This was Brooks Brothers' third location. An earlier site was at 466–468 Broadway [*see* pages 202 and 203].

Return to Lafayette Street again, and continue east on Bond Street.

4. No. 26 Bond Street is an unusually large late Federal-style house, and was probably the residence of an affluent family.

5. At the northwest corner of the Bowery, the **former Bond Street Savings Bank** is pure wedding cake in cast iron. Built in 1874 from plans by Henry Engelbert, it is another attractive example of the French Second Empire style. With the influx of many German immigrants into the neighborhood, it later became the German Exchange Bank; and with its subsequent failure in the early 20th century, it ended its banking career as a deteriorating loft building. But in 1963, with the growing popularity of off-Broadway theater, it gained a new lease on life as a playhouse. The newborn **Bouwerie Lane Theater,** home of the Jean Cocteau Repertory Company, won additional recognition when it was designated an official New York City Landmark. Note the lovely façade with its rows of paired Corinthian and Ionic columns flanking the windows, the ornate modillions under the cornices of the roof and surmounting pediment, and the stately entranceway guarded by paneled cast-iron newel posts. Diagonally across the Bowery is the Amato Opera, long a cultural landmark in the East Village.

Walk north one block on the Bowery.

Originally **"Bouwerie"** in Dutch, the street's name hearkens back to the days of Peter Stuyvesant, when he had it built as a road from the lower city past the "bouweries," or farms, to his own estate a half-mile north. Although the Bowery is now synonymous with the less fortunate of society who inhabit much of this now-dismal thoroughfare, it was for a time a lively center of entertainment. Music halls, theaters, and beer gardens were numerous in the late 19th century, and the street is recalled in the humorous lyrics of the Gay '90s song "The Bowery—I'll Never Go There Anymore!"

The building on the east side, across the Bowery (do not bother to cross the street!), is the **Men's Shelter,** administered by the City's Social Services Administration. It offers a free bed and meals to the indigent. Careful scrutiny of the near wall reveals an old sign indicating that this was once the Bowery Branch of the Y.M.C.A.

Turn left (west) on Great Jones Street.

There never was anyone named "Great Jones"! The land for the street was deeded to the city by Samuel Jones, a lawyer and New York's first comptroller. The agreement called for the street to be named for him; however, there was

The Broadway Central Hotel, built in 1871 in Second Empire style by Henry Engelbert, built on an earlier hotel called the LaFarge House. A year after it opened, it witnessed the sensational shooting of Jim Fisk. The enormous hotel deteriorated badly in its last years and gave up the ghost in a spectacular cave-in of its north wing in 1973. The site is now occupied by an N.Y.U. Law School dormitory. (New York City Landmarks Preservation Commission)

already a Jones Street (in Greenwich Village), and it was named for his brother-in-law, Dr. Gardiner Jones. Neither would relinquish his prerogative, so for a time there were *two* Jones Streets. To resolve the dilemma, Samuel Jones suggested that *his* street be named Great Jones Street. (Logically, it should have been called East Third Street, which it really is, anyway!)

6. Midway down the block, at No. 44, is the home of **Engine Company 33 and Hook & Ladder 9.** Formerly the headquarters of the New York City Fire Department, it is a splendid example of the French Beaux Arts style and was designed by Ernest Flagg and W. B. Chambers in 1898. At the time of its construction, it was the headquarters of the chief of the Fire Department, so it is appropriately flamboyant in appearance. Imagine the excitement and thrill when the scarlet and gold horse-drawn engines, their steam boilers belching smoke, would dash out to answer the calls!

Across the street, at **Nos. 31 and 33,** are two mid-19th-century commercial buildings. A glance at the pediment reveals that they were once a pair of livery stables. Serving a similar purpose as today's public garage and rent-a-car establishment, Bienecke's boarded horses and also rented various types of rigs to those who were unable to maintain their own private stable.

7. Reaching the corner of Lafayette Street, look through the parking lot on the northeast corner, and seek out the apse of an old neo-Gothic church protruding from the rear of a nondescript commercial building. About a hundred years ago it was the Mission Chapel of the Immaculate Virgin. With the industrialization of the neighborhood, the congregation departed, and the building was sold. Don't look for the front of the church on the East 4th Street side...it isn't there any more.

8. No. 376–380 Lafayette Street (on the northwest corner) is a solid and imposing Romanesque Revival–style loft building. It was built in 1888, from plans by Henry J. Hardenbergh, who designed, among others, the Plaza Hotel, the Dakota Apartments, and the Consolidated Edison Building. The ornamental detail is in brick and terra-cotta—a remarkably handsome structure for an industrial building.

Turn right (north) on Lafayette Street, then right into East 4th Street.

9. The Old Merchant's House, at 29 East 4th Street, is probably the only surviving Greek Revival–style house in the city—intact *within* as well as outside. Built in 1832 by Joseph Brewster from plans attributed to famed architect Minard Lafever, it was purchased in 1835 by Seabury Tredwell, a wealthy merchant. It remained in the Tredwell family until the last surviving member, Gertrude Tredwell, died in 1933. To save the house and its original furnishings from the auctioneer's block, the property was then purchased by George Chapman, a distant relative, whose sole interest was to maintain it as a unique example of a New York City family's house and style of living. Among the furnishings are the original furniture, mirrors, carpets, draperies, chinaware, and a collection of dresses, shawls, and bonnets. The interior architectural elements also preserved are the mantelpieces, wainscoting, moldings, columns, banisters,

Lafayette Place (now Lafayette Street) was an elegant, tree-lined cul-de-sac around 1870. Not visible on the left of the street are the imposing façades of Colonnade Row, the houses of the wealthiest citizens in town. Note the raised pedestrian crosswalks and Greek Revival–style fence in front of old St. Bartholomew's Church. The view is north from Great Jones Street. (New-York Historical Society)

and the kitchen. There is even a secret passageway that leads under the house from an upstairs closet. Chapman organized the Historic Landmark Society to maintain the Old Merchant's House as a public museum.

To protect and restore the house which had suffered badly, the Decorators Club took it on as an official project, and a major renovation was undertaken in 1973–79 under the supervision of New York University architect Joseph Roberto; and now the Old Merchant's House, completely restored with all its furnishings, is open for all to enjoy. (Open Sunday through Thursday 1–4 P.M., adults $3.00, students and seniors $1.00.)

10. At 37 East 4th Street, a few doors east, is the **Samuel Tredwell Skidmore House.** Built in 1844–45 for a cousin of Seabury Tredwell, it is a late Greek Revival–style house, and much less imposing than its nearby neighbor. At one time the entire block was lined with similar houses.

Return to Lafayette Street.

11. On the northeast corner, at No. 393–399 Lafayette Street, stands the massive **De Vinne Press Building.** One of the great printing "giants" of the late 19th and early 20th centuries, Theodore L. De Vinne was the founder of the Grolier Club and the publisher of such popular magazines as *Scribner's, Century,* and *St. Nicholas.* The De Vinne Press was famous for its innovative typefaces and high-quality books. The architects, Babb, Cook, & Willard, designed this "Romanesque Utilitarian" structure in 1885, in a style reminiscent of the aqueducts of Ancient Rome. Notice how thick the masonry bearing walls are, since it was built before the advent of steel skeletons. The name of the old establishment is still visible on the upper façade.

12. No. 411 Lafayette Street demonstrates how different building mediums can be employed together successfully (in this case, cast iron and brick) to produce a functional and aesthetic effect. Viewed from a distance, the ornate two-story-high cast-iron columns of the **Durst Building,** designed in 1891 by Alfred

Zucker, are an imposing base for this former men's clothing store and factory. The "squared" style of the larger columns adds a feeling of strength, while lightness results from the beaded bands on all the columns, the ornate design on the spandrel panels above the ground floor, and the round-arch windows on the second floor; while slender iron columns divide the paired windows above.

13. The superb Corinthian colonnade across the street (Nos. 428, 430, 432, and 434) is all that remains of one of the most magnificent rows of Greek Revival town houses in America. On the site of John Jacob Astor's Vauxhall Gardens Amusement Park, and completed in 1833 by developer Seth Geer, probably from his own plans, **Colonnade Row** is an architectural treasure and an outstanding example of early urban design. Originally named LaGrange Terrace, after the Marquis de Lafayette's country estate in France, the group consisted of nine mansions on what was then Lafayette Place. (Lafayette Street was not opened till much later; Lafayette Place was a shady, cobblestoned cul-de-sac extending only to where Great Jones Street is now. *See* photographs below and on page 125.)

Constructed of Westchester marble and set back behind a 30-foot courtyard, the impressive row was separated from the street by an iron fence. The nine houses were reduced to four when the John Wanamaker Department Store callously destroyed them early in this century to make way for a garage for their delivery trucks. When he built the row, Geer was criticized for speculating "so

Colonnade Row, on the west side of Lafayette Street, was a group of nine marble town houses built in 1833, which became the most fashionable addresses in the city. Today only four of these survive. (Museum of the City of New York)

far out in the country," but his plan was vindicated when possession was taken by such notables as John Jacob Astor, Cornelius Vanderbilt, Warren Delano (Franklin Delano Roosevelt's grandfather), and other wealthy citizens. Washington Irving stayed here for a time, as did two distinguished visitors from England, William Makepeace Thackeray and Charles Dickens. In 1844, then-President John Tyler secretly married the daughter of resident David Gardiner. John Jacob Astor died nearby in 1848 at the age of 85, leaving a fortune of $20 million. An interesting reminder of John Jacob Astor's lucrative fur business can be seen in the colorful ceramic panels depicting beavers, set in the tile walls of the recently restored **Astor Place subway station,** one block north.

The houses, now subdivided into apartments and commercial properties, are in a rather depressing state. The original stoops have been removed, outrageous disfigurements have sprung up on the roof, and many of the ornate details are either damaged or missing (observe what is left of the lovely row of anthemions on the cornice). In addition, a patina of a hundred years of neglect covers the entire façade. Some attempt at preservation and restoration is being undertaken by a few of the owners, which may possibly return this landmark to a modicum of its former opulence.

14. Facing the beautiful row is the **former Astor Library,** now the **Joseph Papp Public Theater.** Begun in 1849 as Astor's bequest to the City of New York, the library was built in three stages (south wing, by Alexander Saeltzer, completed in 1853; center wing, by Griffith Thomas, in 1859; and north wing, by Thomas Stent, in 1881). It was the city's first major library accessible to the public, and was combined in 1895 with the Tilden Foundation and the Lenox Library to form the nucleus of the New York Public Library.

From 1921 to 1965 the building was the headquarters of the HIAS—the Hebrew Immigrant Aid & Sheltering Society—which since 1884 has been a worldwide migration agency responsible for the rescue of almost four million refugees and their settlement in lands of freedom. When the HIAS moved uptown to larger quarters, the survival of this lovely Italian Renaissance *palazzo* was seriously threatened. Virtually at the eleventh hour it was saved through the efforts of impresario Joseph Papp and a group of concerned citizens who ultimately convinced a skeptical City Council to recommend municipal purchase of the building as a permanent home for the New York Shakespeare Festival.

Renovation began in 1967 under the supervision of architect Giorgio Cavaglieri (who restored the Jefferson Market Courthouse; *see* Greenwich Village, 34), and was completed several years later. The Public Theater is an ideal example of adaptive reuse, proving that one can deal with old spaces and make them work. Contrary to the custom of gutting the interior and merely preserving the façade, Cavaglieri saved the elaborate interior, converting the two-tier skylit atrium of the former main reading room into the 300-seat Anspacher Theater. Two other large spaces were likewise made into theaters. The entrance and lobby remains a classic Corinthian colonnade. (Walk in, look around...and purchase a subscription to a performance series! Public restrooms are available.)

15. No. 436–440 is a large cast-iron commercial building in virtually pristine condition. Although no architectural beauty, it is typical of this type of construction [see SoHo Cast-Iron District walking tour]. It was designed by Edward Kendall in 1870 for Alfred Benjamin & Company, which manufactured men's clothing. Note their initials on the six escutcheons mounted on the pilasters. Interesting are the ram's horn volutes on the capitals, and full ram's horn on the shields.

Adjacent **No. 442–450,** occupying the corner lot, is maintained in almost original appearance by appreciative owners. Built in 1875 from plans by Griffith Thomas, it was for many years the headquarters of book publisher J. J. Little & Company (now Little, Brown & Co.), and is another example of the pleasing wedding of cast iron and masonry.

16. The **District 65 Building,** formerly Clinton Hall, and before that the Mercantile Library Building (George E. Harney, 1890), has little to recommend it architecturally; however, it occupies the site of the old Astor Place Opera House, and "thereby hangs a tale..."

A black page in New York City history was written on the evening of May 10, 1849, when a rampaging mob of thousands stormed the theater in one of the city's bloodiest outbursts of violence. **The Astor Place Riot,** as the event came to be called, stemmed from a bitter rivalry and ongoing feud between English tragedian William Macready and America's greatest actor, Edwin Forrest. Against a background of anti-British sentiment and a general antipathy toward foreigners as well as home-grown aristocrats, feelings had been running high for a number of weeks—spurred in great measure by rumormongers, know-nothings, and a sensationalist press.

That evening, when the curtain rose on the English actor's performance of *Macbeth,* a large and noisy crowd gathered in Astor Place, spilling over into the adjoining streets from Broadway to the Bowery. During the play, Macready was pelted with a steady stream of rotten eggs, copper pennies, and an assortment of vegetables. In the third scene a group of gangsters, led by small-time politician Isaiah Rynders, interrupted Macready's performance with screams and epithets, while a group of supporters of the English actor hurled back abuse with equal vigor. When the play was able to resume, the continuing commotion drowned out the stage. By the time the third act had begun, the mob outside started to assault the theater with bricks and stones. The police, although forewarned, were hopelessly outnumbered, and could do nothing to quell the screaming, cursing multitude that was now advancing on the theater's entrance. Estimates numbered the raging crowd at between 10,000 and 20,000.

In the meantime, the militia had been summoned from the nearby Tompkins Market Armory, but was restrained from action by nervous Mayor Caleb Woodhull, who feared the political consequences of any drastic action. Woodhull himself quietly fled the scene, leaving decisions to the unit's commanding officer. Finally, the order was given to fire, and after a warning volley over the heads of the rioters, the militiamen reluctantly fired volley after volley at point-blank range, killing 31 persons and leaving 150 wounded, putting an end to the worst theater riot in history.

17. At the time of the riot, Astor Place extended to where the "black cube" now rests, at the juncture with 8th Street (then called Clinton Place). Little St.

Ann's Church occupied the site until Lafayette Street was pushed through to meet Fourth Avenue. Now occupying the traffic island is sculptor Bernard Rosenthal's stabile, **Alamo,** erected in 1967. Just north is the **subway entrance kiosk of the Astor Place Station.** Installed in 1986, it is an exact cast-iron replica of one of the 133 Interborough Rapid Transit subway entrances of the early 20th century.

18. Against the backdrop of a wide-open sky, the stunning **Cooper Union Foundation Building** stands as a most pleasing sight. Completed in 1859, this gift to the people by industrialist-engineer-philanthropist Peter Cooper played a significant role in the development of the city. The "Union" was established as the first free, private, nonsectarian, coeducational college. Dedicated to the fields of science and art, it occupies a special place of respect among American colleges and universities.

Peter Cooper (1791–1883), a self-educated "Renaissance Man," was responsible for the first successful American railway locomotive (the "Tom Thumb"); he worked with Cyrus W. Field in the laying of the Atlantic Cable, and, with Samuel F. B. Morse, developed the telegraph. Cooper also battled corrupt politicians and helped to improve the city's public school system. With the profits from his ironworks and a glue factory, he built Cooper Union. In 1876 he ran unsuccessfully for president on the Greenback ticket, although his son Edward was elected mayor of the city, as was his son-in-law, Abram S. Hewitt.

Watercolor drawing of the Astor Place Riot of May 10, 1849, as militia from the nearby Tompkins Market Armory were firing into the crowd. A rampaging mob of between 10,000 and 20,000 stormed the Astor Place Opera House as the culmination of bitter feelings against English actor William Macready. When order was finally restored, 31 lay dead and 150 were injured. (Museum of the City of New York)

The building, designed in a kind of "Italian Renaissance cum Industrial" architectural style, is a unique achievement in itself, being the first to be constructed with wrought-iron beams as its framework. The exterior is of brownstone and rough-hewn sandstone, with cast-iron columns, pilasters, and arches. It was originally a five-story building, but the "factory-roof" art studios were subsequently superimposed. The street level was built with rows of small shops to provide a steady source of revenue for the institution. On the south end of the roof, the cylindrical protuberance houses the shaft of the original circular elevator. Cooper anticipated a lift system and installed the shaft even before a practical elevator was available. The novel construction of the building, employing steel railroad rails produced in his Trenton foundry, demanded that the supported sections of the "Union" coincide in measurement with the standard length of these rails. The rails spanned the brick bearing walls and supported the brick floor arches. In a recent renovation, architecture students were fortunate in obtaining a first-hand view of the original rail placement, as the central section of the interior was literally jacked up several floors while the old masonry walls

Diagonally across from Clinton Hall and the former Astor Place Opera House was Aberle's Theater, previously St. Ann's Roman Catholic Church. The theater opened in 1879, changed its name to the Germania in 1894, and was demolished in 1903. St. Ann's, a national Catholic shrine, is now located at 110 East 12th Street. (The J. Clarence Davies Collection, Museum of the City of New York)

The Astor Place Opera House at the intersection of Astor and Clinton places (later 8th Street) was rebuilt after the riot of 1849 and later became Clinton Hall and the Mercantile Library. In this photo taken ca. 1868, the building also houses auction rooms and the Sixpenny Savings Bank. The present building on the site, the District 65 Center, was also called Clinton Hall. (New-York Historical Society)

were replaced by more modern steel and reinforced concrete. Note the historical plaques on the north side.

The showpiece of the interior is the **Great Hall,** a magnificent auditorium, crisscrossed by arcades of supporting columns topped by granite arches. It was in the Great Hall that the Institution's inaugural lecture was given by Mark Twain in 1859. A year later Abraham Lincoln delivered his momentous "Right Makes Might" speech, establishing a Cooper Union lecture tradition followed by every president up to Woodrow Wilson.

The reconstruction, adhering essentially to the original plans of architect Frederick A. Peterson, was carried out by Cooper Union graduate architects under the direction of architecture department head John Hejduk.

Walk south along the Cooper Union Building to the small park on Cooper Square.

19. The **statue of Peter Cooper** was executed in 1894 by one of the country's foremost sculptors, Augustus Saint-Gaudens. Among his best known works are the equestrian statue of General Sherman near the Plaza Hotel, the statue of

An engraving of Cooper Union, with the Tompkins Market (right) and Bible House (left), enlivened by prancing horses and richly clad citizens as seen in Valentine's Manual *of 1861, looking north from Fourth Avenue and 6th Street. (Museum of the City of New York)*

David G. Farragut in Madison Square Park, the marble altar relief in the nearby Church of the Ascension, as well as the design of one of our former 20-dollar gold pieces. The base and canopy of the monument are by Stanford White.

Notice the attractive, and very visible, Cooper Union clock with its seven-foot frosted glass face. Once driven by an enormous weight and pendulum, it is now powered by a tiny electric motor.

The Bowery, which becomes Third Avenue at this point, was once darkened by the **Third Avenue El,** which rumbled by overhead from 1879 to 1950, on its way from South Ferry and Chatham Square to several points in the Bronx. Old-timers still look back with relish at the speedy, open-air ride provided by the old El. Although the Bowery and Third Avenue were never thoroughfares of scenic beauty, the exciting cityscape panoramas provided by these elevated trains cannot be duplicated by the much slower-moving ground-level buses.

20. The **Abram S. Hewitt Memorial Hall** of Cooper Union (Clinton & Russell, 1905), named for Peter Cooper's partner and son-in-law, occupies the site of the Tompkins Market Armory. Before it burned down, the old barnlike structure was a public market on the ground floor and an armory above. It was from here that the 27th Regiment of the New York National Guard was summoned to quell the Stone Cutters' Riot at the Washington Parade Ground [now Washington Square; *see* Greenwich Village, 7]; some years later, the Astor Place Riot; and in 1863, the Draft Riots (although in the latter disturbance, the militia had to be hastily called back from the just-ended Battle of Gettysburg). The unit later became the 7th Regiment and is now based in the landmark Seventh Regiment Armory, at Park Avenue and 67th Street.

Cross Cooper Square to the northeast corner of East 7th Street.

The area east of the Bowery, roughly between Houston Street and East 14th Street, and extending almost to the East River, is the **"East Village,"** formerly considered part of the Lower East Side.

From the early 19th century, successive waves of immigrants occupied the crowded tenements, leaving their individual ethnic stamp on the neighborhood. First came the Irish, followed by Germans, Jews, Poles, Ukrainians, and after World War II, the Spanish-speaking, mainly from Puerto Rico. In the 1950s and '60s the low rents attracted artists, writers, "beatniks," "hippies," and many who just liked the ethnic mix.

In the several-square-block area just east of the Bowery, centered on East 7th Street, there remains an active, tight-knit **Ukrainian enclave.**

21. The **former Metropolitan Savings Bank** is an ornate pile of marble, very similar in style to the cast-iron buildings for which it served as a model. Attributed to architect Carl Pfeiffer and built in 1868, its stately French Second Empire façade must have presented a convincing appearance of strength to its depositors, and it was one of the city's first fireproof buildings. It is now a church, serving congregations of both a Ukrainian and a Chinese Assembly of God.

22. At 11 East 7th Street is **Surma's Ukrainian Shop**—a fascinating emporium offering Ukrainian books, music, and records, colorful "peasant" clothing, painted (real) eggs, jewelry, and owner-cultivated honey.

23. McSorley's Old Ale House (No. 15) antedates the Ukrainian influx by many years, and claims to be the oldest saloon in the city (1854). Formerly a man's domain, it now permits women to share the authentic old-time atmosphere. In the dimly lit tavern, dozens of aging photographs and yellowing newspaper clippings hang on the grimy sheet-tin walls.

24. St. George's Ukrainian Catholic Church (Apollinaire Osadca, 1977) replaced an earlier church which was situated on an adjacent lot. St. George's, with its large school, is the religious and cultural center of the Ukrainian Catholic community. The adjacent short street, formerly Hall Place, has been renamed in honor of the 19th-century Ukrainian poet, Taras Shevchenko.

Continue toward Second Avenue.

At No. 31, on the north side, is the Hebrew Actor's Union and Actor's Club, which hearkens back to the golden age of the Yiddish theater at the turn of the century.

At the height of the Jewish immigration, Second Avenue from Houston Street to 14th Street was known as the **Yiddish Rialto.** Little now remains of the once lively Yiddish theater except for an occasional on-Broadway production. The old playhouses that once lined Second Avenue were either demolished or stand vacant. One of a small handful of surviving buildings is the ornate little **Orpheum Theater,** around the corner at 126 Second Avenue. It still hangs in as a legitimate theater, but no longer as a Yiddish playhouse.

Perhaps the most famous survivor of the heyday of the Yiddish Rialto is the Moorish-Revival–style **Louis N. Jaffe Art Theater,** formerly the Yiddish Art Theater/Yiddish Folks Theater, at the corner of Second Avenue and East 12th Street (*worth a five-minute detour to see it!*). The building was commissioned in 1925 by prominent Jewish civic leader Louis N. Jaffe as the permanent home for the Yiddish Art Theater, under the direction of preeminent Yiddish actor Maurice Schwartz. Yiddish theatrical performances continued until 1945, although there was a brief reprise between 1961 and 1965 and intermittently thereafter. With no fewer than 20 name changes through the years, including its longest tenure as the Phoenix Theater, it witnessed a variety of productions from burlesque to musicals and off-Broadway stage shows. The theater closed in 1988 and was converted three years later into a complex of seven movie theaters. The interior has been designated a landmark because of its elaborate polychrome ornamentation (Harrison G. Wiseman, architect, and Willy Pogany, designer). The extravagant motifs of Moorish, Alhambraic, Islamic, and Judaic styles are splendid, particularly in the ceiling, which displays some of the most remarkable plaster craftsmanship in the city. The Jaffe Art Theater is listed on the National and New York State Registers of Historic Places. Walk back down Second Avenue to Nos. 135 and 137 to rejoin the tour.

The tour continues on Second Avenue, just north of St. Mark's Place.

Side by side, at Nos. 135 and 137 Second Avenue, are the **Ottendorfer Branch of the New York Public Library** and the **Stuyvesant Polyclinic.** Both were donated by Ann and Oswald Ottendorfer, German-American philanthropists who were deeply concerned with the cultural and physical welfare of the large German community of the Lower East Side. Both buildings were designed by the same architect, William Schickel, and were erected in 1883–84. The library and clinic, formerly the *Freie Bibliothek und Lesehall* and the German Dispensary, respectively, are a unified pair, the former in Victorian style, with some elements of neo-Italian Renaissance and Queen Anne; and the latter in an exuberant version of neo-Italian Renaissance style, with innovative and decorative use of terra cotta.

Walk west on St. Mark's Place.

25. St. Mark's Place is the "main drag" of the East Village and it was the center of New York City's "counterculture." It is difficult to conceive that this was a most fashionable residential block in the early 19th century, with rows of elegant Federal and Greek Revival–style town houses. Vestiges still survive here and there along the block, covered by coats of garish paint and hidden by all manner of "improvements."

No. 20 was once the **Daniel LeRoy House** (1832). The last holdout of the row of town houses on the south side of the street, it shows many late Federal-style features. (Note the historical plaque.)

Sprawling **Nos. 21–25,** a group of old Federal houses joined together to form a single large hall, were until the 1960s the *Dom,* or Polish National Home, a social and cultural center for the Polish community of the Lower East Side. It later went commercial and housed the Electric Circus, a major rock 'n' roll establishment.

No. 12 was built for the **German American Shooting Society** in 1885. Like the *Dom,* it was also a social club. (The beer drinking was done here, the shooting elsewhere.)

No. 4 (1830–31) still retains a few of its Federal-style elements, including a stone molding and fanlight over the entrance.

26. Diagonally across St. Mark's Place, between 8th and 9th streets, is the modern **Cooper Union Engineering Building** (Voorhees, Smith, Smith, and Haines, 1961). It occupies the site of the old "Bible House," headquarters of the American Bible Society from 1852 to 1956, when it moved uptown to the Lincoln Center area—probably the last publishing house to move from the district.

Continue east to Fourth Avenue and turn right to 9th Street.

27. With the large number of local institutions dedicated to books and book production (Astor Library, Mercantile Library, Cooper Union, Scribner's, Bible House, the many publishing houses, as well as nearby New York University), it was no surprise that Fourth Avenue north to 14th Street became the second-hand book center of the city. The five blocks that once comprised **"Booksellers' Row"** boasted no fewer than two dozen book dealers. Sidewalk stands in front of the shops were always piled high with cheap books of every description, but the *cognoscenti* would seek out the real "finds" on the dusty shelves of the dark, labyrinthine interiors. Only two of the booksellers remain: Pageant Book & Print Shop, 109 East 9th Street, and Strand, at 828 Broadway. As in the past, browsers are always welcome.

28. On the west side of Fourth Avenue, between 10th and 11th streets, is the charming Gothic Revival–style **Grace Church Houses and School.** Enriching the appearance of the street, it was built in harmony with the landmark Grace Church, around the corner on Broadway. [For a description of Grace Church, *see* Ladies' Mile and Fashion Row, 2.] The attractive neo-Gothic-style group of buildings were erected in sections over a 35-year period: **The Clergy House,** No. 92 (Heins & LaFarge, 1892); **Grace Memorial House** (Huntington House), No. 94–96 (James Renwick, Jr., 1882–83); **Neighborhood House,** No. 98 (Renwick, Aspinwall & Tucker, 1906–07). In 1974–75 the church sought to demolish Nos. 92 and 94–96 to enlarge its school, and became engaged in a bitter struggle with preservationists. The matter was resolved by gutting the interiors but preserving the façades.

End of tour.

Although the tour ends here, an optional side trip may be made to the nearby **St. Mark's Historic District** [*see* map on next page]:

Return to 9th Street and turn left, passing Third Avenue, and enter Stuyvesant Street.

This diagonally running street was once the driveway from the Bouwerie Road to Peter Stuyvesant's estate. No. 21, the **Stuyvesant-Fish House,** is a rare early Federal residence (1803–04), and was built by the great-grandson of the governor as a wedding gift for his daughter Elizabeth, when she married Nicholas Fish.

The houses Nos. 21–35 and 42–46, plus 106–128 and 109–129 East 10th Street, are a unified group of Anglo-Italianate row houses which form part of the **"Renwick Triangle."** These handsome brick houses were erected in 1861 by Mathias Banta, a well-known speculative builder, who had purchased the property, once the site of Elizabeth Fish's garden, from her son, Hamilton Fish. The

ST. MARK'S HISTORIC DISTRICT
MANHATTAN

scale: 1" = 160'

**Designated January 14, 1969;
extension designated June 19, 1984**

(numbers show buildings inside boundary of district)

restoration of the buildings, which had begun to deteriorate badly after years of rooming-house occupancy, began in the mid-1960s. **No. 118 East 10th Street** was the childhood home of Stanford White in the 1850s.

Georgian-style **St. Mark's-Church-in-the-Bowery** at Second Avenue and 10th Street was built in 1799 on Governor Peter Stuyvesant's *Bouwerie* (farm). The Greek Revival belfry, clock tower, and steeple were added by Ithiel Town in 1828, and the Italianate cast-iron portico in 1854, contributing harmoniously to the appearance of the church. The governor himself is buried in a vault adjacent to the east wall, and it is said that his private chapel was located at this precise spot. His manor house was across what is now the intersection of Second Avenue and East 10th Street. A disastrous fire in July 1978, which heavily damaged the interior of the church and caused the roof to collapse, virtually wiped out the landmark, but the dedicated and activist minister and congregation vigorously sought funds through a series of promotional campaigns, and the church has been completely restored. Walk through the churchyard and note the various monuments and plaques, including those honoring American statesman Daniel D. Tompkins (once Governor of New York and Vice President under James Monroe) and Queen Wilhelmina of the Netherlands.

The No. 6 Lexington Avenue line is at Astor Place and Fourth Avenue.

LOWER
EAST
SIDE

STANTON ST.

RIVINGTON ST.

DELANCEY ST.

WILLIAMSBURG
BRIDGE

BOWERY

CHRYSTIE ST.

FORSYTH ST.

ELDRIDGE ST.

BROOME ST.

ALLEN ST.

ORCHARD ST.

LUDLOW ST.

ESSEX ST.

NORFOLK ST.

SUFFOLK ST.

CLINTON ST.

GRAND ST.

HESTER ST.

CANAL ST.

DIVISION ST.

EAST BROADWAY

HENRY ST.

PIKE ST.

RUTGERS ST.

JEFFERSON ST.

MANHATTAN BRIDGE

START

6. The Lower East Side

[F line to East Broadway, walk one block east on East Broadway to Jefferson Street]

The first tides of mass immigration to this country began sweeping across our shores just before the mid-19th century, with millions of refugees, mostly from Europe, seeking a haven from famines, wars, economic and political repression, and religious persecution. In successive waves they came—Irish, English, Germans, Swedes, Jews, Italians, Slavs—from northern Europe to the eastern Mediterranean, enduring the hardships of a long steerage voyage in crowded, foul ships. Mostly poor and strange to our ways, they would frequently gather together in the larger cities, creating with their fellow countrymen sprawling ghettos that were to become a kind of staging area in the gradual process of assimilation into the new culture.

Among the largest of the immigrant groups were the Jews from eastern Europe, who after 1870 began arriving in ever increasing numbers, fleeing the widespread pogroms and economic restrictions that had become commonplace throughout Poland, Hungary, Bohemia, Russia, and the Balkans. Settling largely on the Lower East Side—a four-square-mile corner of Manhattan bounded roughly by 14th Street on the north, Catherine Street on the south, the Bowery on the west, and the East River on the east—they moved into the squalid, hastily constructed tenements that filled every block in the area. As new arrivals continuously swelled the teeming ghetto, it became the most densely populated district in the world. By 1894, the population reached an astonishing 986 people per acre—one-and-a-half times that of Bombay, India! The immigrant Jews, seeking to maintain their Old World ties, also tended to band together by country of origin, thus creating within the Lower East Side enclaves of Russians, Poles, Rumanians, Lithuanians, Hungarians, and Levantines. In common, however, they shared their religious beliefs and rituals, their miserable living conditions, and their hopes for a better life. Many of the immigrants were drawn to the needle trades, and eked out a meager existence working in the unregulated sweatshops,

139

or laboring in their tiny, crowded cold-water flats in what soon became a cottage garment industry centered about the family sewing machine. Others were employed in the numerous small retail shops and factories that proliferated on the street floors of the tenements, while many chose "private enterprise" as pushcart vendors, hawking an endless variety of wares from these peripatetic two-wheeled establishments that lined the main thoroughfares of the Lower East Side.

In spite of their grinding poverty, the struggle for survival, and the drudgery of daily life, Jewish institutions flourished. More than 500 synagogues and *talmud torahs* (religious schools) were constructed: a Yiddish theater was founded; Hebrew and Yiddish book publishers flourished; and more than a dozen Yiddish newspapers appeared on the newsstands. Rapid naturalization was the immediate goal of all immigrants, and evening classes in English and Americanization at the neighborhood public schools were always jammed to overflowing. Every newcomer dreamed of the day when, no longer, a greenhorn, he could climb the economic ladder, become a "real American," and make a better life for himself and his children.

With the passage in the 1920s of restrictive laws, the great flood of immigration was finally halted and the growth of the ghetto stemmed. As families moved to better neighborhoods in the city, the "old neighborhood" began to decline, and the Jewish ghetto is now largely gone. The depressing tenements are being replaced by high-rise apartments; the small family-run shops are giving way to supermarkets and large retail stores; the hundreds of synagogues—many of them awesome architectural masterpieces—are reduced to a scant, crumbling handful; and the *lingua franca,* once exclusively Yiddish, is yielding to a babel of Spanish, Chinese, and Hindi.

The walking tour of the Lower East Side is largely an imaginative glimpse of the past through a number of the vestiges and surviving artifacts of that era of Jewish immigration—a sort of last look at the remnants of the old neighborhood, which in a few short years will be no more. It was a wonderfully rich and fruitful period of American history in which millions of Jews came to the United States through the port of New York and spread across the entire country making their contributions to the total fabric of American life.

Begin the Lower East Side tour at the corner of East Broadway and Jefferson Street (on the park side), one block east of the East Broadway subway station. (The tour is best made on a Sunday.)

1. The Educational Alliance (197 East Broadway) was known as the Hebrew Institute when the building was erected in 1891 from plans by the Jewish architectural firm of Brunner & Tryon. It was organized by a group of "uptown Jews" as an educational, cultural, intellectual, and social service center for the residents of the Lower East Side. It provided training in Americanization for the newly arrived immigrants, and is credited with helping speed up the immigrants' process of assimilation with its day and evening classes in English and citizenship. It housed a free library at a time when no public libraries existed in the city, and its classes were later used as models for the New York City

Board of Education's citizenship program for the foreign-born. The Alliance also distributed clothing and food to the needy. Classes for children were also offered in Jewish religion and history, and the Alliance conducted free Sabbath and High Holy Day services for those too poor to be members of a synagogue congregation. It was also a pioneer in the concept of summer camp for children.

Through the years the Alliance has expanded its educational work, offering free courses in a wide spectrum of disciplines: art, music, philosophy, drama, science, and vocational skills. Although its original constituency is largely gone, it holds classes for Chinese and other children whose parents work during the day. It is also very active in community social service projects, and conducts many programs for senior citizens, including a daily lunch.

The Lower East Side's population is now approximately 40 percent Puerto Rican (and other Spanish-speaking groups), 30 percent Chinese, 10 percent Black, 5 percent others (Indian, Ukrainian, Polish, Albanian, and Italian), and only 15 percent Jewish. The original East Broadway building of the Alliance was modernized in 1970–71 and renamed the David Sarnoff Building. Adjoining the Educational Alliance on Jefferson Street is the David L. Podell Residence for Senior Citizens. This new annex contains subsidized efficiency apartments for the elderly, and has a direct connection into the Alliance building.

2. To the left (in the park) is the **Seward Park Branch of the New York Public Library.** Built in 1910, it was one of the early branches of the newly established free municipal library system. The public library was founded by Andrew Carnegie, who was instrumental in merging the Astor, Tilden, and Lenox Trust libraries—the three largest private collections in the city.

So great was this free library's popularity with the immigrants when it opened that it was not uncommon to see long lines of adults and youngsters patiently awaiting their turn to enter the crowded building. Until recently this branch had the largest Yiddish collection in the city. Next to the library, at the turn of the century, stood the office of *Der Groisser Kundess* (The Big Stick), a popular Yiddish weekly that published humorous stories and cartoons, and offered a bit of comic relief from the grim realities of immigrant life.

3. Across the street, at 175 East Broadway, towers the ten-story **former Jewish Daily Forward Building** (George A. Boehn, 1911). The building is no longer occupied by the *Forward,* as the newspaper has moved its offices uptown, where it continues to publish, with an annual deficit made up by contributions from loyal supporters. Founded in 1897 by Abraham Cahan, the *Forward* became the most influential newspaper in the Jewish community, and was read with a dedication second only to that given to the religious books. As an ardent campaigner for the improvement of the human condition, Abe Cahan and the *Forward* supported the labor movement, fought dishonest politicians, and led in the battle to eliminate the sweatshops, at the same time helping the immigrants adapt to the New World and encouraging them to become informed, loyal citizens. The *Forward* always lent a sympathetic ear to the problems of its readers, and until 1982 conducted a daily column called the *Bintel Brief* (Bundle of Letters), in which problems of readers were printed and answered by the editor. (The column has yielded to one on Social Security.) The paper has always provided a forum for the greatest Yiddish writers (Isaac Bashevis Singer was a regular contributor), and maintains a small staff of foreign correspondents who provide material not available from the usual wire services. Its present circulation is less than a fifth of the 1924 peak of 200,000, and it's now a weekly, published uptown, but there is still sufficient interest in Yiddish with support from contributions to keep it alive.

The building, which housed not only the *Forward* but also an active Yiddish theater and the offices of many Jewish labor organizations, is now in the hands of the Unification Church. To the east of the Forward Building, at No. 183, in a structure which now houses a Chinese noodle factory, was the home of the large-circulation *Morning Journal–Day,* once two Yiddish dailies that merged in the late 1920s. Its closing in 1972 was mourned by many faithful readers. The *Tageblatt,* an even older daily, stood at the corner of Jefferson Street.

4. Triangular **Nathan Straus Square** (formerly called Rutgers Square) is named for the Jewish philanthropist who in 1919 sponsored a program of free sterilized-milk stations for children throughout the country. Nathan Straus, a partner in the R. H. Macy enterprise with his brother, Isadore, was active for many years in charitable causes. (Isadore and his wife went down on the *Titanic* in 1912.)

The circular marble shaft was erected in tribute to the servicemen of the Lower East Side who gave their lives in both World Wars.

5. At the corner of East Broadway and Rutgers Street is **the site of the former Garden Cafeteria.** A local landmark for many years, it had been a favored gathering place of the local "intelligentsia," especially for the staff of the nearby *Forward.* At the turn of the century when the immediate area was known as the "Athens of the Lower East Side" because of the number of newspapers, publishers, and bookstores located close by, an earlier restaurant on the site was the gathering place of journalists, authors, and celebrated actors of the then very active Yiddish theater. In its final years after the departure of the *Forward,* the "Garden" was just a popular and inexpensive dining spot, and a convenient place to meet for an assortment of East Side characters. Changing demographics and economic realities made it more and more difficult for the restaurant to survive, and as the last owner once commented dryly, "How can we stay in business when people come in and spend a whole day over one cup of coffee?" The present Chinese fast-food establishment, replete with typical roast fowls hanging in the window, is dramatic evidence of the changes that are taking place throughout the East Side.

6. Seward Park, carved out of a former slum district, provides a pleasant retreat for the inhabitants of the surrounding crowded and shadeless streets. A small but busy "thieves market" near the Essex Street entrance should be avoided.

7. St. Teresa's Roman Catholic Church, at the corner of Rutgers and Henry streets was founded in 1863 to serve the growing Irish immigrant community that at the time occupied much of the Lower East Side. Built in 1841 as the First Presbyterian Church of New York, it was purchased through the efforts of then-Archbishop Corrigan, and now serves new immigrant groups. It is possibly the only trilingual Catholic church in the city, offering masses in English, Spanish, and Chinese. The church is typical of the Gothic Revival style that

Hester Street was the main shopping thoroughfare of the Lower East Side, with pushcarts, shops, and stalls lining both sides of the street. This view, looking east from Essex Street to Norfolk Street, was taken in 1899, at the height of Jewish immigration. (Museum of the City of New York)

gained so much popularity in the decade of the 1840s. Its adjacent parking lot was once the site of the Hebrew National *Wurstfabrik.*

Rutgers Street is named for the Henry Rutgers family, whose farm occupied much of the land from this point to the East River during the Colonial period. Their property bordered the James DeLancey farm, and the boundary, once a country lane, is now appropriately called **Division Street.** Division Street beyond the Manhattan Bridge was famous early in the century for its millinery district and its very aggressive "pulleresses"—women employees who stood outside the store and pulled in the unwary to get "bargains." From the 1920s until the early 1970s it was a well-known center for women's outerwear.

8. The nameless square (or triangle) formed by the confluence of Canal and Division streets is particularly colorful during the Jewish festival of Succoth, or Feast of Tabernacles, which according to the lunar calendar can fall anywhere from late September to mid-October. The sidewalks are lined with vendors, many in Hasidic garb, selling myrtle leaves, palm fronds, and citrons imported from the Holy Land. These are bought by religious Jews to decorate their *Succah,* or outdoor lattice hut, where meals are taken during the holiday in celebration of the harvest.

9. Walk one block west on Canal Street, noting the number of Hebrew and Yiddish bookstores as well as some new East Indian retail establishments. Canal Street has also become a center for discount merchandise, watchmakers, and a variety of Chinese shops.

Turn right on Ludlow Street. On the right is the massive structure of the now-defunct **Loew's Canal.** When you return to Canal Street, see if you can discover the somewhat altered but still ornate former entrance to this defunct silent-film movie house. It is now occupied by a discount electrical appliance store, and the dark recesses of the theater are used as a warehouse.

At No. 5 Ludlow Street is the equally defunct **Independent Kletzker Brotherly Aid Society** building (1910), whose name and founding date may be read in the pediment. It was customary for newly arrived immigrant groups to maintain association with those from the same *shtetl,* or small town. If the group was large or wealthy enough, they might build a synagogue and a *talmud torah,* purchase a cemetery lot, and sometimes establish a benevolent or mutual-aid society, called a *landsmanshaft,* for their members. This is the only such surviving building in the neighborhood, and was constructed for an immigrant group from the Polish village of Kletsk. The L-shaped building was sold early in this century to Max Kobre's Bank, a private Jewish bank which failed after World War I. (Note the beehives on the second-floor ledge.) In recent times it was the Zion Funeral Chapel; however, changing population patterns forced Zion to move and sell out to two other morticians, one Italian and the other Chinese, and the main floor was then divided in half. The upper stories, which once housed the *landsmanshaft*'s synagogue, have been converted into co-op apartments.

Return to Canal Street and continue west to Orchard Street.

10. Orchard Street for the seven blocks north of Canal Street has been the principal commercial thoroughfare for many years. For those living outside the neighborhood, Orchard Street, originally the location of the DeLancey estate's orchards, is now synonymous with the Lower East Side. Hectic, bustling, and noisy, it is the closest thing to a "native market." Before the pushcarts were ruled off the streets by city ordinance, it was even busier. Here on Sundays come thousands of bargain hunters from all over the New York metropolitan area, taking advantage of the discounts—real and fanciful—offered by the endless row of small retail shops. It is said that the Lower East Side is the only complete mercantile district in the city, where virtually anything can be purchased, and at a lower price than anywhere else. (A stroll along Orchard Street comes later in the tour.)

11. On the southwest corner of Canal and Orchard streets looms the tallest structure on the Lower East Side—the **former Jarmulovsky's Bank** building (Rouse & Goldstone, 1912), now a multi-use loft building. Only a few old-timers remember that active financial institution, founded in 1873, which served as the local Baron Rothschild for more than 40 years, ultimately bringing grief to thousands of unlucky depositors when it collapsed in 1917. Federal banking regulations were quite lax in those days, and private banks flourished throughout the country. Sender Jarmulovsky, who died in 1912 and left the management to his sons, was a shrewd financier whose success was climaxed in the construction of this imposing building at the height of the immigration period. However, mismanagement and a run on the bank by depositors wishing to send money to relatives as World War I threatened forced it into insolvency, owing its creditors millions and ruining thousands of trusting immigrants. The State Banking Department then took it over.

In 1991 the owner of the building demolished a circular, temple-like structure which crowned the building, thus destroying what was once one of the neighborhood's most prominent skyline features and forfeiting any possibility for future landmark status.

12. Allen Street, one block west, was once a dark and dingy thoroughfare, echoing with the rattle of the former Second Avenue Elevated, and boasting one of the largest red-light districts in town. With the El gone and the street widened in 1930 (note the absence of building fronts on the east side), it is a main north-south artery of the city, and above Houston Street it becomes First Avenue. Little remains of its once lusty past. In recent times it was a popular center for copper-and-brass antique merchants, but now all but Mr. J. Kleinstein (No. 32) have vanished—replaced by Chinese wholesale food dealers and restaurants.

Canal Street is named for the 40-foot-wide drainage ditch, or canal, that was dug in 1805 to drain the Collect (the fresh water pond on the site of Foley Square [*see* page 95], a former city water source that had become polluted). The canal emptied into the Hudson River and was crossed by a bridge at Broadway. It was filled in and paved 15 years later, adding another busy thoroughfare to the ever-growing city.

At Eldridge Street turn south (left).

13. The Old Law tenement at **Number 19** is purported to be the birthplace of actor Eddie Cantor. Old Law tenements prevail throughout most of the Lower East Side. Prior to the passage of the "Old Law" in 1879, and modifications in 1887, there was little regulation of the construction of multiple dwellings. Houses were often built of wood, without fire escapes, toilets, or water supply; and there was no provision for the ventilation of interior rooms, as only the front and rear rooms had windows. The 1879 law corrected many of these evils, and included among its requirements that an airshaft be built between adjacent tenement houses to provide (some) light and air for inside rooms, that hallways and stairways be wider and constructed of fireproof materials, that water be piped into each apartment, and that there be a toilet for each two apartments. Thus backyard privies and curbside water pumps became a thing of the past, and the tenements became a bit safer, and possibly a trifle more comfortable. Another prohibition was the construction of the so-called "backyard houses"—multiple dwellings that were built behind other houses, without direct access to the street. The addition of the airshaft to the tenement changed the overhead shape of the building from a simple rectangle to that of an exercise dumbbell—and the name "dumbbell tenement" is still applied to those built under the Old Law. In 1901 the "New Law" was passed, further modifying the building code, widening the airshaft and including a provision that houses higher than five stories must be equipped with an elevator. Seven-story walk-ups were not uncommon in the old days!

Compare this row of Old Law tenements with the row of red brick buildings further south (with curved lintels over the windows), built in the 1870s. These are without airshafts and have narrow hallways with sheet-tin walls and ceilings, and wooden floors and staircases. Fire escapes were added as mandated by the 1879 Law, otherwise these nonfireproof buildings would be frightening fire traps. Scores of pre–Old Law tenements still exist throughout the Lower East Side.

14. The imposing synagogue, **Congregation Khal Adath Jeshurun and Anshe Lubz,** at 12–14 Eldridge Street, was once the largest Jewish house of worship in the neighborhood. Built in 1886 from plans by Herter Brothers, it is built mainly in Moorish Revival style with some Gothic elements. Except for missing finials on the cornice, the façade is in an excellent state of preservation. The stained-glass windows, however, had suffered from vandalism and neglect. The interior is exceptional, with a hand-carved ark of Italian walnut, sculptured wooden balcony, enormous brass Victorian chandeliers and candelabra, high-quality stained glass, brightly painted wall murals, and a lofty, barrel-vaulted ceiling. The building had suffered years of neglect, and the effects of weather and vandalism had taken a dreadful toll. The Jewish population of the neighborhood declined through the years, and the congregation dwindled to the point where fewer than 20 active members remained to support this great house of worship. The magnificent sanctuary was abandoned in the mid-1930s, and services were held in the basement whenever a *minyan,* or quorum of ten adult males, could be assembled.

Until recently, the future of the synagogue was very much in doubt; however, a group of interested citizens (including the author) organized a preservation committee, and soon afterward a professional organization, the Eldridge Street Project, was engaged to raise funds and manage the prodigious task of restoration. Under the direction of restoration architect Giorgio Cavaglieri, the work is now in progress. To date, the building has been stabilized, the façade and interior cleaned, the pews refinished, and the stained-glass windows have been removed for restoration. However, much still needs to be done. Over $2.5 million in small and large donations has been spent, but at least another $1 million is needed to return the synagogue to its late 19th-century grandeur. The Project also sponsors cultural events to attract financial support. The Synagogue, the first to be erected by Eastern European immigrant Jews on the Lower East Side, is listed on the National Register of Historic Places and is a New York City landmark. For a tour, call the Project at (212) 219-0888.

Continue south on Eldridge Street, turning left on Division Street to Pike Street.

15. The **Manhattan Bridge** (Gustav Lindenthal and Carrère & Hastings, 1909) was the last-built of a trio of downtown bridges connecting Manhattan with Brooklyn. (The first, the Brooklyn Bridge, was completed in 1883, and was referred to in Yiddish as the *Alte Brick,* or Old Bridge. The Williamsburg Bridge, opened in 1903, was the *Naiye Brick,* or New Bridge.) A three-cent fare was charged on the creaky trolley that shuttled back and forth when the

The Police Court on Essex Street at the corner of Broome was replaced by Seward Park High School. In this view, taken in 1892, the high wall visible in the background was the Ludlow Street Jail, where corrupt "Boss" Tweed had died 14 years before. (New-York Historical Society)

The opening of the Manhattan Bridge in 1909 improved transportation to Brooklyn, and to an extent encouraged further emigration from the Lower East Side. The Manhattan Bridge Three Cents Trolley provided a cheap trip across the East River. (Brooklyn Historical Society)

(Left) This photograph of a poor Jew with his chalah, preparing for the Sabbath in a coal cellar, is touching evidence of the struggle for human dignity under conditions of abject poverty. The sign at left indicated that the man may have been a shoemaker by trade. (Photograph by Jacob A. Riis. The Jacob A. Riis Collection, Museum of the City of New York)

(Left, below) The squalor of tenement life is dramatically apparent in this picture by an unknown photographer, taken, according to the wall calendar, some time in June 1916. The rear room, without window or ventilation, indicates that this is a pre–Old Law tenement, built before 1879. (Community Service Society of New York)

(Below) Sociologist-photographer Jacob Riis visited the old Essex Market School and recorded this crowded little classroom with its coal stoves and gas illumination. The closely-shaven-headed youngsters seem unusually well behaved, doubtless after strong admonition by the usually very strict teachers. (The Jacob A. Riis Collection, Museum of the City of New York)

For youngsters growing up in the crowded, unsanitary Lower East Side tenements, the daily life of grinding poverty left little time to enjoy the pleasures of childhood. They were expected to work in the sweatshops and shoulder their share of the family's struggle for survival. (Museum of the City of New York)

Sweatshops took many forms. Here a family of Bohemian cigar-makers work busily at their trade. (Photograph by Jacob A. Riis. The Jacob A. Riis Collection, Museum of the City of New York)

Tightly parked rows of pushcarts virtually block access to the sidewalk in this Lower East Side street scene taken in the 1890s. Youngsters generally sought the freedom of the streets to escape the overcrowded condition of their squalid tenement homes. (Community Service Society)

A group of three women buying eggs just before the Sabbath, on Hester Street, 1895. (Photograph by Alice Austen, Staten Island Historical Society)

Photographer Jessie Tarbox Beals posed this Italian immigrant family in the kitchen of their East Side flat. Few apartments consisted of more than a kitchen, small in-between room, and a parlor, or "front room." Communal toilets in the Old Law tenements were located in the halls, adjacent to the cold water faucet. Note the tiny bedroom whose only window opens into the kitchen. The gas stove was considered a "modern improvement," and the kerosene lamp on the stove was the room's only source of illumination. (Museum of the City of New York)

The intersection of Delancey and Clinton streets at the entrance to the Williamsburg Bridge was the busiest on the Lower East Side when this photo was taken in 1919. Motor vehicles and horse-drawn wagons shared the bridge with trolleys and the BMT subway. Then, many more pedestrians than now used the wide bridge walkway, saving themselves the 2¢ carfare. The ornate square buildings in the foreground were entrance kiosks to the underground bridge trolley station. Few of the Old Law tenements along the north side of Delancey Street are still lived in. (The Edward B. Watson Collection)

A smoky elevated train has just passed the Chatham Square junction of the 2nd and 3rd Avenue Els in the mid-1880s. The station was later rebuilt with an upper level to eliminate the dangerous rail crossovers. The train is headed for South Ferry, while the tracks on the left lead to City Hall. Below the elevated structure are Park Row (left), East Broadway (right), and the Bowery (rear). The 2nd Avenue line swings around the left side of Congress Hall up Division Street. (Museum of the City of New York)

Manhattan Bridge was opened. In addition to four lanes of motor-vehicle traffic, it also carries several subway lines.

At the corner of Allen Street (called Pike Street as it curves toward the East River) is the **former power house of the Second Avenue El.** Note the old metal letters on the wall of the original Manhattan Elevated Railway building, as well as the row of holes for the power cables. Since the El made a sharp curve at this point to swing into Division Street, the corner of the power house was flattened. It is now a Chinese-owned warehouse.

Diagonally across the street at 15 Pike Street is an abandoned synagogue, the **Congregation Sons of Israel Kalwarie,** built in 1903. This Classic Revival–style building also suffered from a dwindling congregation, and at present is sealed, with its future uncertain.

Continue north on Pike Street (which becomes Allen Street as it passes Canal Street), to Hester Street.

16. By the 1880s **Hester Street** had become the busiest market in the Lower East Side. With both sides of the street lined with pushcarts and the wares of all the shops piled high on the sidewalks, the crowded street took on the atmosphere of an Oriental bazaar. Especially on Thursday evenings, the congestion and clamor reached its weekly peak, as Jewish housewives shopped for the Sabbath. Anything could be bought on Hester Street—dry goods, food, housewares, books, jewelry, furniture—and haggling was always the rule. On hot summer days the lack of refrigeration was very much in evidence, as fish peddlers pressed to sell out before nature took its course. Everywhere was the smell of decay as the gutters and sidewalks accumulated "mountain ranges" of fruit peels, paper, fish scales, nutshells, rotting vegetables, and rubbish of all sorts. The horses that pulled the many wagons added an immense contribution, too.

Turn right on Hester Street and left on Orchard Street.

17. Note the **seven-story walk-up** on the west side of Orchard Street (No. 45), a short distance from the corner. One can only speculate on the number of unfortunate souls whose hearts were surely overtaxed by the wearying daily ascents to the upper floors. Jewish stars in terra cotta appear on the adjacent building to the right and on the façades of a number of tenements—no doubt a ruse by the builder to attract religious, but naïve, tenants.

18. At the southwest corner of Orchard and Grand streets is the **former E. S. Ridley Department Store.** Its imposing rounded corner and ornate cast-iron façade are all that remains of one of the most fashionable stores in the city during the Gay '90s. Together with competitor Lord & Taylor's, four blocks west on Grand Street, they presented an almost incongruous element of elegance in a neighborhood that could ill afford their wares.

Ridley's, established in the early 1870s, gave up the ghost in 1901, and a year later, Lord & Taylor's moved all of its retail operations to its main store at Broadway and 20th Street [*see* Ladies' Mile, 27]. A bizarre epilogue to the Ridley story took place in 1964, when the proprietor of the store occupying the old

The Yiddish Theater was an important aspect of Lower East Side cultural life. The Grand Theater, the first built in New York expressly for the Yiddish theater, which stood on the southeast corner of Grand and Chrystie streets until the blocks between Chrystie and Forsyth streets were leveled for the construction of Sara Delano Roosevelt Park, boasted many famous actors. In this 1908 photo, Jacob Adler stars in the Yiddish version of King Lear. *(Museum of the City of New York)*

Ridley building was handed an envelope by the letter carrier who inquired if it was addressed to him. On examining the letter they were astonished to see that it was a Ridley business-reply envelope, recently postmarked, and addressed to the mail order department. On opening it they found a yellow slip of paper on which a message was scrawled from a man in Florida inquiring why Ridley's had not sent their catalog "for some time"—63 years after the firm went out of business!

Take a brief detour by continuing north on Orchard Street to No. 97, the **Lower East Side Tenement Museum.** Established in 1988 in a hundred-year-old typical tenement that is being rehabilitated, the Museum conducts programs and tours, including a "living history" experience, with actors portraying the various immigrant nationalities that lived in the building. Information: (212) 431–0233.

Return to Grand Street and turn west (right).

19. On the north side of Grand Street between Orchard and Allen streets, the large gray building was formerly a very popular **sports arena** when it opened in the mid-1880s. Indoor sports at that time were mainly confined to boxing.

20. Look across Allen Street, about 100 yards to the left of Grand Street. The tall building now housing a public garage was **formerly the wagon house and stables of Ridley's Department Store.** Notice some of the features of this industrial Romanesque Revival–style structure, such as the rows of round-arch windows and the generous use of terra-cotta ornamentation in the window mouldings and wall plaques.

21. Continue west on **Grand Street,** which for many years was one of the city's major east-west thoroughfares. Its double horsecar line connected the New Jersey ferries on Manhattan's West Side with the East River ferries to Long Island. On the north side of Grand Street, between Allen, Eldridge, and Forsyth streets, are four diminutive **Federal-style houses** of the 1820s. No longer residences, these old houses with peaked roofs and twin dormers somehow managed to survive.

The Third Avenue El looking north from the Grand Street station in 1895. Before the Els were electrified, the little steam locomotives created problems for those below, spewing hot cinders and oil, and littering the streets with ashes. In this photo, made from a magic lantern slide, the buildings on the left are still standing today, from the Bowery Savings Bank building (extreme left), the early nineteenth-century houses with dormers, the long-defunct Germania Bank (tall white structure), to distant Cooper Union. (The Picture Decorator, Inc., N.Y.C.)

22. At the corner of Eldridge Street, look left at No. 87, formerly a synagogue, and in the late 1970s, a black church. It is now an apartment house. Jewish symbols still remain in the façade.

23. Across Grand Street, at 107 Eldridge Street (now a fabric store), is the **former Eldridge Street Police Station.** The building is in surprisingly good condition, and except for first-floor modifications, looks very much as it did when built as the local station house in the late 1870s.

24. Seven blocks of tenements were demolished between Forsyth and Chrystie streets in the late 1930s to make way for **Sara Delano Roosevelt Park,** named for the mother of F.D.R. The Lord & Taylor store stood at the southwest corner of Grand and Chrystie streets from 1853 until 1902.

25. One block farther west on Grand Street, at the Bowery, the theatrical district of New York in the mid-19th century, is **"Bank Corner."** The landmark former **Bowery Savings Bank** (now Home Savings of America), occupying the L-shaped plot on the northwest corner, was built in 1894 by the famed architectural firm of McKim, Mead & White, and represented the newly popular Classical Revival style. Stanford White is credited with setting the trend for future bank architecture with this popular Roman Classical style. On the same corner, surrounded on two sides by the Bowery's "temple of savings," is the former **Bowery Bank** (note the old insignia in wrought iron), now a branch of Citibank. Across the street on the southwest corner, in a building now occupied by the Manufacturer's Hanover Trust Company, was another victim of the Depression, the **Chatham & Phenix Bank.** Disgruntled depositors sometimes referred to it as the "Cheat 'em & Fix 'em" Bank.

26. Turn north on the Bowery, observing the number of Federal-style houses remaining, particularly **Nos. 133, 134, 136,** and **140.** For years this block has been the "interior lighting center" of the city. Formerly specializing in gas lighting equipment, the dozen or so brilliantly lit stores now offer just about every possible type of electric lighting fixture.

27. Turn right into **Delancey Street.** Once a rather fashionable retail center, it is now shabby and forlorn, serving mainly as an approach route to the Williamsburg Bridge, a half-mile to the east. In its heyday, the city fathers renamed it Schiff Parkway in honor of philanthropist Jacob Schiff; but the name didn't stick, and so it again honors James DeLancey, the original 18th-century landowner. DeLancey chose the wrong side in the American Revolution, and at the conclusion of the war, his property was confiscated and he left for England. Delancey Street is the sole public reminder of his name.

28. On the southeast corner of Forsyth and Delancey streets is the **former Forsyth Street Synagogue,** Congregation Anshe Ileya (J. Cleveland Cady, 1890), now occupied by a Dominican Seventh-Day Adventist Church. The old synagogue was once one of the wealthiest and most exclusive *shuls* on the Lower East Side. The designers of the building, shrewdly planned for future financial security by having a row of stores built into the Delancey Street side. Continue east on Delancey Street.

29. At Allen Street take a short detour north to the **former Municipal Bathhouse.** Built in 1905, it was the last of the free public bathhouses in a city

Looking west on Hester Street at the turn of the century. The excavation at left is for Seward Park, which was to become a welcome oasis in the maze of crowded, depressing tenements. In the background, a horsecar passes on Essex Street while in the distance, the Second Avenue El structure can be seen on Allen Street. (New-York Historical Society)

that had 15 such facilities at the beginning of the century. There were 54 men's showers and 34 women's showers in the white brick and limestone building. Few residents of any poor neighborhood had the luxury of bathing facilities in their dismal apartments, so the city built a series of public baths in the more densely populated districts. To this day, occupants of most of the tenements still do not have adequate bathrooms. Some have a bathtub in the kitchen, but must share a common toilet in the hall. Central heating and landlord-supplied hot water are the exception. The bathhouse was closed in 1988, auctioned by the city in 1992, and converted into a Chinese church.

30. The tall building with templelike columns at the southeast corner of Delancey and Allen streets was once the home of the **Hebrew Publishing Company.** Founded before the turn of the century to cater to the immigrants' thirst for Yiddish and Hebrew reading material, it is still the world's largest publisher of prayer books, language texts, and literary works in both languages, although no longer in the retail business. Stand directly in front of the building, near the curb, and examine the wide concrete panel above the first floor. With a little squinting one can discern the old sign, *Bank of the United States.* This was originally the Lower East Side branch of a largely Jewish-owned bank. Doing business with branches throughout the city, it prospered for many years. It is said that part of its success was due to immigrants' belief that because of its name, the Bank of the United States was actually a government institution, hence safe beyond a doubt. Its failure in 1932 was caused by the collusion of several big city banks that refused to grant it short-term credit. It was customary for banks to help each other when one was momentarily short of working capital, but in this case it was felt that anti-Semitism was the reason. Depositors ultimately received most of their money, but the bank's collapse was a sensation for a number of years.

31. Across the street, the crumbling **Delancey Theater** is the last of the neighborhood's old silent-film playhouses. Its roof has collapsed and a portion of the theater's proscenium arch is visible through the ruins of the interior.

32. Turning north on **Orchard Street,** the atmosphere suddenly changes. Formerly identical in character to the blocks to the south, it has in recent years become a largely Hispanic neighborhood. The sights, sounds, and smells are reminiscent of a typical "south of the border" public market. There is a gaiety and liveliness absent until now, with Latin rhythms blaring from record shops, storekeepers aggressively peddling their merchandise on the sidewalk, and the

Busy Grand Street at the turn of the century was the major east-west artery of Manhattan, as its street cars connected with both New Jersey and Long Island ferries. In this view looking west, a trolley is turning north into Forsyth Street. Directly behind it is the Grand Theater, and in the distance, the Third Avenue El. In the foreground, a policeman keeps a stern eye on a group of schoolboys. (Community Service Society of New York)

aroma of an assortment of savory, exotic delicacies being cooked by street vendors. So busy is this street that vehicular traffic is banned on Sundays. Walk north to Rivington Street and turn right.

33. The First Roumanian Congregation in America, *Shaari Shamoyim* (89 Rivington Street), was organized in 1885. Only the name is Rumanian now, as the synagogue serves a different constituency. The building, in Romanesque Revival style, was built as the Allen Street Methodist Church in 1888, four years before its purchase by the Hebrew congregation. The sanctuary is very spacious, with a particularly beautiful pulpit set against an array of brightly colored stained-glass windows. This small building to the left of the synagogue, once the rectory of the former church, later became *Talmud Torah,* (a Jewish religious school). The dwindling synagogue's congregation was forced to sell it, but the school's carved sign still remains.

Rivington Street is named for James Rivington, a well-known printer and newspaper publisher during the late 18th century. Thought to have been a Tory during the American Revolution, recent historical discoveries show that he was a very successful spy for General Washington, and is credited with breaking the British naval code.

34. Near the corner of Essex Street is another gastronomical landmark, **Economy Candy,** No. 108. The counters, both inside and on the sidewalk, are stacked high with such goodies as dried fruit, nuts, gelatin candies, and halvah.

Farther down on Rivington Street (across Essex Street) are two other food landmarks: **Schapiro's Wine Company,** at the corner of Norfolk Street; and **Streit's Matzoth Company,** one block farther at Suffolk Street. The winery and matzoth bakery are the only ones left in Manhattan. Schapiro's gives free tours and wine-tastings every Sunday. Try not to miss the underground tour past countless enormous vats and casks extending far beneath the buildings on the block, accompanied by an explanation of the kosher winemaking process. But go easy on the generous samples if you intend to continue the walking tour with some degree of sobriety! Return to Essex Street, and turn left (south).

Along the east side of Essex Street, extending for several blocks, is the **Essex Street Market,** built by the city just before pushcarts were banned from the streets.

35. Continue south on Essex Street to **Delancey Street.** This busy intersection, with its approach to the Williamsburg Bridge, was once even busier! When the bridge was opened in 1903, Delancey Street became a major artery, not only for the horse-drawn vehicles and early motorcar traffic, but for horsecars and the new electric trolleys as well. A few years later, the newly built Brooklyn & Manhattan Transit extended its subway line over the bridge, and beneath the intersection a new station was constructed for the train and bridge trolleys. The bridge trolleys have long since disappeared, their elaborate subway entrance kiosks have been demolished, and the large underground station lies dark and abandoned. [*See* photo, page 154, top.]

To the left, the **former Loew's Delancey** was one of the grandiose movie and vaudeville palaces of the early 1920s, its façade still showing traces of the then-popular Moorish Revival style. Adjacent is **Ratner's** (138 Delancey

Virtually every tenement had its share of "sweatshops," operating in crowded apartments from dawn to late night, six days a week. In this view taken around 1905 in a Ludlow Street tenement, renowned photographer Jacob Riis captured the activity and working conditions of a group of cloth cutters. (The Jacob A. Riis Collection, Museum of the City of New York)

Street), a well-known and highly popular Jewish dairy restaurant, the last of many famous dining places that were once located here.

Continue south on Essex Street to Broome Street.

36. The Italianate building on the northwest corner was formerly the **Eastern Dispensary** (ca. 1895), later the Good Samaritan Dispensary, and was one of four large privately endowed clinics that provided free medical care for the needy. Only the Northern Dispensary now remains [*see* Greenwich Village, 28].

Seward Park High School occupies the entire block between Broome and Grand streets. The school was built in 1929 on the site of the Essex Market Court House and the Ludlow Street Jail. Infamous politician William Marcy "Boss" Tweed died there as a convicted felon in 1878. Among the school's alumni: Zero Mostel and Walter Matthau.

37. Walk east on Broome Street to Norfolk Street, and turn right to the **Beth Hamedrash Hagodol** (*Greater House of Study*) **Synagogue** (60 Norfolk Street). This austere Gothic Revival building was built in 1850 as the Norfolk Street Baptist Church and was sold to this congregation in 1885. Priding itself on having been the largest Russian synagogue in the country for many years, its membership is now quite small. Open for daily prayer, the sanctuary is magnificent and should be visited. Most attractive are the ornate ark and pulpit, center *bimah* (reader's platform) with etched glass lamps, cantilevered balconies, Gothic vaulted ceiling, and colorful wall paintings. When the converted gas fixtures are illuminated at twilight, the atmosphere is awesome!

Walk south on Norfolk Street to Grand Street and turn right to Essex Street. Delicious bagels, bialys, and other exotic breadstuffs can be purchased at **Kossar's Bialystoker Bakery** (367 Grand Street).

38. In the two blocks of Essex Street between Grand and Canal streets are a variety of small retail establishments catering to the Orthodox Jewish community. Working in ground-floor tenement shops, much as they did almost a hundred years ago, are the *yarmulke* (skull-cap) makers, torah scribes, *talith* (prayer-

The synagogue was the center of spiritual and cultural life of most Jewish immigrants in the Lower East Side. At times, the need for new houses of worship could not keep up the influx of new worshipers. Typically, a new congregation would purchase and recondition an old church. The Sineerer Shul, which stood at Madison and Montgomery streets until destroyed by fire in 1972, was formerly the Madison Street Presbyterian Church. (New York City Landmarks Preservation Commission)

shawl) manufacturers, *tefillin* (prayer-phylacteries) repairers, and vendors of religious articles and books. There are also *glat* (strictly) kosher groceries and restaurants. The proprietors, many belonging to the Hasidic sect and wearing their traditional garb, will often stop business operations, close their doors, and with the shop filled with patrons, pause to conduct afternoon prayers. A few steps before the corner of Hester Street is **Essex Street Pickles,** formerly Guss' Pickles, and featured in the film *Crossing Delancey* (follow your nose!). Dozens of varieties of tasty pickles are dispensed from large casks on the sidewalk.

At No. 39 Essex Street is **Leibel Bestritzky's Kosher Gourmet Foods,** a determined survivor of what was once a street lined with Jewish food shops.

Around the corner on Hester Street are more food shops to tempt the palate of those wishing to explore further the world of Jewish appetizers. Stop in at **Gertel's** for what some consider the best Jewish pastry in New York. Continue to Ludlow Street.

This corner had another function during the sweatshop era. It was here that the garment industry contractors would gather every morning to hire their daily contract laborers. The noise and commotion was so great that the intersection and its surroundings earned the rather paradoxical name, **Khazzer Mark,** or Pig Market. Return to Essex Street and turn right.

At No. 13 $\frac{1}{2}$, is the small workshop of a *sofer,* or torah scribe. The craftsmen can be seen repairing Torah scrolls or phylacteries, or even writing delicately on a piece of parchment with the traditional quill pen made from a turkey feather.

At Essex Street, turn right to Canal Street, to the East Broadway subway station.

Two additional short tours can be made to other Lower East Side points of interest. Supplementary Tour "A" is a visit to the old Chatham Square Cemetery and a few other landmarks. Tour "B" visits the Henry Street Settlement, the remaining great synagogues, and some additional points of interest.

SUPPLEMENTARY TOUR "A"
TO THE HISTORIC CHATHAM SQUARE CEMETERY

From the original starting point, follow East Broadway about a half-mile west to Chatham Square. At 145 East Broadway is the **Mesivtha Tifereth Jerusalem,** one of the oldest and most prestigious Orthodox rabbinical seminaries in America.

This once-Jewish area has now become exclusively Chinese, and the east side of East Broadway is one continuous colorful market. No. 33, the Classic Revival–style **Chatham Square Branch of the N.Y. Public Library,** was designed in 1903 by McKim, Mead & White. In the distance is a striking panorama of new and old New York, with the Municipal and Woolworth buildings set against the twin towers of the World Trade Center and the gilt pyramid of the U.S. Court House; while almost hidden below is the dark spire of St. Paul's Chapel.

At Chatham Square, with its Chinese-American War Memorial, turn left into St. James Place. Just beyond Oliver Street is the **First Cemetery of the Spanish & Portuguese Synagogue, Shearith Israel.** Built in 1682, this National Historic and New York City Landmark is the burial ground of the first Jewish congregation in the United States, which arrived in 1654 [*see* page 34]. It also has the distinction of being the oldest surviving man-made artifact on Manhattan Island! An earlier cemetery was consecrated in 1656 farther downtown, but no trace of it exists today, and its exact location is uncertain.

The historic burial ground is still maintained by the descendants of the original Sephardic congregation, *Shearith Israel,* the Spanish & Portuguese Synagogue, at 8 West 70th Street. The cemetery contains the graves of many of the early founders, including Gershon Mendes Seixas (1745–1816), the first American-born Jewish minister. Seixas served as a trustee of Columbia College and represented the Jewish community at Washington's inauguration. His brother Benjamin, also buried here, was a lieutenant in the New York militia and a founder of the New York Stock Exchange. The graves of 18 Jewish soldiers who fought for our independence have been marked by the Daughters of the American Revolution. The tombstone of Benjamin Bueno de Mezquita (1683) is the city's oldest. The site also played a role in the defense of the city during the early days of the Revolutionary War, when General Charles Lee mounted two batteries of cannon in the burial ground in an attempt to thwart the British invasion. The cemetery was closed in 1831, and two subsequent burial grounds were opened [*see* Greenwich Village, 33; and Ladies' Mile, 16].

Return to Oliver Street, and turn right to the **Mariners' Temple.** Now an active Baptist Church, this brownstone Greek Revival–style church was designed in 1844 by architect Isaac Lucas for the Oliver Street Baptist Church. The attractive building replaces three earlier churches that were destroyed by fires, and in 1863 it became the Mariners' Temple. The enormous ship's bell to the right of the portico recalls the days when this was primarily a seamen's house of worship. It is Manhattan's oldest Baptist church.

Turn left at Henry Street. This block was known as **"Doctor's Row"** in the 1840s. Don't miss the name *Dr. Naughton* carved into the wall of No. 46. **St. Christopher's Chapel** (No. 48), now the Chinatown Mission of the Episcopal Church, was once an elegant Federal-style residence. At the site of 97 Henry Street, Beth Israel Hospital was founded by Jews in 1889–92, in a simple four-story building with a stoop in front.

At the corner of Market Street is the landmark **Sea and Land Church.** Another "mariners' temple," it was built in 1817 of local Manhattan schist in Georgian style for the Northern Reformed Church, but with some elements that anticipated the later Gothic Revival period. In 1866 it became the Sea and Land Church, but now is the **First Chinese Presbyterian Church.**

Detour right to **51 Market Street,** the former William and Rosamond Clark House. Built in 1824–25, it is a late Federal-style house of rather large proportions, retaining much of the original architectural detail, including a fine doorway.

Follow Henry Street, past Mechanics Alley (the origin of the name is unknown), **under the Manhattan Bridge to Pike Street; turn left one block to East Broadway, then right to where the tour began.**

SUPPLEMENTARY TOUR "B"
TO OTHER LOWER EAST SIDE LANDMARKS

From the original starting point, turn east on East Broadway (the opposite direction of Chatham Square), past the Educational Alliance building. In the block between Jefferson and Clinton streets are over a dozen small synagogues incorporated into the row of apartment houses that line the street. Some belong to small ultra-Orthodox groups. The **Young Israel Synagogue** (No. 225) was founded in 1913 at the Kalwarier Synagogue on Pike Street, as an Orthodox movement for young people, with one of its main goals to combat the growing liberalization of the religion as exemplified by Reform Judaism, and it is still very strong to this day. Many of these storefront synagogues, or *shtiebls,* however, belong to Hasidic groups, of which there are two major communities, the Lubavitcher and the Satmar sects. The *Hasidim* are a very special ultra-Orthodox group (*hasid* means "pious one") who dress distinctively and stay apart from other Jewish groups, mingling with the outside world only when necessary. Modern Hasidism was founded in 18th-century Poland by Israel ben Eliezer, called *Baal Shem Tov* ("Master of the Good Name") by his followers. The movement began as a reaction to the overly academic attitudes of Jewish religious leaders at the time. The essence of the Hasidic spirit is in their intense concentration while performing religious acts and their unbounded joy in devotion—

A cigarette factory sweatshop, ca. 1910. The worker in shirtsleeves at the extreme left is the author's grandfather. (Photograph courtesy Samuel Wolfe)

believing that to be truly religious, one must enjoy his relationship with God. The Hasidim frequently sing, sway, and dance during prayers. Although considered extremists by fellow Jews who do not accept their fundamentalist philosophies, dress, and attitudes toward worldliness and women, the Hasidic movement has nevertheless been growing in popularity since the arrival in this country of so many Hasidim after World War II. The Lubavitchers came mostly from Poland, while the Satmar Hasidim are Hungarians who fled their country after the 1956 Russian invasion.

While there are variations, the traditional Hasidic attire is adapted from the costume of the Polish nobleman of the 18th century, with a long black coat (*kapote*) and a broad-brimmed beaver or sable hat. Hasidim wear the traditional side locks and do not shave their beards. Married women shave their heads and wear a wig, and never expose bare arms or legs.

No. 235 East Broadway was until the mid-1970s the home of the *East Side News,* the Lower East Side's only newspaper. Today one of the tenants is the United Jewish Council of the East Side, a charitable organization which helps the aged sick and poor of the neighborhood. Across the street is the Art Deco–style Bialystoker Home for the Aged, erected in 1929.

At Montgomery Street, turn right to Henry Street, then left. Nos. 263, 265, and 267 are a trio of 1827 Federal-style houses and the home of the **Henry Street Settlement.** In 1893 when nurse Lillian Wald discovered the appalling conditions in the tenements, she devoted her life to caring for the sick and their families. She organized the **Visiting Nurse Service** and later, with the aid of philanthropist Jacob Schiff, the Henry Street Settlement. It was the pioneer social agency on the Lower East Side, and a model for later neighborhood settlement houses throughout the country.

The adjacent firehouse has an interesting history. In 1854 a brownstone on the site was remodeled to be the home of a volunteer fire company known as Americus 6, **William Marcy "Boss" Tweed's own fire company.** His membership helped launch his infamous career, since city volunteer firemen were a potent political power. The fire engine sported a painting of a tiger, which political cartoonist Thomas Nast seized on to identify with Tammany Hall and the Tweed Ring. The successor Engine Company 15's building was rebuilt in the 1890s. Return to East Broadway, turn right to Grand Street.

The Classic Revival building at the intersection of East Broadway and Grand Street (311–13 East Broadway), formerly the Young Men's Benevolent Association (1904), is now a **ritualarium,** or *mikveh.* Among Orthodox Jews it is customary for the bride-to-be to take a ritual bath prior to the wedding ceremony, and for all women to go to the *mikveh* at least once a month. In former times, many synagogues had their own ritual bath chamber, although there were many nonaffiliated *mikvehs* such as this.

Turn west on Grand Street to Willett Street, then right (Marinus Willett was a patriot in the Revolutionary War, and mayor of New York City in 1807–08). Standing alone in the middle of the block is the **Bialystoker Synagogue** (7 Willett Street). Built in 1826 in Federal style, its fieldstone construction gives it a simple but rugged appearance. Originally the Willett Street Methodist

Episcopal Church, it was sold in 1905 to an immigrant Jewish congregation from Bialystok, Poland, which had arrived in the late 1870s. Still serving an active constituency mostly from the adjacent Sidney Hillman Houses, the East River Houses, and the Seward Park Houses, the synagogue is well maintained and has an impressive interior. A three-story-high carved wooden ark dominates the simple sanctuary. Colorful ceiling and wall paintings represent the signs of the zodiac and views of the Holy Land, while sparkling rays of blue and red stream down from a huge, arched stained-glass window. Contrary to the custom of facing east, the Bialystoker Synagogue must, because of its original design, face west.

Returning to Grand Street and continuing west, we pass the **Arts for Living Center and Neighborhood Playhouse of the Henry Street Settlement** (Prentice & Chan, Olhausen, 1975), and turning down Pitt Street toward the Williamsburg Bridge we see the **Police Station and Fire House,** completed in 1974. The new 7th Precinct building replaces the former Clinton Street station house, which for over 70 years stood at the southeast corner of Delancey and Clinton streets, near the end of the Williamsburg Bridge.

Walk under the bridge, turn left on Delancey Street to Attorney Street, then right to the small synagogue in the middle of the block.

This diminutive Greek Revival building was erected about 1845 as the First Protestant Methodist Church. Some years later it was acquired by a black congregation, which renamed it the Emanuel African Methodist Episcopal Church. The adjacent house, which now stands abandoned, served as the former church's rectory. With the influx of Jewish immigrants in the 1880s the church was sold and converted to a synagogue. **Congregation Beth Haknesseth Mogen Avraham** ("Synagogue of the Shield of Abraham") (87 Attorney Street) is little changed, however. Only a *bimah* (reader's platform) was added in the sanctuary, and the brightly painted walls give the interior a cheerful and cozy atmosphere. The downstairs *beth medrash* ("house of study"), reached by a narrow wooden staircase, is used for weekly services. On Sabbath eve, when the handful of elderly worshipers gather together in the small, dimly lit room, the somber scene is reminiscent of a Rembrandt canvas. Despite the changing population patterns, the synagogue still "hangs in" and serves a small but loyal congregation.

Walk north on Attorney Street to Rivington Street, then turn left one block to Clinton Street, and turn right.

At the beginning of the century, **Clinton Street** was a busy commercial street and the center for religious-goods merchants. Store after store offered such articles as prayer books, prayer shawls, *yarmulkes, mezzuzahs,* phylacteries, torahs, candelabra, and ceremonial wine goblets. The street is now almost entirely Spanish-speaking. Walk north one and one-half blocks to the **Chasam Sopher Synagogue** (8 Clinton Street). Built in 1853 for the German congregation Rodeph Shalom, it is the second oldest surviving synagogue building in New York. Its design, rather unique for a synagogue, is of the Round-Arch Romanesque Revival style. In 1886, Rodeph Shalom moved uptown and sold the building to a Hungarian immigrant congregation which renamed the *shul* in honor of a 19th-century religious leader. The exterior has suffered many alterations through the years, losing an ornate iron balustrade and the street-level doors that gave access to the women's galleries. The sanctuary, however, is virtually unchanged—spacious, bright, and unpretentious, its quiet atmosphere a relief from the tumult of busy Clinton Street. The design of the hand-carved ark is a model of the synagogue's front façade, with most of the architectural details faithfully reproduced in miniature. The synagogue is named for Moshe Schreiber (1762–1839), a highly respected rabbi and talmudic scholar who traveled widely through eastern Europe founding religious institutions, and who left over 100 manuscript volumes of his writings.

Too poor to afford a rabbi of its own, Chasam Sopher is now served by an unpaid rabbi from a nearby religious school. The diminutive congregation in this once-predominantly Jewish neighborhood is held together by an elderly Holocaust survivor, Moses Weiser, and his son Eugene, whose dedication and persistence have thus far managed to attract some support to keep the struggling synagogue alive.

Return to the corner of Stanton Street, turn right, walk two blocks west to Norfolk Street and turn right again.

Halfway down the block, almost hidden by its taller neighbors, is the **former Congregation Anshe Chesed** synagogue. Little evidence remains of the past glory of this, the oldest synagogue in New York, and one of the oldest in the country! The smashed windows and doors, peeling stucco, broken fence, and overall state of deterioration are a melancholy end for such a historic building. Designed by architect Alexander Saeltzer in 1849 for the first Reform Congregation in America, Anshe Chesed, it was for a time the largest synagogue in the city. Gone now are the polygonal pyramids that once graced the twin towers of this Gothic Revival–style building, as well as the elaborate windows, traceries, and other medieval details of the façade. It is said that the architect was influenced by Germany's Cologne Cathedral, which had just celebrated its 600th anniversary the year before. In any case, the decade of the 1840s *was* the period of the Gothic Revival. Saeltzer's reputation as an architect was assured two years later when he designed the famous Astor Library on Lafayette Street, later the Hebrew Immigrant Aid Society building, now the famous Joseph Papp Public Theater [*see* Lafayette Historic Group and East Village, 14]. As with neighboring Rodeph Shalom, the German Anshe Chesed congregation also moved uptown, and the building eventually passed to a Hungarian Immigrant group, Ohab Zedek. Changing names several times as different congregations took over the building, it ultimately became Anshe Slonim in 1922, taking its name from a tiny village in Poland. By the early 1970s the neighborhood had declined badly; faced with unremitting vandalism and repeated violence, the members were forced to seek safer places for worship. The venerable building, abandoned and padlocked, and under a city demolition order, seemed doomed. Then in late 1986, as if by a miracle, Spanish sculptor Angel Orensanz, himself a Sephardic Jew, purchased the old synagogue from the city with the intention of converting it into apartment-studios for artists; and a few months later, with its future more secure, the Landmarks Commission granted it landmark status.

Walk back on Norfolk Street, past Stanton Street, to Rivington Street. Turn right one block to Essex Street. The F line Delancey Street station is one block south.

7. SoHo Cast-Iron District

[J, M, N, R, Z lines, or Lexington Avenue line to Canal Street; Broadway No. 6 bus to Canal Street]

Cast iron as a building material had its origins in England in the mid-18th century. It was discovered that pig iron could easily be heated to the melting point by the use of coke, later coal, thus freeing it of impurities while maintaining the proper carbon content needed for strength. The molten mass could then be cast into sand molds of the desired size and shape. In 1779 a cast-iron bridge was completed in England over the River Severn, and in the last decade of the century a number of iron-framed buildings, mostly textile mills, demonstrated the feasibility of this type of construction. Subsequently, the use of cast iron to support large glass greenhouses became very popular, and in 1851 the world was treated to the awesome spectacle of architect Joseph Paxton's London Crystal Palace Exhibition Building. Two years later New York City was witness to another Crystal Palace Exhibition, which was built on the present site of Bryant Park on 42nd Street. The style lent itself successfully to the construction of the dome of the U.S. Capitol, completed in 1865, and to numerous railway train sheds around the world. A number of those expansive iron and glass stations are still in use today.

Cast iron, however, achieved its greatest popularity here in the United States during the period 1860–90, when more commercial buildings with iron fronts were built in New York City than anywhere else in the world! A surprising number of these structures still stand, the majority of which can be seen in the **SoHo Cast-Iron Historic District.**

Recognizing the importance of cast-iron architecture to the growth and development of city, as well as its aesthetic and historic importance, the New York City Landmarks Preservation Commission in 1973 designated a 26-block area as a Historic District—the first such commercial district to be so named. "SoHo" is an acronym for the area SOuth of HOuston Street. Although still a commercial neighborhood, it has become in recent years a popular center for artists and sculptors who find the high-ceilinged loft buildings ideal for studios and workshops. The influx of these artists has given the area a new dimension, demonstrating that with imaginative zoning, industry and art can coexist successfully.

Until the end of the 18th century the area was largely rural, difficult to reach by road from the lower city because of extensive marshlands. With the filling in of the Collect Pond (now the site of Foley Square), the draining of Lispenard's Meadow, and the subsequent paving of Broadway to Astor Place in 1809, the character of the area soon changed to middle-class residential.

By 1825 it had grown to be the most populous ward in the city, with a large freed-slave population. Large, fashionable retail emporiums with such familiar names as Arnold Constable, Lord & Taylor, and Tiffany's, established themselves along Broadway, while elegant hotels were soon erected alongside. For years to come, such hotels as the St. Nicholas, the Metropolitan, and the Prescott House would be synonymous with extravagance and luxury. An array of theaters and music halls soon followed, and by 1850, the Bowery was displaced by Broadway as the entertainment center of the city. And around it grew one of the biggest red-light districts in town.

But the glitter and gaiety lasted only ten years. Keeping pace with the northward growth of the city, the entertainment district moved up to 14th Street, and what was left of the former residential section gradually disappeared. In its place came large textile and other mercantile establishments which commissioned the construction of new buildings, selecting for the most part the new cast-iron-front designs. For the next 30 years some of the largest and most prestigious textile firms in the country were housed side-by-side in those cast-iron "palaces" whose surviving rows of Renaissance Revival–style façades are reminiscent of Venice's Grand Canal. By the early 20th century, the industrial pattern changed again, as the district became New York's millinery manufacturing center. And with the felt hat makers came the fur and feather processors to add the essential details to milady's headgear.

Until recently the area was devoted exclusively to diverse light manufacturing and warehousing; but with the rapidly growing colony of artists, it has achieved a new and charming atmosphere not seen in any of the city's other commercial districts. Many claim that SoHo has now replaced Greenwich Village as the center of artistic creativity. However, with the enormous popularity of SoHo as a place to live and work, there followed the usual skyrocketing rents which have driven out young artists and craftsmen. In their place came the elegant galleries, "chic" bars, noisy discos, expensive restaurants, pretentious boutiques, so-called antique shops, and the usual health-food and fast-food establishments. The resulting "gentrification" of the artist community poses a serious threat to the future of SoHo as a center of creative inspiration. And while the area now houses the largest concentration of art galleries in the city, much of the talent that supplies the galleries has departed to less expensive and more distant neighborhoods.

The characteristics of cast-iron construction: in a masonry building, the weight (load) is borne by the exterior and interior walls, which must be built of a

The aesthetics of cast-iron architecture are shown to advantage in the Dittenhoffer Warehouse, 427–429 Broadway, erected in 1870. (Photo by author)

thickness corresponding to the height of the building. On the other hand, in pure iron construction, the load is borne by a skeleton of vertical and horizontal rolled iron beams, with the exterior brick walls attached to the framework, serving only as a "skin." The cast-iron parts making up the façade are then attached to the street wall. Cast iron, in effect, anticipated the principle of modern skyscraper construction, where similar "curtain walls" surround a structural steel frame.

Cast iron was employed not only functionally, but decoratively as well. Each foundry employed its own architect who designed the building details. At first, architects imitated the style of stone buildings, copying in cast iron the ornate French and Italian Renaissance motifs which were so fashionable in the mid-19th century. Some went so far as to add sand to the beige-colored paint to give the finished product the look of rough stone. It is interesting to note that after cast iron achieved widespread popularity, many builders copied the ornate cast-iron fronts in masonry! It is therefore difficult at times to visually determine if a façade is of iron or stone—unless, of course, one has a magnet handy.

Most of the iron-front buildings erected from the late 1850s through the mid-1870s were essentially Renaissance in style, followed later by the influence of the French Second Empire. The French neo-Grec style, characterized by incised floral and geometric designs, using slender columns and mostly Ionic capitals,

Representation of the first cast-iron building erected in 1848–49 at the corner of Centre and Duane streets by James Bogardus for his Eccentric Grinding Mill. (Museum of the City of New York)

became popular in the 1880s. By the '90s, cast iron began to fall out of fashion, and only an occasional example can be found of that decade. With the introduction of structural steel, the skyscraper era soon followed.

There are many advantages to the cast-iron medium. In 1835 New York suffered a disastrous fire that literally burned off most of the buildings in the south end of Manhattan. Again in 1845 another conflagration occurred, this one consuming 300 buildings! Less combustible building materials were sought (masonry was expensive), and cast iron seemed to offer the solution. It could be melted only in a blast furnace. It was also lightning-proof; the iron framework, acting as a "Faraday's Cage," conducted the electricity safely to the ground. Cast iron was lighter and cheaper than stone, and much cheaper to erect. It could be mass-produced from standardized molds—the iron parts being interchangeable and easily replaced from the foundry's catalog. Cast iron, once painted, was weatherproof and required little maintenance. The building's appearance, could be "renewed" with a different color paint. Iron's coefficient of expansion and contraction was similar to that of the brickwork to which it was attached, obviating the danger of separation under extremes of weather. In addition, an iron framework had greater structural integrity than other building materials, and could withstand stresses that would collapse wood or stone structures. A particular advantage was the space gained by the elimination of massive bearing walls. With a cast-iron façade, large windows were now possible for the first time, affording light and ventilation hitherto impossible. Finally, the simplicity of erection was such that an iron front could be raised almost overnight, with no more tools than a wrench, much like a child's Erector Set, since all parts were fastened together with nuts and bolts.

There were, however, some disadvantages. Although the builders described iron structures as fireproof, in reality they were not. Flooring, beams, joists, and staircases were frequently made of wood; and while a fire would not damage the cast-iron front, it could gut the interior. Cast iron, although highly compressible, was brittle, lacking the tensile strength of modern steel. Rusting was always a problem, as moisture frequently seeped into the iron sections. The iron panels, which could withstand the heat of a building fire, would often crack under the shock of cold water from the firemen's hoses.

The success of cast iron as a structural and architectural medium is credited to two contemporary engineers, Daniel D. Badger and James Bogardus. Badger's foundry mass-produced the first complete iron-front building. Bogardus, who invented the I-beam, designed the oldest surviving cast-iron building in New York, the famous Edgar Laing Store, which stood on the corner of Washington and Murray streets from 1848 to 1971, about a mile from the Historic District. The store was carefully dismantled when the neighborhood was urban-renewed, to be re-erected later on the new campus of the Borough of Manhattan Community College. Measured drawings were made by students in a Restoration and Preservation of Historical Architecture program of Columbia University, and the pieces were inventoried, all under the supervision of the

The former Edgar Laing Store, until recently the oldest surviving cast-iron building in New York. Built in 1848 at the corner of Murray and Washington streets, it was dismantled in 1871 for future re-erection. Thieves subsequently made off with most of the iron sections. (Photo by author)

Landmarks Commission. Unfortunately the remains fell to thieves, and most of the parts were stolen and sold as scrap iron! Hopefully, molds will be made from the drawings so that replacement parts can be recast and the landmark Bogardus Building erected again. Bogardus's original warehouse, however, still stands at 85 Leonard Street, a few blocks south of Canal Street. Badger and his Architectural Iron Works left us with possibly the finest example of commercial cast-iron architecture in America, the Venetian Renaissance–style Haughwout Building at Broadway and Broome Street. Completed in 1857, it is the city's oldest surviving iron-front building, and a designated city landmark.

Within a few years at least three dozen iron foundries were busily producing façades and decorations for the hundreds of new buildings going up in the area. The names of these iron works can be seen embossed in the base blocks of many of these structures: Aetna, Architectural, Atlantic, Cornell, Excelsior, Jackson, etc. With the lone exception of the Cornell Iron Works, which now casts other kinds of iron products, all the original building foundries are now gone. The advent of the "iron age" also brought immortality to such architects as Isaac F. Duckworth, Henry Fernbach, Robert Mook, Jarvis Morgan Slade, John Snook, Griffith Thomas, and Samuel Warner.

The walking tour map indicates *every* building with a complete cast-iron front; however, there are at least as many masonry buildings whose ground floors are full cast iron. Some stone buildings have only cast-iron ornamentation, such as columns, cornices or simply designs. Notice the iron loading docks, light platforms, and sidewalk vault covers. Watch also for old bishop's crook lampposts, built of cast iron and once prevalent throughout the city.

Note: A glossary of architectural terms appears on pages 207 to 209.

BROADWAY TO GREENE STREET (along Canal Street)

The tour begins at Canal Street and Broadway. Named for the drainage ditch that was built in the late 18th century to connect the old Collect Pond with the Hudson River, Canal Street was paved in 1820, and has grown to become one of the city's busiest crosstown thoroughfares. In recent years, Canal Street between Broadway and West Broadway has become one of the city's lively markets, specializing in such unusual used and surplus items as machinery, electrical supplies, hardware, and plastics of every description. The frenetic street scene reaches a fever pitch on weekends when the sidewalks are jammed with displays of merchandise and throngs of bargain hunters and sightseers.

Walk west on Canal Street to **No. 307–311.** Built in 1856–65 for the Arnold Constable "Marble House" [*see* Ladies' Mile, 29], this stone building is in a good state of preservation. It has an Italianate marble façade on Canal Street, and brick on the Mercer and Howard street sides. Note the second-story round-arched windows with decorative keystones, flanked by pilasters with Corinthian capitals. The windows on the third through fifth floors are topped by segmental arches. Above the fifth-floor windows, paired volutes rise toward the center,

The Arnold Constable Store, called the "Marble House," was erected in 1856 when the firm moved to Canal and Mercer streets, to open one of the city's most elegant dry goods emporiums. Constructed of brick and stone, the Italianate building survives today in a surprisingly good state of preservation. (The Edward W. C. Arnold Collection, lent by the Metropolitan Museum of Art. Museum of the City of New York)

forming a modified pediment. The building is capped by a simple cast-iron cornice. Walk around this old department-store building and compare the three façades; then continue west on Canal Street to Greene Street and turn right (north), past one of the city's busiest weekend flea markets.

CANAL STREET TO WEST HOUSTON STREET (along Greene Street)

Greene Street, named after Revolutionary War hero General Nathanael Greene, was opened just after the turn of the 19th century. It is still cobblestoned (they are actually called Belgian blocks), and boasts the largest aggregation of cast-iron buildings in the world! On a Sunday, when few automobiles are to be seen, the street is virtually the same as it was in the latter half of the 19th century. Even the street between Canal and Houston streets has been repaved with the original Belgian blocks, and the street lights are the old bishop's crook lampposts.

Another much-less-admirable feature that hearkens back to the turn of the century is the vast proliferation of sweat shops that can be seen throughout SoHo. These are mainly Chinese-owned, employing recent Chinese immigrant labor at minimum or below-subsistence wages.

The row of ten buildings on the east side of the street, from No. 8 through No. 32–34, is **the longest continuous row of such iron-front buildings anywhere. No. 8** dates from 1883, and **Nos. 10–14** from 1869—all four designed by architect John B. Snook. **Nos. 16** and **18,** built in 1882, and **No. 20–26,** built in 1880, were designed by Samuel Warner, and were joined together and converted into commercial condominiums in 1993. In front of No. 10–12 is the original iron stoop and light platform, which was converted into a loading platform.

Warner also designed **No. 15–17,** across the street, in 1894. A rather late cast-iron building, its "flattened" façade shows the simpler style that supplanted the earlier ornate Renaissance motifs. There is a Cornell Iron Works trademark at the base. Adjacent **No. 19–21** is by Henry Fernbach, and was built as a warehouse in 1872.

No. 23–25, designed in a French Renaissance style by Isaac F. Duckworth (1873), is particularly impressive with its triangular pediment with delicate finials set over two central bays, its iron moldings, partially fluted columns, and stylized designs in the frieze panel and two flanking vertical rows of quoins that extend from the base of the building to the cornice.

The block, however, is dominated by **No. 28–30** on the east side of the street, designed in 1873 by Duckworth (who had a strong predilection for the French Second Empire style) for Picaut, Simon & Capel Company. Note the immense mansard roof with central pavilion, dormers, half-round attached columns, bell-shaped capitals, keystoned and segmental arches over wide windows, and projecting central bays which give a dramatic three-dimensional effect. Notice, too, the light disks in the iron vault covers surrounded by six metal studs. The risers have circle lights with hexagonal frames. These glass disks also permitted sunlight to illuminate the basement. The system was invented by Thaddeus Hyatt in 1845 for installation in sidewalk vaults, and is still to be seen throughout the city. What was formerly the stoop now serves as a loading platform. Except for the removal of the acanthus leaves from the columns' capitals, this imposing building is in as pristine condition as the day it was built, although lack of maintenance is beginning to show in the proliferation of rust, peeling paint, and graffiti.

No. 32, with a small bonnet cornice, is another Duckworth building (1873). Its neighbor, **No. 34,** by Charles Wright, and built the same year, continues the cornice line.

No. 31, across the street (George W. DeCunha, 1876), is interesting because of its neo-Grec details. Note the three square-topped windows on each floor, the freestanding Corinthian columns, flanking pilasters with neo-Grec designs on the terminal blocks at each floor's cornice level, and the repeating rosettes and concave brackets on the entablature. The building, unfortunately, is in a sad state of decay and its future is uncertain. There is another identical building by the same architect at 74 Grand Street (to be viewed soon).

Turn east briefly on Grand Street.

Grand Street got its name from its unusual width, as it was a major east-west thoroughfare when first laid out early in the 19th century.

Nos. 91 and **93** (John B. Snook, 1869), quite unusual in their façades, are not copied from the Renaissance or French Second Empire styles but cast in the appearance of ashlars (large masonry panels). At first glance one would take these for stone buildings. A dead giveaway is the tiny "J. L. Jackson & Bro. Iron Works" label at the base, to the right on No. 91.

Looking north on Greene Street near Broome Street in the heart of the SoHo Cast-Iron District where an almost unbroken panorama of cast-iron buildings presents itself. (Photo by author)

One of James Bogardus's only surviving iron-front buildings, his former warehouse at 85 Leonard Street, erected in 1862. (Photo by David Bishop)

The old New York Life Insurance Company building at 346 Broadway at Leonard Street, built in 1870 from plans by Griffith Thomas, still stands but is hardly recognizable from this early engraving. A turn-of-the-century addition by McKim, Mead & White added nine floors, a clock tower, and winged globe (now removed). The company moved to Madison Square in 1928. (New York Life Insurance Company)

An 1870s steel engraving showing the lavish interior of the New York Life Insurance Company building at 346 Broadway. (New York Life Insurance Company)

The Greene Street side of this neo-Grec-style cast-iron building at 112–114 Prince Street is an enormous trompe l'oeil *painting, by artist Richard Haas, simulating rows of windows—a pleasant solution to a blank brick wall. [See p. 191.] (Photo by author)*

An 1865 advertising poster for Daniel D. Badger's Architectural Iron Works, located between 13th and 14th streets, Avenues B and C. (Museum of the City of New York)

Return to the corner of Grand and Greene streets.

No. 83–87 Grand Street (on the southwest corner) is a rather large structure in a modified neo-Grec style, designed in 1872 by William Hume. The date appears conspicuously over the central bays. The iron for this former silk warehouse was cast by the firm of Lindsay, Graff & Megquier (see label on base).

Across the street, **No. 80–88** Grand Street (B. W. Warner, 1873) was built for a large importing and commission merchant. **No. 78,** alongside, was designed in 1882 by Robert Mook.

No. 72 and **74** (1885), as well as **No. 68–70** (1887) on the northwest corner of Wooster Street, are by George DeCunha, who favored the neo-Grec style. In the latter building, a high cornice is set on paired concave brackets above three wide pilasters.

No. 71–73, on the southeast corner (Mortimer C. Merritt, 1879, corner section 1888), demonstrates how a cast-iron front permits the use of large plate-glass windows. Set between fluted Corinthian columns on paneled bases, the ground floor presents a light and expansive appearance. Each floor has its own cornice, partitioned by ornamental blocks. The bays are framed by smooth pilasters topped by stylized neo-Grec capitals with incised floral designs. The relief panels above the fourth floor serve as a transition to the splendid upper cornice with its paired elongated brackets above each column and similarly elongated modillions. Merritt was the architect of the great Hugh O'Neill Department Store, which still stands on Avenue of the Americas between 20th and 21st streets [*see* Ladies' Mile, 15].

Make a brief detour north on Wooster Street to **No. 80** (Gilbert Schellenger, 1895). This seven-story former warehouse is considered to be the first conversion to artists' lofts in SoHo. In 1967 the new owner began selling co-ops to artists, before it become legal four years later. The building also housed Jonas Mekas's Filmmakers Cinematique and Richard Foreman's Ontological Hysteric Theater. Although many artists have left SoHo because of its skyrocketing rents and popularity as a tourist mecca, many still remain. Note the initials of the original developer, Boehm & Coon, in an escutcheon on the seventh floor. Return to Grand Street and turn left (east).

Return to Greene Street and turn left (north).

No. 37–43 (Richard Berger, 1884) is undistinguished and has lost its cornice.

No. 45 (J. Morgan Slade, 1882) is another typical neo-Grec–style iron front building. The pilasters and columns are topped by Ionic capitals. Note the egg-and-dart molding above the windows, the deep columnar base blocks and connecting panels, and the architrave above the ground floor in the form of a scrolled grillwork strip. The economy of cast-iron construction can be seen in the similarity of sections on each floor—all cast from the same mold.

Although **No. 49** is a stone building, its street number is a lovely cast-iron plaque set into a fluted iron column. Look for D. D. Badger's "Architectural Iron Works" label on the plinth, to the left of the entrance.

Across the street, **Nos. 42–44** and **46–50** are both masonry buildings that have attractive ornamental ironwork details. The former has an iron storefront with fluted columns and pilasters. Its neighbor to the north is far more ornate. Observe the twin iron pilasters on the ground floor with bolted-on scrollwork and medallions, and the small stone pediment on the second floor. With all the surviving details on the lower façade, one can only speculate on the appearance of the now-missing cornice.

Turn left (west) on Broome Street.

Broome Street is named for John Broome, the city's first alderman after the Revolution and lieutenant governor of New York State in 1804. He is also credited with initiating the lucrative China tea trade when he imported the first two million pounds of tea.

One of the best-preserved cast-iron "palaces" in the city is the imposing Gunther Building, on the southwest corner, **No. 469–475** Broome Street. A Griffith Thomas masterpiece, it was built by the Aetna Iron Works in 1871–72 as a warehouse for William H. Gunther, a leading furrier. (The building that housed his old showroom still stands on the west side of Broadway just south of 23rd Street, near Madison Square.) Among its outstanding features are the impressive curved corner with unusual curved windowpanes flanked by columns of quoins, the bold cornice at each floor level, the rows of flat-arched windows, and a simple but firm roof cornice supported by heavy brackets over symmetrical rows of pilasters. The protruding pedestal blocks on both sides of the "Gunther Building" plaque once supported life-size statues (draped in furs?). A balustrade, similar to the one on the second floor, once graced the roof cornice. A significant architectural feature—handed down by the ancient Greeks—is the foreshortening of each successive story. By progressively diminishing the height of each floor, an illusion of greater height is achieved. The Aetna Iron Works was located in former times at 104 Goerck Street, near the corner of Grand Street, on the Lower East Side. Goerck Street has long since disappeared, demapped for a large housing project.

The adjacent building to the west, **No. 477–479,** was erected in 1872–73 by the Excelsior Iron Works from plans by Elisha Sniffen. A very classical building in the French manner, it was built for the Cheney Brothers Silk Mills. While the neighboring Gunther Building has a uniform treatment of the windows, this building shows great variety. Some bays are flanked by engaged columns with Corinthian capitals, others are capped by keystones, and still others are decorated with balustrades. Twin pediments surmount a bracketed cornice, giving the structure an appearance of great width. No. 477 has a four-step iron entrance stoop while 479 has five steps. Note the circle lights surrounded by six raised metal studs, and the name of the iron works.

Across the street, **No. 470** is a typical Griffith Thomas building in stone, completed in 1867. The ground-floor columns and the entablature, however, are of cast iron.

No. 472–474 was built by Thomas two years later, and was probably one of his last stone buildings, for from late 1869 on, he devoted himself exclusively to cast iron.

No. 476–478 is still another Griffith Thomas building (1872), now representing his cast-iron period. L-shaped, it wraps itself around No. 480 to become No. 62 Wooster Street, around the corner. Typical Thomas touches are a cornice line at each floor, flattened window arches, flanking three-quarter round Corinthian columns in the center section with connecting balustrades, and flat pilasters at the sides of the façade.

No. 480 was designed by Richard Berger in 1884.

Return to Greene Street and continue east on Broome Street.

Broome Street in former times was a major east-west artery, and is somewhat wider than its parallel neighbors. It is still a fairly busy thoroughfare, providing an alternate route to the nearby Holland Tunnel.

Situated in one of the finest cast-iron blocks in the district, **No. 465–467** Broome Street is another product of the Aetna Iron Works and was designed by Isaac F. Duckworth in 1872. The beauty of the building is severely diminished by the ground floor "modernization."

The stone building at the northwest corner of Broome and Greene streets, **No. 464–468,** designed in 1860 (architect unknown), was built for Aaron Arnold of the Arnold Constable emporium. Nine bays wide on Broome Street, it is divided into three sections of three windows each. The two-story-high columns flanking the windows are in the "sperm candle" style, for they resemble candles made from sperm whale oil. (More buildings, in both iron and stone, employing the "sperm candle" feature will be seen later on Broadway.) The graceful fluted iron columns on the ground floor were cast by the nearby Nichol & Billerwell Foundry on West Houston Street. The building is extremely handsome, and was a prototype for many later cast-iron copies.

No. 461 (1871) is another Griffith Thomas "iron-fronter."

Still in "Griffith Thomas Territory," **No. 457–459** (1871) is somewhat simpler than the adjacent corner building. Quoined pilasters are set at each end of this six-story, six-bay edifice. The windows are separated by modified Doric columns with egg-and-dart and floral-motif moldings above. Note the balustrade at the bases of the second-story windows. Above the cornice is a rather large pediment.

No. 453–455 (Griffith Thomas again, 1872–73) was built for the Welcome G. Hitchcock silk and veilings store. Two of Hitchcock's early partners were Aaron Arnold and James Constable. Five stories of foreshortened Corinthian columns, wide flat-arched windows, a cornice line at each floor, and quoined pilasters flanking the end bays give a bold look to this well-preserved cast-iron building. Lightness and charm result from the delicate Corinthian capitals, the second-story balustrade, the floral motifs and the intricate modillions and brackets under the ground-floor and roof cornices. Above the fifth floor is a classic attic that once sported finial-tipped cast-iron urns.

No. 448, on the north side of Broome Street, just beyond Mercer Street, is an outstanding cast-iron creation. Designed in 1871 by the firm of Vaux & Withers,

The "Queen" and "King" of Greene Street cast-iron architecture: (left) No. 28–30, in Second Empire style; (right) No. 72–76 in Renaissance style; both designed by Isaac F. Duckworth in 1873. (Left, photo by author; right, New York City Landmarks Preservation Commission)

it has a style of ornamentation not seen elsewhere in the city. Capped by delicately ornate friezes and outlined by pellet moldings, the windows with their flanking triple groups of colonnettes are the most unusual feature of the building. The fifth-floor windows are subdivided into round-arched groups of two, separated by colonnettes. The intervening spandrels repeat the floral motifs. Observe the striking entablature with its rosettes set in panels in a concave architrave and the upper frieze; while "sprouting" from the fifth-floor colonnettes are elaborate brackets. One cannot but condemn the first-floor alterations. Calvert Vaux and Frederick Clarke Withers designed the landmark Jefferson Market Courthouse (now Library) in Greenwich Village [*see* Greenwich Village, 34]. Vaux also teamed up with Frederick Law Olmsted to give us Central Park and Prospect Park.

Returning to Greene Street, note **No. 458,** a three-bay stone building between Mercer and Greene streets. Built in 1867 by David and John Jardine, who shortly thereafter were "converted" to the cast-iron medium, the structure has interesting molded drop-lintels over the windows whose keystones incorporate an incised fleur-de-lis. The ground-floor stone entablature, and its row of columns beneath, divides the building into two distinct sections. The decorative main entablature is of cast-iron capped by a raised, curved pediment. It appears that this former store and warehouse is a kind of structural parasite as it has no side bearing walls of its own, and relies on its two stalwart neighbors for support. D. and J. Jardine ten years later designed the palatial B. Altman store that still occupies the northwest corner of Avenue of the Americas and West 18th Street [*see* Ladies' Mile, 10].

Turn right (north) on Greene Street.

The block from Broome to Spring Street has no fewer than 13 full iron-front buildings, representing the height of cast-iron architectural development.

No. 58–60 (1871) is one of nine buildings in the block designed by architect Henry Fernbach.

No. 62–64, erected one year later, is also by Fernback. Observe how the first-floor columns are fluted on the lower section and topped by Ionic capitals. Each floor has its own entablature with Tuscan columns separating the four central bays. The ornamental double brackets in the roof entablature are a very dominant feature. The restrained curved pediment above the cornice shows the date of construction, 1872.

In front of No. 62–64 is a **"bishop's crook" lamppost.** The lamppost weighs 835 pounds, almost twice that of today's modern aluminum tubular posts. The base shows the ornate fluting and the acanthus-leaf motif. In the "crook" above is the traditional curlicue known as a *feuille rinceau,* French for curling leaf. The next time you pass an older fire-alarm box, note the cast-iron flambeau above and the palmetto-leaf design of the shaft.

No. 66 (John B. Snook, 1873) was built as a store for the Lorillard (tobacco) Company. **No. 68,** identical in appearance, is also by Snook, and was built later in the same year.

Across the street, **No. 65** and **67** (1872) are another look-alike pair, although the former is by John B. Snook and the latter by Henry Fernbach. It appears that both buildings were ordered from the same catalog.

Looking to the east side again, we are confronted by the most regal cast-iron building in the block, **No. 72–76,** known as the "King of Greene Street." Considered to be the finest example of French Renaissance style in the district, this masterpiece was designed by Isaac F. Duckworth and completed in 1873 for the Gardner Colby Company, whose initials can be seen at the entrance. From its pedimented portico to its pedimented cornice, this stately "commercial palace" must have been considered the last word in cast-iron elegance. This ten-bay structure gives an imposing three-dimensional effect with its ranks of free-standing Corinthian columns—each group supporting its own cornice, with projecting centrally paired bays, as well as side bays that are set off on rusticated piers separated by Ionic pilasters. The broken pediments over the entrance and on the roof with their ornate iron urns further accent the central projection. In the roof pediment are decorative birdlike ornaments topped by a fleur-de-lis motif.

No. 69–71 on the west side (Henry Fernbach, 1876) is identical to **No. 73,** its next-door neighbor. Both were erected at the same time, designed by the same architect, are from the same Cornell Iron Works foundry...and were built for the same owner! **No. 75** is another member of the family, with only minor differences in the façade. **No. 77** is a "younger brother," completed in 1878 as the office for the Jennings Lace Works, the firm that introduced Chantilly, Point d'Alençon, and Breton lace to this country. Unfortunately, the cornice on 69–71 has been removed. And **No. 81** is the fifth member of the Fernbach family, built in 1877.

No. 80–82, on the east side, was built as a store and warehouse (Griffith Thomas, 1872).

No. 84–86 (122–124 Spring Street) is a Henry Fernbach building in stone (1883), with brickwork trimmed with cast-iron ornamentation. It has an interesting, restrained façade, with such features as wide stone window lintels and sills, segmentally arched lintels with keystones on the sixth floor, with alternating soldier courses of brick under each window.

Turn right (east) on Spring Street.

Spring Street is named for a fresh-water spring that once flowed nearby.

On the north side of the street are a trio of late-1870s iron buildings. **No. 119** (1878) is by Robert Mook, **Nos. 115–117** and **113** (1878) are by Henry Fernbach. Typical of the Fernbach touch are the separate cornices on each floor ending in a heavy terminal block supported by double brackets, windows flanked by columns with egg-and-dart molding, plus paneled pilasters delineating the buildings. Note the Excelsior Iron Works plaque on No. 111 (although no house number is visible).

At the northwest corner of Mercer Street stands the **oldest house in the neighborhood, No. 107,** built *before* 1808! Its brickwork has been covered by stucco, but it shows its splayed lintels and keystones over the windows.

Across Mercer Street, on the northeast corner, is lovely **No. 101** (Nicholas Whyte, 1870). See how the expanses of plate glass, framed by slender columns, give it a light and airy look. Unusual decorative motifs appear in the clustered corner columns, which rest on piers with a unique rectangular design. Bizarre motifs also appear in the corners of the upper windows, while the ground-floor columns have leaf-ornamented capitals. The whole is an outstanding example of the success of cast iron as a functional and decorative medium.

Adjacent **No. 99** (D. and J. Jardine, 1871), a brick structure with an iron storefront, was built as a hotel. It has several architectural features worthy of note: all the windows have cast-iron drop lintels with a spiral molding and foliate design; above the storefront windows, two panels of stained glass still survive; and the roof displays an intricate iron cornice.

Return to Greene Street and continue west on Spring Street.

Wander down Spring Street to West Broadway to see the variety of new establishments that have taken root. West Broadway was once the heart of the art gallery district of SoHo, but high rents and high-priced boutiques have displaced many of them.

An interesting and entertaining deviation from the tour can be made by walking a few short blocks west to 278 Spring Street to the **New York City Fire**

A 1912 American La France "Metropolitan" steam fire engine with front-wheel drive was one of the first steamers to replace the horse-drawn rigs in the city. Engines similar to this one were the first to respond in the tragic Triangle Shirtwaist Company fire of the year before. It is on exhibit at the New York City Fire Museum, 278 Spring Street. (Photo by Steven Scher)

Museum. The museum was opened in 1987 and occupies a former 1904 Beaux Arts–style firehouse, designed by Paris-trained architect Edward Pierce Casey. The collection was brought from the old Firehouse Museum on Duane Street and was augmented by the collection of the former Firefighting Museum of the Home Insurance Company, on Maiden Lane. The museum's highlights include beautifully preserved hand- and horse-drawn apparatus, fire buckets, helmets, trumpets (a kind of early megaphone for giving orders), toy and working models, portraits, prints, photographs, and an important collection of fire marks. Another of the museum's functions is its Fire Safety Education Program. There is also a small gift shop; and for a snack, their Courtyard Café. (Open Tues. through Sat. 10:00 A.M. to 4:00 P.M.; adults $3.00, children 25¢; 691–1303.)

Return to the corner of Spring and Greene streets and turn left (north) on Greene Street.

Just up the street to the left, on the south wall of No. 93 Greene Street, is the **"ghost" of an old Federal House** which once occupied the adjoining site. Clearly visible are the outlines of its walls, chimney, and peaked roof.

On the west side, **Nos. 93–95, 97, 99** all are neo-Grec–style buildings designed in 1881 by Henry Fernbach. At the base of the second-story windows is a row of vertically incised panels with a neo-Grec motif that, from a distance, simulates a balcony.

Across the street, **No. 96** is by Henry Fernbach (1879), while **Nos. 98** and **100** are by Charles Mettam (1880). The latter two are identical although built for different clients. The pair are flanked by two designed by Fernbach. Both Mettam and Fernbach were contemporaries, and quite similar in taste, but Mettam's work is lighter and somewhat more imaginative.

No. 103–105 (Fernbach again, 1879), occupying a double lot, was formerly one-third larger. **No. 101,** originally an iron-front building, was destroyed in a 1957 fire. The three central bays are framed by Corinthian columns, and each floor has a simple molded cornice. In spite of its present asymmetry it is a pleasing Fernbach building.

No. 112 across the street (1883) is another in the Fernbach line, but its neighbor, **No. 114–120,** is a superlative example of his work. Occupying four lots, it is six stories high and ten bays wide. It was built in 1881 as a branch of the Brooklyn-based Frederick Loeser Department Store (which went out of business shortly after World War II). This is an appropriately elaborate building with a typical Fernbach cornice and entablature. The ground-floor piers are quite ornate, as is the treatment of the broad square windows, which are separated by fluted Ionic columns. Note the different arrangement of the top floor, with segmentally arched lintels separated by columns with egg-and-dart motifs. Imitation fanlights appear between the cornice brackets. Dominating the cornice are stylized acanthus-leaf antefixes located above the pilasters in the middle and at the ends.

(For refreshment, there are a number of restaurants on Spring and Prince streets, and soon on West Broadway, running the gamut from prosaic diners to ethnic and organic food establishments.)

Turn right (east) on Prince Street.

The origin of Prince Street's name is unknown. It may possibly be a reference to Prince William, who later became King William III of England (with Queen Mary II) in 1689.

No. 102–104 (Henry Fernbach, 1881) was also built for Frederick Loeser & Company, and was connected to No. 114–120 Greene Street in the rear. **Nos. 100** and **96–98** were also designed by Fernbach and completed in 1882.

Cross to the northeast corner of Prince and Greene streets.

By now you must have noticed the astonishing *trompe l'oeil* painting covering the entire east wall of No. 112–114. The details are so accurate that passersby often fail to realize that an entire wall of windows has been painted, complete with all the traditional cast-iron details, where none exists. The painstaking work even includes a window air conditioner and a cat! The painting was done by illusionist artist Richard Haas, with the assistance of City Walls, Inc. Alas, this great deceptive mural is fading and losing its visual affect. Even the cat could use a bath! So don't look too closely. Much of the building is occupied by the SoHo Center for Visual Artists. This is a rather late cast-iron building on the south side of the block. Among its graceful elements are the banded pilasters at each end of

Iron foundries took pride in their prefabricated cast-iron buildings and frequently mounted a distinctive builder's plaque at the base. (Photos by author)

the building, fluted colonnettes with neo-Grec capitals flanking the windows, lintels with acanthus-leaf designs, an entablature dividing each story, and each cornice surrounded by incised terminal blocks and elaborate brackets. Above, the raised pediment encloses a fanlight motif. Continue west on Prince Street.

The corner building, **No. 109–111** Prince Street, is discussed later as No. 119 Greene Street. **Nos. 113–115, 117–119,** and **121** share a common façade. The three were designed by Cleverdon & Putzel for the Frank Seitz Warehouse in 1890. The whole is replete with French Renaissance designs in its frieze motifs, medallions, and leaf ornaments. Note how the design changes at each successive story. Only No. 113–115 retains its original entablature; nonetheless, the unity of the group is striking. A local landmark is the Prince Street Bar at the corner of Wooster Street.

If you would like to spend a little time exploring the **"art scene in SoHo"** before continuing the tour, walk one block west to West Broadway, where most of the galleries are located, and make a small loop by walking south almost to Broome Street, and returning on the opposite side, past Prince Street to Houston Street. Visit any gallery and pick up a free copy of the monthly *Gallery Guide,* which has a map of the SoHo galleries and museums and lists current exhibitions throughout the city. If you are following the "Optional Gallery Loop," continue north on West Broadway to the northeast corner of Houston Street.

The quarter-acre plot of land, called **Time Landscape,** is a re-creation of a pre-Colonial mixed forest, showing Manhattan's topography and plant life as it would have existed before the arrival of European settlers 350 years ago. The landscaping and plantings, made possible through private and corporate contributions and the work of local artist Alan Sonfist, include oak, sassafras, maples, evergreens, and a variety of wild grasses and flowers typical of the dozens of plants that thrived in the primeval forest.

You may either return to Greene and Prince streets (see below), or walk east to Broadway and resume the tour on page 194.

No. 119 Greene Street (Jarvis Morgan Slade, 1882) is beautifully adapted to its corner site. The diagonal bay was once the grand entrance. Slade used French Renaissance motifs very effectively. Note how the projecting cornices separate each floor, and how all architectural features are simply realized. The main cornice is plain, as are the pilasters and window groupings. A circular design appears in the paneled frieze in the entablature.

No. 121–123 (Henry Fernbach, 1882) is doubtless the most ornate structure in the block. With its fluted pilasters with acanthus-leaf design, its columns with ornamented capitals, an elaborate "Fernbachesque" cornice topping the whole, we have a wedding of the architect's skill with the founder's technique.

Nos. 125 and **127** are twins. The former was one of Fernbach's last works, completed in 1883. The latter is credited, however, to William Baker, and was not completed till the following year. Possibly Baker was an associate of Fernbach, carrying out the design after his death. Again we have the typical Fernbach style: pilaster moldings with egg-and-dart; fluting; acanthus-leaf and pellet details separating the two buildings; and the cornice above also ornamented with egg-and-dart, as is the upper frieze with rosettes.

Across the street, **No. 130** (Richard Berger, 1888) is an almost perfect example of the neo-Grec style. The designs on the pilasters and pier capitals are clear and precise. The colonnettes are delicate and topped by huge Ionic capitals with egg-and-dart motifs. They are attached to the building wall by means of a screenlike element, pierced with a stylized flower-and-leaf design. Each story is separated by a simple cornice, and even the upper cornice is simply detailed, supported by curved brackets above the colonnettes and pilasters with a row of dentils under its molding. The slender colonnettes emphasize the verticality of the building and demonstrate the decorative possibilities of cast iron.

Nos. 132–134, 136, and **140** share a common façade. All are by Alfred Zucker (1885).

No. 142–144 (1871) is another by Henry Fernbach.

No. 146 is a stone building, but still retains its cast-iron vault covers. Note the "S. B. Althause & Co." foundry name on the edge of the covers, and the "Galls & Mark" trademark on the edge of the light platform. The light platform has the typical circle lights surrounded by six metal studs.

Back across the street, **Nos. 133–135** and **137** are others by Henry Fernbach (1882).

No. 143, a brick, stone, and iron building, was designed by the architectural firm of DeLemos & Cordes in 1887. Nine years later they drew the plans for the famous Siegel-Cooper Department Store, the world's largest store at the time. Their professional skill can still be admired on the northeast corner of Avenue of the Americas and West 18th Street [*see* Ladies' Mile, 11].

GREENE STREET TO BROADWAY

Water tanks. By now you must have noticed the ubiquitous water tanks perched on the roofs of so many of New York's buildings. Since city water pressure is not great enough to rise more than six stories, most taller buildings require the installation of water tanks. Water is pumped up mechanically to fill them, and gravity then takes over and distributes it through the plumbing lines. Wood has been found to be the most durable and economical material. Since 1896 the Rosenwach Tank Company has built the greatest number of rooftop water tanks in the city. While other companies prefabricate their tanks, then hoist them up, the Rosenwach tanks are built on the roof in much the same way as a conventional wooden barrel—with tight-fitting staves held securely by encircling metal bands. The bands are closer together at the bottom because of the steadily increasing pressure of the liquid contents. The conical top usually contains electric heating coils to keep the water from freezing. Later in the tour, look for the conspicuous water tank atop the Haughwout Building (Broadway and Broome Street).

Turn right and walk two blocks to Broadway.

Houston Street was named for William Houstoun by Nicholas Bayard III (a street is named for Bayard, also, near Foley Square). His daughter, Mary, married Houstoun in 1788 after he served three terms as Georgia delegate to the Continental Congress. The current spelling is an error. Out-of-towners frequently associate the name with the Texas hero, Sam Houston, who was not even born when the Houstoun-Bayard wedding took place. And the street is pronounced HOUSE-ton! The buildings along the south side of the street were razed in 1963 when the thoroughfare was widened.

Broadway in the last few years has undergone a swift and dramatic metamorphosis. For nearly a century since the entertainment district moved uptown, it remained a manufacturing wholesale and warehousing area—dark and rather dingy. The lack of major development was fortuitous however, as the buildings were not "modernized," and the fine array of industrial architecture was preserved. The thoroughfare suddenly has come to life as a center for the arts, as many galleries found the loft space and rents attractive, and a spate of new museums opened their doors. And to feed the throngs of visitors, a variety of food emporiums offer many choices. Even new bank branches are taking advantage of the increase in economic activity.

The enormous building at the northwest corner of Broadway is McKim, Mead & White's **Cable Building,** 611 Broadway. Designed in 1894 by Stanford

White, it was the headquarters of the Broadway Cable Traction Company, whose initials in wrought iron can be seen over the entrance. Above the entrance are two relief sculptures, and topping the main cornice is a row of antefixes in the typical Greek anthemion design.

Across the street, **No. 620** (John B. Snook, 1858) may be the second-oldest cast-iron building in New York. A gem of the Italian Renaissance *palazzo* style, this delightful former gaslight-fixture factory building has somehow survived intact, except for some ground-floor modifications. The façade, in imitation of rusticated blocks, gives a three-dimensional effect behind the rows of paired, free-standing Corinthian columns. Each pair of fluted columns supports its own entablature and is joined to its neighbor by ornate semicircular arches rich in design. The structure is a tribute to Daniel D. Badger's Architectural Iron Works. A larger version of this delightful structure is the Cary Building, located at 105 Chambers Street, downtown.

No. 622–626 (1882) occupies the site of the former Laura Keen's Varieties Theater, later the Olympic Theater, a popular entertainment spot from 1856 to 1880, when it was destroyed by fire. Having suffered the ravages of "modernization," little remains except for the five floors of columns, and a rather attractive upper story. Curved-arch windows with keystones and an intricate cornice give some idea of its original ornamentation. Oddly, the building is unevenly divided into two sections of four and six bays, possibly because it was first planned as two separate entities.

No. 628–630 (1882) was designed by Philadelphia architect Henry Schwarzmann, the supervising architect of the 1876 Centennial Exposition. Built for Henry Newman's New York Mercantile Exchange, it has a rather flat but pleasing façade, with bamboolike colonnettes and extensive floral designs. The firm name emblazoned across the front adds to the overall effect. The decorative cornice is made of galvanized iron, and the wrought-iron cresting has disappeared.

Return to Houston Street and continue south on Broadway.

HOUSTON STREET TO CANAL STREET (along Broadway)

Broadway, in the six long blocks south to Canal Street, offers as diverse an array of commercial architecture as can be found anywhere. Virtually every style is represented, in both cast iron and masonry, dating from the period of the late 1850s to the early 20th century. Although the tour is concerned primarily with cast-iron architecture, one should not overlook the great variety of brick and stone buildings—some of which were the forerunners in style of the early cast-iron edifices, as well as those later steel-framework behemoths whose overornateness often approaches decadence. As if searching for an architectural style of their own, the enormous commercial loft buildings of the 1890s through the 1900s cling tenaciously to all the old classic motifs, draping themselves in reckless abandon with a profusion of carved stone and terra-cotta adornments, apparently unwilling to face the stylistic demands imposed by the new "skyscraper" technology.

With the widening of Houston Street, **No. 600–602** Broadway is now the corner building. Built in 1882 from plans by Samuel Warner, each floor is built successively shorter to give the impression of greater height.

Across the street, **No. 597,** a marble building (John Kellum, 1867), looks so much like a typical early cast-iron building that one is tempted to test it with a magnet. **Nos. 593** and **591** are also an interesting pair. The former is an attractive Classical-style building dating from 1860.

No. 591, extensively altered about 1890, still has a great deal of charm. The iron arched doorways and ground-floor window seem to be original, and the window treatment is light and cheerful. Look up to the sixth floor with its attractive entablature and surmounting pediment.

No. 593 is the site of the new **Museum for African Art,** which extends through to Mercer Street. The Museum mounts two major exhibitions each year and a series of smaller ones. The interior was designed by Maya Lin, the architect responsible for the Vietnam Memorial in Washington, D.C., and the Martin Luther King Memorial in Atlanta. (Open Wed., Thurs., and Sun., 11 A.M.–6 P.M., Fri. and Sat., 11 A.M.–8 P.M.)

No. 594 houses the **Alternative Museum.** A new arrival on Broadway, the Museum presents exhibitions of humanitarian significance that explore issues of political and social concern. In its mission statement, it "facilitates a forum in which artists and the public can together challenge tradition and explore new ideas toward a shared ideal of a more equitable society." The Museum seeks to exhibit the work of those artists who have been disenfranchised because of ideology, race, gender, or economic inequality. (Hours: Tues.–Sat., 11:00 A.M. to 6:00 P.M. Suggested admission fee, $3.00.)

No. 583, Astor Building (Cleverdon & Putzel, 1896) houses the **New Museum of Contemporary Art,** which presents changing exhibitions of works of the past decade only. (Open Wed., Thurs., Fri., Sun. 12–6 P.M., Sat. 12–8 P.M. Admission $3.50; seniors, artists, students, members, and children under 12, free.) John Jacob Astor died in his house on the site, in 1848.

No. 568–578, a typical structure of the mid-1890s, not unlike many in this four-block length of Broadway, was designed in Renaissance Eclectic style by noted architect George B. Post, who produced buildings of much greater interest: the New York Stock Exchange, City College north campus, the Long Island Historical Society, the Williamsburg Savings Bank, etc. On the northeast corner, from the mid- to late-19th century, stood the large and fashionable **Metropolitan Hotel,** one of the city's largest. Behind the hotel, extending to Crosby Street, was **Niblo's Garden Theater,** a popular entertainment spot, whose entrance was through the basement of the Metropolitan Hotel.

No. 575 houses the new **Guggenheim Museum SoHo,** and Museum Store, a branch of the Frank Lloyd Wright–designed Solomon R. Guggenheim Museum, at 1071 Fifth Avenue. The interior was designed by renowned architect Arata Isozaki, and opened in 1992. The museum showcases selections from the permanent collection, as well as special exhibitions that complement those at the Guggenheim uptown. The museum also offers gallery talks and a variety of public programs. (Open Sun., Mon., Wed., 10:00 A.M.–6:00 P.M., Thurs.–Sat., 11:00 A.M.–10:00 P.M. Closed Tuesdays, Thanksgiving, December 25, and January 1. Admission: $5.00; over 65 and students with valid ID, $3.00; children accompanied by an adult, free.)

(Look east on Prince Street to the diminutive red brick Federal-style house at the southeast corner of Crosby Street, a surprising remnant of the former residential district of the early 19th century.)

One of the outstanding architectural achievements of the early 20th century is **No. 561–563,** occupying an L-shaped plot on the southwest corner of Prince Street. Known as the **"Little Singer Building,"** it was designed in 1903 by architect Ernest Flagg as an office and loft building for the Singer (sewing machine) Manufacturing Company. Flagg was also responsible for their famous tower—once the tallest skyscraper in the world—which was located at the corner of Broadway and Liberty Street until its unfortunate demolition in 1967. One of the most avant-garde uses of iron, the "Little Singer" presents an innovative 12-story façade of cast iron, decorative terra-cotta panels, and broad expanses of plate glass. Delicate balconies and balustrades with wrought-iron traceries, supported by fragile cast-iron colonnettes, are surmounted by a graceful, lacy arch; while above, curved wrought-iron brackets support the 11th-story cornice. The Prince Street side has a narrower but similar façade.

No. 560-566 (Thomas Stent, 1883), a six-story brick and stone building, occupies the entire Prince Street side to Crosby Street. Heavy brick piers flank both the end and center bays; and at the first, second, fourth, and sixth floors, the piers are decorated with floral capitals. Foliated iron pilasters separate the windows, which have curved lintels, and the entablature between each floor has its own foliated frieze. No. 560 houses the expanded facilities of that famous SoHo landmark, **Dean & DeLuca,** a food specialty store whose delectable wares defy adequate description. Go inside and browse!

On the west side of Broadway, **No. 549–555,** in gray granite with cast-iron colonnettes and spandrels, is the massive **Rouss Building.** Designed in 1889 by Alfred Zucker for Charles Rouss, it stands as a symbol of success of the self-made millionaire who arrived penniless in New York from Maryland shortly after the Civil War. Making his fortune as a wholesale merchant, Rouss attributed his success not only to hard work, but to the opportunities afforded him by Broadway, and in gratitude, he took "Broadway" as his middle name, emblazoning it for all to see in the scrolled pediment above. When an identical section was built in 1900, the roof was altered and the triangular mansardlike attic dormers added. The windows of the façade are divided into groups of three by heavy quoined pilasters, each window grouping having a pair of intervening slender colonnettes. Cast-iron spandrels separate each pair of stories. Although the much-altered ground floor spoils the unity of the building, it is, nonetheless, a bold and impressive structure.

Nos. 552–554, across the street, are among the oldest on Broadway (John B. Snook, 1855). Both are of stone and have two-story iron fronts, joined together later in 1897. Note the wide central window on the second floor, the four large console brackets that support the second-floor cornice, the rounded window lintels with incised keystones, and the elaborate upper cornice with its modillions and decorated brackets.

No. 550, alongside, completed in 1854, was **formerly the Tiffany & Company store.** However, little can be seen of the original façade as it was refaced with cast iron in 1901, probably one of the last such fronts to be erected.

On the west side of Broadway, much altered No. 545 (1885) is by Samuel A. Warner.

Just north of Spring Street, don't miss the attractive wood-and-glass storefront on No. 546! It is a replacement designed by Guy Lindsay Kohn in 1993 to lend authenticity to the Beaux Arts–style building, which had undergone a number of modifications. The structure dates from 1866 when it was built of brick and stone as a loft, replacing the Fourth Universalist Church on the site. In 1901 architect John Correja added a cast-iron front; then in 1930 it was "remuddled" with a sheet-metal ground-floor front. The new addition harmonizes with the Beaux Arts façade and is an asset to Broadway and the historic district.

In front of No. 542 is another "bishop's crook" lamppost.

Nos. 537–541 are a pleasing trio in cast iron (Charles Mettam, 1868). If one ignores the remodeled ground floor, the beauty can be seen in the harmonious treatment of the eight-bay façade set off by three-quarter round columns with Corinthianesque capitals and the flat arches with rope moldings. In the spandrels are rosettes above each column. The roof line, however, dominates the building. Above a paneled frieze are three pediments—two curved, and one triangular—supported by scrolled brackets and modillions. Ornate urns further highlight the intricate cornice.

Back across the street, No. 542–544, built of marble in 1864, has undergone several modifications; nevertheless the arrangement of the upper floors is quite eye-catching. The bays are separated by Corinthian columns, but on the very top floor they are separated by caryatidlike figures. The cornice, topped by two urns above the outer figures, is supported by large scrolled brackets.

No. 540 (D. & J. Jardine, 1867), built of marble, was once a store and warehouse. It has a most unusual two-dimensional effect created by the flatness of the pilasters, "capitals," window arches, lintels, and keystones—all with carved fleur-de-lis designs. Above the cornice, set in a small semicircular pediment, is the date of construction. Again, one can only speculate on how the motif was handled on the original ground floor.

The northwest corner of Broadway and Spring Street is the site of the luxurious Prescott House, built in 1852.

No. 521–523 is all that remains of the once opulent St. Nicholas Hotel. Completed in 1854 at a cost of over $1 million, it was one of the most elegant hotels in the city, competing in luxury only with the Astor House on lower Broadway. There is some controversy over who the architect was. Whether it was Griffith Thomas or John B. Snook, no one knows for sure. The 1,000-bed establishment occupied 11 lots from 507 through 527 Broadway, extending to the corner of Prince Street, opposite the Prescott House which was built two

The remains of the once opulent St. Nicholas Hotel, this pair of stone buildings at 521 and 523 Broadway. Completed in 1854, the million-dollar hotel was second in luxury only to the Astor House downtown. The window lintels and ornamental cornices on No. 521 (left) have been removed since this photo was taken in 1975. (Photo by author)

years earlier. During the Civil War, the St. Nicholas was taken over by the War Department as a headquarters, becoming one of the nerve centers of the Union Army. The life of the hotel, however, was relatively short. With the uptown move of the entertainment district, the plush hotels soon followed, and by the mid-1870s it closed its doors. This remaining section of the old hotel is faced with stone, showing only a trace of its former appearance. The old cast-iron Corinthian storefront has long since been removed. Virtually nothing remains of the original façades of Nos. 521 and 523.

Take a brief detour east on Spring Street to **No. 72,** the **Children's Museum of the Arts.** In this museum designed to introduce youngsters to the arts through active participation, there are a variety of exhibits, and tables where the children can experiment with several art mediums. There are structures to crawl through, and jigsaw puzzles illustrating the works of the great masters. Parents seem to have as much fun as the kids. (Open Tues.–Sun., 11:00 A.M. to 5 P.M. Closed Mon. except on school holidays. Admission charge, but free Thurs. 4:00 P.M. to 7:00 P.M.) Return to Broadway and continue south.

No. 513–519, designed by Samuel A. Warner in 1884 (on the site of part of the old St. Nicholas Hotel), is a 13-bay-wide commercial building in the then-popular Queen Anne style. It incorporates newly adopted terra-cotta elements into the building's multicolor façade. Heavy brick pilasters adorned with terra-cotta plaques and topped with ornate capitals divide the bays into three groups between the first, second, and fifth floors. The windows in the outer bays are separated by delicate cast-iron Ionic pilasters, while the center bay sections have iron columns with very ornate capitals. Scrolled brackets supporting the iron cornice alternate with terra-cotta plaques in the frieze. A half-story mansard roof is offset by three pediments—the center one enclosing an elaborate design. The dark red brick throughout is also typical of the Queen Anne style and became very popular in the contemporary Romanesque Revival style of the 1880s.

A "bishop's crook" lamppost stands in front of No. 515.

Nos. 503–505, 507–509, and **511** were all designed in cast iron by John B. Snook in 1878 to form a harmonious grouping, after the demise of the St. Nicholas Hotel. So many alterations have taken place that only the ornate entablature is really worth of note. A row of vertical pseudo-brackets stretch across the broad concave frieze below the narrow cornice, with larger brackets topped by neo-Grec terminal blocks above the pilasters supporting the cornice.

Across the street, **No. 502–504,** designed by Kellum & Son in 1860, presents a striking façade with its "sperm candle" style. Named after the shape of old whale-oil candles, the motif is credited to Daniel D. Badger, whose Architectural Iron Works constructed the original storefront, and who used the design in full cast iron on a building erected in 1861 at 55–57 White Street (two blocks below Canal Street). The smooth white marble columns separate each window grouping into two-story units, forming a giant "double arcade." Under the cornice is a row of "inverse crenelation," and rising above the molded end brackets are small urns. Architecture buffs have long been arguing whether the "sperm candle" style originated in stone or cast iron.

Cross to the southwest corner of Broadway and Broome Street for the best view of the most beautiful commercial cast-iron building in the country, the **Haughwout Building** (*pronounced* HOW-out), at **No. 488–492** Broadway. Referred to as the "Parthenon of Cast-Iron Architecture in America," this impressive building was one of the first designated New York City Landmarks. Architectural writer Ada Louise Huxtable said of it: "The Haughwout Store's iron elegance contained all the seeds of the future; its metal façade was to lead in turn to the metal frame; the elevator, combined with the metal frame, was to produce the skyscraper; and its repetitive Palladian rhythms were to become the basis of today's aesthetic of pre-fabricated, mass-produced structural units." In 1856 Eder V. Haughwout engaged architect John P. Gaynor to design an appropriate store and showroom for his china and glassware business. The result a year later was this superb Venetian Renaissance *palazzo*. The finely detailed iron façade was cast by Daniel D. Badger's Architectural Iron Works, and later appeared in his illustrated iron works catalog [*see* Recommended Reading]. Haughwout's chinaware was so highly esteemed that it was used in the White House and was displayed at New York's Crystal Palace Exhibition, 1853–54. He also commissioned Elisha Graves Otis to install a steam-driven passenger elevator—the first of its kind anywhere—which years later was to make skyscrapers feasible, at the same time launching the industrial empire of the Otis Company. The basic design motif, repeated on each level, is a keystoned round arch set on fluted Corinthian columns, flanked by taller columns supporting a full entabla-

Considered to be the "Parthenon of Cast-Iron Architecture" is the landmark Haughwout Building at Broadway and Broome Street. This superb Venetian palazzo was cast by Daniel D. Badger's Architectural Iron Works in 1856, and was equipped with the first commercial steam elevator by Elisha Graves Otis. It is probably the oldest extant cast-iron building in the city, and certainly one of the best preserved. (Photo by author)

ture, with an underlying balustrade in each bay. A delicate cornice rises above several bands of elaborate friezework; and in the center bay of the second floor hangs a large iron clock, now minus its hands. The building is in virtually pristine condition (although a restored clock would help); the ground floor, so often altered, is completely intact. Because of its architectural and historic significance, the Haughwout Building has been listed in the National Register of Historic Places.

Cross to the east side of Broadway to get a better view of **No. 491, The New Era Building** (Buchman & Deisler, 1897). Here is an unusual art nouveau variation on the turn-of-the-century industrial architecture theme. The building, with its short and stubby Doric columns and multistory verdigris copper mansard roof, was built for a printing firm, and simply exudes strength and solidity.

No. 477–479 (H. W. Smith and Sons, 1869) contrasts strongly with its neighbors. A center molded pilaster divides the bays into two distinct groupings. The bays themselves are separated by columns with hexagonal bases and stylized Corinthian capitals. The windows have rounded lintels, and abstract geometric detail decorates the spandrels. Simple cornices separate the upper stories. Note the fine leaf-pattern design on the brackets of the upper cornice. And the storefronts survive intact.

The **Roosevelt Building** across Broadway, at **No. 478–482,** is the only surviving Richard Morris Hunt commercial building in New York. The Paris-trained architect also designed the Metropolitan Museum of Art, the base of the Statue of Liberty, the bronze doors of Trinity Church, and the lovely old New York Tribune Building, which dominated Park Row, downtown. This unusual neo-Grec–style building, owned by Roosevelt Hospital, was built as a store for income-producing purposes in 1873. The visual impact of this original statement in cast iron is often lost on the thousands of riders and pedestrians who pass it daily, as *few New Yorkers are in the habit of looking any higher at buildings than ground-floor level.* Built to utilize the advantages of iron architecture to the utmost, it resembles no masonry predecessor nor any other cast-iron building either. The enormous front is divided into three main sections by four fluted pilasters at the tall ground-floor level and continued by bold Ionic columns for the next three levels. Slender colonnettes separate the triple windows, disappearing behind a curved screenlike tracery arch set over each group. The top floor, which repeats the three-window pattern, is shaded by a broad projecting cornice, now minus much of its former decoration. On each incised pilaster is mounted a large circular escutcheon with the street address in bold numerals. A single section of the building extends back to Crosby Street (No. 40), where its one-third-smaller front is graced with a proportionately scaled version of the Broadway façade.

Nos. 466–468 and **462–464** at the northeast corner of Grand Street combine to form a striking pair. Built from plans by John Correja in 1879, the pair was leased by the large textile importing firm of Mills & Gibb, specializing in linens and laces. An earlier tenant on the site was the **Brooks Brothers Store,** which during the Civil War had established its reputation by supplying uniforms for the Union Army. An interesting variation on the decorative theme is the sawtooth motif that embellishes the window lintels, and the rows of incised banding on

Now a vacant lot on the northwest corner of Broadway and Grand Street, the Lord & Taylor store occupied the site from 1860 until fire destroyed it a hundred years later. The firm sold the building shortly after the turn of the century when the retail district moved uptown to "Ladies' Mile." (The Edward S. C. Arnold Collection, lent by the Metropolitan Museum of Art. Museum of the City of New York)

the second- and fourth-story entablatures. On the third, fifth, and sixth floors, the pilasters have unique scallop-and-bandwork capitals, with a medallion motif halfway up the shaft. The cornice is rather heavy and is supported by brackets, while a row of modillions lines the architrave.

The parking lot across the street is the **site of an early Lord & Taylor department store** (1860–72). The original Griffith Thomas–designed building suffered a disastrous fire in 1967 and had to be demolished. During the Draft Riots of 1863, Lord & Taylor armed its employees for protection against the raging mobs that were surging down Broadway (the rioters were finally dispersed by Union Army artillery about a mile north, at what is now 3rd Street). In 1865, when President Lincoln's funeral cortege moved slowly up Broadway, the store was draped in mourning, with merchandise removed from the windows and seats installed for the viewing of the procession.

Midway down the east side of the next block are **Nos. 452, 450, 446–448, and 444**—an interesting quartet in cast iron. The two outer buildings (Nos. 452 and 444) are identical (by Schweitzer & Gruwé); while the inner pair (Nos. 450 and 446–448) share a common façade (John B. Snook). All were completed in the same year, 1877. The flanking outer buildings immediately bring to mind Hunt's Roosevelt Building (at 478–482 Broadway), with their pierced stylized arches and wide spandrel panels, together with the slim colonnettes separating the windows. Crowning the front is a bold projecting cornice decorated with anthemions alternating with raised circular motifs, with neo-Grec console brackets at the ends. Look for the foundry label, which unexpectedly gives the names of the architects along with the Long Island Iron Works. The inner group of buildings is distinguished by quoined pilasters at each end, Corinthian columns defining the window bays and ground floor openings; while above, the entablature is flanked by large console brackets topped by neo-Grec terminal blocks, a common cornice stretches above a paneled frieze, and additional concave brackets with their own incised terminal blocks alternate with frieze panels. The cast-iron fronts were supplied by the J. B. & J. W. Cornell Iron Works (see label).

A "bishop's crook" lamppost stands in front of No. 446–448.

Across the street, **No. 447** (architect unknown, 1860) has an iron storefront listed in D. D. Badger's Architectural Iron Works catalog of 1865.

No. 443–445 (Griffith Thomas, 1860) gives a very aesthetic appearance. Rows of pleasing round-arch windows are topped by individual projecting cornice slabs supported by brackets. A projecting balustrade runs along the second floor, with decorative urns at each end. Ornate scrolled brackets support the main cornice, above which a pediment adds the final touch.

Except for No. 441, built in 1876, the entire west side of the block dates from the 1860s.

"The Bank in the Park," No. 433, at the northwest corner of Howard Street (Eggers & Higgins, 1967), offers an unexpected oasis of restful greenery. In spite of its fake Georgian style, the effect of the diminutive EAB (European-American Bank) and its landscaped plot is quite successful.

Howard Street is named for Harry Howard, a volunteer "fire laddie" of the early 19th century. It was called Hester Street until 1825, which, incidentally, is still the street's name after it makes a small zigzag at Centre Street on its way toward the Lower East Side.

Turn left (east) on Howard Street for a brief glance at **No. 27** and **29.** The former, a modified neo-Grec–style building, was designed by Samuel Warner in 1888. No. 29, 20 years its senior, is by the firm of Renwick & Sands. One must look beyond the added fire escape and the dingy atmosphere, abetted by the narrow and dark street, to enjoy the profusion of decorative elements. The rolling iron shutter in the center window was a novelty introduced in the "iron age." Amazingly, both buildings' ground floors remain completely intact. In front of No. 30, on the north side, is a large cast-iron light vault (Excelsior Iron Works), to admit sunlight into the basement.

Return to the northeast corner of Howard Street and Broadway.

Diagonally across the street is the exquisite **Dittenhoffer Warehouse, No. 427–429,** built (as emblazoned in the ornate triangular pediment) in 1870. The successive shortening of each story clearly creates a feeling of much greater height than would be expected from a five-story building. Architect Thomas Jackson used both Venetian and French motifs to highlight this palatial edifice. Particularly noteworthy is the beautifully ornate façade, as exemplified by the spandrels between the window arches, the decorated column shafts, the

Corinthian capitals, the keystoned arches over the windows, and the frieze below the bracket-supported cornice, which repeats the florid details of the spandrels. Except for one remaining show window on the Howard Street side, most of the ground floor has been altered beyond recognition. The corner was the site of the City Hotel from 1852 to 1869.

Adjacent **No. 425,** erected in 1869, is one of the architect Griffith Thomas's first full iron-front buildings (Aetna Iron Works). How different from its neighbor are the square-headed windows with curved corners, the unadorned entablatures, the almost bare columns, and curved broken pediments. It was built for the LeBoutillier brothers, who later moved their store uptown, opening one of the most fashionable women's wear emporiums during the gaslit era. [*See* Ladies' Mile, 20.]

Continue west on Howard Street.

No. 48, a stone building with a cast-iron storefront, was built in 1860 as an annex to the Arnold Constable "Marble House" across the street. The façade with its rows of round-arched windows, pilasters, heavy entablature, and elaborate cornice is a typical example of the masonry prototypes of early cast-iron buildings.

No. 50–52 was built in 1860 as a store for a gun dealer. A stone building with a cast-iron storefront, it is more imposing than No. 48. The ground level has lovely fluted Corinthian columns, above which are rows of French-style segmental-arch windows in a kind of "recessed" style that creates a flat, two-dimensional effect. The overall restrained appearance ends at the cornice, which is disproportionately ostentatious. During the Civil War, the building became the **New York State Soldiers' Depot,** a rest home and hospital for troops on leave.

Howard Street ends at Mercer Street (named for General Hugh Mercer, killed in the Battle of Princeton in 1777).

End of tour. Canal Street, the starting point of the tour, is one block south and one block east. [*See* following Supplementary Tour.]

SUPPLEMENTARY TOUR BELOW CANAL STREET

A short walk through the neighborhood from Canal Street to Chambers Street, using Broadway as an axis, reveals a number of additional cast-iron buildings of more than casual interest. A few are listed below. *Except where indicated, all cast-iron buildings are located in the one block west of Broadway.* [*See* street map.]

CANAL STREET:	**No. 268** (one block east) (1886, Lansing C. Holden), and **No. 351–353** (two blocks west) (1971, W. H. Gaylor).
LISPENARD STREET:	**Nos. 48–40.** See also cast-iron decoration on **No. 39–41** Clark Building.
WALKER STREET:	**Nos. 57, 49–43, 42.**

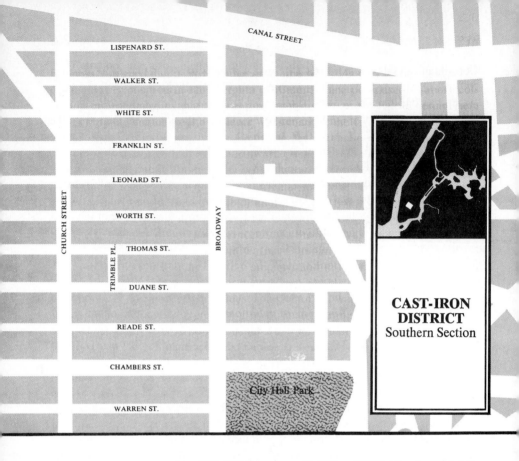

CANAL STREET

LISPENARD ST.

WALKER ST.

WHITE ST.

FRANKLIN ST.

LEONARD ST.

CHURCH STREET

WORTH ST.

BROADWAY

TRIMBLE PL.

THOMAS ST.

DUANE ST.

READE ST.

CHAMBERS ST.

City Hall Park

WARREN ST.

**CAST-IRON
DISTRICT**
Southern Section

BROADWAY:	**No. 385–387** Grosvenor Building (1875, Charles Wright).
WHITE STREET:	**Nos. 57-55, 60, 41, 37–35,** and the avant-garde **Civic Center Synagogue.** Not cast iron, but astonishing! (1967, William N. Breger, architect, and Paul Gugliotta, structural engineer).
FRANKLIN STREET:	**Nos. 81–83.** Only the lower part is cast iron (west of Broadway).
BROADWAY:	**No. 361 James S. White Building** (1881, W. Wheeler Smith).
LEONARD STREET:	**No. 85 James Bogardus's former warehouse** (1860).
BROADWAY:	**No. 346** (east side). Not cast iron, this was the **former New York Life Insurance Company Building** (1870, Griffith Thomas, enlarged 1896, McKim, Mead & White).
BROADWAY:	**No. 319** (corner of Thomas Street) (1869, D. & J. Jardine).
	No. 287 (corner of Reade Street) (1871, John B. Snook).
READE STREET:	Walk one block farther to Church Street to admire the splendidly preserved **Cary Building** at **No. 89–91** (1856, Gamaliel King & John Kellum); castings made by Daniel D. Badger's Architectural Iron Works.
	No. 93.

CHAMBERS STREET: **No. 105–107** (the rear façade of the Cary Building).

No. 120 (just a bit farther west). Only the upper floors are worth looking at; however, to get a good picture of its original appearance, go around the corner to see the rear of the building and its well-preserved façade at 50 Warren Street (ca. 1860, architect unknown; cast by D. D. Badger).

If you are still interested in cast iron...

There is a small but active organization, Friends of Cast-Iron Architecture, which conducts walking tours, sponsors lectures, and fights determinedly for the preservation and restoration of our cast-iron buildings. It is primarily to this group of dedicated cast-iron buffs that credit is due for the designation by the Landmarks Commission of the SoHo Cast-Iron Historic District. (For more information, write to the Friends at 235 East 87th Street, New York, N.Y. 10128).

GLOSSARY OF TECHNICAL TERMS USED IN THE SOHO CAST-IRON DISTRICT WALKING TOUR

ANTEFIX, an ornament projecting above a roof cornice, frequently incorporating an anthemion motif

ANTHEMION, a conventionalized leaf motif based on a honeysuckle or palmette form, originating in Greek ornamental forms

ARCHITRAVE [*see* ENTABLATURE]

BALUSTRADE, a row of baluster columns topped by a railing, forming a parapet, usually set on a cornice or in front of a window

BAY, the general term for the window section

BEARING WALL, a wall upon which the structural load of a building rests

BRACKET, a projecting L- or S-shaped support used frequently in the form of an S-curve

CARYATID, a decorative column in the form of a female figure

CLASSICAL ORDERS. In discussing the buildings dating from the second half of the 19th century within the Historic District, references to the classical orders must be interpreted loosely. The architects of these buildings took great liberties in adapting Greek and Roman forms to commercial buildings. Reference to a specific order refers only to the capital (the design element at the top of the column shaft)

TUSCAN CAPITAL, a very simple unadorned capital, resembling the Doric, but frequently of heavier proportions

DORIC CAPITAL, a relatively simple capital with a flat topmost member

IONIC CAPITAL, a capital with spiral volutes beneath its topmost member

CORINTHIAN CAPITAL, a capital embellished with carved acanthus leaves

CORINTHIANESQUE CAPITAL, a capital incorporating stylized leaf forms

COMPOSITE CAPITAL, a capital combining volutes and acanthus leaves (a composite of the Ionic and Corinthian orders)

CONSOLE BRACKET [*see* BRACKET]

CORNICE [*see* ENTABLATURE]

CORNICE SLAB, a cornicelike projection placed above a window

CURTAIN WALL, an exterior wall, separate from the structural framework, that supports only its own weight

DROP LINTEL [*see* LINTEL]

EGG-AND-DART MOLDING, a classical molding consisting of alternating egg-and-dart-shaped forms

ENTABLATURE, the group of horizontal members directly above column capitals. It consists of:

ARCHITRAVE, the lowest member resting upon the column capitals. An architrave is also occasionally extended to enframe the sides of a door or window opening that is topped by an entablature

FRIEZE, the middle member of an entablature, which in 19th-century architectural styles is frequently embellished by panels or medallions, and interrupted by large cornice brackets; 19th-century adaptations of classical orders often combine a frieze and cornice without architrave

CORNICE, the horizontally projecting topmost member of an entablature. It is frequently found by itself as the crowning motif of a façade

FANLIGHT, a semicircular window placed over a door, with bars radiating from its center like spokes of a fan

FINIAL, an ornamental form at the top of a pediment, spire, pinnacle, etc.

FRIEZE [*see* ENTABLATURE]

IRON VAULT COVERS, a number of iron plates with lights (*see below*) that lie over the vaults, and are on the same level as the sidewalk

KEYSTONE, the central voussoir (block) of an arch

LIGHT, generally, a pane of glass, but in this district it refers to pieces of hardened glass of various shapes, sizes, and colors that are inserted in iron plates

LIGHT PLATFORM, a flat, raised area in front of the façade of a building that is made up of a number of iron plates with lights, and which stands on the vault

LINTEL, a horizontal member placed over a window or door to support the superstructure

MODILLION, a small ornamental bracket used in a closely spaced, regular series below a projecting cornice

PALAZZO, an Italian "palace," usually associated with those from the Renaissance. When referring to 19th-century styles, however, a *palazzo* can be any large, impressive building whose style was derived from the Italian Renaissance.

PEDIMENT, a low, usually triangular gable constructed in a classical style that is often filled by sculpture and usually framed by a cornice. It is used decoratively to crown central bays, porticoes, and important windows of a façade, and is sometimes segmental in shape or broken away in the center.

PIER, in masonry architecture, an upright supporting member carrying a structural load. When interpreted in cast iron, an exterior pier is, in most instances, merely a solid part of the curtain wall placed between the windows and/or on either side of a façade.

PILASTER, a shallow, flat engaged (attached) column, normally serving only a decorative function

QUOIN, in masonry architecture, large stones used to reinforce a corner or salient angle of a building. When interpreted in cast iron, rusticated quoins were used decoratively to emphasize the flanking piers.

RISER, the vertical member between the treads of a stair

RUSTICATION, in masonry architecture, an emphasis of individual (usually large) stones by recessing their connecting parts

SEGMENTAL ARCH, an arch in which the curvature is a segment of a circle, but less than a semicircle

SOLDIER COURSE, a course (row) of bricks set on their ends

SPANDREL, the space between the outer curve of an arch and its rectangular enframement, or between two adjacent arches and a horizontal member above them

SPANDREL PANEL, in skeleton-frame construction, the wall panel between the head of one window and the sill of a window directly above it

TERMINAL BLOCK, a decorative block placed at the extreme ends of a cornice between floor levels, thus interrupting the quoin lines or flanking piers of a façade

TREAD, the horizontal surface of a step

VAULT, a cellar room used for storage, often extending under the sidewalk

VOLUTE, a spiral or scroll-like form, as with the Ionic capital

VOUSSOIR, a wedge-shaped stone forming part of a masonry arch

LADIES'
MILE
and
FASHION
ROW

c. 1900

Fint &
Horner

James
McCutcheon

Western Union
Bldg.

23RD ST.

⑲ ⑳ ㉑ ㉒ ㉓

Riker's

Stern
Bros.

Ehrich
Bros.

⑱

Site of
Best & Co.
and
Bonwit Teller

Flatiron
Building

22ND ST.

Site of
James McCreery

Adams
Dry
Goods

⑰

Sohmer
& Co.

㉔

BROADWAY

21ST ST.

⑯

3rd
Spanish
& Port.
Cemetery

Scribner's

ugh O'Neill

Church of
the Holy
Communion

156
Fifth Ave.

⑮

903

20TH ST.

⑭

㉕

㉖

Simpson-
Crawford

⑬

Cammeyer's

Lord &
Taylor's

Goelet
Bldg.

㉗

150 5th Ave.
Methodist
Book Concern

Gorham
Mfg. Co.

㉘

19TH ST.

⑫

B. Altman

⑪

Siegel-Cooper

Arnold Constable

㉙

㉚

W. & J.
Sloane

⑩

18TH ST.

SIXTH AVE.

17TH ST.

UNION SQUARE N.

FIFTH AVE.

16TH ST.

Union
Square

UNION SQUARE WEST

PARK AVE. SOUTH

15TH ST.

Dead Men's
Curve

⑨ ⑧

14TH ST.

⑦

⑥

Macy's

Hearn's

Bau-
mann
& Co.

Rogers
Peet

13TH ST.

⑤

(Site of Wallack's Theater)

UNIVERSITY PLACE

12TH ST.

④

BROADWAY

4TH AVENUE

James
McCreery

11TH ST.

Hotel
St. Denis

③

10TH ST.

②

Grace
Church

Site of A. T.
Stewart
Cast-Iron
Palace

9TH ST.

WANAMAKER PL.

①

John
Wanamaker

8TH ST.

start

8. Ladies' Mile and Fashion Row

[Broadway R line to 8th Street; Lexington Avenue line No. 6 to Astor Place, walk west one block on 8th Street; Broadway M6 bus to 8th Street]

The department store as we know it today had its genesis in the small whole-sale and dry-goods shops that began to proliferate along the busier thoroughfares of lower Manhattan during the 1820s. With the upsurge of immigration in the following decades, and the rapid growth of commerce and industry, many keen merchants seized the opportunity to expand and diversify, making fortunes by catering to the changing tastes and increased demands of the burgeoning city. By the 1870s and 1880s, the main shopping center of the city had moved uptown, following the northward growth of the city, to an area between 8th and 23rd streets along Broadway, and also on Fifth and Sixth Avenues. With women shoppers always in the majority, it did not take long before this bustling row of large retail stores was known as Ladies' Mile.

Today not one of those fine old establishments can be found on the Mile. The stores either relocated farther uptown to keep abreast with the inexorable north-ward tide, or, unable to update their merchandising techniques, closed their doors forever. Astonishingly, most of the buildings that housed those elegant department stores still remain intact, now the city's latest hot shopping spot.

Our itinerary takes us on a "shopping tour" of those glamorous "ghosts" of a bygone era, and using a little imagination, we can return to the bustling streets of those gaslit days. Listen carefully for the rhythmic clip-clop from the profusion of horse-drawn vehicles and the clatter of their iron-clad wheels on the cobble-stoned street, the persistent bell-clanging of horsecars caught in the tangled traf-fic—their impatient conductors exchanging abuse with draymen and carriage drivers—and the shrill cries of "Extra! Extra!" from little boys hawking their penny papers at the street corners. When we reach Sixth Avenue, our walk will take us under the gloomy structure of the old El, whose wooden trains roar by overhead in an endless, ear-splitting clatter, their smoky locomotives spewing hot cinders and oil on the unwary below. Standing stiffly at the entrance portals to the fancy "magazines" that line the Avenue, liveried doormen await the arrival of the "carriage trade," and as a coach draws up, rush forward to escort the affluent patrons to the door. And clustered about the elaborate show windows, we glimpse elegantly clad women in trailing dresses, billowy hats, and frilly parasols, pressing to catch the latest fashions in furbelows, veils, shirtwaists, millinery, and high-button shoes.

1. The tour begins at 8th Street and Broadway, the southerly end of Ladies' Mile. The huge building at the northeast corner was formerly the **Wanamaker Department Store,** now known simply as 770 Broadway. Construction of this 16-story giant began in 1902 and took five years to complete. Designed by Daniel H. Burnham, architect of the Flatiron Building [*see* Madison Square, 24], the structure was planned as a modern extension to the older "Cast-Iron Palace" that occupied the block directly north. John Wanamaker came to New York in 1896 to open a branch of his Philadelphia store, and purchased the old cast-iron building from the successors of the faltering A. T. Stewart Company. Alexander Turney Stewart, who had been considered a merchandising genius, in 1846 opened New York City's first large department store, at Broadway and Chambers Street. Called "The Marble Dry-Goods Palace," the building still stands today [*see* City Hall, 15]. In 1862 he leased a portion of the old Randall Farm in Greenwich Village, and while maintaining his Marble Dry-Goods Palace as a warehouse, built the first large store in what was to become Ladies' Mile. His new emporium, employing the novel architectural medium of cast iron, occupied the entire block from 9th to 10th streets. Each of the six stories was supported by iron beams, the roof area enclosed by an enormous glass dome over a central court. Rows of cast-iron columns lined the façade, permitting sunlight to stream in through the wide intervening arched windows. A grand staircase and six steam-driven elevators provided easy access to all shopping floors. The exterior, painted a mottled white and sparkling like an architectural gem of the Italian Renaissance, was an immediate success.

When Stewart died in 1876, he was the second richest man in America, although his wealth had come mostly from real estate investments. His fashionable emporium, so successful during his lifetime, was now under the management of a former business associate, and the store was renamed Hilton, Hughes & Company. Later it was taken over by a firm called Dennings, and the once-great Stewart store began to founder. It would have gone under altogether were it not for an eleventh-hour reprieve from John Wanamaker who purchased it in 1896. The establishment was completely reorganized, a new building erected alongside (connected to the "Cast-Iron Palace" by a double-decker "Bridge of Progress" and three subterranean passageways, as well as a direct entrance from the newly built IRT subway station at Astor Place). Business began to boom again, and for nearly half a century the name Wanamaker's was synonymous with the ultimate in department store merchandising.

By 1952, the center of retail trade had moved uptown, and patronage fell off rapidly. Although the southbound end of the Fifth Avenue Bus line was still called the Wanamaker Terminal, few customers were to be seen getting off. The older store building was vacated and all operations shifted to the newer facility

The great Palladian cast-iron palace which had been the A. T. Stewart Store on Broadway at 9th Street was under the operation of Hilton, Hughes & Co. when this photo was made in 1889. In the distance is Grace Church, the Gothic-style landmark which still stands at Broadway's bend at 10th Street. (New-York Historical Society)

next door. Time was running out for the once-popular Wanamaker Store. Two years later the end came, and all retail business was transferred to a small downtown shop and to their suburban stores. In a rather dramatic exit, the old cast-iron building, which occupied the entire block between 9th and 10th streets, fell victim on July 15, 1956, to one of New York's most spectacular conflagrations, blazing out of control for two days in a fiery farewell to the old merchant prince. The apartment building that now occupies the site of the "Cast-Iron Palace" is named Stewart House.

2. Grace Church, at the northeast corner of Broadway and 10th Street, is an outstanding example of the Gothic Revival style. This lovely church, built on land formerly owned by Henry Brevoort, was designed in 1846 by James Renwick, Jr., when only 23 years of age. Renwick was also the architect of St. Patrick's Cathedral and the Smithsonian Institution, but many consider Grace Church to be his crowning work. Renwick himself was a parishioner and later vestryman. Particularly beautiful are the 46 medieval stained-glass windows and the intimate Chantry. The garden beside the Chantry is the site of the former Fleischmann's Vienna Model Bakery, a popular continental café in the days of Ladies' Mile. Bought by Grace Church and named Huntington Close, after a former rector, the plot adds much charm to the setting. The steeple is illuminated at night and can be seen for miles down Broadway. Among the scores of architecturally notable structures of the city built before 1930, the Municipal Art Society places Grace Church in its first category of seven buildings "of national importance to be preserved at all costs."

The view of Grace Church is a debt to early settler Henry Brevoort, whose family owned the lands where Grace Church now stands. He was so intent on preserving a much loved apple orchard that stood in the way of Broadway's

Fleischmann's Vienna Model Bakery, at the northeast corner of Broadway and 10th Street, photographed in 1898 by Percy C. Byron. Conveniently located between Grace Church and the former A. T. Stewart Store, it was a European-style café which produced its own baked goods and was one of the most popular places of refreshment along Ladies' Mile. (The Byron Collection. Museum of the City of New York)

northward march that he succeeded in forcing the city fathers to divert the street to the west, and blocked 11th Street from penetrating to Fourth Avenue.

3. On the southwest corner of 11th Street and Broadway stands a rather non-descript 19th-century building, whose extensively altered façade masks its former identity. **The Hotel St. Denis,** built in 1848 and renovated in 1875, was one of the more fashionable hostelries in the city. *King's Handbook of New York,* 1893 edition, praises the attractiveness of this 250-room hotel and adds, "The equipments of the house, as to steam heating, electric lighting, ventilating, and hydraulic elevators, are supplemented by a perfect corps of polite and well-disciplined attendants." In its heyday, it hosted Presidents Lincoln, Grant, and Arthur, as well as Sarah Bernhardt, P. T. Barnum, and Col. William "Buffalo Bill" Cody. Probably the most significant date in the hotel's history was May 11, 1877, when Alexander Graham Bell gave a preview demonstration of his telephone to a spellbound audience of prominent guests in the second-floor parlor room. The wire was strung from the hotel across the Brooklyn Bridge. The St. Denis closed in 1917, and shortly thereafter was converted to commercial use.

At that time all the adornments were stripped from the façade. Enter at the 11th Street door, walk almost to the bank of elevators, turn right and admire the original cast-iron staircase.

4. Across 11th Street is the Palladian cast-iron establishment of the former **James McCreery & Co. Store.** Arriving in this country as a 20-year-old immigrant from Ireland in 1845, McCreery started in business opening a small shop selling Irish lace. Gradually expanding to larger quarters, and following the uptown tide, he commissioned architect John Kellum to build this large dry-goods store in 1868. He was reputed to be a kindly, tolerant man, whose flowing white beard and long shock of hair, together with a thick Irish brogue, made him a very striking figure. He always showed great concern for the welfare of his employees in an era when social conscience in business was relatively unknown. McCreery, self-educated, became a patron of the arts and dedicated much of his later fortune to philanthropic and artistic causes, including helping to found the Metropolitan Museum of Art.

In 1895 he moved to an even larger building at the northern end of Ladies' Mile, at Sixth Avenue and 23rd Street. The present building miraculously survived years of occupancy by a variety of users, but a few years ago suffered a

The St. Denis Hotel and Taylor's Saloon at the southwest corner of Broadway and 11th Street, ca. 1875. It was in the corner parlor room on the second floor that Alexander Graham Bell demonstrated his "speaking telephone" to a group of prominent New York citizens May 11, 1877. The hotel closed in 1917, but the building, much altered, still stands. (Museum of the City of New York)

disastrous fire, which all but sealed its fate. Demolition seemed the only alternative until a developer, sensing the value of such a rare example of cast-iron elegance, converted it into an apartment house. The interior was gutted, but the beautiful façade was restored to its original appearance. Except for the ugly two-story addition on the roof, it looks much the same today as when it was first built. Since the interior vertical iron beams had to be retained, a curious result is that many tenants have an ornate Corinthian supporting column adorning the middle of their living room! This creditable restoration is an excellent example of adaptive (and profitable) reuse.

5. The building with the smooth mansard roof at the northeast corner of Broadway and 13th Street marks the location of the famous partnership of Marvin N. Rogers and Charles B. Peet. Although both gentlemen died before the firm moved into this building, **Rogers Peet Company** (Clinton & Russell, 1902) had been in business manufacturing men's clothing and army uniforms since 1874 at two previous lower Broadway addresses. A relative latecomer to Ladies' Mile, the company was the last to leave (1970), moving its executive offices to one of its Fifth Avenue stores uptown; now they too are gone.

From 1861 to 1881, the site was occupied by famed **Wallack's Theater.** John Lester Wallack, who managed the playhouse, was also a leading actor, performing in many of the old comedies and contemporary English dramas which were so popular in the late 19th century. When Wallack's moved to the new Rialto district on 30th Street, the house was renamed the Star Theater (1893) and continued to offer dramatic productions until its razing for the Rogers Peet building.

6. Turn west on 14th Street and pause briefly at **Union Square.** Called "Union Place" in the Commissioners' Plan of 1811, its present attractive layout was not achieved until 1831, a credit to Samuel B. Ruggles who planned nearby Gramercy Park [*see* Gramercy Park, 8]. The name "Union" derives not from Civil War days, nor from any association with the labor unions whose activities were later identified with the square, but merely from the fact that this was the "place of union" of the Bowery Road with the northbound Bloomingdale Road. Until the early 1860s it had been a beautiful residential district; then business took over the area. The statuary in the park is particularly worth seeing (return another time, however, for a closer view of the greatest equestrian statue in America and for other great works of sculpture). Gone from the west side of the square are the well known establishments of Tiffany & Company and Brentano's, as well as the array of piano manufacturers that lined the north side of 14th Street east and west of Union Square, from Irving Place to beyond Sixth Avenue.

At the southwest corner of Union Square, on a small triangular plaza, is the **statue of Mohandas Gandhi,** executed by Kantilal B. Patel in 1986. Here we see Mahatma Gandhi dressed in his dhoti and carrying his familiar walking stick. The Parks Department chose this site because of Union Square's tradition of public protests.

For the Broadway horsecars and omnibuses, making the detour around Union Square presented no problem; but when the later cable cars were installed

The equestrian statue of Washington, by Henry Kirke Brown and John Quincy Adams Ward, executed in 1856 and considered one of the finest in America, is seen here at the intersection of Fourth Avenue (now Park Avenue South) and 14th Street. With the advent of the motor age, it was moved into adjacent Union Square. (Museum of the City of New York)

a major traffic hazard was created. The forward progress of the Broadway Cable Traction Company's cars was controlled by continuous sections of underground cable laid in a slot between the rails. To negotiate a sharp curve, the operator of the car, called the grip-man, had to get up speed, release his hold on the 14th Street cable section, stamp furiously on his warning bell as the car swung wildly around the bend, then catch the next underground cable section on Broadway. This repeated act of derring-do always attracted crowds of onlookers, and resulted in numerous accidents—some fatal—and the spot was soon called **"Dead Man's Curve."**

7. Continue west on 14th Street, passing the former **Baumann Brothers & Co.** store, at 22 East 14th Street (D. & J. Jardine, 1881), a large cast-iron edifice whose "modernized" ground floor belies its Classic-style upper façade. Baumann Brothers was a furniture dealer whose business lasted well into the 20th century.

8. Midway between Fifth and Sixth avenues, on the south side of 14th Street (Nos. 34–40), a small vestige remains of what was once a prosperous and dynamic enterprise, **James A. Hearn & Son.** Arriving on 14th Street in 1879 after a brief association downtown with his uncle Aaron Arnold (later of Arnold, Constable & Company), James A. Hearn built up a large dry-goods business, and soon became an aggressive rival of R. H. Macy, then at the corner of Sixth Avenue. The two merchants often indulged in cutthroat competition, to their mutual detriment and the customers' delight. It is said that Japanese silk, a favorite with the ladies of the day, was offered by Macy at 41 cents per yard, whereupon Hearn immediately dropped the price by a few cents; and Macy followed suit. Again and again the price was slashed, until at the next day's closing, the fabric was being "sold" at 11 yards for 1 cent!

Son George, who inherited the business on his father's retirement in 1886, followed the same merchandising path. He, like neighbor James McCreery, was very philanthropic and also became a benefactor of the Metropolitan Museum of Art.

The original building, with an immense cast-iron façade, was many times the size of the present relic. An apartment house to its left now occupies much of the old site, but still remains "tied" to Hearn's by a series of exposed reinforcing girders. For three-quarters of a century Hearn's remained a family "bargain" store. Older New Yorkers still recall the annual mini-riot at the Washington's Birthday Sale, when thousands of bargain-hungry shoppers pushed their way into the store, smashing plate-glass windows and doors, in their stampede to purchase a television set or major appliance for one cent! The store closed in 1955, although it did operate a liquor store for a brief period. Its name is still preserved in a store in the Bronx at East 149th Street and Third Avenue, now run by a department store chain.

9. No. 56 West 14th Street was one of a group of buildings that formed the original Macy's department store. This narrow Beaux Arts–style building is all that remains of a cluster of buildings that marked the early days of what was later to become the world's largest department store.

After a brief career as a whaler, Rowland Hussey Macy tried and failed three times to establish himself in the dry-goods business. His fourth attempt in 1858 with a small shop around the corner on Sixth Avenue, "buying and selling for cash," met with more success; and within a few years he acquired several adja-

The perils of Dead Man's Curve at Broadway and 14th Street are depicted in this woodcut from Harper's Weekly *of March 27, 1897. (New-York Historical Society)*

A rare old photograph of Lord & Taylor's dry-goods store at 47–49 Catherine Street on the Lower East Side, just before the move to Grand and Chrystie streets. At this address Samuel Lord founded the oldest retail store in New York in 1826, taking on partner George Washington Taylor in 1838. Judging from the "selling off" signs, the picture by an unknown photographer was probably taken in 1853. (The Consolidated Edison Company of New York)

Fourteenth Street decked out in patriotic bunting for the presidential election of 1892. The north side of the street, just west of Union Square, displays the signs for at least six different piano manufacturers as this was the music center of the city in the Gay '90s. Steinway Hall and the Academy of Music were just a few blocks east. (New-York Historical Society)

cent buildings, connecting them with passageways, and offering a wide selection of merchandise. The store prospered, and by 1877 when Macy died, it had grown to a row of 11 buildings, with an annual sales volume of well over a million dollars. The store's well-known emblem, a large red star, was adapted by Macy from his arm tattoo, a reminder of his whaling days. The whale motif is still used to promote big sales.

After several changes in management, direction of the store was assumed by brothers Isadore and Nathan Straus who earlier had obtained from Macy a concession to operate a china and glassware department. Under their leadership, business boomed, and R. H. Macy & Company became the city's largest department store. Its more than 500 red-and-black delivery wagons could be seen all over town. Using novel sales and advertising techniques, manufacturing many products under its own name, and offering a wide selection of merchandise sold at highly competitive prices, Macy's set the trend for the future retail industry. Its stock ranged in variety from five-cent ice-cream sodas, straw hats, fabrics of all kinds, furniture, and men's and women's clothing, to the newly popular bicycle. Bicycles, by the way, were demonstrated by professional riders on a specially designed track where customers could give their new "wheels" a trial spin.

Looking north from the 18th Street station of the Sixth Avenue El are Simpson, Crawford & Simpson (extreme left), the domes of Hugh O'Neill, and to the right, Cammeyer's, all bedecked with flags. The El, which gave so much impetus to the growth of Fashion Row, had its origin in the Gilbert Elevated Railway, later the Metropolitan Elevated Railway, then the Manhattan Railway Company, and finally as part of the Interborough Rapid Transit. The photo, taken in 1899, shows a train approaching with its locomotive running backward. (New-York Historical Society)

Another innovation, soon copied by other stores, was the annual Christmas toy display—an event that attracted thousands of visitors.

By the turn of the century it became evident that newer and larger quarters were essential. Fourteenth Street's popularity as a shopping center had begun to wane, and in 1901 a site was chosen for a new building. Purchasing Oscar Hammerstein's Manhattan Opera House, located on the north side of 34th Street west of Sixth Avenue, Macy's demolished the theater and erected the first of its present buildings, opening its doors three years later.

Turn right on Sixth Avenue (Avenue of the Americas) to the northwest corner of 15th Street, and look back at the old Macy's store. On the west wall of the building one can still discern part of a 100-year-old advertisement, proudly claiming in letters several stories high, "Macy's—World's Largest Store."

Proceed north to the northeast corner of Sixth Avenue and 18th Street.

The old Sixth Avenue El, which cast its dark shadows from 1878 to 1938, is now just a memory. Its demolition, however, opened a vista not possible in the gaslit era. Lining both sides of the street in a five-block silent array from 18th to 23rd streets, stand "The Ghosts of Sixth Avenue." Huge, overbearing, and pretentious edifices—in stone, brick, or iron—they evoke the spirit of another day.

10. Across the street (northwest corner of 18th Street), the freshly painted cast-iron building was once **B. Altman & Company**—"The Palace of Trade," erected from plans by D. & J. Jardine in 1876. Until 1906, Altman's was the trend-setter of women's fashions, specializing in the finest silks, satins, and velvets. Ceramics and sculpture, too, graced the show windows and shelves, for Benjamin Altman was not only a keen entrepreneur, but a lover of objets d'art. A collector himself, he presented his accumulation of art works, worth over $15 million, to the Metropolitan Museum of Art shortly before his death in 1913.

As the age of the sewing machine had just arrived, women flocked to his block-long emporium in quest of the high-quality dress goods that made Altman's famous. Benjamin Altman, a solitary man who remained a bachelor all his life, devoted himself exclusively to his enterprise. He took particular pride in appearances. His home-delivery wagons, seen in the more affluent precincts of the city, were rubber-tired, painted a shiny maroon, decorated with brass carriage lamps, and pulled by a matched team of horses driven by a pair of nattily uniformed men. Altman was a considerate employer who shortened the generally accepted 64-hour work week and installed restrooms and a subsidized cafeteria for his workers. In 1906 the store moved uptown, where Ben Altman built a striking Beaux Arts–style building on a full block site between Fifth and Madison avenues, 34th to 35th streets. To the sorrow of many New York shoppers, B. Altman & Company, after enduring several acquisitions, and a leveraged buy-out, closed its doors forever in the late 1980s. After years of neglect, the restored gleaming white building now houses a bright new retailer—Today's Man. Directly across the street stood one of Altman's biggest competitors—Siegel-Cooper & Company.

11. New York was never the same after Henry Siegel arrived from Chicago! Fresh from successful participation in the 1893 World's Columbian Exposition, he joined with partner Frank H. Cooper to found a profitable department store in the windy city, and now sought to build the greatest one of them all in New York City—which he did in five short months! Six stories high and capped by a tall tower, the block-wide store extended almost to Fifth Avenue. Designed by architects DeLemos & Cordes in a grandiose style reminiscent of the Exposition, the new store was unprecedented in proportions. With great fanfare and a record-breaking crowd of 150,000, **Siegel-Cooper & Company** opened its doors on Saturday evening, September 12, 1896.

Its motto "The Big Store—A City in Itself" was no exaggeration. Henry Siegel soon earned the reputation as "the father of merchants," for he was shrewd, innovative, and bold. Never before had such a variety of merchandise been seen under one roof. The central feature of the main floor, however, was the fountain. A circular marble terrace surrounded an enormous white marble and brass statue of *The Republic,* a replica of Daniel Chester French's towering sculpture at the Chicago Fair. Jets of water, illuminated by myriad colored lights, played around the granite pedestal; and from the open "well hole" in the second floor, protected by a mahogany balustrade, customers looked down in awe. The fountain was not only the prime attraction, but the major rendezvous place for shoppers, businessmen, lovers, and tourists. For Gothamites, "Meet Me at the Fountain" became an institution for years to come. To this day, old-timers will quote the slogan without hesitation when asked if they remember Siegel-Cooper.

When the great Siegel-Cooper & Company opened its doors in 1896, it seemed that all New York flocked to the event. In this Byron photo, overflow crowds jam Sixth Avenue between 19th and 18th streets, as El trains bring even more sightseers. (The Byron Collection. Museum of the City of New York)

Siegel showed great understanding of human nature when he introduced the "free sample," especially in his novel food department. After a round of taste-tempting goodies, people *did* buy. He also began the very effective demonstrator system, illustrating the possibilities of such disparate items as kitchen gadgets, wing collars, and sheet music. Among other revolutionary ideas, he installed an air-cooling system, which really brought in the masses on stifling summer days; he hired women in many of the sales departments; and he advertised widely in the daily newspapers and on billboards all over town.

So great was the variety of the store's inventory that one of its advertising slogans was "Everything under the Sun." In this connection there is a long-enduring legend that tycoon and inveterate gambler John W. ("Bet-a-Million") Gates made a wager with John Pierpont Morgan that Siegel-Cooper's boast was mere puffery. To prove his contention, he went to the store and asked a floor-walker if it sold elephants. He was directed to the fifth-floor toy department, but Gates insisted that he wanted a *live* elephant. The unflappable employee then asked what color elephant he wanted. Gates, somewhat taken aback, replied "white." "Fine, sir, we'll let you know the delivery date."

Some weeks later Gates received a telegram informing him that a freighter would be docking the next day with his order. He arrived at the pier in time to wit-

LADIES' MILE HISTORIC DISTRICT
Designated May 2, 1989

N

Numbers indicate addresses within district

ness the unloading of an albino elephant from Ceylon. The chagrined Gates paid his debt to Morgan and ordered the pachyderm delivered to the Central Park Zoo.

By the first decade of the 20th century the inevitable uptown exodus of the shopping trade had begun again. Henry Siegel, however, had resolute faith in his magnificent palace of retailing. Surely the fountain would always remain the favorite meeting spot in town. Alas, time proved otherwise, for the crowds were now meeting at Macy's and Altman's, and the great empire was beginning to

The latest styles are worn by mother and children entering the Siegel-Cooper store. Elaborate bronze columns and lanterns flank the Sixth Avenue entrance. The imposing entrance remains unchanged today. (Photograph by Byron. The Byron Collection. Museum of the City of New York)

Siegel-Cooper advertisement in Pearson's *Magazine for September 1908 advertises the latest styles at prices which today seem unbelievable. Note the shirtwaists for only $1.00. (Author's collection)*

The business office of the Siegel-Cooper Department Store in a photograph taken ca. 1899 by Byron. (The Byron Collection. Museum of the City of New York)

The sales staff of Siegel-Cooper's sheet music counter poses for photographer Percy C. Byron with the latest tunes of 1899. (The Byron Collection. Museum of the City of New York)

An 1861 lithograph of Wallack's Theater, at the northeast corner of Broadway and 13th Street. The site is now occupied by the former Rogers Peet Building. (Museum of the City of New York)

The Eden Musée, an amusement hall and wax museum, stood in the middle of the north side of 23rd Street between Fifth and Sixth avenues. It was so popular in the gaslight era that all street cars made a special stop at the door. The Eden Musée was opened in 1884 and survived until 1916. Robert J. Horner's Furniture Store is at left, and is still there but no longer as Horner's. (The J. Clarence Davies Collection, Museum of the City of New York)

crumble. A reorganization with the backing of financier Joseph B. Greenhut failed to pump new life into the faltering enterprise, and by World War I, the great emporium, now called Greenhut-Siegel-Cooper, was no more.

A recent ground-floor tenant, Bed Bath & Beyond, has remodeled the interior and restored the front, including the splendid bronze portal. And to greet customers, the establishment has installed a *liveried doorman*—the first on Ladies' Mile since the heyday of the grand emporiums, almost 90 years ago!

The best view of the Big Store is from across Sixth Avenue. Note the intricately designed terra-cotta plaques with the firm's monogram, the huge bronze columns set in dramatic archways, and the overall effect of grandeur.

On the north side of West 17th Street, between Seventh and Eighth avenues, Siegel-Cooper's enormous wagon house and stable can still be seen. It, too, is heavily ornamented with distinctive terra-cotta S-C emblems and the company name in large letters on the parapet. During World War I, the store served for a time as a military hospital. And what of the famous statue that graced the fountain? It now rests in Forest Lawn Memorial Park ("The Happy Cemetery"), in Glendale, California.

12. The large, somewhat restrained granite and limestone building occupying the whole block on the west side of Sixth Avenue between 19th and 20th streets reflects the type of establishment it was; for **Simpson Crawford & Simpson** catered exclusively to the "carriage trade." Partners Thomas and James Simpson and William Crawford opened their first retail store on the site in 1879, aiming for the patronage of the conservative moneyed classes, and dealing mostly in high-priced merchandise. A new building, designed by architects William H. Hume & Son, was opened in 1900—the first on the avenue with the newfangled Otis Escalators. It still shows evidence of the very large show windows, and even a trace of the mosaic floor (at the entrance). Price tags on the merchandise and in advertisements were considered superfluous, as their elite clientele would never think of asking anyway. This led to Henry Siegel's sarcastic remark that this was indeed a "priceless" store. Tailor-made dresses were a specialty of the house, with men tailors working overtime to make up the orders for delivery in 24 hours! After James Simpson died, the name was shortened to Simpson Crawford Company, and in the ensuing reorganization, Henry Siegel became president. After the demise in 1914 of the great Siegel-Cooper store across the street, Simpson Crawford limped on for another year, then expired.

13. The red brick and limestone Italianate building occupying most of the block across the avenue was built in 1893 for the largest shoe "department" store in town, **Cammeyer's.** The stately, well maintained *palazzo* remains as a tribute to the imagination and industriousness of Alfred J. Cammeyer and later partner Louis M. Hart. Together they raised the standard of the retail shoe business from the early custom of stringing up pairs of shoes on storefront poles to a distinguished and reputable enterprise on a scale comparable to their department-store neighbors. The store prided itself in its "standard of merit" slogan, which became synonymous with quality footwear. When the uptown exodus put an end to Ladies' Mile, Cammeyer's, still in the forefront of retail merchandising, moved to 34th Street in 1917, and four years later opened an elegant branch on

Fifth Avenue. The pitfalls of specialization, however, ultimately doomed the firm, which disappeared after the Depression.

● ★ **14. The former Church of the Holy Communion,** on the northeast corner of 20th Street, dates from 1846, when the busy shopping center was a quiet and somewhat remote residential district. Architect Richard Upjohn, who designed the church—one of his lesser works—was one of the best-known advocates of the popular Gothic Revival style of the 1840s. The church was closed in the mid-1970s, and has seen a variety of uses—the most recent as a disco!

15. When the **Hugh O'Neill store,** designed by Mortimer C. Merritt, opened in 1876, it must have been a dazzling sight to its first visitors. With flamboyant round towers topped by huge bulbous domes, an imposing pediment rising high above five stories of Corinthian columns and pilasters, and a building almost unrivaled in size, O'Neill's began a tradition that was to cause amazement and surprise to patrons and competitors alike for years to come. Hugh O'Neill was no ordinary merchant, but an aggressive, extravagant, and colorful salesman. Hardly a week went by without a dramatic sale accompanied by much hoopla and publicity, for his appeal was not to the staid, conservative clientele of his neighbors, but to the working classes. With the advent of Elias Howe's great invention, the motto of O'Neill became "Put a Sewing Machine in Every Home!" He offered the machines as loss-leaders and was thus able to move his tremendous stock of piece goods at a healthy profit. His tactics of undercutting and doing battle with his competitors earned him the name, "The Fighting Irishman of Sixth Avenue." Although a bit crusty and brusque, he was a deeply religious man who commanded the love and respect of his employees. He always insisted that they observe their religious holidays, no matter what their faith, and would give them time off with full pay; nor was he ever above discussing their personal problems with them. A special source of pride to Hugh O'Neill was his shiny fleet of delivery wagons; he frequently would be seen making an early morning inspection round, like a general reviewing his troops, as the teams lined up for the day's deliveries. After he died, there was no one to carry on in the same spirit. To save the store, a merger was arranged with its neighbor to the north, the Adams Dry-Goods Company, resulting in a most unlikely partnership that was destined to last only for a few years. Adams had a different retailing style and an even more dissimilar clientele, so the O'Neill-Adams alliance disintegrated and collapsed completely in 1915.

16. Around the corner on 21st Street, seemingly hidden and protected by the L-shape of the Hugh O'Neill store, is the diminutive **Third Cemetery of the Spanish & Portuguese Synagogue.** This shady burial plot is the northernmost of three early cemeteries of this first Jewish congregation in America, and was in use between 1829 and 1851. [*See* Lower East Side *Supplementary Tour A*; Greenwich Village, 33.]

17. The ornate Beaux-Arts **Adams Dry-Goods Store,** designed by DeLemos & Cordes, the architects of the Siegel-Cooper store, reflects the architectural style that came into vogue around the turn of the century. A relative latecomer to the avenue, A.D.G. tried to capture the fancy (and patronage) of the "carriage trade" through conservative merchandising and high-priced inventory. One of its novel offerings was men's ready-to-wear and made-to-measure clothing. Its founder, Samuel Adams, started in business much earlier, but did not erect this building until 1900 (note the date, set near the cornice). Since most department stores were family enterprises, Adams had no one to carry on the name. His only daughter, Eileen, showed no inclination for the retail trade, and married the son of march-king John Philip Sousa. When he sold out to Hugh O'Neill, the newly formed O'Neill-Adams Company made a desperate attempt to create a new image. The two firms now were connected not only by a hyphen, but also by an underground tunnel beneath 21st Street; and great sums were spent in promoting the new venture—but all in vain when it collapsed in 1915. Now recently renovated, Barnes & Noble has moved in, opening its largest superstore while Mattel Toys occupies several floors as well. Owner Israel Taub accepted an award for this restoration.

18. Ehrich Brothers, the last of the old-timers in the Sixth Avenue row, was erected in 1889 from plans by Alfred Zucker, and stands dark and dingy, straddling the southwest corner of 23rd Street. The small corner plot, occupied by a polychrome cast-iron building that juts into the old department store, was always a thorn in the Ehrich Brothers' side—they were unable to acquire the property and had to build around it (much the same as the problem that later faced Macy's when they purchased the 34th Street and Sixth Avenue site in 1904). This corner building, recently restored almost to its original appearance after a destructive fire, shows what cast-iron structures looked like when new. It was formerly a branch of the **Riker's Drug Company,** later absorbed into the Liggett chain.

Ehrich Brothers (Julius S. and Samuel W.) was known as a "bargain store," perhaps even more so than Hugh O'Neill. The store was famous for its sales of manufacturers' closeouts and for its "omnibus advertising" (many categories of merchandise grouped into a single large advertisement). Saturdays were "Children's Days" at Ehrich's, when mothers could leave their young ones to enjoy specially provided entertainment and be free to shop at leisure. One of Ehrich Brothers' young trainees learned the trade quite well, and after the store ultimately closed, went into business for himself, establishing the name of Nathan Ohrbach as one of the city's successful retail merchants.

In 1911 Ehrich's ceased operations for much the same reason as its neighbors. The brothers tried their hand briefly in a "horseless carriage" dealership, but that, too, proved a failure. On the 23rd Street side, one can still see the faded name "Ehrich Brothers" on a rusty panel above the ground floor.

19. On the southeast corner of 23rd Street and Avenue of the Americas from 1869 to 1883 stood the **Edwin Booth Theater,** designed by Renwick & Sands, with Booth himself as manager and frequent star performer. When **James W. McCreery,** known as the "Dean of the Retail Trade," acquired the site, he demolished the theater, and in 1895 opened his second department store. In 1907 he joined his competitors in the great move uptown, building his newest emporium on 34th Street at Fifth Avenue. McCreery's went out of business unexpectedly in 1954 and the store was purchased by Ohrbach's. The 23rd Street structure survived until 1975 as a loft building. When McCreery opened the store in 1895 he installed a marble bust of Shakespeare into the façade—a memento from the Booth Theater, together with a bronze commemorative plaque honoring

Simpson Crawford Company occupied the west side of Sixth Avenue from 19th to 20th streets and opened a new building in 1900. In this 1905 view of their unusually large show window, photographer Percy C. Byron captured the latest fashions of the day. The building is still there, although the company closed in 1915. (The Byron Collection. Museum of the City of New York)

The James W. McCreery store on the southeast corner of Sixth Avenue and 23rd Street, erected in 1895, replaced the Edwin Booth Theater. The company moved uptown in 1907, and in 1975 this building was razed. (Photo by author)

the theater. Both the bust and plaque were rescued by the author when the building came down and were donated by the former owner to New York University. It is said that Booth, dressed as Shakespeare, posed for the sculpture.

20. About 200 feet farther east on 23rd Street, and adjoining what was then the McCreery store, stood the twin buildings of **Best & Company,** which came to 23rd Street in 1881. Specializing in children's wear, it was known by its more popular name, "The Lilliputian Bazaar." McCreery once boasted that he could easily take over Best by merely "punching a few holes in the wall." The store departed in 1910, moving to Fifth Avenue and 35th Street (the impressive building still occupies the southwest corner); and later to 51st Street, where to the dismay of many New York shoppers, it closed its doors forever in 1970. The new Olympic Tower now stands in its place.

Alongside, at what was 58 West 23rd Street, was the famed partnership of **Paul J. Bonwit and Edmund D. Teller.** "Bonwit's" began in 1895 at 289 Sixth Avenue, just south of 18th Street, selling fine-quality apparel for women. It opened its 23rd Street store three years later, then in 1908 Teller sold out to Bonwit, and three years later the store moved uptown to Fifth Avenue and 30th Street. In 1930 it moved again, into a large building at the corner of 56th Street. In the late 1970s, the firm almost disappeared, as its building had to be demolished; but phoenixlike, it arose again, around the corner on 57th Street in the Trump Tower next to Tiffany's, only to "give up the ghost" in the late 1980s.

The third member of the departed triumvirate was fashionable **LeBoutillier Brothers** (pronounced by all "Le-boo-ti-LEER"—even by founder Philip LeBoutillier himself). Arriving in 1898, the store soon became a mecca for the latest in women's styles. By 1913, hard times struck again, and Philip LeBoutillier, the only brother left in the business, closed his shop and joined Best's, ultimately rising to the rank of president of the company.

Across 23rd Street, No. 61–65 is another venerable cast-iron-front building, looking not much different from when it opened in 1877 as Robert J. Horner's Furniture Store. Designed by the noted architect of cast-iron buildings John B. Snook, it later merged with the Flint Furniture Company, whose building still stands at 45–47, to become the well known **Flint & Horner Furniture Company.** Occupying the building until 1912, the firm moved uptown to 34th Street. Like Wanamaker's, Stern's, and Arnold Constable, the company abandoned the city and moved its operations to a suburban location, in this case, Manhasset. Cast iron was ideally suited to the retail trades, as the showrooms could be well illuminated by the large areas of window glass that an iron front permitted. Note the building's feeling of height created by the successive diminishing of each story—an illusive device credited to the architects of ancient Greece.

21. In the middle of the block is the gargantuan white cast-iron building of the former **Stern Brothers Department Store** (best viewed from the parking lot across the street). From humble beginnings when they arrived from Buffalo in 1867, the children of poor immigrants, Stern brothers Isaac, Louis, and Bernard, plus three sisters, opened a small dry-goods shop around the corner on 22nd Street. Business prospered, and in 1878 they engaged architect Henry Fernbach to design the original store, which in turn was greatly enlarged in 1892 by

William Schickel, and extended through to 22nd Street. Until the opening of the
Siegel-Cooper Store 18 years later, it was New York's largest. A far cry from the
little family shop was this luxury store, in front of which were posted blue-liver-
ied doormen with top hats, giving the establishment a touch of class that it was
to retain for years to come.

Although priding itself in its appeal to the carriage trade, Stern Brothers did
not overlook the working classes, for their merchandise was priced for both
extremes of the economic spectrum. Isaac, the guiding spirit of the firm, was frequently to be seen greeting customers by name; and it is said that on occasion he
would make an urgent home delivery in his own carriage. A fourth brother,
Benjamin, joined the partnership after Bernard's passing in 1884. A number of
men working in the department stores of the gaslit era achieved later fame as
merchandisers in their own right. One of them, a 13-year-old youngster starting
as a stockboy, worked his way up in Stern's, eventually opening a store on 34th
Street in 1902 bearing his own name, Franklin Simon.

By 1913, seeing the handwriting on the wall, Stern Brothers built a new store
on 42nd Street and Sixth Avenue and joined the "uptown club." To the regret of
many, the store ceased operations in 1970, leaving only its suburban branches to
carry on the name.

Note the company monogram and the ornate design motifs in the well-preserved façade. It is apparent that the present owners of the building take pride in
the historic and aesthetic value of this beautiful cast-iron front.

*Stern Brothers' original store, in an 1878 print, shares the south side of 23rd Street with
residences, a church, and the Edwin Booth Theater, as well as the recently completed Sixth
Avenue El. (Museum of the City of New York)*

West 23rd Street looking east from Sixth Avenue, ca. 1905, shows the northern limit of Fashion Row. Right to left are the stores of Best & Company, Bonwit Teller, LeBoutillier Brothers, and the enormous white cast-iron front of Stern Brothers. The newly completed Flatiron Building appears in the distance. The Stern Brothers building still remains in a good state of preservation. (Museum of the City of New York)

22. At 14 West 23rd Street is a small iron-front building, now rather woebegone in appearance, which was once **James McCutcheon & Company.** Known as "The Linen Store," it arrived in Ladies' Mile in 1886 after progressive moves uptown, having started 31 years before at Broadway and Astor Place. Dealing exclusively in fine linens, its tablecloths, napkins, doilies, sheets, pillowcases, and such were in great demand from the moneyed classes. In 1907 the store moved to more fashionable quarters on Fifth Avenue. Ultimately it merged with Plummer & Company, becoming Plummer-McCutcheon. More recently it was taken over by Hammacher Schlemmer on 57th Street, and for a time functioned as one of its departments. The building, incidentally, was the **birthplace in 1862 of novelist Edith Wharton.** It was then a brownstone, and was converted in 1882 to a retail store by architect Henry J. Hardenbergh (the Dakota, Plaza Hotel, etc.). The cast-iron front was installed ten years later by another architect, George H. Billings, for the new occupant, James McCutcheon's Linen Store.

23. Just before reaching Fifth Avenue, pause briefly at the red brick Queen Anne–style building also designed by Henry Hardenbergh that **The Western Union Company** built in 1883 as its uptown office. A terra-cotta plaque above the second floor bears the company name. Across the street is the unique **Flatiron Building,** erected in 1902 [*see* Madison Square, 24].

24. Turn south on Fifth Avenue to No. 170 (Robert Maynicke, 1897). The interesting cupola atop this narrow building, which can be seen from quite a distance, marks the location of the former offices and showroom of **the Sohmer Piano Company.** The building, freshly painted white with its dome gilded, is floodlit at night, adding a delightful touch to the nighttime panorama of illuminated buildings. The former Sohmer piano factory on the East River shore in Ravenswood, Queens, is clearly visible from Roosevelt Island. [*See* Roosevelt Island tour at the end of Chapter 13.]

Across Fifth Avenue is an Italianate brownstone building that recalls a more tranquil era. Although now a commercial building, it was originally the **Hotel Glenham,** built in 1861. Relatively unchanged in appearance, it gives a good idea of the style and scale of neighborhood buildings of the time.

At No. 153 was the **Charles Scribner's Sons** store, built in 1894 from plans by Ernest Flagg. Look for the "S" on the fourth-floor balcony. Not only was the firm a well-known book dealer (as it is today), but the publisher of one of the most popular periodicals of the time, *Scribner's Magazine.* The building was purchased in 1973 by the United Synagogue of Conservative Judaism.

At the southeast corner of 21st Street (No. 141 Fifth Avenue) is the imposing **Merchants Central Building** (Robert Maynicke, 1897), a highly ornate Renaissance Eclectic structure, with an enormous cupola.

25. No. 150 Fifth Avenue (southwest corner of 20th Street) is a particularly handsome building in a blend of Queen Anne and Romanesque Revival styles. Emblazoned on the cornice are the letters M.B.C., proclaiming the former home of one of the largest religious book publishers of the "Mauve Decade," the Methodist Book Concern. It was also the headquarters of the Methodist Church in New York. There were, in fact, so many publishers of religious books along the avenue that the district came to be known as **"Pater Noster Row."** Except for the dreadful "modernization" of the entrance, the building, designed by Edward Kendall in 1888, is in pristine condition. By contrast, note the splendid entrance to **No. 156,** on the northwest corner, the former Presbyterian Building (James Barnes Baker, 1894), built in Romanesque Revival style.

Take a brief detour south one block and turn right to **No. 11 West 19th Street,** the Goodstein Building. Viewed from across the street, this 11-story loft building boasts an unusually complete Beaux-Arts façade, and in its excellent state of preservation, it offers a vivid impression of the style of commercial architecture so prevalent at the turn of the century. Its principal tenant is a division of the McGraw-Hill Book Company, which is now in an area that was once the center of the book publishing industry prior to World War I. Return to 20th Street.

Walk east to the corner of Broadway and 20th Street.

26. Both the northwest and southeast corners boast a Stanford White building! **No. 903 Broadway,** the Warren Building, in yellow brick and terra-cotta, was designed in 1887 in Renaissance Revival style; while diagonally opposite is **No. 900,** the Goelet Building, built the year before in a "commercial eclectic" style. A rather unique structure, with its rounded corner and massive polychrome arches, it is missing its cornice and many decorative elements. This may be the only site where two such distinctly different McKim, Mead & White buildings stand face to face.

27. One of the most enduring partnerships in the retail trade was that of Messrs. **Lord and Taylor.** The spectacular structure on the southwest corner of 20th Street is a tribute to the courage and resourcefulness of these two English immigrants who together built one of the most respected fashion establishments in the trade. Opening a little shop on Catherine Street in 1826, Samuel Lord joined the growing number of dry-goods merchants; 12 years later he took on as a partner his wife's cousin, George Washington Taylor, and soon the firm of Lord & Taylor had the reputation for honest business practices and quality merchandise. A year after Taylor retired in 1852, the much expanded firm opened its first "department store" on the corner of Grand and Chrystie streets, a large gray stone building capped by an imposing glass dome, which was a Lower East Side landmark for almost 50 years. Grand Street at the time was one of the busiest shopping streets and a major east-west thoroughfare whose crosstown horsecars connected with the New Jersey and Long Island ferries.

Rapid development of business encouraged the firm to open another branch farther west on Grand Street, at the corner of Broadway; however, it lasted only 12 years. During the 1863 Draft Riots, some 100 employees rushed to secure arms and ammunition from an uptown armory, and barricaded the building, to discourage any attempt by the unruly mobs to sack the store.

In 1869 this extraordinary five-story iron-front building, designed by James Giles in what was described as Bohemian Renaissance style, was opened to the public. Equipped with a steam elevator and other "modern" conveniences, it was an instant success. Surviving the Panic of 1873 four years later, Lord & Taylor continued to be one of the most fashionable women's stores on the newly developing Ladies' Mile. When the store at Grand and Chrystie streets closed in 1902, the present building was greatly enlarged. Much of the elaborate emporium, however, has disappeared. An open lot on the 20th Street side now separates the main building from a segment that once extended to Fifth Avenue. (That amputated vestige is now a garishly painted cooperative apartment house which, after conversion, has taken for itself a Fifth Avenue address.) Particularly attractive is the mansard roof on the corner pavilion, complete with dormers, and all in cast iron.

The year 1914, when so many of these great establishments either failed or departed, saw Lord & Taylor move to its present location at Fifth Avenue and 38th Street.

28. The building at the northwest corner of 19th Street, whose irregular and picturesque roof is reminiscent of an English Victorian castle, was the sales office of the **Gorham Manufacturing Company.** The name survives today and is still synonymous with fine silver. The structure, designed by architect Edward H. Kendall in 1883 in Queen Anne style, housed the company whose specialty was custom-designed silverware and a wide variety of ecclesiastical metalwork. The firm subsequently moved its operations uptown, erecting an appropriately impressive building on the southwest corner of Fifth Avenue and 37th Street.

29. A year after Lord & Taylor opened its magnificent store on 20th Street, its die-hard competitor **Arnold Constable** followed suit one block south. The saga of Arnold Constable, New York's oldest department store, began with Aaron Arnold, a young English immigrant, opening a small dry-goods shop on Pine Street in what is now the financial district. With business flourishing, he moved to progressively larger sites; and taking in two nephews, George and James Hearn, the partnership became Arnold, Hearn & Co. [*see* 8]. A recently hired friend of the Arnold family, James Mansell Constable—in typical Horatio Alger fashion—fell in love with the boss's daughter, married her, and was taken into the partnership. Apparently disgruntled by the sudden rise of Constable, the Hearn brothers left Arnold and went into business for themselves. After another change in location, the firm built a large establishment at the corner of Canal, Mercer, and Howard streets, with an impressive white marble façade which Arnold referred to as his "Marble House." It was here that he renamed his firm Arnold, Constable & Company, and made his reputation selling luxury merchandise, soon becoming the darling of the carriage trade—with a customer list reading like the social register. The building, stripped of its fancy trappings, still stands. [*See* pages 178 and 179.]

In 1869 Arnold retired, leaving the reins of the company in the hands of James Constable. The same year marked the move to the 19th Street site. In a series of land acquisitions, the store, which was designed by Griffith Thomas, grew in size until 1877 when it covered the whole block to Fifth Avenue. The five-story brick and limestone structure, topped by an enormous French Second Empire mansard roof, was a sensation. Devoting itself exclusively to the sale of fabrics, carpets, and upholstery materials, it remained a prestige store for years to come. The vast selection of its dry goods, ranging from children's wear to mourning apparel, led to the comment that "Arnold Constable provides elegant clothing, from cradleside to graveside." The *New York Daily Graphic,* in its January 8, 1877, edition, described the store as "a new Emporium of Trade—a dominant and ornamental addition to the street architecture of New York."

In 1914, that famous "uptown moving year," the company abandoned its pretentious building and moved to its final location at Fifth Avenue and 40th Street. It is interesting to note that from 1860 to 1975, the two fierce competitors, Arnold Constable and Lord & Taylor, had never been more than two blocks apart! With the demise of Arnold Constable after 150 years, its rival survives as the oldest retail store in the city. Arnold Constable's last building is now the New York Public Library's Mid-Manhattan branch.

30. "The house of **W. & J. Sloane** stands indisputably at the head of the carpet and rug industry of this country," wrote Moses King in his *Handbook of New York* for 1893. Unlike the other department stores that had their origin in the dry-goods business, Sloane's dealt almost exclusively in rugs and floor coverings.

Arriving on a sailing ship in 1834, William Sloane, a young weaver from Scotland, found work in a Connecticut mill, learning American weaving techniques. Nine years later he established a small "Carpeting and Floor Cloth Shop" on lower Broadway, using the slogan "Dependable Merchandise at an Honest Figure." In 1852, brother John, the "J" of W. & J. Sloane, was taken into the business, but stayed with William for only nine years. At the closing of the 1876 Centennial Exposition in Philadelphia, William Sloane purchased a superb collection of Oriental rugs that had been a major display at the Fair, offering them to his growing list of wealthy clients. This marked the first time Oriental rugs were sold by a retail house. In the meantime, he had moved up Broadway twice, keeping abreast of the familiar northward push, and a few years later accomplished another "first," contracting with a weaving firm in India to become the only American rug store with its own Oriental source of supply.

William Sloane achieved fame of another sort a few years earlier, when the criminal jury of which he was foreman convicted "Boss" Tweed. While on the jury he learned that merchant-prince A. T. Stewart was about to foreclose a mortgage on the Alexander Smith Carpet Company in Yonkers, N.Y. Sloane raised the money, saved the Smith Company, and in return received an interest and became its exclusive agent for many years. On his death in 1879, the firm's direction was taken over by his eldest son, John II. It was under John Sloane that the company achieved its greatest growth, inaugurating in 1881 the large store across the street from Arnold Constable and an equally spacious outlet in San Francisco. W. & J. Sloane achieved national fame with a contract to carpet some of the swankiest hotels in the city, including the newly opened Waldorf-Astoria on 34th Street; and the company won international fame with the commission to supply all the carpeting for the coronation of Czar Nicholas II. At the same time, the store expanded its operations into home decoration, selling antiques, and manufacturing "registered reproductions" of antique furniture. The building was designed by W. Wheeler Smith and erected in 1881.

As the gaslit era waned, Sloane's moved in 1912 to Fifth Avenue and 47th Street, where they remained until 1962. In a subsequent move down the avenue to 38th Street, they sold their building to E. J. Korvette, acquiring the store formerly occupied by Franklin Simon; and in a late 1982 move Sloane's abandoned their Fifth Avenue address for an adjacent smaller location farther west on 38th Street. Two years later they "gave up the ghost" and moved their operations to the three W. & J. Sloane suburban stores. Interestingly, the present owner of the 881 Broadway store is also a rug and carpet retailer, and has restored the exterior and interior to re-create the aura of elegance of the 1880s.

Find the "S" monogram on a small cast-iron shield set high on the building, as well as the date of construction in terra-cotta Roman numerals.

End of tour. The Union Square subway station is a few short blocks south.

9. Gramercy Park

[Lexington Avenue line to 23rd Street; R Broadway line to 23rd Street; Broadway (M1, M6, or M7) bus to 20th Street]

In Dutch Colonial days the locality was known as *Crommessie* (*krom* = crooked, *mesje* = small knife; the "knife" for the shape of a nearby brook), an area of woods and marshes situated just above the country estate of Governor Peter Stuyvesant. It later became the property of James Duane, mayor of New York City from 1784 to 1789, who named it Gramercy Seat. In 1831 land developer Samuel B. Ruggles purchased a substantial parcel from the Duane Farm and laid out the residential lots and park. Ruggles also laid out lower Lexington Avenue, naming it after the Revolutionary Battle of Lexington, and Irving Place, which he named for his friend Washington Irving. In spite of the growth of the surroundings and the encroachment of high-rise buildings, Gramercy Park has managed to remain one of the most charming residential districts of the city.

1. The tour begins at 28 East 20th Street, just east of Broadway, at the **birthplace of one of Gramercy Park's most illustrious residents, Theodore Roosevelt.** The original brownstone house in which he was born in 1858 was demolished in 1916 and replaced by a commercial building. After T.R.'s death in 1919, however, prominent citizens decided to purchase the site, raze the structure, and create a memorial by reconstructing Roosevelt's boyhood home as it appeared during the years 1865–72. The adjoining lot, No. 26, where T.R.'s uncle Robert had his residence, was also acquired and made into a museum. The birthplace was opened to the public in 1923, and in 1963 both sites were donated by the Theodore Roosevelt Association to the National Park Service. The rooms have been restored to the period of "Teedie's" boyhood. The parlor is furnished with crystal chandeliers, magnificent mirrors, and blue satin hangings, characteristic of the elegance of the day. The master bedroom in which he was born contains the original furniture and a portrait of his mother, Martha Bulloch Roosevelt. Next to it is the nursery and, beyond, the open porch that was used as a gymnasium. In addition to his widely known political accomplishments, Theodore Roosevelt was also an effective, reform-minded Police Commissioner of New York City. (The Birthplace is open Wed.–Sun., 9 A.M.–5 P.M., closed federal holidays. Admission: $2.00; under 17 and over 62, free.)

Proceed east to Park Avenue South, known formerly by its more prosaic name, Fourth Avenue.

2. 250 Park Avenue South (Rouse & Goldstone, 1912) is a large industrial building in neo-Gothic style. But the most striking of these early 20th-century behemoths is No. 257, the **Gramercy Park Building** (Warren & Wetmore, 1912)—its façade divided into five sections by elaborate courses. The restored lobby is a gem!

3. Across the avenue, one block north, is **Calvary Church.** Designed in 1846 by James Renwick, Jr., architect of Grace Church and St. Patrick's Cathedral, it is in the tradition of the Gothic Revival so popular in the 1840s. The wooden steeples, however, were dismantled by the architect in 1860; the octagonal bases were removed in 1929. Eleanor Roosevelt was baptized here in 1884.

4. No. 281 is the **former Church Missions House** (R. W. Gibson & E. J. N. Stent, 1894), now the Protestant Welfare Agencies Building. A flamboyant Romanesque Revival–style edifice, it once housed the missionary societies of the Episcopal Church. Above the entrance, the reliefs in the tympanum depict St. Augustine preaching to the Barbarians of England, and Bishop Seabury preaching to the Barbarians in America.

5. Across the street, at the southwest corner of 22nd Street, in an odd reincarnation, is the **former Bank for Savings,** now the base of a 27-story condominium, with the old bank section converted into a supermarket! The original Classic Revival–style structure (Cyrus L. W. Eidlitz, 1894) was the home of the city's oldest savings bank, chartered in 1819 in Greenwich Village. With the bank's departure, the building was slated for demolition, but it was rescued at the eleventh hour by an association of Gramercy Park residents.

6. The former United Charities Building, at 105 East 22nd Street, was erected in 1891–93 from plans by R. H. Robertson and Rowe & Baker in a modified Romanesque Revival style, for the New York Association for Improving the Condition of the Poor, now the Community Service Society, "...to improve the condition of the working classes, and to elevate their physical state." It also houses, among other charitable institutions, the Children's Aid Society. Turn east on 22nd Street to Lexington Avenue.

7. The lavish Renaissance-style *palazzo* on the southwest corner was designed for the **Russell Sage Foundation** in 1914 by Grosvenor Atterbury. Sage, a financier and philanthropist, died in 1906, leaving an enormous fortune to charity. Among the legatees was Russell Sage College, in upstate Troy, N.Y. He was known to be strongly opinionated and it is said that upon being approached by August Belmont to share in the financial backing of the newly begun subway, he turned to the president of the Rapid Transit Construction Company and commented scornfully that "New Yorkers would never go into a hole to ride it." In more recent years the building was occupied by Catholic Charities, then in 1975 it was purchased by a developer who converted it into condominium apartments, called Sage House.

Across 22nd Street is the **Mabel Dean Bacon Vocational High School,** formerly the Manhattan Trade School for Girls. It was built in 1917 from plans by

The Abram Hewitt House at 9 Lexington Avenue, built in 1851 by Peter Cooper, and later occupied by his son-in-law Abram Hewitt, Mayor of New York, 1887–88. Hewitt commissioned his nearby neighbor Stanford White to redecorate the house and design the mayor's lamps in front. It was demolished in 1939. (Museum of the City of New York)

C. B. J. Snyder, whose Collegiate Gothic style for school buildings was very popular early in the century.

Walk south one block to 21st Street. The northeast corner is the **site of the Cyrus W. Field Residence.** Field, with help from Peter Cooper (who lived just a few doors north, at 9 Lexington Avenue), promoted the Atlantic Cable, which after some initial failures was laid successfully in 1866. He was also responsible for the buildings of most of the elevated railroads in the city during the late 1870s, only to lose them a few years later to railroad tycoon Jay Gould.

8. Gramercy Park, whose name, as mentioned, probably derives from the original Dutch *Crommessie,* is a tribute to Samuel B. Ruggles's foresight, and is an excellent example of urban planning. By taking the 42 lots that comprise the 1 1/2-acre park and deeding the parcel to the 60 surrounding lot owners, he established, in 1831, the only surviving private park in the city. (An earlier private plot, St. John's Park, owned by Trinity Parish, was destroyed by the takeover of adjacent land by the Hudson River Railroad, and ultimately obliterated by the entrance ramps to the Holland Tunnel.) The wrought-iron fence was erected soon after, with extensive planting undertaken thereafter. Although formerly restricted to adjacent property owners, this private park is now accessible to all who live close by and who pay the annual fee. The Park and surrounding lots, including Calvary Church and a stretch of property on 18th and 19th streets, were designated in 1966 by the Landmarks Preservation Commission as the **Gramercy Park Historic District.**

The perimeter sidewalk of Gramercy Park itself has been restored to re-create the original bluestone paving. The repaving was done by the city using some of the original bluestones, plus some newly cut contemporary bluestones. Also, many of the ugly cobra-head lampposts in the historic district have been replaced by bishop's crook lampposts. Six of them were surplus and a gift from the city; about 18 additional were purchased by members of Gramercy Park Associates, Inc. and installed as gifts *to* the city. More are expected to be installed in the surrounding neighborhood.

Turning west at the Gramercy Park Hotel (1925), we pass **the site of Stanford White's residence** (at the corner) from 1901 until his untimely death in 1906. White was murdered by deranged millionaire Harry K. Thaw, who was jealous of his wife Evelyn Nesbit's former relationship with White. Stanford White is acknowledged not only as an exemplary architect, but as one who established the American tradition of art collecting. His private collection of paintings and sculpture is now distributed among several museums. The house was stripped of its art treasures and acquired by the Princeton Club. It was razed in 1923 for the construction of the hotel.

Charming Nos. 3 and 4 Gramercy Park West still remain, adding to the pleasant atmosphere of the neighborhood. This pair of houses, built in 1847, are attributed to architect Alexander Jackson Davis. Twin lanterns in front of No. 4 denote the residence of former Mayor James Harper. (Photograph by Berenice Abbott. Federal Art Project "Changing New York." Museum of the City of New York)

At what would be No. 55 stood the home of diarist **George Templeton Strong,** the peripatetic chronicler of mid-19th-century life and events, who was given the house as a wedding gift when he married Ruggle's daughter. One door east lived Robert "Bob" Ingersoll, orator and lawyer, who, because of his highly publicized lectures on religion, was dubbed "The Great Agnostic."

Rounding the corner, **Nos. 1 and 2 Gramercy Park West** date from 1849–50. Dr. Valentine Mott, probably the most renowned surgeon in the days just before the Civil War, lived in No. 1. He was responsible for the founding of the New York University Medical College and Bellevue Hospital.

The imposing iron fence that encloses the park was the scene (directly opposite No. 2) of a dramatic encounter between novelist-muckraker David Graham Phillips and one Fitzhugh Coyle Goldsborough, the neurotic scion of a wealthy Washington family, on January 23, 1911, as Phillips was on his way from his 19th Street apartment to the Princeton Club. Goldsborough had become obsessed with the idea that Phillips had used his sister as the target of sarcastic barbs in a recent novel. When the two met, Goldsborough drew a revolver and fired three shots, Phillips collapsed against the fence and later succumbed. The young man then pointed the gun at his own head and blew his brains out.

Lovely **Nos. 3 and 4,** with their lacy ironwork porches, were built in 1847 and are attributed to famed architect Alexander Jackson Davis. The pair of lanterns in front of No. 4 indicate that it was once a mayor's residence. James Harper, founder of the J. & J. Harper publishing house, was elected to the city's highest office in 1844, where he fought corruption and organized the Police Department. He bought the house in 1847, but after a fatal carriage accident in 1869 the house went to his children.

No. 10 was the site of the studio of painter **Robert Henri** (1865–1929). As a member of the group of artists known as The Eight, he was a progenitor of the Ashcan School of American Painting, and teacher of such famous artists as George Bellows, Rockwell Kent, and Edward Hopper. His final years were spent here, and his studio's huge north light is still intact.

Turning east at the corner, we see the large double brownstone mansion of the **National Arts Club** at 15 Gramercy Park South. Built in 1845, the two single houses were remodeled from about 1881 to 1884 by Calvert Vaux for Samuel J. Tilden (Vaux, with Frederick Law Olmsted, designed Central and Prospect parks). Although the brownstone façade has weathered badly and is deteriorating, it is nonetheless an engaging example of Ruskinian Gothic, inspired by the Medieval Revival style made famous by the 19th-century English author and artist John Ruskin. Tilden, an eminent lawyer and reformer, was governor of New York in 1875–76, but resigned the office to run as Democratic presidential contender against Rutherford B. Hayes. History records that he won the popular majority by a quarter of a million votes but lost the election—defeated by a group of Southern Republican electors. The National Arts Club purchased the landmark building in 1906.

The National Arts Club is private, but visitors are welcome to visit the art gallery on the second floor during the frequently changing exhibitions. Before entering the gallery, which once was Tilden's dining room, peek into the private rooms on the right and you will be transported back to the late 19th century! Vaux's superb remodeling was inspired by the Aesthetic Movement. Note how he made ample use of carved wood paneling and furniture, stained glass, and tiles. A photo on the wall shows the dining room as it was after the remodeling. The Club was founded in 1898, and early members were Robert Henri, Frederic Remington, and Daniel Chester French, as well as non-artists Woodrow Wilson and Theodore Dreiser.

Adjacent is **The Players,** 16 Gramercy Park South, built for a banker in 1845. It was later purchased by actor Edwin Booth, who in 1888 commissioned Stanford White to remodel it as a private club for the theatrical profession. The huge Tuscan stone porch and elaborate ironwork, including the two graceful lanterns, are some of White's additions. Not all the great "Players" were actors, however. The membership included such notables as Walter Damrosch, Thomas Nast, Mark Twain, Booth Tarkington, Stanford White, Winston Churchill, and even General William Tecumseh Sherman. But they were all *men,* as the Players' Club was until recently "no-woman's land."

"No-man's-land," on the other hand, is still next door at **No. 17,** the **Salvation Army's Parkside Evangeline Residence Hall** for women, built in 1926.

Before crossing Irving Place, look through the park gates at the **statue of Edwin Booth** as Hamlet, sculpted by Edmond T. Quinn and unveiled in 1918.

No. 19 Gramercy Park South is the **Stuyvesant Fish House.** Built for a Horace Brooks in 1845, it was acquired in 1887 by Stuyvesant Fish, wealthy socialite and president of the Illinois Central Railroad. The line had so many of the "400" on its board of directors that it was called the "Society Railroad." His wife, Mary "Mamie" Fish, succeeded Mrs. William Astor as the head of New York society. It is said that Mamie Fish curtailed the traditional dinner hour from a several-hour affair to a mere 50 minutes; she was also responsible for a new informality among members of society, by encouraging the use of guests' first names. The Fishes commissioned Stanford White to remodel the house in 1888. In 1909 the adjoining stable was demolished and rebuilt as No. 20 and connected to No. 19.

In 1931 the house was acquired by Benjamin Sonnenberg, the great public relations man, whose rise from "rags to riches" is vividly recounted in Rev. Stephen Garmey's seminal work, *Gramercy Park* (New York, 1984). The Sonnenbergs meticulously restored the house to its former grandeur and, as Garmey quotes Brendan Gill, it became "a work of art in its own right." No. 19, according to the author, "struck one as the coziest, most colorful, most opulent place one had ever seen." Sonnenberg died in 1978, and the house has changed hands several times, but it still remains the most beautiful on the Park.

No. 19 also figured in the historical novel *Time and Again,* by Jack Finney. In the thoroughly engaging story, which accurately portrays New York life and events in 1883, the building faced Gramercy Park and was a boarding house and the focus of the plot. (Read it and find out what happened there!).

No. 21, next door, built in 1853–54, was the residence of John Bigelow, author and diplomat. Bigelow was co-owner with William Cullen Bryant of the

New York Evening Post from 1848 to 1861, when he gave up his newspaper business to become minister to France during the Civil War. He is credited with depriving the Confederacy of recognition by the French Government, and with stopping the construction of rebel warships.

Ignoring several nondescript remodelings, we come to the former **Friends' Meeting House,** 144 East 20th Street. Designed by King & Kellum in 1859, it is a fine example of the dignified Italianate style so popular in the 1850s. For a time the fate of the Meeting House was uncertain, as the Friends had merged their meetings with the Stuyvesant Square congregation, selling the house to the United Federation of Teachers. There was even talk of demolition and the erection of a high-rise apartment house, in spite of its designation as a New York City Landmark. But early in 1975, the **Brotherhood Synagogue,** which had been sharing quarters with the Village Presbyterian Church on West 13th Street, purchased the building from the U.F.T. Under the direction of architect James Stewart Polshek, working pro bono, the beautifully proportioned building was painstakingly restored. Visit the lovely sanctuary—a space of great simplicity and classical elegance.

At the northeast corner of 20th Street is the turreted red-brick Victorian apartment house, **The Gramercy,** erected in 1883 from plans by George da Cunha, and the first cooperative apartment house in New York City. Peek into its luxurious lobby! The foyer is adorned with stained glass and Minton tiles, and the building is equipped with Otis hydraulic elevators installed in 1883, and among the oldest of their kind still in service. Originally there was a Louis Sherry restaurant on the eighth floor, which, according to Rev. Garmey, was placed so high up in the building "so that residents would not be disturbed by kitchen smells. (Only servants' and bachelor quarters were above it.)"

No. 36, alongside (James Riely Gordon, 1909), in Francis I style, has a white terra-cotta façade replete with gargoyles and elaborate regal motifs; and guarding the entrance, a pair of knights in armor.

Return to Irving Place, walk south one block to 19th Street, and turn east.

9. The tree-lined and serene block between Irving Place and Third Avenue is known as the **"Block Beautiful."** Frederick Sterner was the prime mover in the rehabilitation of many of the old houses. Although none are particularly outstanding by themselves, they form a unity of "harmonious differences." Note the three "Gothic" conversions at **Nos. 127** (1854), **129** (1861), and **135** (1845). **No. 139** (1842–43), in a Tuscan style, earned Sterner his initial popularity. **No. 141** (1843), with its jockey hitching posts, belonged to the late sportscaster Ted Husing. **No. 132** (1910) was the residence of silent film ingenue Theda Bara, and of Mrs. Patrick Campbell, who in 1912 created the role of Eliza Doolittle in Shaw's *Pygmalion*. It was also the home of "muckraker" Ida M. Tarbell, who wrote the highly critical two-volume *History of the Standard Oil Company*. The ceramic reliefs over the entrances of **Nos. 147–149** (1861) are the work of resident artist Robert Winthrop Chanler. Note also **Nos. 144** and **146.** It was in No.

146 that renowned painter George W. Bellows lived from 1910, when he purchased the house, until his death in 1925. The skylight of his third-floor studio is still visible.

Return to Irving Place and continue south to 18th Street.

10. Pete's Tavern, at 66 Irving Place, dating from 1864 when it was called "Healy's," boasts to be the oldest saloon in New York City. The assertion, however, is strongly disputed by McSorley's Old Ale House, on East 7th Street, which opened ten years earlier. Pete's also claims to have been a favorite haunt of O. Henry; but, knowing his proclivities, almost any saloon could have earned that distinction! Legend (and a few faded newspaper clippings) maintains that he wrote *The Gift of the Magi* in the second booth on the right (this is also disputed by a restaurant down the street at No. 55—in fact, they have a plaque on the building to "prove" it). Be that as it may, the Tavern has been a popular local

The Academy of Music, built in 1854 at the corner of Irving Place and 14th Street, was New York's most popular and fashionable opera house until the advent of the Metropolitan Opera House in 1883. In 1926 it was razed to make way for Con Ed's new office building. Note the ad for Drake's Plantation Bitters painted on the curb. (The Consolidated Edison Company of New York)

landmark for many years. Two old carriage houses in the rear have been absorbed into the expanded establishment, and much of the flavor of the gaslit era remains.

11. Around the corner, **Nos. 135–143 East 18th Street** are a row of pre–Civil War houses (1855), each only two bays wide. Note the conspicuous hooded lintels over the windows. All but No. 141 retain their original cast-iron newels, balusters, and fences. **Nos. 145–151** date from the same period (1853–54).

12. No. 55 Irving Place is the site of William Sidney Porter's (O. Henry's) residence. Now an apartment house, little remains of the original building or the old Blue Bell Tavern at the corner (another purported "favorite" of the author). The plaque at the entrance to the restaurant claims *this* to be the location of the writing of *The Gift of the Magi.*

13. The charming little red brick house on the southwest corner of 17th Street, **No. 49 Irving Place,** claims (on its bronze plaque) to have been the residence of Washington Irving. The house was actually built (ca. 1845) for his nephew, John T. Irving, but Washington Irving *was* a frequent visitor. (His home for a time was at 11 Commerce Street, in Greenwich Village.) From 1894 to 1911 the house was occupied by two remarkable women, Elsie de Wolfe and Elisabeth Marbury. Miss de Wolfe was considered "the best-dressed woman in town," and later shocked the interior design profession by becoming the first

Tammany Hall, on the north side of 14th Street between Irving Place and Third Avenue in a ca. 1870 photograph. Chief Tamanend, above, presides over the Society which was founded in 1789 as an outgrowth of the Sons of Liberty. Tammany became a political power through the efforts of Aaron Burr. (New-York Historical Society)

"lady decorator." Her friend Miss Marbury was a noted literary agent, representing authors such as Oscar Wilde and George Bernard Shaw. Their Sunday afternoon socials for the literary world were the talk of the town. In adjacent **No. 47,** Oscar Wilde spent time in 1883 for the performance of his first drama in America, *Vera*. It premiered in the Union Square Theater, but was a flop.

14. In front of Washington Irving High School, built in 1912, is an enormous bust of the school's namesake, executed by Friedrich Baer in 1885 and originally placed in Bryant Park.

15. A short detour to the right on East 15th Street reveals a pleasant architectural surprise, at No. 109–111, the **former Century Association clubhouse.** The Association acquired the venerable building in 1857, ten years after its founding, and in 1869 looked to two clubmember-architects to design a major reconstruction. The plans fell to the renowned Henry Hobson Richardson,who was assisted by Charles Gambrill. The result was a clubhouse in the then-fashionable neo-Grec style.

The Century Association, a social club dedicated to "promote the advancement of art and literature," was founded by William Cullen Bryant, and took its name from the 100 original male members [*see* Chapter 12]. In 1891 the club moved to its present quarters on West 43rd Street. Until recently it had been assumed that their former building had long-since been demolished, but researchers discovered that the street had been renumbered, and it was the house bearing the old number that had disappeared. It now remains the only building in Manhattan by H. H. Richardson, as well as the oldest surviving private clubhouse. Recognizing its cultural, social, and historical significance, as well as its architectural interest, the former clubhouse was designated a landmark by the Landmarks Commission in 1993.

Return to Irving Place.

Occupying the entire block, from 15th to 14th streets, and Irving Place to Union Square, is massive **Zeckendorf Towers** (Davis, Brody & Assocs., 1987), a 670-unit condominium in four 29-story towers, topped by open-framework pyramids. The towers are set on a seven-story base that fills the triangular plot, while maintaining the orientation to the city street grid. Original plans called for much taller buildings, but fierce community opposition persuaded the Zeckendorf Company to scale down the height, thus reducing the "darkening and overwhelming" effect on the park below and respecting the scale of Union Square's surroundings. Recently on the site were the Amberg Theater (northeast corner), and on the western third of the block, the unforgettable **S. Klein department store,** whose slogan, "On the Square," was familiar to New York shoppers for 70 years. The northwest corner of Klein's building was the site of the posh Union Square Hotel, an establishment that catered to celebrities when this was the theater district.

16. Situated on the entire block to Third Avenue, between 15th and 14th streets, is **the headquarters of "Con Ed."** The main building was designed by Henry J. Hardenbergh (architect of the Plaza Hotel and the Dakota Apartments).

Begun in 1911, the structure and its extensions developed in stages, and took 18 years to complete. The unique clock tower, a pleasing contribution to the cityscape, was planned by Warren & Wetmore (architects of Grand Central Terminal) and completed in 1926. The company's predecessor, the Manhattan Gas Light Company, was located near the corner of 14th Street from 1885 to 1910; and at the corner was the **Academy of Music,** built in 1854. Farther east in the block was Tammany Hall, and at the Third Avenue corner, the popular entertainment spot, Tony Pastor's Music Hall. The Academy of Music hosted such greats as Jenny Lind, Adelina Patti, Helena Modjeska, E. H. Sothern, Edwin Booth, and Julia Marlowe. When the Metropolitan Opera House opened at Broadway and West 39th Street in 1893, the Academy of Music soon declined, and for a number of years presented only vaudeville and silents. In 1926 it finally surrendered to the wrecker's ball, making way for the Consolidated Edison Company's main building extension. A description of the interior of the Academy of Music appears on the opening page of Edith Wharton's Pulitzer Prize–winning novel, *The Age of Innocence,* where she observes that "the world of fashion was still content to reassemble every winter in the shabby red and gold boxes of the sociable old Academy."

Walk a few steps left to 145 East 14th Street, the **Con Edison Energy Museum** (open Tuesday through Saturday, 10 A.M. to 4 P.M.). In a series of exhibits and dioramas, the age of electricity comes alive. On display with recorded narrations are a working model of Thomas Edison's 1882 generating station on Pearl Street in lower Manhattan, factories and offices of the 1890s and 1920s, antique kitchen appliances, and a cutaway view of a typical New York City street. (Admission free.)

17. Walking back west, stop in front of 110 East 14th Street. Until June 1982 this was the site of the famous **Lüchow's** restaurant. The Victorian-style building dates from 1840 when the neighborhood was still residential, but on May 1, 1882, when 14th Street had become the heart of the entertainment district, August Lüchow purchased the ground-floor beer hall from owner Baron von Mehlbach, and expanded it into what was to become the most popular German restaurant in the city. Concertgoers from the nearby Academy of Music and Steinway Hall (across the street) packed the mirrored and wood-paneled rooms, the oompah bands played night after night, and the beer flowed like the Rhine. Lüchow's soon became a mecca for the big names in the music world. Distinguished habitués were Paderewski, Caruso, and Fritz Kreisler; and in later years, Cole Porter, Sigmund Romberg, Richard Rodgers, and Leonard Bernstein. Frequently seen at the turn of the century were Lillian Russell, William Steinway, and even Theodore Roosevelt, who preferred venison and champagne to the traditional fare. It was here that Victor Herbert founded the American Society of Composers, Authors & Publishers (ASCAP); and songwriter Gus Kahn penned "Yes Sir, That's My Baby" on a Lüchow tablecloth. But 14th Street no longer drew the crowds, so the owners felt that the establishment should be closer to the theater district that had departed 80 years before, and the restaurant was moved uptown opposite the Winter Garden, on Broadway, but it, too, has since closed. A local civic group, the Union Square Park Community Coalition, had hoped to save the venerable landmark which sits vacant and decaying; however the Lüchow's building is not protected by official city landmark status, and the owner has shown no interest in preserving it despite promises to the contrary. Adding to its misfortune, the rear wall of No. 108 recently collapsed, making the outlook for saving the old building even more grim.

End of tour. The Union Square subway station is one block west.

10. Madison Square

[Broadway R line subway to 28th Street; Fifth Avenue–Broadway buses M6 or M7 (southbound) to 28th Street]

Along Broadway from 23rd to 42nd streets, during the 1880s and 1890s, was the Rialto of New York—the celebrated Great White Way. Keeping pace with the northward drive of the city, the theater district, in a series of moves up Broadway, now reached to Longacre Square (called Times Square after 1904). Our uniquely American theater idiom, the musical comedy, was coming into its own, and the heyday of songwriting had begun. Along 28th Street, music publishers and tunesmiths by the score worked around the clock in a cacophony of musical sounds, to give birth to the appropriately named Tin Pan Alley. Facing nearby Madison Square arose Stanford White's monumental "Garden" to present a variety of entertainment on a scale hitherto unheard of by American audiences. Competing with the live entertainment of Broadway came the infant motion-picture industry, grinding out its silent films in hastily constructed studios in the West 20s.

Gone now are the legitimate theaters and music halls, the budding film industry, and the opulent hotels, restaurants, and cafés that lined Fifth Avenue and Broadway. Gone, too, is the din, glitter, and excitement that drew the throngs of nightly visitors. Even lavish Madison Square Garden bade farewell to its namesake site in 1925 and moved (twice) to other locations.

Broadway and adjacent Madison Square have quite a different flavor now. The 20th century witnessed the development of a bustling business district, bringing with it some of the most imposing commercial structures in the city. The area now between 26th and 32nd streets is primarily an export-import center, with a wide variety of mostly wholesale businesses. The owners represent many of the recent larger immigrant groups—Koreans, Indians, Arabs, Africans, etc. Have you ever wondered where the ubiquitous street vendors obtain their merchandise? It is here in this colorful bazaar which exudes a different sort of liveliness than did the theater district a century ago.

Shady Madison Square Park, however, still retains its quiet elegance—a refuge from the congestion and clamor of surrounding streets. And here and there, dwarfed by modern, multistoried neighbors, some architectural vestiges of the past still survive—mute reminders of that vibrant, exciting era of 90 years ago.

1. The tour begins at **West 28th Street and Broadway,** the former heart of "Tin

255

Pan Alley," where most of the popular music publishers were located at the turn of the century. The cacophony of music emanating from all the buildings in the block to Fifth Avenue gave rise to the name. Notice the typical turn-of-the-century skyscrapers, **No. 1170 Broadway** (DeLemos & Cordes, 1903) and **No. 1181,** The Baudoine Building (Alfred Zucker, 1896), in which architects still displayed that *horror vacui,* or abhorrence of leaving any part of the building undecorated; hence the façades were usually divided into three distinct sections, similar to a Classic column: the "base," usually the first three or four stories; the "shaft," the tall, relatively unadorned center section; and the "capital," the top group of stories, frequently very ornate and topped with a projecting cornice. This "Tripartite" style of commercial building architecture remained popular until about 1910. Note the dome on No. 1170.

   2. On the northeast corner of West 29th Street and Broadway is the charming **Gilsey House** (Stephen D. Hatch, 1869). Built of marble and cast iron, it is a splendid example of the French Second Empire style. It was the favorite hotel of Oscar Wilde during his American lecture tours, and was also a frequent haunt of James Buchanan "Diamond Jim" Brady, the financier and *bon vivant* of the Gay '90s. The hotel, built for Peter Gilsey, opened in 1871, and was the first in the city to boast a telephone. The sympathetic and precise restoration of this magnificent pile is a credit to the developer, who purchased a deteriorating commercial building and converted it into a profitable and desirable co-op. Just up Broadway two blocks, its dark mansard roof almost hidden, is **the former Grand Hotel.** Built in 1868 from plans by Henry Engelbert, it was considered one of the great hostelries of New York. In its present state it is but a ghost of its former elegance. The owner recently painted over the natural marble façade and distinctive tile mansard roof, in violation of the Landmark law. Removal of the paint, however, would be too damaging, and it will likely have to remain. Turn east on West 31st Street to the Herald Square Hotel.

   3. The refurbished Herald Square Hotel, until recently the Hotel Clinton, is **the former home of Life Magazine.** Before its purchase by the Time-Life Corporation in 1936, *Life* was a rather sophisticated humor weekly. Visible on the upper stone balcony is its name, as are groupings of L's on the ornate cast-iron balconies, together with the sculptured cherub and the inscriptions of "Wit" and "Humor." The building, with its Classical façade, was designed in 1893 by the noted architectural firm of Carrère & Hastings.

   4. The Wolcott Hotel, at 4–10 West 31st Street, is a fine example of Renaissance Eclectic–style hotel architecture so popular at the turn of the century. In its recent remodeling, the interior designers may have gone a bit too far in attempting to recreate a *fin de siècle* lobby. (Take a look, anyway!) Turn south on Fifth Avenue to the southwest corner of West 27th Street. (Incidentally, Fifth Avenue is the east-west dividing line of all numbered streets in Manhattan, from 8th Street north.)

   5. The dark red apartment house across the street (284 Fifth Avenue, entrance on West 30th Street) is the **Wilbraham Apartments.** Built in the mid-1880s, it was one of the first "French Flats," or residential apartments for the wealthy. Actress Lillian Russell occupied the top floor during the heyday of her career.

   6. The building at 276 Fifth Avenue was **formerly the Holland House** (Harding & Gooch, 1891). Named for a similar hotel in the Kensington section of

London, it was a gathering place for intellectuals and gourmets. The staircase of Siena marble and bronze and its famous restaurant made it a showplace until its closing in 1920. In its 1903 edition, *King's Views of New York* called it "the peer of any hotel in America...where the most fastidious people are its 'instant guests.'"

7. At the northwest corner of 29th Street is the well-known **Marble Collegiate Reformed Church,** where Dr. Norman Vincent Peale's Sunday sermons originated to reach a nationwide radio audience. Built in 1854 from plans by architect Samuel A. Warner, the church is a fine example of early Romanesque Revival style applied to what is essentially a Gothic Revival–style building. The congregation dates back to the founding of the Dutch Reformed Church in America in 1628. Note the huge bronze bell in front of the church. Cast in Holland, it summoned the faithful while it hung in the old North Church downtown on William Street in the 18th and 19th centuries.

8. Turn east on 29th Street to the landmark Episcopal Church of the Transfiguration. Known as the **"Little Church around the Corner,"** it dates from 1849–1856, and is New York City's unique example of the Cottage Gothic style of the 14th century. It earned its nickname from an incident that occurred in 1870. When actor George Holland died and was refused burial rites at a nearby church, a friend, Joseph Jefferson, was informed that there was a *little church around the corner* that would perform the rites—and the name stuck. The church has been closely connected with the acting profession since that time. The lich-gate at the entrance recalls the custom of conducting a preliminary burial service outside the church (*lic* is the Anglo-Saxon word for "body"). The interior is unusually beautiful, with a quiet, intimate atmosphere. Look for the stained-glass window (in the south transept) of actor Edwin Booth as Hamlet, done by John LaFarge. The reredos of the *Last Supper,* as well as the lich-gate, were designed by architect Frederick Clarke Withers. Note also the Chantry with its Brides' Altar, the carved wooden screens at the entrance to the nave, the Joseph Jefferson Memorial Window, the Mortuary Chapel with stained-glass copy of Raphael's *Transfiguration,* and the little chapel dedicated to actor José María Muñoz. The church takes pride in its history of helping the less fortunate. During the Draft Riots of 1863, it sheltered runaway slaves, and in the depressions of 1907 and the mid-1930s, it operated bread lines. It is still very active in community service, and also supports a small professional theater company, appropriately called "The Jefferson Players." The Little Church around the Corner is both a New York City landmark and a National Historic Landmark, and listed as a "National Shrine of Church and Theater."

Return to Fifth Avenue.

9. 256 Fifth Avenue, above the ground floor, is pure fantasy—a mixture of Venetian Gothic, Moorish, and whatever; the builder of the early 1890s went "hog wild" with the new terra-cotta medium.

250 Fifth Avenue (McKim, Mead & White, 1907) was built for the Second National Bank of the City of New York, and is not considered one of the firm's best designs. Now a branch of Citibank, the building cries out for restoration.

The first Madison Square Garde building was originally the Union Depot of the New York & Harlem Railroad at 28th Street and Madison Avenue. It served for a time as P. T. Barnum's Hippodrome, then in 1879 it became the "Garden." It lasted only until 1890, when Stanford White's great masterpiece replaced it. (New York Life Insurance Company)

10. The **former Brunswick Building** (Francis H. Kimball, 1907), southeast corner of 27th Street, is one of the city's most attractive commercial structures. Now called the Gift Building, it is notable for its red-brick façade and contrasting limestone trim, its splayed window lintels, swags and consoles, paired balconies, and ornate designs above the 10th floor's round-arch windows. An intricate wrought-iron balcony wraps around the building one floor higher, just below a verdigris cornice. The predecessor on the site, the fashionable Brunswick Hotel, was favored by the sporting crowd and particularly by the New York Coach Club, whose well-heeled members conducted an annual parade of their sumptuous horse-drawn carriages.

Further east on 27th Street is the **Prince George Hotel** (Howard Greenley, 1906). Once one of the city's most posh, it was the first with a private bath in every room, and catered to such flamboyant personalities as "Diamond Jim" Brady and Lillian Russell. Today it is an embarrassment, having recently suffered the indignity of being a welfare hotel, and at this writing, it is abandoned and for sale. Return to Madison Avenue and turn left (south).

11. The New York Life Insurance Company Building, designed by Cass Gilbert and built in 1926–28, is a most imposing structure. Although of no particular architectural style, the *AIA Guide to New York* refers to it as "Limestone Renaissance at the bottom, Birthday Cake at the top." The gilt pyramid that caps this mammoth structure is similar to the one Gilbert later designed for the top of the U.S. Court House on Foley Square, and is illuminated at night. The lobby of the New York Life Building is particularly attractive. Its coffered ceiling, enormous hanging lamps, and ornate doors and paneling—all of bronze—make it one of the great interiors of the city. The "grand staircase" leading to the subway station belies what is below. Compare this lavish lobby with Cass Gilbert's treatment of his Woolworth Building, built 13 years before.

This is the **site of the first two Madison Square Gardens.** Originally, the Union Depot of the New York & Harlem Railroad was built here after it had been moved uptown from its earlier location near City Hall. (The city fathers objected strenuously to the noise and air pollution of the old steam locomotives.) In 1871 the railroad terminal was shifted to the present site of Grand Central Terminal, and the Depot was sold to P. T. Barnum, who converted it into his popular Hippodrome. Nine years later it became the first Madison Square Garden.

In 1890, Stanford White designed the second Madison Square Garden, an imposing Spanish Renaissance–style structure, which occupied the entire block. Its central tower, modeled after the *Giralda* in Seville and topped by Augustus St. Gauden's statue of Diana, would be a dominant feature of the city skyline for 35 years. Complete with the largest amphitheater in the country, Garden Theater, Roof Garden, concert hall, café, and even an immense swimming pool, it was an immediate sensation. Among some of the events staged in the Garden were operatic concerts, prize fights (Jack Dempsey knocked out Bill Brennan), Wild West Shows, aquatic exhibitions, the first American automobile show, six-day bike races, and Barnum & Bailey's circus. Diana now resides in the Philadelphia Museum of Art.

Planned at first to be the site for annual horse shows, Stanford White designed Madison Square Garden to include a theater, concert hall, roof-garden, and restaurant, graced with a dramatic tower—the second highest in the city—and surmounted by a gilt statue of Diana. (New York Life Insurance Company)

Architect White had an eye not only for beautiful buildings, but for beautiful women as well. His two homes nearby were the scenes of frequent and wild all-night parties. Rumor had it that White had installed a high red-velvet swing on the top floor of his West 24th Street love nest, on which girl friends were offered all manner of inducements to oscillate "in the altogether." One of these steady "swingers" was young Evelyn Nesbit, a former *Floradora* show girl who later married eccentric millionaire Harry K. Thaw. On the evening of June 25, 1906, Stanford White entered the Roof Garden theater and was observed by Thaw and his recent bride, who were dining at a nearby table. Evelyn whispered something about White to her husband that infuriated him; whereupon he leaped up from the table, stalked across the floor, drew a revolver, and fired three fatal shots at the architect. After nine years and three prolonged trials, Thaw was acquitted.

After its demolition in 1925, the Garden was rebuilt at West 50th Street and 8th Avenue, where it remained until 1968. Ironically, its present location at Eighth Avenue between 31st and 33rd streets is on the site of McKim, Mead & White's greatest architectural achievement—Pennsylvania Station—which fell victim to the wrecker's ball and civic short-sightedness in 1963–66!

12. No. 50 Madison Avenue was built in 1896 by Renwick, Aspinwall & Owens for the American Society for the Prevention of Cruelty to Animals (ASPCA).

13. The glistening **Merchandise Mart Building** (Emery Roth & Sons,

The elegant Leonard Jerome Mansion, built in 1859, later the Manhattan Club, graced the southeast corner of 26th Street and Madison Avenue. Daughter Jennie Jerome later became Lady Randolph Churchill, mother of Sir Winston. The Landmark Law came too late to save the beautiful house, and in its place is the enormously out-of-scale Merchandise Mart Building. (New York Life Insurance Company)

"Dr. Parkhurst's Church," as the Madison Avenue Presbyterian Church was called, was built in 1853 when the neighborhood was entirely residential. On this peaceful site of the late 1880s—the corner of 23rd Street and Madison Avenue—now stands the Metropolitan Life Tower. (Metropolitan Life Insurance Company)

Madison Square has managed to escape most alterations made in the name of progress. The drinking fountains and pavilion are gone, but the trees remain, sporting the foliage of almost a century of growth since this 1901 photo was taken by Byron. (The Byron Collection, Museum of the City of New York)

The young boy drinking from the common cup was a participant in a Madison Square clean-up campaign sponsored by the Metropolitan Life Insurance Company in 1913. (Metropolitan Life Insurance Company)

An early 1900s sightseeing bus in front of No. 1 Madison Avenue. (Metropolitan Life Insurance Company)

The triangular site of the Flatiron Building, the intersection of Broadway and Fifth Avenue at 23rd Street, as seen from the Fifth Avenue Hotel in 1884. Note the white Broadway omnibus at left. (New-York Historical Society)

The expression "Twenty-Three Skidoo!" is said to have come from the efforts by Officer Kane, stationed at Fifth Avenue and 23rd Street, to "shoo" away the young men who gathered at the breezy corner to catch a glimpse of a lady's ankle. (Metropolitan Life Insurance Company)

The 28th and 29th Street crosstown car was one of the last to exchange horsepower for electric. In this undated photo, a two-horse team passes in front of 45 East 29th Street on its way to the New Jersey ferry terminal at West 23rd Street. (Metropolitan Life Insurance Company)

Prim young ladies serving tempting desserts in Maillard's elegant confectionery shop, on the ground floor of the posh Fifth Avenue Hotel. (Photograph by Byron. The Byron Collection. Museum of the City of New York)

1974), on the southeast corner of 26th Street, is a shocking example of utter disregard for scale. It would appear that the designers cared not at all about the height, shape, and style of adjacent buildings when they planned this one. By acquiring the air rights from the Court House to the south, they were able to raise this enormous dark shaft to an eye-boggling height, thus overwhelming its neighbors, destroying a pleasing skyline, and casting a visual pall over the park below. To make the picture even more dismal, the former occupant of the site was the Leonard Jerome House (Jerome's daughter, Jennie, became Lady Randolph Churchill—Winston Churchill's mother). The attractive mansion, built in 1859, later became the Manhattan Club where, it is said, the Manhattan cocktail was invented. Demolition took place with indecent haste, just before the passage of the Landmarks Preservation Law, and New York suffered another irretrievable loss.

   14. The Appellate Division, New York State Supreme Court is a Beaux Arts–style gem of a building, and is a tribute to its architect, James Brown Lord. Built of limestone in 1896–1900, this exceptional building miraculously escaped the fate of its ex-neighbor, the Jerome House, when public outcry prevented the Court's consolidation into the Foley Square complex.

   The exterior, with its projecting Corinthian porticos, supports an astonishing display of sculpture by 16 artists, each figure representing a person noted for achievements in the history of law. On the Annex is a three-story-high half-column, placed in 1990 as a Holocaust memorial. Note the inscription, "Indifference to Injustice is the Gate of Hell..."

   Take a moment or two to examine the sculpture:

Madison Square side:

   Balustrade (left to right): *Confucius* (Philip Martiny), *Peace* group (Karl Bitter), *Moses* (William Couper)

   Four caryatids: *The Four Seasons* (Thomas Shields Clarke)

25th Street Side:

   Entrance: *Force* and *Wisdom* (Frederick Ruckstull)

   Above portico windows: *Morning* and *Night, Noon* and *Evening* (Maximilian M. Schwartzott)

   Pediment: *Triumph of Law* (Charles H. Niehaus)

   Surmounting pediment: *Justice* flanked by *Power* and *Study* (Daniel Chester French)

   Balustrade (left to right): *Zoroaster* (Edward C. Potter), *Alfred the Great* (Jonathan Scott Hartley), *Lycurgus* (George E. Bissell), *Solon* (Herbert Adams), *Louis IX* (John Donoghue), *Manu* (Augustus Lukeman), *Justinian* (Henry Kirke Bush-Brown), *vacant* (formerly *Mohammed,* Charles Albert Lopez; removed at the request of the Moslem community of New York City)

A visit to the interior is most rewarding (open weekdays only). The furniture was designed by the architectural and interior design firm of Herter Brothers, the cabinetry by George C. Flint Company, the sculpture of Charles O'Connor by James W. A. MacDonald, and the stained-glass windows by the Maitland Armstrong Company. There are also splendid murals painted by a number of famous American muralists. Nothing was spared in making the Appellate Court House an aesthetic, architectural masterpiece.

 15. The Metropolitan Life Insurance Company buildings complete the panorama of the east side of Madison Square. The original main building, at the corner of 23rd Street, was built in 1893. Its crowning glory, however, came in 1909 with the 700-foot tower addition, making it the tallest building in the world at the time, and the identifying symbol of the company—"the Light that Never Fails." Designed by the firm of Napoleon LeBrun & Sons, the tower is based on the *Campanile* of St. Mark's Square in Venice. Four years after its completion, its height record was surpassed by the 60-story Woolworth Building, downtown. In the mid-1950s, the original main building was demolished and the present 12-story structure erected in its place. The tower was given a "facelift" as part of the overall modernization project, with most of the ornamentation stripped off the façade. Only the four three-story-high clocks and the surmounting gilded lantern escaped the butchery. Yet the tower glitters like a jewel in its nighttime illumination. It is floodlit in a variety of colors corresponding to holidays—red, white, and blue on July 4th; green on St. Patrick's Day; and at Christmas, red lamps shine in the tower windows, simulating a holiday tree.

An interesting event in the history of the 50-story tower occurred on election night 1908, one year before its completion. The *New York Herald* installed a giant searchlight among the still-exposed girders near the top of the spire to signal the election results far and wide. A northward-swinging beam would indicate a majority for the Republican presidential candidate William Howard Taft, and a southward beam for Democrat William Jennings Bryan. As the first returns showed a plurality for Taft, the beacon moved slowly up and down in a northward direction. By a little after 8 P.M., as the telegraphed vote count gave a clear majority to the Republican, the searchlight's rays were held steadily northward. Thus New Yorkers and suburbanites for miles around were the first to get the election results transmitted from the tall tower's beacon.

The **North Building,** occupying the block between 24th and 25th streets, was designed by Wald, Corbett, & Angilly, and built in three stages from 1932 to 1950. A striking example of the Art Deco style, the massive Alabama limestone exterior was planned to conform to the city's building regulations requiring extensive setbacks on tall buildings. Their "stepped" arrangement, along with the interesting angular upper walls and chamfered corners, can best be appreciated from across the square. Arched loggias at the four corners provide entrance arcades that lead to central elevator halls, and the huge building is connected to the Home Office Building by a skywalk and a tunnel. The lobby walls are faced with handsome Italian cremo marble. Just before the outbreak of World War II the company stockpiled huge blocks of this marble for fear that a war might destroy the northern Italian quarries and prevent a uniform completion of the building's interior. The North Building holds the distinction of being the first commercial structure in New York City to have central air conditioning.

On the site of the adjacent Metropolitan Life Tower stood the brownstone Gothic Revival–style Madison Square Presbyterian Church, built in 1853. Its outspoken minister, the Reverend Charles H. Parkhurst, led a vociferous campaign from 1892 to 1894 against citywide crime and police corruption. Accused by angry Tammany politicians of being self-serving, Dr. Parkhurst documented his charges by personally visiting the dens of iniquity that City Hall denied existed and proving complicity and brutality by the police. After these revelations from Parkhurst's pulpit, the State Legislature convened the Lexow Committee, whose subsequent investigation corroborated Dr. Parkhurst's accusations and led to the defeat of Tammany Mayor Hugh Grant, a major shakeup in the Police Department, and the appointment of Theodore Roosevelt to the Board of Commissioners. The Metropolitan Life Insurance Company acquired the church property for needed building expansion, and in exchange for the corner plot, agreed to build a new house of worship across the street for Dr. Parkhurst's congregation. Stanford White was commissioned to design the new church, which was completed in 1906 in Italian Renaissance style. The bright, white granite New Madison Square Presbyterian Church was White's last public building and is considered by many authorities to be the most beautiful building he ever designed. In 1919, the ever-expanding company purchased the property and demolished the lovely church. (The parishioners had, for the most part, moved to more fashionable precincts uptown anyway, as the neighborhood by that time

For a brief period in 1906 there were two Madison Square Presbyterian Churches standing side-by-side. Needing additional land to erect its famous tower, the Metropolitan Life Insurance Company bought and razed the older Gothic Revival–style church and built another for Dr. Charles H. Parkhurst's congregation. The neoclassic "temple," Stanford White's last major commission, survived only until 1919 when the Insurance Company again acquired the property to build its North Building. (Metropolitan Life Insurance Company)

was almost exclusively commercial.) A "new" annex to the Home Office was erected, but it, too, was razed when the new North Building was designed.

16. Madison Square Park became the pleasant oasis it is now in 1870. At the time of the Revolution it was a swampy grassland traversed by a meandering stream, abounding with game. Later it became a paupers' burial ground. By the first decade of the 19th century, a military outpost was established as part of the defenses of the lower city at the junction of the Eastern Post Road and Bloomingdale Road—now Broadway—near the present intersection of Fifth Avenue. In 1811, the famous New York City Commissioners' Report officially designated the street pattern of much of Manhattan Island, and a "Parade" was laid out between 23rd and 34th streets and Third and Seventh avenues. A few years later it was greatly reduced in size and named in honor of the then fourth president, James Madison. In 1844 the Square was again reduced, to its present size. In its concept the plan was a forerunner of the one that subsequently gave us spacious Central Park. The park underwent a major restoration in the early 1990s. A significant change was in the park's paths, which are now aligned with the street grid, so that one can now walk from Madison to Fifth Avenue without a detour. The atmosphere in the renovated park now more closely evokes its gracious past.

Enter the Park at the Statue of Roscoe Conkling, near 23rd Street.

Elected as a Republican to the U.S. Senate in 1867, Conkling served the Empire State for 14 years. He resigned in 1881 after a dispute with President Garfield and retired to law practice. During the Great Blizzard of March 12, 1888, he was caught without transportation home from his downtown office, and set out on foot against the mounting drifts and sub-zero cold. He became lost in Madison Square, but was rescued and carried to his nearby home. The effects of the exposure, however, were fatal, and he died six weeks later. This bronze memorial statue, by sculptor John Quincy Adams Ward, was erected in 1893 through contributions by friends, and stands near the site where he was felled by the blizzard.

Hansom cabs line the west side of Madison Square, across from the fashionable Fifth Avenue Hotel, as two young ladies stroll toward the camera of Percy C. Byron, 1905 (The Byron Collection, Museum of the City of New York)

Three types of horse-drawn carriages wait outside Delmonico's, at Fifth Avenue and 26th Street, in 1888, then the most fashionable dining place in town. A number of years later, the restaurant moved up Fifth Avenue to 44th Street where it finally closed in 1923. The restaurant on the site of Delmonico's first establishment, at Beaver and South William streets, seeks to preserve the name and tradition. (New-York Historical Society)

Walking north along the park path, we pass *Skagerrak* on the left (Antoni Milkowsky, 1972), a "minimal" sculpture of weathering steel cubic rectangles. Continue to the north end under the broad elms and horse chestnuts, to the imposing **statue of Admiral David Glasgow Farragut,** dedicated in 1881. In a dramatic posture as a rugged sailor facing the wind, Farragut is memorialized as the great naval hero of the Civil War. His victories at New Orleans and Mobile Bay finally closed all Gulf ports to the Confederacy. One can almost hear him shout that celebrated order, "Damn the torpedoes, full speed ahead!" He is represented in one of the great 19th-century statues by famed sculptor Augustus St. Gaudens, with Stanford White as the designer of the beautifully rendered pedestal bench.

A short distance to the west is the **statue of Chester A. Arthur,** 21st president, who assumed the office after the assassination of James Garfield in 1881. The monument, by George E. Bissell, was unveiled in 1899 and was a gift of Catherine Lorillard Wolfe, who lived in a brownstone on the site of the Metropolitan Life Tower.

17. The southwest corner of Fifth Avenue and 26th Street marks the **site of Delmonico's restaurant,** between 1876 and 1902, before its ninth and final move uptown to 44th Street [*see* pages 62 and 318]. When Charles, and son Lorenzo,

Delmonico opened their newest dining salon, it achieved instant popularity with the "400" and became a formidable rival to the Café Brunswick, across the avenue. Its world-renowned chefs, lavish menus, impeccable service, and elite clientele made it the gourmet landmark *par excellence* well remembered to this day.

18. One block south is the **General William J. Worth Monument.** Designed by James C. Batterson and erected in 1857, this obelisk marks the only burial site of a public figure under a Manhattan thoroughfare. Worth fought in the Seminole and Mexican wars, and the names of some of his famous battles are carved on the granite shaft. Although a downtown street is named for him, he is perhaps more of a hero in the state of Texas, where the city of Fort Worth honors his memory. Interesting is the cast-iron fence with repeating sword motifs, now being restored. The mysterious marble-faced structure behind the monument is a city water-metering station. The Catskill Water Supply tunnel passes just below.

Along Fifth Avenue and adjacent Broadway stood many famous hotels of the gaslit era. On the southwest corner of Broadway and 26th Street stood the St. James Hotel, whose name is borne today by the neo-Gothic skyscraper on the site. Occupying the west side of Broadway between 24th and 25th streets was the Hoffman House, an elegant hostelry of the time, whose bar was also a noted art gallery. Remembered particularly is Adolphe Bouguereau's huge, somewhat risqué painting. *Nymphs and Satyr,* which created quite a sensation in those

Looking north on Fifth Avenue at Madison Square Park. In 1876 the arm of the Statue of Liberty was brought from Philadelphia's Centennial Exposition to New York as a means of raising money for the base and the costs of assembling France's gift to America. The statue was finally erected ten years later. (New-York Historical Society)

Victorian days. The painting can be seen today, no longer causing a stir, at the Sterling and Francine Clark Art Institute, in Williamstown, Massachusetts.

19. Make a brief detour along West 25th Street to the **Serbian Orthodox Cathedral of St. Sava.** Designed in 1855 by Richard Upjohn, it was built in Gothic Revival style as the Trinity Protestant Episcopal Chapel, and was the site of Edith Wharton's wedding in 1885. Alongside is the 1860 **Parish House,** in Victorian Gothic style, by J. Wrey Mould. The buildings were purchased by the Serbian Church in 1943.

Walk through the alleyway between the buildings and return to Broadway, turning south to the corner of 24th Street.

20. The building occupying the entire block to 24th Street, as well as its neighbor to the south, is linked together not only by a skywalk, but by the same street number: **200 Fifth Avenue.** This pair of commercial buildings is the Toy Center, home for most of the city's wholesale toy manufacturers and distributors.

A few yards down 24th Street stood the Madison Square Theater, famous at the turn of the century for its hydraulically operated double stage.

Across the street, at the edge of the park, is the **Eternal Light Monument.** Erected in 1924 from plans by Thomas Hastings (of the architectural firm of Carrère & Hastings) and Paul W. Bartlett, its star-topped light honors the fallen of World War I. At a point just to the left, the arm of the Statue of Liberty was displayed from 1876 to 1884 while funds were being raise to pay for the base. The arm and torch were first sent by France to the Philadelphia Centennial Exposition, then brought to Madison Square Park. The arm was later returned to France for attachment to the statue which was finally erected in New York Harbor in 1886.

21. The tall **sidewalk clock** in the next block is one of the last remaining on the streets of New York, a vestige of the days when wristwatches were unknown and pocket watches were for the affluent. They were usually placed in front of a commercial establishment as an advertising gimmick. This cast-iron street clock, which still runs perfectly, was built by the Hecla Iron Works in the 1880s with a movement by Seth Thomas—the oldest surviving American clockmaker.

22. The plaque on the massive Italian Renaissance **Toy Center Building** (Maynicke & Franke, 1909), at the corner of 23rd Street, details the long and varied history of the site. The **Fifth Avenue Hotel** was the most luxurious in the city when it was completed in 1859. Earlier in the 19th century, there was a post tavern used for changing horses, and later a road house, known as Corporal Thompson's Madison Cottage. The *New York Herald* of May 9, 1847, carried the following notice about the inn:

> MADISON COTTAGE—*This beautiful place of resort opposite Madison Square, corner of Twenty-Third Street and Broadway, is open for the season, and Palmer's omnibuses drive to the door. It is one of the most agreeable spots for an afternoon's lounge in the suburbs of our city. Go and see!*

In 1853, Franconi's Hippodrome replaced the Cottage, offering a variety of public entertainment in an open-air arena, which included chariot races and circus performances.

The elegant dining salon of the subsequent Fifth Avenue Hotel was a favorite gathering place for the financial and political bigwigs of the day. A nightly spectacle at the main entrance was the steady procession of flashy carriages with matched teams of horses, bringing such giants as Jay Gould, "Jim" Fisk, "Larry" Jerome, Commodore Vanderbilt, and "Boss" Tweed. The powerful politico "Tom" Platt—credited with Theodore Roosevelt's presidential victory in 1898—held court before a coterie of adulating yes-men near the bar, in his so-called "Amen Corner." O. Henry, in his *Voice of the City,* vividly described the life and spirit of the times. The Hotel was also frequented by Mark Twain, Edwin Booth, William Cullen Bryant, and Stanford White.

Cross Fifth Avenue to the park.

23. The Statue of William H. Seward, by Randolph Rogers, was unveiled in 1876. As U.S. Senator from New York before the Civil War, and later as Lincoln's Secretary of State, Seward so distinguished himself as a statesman that President Andrew Johnson retained him in his own cabinet. A wise choice

Madison Square ca. 1916 is no longer dominated by the "Garden" but by the Metropolitan Life Insurance Company buildings rising on the east side. Horse-drawn vehicles are still plentiful, but the age of the motorcar has already begun. (Metropolitan Life Insurance Company.)

indeed, as Seward foresaw the importance of Alaska and was responsible for its purchase. However, the statue was not well received. One critic proclaimed that "Mr. Seward was a man 'all head and no legs,' whereas the statue represents the statesman with unusual length and prominence,"—an observation that lent credence to the legend that the statue originally was not Seward, but *Abraham Lincoln Signing the Emancipation Proclamation!* However, this is not true, although the legend persists from one guidebook to another. When Rogers completed a statue of Lincoln for Philadelphia's Fairmount Park, there were striking similarities between the two figures, and gossipers claimed that to save money he used the same figure twice. Seward was the first New Yorker to be honored with a public monument.

24. Directly across 23rd Street, in the triangle formed by the confluence of Fifth Avenue and Broadway, stands the striking **Flatiron Building.** Newly arrived from Chicago and his successful participation in the planning of the World's Columbian Exposition of 1893, Daniel H. Burnham designed this innovative and daring commercial structure in the Italian Renaissance style. With a towering steel framework and rusticated terra-cotta walls in the shape of an enormous flatiron, it startled even blasé New Yorkers when it was completed in 1902. Visitors at first shunned the rooftop observation deck, predicting that strong winds would soon topple "Burnham's Folly." With fears allayed by the passage of time, the panoramic view attracted crowds of sightseers. On a clear day, the New Jersey Palisades and Coney Island's beaches were easily visible. Although originally designated the Fuller Building, popular insistence on calling it by what it resembled forced the owners to yield and make the building's nickname official. It is now a designated landmark. Note the ornate yet restrained façade, whose undulating walls and sharp corners, topped by a classic cornice, result in a dramatic perspective. The protuberance on the ground floor extending toward 23rd Street was added a few years later, and was dubbed "the cow-catcher."

The busy intersection in front of the Flatiron Building has always been a particularly windy spot, and in the era when skirts trailed on the ground, it was a favorite vantage point for girl-watchers hoping for a glimpse of a trim ankle. It is said that nearby traffic policemen would turn from their task of untangling the confusion of horsecars, omnibuses, wagons, and carriages, to shoo away these young voyeurs—hence the expression, "Twenty-Three Skidoo!"

End of tour. The R line 23rd Street station is at the corner. The Lexington Avenue line is two blocks east on 23rd Street and Park Avenue South.

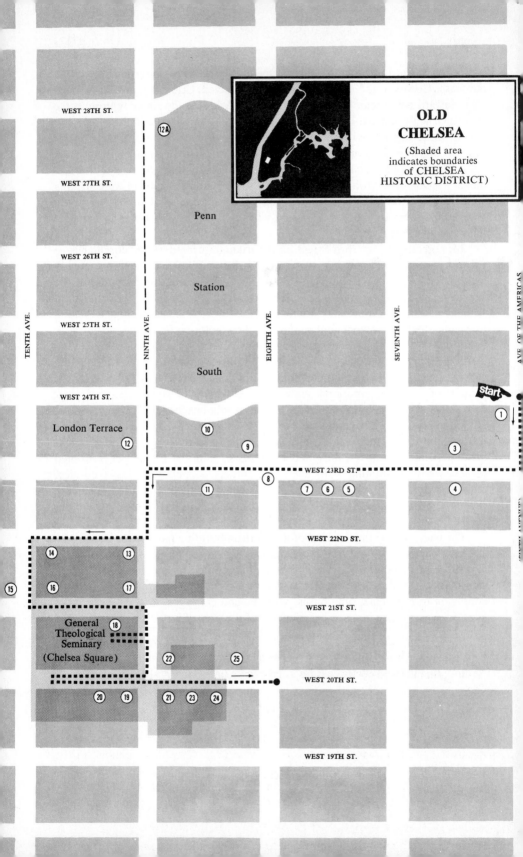

11. Old Chelsea

[Broadway–Seventh Avenue line, Sixth Avenue F line, Broadway R line, PATH to 23rd Street; Broadway, Fifth, Sixth, Seventh Avenue buses to 23rd Street]

The neighborhood now encompassed by 14th to 30th streets and Avenue of the Americas to the Hudson River was rural farmland in 1750 when Captain Thomas Clarke bought a tract of land there and named it after the Chelsea Royal Hospital, an old soldiers' home built by Sir Christopher Wren in the Chelsea borough of London.

It was Clarke's grandson, however, who was to bring fame to Chelsea and immortality to himself. A professor of classics and biblical literature at General Theological Seminary, **Clement Clarke Moore** is remembered less for his scholarly *Compendious Lexicon of the Hebrew Language* than for his inspired poem, "A Visit from St. Nicholas," composed in 1822 while he was driving in a sleigh from the lower city, bringing goodies for the Christmas dinner. In addition to popularizing Santa Claus, Moore did much to influence the development and character of the neighborhood through foresight and wise urban planning. He served as vestryman at St. Luke's Church in Greenwich (Village), and was a founder of St. Peter's Church in Chelsea. He also donated the land for the General Theological Seminary and established guidelines for local residential zoning that in great measure contributed to the charming atmosphere of much of Chelsea today.

Moore is buried in uptown Trinity Church Cemetery (155th Street and Riverside Drive), where, every Christmas Eve, a candlelight procession of children carolers lays a wreath on the grave of the author of "'Twas the night before Christmas...."

By the mid-19th century Chelsea had grown into a peaceful residential area. Only the chugging of the locomotives of the Hudson River Rail Road on Eleventh Avenue, and the rattling Eighth Avenue horsecar—Chelsea's first "rapid" transit—disturbed the quiet of the streets. But the tranquility of the neighborhood was shattered some 20 years later with the arrival of the city's liveliest entertainment district. Once-sedate 23rd Street now echoed to the sounds of music halls and late-night revelers. The Ninth Avenue El, the city's first overhead railway, pushed through the Chelsea district in 1871, and the noisy steam-driven trains competed with the furor of iron-tire dray wagons,

275

horse-drawn omnibuses and clanging bells of a proliferating network of horsecar lines. Along Sixth Avenue, a new and enormous shopping center was developing, as huge, palatial department stores opened their doors in what was to be the most popular retail district in the city. A year later the Sixth Avenue El added its roar to the growing clamor, and in the shadow of the El, at 30th Street, the "Haymarket" enjoyed the reputation of being the most-raided den of vice in the city's history.

As the century drew to a close, a new dimension was added to Chelsea with the birth of the motion-picture industry, as studios ground out silents in enormous, barnlike buildings east of Sixth Avenue.

Chelsea has become relatively quiet again. The music halls are all gone, the theaters have moved uptown, the great department stores either folded or relocated elsewhere, the film industry discovered Hollywood, and the Els were sent as scrap iron to Japan. And with the departure of commerce, the neighborhood began to decline. The lovely row houses deteriorated, and the area took on an air of neglect and decay. Then, at the last minute, Chelsea received a reprieve. With the shortage of housing and skyrocketing real-estate values, a new population entered the scene. Writers, actors, advertising executives, teachers, and other professionals discovered Chelsea and began buying up the aging town houses, restoring them with loving care. Overnight a "restoration revolution" began and the neighborhood has once again become an eminently desirable place to live— and just minutes from the heart of town. The designation by the Landmarks Commission of a part of Chelsea as a Historic District has added even greater impetus to maintaining the appearance and traditions of this charming quarter.

Many vestiges of the past are still to be seen: the old department store buildings, bits and pieces of the old theater district, several lovely churches, the delightful campus of the General Theological Seminary, and the row upon row of splendid town houses. But the special quality of Chelsea—still very much in evidence on almost every block—is the charming 19th-century atmosphere, all within the shadow of midtown Manhattan.

The tour begins at the corner of Avenue of the Americas (formerly Sixth Avenue) and West 24th Street.

1. The small red brick building on the southwest corner (best seen from across the street) is all that remains of one of the most popular entertainment spots of the gaslit era, Koster & Bial's Concert Hall. The hall itself used to face 23rd Street, and is long since gone, but this structure, once the beer-garden annex, was known as **The Corner.** Its name still survives in the upper cornice, and is the sole reminder of a once frenetic entertainment career.

Koster & Bial's opened in 1879, and was probably the liveliest vaudeville house in town. Here Victor Herbert conducted his 40-piece orchestra, and between the music, the free-flowing liquor, and imported talent, the Concert Hall became *the* place during the "Naughty '90s." Seeking a larger theater and anticipating another uptown move by the entertainment district, Koster & Bial closed their popular establishment and entered into a short-lived partnership with impresario-composer Oscar Hammerstein at his 34th Street Manhattan Opera House (on the present site of Macy's). The relationship was tempestuous at best, and ended in a court battle that saw the exit from "show biz" of Koster & Bial, while Hammerstein's star continued to rise.

2. On the southeast corner of 23rd Street and Avenue of the Americas from 1869 to 1883 stood the **Edwin Booth Theater,** with Booth himself as manager and frequent star performer. In spite of brother John Wilkes Booth's assassination of President Lincoln, Edwin remained one of the country's most popular actors. When James W. McCreery, known as the "Dean of the Retail Trade," acquired the site, he demolished the theater and erected his second department store. (The first still stands at Broadway and 11th Street, a cast-iron building converted into an apartment house.) In 1907 the firm moved uptown again, but his building remained until 1975. [For a detailed description of the department stores of the gaslit era, *see* Ladies' Mile.]

Across the avenue, on the southwest corner, is a small cast-iron building that once housed **Riker's Drug Company** and was later absorbed into the Liggett Drug chain. When the building suffered a disastrous fire, it was rebuilt by the owners and restored (except for the cornice) to its original appearance.

Note that the name of **Ehrich Brothers,** another of the great emporiums, can barely be made out through a new layer of ivory paint on an iron panel on the adjoining building on 23rd Street. The huge store which faced both 23rd Street and Sixth Avenue, surrounding Riker's corner, gave up the ghost in 1911.

Des Morgens schmeckt der Brandewein,
Desgleichen am Mittage,
Doch wer ihn Abends trinken thut,
Ist frei von jeder Plage;
Hingegen soll ein Brandewein,
Um Mitternacht
nicht schädlich
sein.

Koster & Bial's "The Corner," a beer-hall annex to the famous 23rd Street Music Hall, still stands at the southwest corner of Sixth Avenue and 24th Street. This photo was taken in 1904. (Museum of the City of New York)

Cross to the north side of 23rd Street and walk west.

3. At what is now No. 135 West was **Proctor's Twenty-Third Street Music Hall.** Another of the great vaudeville showplaces, Proctor's opened in 1888, in a large Flemish-style building, packing them in with such topflight stars as "Jersey Lily" Langtry, the inimitable Lillian Russell, Scotland's idol Harry Lauder, female impersonator Julian Eltinge, Eva Tanguay, the "I Don't Care" girl, and sparkling Lottie Collins, who never failed to stop the show cold with her rendition of "Ta Ra Ra BOOM De Ay!" E. F. Proctor later opened other theaters throughout the city as well as out of town, and when he died, his chain was sold to R.K.O. for a reported $16 million.

4. Continue west on 23rd Street, noting **No. 148–156,** a large Gothic Revival-style former commercial building, converted to a condo, named Chelsea Mews. Again on the north side, fanciful **No. 167** is a curious piece of Victoriana that hearkens back to 1898 when 23rd Street was the entertainment district. Its original function is uncertain, but what is left of the façade after a recent "modernization" is interesting. Above the cast-iron front is a sheet-metal cornice and an amusing tower. Farther down the street at No. 209 is the **Muhlenberg Branch of the New York Public Library,** named for a former pastor of the Church of the Holy Communion (Avenue of the Americas and West 20th Street). Two doors beyond is the busy **McBurney Branch of the Y.M.C.A.,** built in 1904.

Proctor's became the most famous music hall in the city when it opened in 1888, and featured only topflight entertainers. In this Byron photograph, taken ca. 1910, Lillian Russell is the starred performer. (The J. Clarence Davies Collection. Museum of the City of New York)

5. On the south side of the street, midway between Seventh and Eighth avenues, is a proud survivor of the quarter's Golden Age—the striking **Hotel Chelsea.** When opened in 1883 as a cooperative apartment house, it was a most luxurious address for those well-to-do artists who sought a quiet and elegant atmosphere to inspire creativity. In 1905 it became a hotel, and its guest register through the years reads like an artistic and literary *Who's Who.* Notice the bronze plaques honoring such greats as Mark Twain, Thomas Wolfe, Dylan Thomas, and Brendan Behan. Other notables who have graced the Hotel Chelsea are O. Henry, Sarah Bernhardt, Lillian Russell, Edgar Lee Masters,* John Sloan, Larry Rivers, James T. Farrell, Arthur Miller, Tennessee Williams, Virgil Thomson, Jackson Pollock, and Yevgeny Yevtushenko. It was Andy Warhol, though, who brought the Chelsea to the world of moviegoers when he filmed artist Brigid Polk in her hotel room. This formed the basis for his screen classic, *The Chelsea Girls,* thought to be Warhol's best film and his first financial triumph. The hotel also figured in the British film *Sid and Nancy.*

Designed by Hubert, Pirsson & Company in a style that has been described as Queen Anne or Victorian Gothic, its outstanding architectural features are its exuberant roofline with dormers and tall chimneys, and its richly ornamented iron balconies and interior grand staircase. The labels at the base show that the iron was cast by the J. B. & J. M. Cornell Iron Works. When built, its 11 stories made it one of the tallest structures in the city. Studios were added on the roof, making it the first such building to have duplexes. It also boasted the first penthouse in town. The lobby has been altered considerably and now doubles as a contemporary art gallery, presided over by managing director Stanley Bard, himself a patron of the arts. The broad iron staircase, which used to open with a wide sweep into the lobby, has been closed off at the ground-floor level because of fire laws. Its ten-story spiral ascent to the roof can, however, be admired from the second floor. Time has been kind to the old dowager. Its Edwardian charm still remains, just as faithfully as its worldwide devoted clientele.

6. The synagogue **Congregation Emunath Israel,** at No. 236–238, occupies the former house of worship of the Third Reformed Presbyterian Church.

7. No. 252–256, a new Cineplex Odeon theater, sits on the **site of Cavanagh's Restaurant,** which opened in 1876. A favorite dining spot for the elite in the heyday of Chelsea's entertainment era, it hosted such personalities as Lillian Russell, "Diamond Jim" Brady, and John L. Sullivan. It was also the hangout of powerful turn-of-the-century Tammany Hall politicians. The exclusive establishment fell on hard times and had to close its gaslit-era dining room in 1970.

---

*Edgar Lee Masters, known mainly for his *Spoon River Anthology* (1915), also wrote a short poem entitled "The Hotel Chelsea":

> Today will pass as currents of the air that veer and die.
> Tell me how souls can be
> Such flames of suffering and of ecstasy.
> Then fare as the winds fare?

The Grand Opera-House, on the northwest corner of 23rd Street and Eighth Avenue, was not only a theater, but the headquarters of Jim Fisk's Erie Railway. After Fisk was shot by Edward S. Stokes over a lover's quarrel and lawsuit in 1872, the Opera House was taken over by Jay Gould. The Grand Opera-House later featured silent films and degenerated into a second-rate movie house, falling under the wrecker's ball in 1960. (The J. Clarence Davies Collection. Museum of the City of New York)

8. The intersection of Eighth Avenue and West 23rd Street marks the approximate **site of the original Thomas Clarke house.** The farm, named "Chelsea," was situated between the Fitzroy Road (which ran parallel to and just west of Eighth Avenue) and the Hudson River, from 19th to 24th streets. The Fritzroy Road was the principal north-south thoroughfare and began about two blocks south, at Love Lane, between the present 21st and 22nd streets. Love Lane ran east to the Albany Post Road (later Bloomingdale Road; now Broadway), the only route to the lower city. When the Clarke house burned down in 1777, his widow had it rebuilt farther west, on a bluff overlooking the Hudson, between the present Ninth and Tenth avenues. Two years later, a grandson, Clement Clarke Moore, was born there.

9. When Pike's Opera House opened on the northwest corner in 1868 with a performance of Verdi's *Il Trovatore,* it was an instant success...so successful that financiers Jay Gould and Jim Fisk bought it within the year. They changed its name to **The Grand Opera-House** and enlarged its repertoire to include all kinds of theatrical entertainment. Some of the productions were tailor-made for the talents of Josie Mansfield, Fisk's mistress. Josie lived in an adjacent mansion, connected to the Opera-House by an underground tunnel. The two partners even moved the offices of their Erie Railway into the theater. Next year, when Fisk and Gould attempted to corner the gold market, causing the "Black Friday" panic, it is said that Fisk, himself in a panic, hid in the vault of the Opera-House to avoid the wrath of the surging crowds. In the meantime, Josie, tiring of "Jubilee" Jim, began taking up with a former partner of his, Edward S. Stokes. This led to a series of lovers' quarrels and a sensational lawsuit, all paraded across the front pages of New York's dailies. An angry Stokes then waylaid Fisk on the staircase of the old Grand Central Hotel on January 6, 1872, and shot him twice with a revolver. Fisk died the following day, and as one of the most influential politicos in the city, was given a state funeral. Stokes was convicted after several trials and served four years in prison. Jay Gould continued to operate the theater for a number of years. During the first decade of the 20th century, the Opera-House inaugurated the "Subway Circuit," offering first-run productions shortly after their initial Broadway openings. By World War I, the theater, like so many of its contemporaries, switched to silent films with vaudeville, and continued as a movie house until 1960, when it was demolished to make way for the sprawling Penn Station South housing development.

10. Penn Station South (Eighth to Ninth avenues, 23rd to 29th streets) was built in 1962 from plans by Herman Jessor by the ILGWU (International Ladies' Garment Workers Union) as a middle-income housing co-op. Appropriately close to the Garment District, this mammoth urban-renewal project occupies 12 square blocks of former tenements, injecting new life into the Chelsea area.

11. The solid-looking Classic-style building across 23rd Street, **No. 322–324,** was built for the American Jersey Cattle Club. Look above for the stone escutcheons that represent the U.S. and the British island of Jersey. In recent years additional floors were added, and the building was converted to a condominium.

The **James N. Wells Real Estate Company,** at No. 340, is the oldest of its kind in Chelsea and dates back to 1819, when Wells began developing parts of Greenwich Village and later worked with Clement Clarke Moore on plans for Chelsea. He was also a skillful builder and was responsible for the construction of St. Luke's Church in Greenwich Village (where both Wells and Moore served as vestrymen). (More about James N. Wells later.)

12. Before the construction of the present **London Terrace Apartments** (occupying the entire block, Ninth to Tenth avenues, 23rd to 24th streets) in 1930, an earlier "London Terrace" stood on the site. Designed by famed architect Alexander Jackson Davis in 1845, the original row of Greek Revival buildings was set back from the street behind a shady garden and protected by an iron fence. A three-story-high colonnade ran the entire length of the row, giving the town houses an air of stately elegance. With the wealth of its prominent tenants, London Terrace was soon known as "Millionaires' Row." On the 24th Street side was a similar row of town houses, but only two stories high, called the Chelsea Cottages.

The new complex, built by Farrar & Watmaugh, is in reality two separate rows of interconnecting apartment buildings surrounding a central garden. In addition to the 1,670 units, there is a swimming pool, solarium, a number of stores, a bank, and a post office. When the new London Terrace opened in 1930, the doormen were uniformed as London "bobbies"—a touch of charming snobbery. After all, Chelsea was a London suburb, and this was thought to add upliftment to the area.

The Clement Clarke Moore residence stood alone in the block to the south until 1854 when land development forced the demolition of the large three-story house. (A plaque on No. 420 marks the site.) Dr. Moore spent his summers at Chelsea, his winters on Charlton Street in Greenwich Village, and occasionally stayed at a third home in the village of Newtown (now Elmhurst) in what is now the Borough of Queens.

12A. An optional side trip may be made to the landmark **Church of the Holy Apostles,** at Ninth Avenue and 28th Street. The church, designed by noted architect Minard Lafever in 1848–49, is quite handsome but fits into no particular architectural style; although some say it was a forerunner of the Italianate. Dominating the structure is the greatly oversized bronze and slate steeple, yet it is not incongruous among the towering apartment houses that surround it. Most attractive are the splendid stained-glass windows by William Jay Bolton, America's greatest stained-glass artisan of the time. The square glass panels with delicately painted circular medallions present a dazzling spectacle when

A rare view of the original London Terrace, on West 23rd Street between Ninth and Tenth avenues, designed in 1845 by Alexander Jackson Davis, and known then as "Millionaires' Row." A year after this photo was taken in 1929, the "Row," no longer favored by millionaires, was demolished and the new London Terrace Apartments were built. The old Ninth Avenue El in the background, as well as the crosstown trolley, are also gone. (The Consolidated Edison Company of New York)

The house of Clement Clarke Moore, author of "'Twas the Night before Christmas...," which stood alone on high ground between Ninth and Tenth avenues, 22nd to 23rd Street, until 1854, in a lithograph from Valentine's Manual *of the same year. (Museum of the City of New York)*

brightened by the rays of a late afternoon sun. The transepts were added in 1858, and were designed by another well-known architect, Richard Upjohn (& Sons). The Ninth Avenue El once clattered overhead and darkened the avenue, from the late 1870s to 1940. The church today is well-known for its program of feeding the poor and homeless.

In April 1990 the church suffered a devastating fire. Some of the magnificent Bolton stained-glass windows were lost and many were severely damaged, including the rose window. The church then undertook a major restoration project, including a careful replication of the missing glass. By the summer of 1993 work was completed, and once again the interior glistens in the afternoon sunlight.

Return to 23rd Street and continue south. Turn west (right) on 22nd Street. The tour route now enters the Chelsea Historic District.

13. Nos. 400–412, built in 1856 in the Italianate style, are known as the **James N. Wells Row.** These narrow houses were each designed with an English basement and small entranceways, and form a harmonious unit with their original roof cornice. All but one still retain their dormer windows; No. 408 is probably the best in the row, except for its modified windows; however, only No. 404 has its original doors.

No. 419–421, on the north side, were also built in 1856.

No. 414 (1835) dates from the decade of the Greek Revival, and was the residence of James N. Wells. An elegant mansion in its heyday, albeit in sad disrepair, it is the last surviving Greek Revival house with five bays (windows) in Manhattan.

It was remodeled 1864–66 in Italianate style, and in 1875 it was sold to the Samaritan Home for the Aged. In the 1930s the Salvation Army acquired it for a women's shelter. It is now a multiple-dwelling house, in rather rundown condition.

No. 436 was the **residence of actor Edwin Forrest** [*see* East Village, 16, for more about Edwin Forrest and the Astor Place Riot]. Built in 1835 in Greek Revival style, it was bought by Forrest in 1839 together with the adjoining properties, Nos. 430–434. It was rumored that Forrest wanted the house as a sanctuary from his numerous in-laws who had moved in with him and his new bride when he lived downtown. Some years later the house was acquired by Christian Herter, the former Secretary of State. Sadly, the house has suffered too many "modernizations" through the years and is now barely a shadow of its former self.

No. 444 (1835–36) is a well-restored Greek Revival–style house, and was the property of Clement Clarke Moore. Note particularly the charming attic windows set in a wooden frieze (fascia) board below the cornice.

Nos. 446 and 448, the Berrian-Walker Houses, were built in 1854 in the popular Italianate style of the middle decade of the 19th century. No. 448 unfortunately suffered a major renovation when its front wall was reconstructed with the addition of one bay per floor, instead of two, as with No. 446.

No. 450 is a handsome Greek Revival house with a high stoop and typical

Actor Edwin Forrest purchased this stately town house (No. 436 West 22nd Street) four years after it was built in 1835, allegedly as a sanctuary from bothersome in-laws. In more recent times it was the home of former Secretary of State Christian Herter. Unfortunately, a series of mindless "modernizations" have all but obscured its original appearance. (Museum of the City of New York)

The interior of No. 436 West 22nd Street after Edwin Forrest's death, when it was owned by I. W. Drummond at the turn of the century. (Museum of the City of New York)

basement windows. It has been very nicely refurbished and restored to its original appearance. It is gratifying to see a building correctly remodeled, rather than the more common "remuddled."

No. 453, across the street, is from the mid-1850s and has interesting ornate hooded lintels over the windows. **Nos. 457–477** are a splendidly restored row.

The L. Monette apartment building, **No. 454,** was built in 1897 in a neo-Renaissance style, and although a multifamily tenement house, is not an unpleasant addition to the street.

14. Clement Clarke Moore Park, on the southeast corner of Tenth Avenue, was designed by landscape architect Paul M. Friedberg as a multilevel play park, and was opened in 1968.

Turn left (south) on Tenth Avenue.

Before the successive landfill projects of the 19th century, the Hudson River shoreline extended to where the east side of Tenth Avenue is now. As the streets and avenues were pushed through, the hills were leveled, and the earth was used to reclaim the land to the west.

15. The Guardian Angel Roman Catholic Church (John Van Pelt, 1930), known familiarly as the Shrine Church of the Sea, was built in a fanciful Italian

Romanesque Revival style when the port of New York was much busier than it is now, and when much of the church's constituency came from the ships from far-flung parts of the world. It still serves a sea-oriented community.

On the east side of the avenue, **No. 188–192** (Andrew Spence, 1891) is a well-kept small tenement built in the Queen Anne style, still preserving its original storefronts. Note the oversize spandrels running the full height of the building, which may have covered chimney flues.

Turn east (left) on West 21st Street.

A pleasant feature of the north side of the street is the set-back arrangement of the houses, with a lush front yard complementing the dignified "halls of ivy" of the General Theological Seminary, across the street.

16. Nos. 473–465 are a well-preserved row of Greek Revival–style houses, built in the year 1853. **No. 471** is the best in the group, closest to the original design. Note the following architectural features of the houses: the bracketed entablature over the doorways, bracketed roof cornices, double-hung windows, the window lintels and window guards, cruciform paneled doors, and low stoops with cast-iron railings. Note the old Chelsea Square house numbers.

No. 463 was the first to be built on the block (1836) and dates from the Greek Revival period. Its brickwork is laid in Flemish bond (alternating short and long bricks, called "headers" and "stretchers"). Pedimented lintels cap the windows, and the attic windows are set in a wooden fascia board.

Nos. 461–459, two rowhouses converted to apartments, were built separately in 1854. The pair is called the William Cummings House after a descendant of the original owner of No. 461, Thomas Cummings, and both are typical brownstones in the Italianate style. Compare them with adjacent **457** and **455**. The latter two, built in the same year, are of a somewhat different style. Note the difference in height of the stoops. Thoughtless renovations over the years have destroyed the symmetry of the row of houses.

 No. 453 (1857) still preserves its splendid entranceway. Crowning the stoop with its cast-iron railings is an arched doorway, above which a huge cornice slab rests on stuccoed consoles. The house has been listed on the National Register of Historic Places.

No. 445 (1898) is another neo-Renaissance-style apartment house. Built of Roman brick and stone, it is typical of the so-called Eclectic Period of the late 1890s. **No. 441** has been well restored and maintained.

The brownstone doorway of **No. 407** (1852) is well preserved, although little else on the façade is. Note the carved head in the keystone of the arch and the doorway pediment supported by a pair of ornate consoles.

No. 405, the last in the row of set-back houses, has been refaced with "brownstone" concrete which thoroughly destroyed all the former Italianate features. How this disaster escaped the watchful eye of the Landmarks Commission is a mystery, especially since the Commission had called it "one of the purest examples of this style in Chelsea."

17. Delightful No. 401, listed officially as **No. 183 Ninth Avenue,** was built in

1831–32, and is the second oldest house in the Historic District. It still preserves much of its original Federal-style appearance, and can best be viewed from across the street. The four-sided pitched roof, dormer windows, simple cornice above an equally simple fascia board, and side entrance are typical elements of the Federal style. The brickwork is in Flemish bond, the more expensive way of laying bricks, evidence of a wealthy original owner. Look up at the painted sign on adjacent No. 191 Ninth Avenue, advertising the James N. Wells & Son Real Estate firm. Wells lived in No. 183 in 1833–34 and maintained his office on the second floor, where his descendants carried on for many years. The sign itself is probably over 100 years old. The ground-floor store was incorporated into the building very early in 1835. Note, too, the Historic District plaque on the 21st Street side.

The three small wooden houses to the right, **Nos. 185, 187, and 189,** were all built for Wells, No. 185 in 1856, the other pair in 1857. Wooden houses are now a rarity in Manhattan, and these three, while not as old as they appear, add considerable charm. In 1934 the Wells office moved to the 23rd Street site.

18. The General Theological Seminary, No. 175 Ninth Avenue, occupies the entire block from Ninth to Tenth avenues, and 21st to 20th streets. The plot, known as **Chelsea Square,** was donated to the seminary by Dr. Clement Clarke Moore, himself a professor of Biblical Learning at the institution. The lovely campus with its shady lawns and small-town college atmosphere is a veritable oasis in the city; it is open to the public Mon.–Fri. 12 noon to 3:00 P.M., Sat. 11 A.M. to 3:00 P.M., Sun. 2:00 P.M. to 4:00 P.M.

The modern building facing Ninth Avenue houses the administrative offices and the excellent St. Mark's Library; but one must first pass through the large entranceway into the inner quadrangle to appreciate the old-world quality of the campus.

Construction of the Episcopal Seminary began in 1825 with a Gothic-style East Building (now demolished), and was followed in 1836 by a counterpart on the west side, which still remains as a fine academic building. Early seminarians

The Gothic-style General Theological Seminary on Chelsea Square in an 1841 lithograph, as seen from Ninth Avenue between 20th and 21st streets. (New-York Historical Society)

had an unobstructed view of the Hudson, as the riverbank reached the western edge of Chelsea Square. The completion of most of the seminary complex was accomplished during the brief period 1883–1902, when Eugene Augustus Hoffman, the third dean of the school, revolutionized the physical setting by engaging architect Charles Coolidge Haight to create a master plan for a campus equal to that of most American colleges of the day. Through Hoffman's own financial contributions and his ability to interest wealthy laymen, an endowment was established for professorships and the groundwork laid for the development of a great theological library.

The St. Mark's Library, which was completed in 1960, replaced Haight's original building and contains 210,000 volumes in its extensive reference collection. It is **the nation's greatest ecclesiastical library** and has the largest collection of Latin Bibles in the world! Among the Rare Book Room's treasures are a number of medieval manuscripts, prayer books, and psalters, and a unique Latin choir book that honors John Hus as a martyr.

Haight's plan called for an arrangement of buildings roughly in the shape of a letter "E" with the spine along West 21st Street. The style of construction was one that he himself pioneered, the English Collegiate Gothic. Centrally placed is the **Chapel of the Good Shepherd,** dominated by a 161-foot-high square **Bell Tower** modeled after that at Magdalen College, Oxford. Interestingly, the interior of the chapel is devoted mainly to choir stalls, since most of the communicants are postulants for Holy Orders. The spectacular bronze doors, by J. Massey Rhind, were executed in 1899, in memory of Dean Hoffman's son.

Sherred Hall, a three-story classroom building flanked by dormitories, was the first to be erected, and expresses beautifully the simple quality and uniform character sought by the architect. Its arched main entrance is especially noteworthy.

The culmination of the building plan came with the opening of handsome **Hoffman Hall,** the refectory-gymnasium building. The enormous dining hall, like a medieval knights' council chamber, re-creates an atmosphere of the Middle Ages. The huge fireplaces at each end, a musicians' gallery, a coffered barrel-vaulted ceiling, and a stained-glass bay window, combine to make it one of New York City's most beautiful interior spaces.

On leaving the Seminary grounds, turn right, and right again into West 20th Street.

19. No. 402, a Renaissance-style apartment house, was designed in 1897 by C. P. H. Gilbert, the architect of mansions for Felix Warburg (Jewish Museum), Joseph A. De Lamar (Polish Consulate), and Otto Kahn (Convent of the Sacred Heart), and a host of other well-heeled clients. The name "DONAC" is an acronym for the original land owner, Don Alonzo Cushman. Tenants have a pleasant view down West 20th Street through their large concave bay windows.

No. 404 is the oldest house in the Historic District. Built in 1829–30, it still retains one clapboard side wall. A Federal-style house, it later received a Greek Revival doorway, had its roof raised one story, and in the 1850s was modified with Italianate parlor-floor windows.

An 1854 engraving of Gothic Revival row houses which once lined 20th Street at the corner of Sixth Avenue before the arrival of the parade of Fashion Row department stores. (Museum of the City of New York)

20. Nos. 406–418, built for Don Alonzo Cushman in 1839–40, ranks among the most beautiful Greek Revival rows of town houses in the country. Equal in many respects to "The Row" on Washington Square North [*see* Greenwich Village, 3, 5], this group of seven pristine houses, called **"Cushman Row,"** displays a wealth of architectural detail. The ten-foot front yards are a most agreeable complement to the greenery of the Seminary across the street. No. 408 has been nicely restored, except for the gable. Notice the pineapples, a traditional symbol of welcome, atop the newels in front of Nos. 416 and 418. Exceptional are the charming attic windows encircled by cast-iron wreaths. Note, too, the well proportioned entablatures over the doorways, set on Doric pilasters, the molded window lintels and the six-over-six windows, typical elements of the Green Revival style.

Don Alonzo Cushman (1792–1875) was a successful dry-goods merchant ("Don" *was* his first name, not a title) who became associated with Clement Clarke Moore and James N. Wells. He was a founder of the Greenwich Savings Bank—one of the first savings institutions in the city, now part of Crossland Savings Bank. With his later involvement in real estate, he helped influence the development and shape the character of the Chelsea neighborhood.

Return to Ninth Avenue.

21. The large Greek Revival–style house on the southeast corner, **No. 162 Ninth Avenue,** was a long-time residence of James N. Wells (he lived briefly at No. 414–416 West 22nd Street, and his offices were seen earlier at No. 183 Ninth Avenue). Built in 1834, it was one of the most imposing residences in Chelsea. Although somewhat modified, it still retains its original wide doorway, fluted Doric columns topped by a large entablature, and pedimented window lintels. The rambling, former *one*-family mansion is now a co-op occupied by many.

Cross Ninth Avenue and continue east on West 20th Street.

22. The group of four Italianate buildings on the north side of West 20th Street (**Nos. 361–355**) were built for Don Alonzo Cushman. No. 361 was built in 1860, the other three in 1858. Although somewhat altered, they present a fine row of houses. The late 19th-century ironwork on the stoops is very attractive, as are the rope moldings on the inner doorways. No. 353 still preserves its original ornate cast-iron railings. Note the dormers, too.

23. On the south side, another Italianate row (**Nos. 348–358**) was built in 1853–54 for the six children of James N. Wells. Each house is only two bays wide and set behind a small front yard. The Landmarks Commission describes it as "one of the longest and most charming of the rows of English basement houses to be found in Chelsea." It is unfortunate that each house has suffered some alteration; however, Nos. 348 and 352 are probably closest to the original design. Note the "ear panels" on the doors of No. 358. The entire row of buildings is unified by its original cornice line, which has survived unscathed.

24. The **St. Peter's Church group,** consisting of rectory, church, and parish hall, was, like its nearby neighbor the General Theological Seminary, built on land donated to the institution by Dr. Clement Clarke Moore. The cornerstone for the original chapel, which is now the **Rectory Building,** was laid in 1832, making it the oldest church building in Chelsea and one of the oldest Greek Revival–style buildings in the city. It once had full-height Doric columns, but these were removed and replaced with unusual brick pilasters.

The **church building** was completed in 1838 in Gothic Revival style, and is considered a fine model of the English parish Gothic church—the first of its style in this country. Dr. Moore served as vestryman and organist for a number of years, and it is said that he was responsible for the selection of the church's design. Among the names on the cornerstone are those of Dr. Moore, James N. Wells, and architect-builder James W. Smith, himself a resident of Chelsea. The church building is virtually unchanged except for the loss of its beautiful Gothic wooden porches, which had to be removed because of rotting. The marks left by the old porches can still be seen on the church walls. Unlike the usual Gothic church built in cruciform shape, St. Peter's is built on the plan of a Greek temple. The pulpit, chancel rail, and lectern were presented as a memorial to Don Alonzo Cushman by members of his family.

The **Parish Hall,** called St. Peter's Hall, completes the group. It was designed in 1871 in the so-called Victorian Gothic style, and now houses the

Atlantic Theater Company. The ornamental **wrought-iron fence** that embraces the three buildings is from Trinity Church downtown and was a gift from Trinity Church in 1837. Two years later the downtown church was razed and the present Trinity Church erected.

25. No. 331, on the north side of the street, is a rather late Greek Revival house, built in 1846. The side door opens on a passageway leading to a rear building. Although it is the only one in the Historic District with such a feature, nearby Nos. 311 to 305 have similar passageways, the latter has a see-through gate. Occasionally called "horsewalks," they also provided access to rear stables.

End of tour. The Eighth Avenue A and E lines are three blocks north at 23rd Street. The Broadway–Seventh Avenue line is at 23rd Street and Seventh Avenue. The F and PATH lines are at 23rd Street and Avenue of the Americas (Sixth Avenue).

UNITED NATIONS

U.N. PLAZA   1ST AVE.

Tudor City Place

2ND AVE.

EAST 43RD ST.
EAST 42ND ST.
EAST 41ST ST.

3RD AVE.

LEXINGTON AVE.

Grand Central Terminal   PARK AVE. VIADUCT

VANDERBILT AVE.

MADISON AVE.

5TH AVE.

N.Y. Public Library

Bryant Park

AVE. OF THE AMERICAS

BROADWAY

Times Square

7TH AVE.   7TH AVE.

BROADWAY

WEST 44TH ST.
WEST 43RD ST.
WEST 42ND ST.
WEST 41ST ST.
WEST 40TH ST.

8TH AVE.

Start

42nd STREET
Eighth Avenue
to Tudor City Place

12. Forty-Second Street

Come and meet those dancing feet,
On the avenue I'm taking you to,
Forty-Second Street.
Hear the beat of dancing feet,
It's the song I love the melody of,
Forty-Second Street.

Little "nifties" from the Fifties, innocent and sweet,
Sexy ladies from the Eighties, who are indiscreet.
They're side by side,
They're glorified.
Where the underworld can meet the elite,
Naughty, bawdy, gawdy, sporty,
*Forty-Second Street.**

[Words by Al Dubin, Music by Harry Warren]

[Eighth Avenue A, C, E lines to 42nd Street; M42 crosstown bus to Eighth Avenue; buses from New Jersey to the Port Authority Bus Terminal]

Few thoroughfares in the world are as well known or as widely diversified as 42nd Street—New York's major crosstown artery for almost three-quarters of a century. Considered by New Yorkers as the center of the city and, at its intersection with Broadway, the center of the world, it slices the middle of Manhattan horizontally from the Hudson to the East River. Although the street was opened

Construction of the Ninth Avenue El (the New York Elevated Railroad) station at 42nd Street, 1875–76. (Museum of the City of New York)

officially in 1836 with the removal of squatters' shanties and the filling in of the *Grote Kil* (Big Stream), the real history of 42nd Street begins late in the 19th century, and will be discussed block by block on the tour.

Before beginning the tour, you might want to take a quick stroll west on 42nd Street between Ninth and Tenth Avenues. On the north side, the twin 45-story **Manhattan Plaza** towers (David Todd & Associates, 1977) provide federally subsidized rents to performing artists. Directly across the street is the off-Broadway **Theatre Row,** a group of ten playhouses carved out of former warehouses, sleazy tenements, and a few disreputable "entertainment" establishments. The project was created by the nonprofit 42nd Street Development Corporation, in cooperation with a group of theater pioneers, the City and State governments, private industry, and concerned citizens. The theaters are a bold experiment and a major phase in the revitalization of a once badly deteriorating neighborhood. Thus, with performing artists living in close proximity to a new and lively extension of the theater district, the contagion of this development can only spread, for the betterment of the entire area. Along the street are a number of theater-related restaurants and a theater bookshop.

The tour begins in front of the old McGraw-Hill Building, 330 West 42nd Street, west of Eighth Avenue.

New York's "green skyscraper," the **former McGraw-Hill Building,** was completed in 1931 from plans by architect Raymond M. Hood, in collaboration with Fouilhoux & Godley, in a unique variation of the Art Deco theme. The building's shape, with its series of setbacks, was dictated by the Zoning Resolution of 1916, and architect Hood exploited these requirements boldly and effectively. Unusual are the metallic bands of green, silver, and gold that encircle the ground floor and continue into the lobby; while on the façade above, row upon row of bluish-green terra-cotta bands continue the motif. Two other examples of Hood's ingenuity will be seen later. When the McGraw-Hill Publishing Company opened its new office skyscraper at 1221 Avenue of the Americas, fear was expressed for the future of the lovely green tower. However, in late 1974, Group Health Incorporated (GHI) took possession of it for its own corporate headquarters.

When you reach Eighth Avenue, look back at the building and notice the steel-framework sculpture projecting from the 32nd floor—Owen Morrel's *Boomerang.*

The Holy Cross Roman Catholic Church (Henry Engelbert, 1870), with its prominent verdigris dome, hearkens back to the time when the neighborhood was predominantly Irish and known as "Hell's Kitchen." An area of small factories and blocks of festering slums, it was one of the most notorious sections of the city, where even the police walked in fear and only in broad daylight. The church now ministers to a somewhat smaller, if more peaceful community. The simple exterior, in a transitional Byzantine style, belies the ornateness of the spacious interior. In a mixture of styles, primarily Italian Baroque, the architect has created an impressive nave and sanctuary. Observe the high barrel-vaulted ceiling, the wooden balcony, the fine paintings of Peter, Paul, and Jesus in the apse, and the Tiffany windows in the clerestory as well as the circular windows in the transept. The cupola was also decorated by Tiffany. This was famous Father Duffy's Church for many years—Francis P. Duffy, who worked so hard to uplift the old "Hell's Kitchen" neighborhood and break up the tough gangs that gave it such an unsavory reputation. It was Father Duffy who was closely associated with many theater personalities, and who served as chaplain of the "Fighting 69th" Division (actually the 165th Infantry Regiment) in the trenches of France during World War I. He served until his death in 1932, and an appreciative Broadway community erected a statue of him in Times Square.

A surviving row of tenement houses (ca. 1875) ends at No. 319 West, which is painted in "patriotic" colors to advertise the **Kaufman Army & Navy Store.** A local landmark for years, its pair of World War I French Hotchkiss cannons guarding the door are about the only military surplus items not for sale.

The **Port Authority Bus Terminal,** the largest in the world, was opened in 1950, with the striking addition between 41st and 42nd streets completed in 1981 from plans by the architects and engineers of the Port Authority of New York & New Jersey Terminal Department. It has twin levels of bus ramps and serves 190,000 daily commuters from New Jersey, as well as long-distance bus riders. The upper levels are dominated by the dark brown steel trusses which project over sidewalk arcades. Walk up to the main ticketing area of the south wing to see sculptor George Segal's grouping of three white-painted bronze *Commuters* waiting for their bus. (Segal, himself, is a bus commuter.)

The block between Eighth and Seventh avenues until recently was generally referred to as New York's **"Sin Street."** More seedy than sinful, it boasts no fewer than 15 movie houses (count 'em!)—possibly a world record. The theaters—many closed for renovation or for conversion into legitimate theaters, were known for their wide range of films, including first-runs, foreign films, "oldies," and X-rated. Crowded cheek by jowl among the "flicks" are a dismal aggregation of "adult" video stores, peep shows, and X-rated movies. All are gradually being forced out (to open elsewhere, alas), and "Sin Street" will be sinful no more. The block had become a popular promenade with the more earthy elements of New York society and was regularly the target of (unsuccessful) clean-up campaigns by City Hall. Many of the older movie houses were once legitimate theaters and still show architectural traces of their more glamorous past behind garish new marquees. Plans have been drawn to rebuild the east side of Eighth Avenue, north and south of 42nd Street, to a wholesale trade center, and the New York Mart will rebuild the area between 40th and 42nd streets; another developer will work on the blocks to the north.

Walking east we pass the following theaters (those that are among the 45 theaters in the midtown area that have been designated as landmarks are indicated with an asterisk): the **Empire* (formerly the Eltinge), No. 236 (1912); the **Liberty,* No. 234 (1904); the **Harris* (formerly the Chandler, the Cohan & Harris, and the Sam H. Harris), No. 226 (1914); the **Selwyn,* No. 229 (1918); the **Times Square,* No. 219 (1920); and at the same address, but with its façade facing West 43rd Street, the **New Apollo* (1920); the **Lyric,* No. 213 (1903);

The north side of 42nd Street just west of Times Square, ca. 1910, showing the Lyric and Belasco theaters. Oscar Hammerstein's Victoria faces Times Square at right. (Photograph by Byron. The Byron Collection, Museum of the City of New York)

The picturesque Casino Theater was built in 1882 on the southeast corner of Broadway and 39th Street as a concert hall, but played mostly comic operas. In this Byron photograph taken around 1900, shortly before it was acquired by the Shuberts, the Arabesque-style building is covered with advertisements for a long-forgotten musical. The Casino Theater survived until 1930. (The Byron Collection. Museum of the City of New York)

Posing for an unknown photographer in front of the Casino Theater entrance in 1924 is stage-door tender William Reilly. The gas lamp once stood in front of the Hoffman House Café, at Broadway and 26th Street; and was placed at the theater to recognize the 72-year-old Reilly's former career as a member of the city's once vast army of lamplighters. (The Consolidated Edison Company of New York)

Looking west on 42nd Street from in front of the original Grand Central Depot in the late 1890s. Just beyond is the newly opened Hotel Manhattan, at the corner of Madison Avenue, now the site of the Sperry & Hutchinson Building. (Museum of the City of New York)

and the *Victory (formerly the Belasco—not to be confused with the present Belasco Theater on West 44th Street), No. 207 (1900).

Perhaps the finest in the block is the landmark New Amsterdam, No. 214 (Herts & Tallant, 1903), with both exterior and interior designated. Considered the most opulent theater in America, it was the first to be designed with an Art Nouveau interior. Florenz Ziegfeld, owner for a time, remodeled the roof garden into a second theater, the *Aerial Gardens*. Unfortunately, the restoration work on this splendid theater has come to a halt due to the enormous cost of unexpected structural repairs; however, its new owner Disney has promised to rehabilitate the theater by 1996, this may help revitalize the street.

Just to the right of the Selwyn Theater, look north to the fancifully ornate building which rises above 43rd Street with a black peaked roof perforated with little dormer windows, and surmounted by a lantern. Built for the New York Times (Ludlow & Peabody, 1913, additions, 1923 and 1948) when it shifted operations from its Tower on Times Square, it is a handsome structure in German Renaissance style, virtually hidden by its newer neighbors.

Of some architectural interest is the way-out-of-scale Candler Building (No. 220 West), rising high above its sleazy surroundings, and best viewed from across the street. Designed by Willauer, Shape & Bready and completed in 1916, it represents no particular architectural style (some might call it Eclectic) but it does have a pleasing, if somewhat grimy façade flanked by its slanted parapet "shoulder" buildings. The building is named for the owner of the Coca Cola Company, Asa G. Candler, who in 1912 acquired the property and had the structure built for his offices. The ground floor was occupied by a branch of the Exchange Buffet, New York's pioneer chain of "honor system" cafeterias, now long since defunct, in which patrons merely informed the cashier on leaving what they had eaten, and were charged accordingly. (Spotters were stationed inconspicuously to verify diner's purchases.)

Cross Seventh Avenue, turn left and cross 42nd Street, walk past the former Times Tower to Times Square, and proceed north along the east side of Times Square.

Known universally as "The Crossroads of the World," Times Square is the heart of the entertainment district, and has been for almost a century. In the 1880s and 1890s, the two vertical triangles forming the "square" were lined with carriage dealers and called Longacre Square, after a London district (the name lives on in the nearby *Longacre Theater* and *Longacre Hotel*). Then the Rialto arrived! The Metropolitan Opera House opened just to the south, at 39th Street and Broadway, in 1893; Charles Frohman built his large Empire theater across the street in 1894; Oscar Hammerstein (*père*) moved up from his 34th Street Manhattan Opera House site to open the dazzling Olympia Music Hall in 1895. The Olympia, looking for all the world like a Renaissance palace, occupied the entire Broadway blockfront from 44th to 45th streets, had a roof garden, café, concert hall, and theater, and was the talk of the town. Hammerstein also built the lavish Victoria Theater on the northwest corner of 42nd Street, where the

Times Square in 1900—then called Longacre Square—looking south from 45th Street, with the New York and Criterion theaters at left, and Rector's famous restaurant and the Hotel Cadillac in the next block. (Photograph by Byron. The Byron Collection. Museum of the City of New York)

Rialto Theater is now. Others soon followed, one more grandiose than the other, offering not only legitimate theater, but vaudeville, cabaret, and music-hall entertainment. Many even had roof gardens with luxurious restaurants. And to further satisfy the appetites of the new theater crowds came such establishments as Shanley's, Rector's, Churchill's, and the Café de l'Opéra. Broadway is still synonymous with the stage, but only about three dozen legitimate theaters survive in the immediate Times Square area; and very few new theaters have been built in the past 25 years. Most are clustered in the blocks west of Broadway, between 44th and 52nd streets. Little Shubert Alley, connecting 44th and 45th streets, still evokes the glamour of "show biz," surrounded as it is by a number of theaters with brightly illuminated marquees.

With the rise of the film industry in the 1920s, enormous and opulent movie palaces opened along Broadway, displacing the "legit" theaters to the west. Who can forget such names as the Palace, Strand, Capitol, Paramount, Rialto, Rivoli, Warner (where in 1927 New Yorkers were treated to the first sound film, Al Jolson in *The Jazz Singer*), and the most lavish of them all, the Roxy? Some still remain, but mostly in name only. The Paramount Film Corporation erected the massive theater and office building on the west side of the square, between 43rd and 44th streets, a unique addition to the cityscape. The incredible shape of the

New York Paramount Building (Rapp & Rapp, 1927), with nine ascending set-backs on each side, gives it the appearance of a symmetrical pile of gargantuan children's building blocks assembled by some young Gulliver. The setback style resulted from the Zoning Resolution of 1916. The tower clocks and black glass are pure Art Deco, but the rest is neo-Classical. The once-lavish Paramount Theater, however, has disappeared, replaced by office space.

With the arrival of New York's first subway line in 1904, *New York Times* publisher Adolph Ochs astonished his contemporaries by moving out of "Newspaper Row" downtown and erecting his famous wedge-shaped **Times Tower** (Eidlitz & MacKenzie) at the intersection of 42nd Street, Broadway, and Seventh Avenue. Ochs persuaded the city fathers to name the new subway station after the *Times,* and with that, the name of the square soon followed. Built of pink granite in Italian Renaissance style, and decorated with glazed terra cotta, the Times Tower became the dominant landmark on the Square. When the *Times* moved in on New Year's Eve of 1904, its fireworks display was to start a tradition with New Yorkers. Each December 31 since 1908, enormous throngs of revelers gather before the Tower awaiting the descent of the famous illuminated ball announcing the arrival of the New Year. Even after the newspaper moved all of its operations into its former annex on West 43rd Street, and the Times Tower

The Pabst Hotel, on 42nd Street, facing away from Longacre Square. The hotel and adjoining four-story buildings were demolished in 1903 to make way for the Times Tower. (Photograph by Byron. The Byron Collection. Museum of the City of New York)

was reconstructed as the Allied Chemical Tower, the old custom was preserved. Another hallmark of the former building is the electric news **Motogram** with its 14,800 bulbs that flashes headlines around the building. When Allied Chemical vacated the old Times Tower in 1975, the building was purchased by real estate developer Alex Parker and renamed **No. One Times Square.** Renovation plans called for sheathing the east and west walls with 5-by-7-foot mirrors, but the scheme was never carried out. The building is now just an office tower and the old Times Building must now endure the indignity of an advertisement at the very top for *New York Newsday!* On the north side of the building is a new generation of signage, the SONY JumboTron video screen, the largest permanent system of its kind yet to be installed outdoors in the United States.

Hotels also were built in the new theater district. For some 60 years the *grande dame* of them all, the **Hotel Astor,** was a familiar site on Times Square.

Commissioned by William Waldorf Astor, it was built in an exuberant Beaux Arts style with a huge mansard roof, opening its doors in 1904 on the block between 44th and 45th streets. In 1969, it was replaced by the 53-story office tower, designed by Kahn & Jacobs for the now-defunct W. T. Grant Company. By changing its 1515 Broadway address to **One Astor Plaza,** it keeps the old hotel's name alive. From a distance the odd concrete "wings" atop the structure add a gaudy and bizarre (and not wholly inappropriate) touch to the Times Square scene. The building houses one of the new Broadway theaters, the Minskoff, and it has the distinction of being the first structure to take advantage of the new zoning laws which permit greater height in exchange for space set aside for a theater (it has a movie theater as well).

Detour briefly east on 45th Street to the **Lyceum Theater.** Built by Herts & Tallant in 1903 in a florid and strong Beaux Arts style, it is the oldest house in the city still serving the legitimate stage, and possibly the most beautiful; and narrowly missed the wreckers' ball not long ago. Both the interior and exterior are designated landmarks. From its opening and for almost four decades, the Lyceum was managed by impresario Daniel Frohman, who lived above the theater in a private suite, and often kept an eye on the stage below through a small trapdoor. The former Frohman suite is now the office of the **Shubert Archive,** said to be the world's largest theatrical collection housed under one roof.

At the northeast corner of 46th Street is the I. Miller Building, once the showplace of the well-known women's shoe manufacturer. On the south façade (at second-floor level) are a **row of sculptures by A. Stirling Calder,** depicting Ethel Barrymore as *Ophelia,* Marilyn Miller as *Sunny,* Mary Pickford as *Little Lord Fauntleroy,* and Rosa Ponselle as *Norma.* (Are there other figures hidden behind the enormous, ugly sign facing the Square?)

The traffic pattern in Times Square is much saner since the one-way routing was established. Before World War II, the scene was always one of bedlam, or at least total chaos. Adding to the confusion created by the number of intersecting streets were the trolley lines that crisscrossed Times Square on both Broadway and Seventh Avenue. The 42nd Street crosstown car, which either went west to the 42nd Street ferry or turned north on Broadway, contributed further to the disorder.

The upper "V" of Times Square is known as **Father Duffy Square.** His statue (Charles Keck, 1937) in front of a Celtic cross stands close by that of **George M. Cohan** (Georg Lober, 1959), "giving his regards to Broadway." The adjacent **TKTS booth,** established in 1973, sells half-price tickets to Broadway shows to those who line up on the day of the performance. It is a highly popular addition to the square, adding much-needed cultural upliftment to the rather sordid street scene. The attractive canvas and tubular-steel structure was designed by Mayers & Schiff.

At the northern end of Times Square, and virtually hidden by the stack of bright signs, is the new **Renaissance Hotel,** 714 Seventh Avenue (Di Leonardo International, 1992). The dark-glass curtain-wall structure is best seen from the side.

The **"Great White Way,"** as Broadway's theater district has been called, is today brighter than ever. The name is attributed to outdoor-advertising executive O. J. Gude, who in 1901 conceived the idea of erecting very large electrical display signs to promote commercial products and theatrical performances. These signs were to be placed in the busiest and most conspicuous locations, and he settled on Times Square as the most appropriate site. Through the years the neon signs of Times Square have been one of its stellar attractions, particularly at night when the multicolored flashing advertisements create an almost magical atmosphere. Many of the designs were created by Douglas Leigh, who is responsible for the lovely floodlight illumination on many of New York's skyscrapers; and the builder and installer is the Artkraft Straus Sign Corporation. The redevelopment guidelines established by the city for Times Square now require that any new building erected between 42nd and 50th streets devote the first 120 feet of its façade to illuminated signs. By keeping those colorful, blinking, and dazzling neon and laser signs, they will maintain the tradition of the bright lights and glitter that has made Times Square such a glamorous tourist attraction.

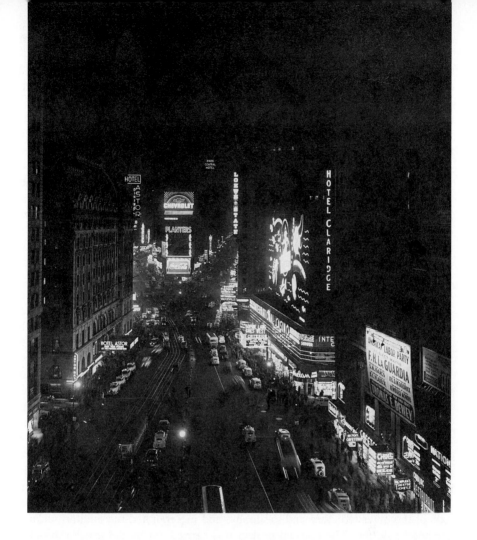

Times Square by night is a scene familiar to all, although there have been many changes since this photo was taken at the outbreak of World War II. Within a few months the bright lights would be dimmed for the duration of the war; gasoline rationing had already reduced the number of autos, leaving half-empty Broadway and Seventh Avenue to the trolleys and taxicabs. At left is the Hotel Astor, and across the Square is the famous Wrigley Chewing Gum sign atop the Criterion Theater. At the lower right, a billboard promotes the re-election campaigns of Mayor Fiorello H. LaGuardia and then–District Attorney Thomas E. Dewey. (Museum of the City of New York)

On reaching the north end of Times Square, turn around and begin walking down the *west* side.

At 1557 Broadway, hidden behind the tacky sheet metal and plastic are the invisible remains of **New York's first Automat.** Joseph V. Horn and Frank Hardart began operations in Philadelphia and came to New York in 1912. Then followed the ubiquitous chain of popular self-serve establishments that dispensed food at the turn of a knob and drinks at the pull of a crank. In its heyday in 1922 there were 21 Automats in the city. By 1991 the last one, at 200 East 42nd Street, albeit an ersatz copy, closed its doors, and the city lost a great amenity.

The first major hotel to be build on Times Square in more than 75 years was the **Marriott Marquis Hotel,** between West 45th and West 46th streets, designed by John Portman and completed in 1985. Its conception created a storm of protest which continued for several years, as plans called for the demolition of five legitimate theaters, the Astor, Bijou, Gaiety, Helen Hayes (former), and Morosco—playhouses that were revered by theatergoers and actors alike. Tumultuous demonstrations and repeated court challenges preceded the bulldozers, which finally leveled the site (including part of the Helen Hayes Theater's façade that was supposed to have been saved) in the spring of 1982. As a result of this tragic loss, and to prevent similar destruction of other legitimate theaters, the Landmarks Commission soon thereafter designated the exteriors and/or interiors of 45 playhouses in the midtown area.

Pause for a moment to study the new construction that has changed the face of the *east* side of Times Square. Occupying the entire block from 45th to 46th street, directly opposite, is the 44-story Bertelsmann Building, **No. 1540 Broadway** (Skidmore Owings & Merrill, 1989–93). A post-modern mixed-use building, it is sheathed in four contrasting bands of blue and green glass, and sports a novel 100-foot-high steel-framed spire. Its predecessor on the site was the 1920 Loews State Theater Building. The new structure continues the film industry tradition by offering not one, but four movie houses as part of a six-level entertainment and shopping complex.

Looking north at the southeast corner of 47th Street and Broadway is the **Embassy Suites Hotel** (Fox & Fowle, 1990). An interesting feature of this 43-story building is how it was designed to accommodate the famous old ***Palace Theater** (1913), whose interior is a designated landmark. The builders removed part of the outer structure and the lobby, and incorporated the auditorium into the hotel's design. The unusual project was carried out by the installation of a 135-foot truss, 45 feet high, set over four massive columns to span across the theater like a bridge.

In the midblock between 44th and 45th streets, halfway down the block toward Avenue of the Americas, is the **Hotel Macklowe** (Perkins & Will, with William Derman, AIA, 1991). The prominent 52-story gray-greeen glass curtain-wall tower has entrances on both streets, and is physically connected to the adjacent ***Hudson Theater** (J.B. McElfatrick & Co., 1903), currently under restoration as part of the compromise for the height of the Macklowe. If time permits, you might want to just skip over there, not only to see how the Hudson Theater was refurbished and tied to the hotel, but also to see the **former Lamb's Club Building,** No. 130 West 44th Street, now home to the Lamb's Theatre and the Manhattan Church of the Nazarene. The neo-Georgian–style building was designed for this famous actors' club by Stanford White of the firm of McKim, Mead & White, in 1905. Playwright **Eugene O'Neill** (1888–1955) was born in the Barrett House, which once stood on the southeast corner of 44th Street. Then return to the west side of Times Square.

At the south end of Times Square, between 43rd and 44th streets, is **1500 Broadway** (Leo Kornblath, 1972), a 33-story tower sheathed in black glass. One of the first high-rises to be erected on Times Square, it underwent a major renovation in 1989. Although it keeps its ground-floor movie house, new additions are a four-story granite portal and a domed rotunda.

Turn west on 45th Street to Shubert Alley. Walk down the Alley and turn left on 44th Street to Times Square again.

In this short loop of part of the theater district, one can see no fewer than 13 playhouses! **The *Booth** (Henry B. Herts, 1913) recalls the name of actor Edwin Booth, America's favorite in the late 19th century. (He built his own theater at Sixth Avenue and 23rd Street, which he managed and acted in from 1869 to 1883.) The ***Sam S. Shubert** (same architect and date as the Booth) honors the great impresario whose name is synonymous with show business.

Return to 42nd Street and cross to the south side, between Seventh Avenue and Broadway. At this writing, plans are still under way to redevelop Times Square, or at least the southern section, into a new overall commercial environment. It is an interesting idea that is supposed to upgrade the area and make it attractive to business and provide an upscale retail shopping district. However, fears have been expressed that the change, which includes the construction of four gigantic towers at the intersection of Broadway, Seventh Avenue, and 42nd Street when the market for office space improves, will create a sterile, dull environment that ultimately will destroy the charm and glitter of Times Square. For the moment, the tower plan is on hold. Plans have been approved, however, for the complete refurbishment of the Times Square subway station, a project that will continue until the end of the century.

At the southeast corner of 42nd Street and Seventh Avenue is the **former Knickerbocker Hotel** (Marvin & Davis and Bruce Price, 1902), commissioned by John Jacob Astor IV. Built two years before his Hotel Astor, it is the sole survivor of many Times Square hostelries built at the turn of the century, and was one of the most fashionable. Its King Cole Bar with Maxfield Parrish mural attracted many luminaries from the entertainment world, including George M. Cohan and Enrico Caruso, who often serenaded appreciative crowds from the balcony of his suite. Note the crowning mansard roof of this red-brick and limestone Renaissance Eclectic building. In a later incarnation it became the Newsweek Building, and now is known merely as 142 West 42nd Street. The Parrish mural was rescued and graces a bar with the same King Cole name at the St. Regis–Sheraton Hotel, uptown.

Continue east on 42nd Street.

The traffic congestion on 42nd Street, which seems to worsen every year, may soon be alleviated if a new plan, presently under serious consideration by the city, is put into effect. The recommendation is to make 42nd Street one-way, with motor vehicle traffic confined to the north side, and to install a new **light**

rail trolley on the south side. Although the last streetcar ran on 42nd Street in 1946, these lightweight, energy-efficient and speedy trolleys—so popular in many cities around the world—should help reduce traffic volume and pollution. If all goes according to plan, they will be running from the United Nations to the Hudson River and the Javits Center by 1995.

Midway down the block, on the south side, stands the cathedrallike **former Bush Terminal Building** (No. 130 West), now the Bush Tower. It was erected in 1918 from plans by Helmle & Corbett; however, the architects seemed to have had a later tenant in mind when they designed this neo-Gothic-style building. For many years until the structure was renovated, it had been the home of the Wurlitzer Music Company. Although gone from New York, it is worthy of mention because of the firm's long and close association with the city. Founded in 1856 by Rudolph Wurlitzer, they made band instruments, and during the Civil War supplied the Union Army bands. They later specialized in keyboard instruments, and for a time also made juke boxes. In the 1930s they built the largest organ in the city, the "Mighty Wurlitzer" for Radio City Music Hall, and another almost as large for the Brooklyn Paramount Theater.

Notice the *trompe l'oeil* effect on the side walls of the building, where vertical bands of tan and brown bricks are paired to give an illusion of depth. The

The 42nd Street crosstown horsecar makes its way eastbound across from Reservoir Square (now Bryant Park) in this 1889 photo. The tall building with the mansard roof is the Harmonie Club, the site of the present W. R. Grace Building. In the background the Sixth Avenue El and its 42nd Street station span the rather quiet thoroughfare. 42nd Street may again see rails running down the middle, if plans are successful for the construction of a light-rail crosstown trolley line. (New-York Historical Society)

Looking north from the top of the just-completed Times Tower, 1905. To the left is the then brand-new Hotel Astor with its fashionable roof garden. (Museum of the City of New York)

sheer verticality of the structure is emphasized by its 480-foot height on a plot of ground only 50 feet wide.

The gleaming white marble and black glass **New York Telephone Company Building,** at the southwest corner of Avenue of the Americas, is one of a number of skyscraper office towers erected by "Ma Bell" for local corporate headquarters. Completed in 1974 from plans by Kahn & Jacobs, it serves as the "anchor" for a growing line of new "glass boxes" springing up along the avenue north of 42nd Street. The narrow plaza to the west of the building with its mini-waterfalls and tree plantings is a pleasant oasis between the tall towers—a concession to the zoning laws that require open space in proportion to building height. Above the new subway entrance in the west lobby is an attractive and colorful mosaic mural by Richard Kirk (but why hidden away from the main entrance?).

Avenue of the Americas, formerly called Sixth Avenue, was renamed by former Mayor Fiorello H. LaGuardia. In spite of the decorative coats of arms of the Latin American nations mounted on the Avenue's lampposts, most New Yorkers rejected the mayor's flamboyant gesture, and still refer to the thoroughfare by its original name.

From 1878 until 1938 the Sixth Avenue El rattled overhead, keeping the busy avenue in perpetual twilight. The broad vistas from the old wooden platform cars, however, were superb.

You might want to make an optional detour to visit the midtown branch of the **International Center of Photography**, one block north at 1133 Avenue of the Americas (northwest corner of 43rd Street). At New York City's only museum dedicated exclusively to photography, there are frequently changing exhibitions on a variety of subjects, ranging from early vintage to avant garde prints, but the emphasis is on contemporary photographic art. The main center is located at 1130 Fifth Avenue, at 94th Street (Hours: Tues. 11 A.M.–8 P.M., Wed.–Sun. 11 A.M.–6 P.M. Admission $4.00, students and seniors $2.50, children under 12, free.)

One of the unusual additions to the city's ever growing skyline is the slope-fronted **W. R. Grace & Company Building** (No. 43 West), completed in 1974. The revolutionary profile derives from the architects' (Skidmore, Owings & Merrill) interpretation of the zoning regulations, which stipulate the ratio of a building's verticality to the amount of horizontal setback. The façade is covered with travertine, and although the shape is controversial, it is a relief from the endless rows of unimaginative "glass boxes" erected during the last 30 years. What is objectionable to many is the resultant destruction of the 42nd Street "street wall," considered an essential element in urban design. Also unsuccessful is the rear plaza, designed like an enormous checkerboard. The addition of trees (in boxes) has not helped much. To enter from the 43rd Street side, one is forced to cross the full length of the plaza. The two-story private reception area on the 47th and 48th floors (unfortunately not open to the public) is impressive, with a spiral staircase set against broad expanses of city panorama. A similar building (by the same architectural firm) was built simultaneously at 9 West 57th Street.

The Grace Building occupies the **site of the Stern Brothers Department Store,** which stood on the L-shaped plot from 1913 to 1970. (Interestingly, Stern's first store, an immense cast-iron building still in pristine condition, stands on the south side of West 23rd Street, between Fifth and Sixth avenues [*see* Ladies' Mile, 21].)

Adjacent No. 33 West, formerly a commercial office building, is now the **Graduate Center of the City University of New York.** The most striking feature is the renovation of the ground floor by architect Carl J. Petrilli, with its concrete cantilevered "canopy" and the open passageway to 43rd Street. The split-faced concrete walls of the passage are in sharp contrast to the exterior— one can almost forget that the building was erected in 1912. Access is by a glassed-in bank of elevators in the passageway. Pleasant and convenient for pedestrians, the mall is used for exhibitions and has been tastefully planted with shrubbery (although one wonders how they can survive in the cavernous darkness). In the 1920s the building was famous for its third-floor concert hall, Aeolian Hall (note the lyres on the façade), and witnessed the premiere of George Gershwin's *Rhapsody in Blue.* The Graduate Center was dedicated in 1970 after a three-year renovation and has been the recipient of many awards for excellence in design. The Municipal Art Society awarded it a special prize "for improvement of the aesthetic quality of life in New York City," and former *New York Times* architecture critic Ada Louise Huxtable described the Center as "one of New York's most successfully recycled buildings."

No. 11 West, the **Salmon Tower** (York & Sawyer, 1927), is distinguished only in its elaborate entrance and luxurious lobby. Around the ornate arched

The Avenue of the Americas today is a far cry from the dark and dingy Sixth Avenue (as it was then called) of 90 years ago. Looking north from 42nd Street, the Manhattan Elevated Railroad seems to cast a pall of gloom over the avenue. (New-York Historical Society)

entrance on both 42nd and 43rd streets are bas-relief sculptures of the months plus a row of classical figures above, representing the professions, and in the vaulted passage are marble walls and decorative bronze fixtures. Even the two mailboxes are adorned with low-relief bronze sculptures. The building also houses the **Midtown Center of New York University.** The "tower" section actually faces Fifth Avenue, as **No. 500 Fifth,** the two buildings being connected by a second-floor passageway. No. 500, completed in 1931 from plans by Shreve, Lamb & Harmon, was known as the Transportation Building, because it formerly housed the New York offices of virtually every important railroad in the country. In their stead today are numerous foreign airlines.

Cross 42nd Street and return to Avenue of the Americas; turn left at the corner and enter Bryant Park, but before you do, you might consider an alternate route back to Avenue of the Americas:

Just west of Fifth Avenue (on the south side of 42nd Street) is the entrance to the Fifth Avenue station of the No. 7 Flushing line subway. Connecting this station with the D and F Sixth Avenue lines at Avenue of the Americas is an **underground pedestrian passageway,** built in 1973. This well-lighted, brown-ceramic-tiled corridor is enlivened with eight photo murals depicting landmarks that once stood on the site of Bryant Park as well as views of the Fifth Avenue Library building. But it will cost you a transit token to take this unusual subterranean route!

Bryant Park has recently emerged from a four-year major restoration program. The landscaping was greatly enhanced with trees, shrubbery, and plantings; paths were relaid with bluestone paving; the statuary was rearranged and cleaned; new period lighting was installed; security upgraded; and incredibly, clean and functioning restrooms were opened. The design plan was eminently successful, as the junkies and undesirables have decamped, and it is once more a park for the people. Credit for the magnificent reconstruction goes to the firm of Hanna/Olin, Ltd. for the landscaping, and to Hardy Holzman Pfeifer who designed the kiosks and restaurant. In addition, below the great lawn a two-story 120,000-square-foot underground structure was erected that houses 84 miles of stacks and 3.2 million books from the adjacent Central Research Library. The project was developed in 1980 by the Bryant Park Restoration Corporation, which was founded by the New York Public Library and the Rockefeller Brothers Fund, in cooperation with the City and the Department of Parks and Recreation.

HISTORICAL BACKGROUND. The site of Bryant Park was first set aside as a public property by the colonial government in 1686 when the area was still a wilderness and a hunting ground of the Indians. Almost a hundred years later, during the Revolutionary War, it witnessed the hasty retreat of General George Washington's army, as it withdrew up Manhattan Island to avoid superior British forces. From 1823 to 1840 it was used as a potter's field. Two years later the Croton Distributing Reservoir was constructed on the site, as a newly built acqueduct brought fresh water to the city for the first time. The reservoir was an enormous Egyptian-style stone enclosure that covered four acres, with walls 50 feet high and 25 feet thick, along the top of which there was a very popular public promenade. The reservoir was razed in 1911 to make way for the new library.

In 1853 New York City inaugurated the **Crystal Palace Exhibition** on the site adjoining the reservoir. Modeled after London's famous exhibition of two years earlier, it was an enormous domed cast-iron-and-glass pavilion, designed to display fine arts and industrial products from around the world. Like a gargantuan Victorian greenhouse, its pinnacles rose 76 feet above what was then called Reservoir Square. New York's first World's Fair lasted two years and was one of the most spectacular attractions ever to be presented in the city; but it was a financial failure, and five years later the pavilion was destroyed in a disastrous fire.

During the Civil War the site was used as a drill field by the Union Army. In 1894 the name was changed to honor William Cullen Bryant—poet, orator, journalist, and editor of the *New York Evening Post*. But little was done to make the site parklike until 1933, when the city fathers conducted a competition for the development of Bryant Park. The successful entry was submitted by Lusby Simpson, an unemployed architect from Queens. Since the park was dedicated, several pieces of sculpture have been installed, which can be seen on the brief tour below. Bryant Park has become a first-rate urban amenity—a source of rest and inspiration and a hub of cultural and educational activity.

A BRIEF TOUR OF BRYANT PARK. Enter the park at the northwest corner (42nd Street and Avenue of the Americas). The little kiosk on the right is the Bryant Park Cafe; on the left is the kiosk of the Bryant Park Music and Dance Half-

The burning of the Crystal Palace, October 5, 1858. The Exposition, which was held in 1853–54, is now the site of Bryant Park. (New-York Historical Society)

Price Ticket Booth and Ticketron, sponsored by classical music FM station WNCN, where tickets may be purchased (for cash only) for music and dance events throughout the city. Notice the huge bronze lamp standards in turn-of-the-century style that surround the park. To the right (south) follow the path to the Josephine Shaw Lowell Memorial Fountain. The pink Stoney Creek granite fountain honors the pioneer social worker and philanthropist, and was designed by Charles A. Platt and presented to the city in 1912. Turn left and walk down the Great Lawn to *Big Crinkly,* the colorful stabile by Alexander Calder, executed in the last year of his life, 1971. To the left is the statue of William Earle Dodge by John Quincy Adams Ward (1885). Dodge was a merchant and philanthropist who founded the Y.M.C.A. The statue was moved from its original site in Herald Square in 1941 to make place for the James Gordon Bennett Memorial. To the right is a bust of Johann Wolfgang von Goethe, by Karl Fischer, and presented to the city by the Goethe Society in 1932. On the terrace at the east end, to the right, is a bust of author Gertrude Stein, sculpted in 1923 by Jo Davidson, but not cast until 1991. Dominating the park at the east end is the imposing sculpture of the seated William Cullen Bryant, executed in 1911 by Henry Adams, and protected by a Roman-style arch designed by Thomas Hastings. The Beaux Arts–style comfort station is along the 42nd Street edge. (The park is open daily from 6:00 A.M. to 8:00 P.M.)

The skyscraper panorama surrounding Bryant Park is striking. Look particularly south, to the West 40th Street side where, left to right, the following interesting buildings can be seen to good advantage:

The Republic National Bank Building, formerly the **Knox Building** (at the corner of Fifth Avenue). This ornate Classical showpiece with an imposing mansard roof was designed in 1902 by John H. Duncan for the Knox Hat Company. It suffered some modifications in 1965, but still retains much of its charm. Wrapped around the landmark Knox Building on an L-shaped lot is the 27-story **Republic Tower,** world headquarters of the Republic National Bank (Eli Attia, 1982). Israeli-born architect Attia designed the glass-wall structure to serve as a backdrop for the older building, while at the same time preserving its own special geometric richness of form.

The **former Engineers Club** (No. 32 West) is a Renaissance Revival–style building of satisfying proportions, recently converted to a residential co-op.

The American Standard Building (formerly American Radiator Building), designed in a bold, cubic massing of forms by architect Raymond M. Hood in 1923, is the undisputed beauty of the block. With its unique black-and-gold color scheme, it is most impressive. It has been said that its striking color combination, illuminated at night, gives it the appearance of an enormous glowing coal—ideal for the corporate headquarters of the American Radiator Company. In 1926 Talbot Hamlin, the noted architectural historian, described it as "the most daring experiment in color in modern buildings yet made in America." Note how the tower's setbacks terminate in gold-colored cubistic masses— forms often associated with the Art Deco style. The arched and pinnacled form at the top of the tower is a delightful crown to this skyscraper.

No. 50 West 40th Street, now used by Daytop Village, is interesting for its massive segmented column shafts, but for little else above.

Note, too, the Beaux Arts–style former comfort stations at each end of the path, in complement to the style of the library. Bryant Park, because of the high quality of its landscape architecture, its historical and aesthetic interest, and its splendid urban location, has been designated an official Scenic Landmark by the New York City Landmarks Preservation Commission.

Make a brief detour 100 feet south on Fifth Avenue to the bronze plaque set in a decorative niche of the Knox Tower, which depicts the 19th-century **John B. Wendel Mansion** that once occupied the site—one of many such houses of the affluent that lined Fifth Avenue.

Walk back on Fifth Avenue to the main entrance to the Library.

The Central Research Library building is considered the finest example of the Beaux Arts style in America. A majestic, delicate, and supremely aesthetic structure, its location at Fifth Avenue and 42nd Street is ideal. In a competition to select the architect, winning plans were submitted by the firm of Carrère & Hastings, and the building was inaugurated in 1911. Attending the ceremonies were the President of the United States, the governor, and the mayor. Completed at a cost of $9 million, it is one of the truly great libraries of the world. The New York Public Library was the result of the merger in 1895 of the three largest private libraries in the city: the Astor, Tilden, and Lenox libraries, with endowments from each of the trusts, plus a building grant from Andrew Carnegie of $5.2 million. The New York Free Circulating Library joined the consolidation in 1901.

The exterior is built of Vermont marble, and the building, in the traditional Louis XVI Renaissance form, presents an ingratiating rather than imposing appearance. It is built around two inner courts with an immense central reading room occupying a half-acre of floor space. Dominating the grand entrance are the two famous lions designed by Edward C. Potter. The style of the majestic lions is from standard architectural forms, but they have been the source of humorous criticism since their installation, even to the unspeakable pun of "reading between the lions." The 95-foot tapered steel flagpoles are set on exquisite bronze bases designed by Raffaele Menconi and cast by the Tiffany Studios, and were installed in 1941 as a memorial to former reform Mayor John Purroy Mitchell. The sculpted figures on either side of the main entrance are by Frederick MacMonnies: The man seated on a sphinx on the north side represents *Truth;* the woman seated on Pegasus on the south side represents *Beauty.* The six figures on the attic wall over the main entrance are by Paul Bartlett and are executed in Georgia marble for contrast. They depict, from left to right, *Philosophy, Romance, Religion, Poetry, Drama,* and *History.* The two groups in the pediment by George Gray Bernard represent *Art* and *History.*

Enter **Astor Hall** at the top of the stairs—a monumental white marble lobby whose high-arch bays rise on all sides to a segmental vault, flanked by twin grand staircases supported on flying arches leading to the upper floors. Statues of John Merven Carrère and Thomas Hastings are set in niches on the first landing. The walls of the third-floor Central Hall are of dark wood, above which are plaster-paneled barrel vaults. Notice how the ceiling extends over the cornice line at each end to permit light to enter from segmental arch windows. The fine murals were painted by Edward Laning, under the auspices of the Artists Program of the WPA, and were completed in 1940. The four arched murals represent the four stages in the development of the recorded word: *Moses with the Tablets of the Law, The Medieval Scribe, Gutenberg Showing a Proof to the Elector of Mainz,* and *The Linotype—Mergenthaler and Whitelaw Reid.* The murals in the lunettes above the square-headed doors are *Learning to Read* (west side), and *The Student* (east side). The aerial mural on the ceiling, with its *trompe l'oeil* effect, tells the story of *Prometheus Bringing Fire to Men.*

The recently restored main-floor **Gottesman Exhibition Hall** with white marble walls and Vermont marble columns is surmounted by a beautifully carved Renaissance-style oak ceiling. See also the newly restored lecture hall downstairs, the **Celeste Bartos Forum,** with its high elliptical glass dome.

Free one-hour tours of the Library are conducted Tuesday through Saturday at 11:00 A.M. and 2:00 P.M.

Walk north on Fifth Avenue to the corner of 43rd Street.

The Manufacturers Hanover Trust Company Building (No. 510), on the southwest corner, was designed in 1954 by Skidmore, Owings & Merrill, and is an example of the early use of the "glass cage" as a building style. Look through the broad glass pane at the exposed bank vault door.

The ruins of the Crystal Palace as depicted in Harper's Weekly, *October 16, 1858. (New-York Historical Society)*

The transept of the cast-iron-and-glass Crystal Palace Exhibition Hall as seen from the gallery. Many nations were represented in this first American world's fair of science, industry, and art. (New-York Historical Society)

The height of satiety was reached in 1903 when C. K. G. Billings gave his famous Dinner on Horseback at Sherry's for a group of friends from his riding club. Diners were served on trays fastened to the horses' pommels by waiters in footman's livery. (Photograph by Byron. The Byron Collection. Museum of the City of New York)

The Latting Observatory Tower burned to the ground on August 30, 1856, a harbinger of the fate of the nearby Crystal Palace two years later. (New-York Historical Society)

Turn left (west) on West 43rd Street.

The former **Columbia University Club** (No. 4 West) is an example of Italian Renaissance style, but a much finer representation can be seen across the street in **the Century Association** (No. 7 West). Since two partners of the firm of McKim, Mead & White, which planned the club, were members (Stanford White and Charles Follen McKim), one could have safely expected a certain extra touch—an assumption clearly vindicated in the design of this grand old Veronese *palazzo*. The Century was the first of the firm's many Renaissance-style clubs, and was begun in 1889 from plans by McKM&W architect William Kendall, and took two years to complete. Typical Renaissance features are the monumental arched doorway and Palladian window above the third-floor windows, which are skillfully joined to those below. Topping the building is a balustrade and ornate cornice. The Association dates from 1847 and was established "to promote the advancement of art and literature." The name "Century" refers to the original 100 members, among whom was William Cullen Bryant. The former clubhouse of the Century Association may be seen on East 15th Street. [See Gramercy Park chapter.]

Return to Fifth Avenue, turn left, stopping in front of the Morgan Guaranty Trust Company.

The 20-foot-high **Seth Thomas street clock** is probably the oldest artifact on the block. Built of cast iron, these sturdy timepieces were prevalent throughout the country from the 1880s until World War I, when the popularity of the wristwatch eliminated the need of a public clock. Most served as advertising gimmicks for the shops in front of which they were erected. Seth Thomas is still in business—the last survivor of dozens of 19th-century American clockmakers.

The southwest corner of 44th Street was the site of famed **Sherry's,** one of the most lavish and fashionable establishments at the turn of the century. A combination restaurant and residential apartments, it catered to New York's most affluent clientele for 21 years. The building, erected for owner Louis Sherry in 1898 by McKim, Mead & White, was later remodeled for the Guaranty Trust Company, and remained until the early 1950s when it was demolished to make way for the present successor bank.

No less extravagant was **Delmonico's,** Sherry's archrival, which, just six months before, moved up from its Madison Square location into an ornate Beaux Arts building designed by James Brown Lord on the northeast corner. The restaurant with its ballrooms and bachelor residences was closed in 1923, four years after the demise of Sherry's.

Turn left (west) on West 44th Street (walk on the south side of the street).

[The points of interest can best be viewed from across the street.] **The Harvard Club** (No. 27 West) is a modest neo-Georgian-style building, designed by Charles Follen McKim, and completed in 1894. The red Harvard brick is laid in Flemish bond and the trim is in Indiana limestone. The club was extended through to West 45th Street in 1905 from plans by McKim, Mead & White, and was again enlarged in 1915. The interior Harvard Hall is an immense three-story Florentine-inspired "knights' chamber" with two great fireplaces.

The New York Yacht Club (No. 37 West) is one of the city's most romantic buildings. The sculpted design of three 17th-century sailing ships' sterns, complete with waves and dolphins built into the bay windows, is both innovative and aesthetic. The Beaux Arts Eclectic building with its striking limestone façade, was designed by Warren & Wetmore (who helped create Grand Central Terminal) in 1901. Founded in 1844, the New York Yacht Club is the patriarch of all American sailing clubs and the internationally famous "America's Cup Race" held every four years. The Cup was first won by the schooner *America* in 1851, and lost only once (to Australia in 1983), then regained by *Stars & Stripes* of the San Diego Yacht Club in 1987. The Club, now in its sixth home, was built on land donated by J. P. Morgan, the commodore from 1897 to 1899, and his 241-foot-long *Corsair II* became the club's flagship. The interior's Model Room, measuring almost 100 feet long, is surrounded by a balcony with galleon railings and covered by a splendid stained-glass ceiling. Hundreds of ship models are displayed, including every defender of the America's Cup. Interestingly, an ornate wooden pergola that once stood atop the building but was removed many years ago, has been replaced—a faithful reproduction of its turn-of-the-century predecessor and a charming final touch.

The **Hotel Iroquois** (No. 49 West) as well as the just passed **Hotel Mansfield** and **Hotel Royalton** are typical of the turn-of-the-century Renaissance Eclectic–style hotels that sprung up in the midtown area. The Royalton has been remodeled as a classy, upscale hotel. Look inside!

The **Hotel Algonquin** (Goldwyn Starrett, 1902) is of the same Renaissance Eclectic school, and has managed to maintain its *fin de siècle* elegance. The Algonquin has always been a favorite haunt of stage and literary personalities, though, alas, less so now. Enter and settle into one of the soft chairs in the oak-paneled lobby, order a drink, and imagine yourself a witness to the famous "Round Table" of the 1920s, when such figures as Alexander Woolcott, Robert Benchley, George S. Kaufman, Heywood Broun, Franklin P. Adams, Edna Ferber, Dorothy Parker, and others would gather and try to outdo each other in witty chatter, while pretending to act as the arbiters of the American cultural scene. The hotel is now Japanese-owned. Look, too, for Hamlet, the hotel's live-in cat and most famous guest. He is probably the fourth or fifth feline to bear the name.

Return to Fifth Avenue walking along the north side of the street.

The Association of the Bar (No. 42 West, adjacent to the Hotel Royalton) is a majestic structure, appropriate to its distinguished function. Two magnificent fluted Doric columns guard the portico of this Classic Eclectic limestone building, above which rise four pairs of Corinthian pilasters to an ornate cornice supported by finely detailed brackets. The Bar Association was founded in 1870 "for the purpose of maintaining the honor and dignity of the profession of the

Law, of cultivating social relations among its members and increasing its usefulness in promoting the due administration of justice." The building was designed by Cyrus L. W. Eidlitz, and completed in 1895, and contains one of the largest law libraries in the country.

Touro College Law School (No. 30 West) is a typical turn-of-the-century Renaissance Eclectic building with an enormous semicircular roof pediment. The structure, designed in 1930 by Tracy & Swartwout, was built for the Army & Navy Club of America.

The General Society of Mechanics and Tradesmen of the City of New York (No. 20 West) was founded in 1785. It began as a technical institute offering free courses in the mechanical trades. The present building, formerly the Berkeley Preparatory School, was erected in 1891 from plans by Lamb & Rich. Note the equestrian frieze above the row of Ionic columns on its Renaissance Eclectic façade. Within is a library in a converted drill hall, but don't miss its unique **Mossman Collection of Locks** and see the mind-boggling Very Complicated Lock. The building is open Mon.–Thurs., 9:00 A.M. to 7:00 P.M., Fri. 9:00 A.M.–5:00 P.M. Closed weekends and holidays.)

Cross Fifth Avenue and turn right to the southeast corner of 43rd Street.

The Israel Discount Bank (511 Fifth Avenue) remodeled the ground-floor space, preserving the remarkable character of the Renaissance façade and interior. Observe the splendid coffered ceiling. The building was originally the Postal Life Insurance Building, erected in 1917 from plans by York & Sawyer. The renovation in 1962 was designed by Luss, Kaplan & Associates.

Across 43rd Street on the northeast corner, from 1868 to 1927, stood **Temple Emanu-El,** the largest synagogue in the world. Its twin "Moorish" towers were conspicuous landmarks on Fifth Avenue for over half a century, until rising land values and the northward push of the business district forced relocation to the present site, 22 blocks north. It is still the world's largest.

On the northeast corner of 42nd Street and Fifth Avenue is an astonishing 85-foot-high, three-dimensional, multimedia, walk-through "billboard," constructed of aluminum and glass, and designed by the firm of John Burgee. Visitors are whisked to the upper floors by elevator and then walk down on ramps through a variety of high-tech exhibit areas. The developer, Spectacolor, claims that this foreign-backed project "transcends advertising in the conventional sense" and serves as a kind of "World's Fair–class pavilion." On the site until its recent demolition was a six-story Italianate house, from ca. 1870, and familiar to most everyone in the area. It had been built for Levi P. Morton, vice-president in the Benjamin Harrison administration, and later served a variety of purposes, from a residential hotel to a gypsy tea room, remaining an enduring and odd anachronism at this busy intersection until 1992.

Turn left (east) on 42nd Street.

The system of designating streets east and west of Fifth Avenue was inaugurated in 1838.

Temple Emanu-El, at the northeast corner of Fifth Avenue and 43rd Street, with its twin Moorish towers, was the largest synagogue in the world when it occupied the corner from 1868 to 1927. It still maintains the distinction at its present site at 65th Street. (New-York Historical Society)

The Sperry & Hutchinson Building, on the northwest corner of Madison Avenue, is the home of (S & H) Green Stamps. The company was the first to introduce trading stamps as another way for merchants to encourage customer loyalty by giving them a little something extra. The company has been in business since 1896. The present building, which S. & H. leases, was built in 1964 from plans by Kahn & Jacobs. On the site previously was the Hotel Manhattan and later the National City Bank.

The Lincoln Building (No. 60 East) towers 53 stories above 42nd Street, and was built in 1929–30 from plans by the architectural firm of J. E. R. Carpenter. A product of the skyscraper building boom of the late 1920s, it was designed according to the setback requirements of the zoning law. In the 1929 prospectus it claimed that "No other office structure has ever been created where clear fresh air is more abundant or where radiant sunlight is more plentiful....Other buildings are far enough away to give unimpeded ventilation to all floors." On the walls of the vestibule are quotes from speeches by Abraham Lincoln, and in the center of the lobby a miniature bronze sculpture fashioned from Daniel Chester French's original model for the seated Lincoln at Washington's Lincoln Memorial.

The adjacent 26-story **Philip Morris Building,** begun in 1981, blends harmoniously with the 42nd Street "street wall," since architects Ulrich Franzen and Associates chose to have their rough-textured precast gray granite-paneled

Looking across the intersection of Fifth Avenue and 42nd Street, ca. 1875, at the Croton Distributing Reservoir. (New-York Historical Society)

As late as 1902, Fifth Avenue and 44th Street still looked almost rural, with Henry H. Tyson's Fifth Avenue Market and Ye Olde Willow Cottage tavern. Temple Emanu-El is barely visible to the right. The photo was taken from in front of Sherry's. (New-York Historical Society)

building face Park Avenue (No. 120), thus linking it to the axis of new skyscrapers that reach down Park Avenue to 32nd Street. The engaging three-story colonnade provides a covered pedestrian space, with access to street-level shops and a branch of the Whitney Museum. The site was formerly occupied by the noted Art Deco–style Airline Building, built in the late 1930s to serve as the in-town terminal for the newly opened LaGuardia Field. The **Whitney Museum of American Art at Philip Morris** features two public areas, a 42-foot-high sculpture court of 20th-century American works in a garden setting, a smaller gallery for changing exhibits, and a few shops. Take an espresso from the little bar, sit at one of the scattered tables, and enjoy the works of art. (The Sculpture Court is open Mon.–Sat., 7:30 A.M.–9:30 P.M.; the Gallery, Mon.–Fri., 11:00 A.M.–6:00 P.M., Thurs. to 7:30 P.M. The shops are closed on weekends. Admission free.)

Grand Central Terminal, a magnificent Beaux Arts Eclectic structure of mammoth proportions, has provided a dramatic gateway into New York City since its completion in 1913. Designed by Whitney Warren and Charles D. Wetmore plus Charles A. Reed and Allen H. Stem, the master plan combined function, accessibility, and aesthetics, which resulted in a monumentally successful architectural achievement.

(Photo, left) The same intersection forty years later shows a new type of Fifth Avenue omnibus. The "double decker" open-top models ended service in 1946, the closed-top models in 1953. The building on the northeast corner, built ca. 1870 for Levi P. Morton who served as vice-president in the Benjamin Harrison administration (1889–93), survived until 1992! (Photograph by Alice Austen. Staten Island Historical Society)

The broad south façade, with its triple arches, provides great expanses of glass to illuminate the interior. Crowning the center arch is the imposing sculpture group by Jules Coutan, representing Mercury, Hercules, and Minerva, set above a 13-foot-high clock. Below is a statue of the founder of the original railroad empire, Cornelius "Commodore" Vanderbilt (the statue, by Albert De Groot, is visible from the south side of 42nd Street). The terminal covers the three blocks to 45th Street, but below ground are 33.7 miles of track on two levels—66 tracks on the upper, and 57 on the lower level—a practical plan devised by railroad engineer William J. Wilgus. Reed and Stem's ingenious series of ramps connect the two levels with streets, subways, adjacent office buildings, and hotels, separating pedestrians from vehicular traffic. The main concourse, one of the most awe-inspiring interior spaces in the country, is covered with a vaulted ceiling supported by 125-foot-high piers and hung from steel trusses. On the ceiling are illuminated constellations of the zodiac (the ecliptic line, through a designer's error, runs the wrong way). Sunlight entering through the 75-foot-high windows casts long rays across the marble floor, augmenting the feeling of height and grandeur. The upper level was formerly used primarily for long-distance trains and the lower for the hundreds of commuter trains, but with the decrease in passenger business, the lower level is restricted to weekday rush-

Commodore Vanderbilt's Grand Central Depot gave New York its first direct rail link. This sprawling Second Empire building, built in 1871, hid an enormous ground-level train shed. The station was enlarged in 1899 and replaced by the present multilevel terminal in 1913. (Museum of the City of New York)

hour service only. Particularly attractive are the Guastavino hollow tile vaultings in the lower level.

Who can forget the names of such great trains as the "Empire State Express," the "North Shore Limited," or the "Commodore Vanderbilt"? Or the rolling out of the red carpet for the daily departure to Chicago of the "Twentieth-Century Limited"? The terminal is still heavily used, however, with about 120,000 daily Metro-North commuters, but AMTRAK trains now leave from Pennsylvania Station.

In the early 1990s, Grand Central Terminal was given a complete facelift, inside and out. The former proliferation of shops and advertising displays that cramped the main hall and accessways were removed, and the spacious waiting room was restored to its early 20th century elegance. The exterior was cleaned and provided with nighttime illumination that serves to highlight the imposing Beaux Arts details.

The New York & Harlem Railroad, which began chugging down Fourth Avenue in 1832, used a depot at 26th Street [the site of the first Madison Square Garden; *see* Madison Square, 11]. It then used horses to pull the coaches the rest of the way to the end of the line near City Hall. In 1854 the Common Council banned steam locomotives below 42nd Street because of the air and noise pollution, and in 1871 Commodore Vanderbilt had a huge cast-iron and glass terminal built at the present site. The former route down Fourth Avenue (now Park Avenue) cut through Murray Hill to 32nd Street. This "cut" was taken over by the Metropolitan Street Railway for use by its horsecars and later trolleys, and was covered over and converted into a tunnel. Today it is used by automobiles only and connects with an elevated viaduct that encircles the station on its way to upper Park Avenue. The viaduct also bypasses the huge MetLife (ex-Pan Am) Building and passes through the former New York Central Office Building, which was later renamed the New York General Building, and in more recent times, the **Helmsley Building.** A short spur of the Third Avenue El that connected with Grand Central Terminal was demolished when the viaduct was built in 1919.

The old station was enlarged in 1899, but with the 1902 regulation banning steam trains altogether from the city, the company—now the New York Central—had the choice of either relocating outside the city limits, or doing what it so wisely did, electrifying its lines. The railroad then acquired the sub-surface land rights for an underground terminal and yards, and began building the huge station. With the new land and air rights, the Central was able to build itself an attractive office building and two hotels, the Commodore (now the Grand Hyatt) and the Biltmore (rebuilt as the headquarters of the Bank of America). The new terminal also served the former New York, New Haven & Hartford Railroad, allowing trains from New England direct access into the heart of the city. It now serves only the Metro-North Commuter R.R.

Cross the main concourse and take the escalator for a brief visit to the extravagant lobby of the **MetLife Building** (originally the Pan Am Building). Built in 1963 and designed by Walter Gropius, Emery Roth & Sons, and Pietro Belluschi, it did much to destroy the scale of Grand Central Terminal. The enormous office building provided more floor space than any other in the world until

The enormous cast-iron-and-glass train shed of Grand Central Station, ca. 1872.
Electrification did not come until 1902. (Museum of the City of New York)

the construction of the World Trade Center, adding additional traffic and congestion to an already overcrowded area. Its precast curtain-wall construction made it one of the first of its kind in the city. It also created an outpouring of discontent, not diminished by the helicopter landing pad on the roof (since discontinued). Former Landmarks Commissioner Harmon H. Goldstone referred to the then–Pan Am Building's interruption of the broad view of Grand Central Terminal from Park Avenue as "a monstrous bland blanket." There was some regret at the loss of the familiar Pan Am logo atop the building. Some wags suggested that a more suitable logo for the Metropolitan Life Insurance Company, the building owner, would have been a giant Snoopy!

Several years ago the Penn Central transporting Company (a result of the merger of the New York Central, New Haven, and Pennsylvania railroads) sought to obtain permission to construct a 55-story tower above Grand Central Terminal. In denying the application, the Commission felt that such a tall tower would in effect destroy the landmark, reducing it to the status of a "curiosity." The Penn Central then had the temerity to suggest that the front of the terminal should be demolished altogether! The Commission, of course, did not agree that this was an appropriate means of preserving the landmark. A major public outcry, supported by the Municipal Art Society and such public figures as Jacqueline Onassis, helped convince the courts that the destruction of Grand Central Terminal was really not in the best interest of the city or its citizens. However, the ultimate solution came with the transfer of the Terminal's air rights. Exit from the Terminal and cross 42nd Street to the east side of Park Avenue and admire the recently restored south façade.

Although the name **Pershing Square** appears on the **Park Avenue Viaduct**, the square really no longer exists. A rectangular piece of land on the southeast

corner of Park Avenue and East 42nd Street was cleared in 1914 after the demolition of the imposing Grand Union Hotel. Named for the Commander-in-Chief
of the American Expeditionary Forces in World War I, the plot was acquired by
the city for an open plaza. In 1920, it was sold to a developer who three years
later erected No. 100 East 42nd Street, naming it the Pershing Square Building.
A large plaque in the lobby relates the history of the site.

The **former Bowery Savings Bank** (No. 110 East), now Home Savings of
America, was built in 1923 from plans by York & Sawyer. Designed in a
Romanesque basilica style, the imposing arch leads into the huge banking room,
160 feet long and 65 feet high, with a beamed and coffered ceiling. The walls are
of variegated limestone, interspersed with blocks of Ohio sandstone. On each
side wall are six columns of different-colored marble, carrying five stone arches.
Between the columns are panels of unpolished marble mosaic from quarries in
France and Italy. The mosaic marble floors add to the artistic effect. The former
massive bronze doors are hung for ornamentation on the east and west walls.
Another dramatic interior space, it was cited for architectural merit by the
Municipal Art Society and the Society of Architectural Historians. The Bowery
Savings Bank, founded in 1834, was one of the city's oldest and boasts a mag-
nificent Classic-style McKim, Mead & White landmark building in its 130
Bowery office downtown [*see* Lower East Side, 25]. The rich architectural detail
has many lovely motifs, including the bull and bear of Wall Street, a rooster representing punctuality, a squirrel for thrift, and a lion for power. The sculpture is
by Ricci & Zari. Many consider this the finest work of York & Sawyer.

The 56-story Art Deco **Chanin Building** (No. 122 East), is a delightful addition to the city's panorama. Built in 1929 from designs by Sloan & Robertson, it
came at a period when decoration was still considered an essential element of the
architectural whole. Note the wide ornate bronze band on the third floor, with
motifs of birds and fish running the full length of the façade, and the base of
terra-cotta plant forms. The lobby is a gem of Art Deco styling. Bronze is used
tastefully and artistically in the amazing convector grills, the low reliefs on the
elevator doors and mailboxes, the "jeweled" clocks, and even in the "waves" on
the floor at the 42nd Street entrance. One cannot help but rejoice at the excellent
building maintenance and the lack of "modernization" which has helped keep
the Chanin Building in pristine condition. Unfortunately, the top floor observation deck is now closed. A theater on the 50th floor is also closed, as is the former basement bus station of the Baltimore & Ohio Railroad train connection.

Facing, or rather reflecting, the Chanin Building, is the glistening **Grand
Hyatt Hotel** (Gruzen & Partners, with Der Scutt, 1981). This glitzy member of
the Hyatt chain in New York City is, alas, disturbingly out of context with its
neighbor, Grand Central Terminal. The bronze-tone glass sheathing now covers
the entire façade of what was once the Hotel Commodore, designed by architects
Warren & Wetmore as part of the original Terminal project. As a hotel, the Hyatt
is a vast improvement over its predecessor, which had declined so badly in its
later years. The striking Sun Garden cocktail lounge is cantilevered over 42nd
Street, and although intrusive on the street wall, it provides a pleasant view with
a tropical atmosphere. The plant-filled lobby, with its metal geometric sculp-

tures and comfortable seating, is reached from the street entrance by an escalator gliding past a bubbling waterfall.

Perhaps the most unusually shaped building, and certainly one of the most beautiful, is the 1,048-foot-high **Chrysler Building** (No. 405 Lexington Avenue), on the northeast corner of Lexington Avenue. Its graceful vertical shaft tapering into a fine stainless-steel point gives it a distinctive and artistic position in New York's skyline. Designed by William Van Alen in 1929, it became, upon completion a year later, the tallest building in the world, only to be relegated to second place a few months later by the Empire State Building. Close examination of the lovely Art Deco façade readily indicates that this was planned as the automotive tower of the city. At each setback are stylized "motor" designs. The building flares out sharply at the fourth setback into what appears to be shiny radiator caps—for a 1929 Chrysler! At other levels are basket-weave designs and a band of abstract automobiles. The Chrysler Building was one of the first to have exposed metal as an essential part of the design. An interesting event in the history of its construction was the deception of a rival architect by Van Alen as the building neared completion. When they reached a height of 925 feet, everyone assumed that this was the maximum; and when the downtown "40 Wall Tower" (40 Wall Street) also reached that height, architects H. Craig Severance and Yasuo Matsui added another two feet to make their building "the tallest in the world." To their consternation the tall stainless-steel spire of the Chrysler Building was secretly assembled, raised through the dome, and bolted into place, adding a victorious 123 feet. The elegant lobby is faced with African marble, and the ceiling is covered with what is considered the world's largest mural, 97 by 100 feet, depicting transportation themes. Artist Edward Trumbell used as models some of the men who had actually worked on the construction of the building. In its early years, the lobby served as a showroom for Chrysler Motors products. The lavish observation lounge has been closed and now houses electronic equipment; however, the installation of the spectacular illumination in the tower in the winter of 1981 (according to architect Van Alen's original plans, but with modern high-intensity light tubes) has added a brilliant touch to the nighttime city skyline. The successive rows of brightly lit inverted V's have been likened to some ethereal necklace suspended from the clouds. On the ground floor, Con Edison maintains a "Conservation Center," an exhibit open to the public which graphically illustrates ways to save energy.

After examining the unique lobby of the Chrysler Building, exit on the Lexington Avenue side. As you step outside, note the dazzling reflection of the building in the Grand Hyatt Hotel across the avenue. Then turn right and walk to the corner of 43rd Street. Diagonally across is the 33-story **Graybar Building** (Sloan & Robertson, 1927). Although relatively undistinguished architecturally, it was the largest office building in the world when completed. It also provides direct access into Grand Central Terminal, giving the impression that it is a part of the great station. What *is* unusual are the bright polychrome bas reliefs on the lower façade whose motifs are adapted from ancient mythology.

Note the steel canopy over the entrance to the passageway into the terminal. Supporting it from above are three cables designed to resemble ships' hawsers, with an **iron rat** climbing two of the lines, including the usual rat-deflector cones. (A middle rat must have "abandoned ship.") Return to 42nd Street and turn left.

Around the corner on 42nd Street (best viewed from the south side of the street), it will be noted that the east wall of the Chrysler Building's lower set-back is not parallel to the north-south avenues. This is because the property line follows the route of the former East Post Road, which in the 18th century ran approximately between Lexington and Third avenues, wending its way up Manhattan Island.

The massive former **Mobil Building** (No. 150 East), occupies the entire block to Third Avenue. Unusual are the embossed stainless-steel panels that cover the entire building. Originally the Socony-Mobil Building, it was built in 1955 from plans by Harrison & Abramovitz. When opened it boasted three superlatives: the largest steel-sheathed building; the largest air-conditioning system; and on the second floor, the largest floor space in the world. The design of its steel panels prevents warping, and the projecting surfaces are cleansed by the wind. When Mobil Oil abandoned the 42-story building, it was purchased by Japanese interests.

Third Avenue has changed drastically since World War II. For over 70 years the avenue was darkened by the rattling Third Avenue El and, like so many of the El-covered thoroughfares, was lined with dingy tenements, saloons, and cheap little shops. When the El came down in 1955—the last survivor of Manhattan's once extensive overhead railway network—Third Avenue underwent a complete transformation. From 38th Street to 57th Street, modern office buildings were erected; and typical of the 1950s and early '60s, most were box-like carbon copies of each other. There is little relief in the homogeneous and monotonous streetscape. **Second Avenue** was also relieved of its overhead El and enjoyed a similar renaissance, albeit somewhat later.

On the southeast corner of Third Avenue, until 1990, stood New York's **last Automat.** Although a re-creation of the once ubiquitous fast-food Art Deco–style restaurants, it was a pleasant reminder of the days when tasty, low-cost food was dispensed from coin-operated see-through doors and five-cent coffee flowed from brass dolphins' mouths at the turn of a crank. It was a gathering place that knew no social bounds and a homey amenity that is gone forever.

The adjacent **New York Helmsley Hotel** (Emery Roth & Sons, 1981) replaced the former Central Commercial High School, which had occupied the site since 1906. The lofty structure blends well with its modern neighbors, although it adds little architectural excitement to the streetscape. The porte-cochère, a novelty on 42nd Street, helps relieve some of the traffic congestion (unlike its rival, the Hyatt); and its two-story-high, dark-toned, mirrored-glass overhang, while breaking the "street wall," shifts attention from the monotonous verticality of the row of buildings. The Helmsley, newest of six New York City Helmsley hotels, is named for the chairman of the board of the chain, real estate tycoon Harry Helmsley.

Step back across 42nd Street and notice the diminutive five-story Romanesque Revival–style structure (No. 202) tucked between the Helmsley and the corner building. Built in the mid-1880s, it became one of a number of "holdouts" in the city—buildings whose owners either refused to sell to site developers, or who held out for prohibitive sums, forcing architects and builders to work around them. An odd anachronism, this brick and masonry house gives some idea of the scale and type of building that lined the thoroughfare a hundred years ago.

The New York Daily News Building (No. 220 East) was completed in 1930, a year before architect Raymond M. Hood's opposite outpost, the McGraw-Hill Building. Differing sharply from it and from his American Radiator Building of seven years earlier, the News Building uses other means to stress its verticality. In cooperation with John Mead Howells, Hood resorted to rows of brown brick spandrels and windows to create an up-and-down stripe effect. In 1958, an addition was added by Harrison & Abramovitz, wisely following the original style. Not to be missed is the attractive **lobby**, designed as an educational exhibition. In the center is the world's largest interior globe, illuminated from within and rotating slowly on a recessed platform. An excellent geography lesson, the globe's details are constantly kept up to date. On the lobby floor are bronze lines pointing to cities around the world and to the relative positions of the planets. The back wall has various meteorological instruments. The *News* does its printing in Brooklyn, Garden City, and Kearny, N.J., and at one time had the largest circulation of any newspaper in the country. The attractive building was cited by the Municipal Art Society and the Society of Architectural Historians for "originality in design and influence on later work." The newspaper briefly became the *Daily Planet* when it was featured in the film *Superman* in 1978.

The Ford Foundation Building, midway down the north side of 42nd Street, stands as a significant contribution to the quality of life in the city. The L-shaped building arranged around a 130-foot-high "greenhouse" was designed by Kevin Roche, John Dinkeloo and Associates, and was completed in 1967. The architects' plan was "to provide a proper environment for the building's staff—a space that would allow them to enjoy the view, but at the same time, allow them to be aware of the existence of other members of the Foundation, people who share their common aims and purposes." They felt that their building should contribute something to the city, maintaining a low profile and observing "the lines and planes created by other buildings which form the surrounding street." The result was eminently successful. The 12-story glassed-in area is anchored by granite piers and side walls, and shelters a one-third-acre garden. The shrubbery is frequently changed and is centered about a terraced garden with 17 full-grown trees, thousands of ground-cover plants, and aquatic plants in a still pool. Each season brings its own bloomings, and the entire area is floodlit, adding to the natural effect of filtered sunlight. The "greenhouse" also serves the additional purpose of a waste air chamber and thermal buffer. Ada Louise Huxtable, former architecture critic of the *New York Times,* in praising its successful design, called the Ford Foundation Building "a splendid, shimmering Crystal Palace...one of the Foundation's more valid contributions to the arts." (The garden may be visited on weekdays.)

In the late 1920s, many rows of brownstones at the east end of 42nd Street were leveled to make way for Tudor City. This group of houses stood on the south side of 42nd Street near the present Tudor City Place before the thoroughfare was widened. (Fred F. French Investing Company)

Across 42nd Street are the Church of the Covenant, the Hotel Tudor, and the broad Tudor City complex. Not officially part of Tudor City, the **Church of the Covenant** (J. Cleveland Cady, 1871) fits harmoniously into the architectural style of the complex. Cady was a member of the congregation, and the church was one of his first commissions. Built as the Covenant Memorial Chapel to serve as a mission for the working-class neighborhood, it became a regular church in 1893. The interior has great charm, with antique glass, bright stained-glass windows, and delicately carved wood traceries. When 42nd Street was depressed for the construction of Tudor City, the church ended up a full story above street level, requiring the construction of a staircase for access to the entrance.

Climb the stairway on the north side of 42nd Street to Tudor City Place, which spans the street.

Tudor City was developed in 1925–28 by the Fred F. French Company as a "self-contained city within walking distance of the city itself." There are 12 apartment houses with a total of 3,000 apartments, a 600-room hotel, shops, restaurant, post office, and private parks—all designed in a Tudor Gothic, or English Cottage, style. From the north end of Tudor City Place there is a superb view of the United Nations.

The site has had a checkered history, beginning with the rural Winthrop Mansion, "Dutch Hill," in the 18th century. The house was later converted into a tavern and rest stop for the stagecoaches of the old East Post Road. By mid-19th century the area deteriorated badly and became the hangout for gangs of criminals. In the early 20th century, the rocky crags were taken over by the notorious "Rag Gang," led by archfelon Paddy Corcoran. The neighborhood surrounding "Corcoran's Roost" became industrialized with breweries, slaughterhouses, glue factories and a gas works (which explains why there are few windows in the east side of the Tudor City apartment houses that might offer unattractive views or admit unsavory odors). Tudor City has remained a staid and tranquil enclave, enhanced by the arrival of the U.N. in the early 1950s.

Toward the south end of Tudor City Place, turn right briefly into East 41st Street. Alongside the park is a solitary survivor of the mid-19th-century brownstone era. **No. 37,** a three-story plus basement Italianate residence, long a deserted hulk, recently was restored by its new owner to its original pristine beauty.

The two little shady parks on each side of the 42nd Street overpass had been the subject of a long-standing battle between the owners of Tudor City and the tenants. Plans were to erect additional high-rise apartment houses on each site, thus destroying the pair of parks. In 1987, after a fifteen-year struggle, the strong tenants' association negotiated with the general partnership that is converting seven Tudor City buildings to cooperative ownership, and the little parks were turned over to the non-profit tenants' group, Tudor Greens Inc., with development rights held by the Trust for Public Land, a national group. The rights can never be sold or transferred, and the trust also holds a conservation easement to the land, which means that it will forever remain a green oasis. [The United Nations is described at the beginning of the East River Panoramas tour.]

End of tour. The 42nd Street crosstown bus stops at the foot of the north stairs leading down from Tudor City Place.

EAST RIVER
PANORAMAS

United Nations (Turtle Bay)
to Beekman Place

E. 53RD ST.

E. 52ND ST.

E. 51ST ST.

E. 50TH ST.

E. 49TH ST.

E. 48TH ST.

E. 47TH ST.

E. 46TH ST.

E. 45TH ST.

E. 44TH ST.

E. 43RD ST.

E. 42ND ST.

LEXINGTON AVENUE

THIRD AVENUE

(EAST POST ROAD)

SECOND AVENUE

FIRST AVENUE

(First Avenue Tunnel)

UNITED NATIONS PLAZA

TUDOR CITY PL.

Boundary: Beekman Estate
Turtle Bay Farm

Turtle Bay
Gardens
Historic District

De Voor's Mill Stream
(Turtle Creek)

Orig. site
"Mt. Pleasant"
Beekman House

2nd site

BEEKMAN PLACE

MITCHELL PL.

(Site of
Turtle Bay)

United
Nations

start

⑩
⑨
⑧
⑤
⑥
④
③
②
①

13. East River Panoramas and Roosevelt Island

[First/Second Avenue (M15) bus to East 42nd Street; 42nd Street crosstown (M42 or M104) bus to First Avenue. Nearest subway: Lexington Avenue line or 42nd Street S Shuttle to Grand Central]

The walking tour begins at United Nations Plaza, opposite the U.N. Secretariat Building, in Ralph J. Bunche Park, just north of 42nd Street, on the west side of United Nations Plaza (First Avenue), and follows the East River shoreline (with some detours) to Gracie Mansion, ending at the Henderson Place Historic District at East 86th Street.

1. Ralph J. Bunche Park honors the peace efforts of the United States' first black U.N. official, who served as secretary to the Palestine Peace Commission in 1947 and was awarded the Nobel Peace Prize three years later. He was subsequently appointed Under-Secretary General for Political Affairs, a post he held until his death. The aluminum sculpture, *Peace Form One,* is by Los Angeles–born black artist Daniel LaRue Johnson.

The backdrop for the mini-park is the **Isaiah Wall,** given by New York City to the United Nations. It bears the familiar lines from the Book of Isaiah, "They Shall Beat Their Swords into Plowshares...."

Climb the (Natan) **Shcharansky Steps** (named for the Soviet dissident) for a fine view of the U.N., then go back down and head north along the curbside **Raoul Wallenberg Walk** that honors the martyred Swedish diplomat who saved thousands of Hungarian Jews from the Nazis, only to be arrested by the Soviets and vanish. It is now believed that he was executed by the Russians in 1947.

The United Nations. After several years in temporary quarters on Long Island, at the City of New York Building in the Flushing Meadow Park 1939–1940 World's Fair Grounds, and at the former Sperry Gyroscope Plant at Lake Success, the U.N. moved into its permanent headquarters on this Manhattan East River shorefront site in 1952. Technically outside the territorial jurisdiction of the United States, the U.N. complex consists of three main buildings: the 544-foot-high Secretariat, completed in 1950, the General Assembly Building (1952), and the Dag Hammarskjöld Library (1963).

The site that now appears so ideal for the location of the world body was formerly a depressing aggregation of slums, coal docks, factories, slaughterhouses, and breweries. The original plan called for a site north of the city in Westchester County, but a grant of $8.5 million from John D. Rockefeller made it possible to purchase a parcel of land that had already been accumulated by William Zeckendorf for private development. In the earlier Zeckendorf plan, all buildings east of Third Avenue between 46th and 49th Streets were to be razed. The revised proposal proved more practical and saved many beautiful houses from demolition, including the historic Turtle Bay Gardens.

The new plan was approved by Congress in record time and the city rushed through all the enabling legislation, which included the waterfront rights and

View of the United Nations site taken from Tudor City, looking north, December 1946. In the distance, the graceful Queensboro Bridge leaps across Welfare (now Roosevelt) Island. (Official United Nations Photo)

tax-exempt status. An international team of renowned architects, led by America's Wallace K. Harrison, drew up the designs. Among the planners were Le Corbusier (France), Sven Markelius (Sweden), Oscar Niemeyer (Brazil), plus representatives from ten other countries. The library was designed by Harrison, Abramovitz & Harris. The pool was a gift from American schoolchildren, its freestanding stone sculpture by England's Barbara Hepworth, and the Council Chambers a gift from Norway, Sweden, and Denmark.

One of the most unusual sculpture groups is *Good Defeats Evil,* by Tsereteli Zurab, representing a contemporary St. George killing the dragon. The mammoth 40-ton, 39-foot-high monument was presented by the then–Soviet Union to commemorate the 1987 signing with the United States of the I.N.F. (Intermediate Nuclear Forces) Treaty. It consists of parts of a Russian intercontinental ballistic missile and an American Pershing missile, and was erected in 1990.

The buildings and grounds display many beautiful art objects, with such items as a Peace Bell and Shrine from Japan, mosaics from Tunisia, and even a model of Sputnik from the former Soviet Union. At the same time, New York City diverted busy First Avenue into a five-block-long tunnel and widened East 47th Street into Dag Hammarskjöld Plaza. The flags of the approximately 180 member nations line the east side of what was formerly First Avenue, now renamed United Nations Plaza.

2. The west side of **United Nations Plaza** has its own panorama of modern architecture. Among the more interesting buildings are:

No. 771, the Herbert Hoover Building, headquarters of the **Boys and Girls Club of America** (1960).

No. 777, the **Church Center for the United Nations** (William Lascaze, 1962). The impressive stained glass in the sanctuary of this nondenominational church represents *Man's Struggle for Peace and Brotherhood,* by Henry L. Willet.

The United Nations Plaza Hotel (Kevin Roche, John Dinkeloo and Associates, 1976) is one of the most striking additions to the city skyline. This irregularly shaped aluminum and blue-green reflective-glass curtain-wall structure is a dramatic counterpart to the smooth, straight shaft of the U.N. Secretariat Building, and its gridiron skin looks for all the world like a sheet of misfolded graph paper, as it looms skyward from a street-level "skirt" to a sliced-off corner and 45-degree setbacks on the north side. It is a dizzying and exciting visual experience, and a welcome change from the traditional glass boxes of recent times. Visit the Ambassador Grill, whose mirrored skylights create the illusion of a night sky overhead. The 288-room hotel shares space with office tenants, and is managed by the Hyatt International Corporation.

No. 799, the **United States Permanent Mission to the United Nations** (Kelly & Gruzen and Kahn & Jacobs, 1959). It is an attractive, eye-catching building, and appropriate to the U.N.'s host country. The electric wires inside the precast concrete "honeycombs" were installed to shock pigeons into roosting on some other nation's edifice.

No. 809, the **Institute of International Education** (Harrison, Abramovitz & Harris, 1964). Architect Alvar Aalto designed the Edgar J. Kaufmann Conference Room in the penthouse.

The "Old Store House at Turtle Bay, N.Y., 1852" in a lithograph from Valentine's Manual, *1857. The house was the site of a Liberty Boys' raid led by Marinus Willett, on the King's stores, just before the American Revolution. (Museum of the City of New York)*

No. 823 (345 East 46th Street), the **Anti-Defamation League of B'nai B'rith** (Harrison, Abramovitz & Harris, 1952), also Afro-American Institute.

Enter the **United Nations** at the Visitors' Gate, and spend some time exploring the General Assembly Building lobby and lower concourse; then take one of the guided tours (daily 9 A.M. to 4:45 P.M., except on Christmas and New Year's, and when special security measures are in effect). The entrance to the attractive garden is farther up the street at the corner of East 48th Street (*closed in winter*).

On the north side of Dag Hammarskjöld Plaza:

No. 345 East 47th Street, the **United Engineering Center** (Shreve, Lamb & Harmon, 1961).

No. 333 East 47th Street, the **Japan Society Building** (Junzo Yoshimuro and Gruzen & Partners, 1971). Funded by John D. Rockefeller III to the tune of $4.3 million, this striking example of modern Japanese architecture was inaugurated by Prince and Princess Hitachi and is the U.S. headquarters of the Society.

The Holy Family Roman Catholic Church (rebuilt in 1964 by George J. Sole) is dominated by its gray granite and aluminum bell tower. The church was built on the site of a brewery stable.

Return to United Nations Plaza, and turn north to East 48th Street.

In the mid-17th century, the area along the river below the present East 49th Street was the **site of the Turtle Bay Farm.** The origin of "Turtle" is uncertain. Some claim it to come from the many turtles that were once common along the shore or Turtle Bay (where the U.N. is now); others attribute it to the early Dutch word *deutal,* a farm implement, which was later corrupted into "turtle." The original farm dated from 1639. Just before the Revolutionary War, the neighborhood figured in a bold act by a group of "Liberty Boys," under Marinus Willett, who sailed down from Greenwich, Connecticut, in a small sloop, seized a cache of arms from a British storehouse in the lower city, then attacked a small stone fort that stood at the foot of East 45th Street, surprising the guards and making off to Boston with a boatload of supplies for the new Continental Army.

Flowing deep below East 48th Street is **De Voor's Mill Stream,** later called Turtle Creek, which once emptied into Turtle Bay. Because of a cholera epidemic in 1854, the city fathers blocked the now polluted creek and channeled it into a culvert, which still empties into the East River under the present United Nations site.

A short distance west on 48th Street is the soaring tower of **100 United Nations Plaza** (Schuman, Lichtenstein, Claman & Efron, with Der Scutt, 1986). Its 52 stories of glass, stone, and steel rise to an eight-step pyramid, as each floor with its multiple wedge-shaped balconies gives the façade a striking texture.

3. The twin monoliths of **Nos. 860 and 870 United Nations Plaza** (Harrison, Abramovitz & Harris, 1966) are luxury cooperative apartment houses. Originally they were planned to be the IBM World Trade Center, but now only the lower floors are used for commercial purposes.

4. The Beekman Tower (John Mead Howells, 1928) was built as the Panhellenic Hotel, a national meeting place for Greek-letter sororities, and is now a residential hotel. It is a bold Art Deco shaft whose 26-story-high deep

The Abigail Adams Smith House, a museum maintained by the Colonial Dames of America, was built originally in 1799 as a stable for Col. William Stephens Smith. The site has been much improved with the removal in the 1930s of the gas tanks. [See pp. 344–345.] (Museum of the City of New York)

window recesses emphasize the feeling of verticality. The Top of the Tower lounge offers a spectacular view.

5. Beekman Hill. The high ground that dominated the area between 50th and 51st streets was the site of the James Beekman mansion, *Mount Pleasant.* Built in 1763, the beautiful Colonial mansion stood near East 51st Street, but was later moved one block south when First Avenue was opened.

Turn right on East 50th Street to Beekman Place.

6. The Beekman Place District. The two blocks, East 50th Street to Beekman Place, and Beekman Place between 50th and 51st streets, were formerly cobblestoned, and consist mainly of town houses, remodeled in the 1920s. This delightful group of luxury residences has a unique atmosphere of charm and tranquility, in striking contrast to the surrounding neighborhood. Although not startling architecturally, each house has a character of its own, reflecting the individual taste of the original owner and the imagination of its builder.

The town houses were favored particularly by great theater personalities. Alfred Lunt and Lynn Fontanne lived in the house on the northeast corner of East 50th Street and Beekman Place. Among others who enjoyed Beekman Place addresses were Ethel Barrymore, Katherine Cornell, and Irving Berlin. It was also home for members of the Rockefeller family and former Secretary of the Navy and Defense James Forrestal.

Some of the more interesting remodeled town houses on East 50th Street: **Nos. 405, 414–420, 417,** and **419.** On Beekman Place: **Nos. 19–21, 23** (look up at the modern superimposition!), **33** (note its storybook roof and dormers, and the ropelike twisted bronze rainspout), **32–34,** and **35.** Notice the old **bishop's crook lamppost** on the southeast corner of Beekman Place and East 51st Street.

Turn right (east) on East 51st Street, pass through the little Peter Detmold Park, and down onto the footbridge over the East River Drive.

7. An excellent vantage point for a rear view of the Beekman Place District, the bridge is also a perfect site from which to view Cannon Point just to the north, where the Drive disappears under Sutton Place. Just to the south was a pleasant beach, where swimming was frequently enjoyed in the "altogether," and where Edgar Allan Poe came in 1846 to live with his young, sick wife, the former Virginia Clemm. Horace Greeley, the illustrious editor of the *Tribune,* came here to seek solace from the tragic loss of several children. Author Thomas Wolfe lived for a time on nearby First Avenue, and Yiddish novelist Sholem Asch described the neighborhood of the East 40s very vividly in his *East River,* published in 1946. The park is named for a murdered Turtle Bay activist.

To the north is the picturesque **Queensboro Bridge** (Gustav Lindenthal, engineer; Palmer & Hornbostel, architects), leapfrogging over Roosevelt Island. Completed in 1909, this intricately designed steel cantilever bridge connects Manhattan with Long Island City in Queens. The upper roadway once carried the wooden railway cars of the Second Avenue El, and a trolley line shared the lower level with vehicular traffic. The trolley, the last of the city's once-extensive network, shuttled back and forth at a five-cent fare, and was finally removed in 1955. The bridge also provided the backdrop for a number of movies in the 1930s and '40s, particularly the classic *Dead End,* which dealt with the conflicts between the wealthy of Beekman Place and the very poor of the tenements on adjoining dead-end streets. [Roosevelt Island is described on pages 356 to 366.]

The **East River** or **Franklin D. Roosevelt Drive,** begun in the late 1930s during the administration of New York's colorful Fiorello H. LaGuardia, was planned as a link in a projected "Circumferential Belt Parkway." It is built on landfill provided by the rubble of buildings destroyed during the World War II blitz on London and Bristol. Convoys of cargo ships returning from England during the war carried the broken masonry in their holds as ballast.

Return to East 51st Street and First Avenue.

8. On what is now the northwest corner of East 51st Street and First Avenue stood **James Beekman's mansion,** *Mount Pleasant,* from 1763 to 1874. During the American Revolution the house was used by the British for their military headquarters. Patriot Nathan Hale, captured on September 21, 1776, near Huntington, Long Island, was brought to the Beekman House, where he was condemned without trial and taken to the Dove Tavern (which stood on the site of the present Sign of the Dove restaurant), where he was hanged as a spy. [*See* Statue of Nathan Hale near City Hall, Chapter 3.] And it was here four years later that Major John André received his instructions to meet General Benedict Arnold and obtain the plans to the fort at West Point. Intercepted by patriots in Tarrytown, André, too, was hanged for the same offense. With the signing of the Treaty of Paris in 1783, the British Commandant, Sir Guy Carlton, was permitted to rent the mansion to carry out the plans for the British evacuation of the port of New York. A frequent visitor in the following years was newly elected President George Washington. The Beekman family continued to occupy the house until the cholera epidemic of 1854, and it was demolished 20 years later. Fortunately, a number of furnishings were saved and the reconstructed parlor, a bedroom, and three mantelpieces can be seen at the New-York Historical Society (Central Park West at West 77th Street).

★ The present building on the site was erected in 1892 as **Primary School 35.** This yellow brick and brownstone structure, in a mostly Romanesque Revival style, once served as the United Nations International School, for the children of U.N. delegates. The building, which lost out on a bid for *city* landmark designation, has had a varied career: community center, nursery school, and shelter for homeless women.

Across First Avenue, at No. 940, is **Pisacane Mid-Town Sea Food,** an old-style fish market which replaced a similar establishment that had been on the site since the building was built, ca. 1860. Look around inside; little has changed.

You have probably noticed that the east side of First Avenue, between 51st and 53rd streets, is virtually unchanged since the area was developed. The houses with straight window lintels were built in the 1860s, while those with the segmental-arc (curved) lintels date from the 1870s.

Turn east on East 52nd Street.

9. River House (Bottomley, Wagner & White, 1931), 435 East 52nd Street, enjoys one of the best panoramic views of the East River. A luxury cooperative apartment house, its facilities include tennis courts, a squash court, swimming pool, and ballroom, and at one time included a private dock for the convenience of visiting millionaires' yachts.

Return to First Avenue, go north one block, then west (left) on East 53rd Street.

10. Nos. 314 and **312 East 53rd Street** are surprising survivors from the days when the neighborhood was still semirural in character. The pair of wooden houses with their round-topped dormer windows and corbeled entrance hoods were built in 1866 and reflect the influence of the French Second Empire style, which became popular in this country after the Civil War. Only No. 312 has been designated a landmark. (No. 314's "wooden" slats are aluminum imitations.)

Return to First Avenue, turn left (north).

Cross First Avenue and take a short detour east on East 54th Street to **River Tower,** No. 420 (Schuman, Lichtenstein, Claman & Efron, 1981), on the right side. A 38-story "blockbuster" of an apartment house, it is set on an angle to the street, with an odd geometry, beginning with conventional horizontal bands of tan brick and glass and culminating in rows of pointed bay windows on the upper seven stories. And at street level, a Jean Dubuffet sculpture greets visitors at the entrance. In stark contrast is the **St. James Tower,** No. 415 (Emery Roth & Sons, 1982), across the street. A solid vertical cube of dark purple brick with radial corners and flush windows, this condominium building emanates strength, if not innovation, and unlike its ostentatious neighbor, hides its massiveness behind the line of the street wall.

Return to First Avenue, and turn right (north) to East 55th Street.

On the northwest corner of East 55th Street is the Catholic Center Building (1973), which houses, among other offices of the archdiocese, Catholic Charities. While the building is not especially distinguished, the **Church of St. John the Evangelist** is worth a visit. The entrance façade has interesting low-relief sculpture work, and the sanctuary, which has seating on three sides, is dominated by a large carved mahogany reredos. The organ, to the left, is free standing. This is the church's fifth building and the second on the site, replacing an earlier structure of 1881.

Turn right (east) on East 57th Street to Sutton Place.

11. Sutton Place, named for late-19th-century land developer Effingham B. Sutton, was formerly called Avenue A (which now exists only between Houston

and 14th streets). Lined with luxury apartment houses and elegant town houses, the street is another riverside bastion of the "upper crust," and continues north under the Queensboro Bridge approach, where it changes its name to York Avenue. Reminiscent of the Beekman Place district are the charming town houses along the short dead-ends on East 57th and 58th streets. **No. 1 Sutton Place North**, a lovely Georgian-style reproduction, was built in 1921 for Anne Morgan, daughter of J. P. Morgan. **No. 3** is the official residence of the Secretary General of the United Nations.

    12. Walk ahead into little **East River Park** with its endearing bronze statue of the friendly wild boar and its tiny animal friends. The original, from ancient Greece, is in the Uffizi Gallery in Florence, Italy. Sculptor Pietro Tacca made two other copies—one stands in Florence's Straw Market, and the other is in Kansas City's Country Club Plaza. Years of children's caressing fingers have polished the protruding parts.

Return to Sutton Place and turn right (north).

    13. The row of town houses on the east side of Sutton Place is particularly charming, each with its own engaging features. **No. 19** has a carved Medusa's head in the keystone, while in a niche on the second floor of **No. 21,** St. Francis holds a little bird in his hands.

    At the end of the delightful East 58th Street cul-de-sac called "Sutton Square," with its cozy minipark below, is another of New York City's seemingly endless source of surprises—secluded **Riverview Terrace** one of the city's few remaining private streets. With its protective fence and entrance gate with "amputated" goats, and fronted by a lush sunken garden, the six fortunate town houses are quite removed from the bustle of city life. The shady little lane paved with Belgian blocks extends north only to East 59th Street, where a stockade fence keeps out the "injuns."

Continue north on Sutton Place (now York Avenue), and turn west (left) on East 61st Street.

    Immediately to the right, on the north side, is **425 East 61st Street** (Liebman, Liebman & Associates, 1975), an office tower of unusual design. This block-through structure is "framed" between greenish-gray side walls, with the upper two floors successively cantilevered out (and commanding the highest rents). The side walls conceal the ventilation shafts for the floors and underground garage.

    14. Another delightful surprise is the 1799 **Abigail Adams Smith Museum,** headquarters of the Colonial Dames of America. The property dates from a patent granted in 1676 and passed through many hands until 1795, when 23 acres were deeded to Col. William Stephens Smith who had served under George Washington during the American Revolution. Nine years earlier, Colonel Smith married Abigail Adams, daughter of John Adams, who later became the second president of the United States. They began building a country estate which they named *Mount Vernon,* after Washington's Virginia home. However, due to financial problems, their mansion was not completed, and in 1799 the estate was sold to William T. Robinson, a New York merchant who had prospered in the China trade, who completed the structure. The Mount Vernon mansion, one of a number of fashionable residences along the East River, later passed into new ownership and became a hotel. According to an advertisement of the time, it boasted "excellent facilities for fishing, shooting, and salt-water bathing" (the East River shore was then only 50 feet from the door), and offered "every day in season soup made from the fine green turtles fattening in a crawl made for that purpose in the East River."

In 1823 the hotel was converted into a female academy that survived for only three years, when a disastrous fire consumed the building. The property was then divided and sold, and the undamaged stable, built of Manhattan schist, was remodeled as another hotel. One of the new proprietors, Joseph Coleman Hart, completely redesigned the old coach house; but in 1833 it was purchased by Jeremiah Towle, whose family lived in it for over 70 years. In 1905 his daughters sold it to the Standard Gas Light Company.

The lovely old house soon began to suffer from the encroachment of urban blight as the once fashionable rural neighborhood declined, with breweries and warehouses replacing the elegant riverside estates, and three enormous gas tanks rising up in the rear of the property. In 1919 the neglected house was leased by Jane Teller, president of the Society of American Antiquarians, who opened an antique and colonial crafts shop. Five years later the Colonial Dames of America, the nation's first patriotic women's organization, purchased and restored the house, and planted an 18th-century–style garden around it. They then assembled a collection of furniture and artifacts of the Federal period, which are displayed in nine period rooms. The museum has been open to the public since 1939. [Open weekdays 12:00 P.M.–4:00 P.M.; Sunday (Sept.–May) 1:00 P.M.–5:00 P.M.; Tuesday (June and July) 5:30 P.M.–8:00 P.M. Closed in August. Admission $2.00, $1.00 for students and senior citizens; children under 12 free. Phone (212) 838–6878.]

The adjoining building, No. 417 East 61st Street, has been remodeled in a matching Federal style and serves as the office, with an auditorium and exhibit rooms, and facilities for group orientation lectures. It also houses the headquarters of the Colonial Dames of America.

Continue west to First Avenue; turn north to East 62nd Street, then west about 50 feet.

15. On the north side of East 62nd Street, just west of First Avenue, is **No. 367.** Although extensively remodeled through the years, it does give some idea of the typical type of residence that lined the local streets in the 1870s. Built originally as a one-family house, it was later converted to multifamily use.

16. First Avenue in the East 60s and 70s, once quietly residential and later a decaying commercial thoroughfare, has since the early 1960s enjoyed a renaissance as New York's "swingles" district, although of late it has lost some of its luster, and much of the "action" has moved to SoHo, Chelsea, and the Upper West Side. With upbeat bars and restaurants attracting the young (and not-so-young) "unattached" from all over town, the avenue "swings" every night, reaching a crescendo by Saturday evening, as lines form in front of the more popular spots. The rebirth of First Avenue has also encouraged an influx of expensive restaurants, boutiques, antique shops, plant stores, and exotic food emporiums. Among the more flamboyant gathering places are Chippendale's (probably of more interest to women) at East 61st Street, and Friday's, on the northeast corner of East 63rd Street.

17. Between East 64th and 65th streets, on the east side of First Avenue, are the **City & Suburban Homes Company, First Avenue Estate,** designed by James E. Ware & Philip H. Ohm, 1898–1915 as a low-cost multiple-dwelling complex. One of two mammoth (for the time) housing developments on the Upper East Side, these multifamily units were planned to have as much light and air as possible in the days before air conditioning. Walk through the alley between the buildings to East 65th Street, noting how the architect used the areaways both economically and practically for the comfort of the tenants and the services for the buildings. This model tenement complex, the largest built by the company, provided quality living far ahead of its time for working people.

The ornate Third Avenue Railway carbarn between 65th and 66th streets was erected some time before 1873, then rebuilt in 1896 in Victorian style from plans by architect Henry J. Hardenbergh. Today no trace remains of the elaborate structure, its trolleys, nor the Third Avenue El. (Photograph by Berenice Abbott for Federal Art Project "Changing New York." Museum of the City of New York)

Turn right on East 65th Street to York Avenue.

 18. Rockefeller University, a research center for medical and related sciences, was founded by John D. Rockefeller in 1901 on the site of the former Schermerhorn estate. The shady campus is dominated by the Classic-style **Founders' Hall,** opened as a laboratory in 1903. Formerly known as the Rockefeller Institute for Medical Research, the name was changed in 1965, and in 1974 the institution was designated a National Historic Landmark by the National Park Service.

Ask permission of the guard (*on weekdays only*) at the 66th Street main entrance, and walk up the tree-lined hill. To the left, the incongruous hemisphere is the **Caspary Auditorium,** built in 1957 by the firm of Harrison & Abramovitz. Flanking Founders' Hall is the Hospital Building and Flexner Hall. Turn right at the sign that points to the ramp for the handicapped, and walk to the ramp overlooking the peaceful **Theodore H. Berlin Memorial Garden.** Descend the spiral staircase to the garden and walk north along the beautifully landscaped path, past the main entrance walk, exiting at the gate just beyond 67th Street. (If it is locked, you will have to return the way you came.)

Continue north on York Avenue.

19. York Avenue from Rockefeller University to East 72nd Street is devoted mainly to medical institutions:

Facing the University at 1233 York Avenue, between East 66th and 67th streets is the "glassy" **Sloane House Nurses' Residence of New York Hospital–Cornell Medical Center** (Harrison & Abramovitz, 1965).

Between East 67th and 68th streets is the **James Ewing Memorial Building of the Memorial Sloan-Kettering Cancer Center** (Skidmore, Owings & Merrill, 1950); and around the corner at 444 East 68th Street, the main building of the **Memorial Sloan-Kettering Center** (James Gamble Rogers, Inc., 1935).

For the next two blocks, the cityscape is overwhelmed by the massive complex of **New York Hospital–Cornell Medical Center,** designed in 1933 by the firm of Coolidge, Shepley, Bulfinch & Abbott, of Boston. This powerful group of buildings displays a neo-Gothic motif in its pointed-arch windows that rise to the full height of the walls. The medical center also shelters the **city's oldest hospital.** In 1769, Dr. Samuel Bard of King's College (now Columbia University) pleaded to King George III for "an hospital for the sick poor of the Colony which would also serve as a medical training school." Two years later the monarch granted its charter.

A new addition to the ever-growing hospital complex is to rise above the East River Drive on a huge platform between 68th and 70th streets. New York Hospital is constructing a 12-story $908 million building, scheduled for completion in 1998. The 776-bed structure with its one million square feet will have as much floor space as the Chrysler Building and will rise 185 feet above the platform level. The hospital will also build a new pedestrian bridge over the drive to the East River esplanade, at 71st Street, plus a new park at the foot of East 60th

Street. The architects for the new building, Hellmuth, Obata & Kassabaum and Taylor Clark Architects, have produced a design that will complement the neo-Gothic pointed arches of the main buildings.

Between East 69th and East 70th streets, walk into the arcade and see the **carved lions' heads** brought from the former Medical College buildings at 477 First Avenue, and attached to the wall in 1969.

At the northwest corner of East 70th Street stands the towering **Laurence G. Payson House** (Frederick G. Frost, Jr. & Associates, 1966), a residence of the Medical Center which wraps around the attractive **Herman L. Stick Medical Building**; and at 515 East 71st Street, around the corner, the **Cornell University Medical College S Building**, originally the Institute for Muscle Diseases (Skidmore, Owings & Merrill, 1961).

Between 71st and 72nd streets on the east side is **Sotheby's** auction gallery. Once the Eastman Kodak warehouse, the building was given an $8 million face-lift in 1980, and it replaced the gallery's former Madison Avenue facility.

20. Occupying the block between 71st and 72nd streets, on the west side of York Avenue, is the Mary Manning Home (for the aged). It replaced the famous Murry and Leonie Guggenheim Children's Dental Clinic which had been on the block since 1930.

Look east across York Avenue for a reminder of the commercial past of the neighborhood in the **former Purepac Pharmaceuticals Company complex,** an industrial Romanesque Revival–style building (No. 521 East 72nd Street) on the north side. Note **One East River Place,** a recent addition to the block which replaced one of Purepac's old buildings. It has a small sitting area and a simulated waterfall. The firm moved its operations long ago to Elizabeth, New Jersey.

East 72nd Street ends in a terrace overlooking the East River and Roosevelt Island—a convenient place to relax on a park bench and observe Roosevelt Island, the Hell Gate Bridge (described later in the tour), and to the south, the tower of the old Williamsburgh Savings Bank, in Brooklyn.

Just north of East 72nd Street on the east side of York Avenue are a pair of five-story ca. 1870 buildings with **"Alfredo's Casinos"** emblazoned in the cornices of Nos. 1364–66. They were probably joined at street level as a dining saloon, or perhaps as a less-elegant tavern.

Continue north on York Avenue to East 77th Street, and turn right one block to Cherokee Place.

21. The Cherokee Apartments is an enormous multifamily project designed by Henry Atterbury Smith, and is particularly interesting. Walk into one of the Guastavino tile vaulted tunnels leading to a central courtyard. Notice the separate entranceways grouped around the court, each with a semi-enclosed stairway leading six flights to the top. A central alley for building service splits the complex in half; side driveways slope down to the basement, with deep grooves in the pavement to keep horses from slipping. The exterior wrought-iron French balconies add a touch of elegance, as do the Spanish-style overhanging cornices and bronze lamp standards. The large windows are all triple-hung, making each apartment light and cheerful. The entire design is living-oriented—a visionary concept for 1910 when built as the Shively Sanitary Tenements.

22. John Jay Park, named for the nation's first chief justice, is the most popular recreational spot in the neighborhood. The swimming pool, picnic area, and athletic facilities on a site overlooking the river make this one of the most heavily used parks in the city.

Return to York Avenue on East 78th Street.

23. Observe the old carved stone street sign on the wall of Public School 158, hearkening back to the days when this was still **Avenue A.** Note, too, the boot-scrapers on the 78th Street entrance. This is a special school for the language and hearing impaired.

Across York Avenue, at No. 1465, is the **Webster Branch of the New York Public Library.** Built in 1905, it resembles a modest Italian Renaissance villa. The library until recently boasted an enormous Czech collection, as the neighborhood between East 71st and East 75th streets, east of Second Avenue, once was known as "Little Bohemia," but today only a dwindling number of Czechs and Slovaks still live in the area.

Look across the avenue at the three houses on the northwest corner of East 78th Street (Nos. 1477–81 York Avenue), and notice the **sunburst designs** in the cornice pediments. This typical Victorian motif also appears on the adjoining houses around the corner on 78th Street.

Crossing York Avenue, and continuing a few steps farther west on East 78th Street, one is astonished by a pair of beautifully preserved survivors—two aging wooden buildings, numbered **450a** and **450b.** Once part of a row of five similar houses, they date from the 1850s when the area was completely rural. According to local legend, they were occupied by workers from an adjacent duck farm, and were not converted into stores until after the turn of the century.

On the north side of East 78th Street, No. 425, **The Multi-Level Apartments** (William Gleckman, 1972) is a reconversion to end them all! Formerly a remodeled tenement, it was gutted and rebuilt with broad balconies (that double as fire escapes), an interesting lobby and entranceway, and apartments that are either true duplexes or "multi-level" with raised bedrooms or lowered living rooms. The whole building has been stuccoed over, giving it a warm, Mediterranean look. A precursor of many such dramatic reconversions throughout the city, it received the 1975 annual award for "excellence in modernization of a residential building" from the Building Owners & Managers Association.

Return to York Avenue and walk north to East 79th Street. Turn right to East End Avenue.

The City and Suburban Homes Company, Avenue A (York Ave.) Estate antedate the apartment complex with a similar name seen earlier. From their construction in 1901–1913 until the 1930s, the 14-building, 6-story complex was the largest low-income project in the country and was built with funds raised from New York's leading families. Profits were kept low so that high-quality apartments could be made available to the working classes. Yet it was the most successful of the privately financed limited-dividend developments of the time. The buildings, with restrained Beaux Arts and neo-Gothic details, were designed by Harde & Short, Percy Griffen, and Philip Ohm. After being declared a landmark in 1990 over the objections of the owner, the now-defunct Board of Estimate revoked the designation from the easternmost four buildings to allow the developer to erect a tower on the site. An appeal to the Appellate Court by residents, preservationists, and community activists two years later resulted in a reversal of the decision, reinstating landmark status. In 1993 an appeal to New York State's highest court reaffirmed the lower court's decision, and City and Suburban Homes' landmark status was sustained, ending an eight-year struggle to landmark the complex and defend the designation.

East End Avenue, developed as an apartment-house row for the affluent at about the same time as Sutton Place, looks rather similar. Before the street became fashionable in the 1920s, it was named simply Avenue B.

No. 2 East End Avenue, a former electrical underwriters' factory building, was converted in 1979 to apartments under the provisions of the J-51 program, which provided for both property-tax abatements and the forgiveness of property taxes to encourage the renovation of run-down buildings.

At East 81st Street, turn right and enter the promenade, called John Finley Walk.

24. This splendid promenade built over the East River Drive is one of the great pedestrian walkways of the city. It is named most appropriately for **John Huston Finley** (1863–1940), past president of the City College of New York, state commissioner of education, and editor-in-chief of the *New York Times*. He was, in addition, a *great pedestrian,* who believed that "a good walk clears the mind and stimulates thinking." Finley walked to work daily until past the age of 70, and frequently hiked the 32 miles around Manhattan Island, declaring that he enjoyed the sights of the crowded city as much as the scenery of the open country.

Roosevelt Island, directly opposite, is described in a separate tour at the end of this chapter.

Follow Finley Walk to Carl Schurz Park.

25. Carl Schurz Park, dramatically situated on rocky bluffs overlooking a bend in the East River, offers unsurpassed views of the Triborough and Hell Gate bridges, Ward's and Randall's islands, Astoria in Queens, plus an exciting parade of ships sailing close by in the river's deep-water channel. Just off 96th Street is treacherous Mill Rock.

The site during the Dutch Colonial period was known as Hoek van Hoorn ("Hoorn's Hook"), named for the Hanseatic town on the Zuyder Zee. Just before

The ferry Welfare *making its regular three-minute crossing between East 78th Street and Welfare Island, 1948. The elimination of this convenient service shortly thereafter virtually isolated the island for many years. (Gibbs Marine Photos)*

the American Revolution, Jacob Walton built himself a house on the promontory, but his tenancy was short-lived, as the Continental Army set up a battery of nine guns and took over the house as part of the fortifications. Known as Thompson's Battery, it was knocked out of action by a cannonade from British men-of-war seeking to isolate the island of Manhattan as the war began in earnest in 1776. The Americans fled and the site became a British Army outpost. In more peaceful times it became East End Park, and was renamed in honor of Schurz in 1911.

The park has a wide range of recreational facilities distributed about the wooded and hilly terrain, and provides a verdant backdrop to New York City's most famous residence, Gracie Mansion.

Carl Schurz (1829–1906) is considered the most notable German immigrant of the 19th century. Fleeing the unsuccessful Revolution of 1848, he came to America in 1852, learned the language in an astonishingly brief time, and involved himself in politics. He settled in Watertown, Wisconsin, and practiced law there and in Milwaukee. Winning the confidence and respect of President Abraham Lincoln, he was appointed minister to Spain and, soon thereafter, a major general in the Union Army. He was also responsible for helping to shape the new liberal Republican party. After the war he was elected senator from Missouri, and in 1877 was named secretary of the interior in the Hayes administration. Coming to New York he assumed the editorship of the *New York Evening Post* and wrote for *Harper's Weekly*. Schurz settled in the German community of Yorkville, where he remained until his death.

Continue following the promenade, and pause for a few moments at the flagpole marking **the site of Hoorn's Hook.** The East River is usually rather turbulent at this point, as tidal currents flowing up from New York Bay meet those from Long Island Sound, causing eddies and rifts that are hazardous to small boats. The river makes an S-turn as it passes under the **Triborough** (suspension) **Bridge** (O. H. Ammann and Aymar Embury II, 1936) and the lovely arch of the **Hell Gate Bridge** (Gustav Lindenthal, engineer, and Henry Hornbostel, architect, 1917). Both bridges connect Queens with Ward's Island and the Bronx. Hell Gate, once a graveyard of ships, was cleared of most of its rock outcroppings in 1885 by the Army Corps of Engineers. It is the supposed site of a sunken British treasure ship that was wrecked just before the Revolutionary War, and is still the object of occasional diving expeditions.

Hell Gate was also the site of the **General Slocum Disaster,** the second worst inland water catastrophe in American history. On June 15, 1904, the paddlewheel steamer *General Slocum* was sailing up the East River on a charter trip with over 1,300 passengers—mostly women and children—on a Sunday School picnic sponsored by the St. Mark's Evangelical Lutheran Church on East 6th Street. Just as it was passing opposite this point, fire broke out. Realizing that the fire was out of control, and seeing no favorable spot to beach the ship in the Hell Gate passage, the captain ordered full speed ahead with the hope of beaching his burning vessel on the Bronx shore. Lifesaving equipment proved inadequate, and the wind-fanned flames spread rapidly through the ship. In the ensuing panic, hundreds fell or jumped overboard to their deaths. By the time the *General Slocum* finally beached on North Brother Island, just off the Bronx, 1,021 lives were lost. A memorial service for the victims is conducted every year at the Trinity Lutheran Church of Middle Village, Queens, and a wreath-laying ceremony is held at the Slocum Monument in nearby Lutheran Cemetery. The Lower East Side German community was so stricken by the calamity that many moved out, settling uptown in the adjoining Yorkville neighborhood.

Follow the promenade to its end at the FDR Drive, and on the right is the **Fireboat House Environmental Center.** Until recently it was one of 22 fireboat stations that used to guard the harbor; now there are only four. The building and pier have been converted to a solar energy demonstration and education center, although not without considerable difficulty. A tug with barges in tow crashed into the pier, almost destroying it, and later a fire consumed most of the house. The former fireboat house is equipped with passive and active solar collectors, and classes are held in solar energy use; there is also a demonstration tank of harbor marine life. The facility is used by elementary-school science classes, as well as by the sponsoring Neighborhood Committee for the Asphalt Green Project, which conducts classes and seminars in solar energy, seamanship, fishing, the lore of the sea, and art. It also sponsors a Sea Scout group.

Across the FDR Drive, and accessible later in the tour, is the **Asphalt Green Recreational Center,** formerly the **Municipal Asphalt Plant of the City of New York** (erected 1941–44). Architects Kahn & Jacobs, influenced by Le Corbusier, were the first in the country to make successful use of the parabolic arch form in reinforced concrete. An amazing example of form following function (that of concealing the asphalt-mixing machinery), the arresting structure was in use until 1968 for making of asphalt to pave the city's streets. In 1981 the 5 1/2-acre site was taken over by the Asphalt Green Project to be recycled as a swimming, sports training, and rehabilitation center, with extensive athletic facilities, playing fields, and an adjacent swimming pool—the only Olympic-size pool in the city open to the public. Within the landmark building itself is the Murphy Center, which contains two gymnasiums, a track, basketball and volleyball courts, fine art and graphic art studios, a photography studio and darkroom, plus the Asphalt Green Mazur Theatre. The splendid reconversion/adaptive reuse was done by the firm of Hellmuth, Obata & Kassabaum and Pasanell plus Klein. In 1989 additional funding was provided by the City to help bring the project to fruition.

Go back about 100 feet on the promenade and climb the stairs to the right; follow the path to Gracie Mansion.

26. Gracie Mansion. Built as a country manor house in 1799 by wealthy merchant Archibald Gracie, it is one of the best preserved and most striking examples of the Federal style, and is a place of gracious living. The Gracies entertained many famous guests, including Louis Philippe, later King of France; President John Quincy Adams; the Marquis de Lafayette; Alexander Hamilton; James Fenimore Cooper; Washington Irving; and John Jacob Astor.

In 1887 Gracie Mansion was purchased by the city. It was restored by the Parks Department in 1927 with early 19th-century antiques. Four years earlier, it had become the Museum of the City of New York, under the directorship of New York historian Henry Collins Brown. When the museum's new building was opened on Fifth Avenue and 103rd Street in 1932, the mansion lay dormant for a few years until selected by Mayor Fiorello H. LaGuardia to be the official mayor's residence. It now holds the distinction of being the only original county seat in Manhattan still occupied as a home. A ballroom and reception wing were added in 1966 in perfect harmony with the architectural style.

Until recently the mayor's residence, although a national historic landmark, was "off limits" to all but official visitors. Now, however, the Gracie Mansion Conservancy gives tours on Wednesday only, at 10 A.M., 11 A.M., 1 P.M., and 2 P.M., by reservation only. (Phone 570-4751.) Suggested admission: $3.00 general public, $2.00 seniors.

Before leaving the park make a short detour to the south of Gracie Mansion to the circular sunken area opposite East 87th Street, to the **statue of Peter Pan** (Charles Andrew Hafner, 1928). The charming figure once graced the lobby of the New York Paramount Theater on Times Square, and was moved to Carl Schurz Park in 1975, about 30 years after the theater closed.

Exit from the park at East 87th Street.

(If you wish to visit the Asphalt Green Sports and Arts Center, turn right [north] on East End Avenue to 90th Street.)

27. Occupying less than a half acre between East 87th and 86th streets is the charming **Henderson Place Historic District,** a group of 24 homogeneously designed town houses. Begun in 1881 from plans by Hugh Lamb and Charles A. Rich, the quaint little houses are built in what is described as the Queen Anne style.

Originally farmland, the property was acquired at the turn of the 19th century by Archibald Gracie and John Jacob Astor (who also had an estate nearby).

East 86th Street (now Carl Schurz Park) ca. 1890. Barren of trees, Gracie Mansion stands out prominently at the far end. (Photograph by Jacob A. Riis. The Jacob A. Riis Collection. Museum of the City of New York)

After some years it passed into the hands of John C. Henderson, a fur importer and hat manufacturer, who decided to expand into the real-estate business and build homes for "persons of moderate means."

Until the 1830s, the section had been part of the remote hamlet of **Yorkville**, surrounded by large country estates. With the arrival in 1834 of the New York & Harlem Railroad, and a stagecoach line a year later, rapid development took place. Since the 1790s the neighborhood has been predominantly German, and has been swelled by periodic waves of immigration—the largest moving up just after 1900 from the Tompkins Square area downtown. It has also been popular with immigrants from Austria, Hungary, and Czechoslovakia, and much evidence still survives throughout Yorkville of this intermingling of nationalities.

A walk around the historic district takes but a few minutes.

Observe how the design of the individual houses combines to create a uniform effect. A turret marks the corner of each block; roof gables, pediments, parapets, chimneys, and dormer windows are arranged symmetrically; doorways, stoops, and basement entrances are paired under broad arches. The building walls are of smooth red brick, joined by black mortar, rising to meet sloping gray slate roofs. Note, too, the typical bay windows and the double-hung sash, in which the lower is a solid pane, while the upper is divided into smaller squares. In its *Designation Report* for the Henderson Place Historical District, the Landmarks Commission describes the dwellings as having been "designed with the characteristics of the Elizabethan manor house with Flemish classic detail in

A view of Gracie Mansion seen only by invited guests. The north side porch of this 1799 manor house, now the mayor's residence, enjoys a splendid East River panorama. (Museum of the City of New York)

a style developed in England between the years 1870 and 1910, principally by Richard Norman Shaw." Although having little to do with Queen Anne who reigned from 1702 to 1714, Shaw developed the design to create a "comfortable and romantic domestic style." The so-called Queen Anne style achieved its greatest popularity here in the 1880s and '90s. Walk around the corner of 86th Street to lovely **Henderson Place.**

Unfortunately, the scale of little Henderson Place is severely damaged by the towering apartment house on the west side, for whose construction eight of these picturesque town houses were sacrificed. As a final indignity, the apartment house took the Henderson name for itself.

End of tour.

A walk west along 86th Street, the *Hauptstrasse* of Yorkville, is quite interesting. The 86th Street crosstown bus (M86), at the northwest corner of York Avenue, one block west, connects with the Lexington Avenue subway at Lexington Avenue, with the Eighth Avenue subway at Central Park West, and at Broadway with the Broadway–Seventh Avenue subway.

ROOSEVELT ISLAND

[Aerial tram station at Tramway Plaza, on Second Avenue between East 59th and East 60th streets. Departs every 15 minutes, more frequently during rush hours, fare $1.40 each way. By subway, B and Q lines from Manhattan, or 21st Street–Queensbridge station in Long Island City. The Queens Transit Q102 bus leaves from 59th Street and Second Avenue, but goes via the Queensboro Bridge to Long Island City first, then to Roosevelt Island where it circles the island]

Roosevelt Island for many years was called Welfare Island. Prior to that, it was Blackwell's Island, and in Dutch Colonial times, Varcken Eylandt (Hog Island). Two miles in length by no more than 800 feet wide, it was first acquired by Dutch Governor Van Twiller and used for pasturage for hogs. Some years later it was purchased by Captain John Manning, a British officer who surrendered New York back to the Dutch in 1673. It is said that he retired here in disgrace after having had his sword broken over his head for not resisting the invasion with more enthusiasm. Robert Blackwell took title to the island in 1686 after marrying Manning's stepdaughter, and lived here until his death in 1717. The old Blackwell House has been restored as part of the Roosevelt Island development. In the 19th and early 20th centuries, as Blackwell's Island, it was city property used for a hospital, penitentiary, lunatic asylum, and "poor house."

A Currier & Ives lithograph, 1862, showing Blackwell's (now Roosevelt) Island and the East River from 86th Street. (Museum of the City of New York)

The notoriety of these institutions was so widespread that an investigation was conducted in 1921, with the result that the prison was moved to Riker's Island and the name changed to Welfare Island. Two city hospitals (Goldwater and Bird S. Coler) are still in service, and six structures, the octagonal Victorian tower of **the old lunatic asylum, the Blackwell House, the Strecker Laboratory, the Chapel of the Good Shepherd, the Lighthouse, and the Smallpox Hospital,** are designated landmarks.

In 1969, New York State's Urban Development Corporation (UDC) was granted a 99-year lease to develop the island. In the 1970s as part of the Federal Government's New Communities Program, Roosevelt Island became the "new town in town," and in 1973 the island was formally renamed in honor of President Franklin D. Roosevelt.

In 1984, the Roosevelt Island Operating Corporation (RIOC) was created as a state public-benefit corporation to run the island. RIOC runs the tram, sport facilities, minibuses, public safety, the Motorgate parking garage, and the grounds.

Connection to the city proper is by an aerial tramway which carries commuters in small cabins suspended from an overhead cable—much like a ski lift—to a terminal at Second Avenue and East 60th Street, and by a vehicular lift bridge from Ravenswood in Queens. Cars are restricted on the island and must be parked in a central garage near the bridge, where minibuses pick up passengers and make frequent trips on a fixed route around Roosevelt Island.

Roosevelt Island is a planned community of mixed income and multi-ethnic backgrounds, with a special quality of life, and has become one of the favored places to live in the city, as well as a prime tourist attraction. About 7,500 people live on the island in a dense massing of multistory buildings; 3,200 units have thus far been completed, with another 2,000 planned in Southtown, near the tram.

The **Roosevelt Island Tramway** (station designed by Prentice & Chan, Ohlhausen, 1976) glides across the East River at 16 m.p.h., and is controlled automatically from the terminal on Roosevelt Island, although a cabin attendant can override the system if necessary. There is even a rescue car with its own power supply to prevent passengers from being stranded high overhead in case of a power failure. The Swiss-made tram consists of two opposing cabins that soar to a height of 250 feet alongside the Queensboro Bridge, providing a thrilling ride and spectacular river views, from this, the first aerial tramway to be used for urban mass transit. Be sure to see the operating mechanism in the tram dock.

There is a red minibus that runs frequently from Tramway Plaza north to Octagon Park (fare 10¢). The drivers are helpful and usually quite knowledgeable about the island and its facilities.

Walk north past the subway station to just opposite the Blackwell House and Park (on the right). To the left, on the river's edge, are the **Meditation Steps** and **Observation Pier,** which offer a peaceful setting for watching the river traffic or enjoying the panorama of Manhattan's East Side and its hospital complex. The **East River Walk,** popular with strollers, cyclists, and joggers, provides additional opportunities for river viewing or just relaxing.

ROOSEVELT ISLAND, NEW YORK

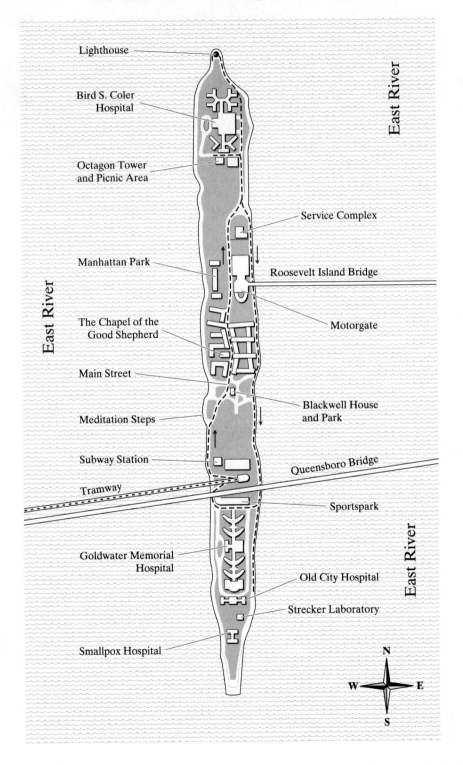

Lighthouse

Bird S. Coler
Hospital

Octagon Tower
and Picnic Area

Service Complex

Manhattan Park

Roosevelt Island Bridge

The Chapel of the
Good Shepherd

Motorgate

Main Street

Meditation Steps

Blackwell House
and Park

Subway Station

Queensboro Bridge

Tramway

Sportspark

Goldwater Memorial
Hospital

Old City Hospital

Strecker Laboratory

Smallpox Hospital

East River

East River

East River

N
W — E
S

The Roosevelt Island Aerial Tramway is the first to be used for urban mass transit. The twin cabins loft commuters across the west channel of the East River to the island's terminal at a speed of 16 m.p.h. The view is looking west toward the tramway's Manhattan terminal on Second Avenue near 59th Street. To the left are the approaches to the Queensboro Bridge. (Photo by author)

The **Blackwell House,** named for James Blackwell who built it in 1796, is one of the few surviving farmhouses in New York City. When the island was purchased by the city in 1828, the house was acquired to serve as the residence for administrators of the various medical and penal institutions that were built on the island. By the 1970s it had become a derelict, but was restored in 1973 by preservation-architect Giorgio Cavaglieri, and in the same year the surrounding grounds were developed into **Blackwell Park,** and includes playgrounds and basketball courts.

Continue north on Main Street, the island community's lifeline, into "town." On both sides of the street are the residential complexes plus a variety of convenience shops and facilities, including a bakery, delicatessen, three restaurants, a library, post office, etc. Note the charming brick paving and the sheer diversity of architecture that gives an integrated feeling to Main Street. The variety of buildings and massing suggests the scale of a European medieval town.

On the right is **Eastwood** (Sert, Jackson & Assocs., 1976), 510–580 Main Street, a Mitchell-Lama project (built with state subsidy) providing 1,003 apartments to low and moderate income tenants, plus specially designed units for seniors and the physically challenged.

Across the street, on the left, is **Rivercross** (Johansen & Bhavani, 1975), 531 Main Street. It is a Mitchell-Lama cooperative with 377 units for moderate-income tenants.

The 18th-century Blackwell farmhouse on Roosevelt Island before its restoration by architect Giorgio Cavaglieri as part of the new development project for the island. (New York City Landmarks Preservation Commission)

The Chapel of the Good Shepherd (Frederick Clarke Withers, 1889) at 543 Main Street, serves not only an active ecumenical congregation, but is a community center and town meeting hall. The lovely red-brick Victorian Gothic country chapel (restored in 1975 by Giorgio Cavaglieri) is the focal point of the town. The old bronze bell (read the inscription!) sits on the beautifully restored red-brick plaza like a piece of sculpture. It is said that the chapel bell rang each morning to wake the poor sleeping on their straw mattresses in the nearby almshouses.

Just beyond the chapel on the left is **Island House** (Johansen & Bhavani, 1975), 551–575 Main Street, a Mitchell-Lama middle-income rental building with 400 apartments.

Westview (Sert, Jackson & Assocs., 1976), 595–625 Main Street, is another Mitchell-Lama middle income rental building with 361 apartments and an indoor pool (visible at the rear).

Northtown Park offers a Little League baseball/softball field plus other sport facilities enjoyed by island residents. The Roosevelt Island Little League team boasts more than 200 participants.

Across the street is **Public School 217,** the island's brand-new innovative elementary school for grades pre-kindergarten to 8th grade (Michael Fieldman & Partners, 1992). After graduation, students must attend high school in Manhattan or elsewhere.

Roosevelt Island's Northtown Main Street residential and business area has been compared in its massing, scale, and variety of architecture to a medieval European town. On the left is the Chapel of the Good Shepherd. (Photo by author)

Manhattan Park (Gruzen Samton & Steinglass, 1989) is a five-building rental complex with 1,107 units. It was the final construction project of the second phase of the island's development. There are four market-rate buildings and one federally subsidized 222-unit building for seniors and low-income families. There is also a large auditorium and outdoor swimming pool with a formal European-style sitting park and several playgrounds.

The huge **Motorgate Garage** provides visitors' parking and a ramp to the Roosevelt Island Bridge. The imposing glass-enclosed structure was designed by Kallmann & McKinnell in 1974. A new addition is a Sculpture Center where young, emerging sculptors can exhibit their work.

The **AVAC Complex,** just to the north, is one of the unique features of the island. Designed by the same firm as the Motorgate, it houses the Automated Vacuum Collection system. Similar to the one in Disney World, it whisks all refuse from the island's residential buildings, at a speed of 55 m.p.h., to this building through underground tunnels. Here the garbage is efficiently compacted to one-fifth its original size, sealed in containers, and carted away by the city's Sanitation Department.

Octagon Park, north of Manhattan Park, is a new 15-acre sports complex, plus 200 community gardens, picnic and barbecue areas, and extensive plantings. The park was designed by the architecture and landscape architecture firm of Weintraub and di Domenico. The big green fence in the middle is construction access for **New York City Water Tunnel No. 3,** begun in 1970 and being built by the city's Department of Environmental Protection. When completed the site will be restored and landscaped. Tunnel No. 3, a vital segment in the water supply system, runs south from the Hill View Reservoir in Yonkers, into the Bronx, to Central Park in Manhattan, and then east under the East River to Long Island City, in Queens. The 20-foot-diameter concrete-lined tunnel was excavated in bedrock, 800 feet below the surface. Here on Roosevelt Island there is a shaft and subsurface valve chamber which permits direct access to the tunnel as well as for the connection of future stages without unwatering or removing any other stage from service.

The **Octagon Tower,** the park's namesake, was once the central hall of New York City's first public mental institution, the Lunatic Asylum. The eight-sided marble structure was designed in 1839 by renowned architect Alexander Jackson Davis; a mansard roof, by Joseph M. Dunn, was added in 1879. Four wings were planned originally, but only two were built, and they were demolished in 1970. Inside is a magnificent five-story rotunda with a cast-iron spiral staircase. The hospital once housed 1,700 patients—twice its designed capacity—and Charles Dickens visited it in 1841 on his tour of the United States. He commented favorably on the architecture, particularly the staircase, but he lamented the "long, listless, madhouse air," and the "terrible crowd with which these halls and galleries were filled." In 1887, reporter Nellie Bly (with a $25 retainer from *New York World* publisher, Joseph Pulitzer) had herself committed as an inmate, and exposed its dreadful conditions as a "human rat trap," with some patients chained to their beds at night. In 1894 it became Metropolitan Hospital, and in 1955 the hospital was moved to Manhattan, and the Octagon

The Lunatic Asylum in its final role as Metropolitan Hospital, as seen in an early-20th-century photograph. The building wing to the left was razed in 1970, leaving only the Octagon Tower, now a preserved ruin. (New-York Historical Society)

was abandoned. The building lost its roof to a fire in the late 1980s, but it was recently rebuilt, and the building will be partially restored as a stabilized ruin for future public access.

Directly north is **Bird S. Coler Hospital;** built in 1952, a many-winged complex with 1,045 beds, it is one of two remaining chronic care institutions on the island and is run by the New York City Health and Hospitals Corporation. Walk around the hospital on the west side and follow the promenade to the northern tip of the island.

The **Lighthouse,** a 50-foot octagonal Gothic Revival–style structure was erected in 1872 from plans by the supervising architect for the city's Commission of Charities and Correction, James Renwick, Jr. (architect of St. Patrick's Cathedral and the Smallpox Hospital at the south end of the island). It is built of a locally quarried granite, called Fordham gneiss. When built, it stood on an islet just off the tip of the island, but was later joined to it. The lighthouse and its site in **Lighthouse Park** is particularly romantic, with excellent views of the upper reaches of the East River and the swirling rifts of Hell Gate. Although an unofficial lighthouse when built, the U.S. Lighthouse Service provided a lamp until it was decommissioned some years ago. Note the lovely crocketed cornice—a tribute to Giorgio Cavaglieri's excellent restoration, in 1975.

There is a legend connected with the construction of the lighthouse. Before work began, there was a small clay fort on the site, made by John McCarthy, one of the inmates of the asylum, who feared an invasion by the British. After some negotiations, he was persuaded to demolish his fort and help build the lighthouse. Until recently a plaque with the following inscription could be seen on the base:

This is the Work
Was Done By
John McCarthy
Who Built The Light
House From the Bottom to the
Top. All Ye Who Pass By May
Pray For His Soul When He Dies.

An interesting story, but no documented evidence exists to confirm it. Even the plaque has disappeared.

To visit the south end of the island, you can either walk or take the minibus in Octagon Park. If you take the bus, get off at the Tram Dock and walk south along the road under the Queensboro Bridge.

On foot, walk south past Octagon Park and bear to the left (west) and follow the road past Motorgate and under the **Roosevelt Island Bridge** which links the island with Long Island City. Originally called the Welfare Island Bridge, it is a lift span erected in 1955, and provides the only motor vehicle access to the island. Across the east channel of the East River is Socrates Sculpture Park in Astoria and the prominent Adirondack Building, formerly the **Sohmer Piano factory** (1886) with its Second Empire cupola. Further downriver is the gigantic Con Edison Ravenswood Generating Station, known as **"Big Allis."** Continue south past the steam plant, until you pass under the **Queensboro Bridge.** [For a description of the bridge, *see* East River Panoramas, 7.]

Just south of the bridge are a pair of tennis bubbles and the adjacent **Sportspark**, with an indoor swimming pool, squash courts, basketball court, and steam room.

Immediately below is the sprawling **Goldwater Memorial Hospital** (Isador Rosenfield, senior architect, NYC Department of Hospitals; Butler & Kohn, York & Sawyer, 1939, addition, 1971). This is the second chronic care hospital on the island, with a full-time staff of 1,800 to care for 900 patients. The hospital was designed with the patients in mind, with a series of chevron-shaped balconied wings extending from a central north-south hall, providing the long-term patients with panoramic views and sunlight.

This is as far as the public can explore at the south end of the island. A tall fence extends from "river-to-river" because the structures below have deteriorated so badly as to pose a serious hazard. "The Ruins," as they are called, will some day be stabilized and accessible, but in the meantime you will have to settle for a brief description:

In the middle of the island, just below the fence is the crumbling **City Hospital,** formerly the Island Hospital, then the Charity Hospital, designed by James Renwick, Jr. in 1859. It was built of locally quarried stone by convicts from the nearby penitentiary (one of several prisons on the island). During the Civil War it was used as a military hospital for Union soldiers, and later it was

Among the many municipal institutions on Blackwell's Island was the Hospital for Consumptives. Doctors, nurses, and patients pose for Percy C. Byron's camera on a summer afternoon in 1903. (The Byron Collection. Museum of the City of New York)

an institution for the poor, as the name implies. Because of its advanced state of decay it was not designated a landmark.

To the south and east is the **Smallpox Hospital** (James Renwick, Jr. 1854–56; south wing, York & Sawyer, 1903–04; north wing, Renwick, Aspinwall & Owen, 1904–05). This Gothic Revival–style structure, built of the familiar locally quarried granite, is now a stabilized ruin; it was constructed during a severe smallpox epidemic in the city. In 1875 it was converted to City Hospital, and in 1905 to a nursing school and residence, the third nursing school in the country. With a binoculars the ruin can easily be seen from the Manhattan side of the river.

On the west side of the Smallpox Hospital is the **Strecker Laboratory** (Frederick Clarke Withers and Walter Dickson, 1892; third floor, William Flanagan, 1905). Originally built as the pathology laboratory for the adjacent Charity Hospital, the small Romanesque Revival–style structure of gray stone and orange brick is now overgrown and possibly even beyond stabilization. When opened in 1892 it was the city's premier laboratory for medical and bacteriological research.

The 3 $^1/_2$-acre tip of the island is planned as the **site of the Franklin D. Roosevelt Memorial Park.** Its location, directly opposite the United Nations,

Ruins of the Smallpox Hospital, designed by James Renwick, Jr. in 1854–56. This Gothic Revival–style structure, with only a few walls remaining, was erected during a smallpox epidemic in the city and later served as City Hospital and a nurses' residence. (Photo by author)

inspired the late architect Louis I. Kahn to produce a unique and unusual design. A drive for private funds is being spearheaded by the Eleanor and Franklin Roosevelt Institute.

End of tour. To return to the starting point, walk north along the west side promenade, past the Queensboro Bridge, to the Tram Dock. The subway station is a short distance further.

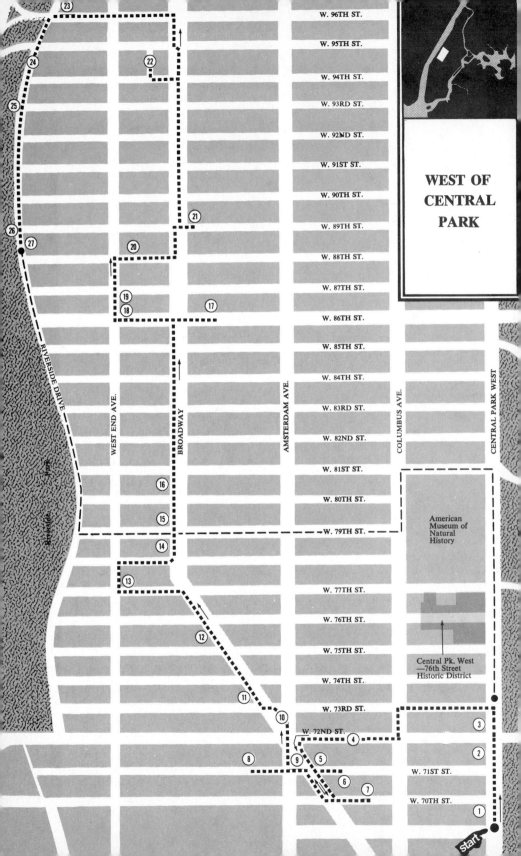

WEST OF CENTRAL PARK

W. 96TH ST.
W. 95TH ST.
W. 94TH ST.
W. 93RD ST.
W. 92ND ST.
W. 91ST ST.
W. 90TH ST.
W. 89TH ST.
W. 88TH ST.
W. 87TH ST.
W. 86TH ST.
W. 85TH ST.
W. 84TH ST.
W. 83RD ST.
W. 82ND ST.
W. 81ST ST.
W. 80TH ST.
W. 79TH ST.
W. 77TH ST.
W. 76TH ST.
W. 75TH ST.
W. 74TH ST.
W. 73RD ST.
W. 72ND ST.
W. 71ST ST.
W. 70TH ST.

RIVERSIDE DRIVE
WEST END AVE.
BROADWAY
AMSTERDAM AVE.
COLUMBUS AVE.
CENTRAL PARK WEST

American
Museum of
Natural
History

Central Pk. West
—76th Street
Historic District

start

14. West of Central Park

[Eighth Avenue A line to 72nd Street; Broadway–Seventh Avenue line to 72nd Street; 72nd Street crosstown M72 bus to West 72nd Street and Central Park West; M10 Central Park West bus to West 72nd Street]

The tour begins at Central Park West and West 70th Street.

Central Park, 59th Street to 110th Street, Fifth Avenue to Central Park West, is a tribute to the foresight of our early city fathers, and particularly to poet William Cullen Bryant, who pleaded the cause of a public park and recreation area close to the inner city. The land was acquired by the city in 1856, and a contest announced for the best plan of development. The winning entry, entitled "Greensward," was submitted by landscape architects Frederick Law Olmsted and Calvert Vaux, who spent the next 20 years supervising the creation of one of the most successful landscaped areas anywhere.

This charming piece of picturesque "country" includes several lakes, forest land, rocky hills, open meadows, secluded glens, a bird sanctuary, footpaths, bridle paths, extensive recreational facilities, an excellent zoo, and an array of artistic public sculpture.* Central Park is listed in the National Register of Historic Places and has been designated a Scenic Landmark by the New York City Landmarks Preservation Commission.

1. The Spanish & Portuguese Synagogue, Congregation Shearith Israel, at the southwest corner of West 70th Street, is the oldest Jewish congregation in the United States. Its first house of worship was erected in 1730 by the descendants of a group of 23 men, women, and children who arrived in Nieuw

---

*Since Central Park is not included in this tour, detailed information, including a map and list of park activities, can be obtained from two organizations that are dedicated to preserving and protecting it: The Central Park Conservancy, 830 Fifth Ave., New York, N.Y. 10021, and The Greensward Foundation, 16 East 8th Street, New York, N.Y. 10003.

Central Park West (then called Eighth Avenue) in 1895, looking north toward the Hotel Majestic on 71st Street and the Hotel San Remo two blocks farther. The hotels have long since been replaced by luxury apartment houses which retain the old names. (Museum of the City of New York)

Amsterdam in 1654—refugees from the Inquisition in Brazil. After three successive moves uptown, this Classic Revival building was built in 1897 from plans by Brunner & Tryon. The interior is very impressive, and can be visited Sunday mornings or during services on Friday evenings or Saturday mornings. The auditorium is arranged according to Sephardic tradition with the benches facing the centrally placed reading desk. The Little Synagogue, a small room in the rear of the building, is an accurate reconstruction of the Mill Street temple of 1730, with many of the original artifacts as well as some from subsequent buildings. Two huge millstones in the hall are from the old Dutch mill, which stood at the corner of Mill Lane and Mill Street (now South William Street), where services were conducted before the construction of the first synagogue. The congregation maintains the three Spanish & Portuguese cemeteries described on other tours [*see* Lower East Side, Supplementary Tour A; Greenwich Village, 33; and Ladies' Mile, 16]. The Synagogue still follows the Sephardic tradition handed down from the Jews of Spain and Portugal, and the ritual and Hebrew pronunciation differ somewhat from that of the Ashkenazic Jews, although Sephardic Hebrew is now the official language of Israel.

2. The Majestic Apartments, 115 Central Park West, was built in 1930 from plans by Jacques Delemarre of the architectural firm of Irwin S. Chanin, and is a fine example of the Art Deco style that became the rage in the late 1920s and '30s. The avant-garde brickwork is particularly attractive, as are the pair of roof towers. (One of the towers hides unsightly water tanks.) One of four twin-tower apartment houses that enliven the cityscape of Central Park West, the Majestic is named for a French Renaissance–style hotel that once occupied the site. The Majestic was originally planned as a 53-story apartment hotel, but the newly enacted multiple-dwelling law, with its severe height restrictions, limited the number of stories to three times the width.

3. The Dakota, on the northwest corner of West 72nd Street, is the West Side's most prestigious address, and has been since it was completed in 1884. Designed by famed architect Henry Janeway Hardenbergh (Plaza Hotel, Con Edison Building, Hotel Martinique, Art Students' League Building, etc.) in a German Renaissance style, its picturesque setting facing Central Park has been the subject of many prints and photographs. The Dakota was the city's first luxury apartment house. Standing dark and dour for many years, the Dakota recently underwent a steam cleaning, revealing its original yellow brick with brownstone and terra-cotta trim. This massive ten-story edifice, which provided servants' quarters and laundry facilities on the eighth and ninth floors, plus a tenth-floor gymnasium and playroom, is considered one of the most notable buildings of its kind in the country. True to the architect's conception of a château, it is surrounded by a "moat," with access to the interior through a dramatic two-story segmental arch guarded by a sentry box. The entranceways to the building are in the four corners of the spacious courtyard, formerly a car-

The Dakota forms a backdrop for the throngs of skaters on Central Park Lake, ca. 1890. (New-York Historical Society)

riageway. On the south façade of the building are two end pavilions with semi-circular oriel windows that extend from the ground floor to the roof. The fanciful roof, with huge gables at each corner and in the center, is perforated with symmetrical dormer windows. The Dakota is indeed a fortress, as the load-bearing walls are several feet thick and each floor is separated by layers of thick concrete. When completed, it had extensive facilities for an army of servants and boasted a private restaurant for the exclusive tenants. The eight hydraulic elevators, although modernized, are still in use and are operated from a huge pump room in the basement. The cast-iron fence that surrounds the building was made by the Hecla Iron Works in Brooklyn, in 1884.

The Dakota was built by Edward S. Clark, heir to the vast Singer Sewing Machine empire and manufacturer of "Clark's O. N. T. Thread." Clark's friends ridiculed the idea of his constructing a luxury house so far uptown and remarked that "it might just as well be in Dakota," which was then Indian territory. The name stuck, but "Clark's Folly" proved to be a sound investment. The Dakota, with its atmosphere of brooding hauteur, was the setting for the film *Rosemary's Baby,* and for the historical science-fiction novel *Time and Again,* by Jack Finney. Home to such notables as Boris Karloff, Lauren Bacall, and Leonard Bernstein, it was also the site of the tragic murder of former Beatle John Lennon, on December 8, 1980.

Clark's Dakota added great impetus to the growth of the neighborhood. Coinciding with its completion, the city changed the name of Eighth Avenue

In splendid isolation, the Dakota rises above Central Park West and 72nd Street, ca. 1890. Completed in 1884 from plans by Henry J. Hardenbergh, the huge apartment building was the subject of jibes for being "so far out of town...it might just as well be in Dakota!" (And the name stuck!) (Museum of the City of New York)

above 59th Street to Central Park West. Until that time the Eighth Avenue horse-car line and a stagecoach on the Bloomingdale Road (now Broadway) provided the only "rapid" transit, but in 1879 the Ninth Avenue El was pushed north on what is now Columbus Avenue, as far as 81st Street, affording quick access from downtown. However, it was not until the late 1880s, that the great building boom began on the West Side.

Walk back to Central Park West, turn left to West 73rd Street, and turn left again.

Clark and Hardenbergh combined their talents in another project, the development of rental row houses on West 73rd Street. The street, the south edge of the former Central Park West–West 73rd–74th Street Historic District, now subsumed by the **Upper West Side–Central Park West Historic District,** is enlivened by these lovely polychrome beauties which are such a change from the unremitting rows of brownstones that lined the city's streets in the 1870s and '80s. Note **Nos. 15A–19** and **41–65** (1882–85). Alas, the symmetry is broken by the intrusion of a hotel in midblock. At the northwest corner of Columbus Avenue, **Nos. 101** and **103** (apartment houses) are also the work of Hardenbergh (1879).

Turn south to 72nd Street, then west.

4. Until the late 1940s **West 72nd Street** was one of the better addresses on the West Side. Some vestiges of former elegance can be seen in the building that was formerly the Hotel Hargrave (**No. 112**), built in the typical Renaissance Revival–style of architecture so favored during the so-called Eclectic Period at the turn of the century. **Nos. 129, 137, 139,** and **141** were elegant town houses, and **No. 166,** with its ornate cornice, was once an opulent apartment house. No. 174 was also a stately residence until the remodelers ("remuddlers"?) arrived.

Turn south on Broadway to West 71st Street.

5. No. 171 West 71st Street, **the Dorilton,** still maintains some pretense of luxury. Built in 1900 from designs by Janes & Leo, it is a grandiose French Beaux Arts–style structure. The original copper sheathing that adorned the roof has been replaced by shingles. Note the pair of sculptured figures on the Broadway façade, the handsome iron gateway on the 71st Street side, the high supporting arch, as well as the very ornate lobby.

6. Farther down West 71st Street is the neo-Gothic-style **Church of the Blessed Sacrament** (Gustave Steinback, 1917). It is more noteworthy for its interior than for its somewhat disproportionately styled exterior. Note how the cleverly designed vaulted ceilings give the nave an impression of great height.

Return to Broadway and turn south to West 70th Street.

7. The **former Knights of Pythias Temple,** 135 West 70th Street, recently a branch of the Borough of Manhattan Community College and now reconverted

The Boulevard, now Broadway, looking north from 70th Street toward Sherman Square in 1907, showing some of the modes of transportation in use at the time. Somewhat blurred in the background is the newly completed Ansonia Hotel. To the right, the arched entrance of the Dorilton is clearly visible. (Photograph by Byron. The Byron Collection. Museum of the City of New York)

and named Pythian Apartments, was erected in 1926. Unfortunately, the developer stripped away most of the Egyptian-style adornments. Architect Thomas W. Lamb drew on ancient Egyptian motifs for the styling of this fraternal organization's Grand Lodge. The polychrome designs, seated Pharaohs, ornate columns, and upper "temple" are straight out of Karnak! An Egyptian Revival style in architecture achieved brief popularity after the discovery in 1922 of the tomb of King Tutankhamen in Thebes.

Returning to Broadway, note the luxury apartment house at the southeast corner, **No. 154.** It began its life in elegance, ca. 1900, deteriorated through the years, and has now come full circle reflecting the changes that are taking place throughout the Upper West Side.

Cross to the west side of Broadway and turn west (left) into West 71st Street.

8. The house, No. 213, is all that remains of the **former Christ Church.** The orange brick and terra-cotta trim of this Romanesque Revival–style old rectory gives some idea of the appearance of the church that was built in 1890 from plans by Charles C. Haight; the rectory three years later by Rose & Stone. The adjacent new high-rise occupies the church site, while the corner office building stands on the former east end and bell tower of the church that were sold years before, in 1925.

The trio of adjacent town houses (**No. 215–219**) was built in 1891 in the Italianate style. Note how these brownstones are deceivingly painted to resemble marble. At Broadway you have an excellent view of the Dorilton.

9. At the intersection of Broadway and West 72nd Street, the **Subway Entrance** on the center "island" (Heins & LaFarge, 1904) is one of the last of such structures remaining in the city. Technically called "control houses," because subway riders were under the control of the transit system once they entered, they date from the original Interborough Rapid Transit subway line built in 1904, when many touches of elegance were included in our first underground railroad. The line's route began at City Hall, ran north to 42nd Street, crosstown to Times Square, then north on Broadway to 145th Street.

The intersection is divided into **Sherman Square** to the south of West 72nd Street, and **Verdi Square** to the north.

At the beginning of the 19th century this busy confluence of major thoroughfares was the sleepy **hamlet of Harsenville,** named for farmer Jacob Harsen, whose house stood approximately at the present intersection. When the Bloomingdale Road was opened in 1701 from the lower city to the Hudson River, the area began to lose its bucolic flavor. Toward the end of the century, the Bloomingdale Road north of 59th Street was renamed the Boulevard. Moses King, in his *Handbook of New York City,* 1893 edition, described the Boulevard as "two capital roadways, separated by a central strip of lawns, trees, and flowers. When finished it will be one of the most beautiful driveways in the world,

Backyard of the Jacob Harsen homestead at the corner of Tenth Avenue (now Amsterdam Avenue) and 70th Street, ca. 1888. The present intersection of Broadway and 72nd Street was the site of the hamlet of Harsenville during the 18th century. The house was built in 1701 for the Dyckman family, and survived until 1893. (New-York Historical Society)

traversing as it does, the remarkably picturesque region between Central Park and the Hudson River, much of the way over high ground, commanding beautiful views." The Boulevard was renamed Broadway early in this century, making it Manhattan's longest traffic artery.

10. Verdi Square Scenic Landmark, named for the great Italian composer, provides a small patch of green along busy Broadway. The benches are usually filled with older adults from the neighborhood who meet to gossip, reminisce, or take in the sun in warmer weather, and who, unfortunately, must compete for space with drunks and undesirables. It was in this neighborhood that the late Nobel Prize winner, Isaac Bashevis Singer, spent most of his life in America. The **Statue of Giuseppe Verdi,** commissioned by New York's Italian community in 1906 and executed in marble by Pasquale Civiletti, stands on a granite pedestal over four life-size figures representing characters from Verdi's operas *Otello, Aïda, Falstaff,* and *La Forza del Destino.* The square is an officially designated New York City Scenic Landmark.

Dominating the north side of Verdi Square is the massive **former Central Savings Bank Building** (now Apple Bank for Savings). Its limestone façade, designed in the style of an enormous Italian Renaissance palace by York & Sawyer in 1928, creates an atmosphere of solid financial security—no doubt the intention of the builders. The wrought-iron window grilles and the large lanterns (by Samuel Yellin) add an artistic touch, while a handsome clock flanked by two lions decorates the 73rd Street entrance. The bank, built on a trapezoidal plot (although the interior is rectangular), is a well designed and dignified structure—a fitting backdrop to Verdi Square.

11. One of the city's truly magnificent buildings is the French Beaux Arts–style **Ansonia Hotel** (Graves & DuBoy) on the northwest corner of Broadway and 73rd Street. Begun in 1899 and completed five years later, it is the dominant landmark of the West Side. When the Ansonia opened, it was one of the most opulent hostelries in town. The builder, William Earl Dodge Stokes, a wealthy land developer and inheritor of the Phelps Dodge Company fortune, brought architect-sculptor Paul E. M. DuBoy from France to carry out his grandiose plans for a sumptuous hotel in the style of the elegant palaces along the Parisian *grands boulevards.* Although its 17 stories would have made it second only to the Eiffel Tower in Paris, its dramatic setting here on Broadway is quite appropriate.

The corner round towers, surmounted by cupolas and railings in harmony with the convex mansard roof, are the most striking feature of the building. Rows of delicately ornate balconies break up the overwhelming verticality caused by tier upon tier of windows, while a series of recessed courts on the Broadway and West 73rd Street sides give a feeling of depth and also provides a maximum of light and air.

Stokes, who owned the construction company, supervised every step in the building of the hotel. Thick masonry walls made it completely fireproof. The building also featured a roof garden, shops in the basement, and *two* swimming pools. The Ansonia is named indirectly for Stoke's maternal grandfather, Anson Greene Phelps, who founded the Ansonia Brass & Copper Company in his namesake town of Ansonia, Connecticut. In 1879, a subsidiary of the firm, the famous Ansonia Clock Company, moved its operations from the Connecticut town to Brooklyn, bringing the Ansonia name to the city 20 years ahead of the hotel. Stokes's most illustrious relative, however, was I. N. (Isaac Newton) Phelps Stokes, the architect-historian who wrote the definitive six-volume *Iconography of Manhattan Island.*

The fine reputation of the Ansonia through the years was due to its world-renowned clientele. Much the same way that the downtown Hotel Chelsea was the favorite of the *literati,* the Ansonia was the bastion of the musical world. The thick walls provided soundproofing that proved a most attractive feature. Among the "greats" who have stayed at the hotel were Enrico Caruso, Leopold Auer, Feodor Chaliapin, Mischa Elman, Geraldine Farrar, Lauritz Melchior, Ezio Pinza, Lily Pons, Yehudi Menuhin, Tito Schipa, Igor Stravinsky, Arturo Toscanini, and even Babe Ruth. It was for a time the favorite of Sol Hurok, Billie Burke, Florenz Ziegfeld, and Theodore Dreiser.

Much of the early splendor of the hotel has now vanished. Several of the crowning cupolas and lanterns are missing, a number of the decorative railings and balconies have been removed, the immense ground-floor archways have been either blocked up or converted into small stores, the spacious lobby has been partitioned into unrecognizability, and there is little of its former grandeur; only a small reminder in the tiny lounge area which displays historic photos of the Ansonia. But from afar, the Hotel Ansonia is still a great lady!

John C. van den Heuvel's country estate, ca. 1819, occupied the entire block now bounded by Broadway, West End Avenue, 78th and 79th streets. (The J. Clarence Davies Collection. Museum of the City of New York)

Pushed by a diminutive steam dummy (which was a locomotive encased in a boxlike structure to shield the machinery from public view for "cosmetic" reasons), a train of the newly opened New York Elevated Railroad (later the Ninth Avenue El) enters the 59th Street station. The name of "Ninth Avenue" above 59th Street was later changed to Columbus Avenue. (Museum of the City of New York)

Continue north on Broadway

On the east side of Broadway near West 75th Street is the **Beacon Theater** (Walter Ahlschlager, 1928). Its front, lost in the façade of the adjoining hotel, should be seen on its 75th Street side. The splendid auditorium, a designated landmark, was saved from conversion to a disco by determined community residents, and now offers theatrical performances, rock concerts, etc. Across from the rear of the theater, the **Berkeley Garage,** 201 West 75th Street (C. Abbott French & Co., 1890), is a striking example of the Romanesque Revival style made popular by architect Henry Hobson Richardson in the 1880s and '90s. Once the stables of the New York Cab Company, the three huge half-round arches provided a grand entrance for the horses and carriages. The heavy stone base conflicts somewhat with the elaborate cornice, but it is nevertheless a worthy survivor. Skip the "modernized" Amsterdam Avenue side, and return to Broadway.

12. The Astor Apartments (Clinton & Russell, 1905), between 75th and 76th streets, on the west side of Broadway, once a luxurious apartment house, was built by real-estate magnate William Waldorf Astor, who owned and developed much of the land in the neighborhood.

Continue north on Broadway to West 76th Street.

Walk a few steps west on West 76th Street to **No. 252,** whose well-restored Renaissance Eclectic façade is an upliftment for the block.

At the southwest corner of Broadway and West 77th Street is the **Hotel Belleclaire** (Emery Roth, 1903). Its ornate wildly eclectic façade, particularly on the 77th Street side, offers an endless variety of dormers, bay windows, balconies with wrought-iron railings, and unusual covered chimneys.

Walk west to West End Avenue.

13. West End Avenue was a "millionaires' row" of town houses until the early 20th century. When the New York Central Rail Road freight line, one block to the west, was covered over and Riverside Drive opened, the affluent residents were lured away to the new street with its unrivaled vistas of the Hudson River. An apartment-house building boom on West End Avenue after World War I and through the 1930s again attracted the wealthy (and near-wealthy); and the street, which declined somewhat after World War II, is again a choice location.

Look down the **west side of West End Avenue, between West 77th and West 76th streets**—a complete blockfront of lively, exuberant town houses (Lamb & Rich, 1891) that gives some sense of the first phase of development of the avenue. An engaging variety of gables, dormers, arches, and bay windows on a row of houses which fortunately escaped the second phase.

The West End Collegiate Church and Collegiate School incorporate both Dutch and Flemish features. Architect Robert W. Gibson created a charming "Nederlandisch" grouping with typical step-gables, pinnacles, and ornate dormer windows, modeling it after the *Vleeschhuis*—the 17th-century public meat market of Haarlem, Holland. This "Collegiate" church, built in 1891–92, is a descendant of the original Dutch Reformed Church, organized in 1628—the oldest Protestant congregation in America; and the Collegiate School is the country's oldest independent secondary school.

14. The entire block, West End Avenue to Broadway and West 78th to West 79th streets, is occupied by the **Apthorp Apartments.** A dignified luxury apartment house, it still preserves its original old-world elegance, despite the surrounding decrepitude of some of its neighboring streets. Built for William Waldorf Astor in 1906–08 from plans by Clinton & Russell, the enormous limestone structure is set around a broad central courtyard with fountain, access to which is through high vaulted passageways. The Broadway entrance is the grandest—a former carriageway whose bronze gates are reminiscent of the portcullis of some medieval castle. At each entrance, set in the spandrels of the façade, are two winged figures, and around the building runs a lovely ornate frieze. A cast-iron portico marks the entrance to each of the four separate units. Except for the addition of ground-floor shops on the Broadway side, the building remains virtually unchanged.

The apartment house is named for Charles Ward Apthorpe (*with an "e"*), who purchased the land in 1763. The property was passed to Apthorpe's son-in-law, Baron John C. van den Heuvel in 1792, and ultimately came into the Astor family in 1879.

Turn east on West 78th Street to Broadway, and north to West 79th street.

15. The First Baptist Church, on the northwest corner of West 79th Street, was built in 1891 mainly in Romanesque Revival style from plans by George Keister. The asymmetry of its twin towers is puzzling, as is the incompleteness of the right member. Contrary to expectation, the auditorium is semicircular in shape, with a quality of intimacy contrasting strongly with the austerity of the exterior.

16. Zabar's, at 2245 Broadway, is a *gourmet* landmark occupying more than half the block; known throughout the West Side (and by *cognoscenti* in all boroughs), it is a unique emporium whose mind-boggling variety of gustatory temptations defies cataloguing.

Across Broadway at 81st Street, a 20-story condominium rises behind the cream-colored Classic Revival–style façade of what was once the **RKO 81st Street Theater** (Thomas Lamb, 1914). Gone for years as a movie palace, it was recently a film studio where "Sesame Street" was first produced. The preserved front formerly had been the main entrance and office block and is now the rather

The original building (1877) of the American Museum of Natural History at 77th Street and Central Park West. This photo, taken ten years later, shows a broad wasteland which was soon to be covered by many new wings of the Museum. [See pp. 385–386.] (Museum of the City of New York)

bizarre entrance to the new apartment tower, whose design came from the firm of Beyer Blinder Belle. It and the nearby Bromley (Philip Birnbaum & Assocs.), between 83rd and 84th streets, are typical of the new upscale apartment houses that sprang up along Broadway in the 1980s.

Continue north on Broadway. At West 86th Street, cross to the east side.

Broadway and West 86th Street marks the **site of the village of Bloomingdale,** the largest settlement on the west side of Manhattan Island in the late 18th century. Its counterpart on the east side was the village of Haarlem (which subsequently dropped an "a" from the spelling).

17. Another massive luxury residence is the **Belnord Apartments,** located between Broadway and Amsterdam Avenue, from West 86th to West 87th streets, in a setting quite similar to that of its "cousin," the Apthorp. Completed in 1908, architect H. Hobart Weekes designed it for gracious living. Its porte-cochère, formal central garden, cast-iron lampposts, and ornate separate entranceways are reminders of the affluent life-style of its former tenants. Present tenants, however, have been battling for years with an intransigent landlady for much-needed improvements. One such tenant was Isaac Bashevis Singer.

Cross Broadway again and walk west on West 86th Street to West End Avenue.

18. On the northeast corner of West 86th Street and West End Avenue is the **Church of St. Paul and St. Andrew** (R. H. Robertson, 1895–97). In its designation report, the Landmarks Preservation Commission called the church "...a brilliant exemplar of the eclecticism that spread through American architecture in the late 19th century." Designed in an unusual combination of Early Christian, German Romanesque, and early Italian Renaissance architectural styles, this striking edifice of yellow brick with buff-colored terra-cotta trim is one of the outstanding church buildings of the city. Built originally for St. Paul's Methodist Episcopal Church, the congregation merged in 1937 with nearby St. Andrew's M. E. Church, which since 1890 had been located on West 75th Street, between Amsterdam and Columbus avenues. (St. Andrew's old building, designed by J. Cleveland Cady, still stands, and is now a synagogue).

The major features of the church are its bold octagonal campanile; the broad entrance porch with triple round-arched doorways, surmounted by ornate ocular windows flanked by terra-cotta reliefs of angels, and topped by a balustrade; a smaller tower with open belfry, set at a 45-degree angle to the façade; the tall clerestory on the 86th Street side with its odd round-arched flying buttresses; and a Spanish tile roof.

When erected, St. Paul's was a significant visual landmark in the area, until the advent of the tall apartment houses that supplanted the rows of town houses. The impact, however, is still quite apparent, and the landmark church is considered a key work in the career of the architect, Robert Henderson Robertson.

Turn north (right) on West End Avenue.

19. Adjacent **St. Ignatius Episcopal Church** (1902), in Gothic Revival style, is another house of worship designed by architect Charles C. Haight, but not one of his better works. This "ecclesiastical block" provides a pleasant break in the monotony of the seemingly endless rows of apartment houses along West End Avenue. Across West End Avenue from St. Ignatius's is the Tudor Gothic Revival–style **Cathedral Preparatory Seminary** in attractive red brick and limestone. The building was built for St. Agatha's School (Boring & Tilton, 1907), and later became a branch of Cathedral College.

Diagonally across West 87th Street, on the northwest corner, is an Art Deco–style apartment house, **565 West End Avenue** (Herman I. Feldman, 1937). Particularly attractive is the bright orange brick, with a course of black bricks in the base and a stainless-steel cornice over the entrance.

Turn east (right) on West 88th Street.

20. Dominating the middle of the block is **Congregation B'nai Jeshurun,** designed by Henry B. Herts and Walter Schneider in 1918. A broad Moorish façade of orange granite and a highly ornate carved limestone portal in Romanesque Revival style give this synagogue a stately and imposing appearance. The richly polychromed interior is well worth a visit. B'nai Jeshurun is the oldest Ashkenazic congregation in the city. It was founded in 1825 by a group of German and English Jews who split with the Spanish and Portuguese Synagogue and adopted the German ritual and language as opposed to the Sephardic Spanish-Portuguese.

Occupying the block on the east side of Broadway between 87th and 88th streets is one of the "mold-breakers" among recently designed apartment houses. In a welcome departure from the traditional (since the 1950s) glass box or white brick "wedding cake," architects Gruzen & Partners, in 1982, have created a twin-tower limestone-trimmed brick building which is reminiscent of the fine old apartments that line Central Park West (the Majestic, San Remo, Eldorado, and Beresford). While maintaining a respectful adherence to the "street wall," the first thirteen stories of **The Montana** step back at the roof line of neighboring buildings, then leap skyward in two symmetrical towers for another thirteen stories.

Turn north (left) on Broadway to West 89th Street.

21. Another of the immense luxury multiple dwellings is the **Astor Court Apartments** (89th to 90th streets, east side of Broadway), designed by Charles A. Platt in 1916. The interior garden courtyard and ornate balconies add grace and charm, but its crowning glory is the superb copper-clad cornice.

Continue north on Broadway to West 94th Street and turn west (left). About 50 yards down the north side of the block is the entrance to Pomander Walk.

22. New York City presents an almost inexhaustible supply of architectural surprises, and delightful **Pomander Walk** is no exception. Constructed in 1921, this diminutive double row of charming houses was designed to imitate a small street in "Merrie England." The idea originated with the stage setting for the English play *Pomander Walk,* which opened in New York in 1911. In the play, the Walk was a small mews in the London suburb of Chiswick. Among the famous who lived here were Gloria Swanson, Rosalind Russell, and Humphrey Bogart.

Until recently it was possible to stroll through Pomander Walk to 95th Street. However, times being what they are, only residents may enter, but an excellent view may be had through the gate.

Return to Broadway.

At the southwest corner of 95th Street is **Symphony Space** (originally Astor Market, then the Symphony Theater). Since 1978 it has presented a wide variety of performing artists, including Garrison Keillor's radio show—all at modest prices.

Continue north on Broadway to West 96th Street, and turn west (left) to Riverside Drive. Walk under the viaduct, turn right and climb up to the Drive.

23. For the past hundred years or so, New Yorkers have been called "cliff dwellers" for reasons that are obvious. The architect of this otherwise undistinguished apartment house (Herman Lee Meader, 1914) displayed a keen sense of humor in the frieze that depicts motifs from the lives of the early Arizona Cliff Dwellers, with masks, buffalo skulls, mountain lions, and rattlesnakes. The interesting designs are more than symbolic to our contemporary "cliff dwellers." (The building faces the Drive on the northeast corner of 96th Street.)

Walk south on Riverside Drive along the west sidewalk.

24. Tree-lined **Riverside Drive** is one of the city's loveliest streets. Much of the dignity and elegance of yesteryear are gone, but the broad panoramic vistas are still unspoiled. As more affluent families moved into the area, elegant town houses and mansions were built, and it was not long before Riverside Drive challenged Fifth Avenue as one of the most fashionable addresses in town. By the 1930s it began to fade; but with the expansion of **Riverside Park** in 1937 when the railroad tracks were covered, much of the charm returned. Vehicular traffic was then diverted to the new Henry Hudson Parkway, close to the riverbank. Riverside Park was designed by Frederick Law Olmsted, the landscape architect who revolutionized our ideas on park planning, and who gave us Central and Prospect parks, among many others. Riverside Drive was pushed north to West 129th Street by 1885, but the 96th Street viaduct was not built until 1902. Along the Drive can be seen the former opulent town houses and the newer luxury apartment houses that sprang up with the completion of the Park and Drive.

25. At West 93rd Street, on a slight crest overlooking Riverside Park, is the heroic **Joan of Arc Memorial Statue,** executed in 1915 by famed American sculptor Anna Vaughn Hyatt Huntington. The statue was commissioned by the Joan of Arc Statue Committee to commemorate the 500th anniversary of the birth of the Maid of Orleans, presumed to be in 1412. Her armor is historically accurate, having been researched by the Metropolitan Museum of Art's curator of armor. Sculptor Huntington has succeeded in capturing Joan of Arc's expression of intense fervor and sense of mission as she rode forth to lead the French troops in battle against the English and Burgundians. The bronze statue was cast by the well-known Gorham Company (which still is in business, but no longer casting huge statues). The Gothic-style pedestal of the monument was designed by architect John V. Van Pelt, and contains fragments from France's Rheims Cathedral (where in 1429 Joan of Arc reached the pinnacle of her career with the coronation of Charles VII) and stones from the Tower at Rouen (where she was burned at the stake two years later).

26. At the corner of West 89th Street stands one of the West Side's most significant public sculptures, **The Soldiers' and Sailors' Monument.** Sculptor Paul E. M. DuBoy and architects Charles W. and Arthur A. Stoughton completed the marble Civil War memorial in 1902 (just after DuBoy put the final touches to his work on the Ansonia Hotel), patterning it after the Choragic Monument of Lysicrates in Athens.

27. The imposing mansion on the southeast corner of the Drive and West 89th Street is the **former Isaac L. Rice Residence** (Herts & Tallant, 1901), now the Yeshiva Chofetz Chaim, a seminary. Rice, a lawyer, publicist, publisher, acclaimed chess player, and renowned pioneer in electric storage battery technology, named the house Villa Julia for his wife (who was the founder of an organization that would be much appreciated today, The Society for the Suppression of Unnecessary Noise). After Isaac's death, Julia Rice presented the city with a number of sports facilities, one of which survives in the Bronx, Rice Memorial Stadium. The mansion was acquired in 1908 by Samuel Schinasi, a partner in the Schinasi Brothers manufacturing firm. A year later, his brother, Morris, commissioned his own residence, which was erected about a mile north on the Drive, at West 107th Street. Coincidentally, these are the only two surviving free-standing mansions from the great number that once graced Riverside Drive. Although some alterations were made between 1906 and 1948, the maroon-colored brick, wildly eclectic house is a sheer delight! Note how the porte-cochère is partly recessed into the structure, and how the positioning of the house on its corner plot adds stature to the whole. Landmark status did not come easily, as the owners vigorously opposed designation, fearing that the restrictions would hamper growth of the institution by prohibiting what they felt were needed alterations.

Continue south to West 85th Street and turn east.

No. 350 West 85th Street, **The Red House** (Harde & Short, 1904), is a romantic gem! Built in the style of an Elizabethan manor house, this six-story apartment building provides a grand climax to the walking tour. The effect is again pure *Merrie England,* from its Gothic detailing right up to the dragon and crown cartouche set high in the brickwork.

Return to Riverside Drive and turn south to West 84th Street.

In the park, directly opposite, is a prominent rock outcropping of Manhattan schist called **Mount Tom,** which Edgar Allan Poe found to be an attractive summer spot for contemplation of the river when he lived here in 1843–44. The site was also the original choice for the location of the Soldiers' and Sailors' Monument. For two blocks, West 84th Street is called **Edgar Allan Poe Street.**

Although this is the end of the walking tour, a pleasant stroll back to the starting point can be made as follows:

Continue south on Riverside Drive [*see* map] to West 79th Street; east to Columbus Avenue; north to West 81st Street; east to Central Park West; then south to West 72nd Street. (Or, alternatively, walk down Broadway to the Lincoln Center for the Performing Arts, West 66th to West 62nd streets.)

Following the first itinerary given above, the block between Columbus Avenue and Central Park West is quite attractive and faces the **Hayden Planetarium** (Trowbridge & Livingston, 1935). Along Central Park West to West 77th Street is the outstanding **American Museum of Natural History,** which houses one of the world's greatest scientific and gem collections and is one of the most frequently visited places in town. The equestrian statue of Theodore Roosevelt flanked by an Indian chief and a Bantu was sculpted in 1939

An artist's conception of the completed American Museum of Natural History was not too far amiss when drawn for Moses King's Views of New York *in 1908. The central tower, however, was never built. (Author's collection)*

by J. E. Frazer. The museum consists of a group of buildings occupying a four-block area formerly called Manhattan Square, whose construction began in 1873 with the original Jacob Wrey Mould and Calvert Vaux building (to be seen shortly). Adjacent to it in the rear is the power house and a wing by Charles Volz (1908). The Central Park West side is dominated by the rather pretentious Beaux Arts–style Theodore Roosevelt Memorial Wing (John Russell Pope, 1935), now the main entrance, with side wings by Trowbridge & Livingston (1924–33). The **West 77th Street side of the museum,** however, includes an impressive entrance and is one of the city's great examples of Romanesque Revival–style architecture. The massive structure of pink Vermont granite, with carriage entrance, arcaded porch, grand staircase, turrets, and corner towers, was erected between 1892 and 1899 under the supervision of J. Cleveland Cady, and later by his firm of Cady, Berg & See. Many feel that this should have remained the main entrance to this great institution. (The original red-brick building by Calvert Vaux and J. Wrey Mould can be seen by looking through the fence on Columbus Avenue and West 77th Street.)

●   **The New-York Historical Society,** on the southwest corner of West 77th Street (York & Sawyer, 1908; with wings added in 1937–38 by Walker & Gillette), was built in Classic style. The Society, founded in 1804, possesses a superb collection of books, prints, manuscripts, paintings, portraits, silver, and other historical memorabilia, including the original Audubon *Birds of America,* the McKim, Mead & White files, and a collection of Tiffany lamps. Sadly, the future of this almost 200-year-old institution is in doubt. Beset by financial woes, it recently closed its library and gift shop, but at this writing promised support from the city will keep the library open at least for a while longer.

●   The two blocks between West 77th Street and West 75th streets mark the
★   eastern edge of the **former Central Park West–76th Street Historic District** (now part of the Upper West Side–Central Park West Historic District), a grouping of 40 town houses of unified scale and general design, plus the New-York Historical Society Building; the neo-Gothic **Universalist Church of New York** (formerly called Church of the Divine Paternity, built in 1897 from plans by William A. Potter); and the Beaux Arts–style **Kenilworth Apartments** (Townsend, Steinle & Haskell, 1908). The church presents a varied and interesting façade with its pointed arch windows, buttresses, finials, and gables, plus two magnificent stained-glass windows. Take a brief detour along quiet, tree-lined **West 76th Street,** and notice the variety of architectural styles with their handsome details—so typical of the late 19th-century period of eclecticism.

●   Continuing south, the two succeeding blocks are occupied respectively by the mammoth and luxurious twin-tower **San Remo Apartments** (Emery Roth, 1930), a fine example of the architect's adaptation of the Italian Renaissance style to a high-rise apartment building; and the stately **Langham** (Clinton & Russell, 1905), with its magnificent roof line.

The Eighth Avenue A line is at 72nd Street and Central Park West. Transfer at 59th Street–Columbus Circle for the A and D expresses and the Nos. 1 and 9 of the Broadway–Seventh Avenue line.

BROOKLYN HEIGHTS
Including All
of the Historic District

East River

Brooklyn Bridge

FURMAN ST.

BKLYN-QUEENS EXPY.

POPLAR ST.

MIDDAGH ST.

CRANBERRY ST.

ORANGE ST.

start

CADMAN PLAZA WEST

HIGH ST. IND Sta.

PINEAPPLE ST.

IRT

CLARK ST.

THE ESPLANADE

COLUMBIA HEIGHTS

WILLOW ST.

HICKS ST.

COLLEGE PL.

HENRY ST.

MONROE PLACE

Brooklyn Piers

LOVE LA.

PIERREPONT ST.

TIERP'T PL.

MONT. TERR.

Henry Ward Beecher Monument

MONTAGUE ST.

BMT

BMT

COURT ST.

REMSEN ST.

CLINTON ST.

GRACE COURT

GRACE CT. AL.

HUNTS LA.

JORALEMON ST.

COLUMBIA PL.

WILLOW PL.

GARDEN PL.

SIDNEY PL.

AITKEN PL.

LIVINGSTON ST.

SCHERMERHORN ST.

STATE ST.

15. Brooklyn Heights and the Fulton Ferry Historic District

[A or C line to High Street–Brooklyn Bridge (use the rear exit, and walk through Whitman Close town houses to Henry Street, turn left one block); Broadway–Seventh Avenue line to Clark Street–Brooklyn Heights. On exiting from the St. George Hotel, turn left to Henry Street, and left again two blocks to Orange Street]

The section of Brooklyn known as Brooklyn Heights was New York City's first suburb. Situated on bluffs that rise steeply above New York Bay, the "Heights" was for over 250 years a relatively remote and rural area, undisturbed by the growth of the burgeoning port city across the East River. Before the arrival of the Dutch in 1626, the western portion of Long Island was inhabited by several tribes of the Algonkian Nation, particularly the Canarsees, who lived in long houses—some actually several blocks in length—on the high promontory facing Manhattan Island. When the first Dutch settlements were built, the Indians abandoned their village of Ihpetonga ("High Sandy Banks"), and in 1646 the village of Breuckelen (named for a town in the Dutch province of Utrecht) was established by Dutch settlers from Manhattan. When the British captured New York, they changed the name to Brooklyn. The beginning of the Revolutionary War saw the crucial battle of Long Island lost by the patriots on August 27, 1776, as Washington's meager forces were overwhelmed by a superior British and Hessian army under Lord Howe. After their defeat at the Flatbush Pass (in the present Prospect Park) and the threat of total annihilation through a flanking maneuver, a small regiment of Maryland Continentals fought

The Plymouth Church in a Civil War–era engraving, showing crowds gathering to hear the fiery oratory of abolitionist Henry Ward Beecher. Except for a later Tuscan-style porch, the barnlike building is unchanged. (Brooklyn Historical Society)

a desperate delaying action at nearby Gowanus, as Washington successfully withdrew the army to Manhattan under cover of a heavy night fog.

Since Dutch colonial days, a small sail ferry operated to the foot of the Old Ferry Road (now Fulton Street) from Peck Slip, in Manhattan. A bell hung at each landing so that prospective "commuters" could summon the boat. However, the opening in 1814 of Robert Fulton's steam ferry *Nausau* signaled the beginning of the area's development as a residential community. Brooklyn Heights by 1820 was thickly settled, with much the same street layout as today. In 1834 the State Legislature granted a charter to the *City* of Brooklyn, and with its rapid growth and subsequent annexation of several other independent villages, by the mid-19th century it became the third largest city in the nation, with a population exceeding 85,000. Brooklyn has always been known as a city of churches and homes. It also has the distinction of having the most cemetery area in proportion to its size, which author Thomas Wolfe was keenly aware of when he said sardonically, "Only the dead know Brooklyn."

Laid out at right angles to the waterfront, the shady streets of Brooklyn Heights provided easy access to the river, and as late as the 20th century there were no fewer than three ferries operating to lower Manhattan (Wall Street to Montague Street, South Ferry to Atlantic Avenue, and the Fulton Ferry connecting both Brooklyn's and Manhattan's Fulton streets). With the rapid development of the City of Brooklyn (which did not merge with the City of New York until 1898) the "Heights" was bypassed and left undisturbed as land speculators and builders moved south and east. Thus, Brooklyn Heights today remains strikingly similar to its early appearance of more than 150 years ago. Of the approximately 1,100 houses in the neighborhood, more than 600 were built before 1860! The only major physical change was made in 1950 when the City of New York built the Brooklyn-Queens Expressway along the Brooklyn Heights waterfront, removing a number of old houses but substituting the magnificent Esplanade over the roadway, which provided residents with one of the most scenic views of New York Harbor. However, with the abandonment of the ferries and the construction of the new highway, the Heights is now permanently separated from the water. Its ties to Manhattan were greatly increased with the opening in 1883 of the Brooklyn Bridge; and by 1908 the first of several subway tunnels reached the Heights, although elevated trains had already been using the bridge for more than a decade. The arrival of the subway caused many of the patrician inhabitants to flee, and a number of their stately mansions were divided into small apartments. The neighborhood is still characterized by rows of lovely brick and brownstone houses—most with a uniform 50-foot height, representing virtually every architectural style of the 19th century. The Heights is also noted for several of its landmark churches designed by famous architects; but it is mainly regarded as one of the most charming and desirable residential sections of the city. In recognition of its aesthetic and historic value, Brooklyn Heights was designated in 1965 as **the City's first Historic District.**

Note: Brooklyn Heights is a rather extensive area with a great number of interesting and important sites. The chapter has therefore been divided into four sections, a **First Tour,** a **Second Tour,** and a **Brief Look at Brooklyn's Civic Center** followed by a **tour of the Fulton Ferry Historic District.**

FIRST TOUR

The first tour begins at the corner of Henry and Orange Streets (one block west of Cadman Plaza).

Orange Street, and its two adjacent neighbors, Cranberry and Pineapple streets, were named by developers John and Jacob Middagh Hicks; or as a story goes, by one of their relatives, a Miss Middagh. Irked by wealthy neighbors who named the streets after themselves, she ripped down the immodest signs and replaced them with ones with botanical names. The city fathers promptly removed them, but after a protracted battle, the Board of Aldermen gave in and allowed her choices to remain. She is also credited with naming Poplar and Willow streets.

No. 69 Orange Street is one of the oldest houses in Brooklyn Heights. Built ca. 1829, it is typical of the wooden clapboard residences erected during the early development of the neighborhood. The mansard roof was added after 1870. Note the ornate brackets and consoles.

Alongside to the west is the famous **Plymouth Church of the Pilgrims.** Founded in 1847 by the fiery Henry Ward Beecher, its first minister, it was designed by architect Joseph C. Wells in an Italianate style and completed two years later. An austere, barnlike structure, it became one of the most influential churches in the nation. Beecher, an outspoken abolitionist, preached for many years and invited many noted public figures to share his pulpit. Among the anti-slavery agitators who shared his pulpit in passionate oratory were William Lloyd Garrison, Charles Sumner, and John Greenleaf Whittier. Abraham Lincoln worshipped here twice and his pew, No. 89, where he worshipped the first time, is marked with a silver plaque. (On his second visit he sat in the balcony.) In 1867 Charles Dickens delivered an address on the occasion of his second visit to America; and through the years such greats as Horace Greeley, Mark Twain, and Booker T. Washington attended services here. In dramatic outpourings of rhetoric, Henry Ward Beecher fought with uncompromising vigor against slavery, and with equal grandiloquence campaigned for women's suffrage, temperance, and general reform. With typical dramatic flair, he once auctioned off a mulatto slave girl named Pinkie before an aghast congregation, using the money to purchase her freedom and arouse the attention of the entire country. Pinkie, actually Mrs. James Hunt, subsequently returned in 1927 to address the congregation from the very same platform where she had been "sold" almost 70 years before. Local Union Army units on their way south to southern battlefronts would stop for services at the Plymouth Church, and at the height of the Civil War, Beecher made a trip to England to win sympathy away from the Confederate cause. President Lincoln later honored Beecher by having him deliver a speech at the symbolic raising of the flag at Fort Sumter. (Incidentally, Beecher's sister, novelist Harriet Beecher Stowe, will always be remembered for her very influential but overimaginative *Uncle Tom's Cabin.*) Beecher, who in a few short years had become a national hero, was later involved in a sensational "page-one scandal," accused of having committed adultery with the wife of a former associate. Although the minister was subsequently acquitted by the jury, his reputation and career suffered irreparable damage.

The exterior of the church is virtually without ornamentation, in the tradition of the New England Congregational Church—even lacking the usual steeple. Inside, the sanctuary is simple, with pale green walls and woodwork. A balcony supported by cast-iron columns surrounds the hall, connecting with the organ in front. There are 19 stained-glass windows designed by Frederick Stymetz Lamb representing the "History of Puritanism and Its Influence Upon the Institutions and People of the Republic," with the broader theme of political, intellectual, and religious liberty. The chairs are contemporary copies of some brought from the Mount of Olives in 1868 by members of a trip to the Holy Land, the occasion made famous by Mark Twain in his *Innocents Abroad.* Adjoining the sanctuary is **Hillis Hall,** a social center, named for a turn-of-the-century pastor. Its middle stained-glass window on the north side is a magnificent representation of the Ascension into Heaven, one of five from the Tiffany Studios. The Church House (75 Hicks Street), was a gift of sugar and coffee magnate John Arbuckle, and was built in 1913 in Classic Eclectic style from plans by Woodruff Leeming. In the connecting arcade is a fragment of the Plymouth Rock brought from Massachusetts in 1840, and portraits of the church's pastors, and a painting of Beecher with Pinkie. In the

68 Hicks Street, at the southwest corner of Cranberry Street, in 1920. Built 100 years before, most changes seem to have occurred in recent years. (Brooklyn Historical Society)

lovely arcade garden is a **statue of Beecher** by sculptor Gutzon Borglum. The church was seriously damaged by fire in 1849, and in the early 20th century a Tuscan porch was added; otherwise the structure is in original condition. The Plymouth Church was merged in 1934 with the Congregational Church of the Pilgrims (whose former building still stands on the corner of Henry and Remsen streets, but is now Our Lady of Lebanon Maronite Cathedral).

Turn right (north) on Hicks Street.

    Hicks Street is named for the family of the brothers John and Jacob Middagh Hicks, early residents and developers of the area.

    No. 68 Hicks Street, at the southwest corner of Cranberry Street, is a two-and-a-half-story frame house topped by a gambrel roof, built ca. 1820. It was originally a grocery store and tavern. The clapboard walls are sympathetic modern replacements made of old wood. Note the Ionic colonnettes at the entranceway.

    Brooklyn Heights was intimately involved in the life of poet **Walt Whitman.** In his childhood he lived on Cranberry Street almost directly behind the Plymouth Church, and some 30 years later his *Leaves of Grass* was printed in a shop just down the street at the corner of Fulton Street. "The Good Gray Poet" also served from 1846 to 1848 as editor of the Brooklyn *Daily Eagle,* whose offices were located a few steps farther north, close to the site of the old Fulton Ferry.

    No. 59, diagonally across the intersection, another frame house of ca. 1820, was the residence and shop of a cooper (barrel maker). The building has also suffered the ravages of modernization, with a stucco front and replacement entrance door. Adjacent **No. 57,** built about five years later, was the home of a merchant. The mansard roof was added during the period of the popular French Second Empire style in the 1870s. Actually, the mansard roof fits rather harmoniously with a number of the revival styles, and, as will be seen later, lent itself quite well to the Italianate brownstone row house also.

No. 51, with arched dormer windows, belonged to a sea captain, and was built ca. 1831. The low front stoop was removed and the entrance door installed on the basement level. The original door lintel is still visible.

Across the street, **Nos. 60** and **56** have been altered considerably. No. 60, a two-and-a-half-story frame house with a gambrel roof, has dormer windows similar to No. 51. The arch of a former fanlight doorway is still visible. No. 56, a three-story frame building, was probably a boardinghouse when built, and has subsequently had an additional floor added. Both houses were constructed before 1829.

Turn left (west) into Middagh Street.

Middagh Street was probably named after early resident John Middagh, either by himself or by relatives John and Jacob Middagh Hicks. One speculates on what the cantankerous Miss Middagh would have said after her successful campaign for botanical street names, only to see a street named after *her* family.

Typical residences of middle-class merchants and artisans of the early 19th century are **Nos. 25–33** Middagh Street. **Nos. 31–33** is a dual house, built in 1820 (note plaque). The former was a "men's hairdressing parlor," the latter, a paint store. Doubtless, the rear and upper floors served as living quarters. **No. 29,** built ca. 1830, was the home of an engineer; the profession of **No. 27's** occupant is unknown, but the house dates from 1829; and the much-remodeled **No. 25,** a laborer's house, and smaller than the others, was built in 1824. It has suffered so many physical changes as to be almost unrecognizable (stuccoed front, lowered entrance, etc.).

Across Middagh Street, **No. 30,** a three-story frame house, was built in 1824, and has a street-level entranceway in Greek Revival style. Alas, the front wall has been defaced with asphalt shingles. Adjoining **No. 28** was erected ca. 1829 for a sea captain. Another unfortunate modernization has rendered this old house an aesthetic nonentity.

As if to make up for the architectural desecrations committed on its neighbors, **No. 24 Middagh Street** is a delightful gem of a house! An amazingly well preserved example of the Federal style, the **former Eugene Boisselet House,** built in 1820, is referred to by the *AIA Guide to New York City* as "The Queen of Brooklyn Heights," and is said to be the oldest house in the neighborhood. The brickwork basement is laid in typical Flemish bond (rows of alternating long bricks, called "stretchers," and short bricks, called "headers"), while the walls are built of clapboard. Two stories plus an attic with dormers is very characteristic of the Federal style, although the roof of this house, rather than peaked, is gambrel. The doorway is artistically carved and flanked by Ionic colonnettes, with leaded-glass side lights (small windows), and surmounted by a transom and sculptured panel. On the attic level, visible from Willow Street, twin quarter-round windows enframe an arched window, and twin chimneys strike a harmonious balance. A board fence connects the house with a small rear-garden cottage, probably a former carriage house. The missing back porch would likely complete the beautifully proportioned building.

Turn left (south) on Willow Street.

Nos. 20 through 26 Willow Street form a pleasing row of simple Greek Revival–style houses, built 1846–48. **No. 22 was the residence of Henry Ward Beecher**. The entranceways are quite handsome, approached by stone stairs with ornate wrought-iron railings that terminate in a vertical swirl. Note the "Greek ears" on the door enframements, which are topped by a low-pitched pediment, and the recessed doors flanked by pilasters and side lights are surmounted by a transom. At the rear (not visible from Willow Street) are a pair of two-story open galleries on Nos. 24 and 26, facing the harbor, a typical and delightful addition to Brooklyn Heights houses facing the river. It's a shame the rest of the galleries were glassed-in.

Nos. 28 and 30 are a pair of Italianate brownstones, four stories high with a common cornice supported by brackets, and arched entranceways. No. 28 was built in 1858, its neighbor a year later.

At the corner of Cranberry and Willow streets stands one of the earliest apartment houses in the city, **"The Willows"** (No. 37). Elements of the Queen Anne style are evident in the high bay window with its classical swags and small broken pediment. This early multiple dwelling house was designed by architect A. F. Norris and erected in 1886. Note the plaque.

Turn right (west) into Cranberry Street.

Nos. 13, 15, and 17 Cranberry Street show most of their original Federal-style details. No. 17 (now numbered No. 19), at the corner of Willow Street, was built in 1833, and still retains its paneled window lintels and arched doorways; however, the glass doors are later additions. Part of the original fence (with Greek Revival anthemion motifs) on the Willow Street side still remains. The cast-iron balustrade on the stoop and the romantic mansard roof were added later. The entrance to No. 13, flanked by paneled blocks, probably supported ornate cast-iron basket newels. The fanlight doorway is enframed by a lovely archway with matching panel blocks; and the cornice, typical of the Federal style, is supported by rows of consoles above a bead-and-reel board. The house dates from about 1829. No. 15 has suffered the most, with the loss of its stoop and cornice and the addition of the extra story.

Return to Willow Street and turn right (south).

Nos. 55 and 57 Willow Street, a pair of Federal-style houses, were built ca. 1832 and 1825, respectively. Both have Flemish bond brickwork, indicative of more expensive construction. No. 57, a two-and-a-half-story house at the northeast corner of Orange Street, is known as the **Robert White House,** after the merchant who first occupied it. Note the handsome dormer windows, which luckily escaped the improvements that destroyed the entrance, railings, and windows. The original size of the windows can be seen in the "blind windows" on the Orange Street side. A lovely frieze with Greek key motif, tooled stone lintels above the windows and doors, and tall twin chimneys add to the charm.

Turn right (west) on Orange Street to the corner of Columbia Heights.

The 12-story Margaret Apartments, 97 Columbia Heights (The Ehrenkrantz Group & Eckstut, 1988), was erected on the **site of the Hotel Margaret,** which was destroyed in a raging fire while under renovation in 1980. The old landmark hotel, designed by Brooklyn architect Frank Freeman in 1889, was a familiar and appreciated building, and had been the residence during the 1920s of etcher Joseph Pennell and novelists Sigrid Undset (Norwegian-born winner of the 1928 Nobel Prize) and Betty Smith, who wrote *A Tree Grows in Brooklyn* in 1943. The conflagration was compared to the one which consumed Underhill's Colonnade at almost the same location in 1853 [*see* engraving on the following page]. The new building was purchased by Jehovah's Witnesses, following a dispute with the city over the zoning laws which limit new building height to 50 feet. Because the former hotel was taller and the developer feared economic loss, a compromise was agreed to on its ultimate bulk. They should also have settled on more subdued colors for this overbearing newcomer.

Turn left (south) on Columbia Heights.

On the left side of Columbia Heights, at No. 107, is the **Brooklyn Heights Residence of the Watchtower Bible and Tract Society,** commonly called Jehovah's Witnesses (Frederick G. Frost & Associates, 1959). The Witnesses have established their headquarters in Brooklyn Heights, and the residence, as well as the apartment house across the street, are some of their ever-increasing number of facilities. Erected before the passage of the Landmarks Law which limited the height of new buildings in this historic district, it overwhelms neighboring buildings. The garden and fountain do provide some relief.

Walk south on Columbia Heights to Pineapple Street, and turn left (east).

Halfway down the block on the north side is a peaceful country-style house, charming **No. 13 Pineapple Street.** Built around 1830, it is a large residence with an interior central transverse stair hall, whose rooms are arranged on either side. A third floor was added to the building in the mid-19th century, requiring a new bracketed cornice; and the front windows were then also enlarged. The stoop, too, is relatively new, as is the reproduction fanlight over the entrance. Nonetheless, it is a pleasant reminder of the past, enhanced by a spacious plot that breaks the monotony of the row houses.

Return to Columbia Heights and turn left (south).

On the southeast corner is a dormitory and library of the Jehovah's Witnesses, and part of the headquarters complex of the Watchtower Bible and Tract Society. Erected in 1970 the building's design won the approval of the Landmarks Commission only after several previous submissions had been rejected. The successful plans for the present structure, by Ulrich Franzen Associates, were accepted only because the Commission found them compatible with the style of the surroundings. (One of the rejected designs called for a 12-story tower, which the Landmarks Commission felt would have been totally out of scale with neighboring buildings.) An appealing aspect of the plan is the adaptation of the house fronts of the three adjacent brick houses to the south into the overall design, and the repetition of their bay-window motif in the theme of the office building's façade.

Across the street, **No. 138 Columbia Heights** is a lovely town house built ca. 1860 and a nice example of the Italianate style. In good condition are its delicate cornice consoles, the segmental arch windows, the frieze and cornice over the window and door enframements, and the curved pediment set on consoles over the doorway. But how did the owner get away with installing a window in the cornice?

Columbia Heights is named for the estate of early landowner Hezekiah Beers Pierrepont, whose mansion "Four Chimneys" and extensive property overlooked the harbor in the early 19th century. Pierrepont owned the Anchor Gin Distillery at the foot of Joralemon Street, which was operated by a large windmill and was conveniently close to the ferry. The wealthy merchant was also

Underhill's Colonnade on the Heights, overlooking the harbor in the late 1830s. The engraving is from the letterhead of a fire insurance company, showing a house on fire (fanciful or otherwise), which was doubtless intended to serve as a graphic warning to those not insured. The Colonnade itself was consumed by fire in 1853. (Brooklyn Historical Society)

Robert Fulton's chief financial backer, helping him establish the first steam ferry in the world. By mid-19th century, Columbia Heights (then Columbia Street) became one of the most fashionable strips in Brooklyn. A row of eight three-story, wooden, Greek Revival–style houses connected by a common colonnaded portico was erected in 1835 on the most prominent point on the Heights, between Cranberry and Middagh streets. Known as General Underhill's Colonnade Row, or simply **Underhill's Colonnade,** it was the area's most significant landmark until one cold December morning in 1853, when it was consumed in a spectacular conflagration. Occupying the east side of Columbia Heights between Pineapple and Clark streets from 1844 to 1904 was the sumptuous **Leavitt Bowen Mansion,** with a monumental Corinthian portico facing the harbor. Another long-vanished landmark was **Dr. Charles H. Shephard's Turkish Bath** which occupied a Greek Revival house on the corner of Cranberry Street from 1863 until 1913.

Turn left (east) at Clark Street to Willow Street.

The **former Towers Hotel,** on the northeast corner of Clark and Willow streets was purchased by the Watchtower Bible and Tract Society to house staff members of its expanding world headquarters office. The Towers, a prominent feature of the Heights skyline since its opening in 1928, was one of Brooklyn's last luxury hotels. Designed by architects Starrett & Van Vleck, the building's four octagonal towers, illuminated at night, were a familiar landmark.

Continue east on Clark Street to Hicks Street and turn right (south).

Nos. 131 and **135 Hicks Street,** on the east side, are rare examples of brownstones in the Gothic Revival style. No. 131 is by far the better preserved of the pair, with its elaborate cornice still intact, and without the abominable penthouse that surmounts its twin. It is referred to as the **Henry C. Bowen House,** after the original merchant-owner who had the house built around 1848. Bowen was a founder of the Plymouth Church as well as the abolitionist newspaper, *The Independent,* which Henry Ward Beecher edited. Both houses share Tudor Gothic arched doorways and ornately carved spandrels, square-topped windows with sashes in imitation of casements, hood (or label) moldings over the windows, cast-iron railings and traceries. The cornice of No. 13 is set above a bead-and-reel molding, and only the missing cast-iron fence would complete this lovely house. (Perhaps the owner could make a deal with his neighbor in No. 135 to obtain its finials.) The Gothic Revival style was in vogue in Brooklyn Heights between 1844 and 1865. (Note the plaque.)

Returning to Clark Street, the **Hotel St. George,** in a massing of several buildings of different styles and eras, occupies the entire block from Hicks to Henry and Clark to Pineapple streets. Built in 1885 by William Tunbridge, a retired sea captain, from plans by August Hatfield, it then grew piecemeal until 1929 and became the largest hotel in the city. The original section is still visible a few steps east of Hicks Street, split into two wings. Few old-timers will forget

The Congregational Church of the Pilgrims on Remsen and Henry streets still had its steeple in this ca. 1880 engraving. In 1934, the congregation moved to the Plymouth Church and the building now houses Our Lady of Lebanon Maronite Cathedral. (Brooklyn Historical Society)

Of these five unusual row houses on Clinton Street and Aitken Place, only two survive (Nos. 140 and 142). Most unusual are the cast-iron lintels, moldings, and cornices. (Brooklyn Historical Society)

Hezekiah Beers Pierrepont's Anchor Gin Distillery in 1823, near the present site of Joralemon and Furman streets, in a painting by an unknown artist. The windmill and boats are reminiscent of a 17th-century Dutch landscape. (Brooklyn Collection. Brooklyn Public Library)

The Fulton Ferry slip in 1746, showing the step-gabled Dutch-style house of the ferrymaster, at right. (Author's collection)

Map showing the five Dutch towns and the one English town (Gravesend) which during the 17th century constituted Kings County. The names of the original Dutch towns are in parentheses. (The Williamsburgh Savings Bank)

The first village map of Brooklyn showing the street patterns, which are virtually the same today, and the estates of the landowners, many of whom were not averse to having their names perpetuated in street designations. (Author's collection)

the once-famous Grand Ballroom; and just about anyone who grew up in Brooklyn in the '30s remembers swimming in the enormous saltwater pool and watching his floating reflection in the room-length ceiling mirrors. It was also the favorite hotel of the old Brooklyn Dodgers. Those were the halcyon days of the St. George as a hotel.

By the mid-1970s the hotel had deteriorated so badly that it became a source of serious concern to the community. But with the skyrocketing real-estate values of a few years later, along came the developers, and within a brief period the property was divided into several parcels and major renovation projects begun. The "Tower" section facing Hicks Street was converted into a co-op. The rear wings on Pineapple Street were rebuilt as cooperative apartments, with the late 19th-century façades sympathetically restored. The east wing on Henry Street, however, remains as the only surviving member to stay as a hotel. The owner, who has been operating the hotel, has been filling the unit with temporary H.I.V. residents, AIDS patients, and the homeless, under contract with the city. This change in status has not contributed much to the ambience of the surrounding neighborhood, and a local civic group, the Brooklyn Heights Association, has been at loggerheads with the city and the owner over the operations and the future of the once-proud St. George Hotel. At this writing, the center section on Clark Street, which once housed the main entrance, is still vacant, with its massive gates sealed. Still in litigation, it lies dark and deserted, the bronze doors sealed with plywood.

The famed ballroom, however, which once echoed to the strains of society music and the din of gala celebrations, now reverberates to the thumps and thuds

This charming residence, the Peck House, stood on the southwest corner of Clark and Willow streets until it was demolished ca. 1905. (Brooklyn Historical Society)

The lavish Bowen-Leavitt mansion was one of the area's most elegant. Razed over a half-century ago, it faced Columbia Heights at the northwest corner of Clark Street. (Brooklyn Historical Society)

of two levels of squash and racquetball courts. And the gargantuan, block-long tiled and mirrored swimming pool, destroyed through the intervening years by neglect and saltwater deterioration, has been divided into two spaces, one for a smaller and more manageable pool which incorporates some of the surviving mosaics, and one a cavernous area rebuilt as a gymnasium.

Take a quick walk around the hotel, then return to the corner of Clark and Willow streets, and proceed south on Willow Street.

Nos. 101 and **103 Willow Street** are a pair of Greek Revival–style houses, both with an added fourth story. No. 101, built 1839, displays the characteristic (for Brooklyn Heights) pedestal blocks flanking the stairway with ornate wrought-iron railing and balusters that descend into ornate swirls. On No. 103, dating from ca. 1848, look for the "Greek ears" at the corners of the entrance door enframement.

Across the street is the **Danish Seamen's Church,** 102 Willow Street, a reminder of earlier days when the busy Brooklyn waterfront was crowded with sailors from many nations, and Brooklyn Heights and adjacent Cobble Hill had a large Scandinavian population. Its neighbor, **No. 104,** was built ca. 1829. A frame house, it has a rather high basement laid in Flemish bond, and was the home of a baker. **No. 106** was remodeled in neo-Grec style.

The best examples of the Queen Anne style in the Heights are the three houses **Nos. 108–112.** More a fashion than a revival, the basic characteristics of

"Queen Anne" are the picturesque massing of different building materials (stone, brick, terra-cotta, shingles, and slate) in a harmonious potpourri of gables, chimneys, bay windows, dormers, towers, rectangular and arched windows and entrances, balconies, and porches—combining elements of the Romanesque, Gothic, and Renaissance styles. The major advocate of the so-called Queen Anne style was English architect Richard Norman Shaw. Its popularity in America became fairly widespread after its introduction at the British Pavilion during the Philadelphia Centennial Exposition in Philadelphia in 1876, and lasted for about 20 years. Actually, Queen Anne of England died in 1714; however, some of the Gothic and Renaissance elements popular during the reign of the last Stuart queen are evident in the design motifs. This group is considered the finest Queen Anne row in the city. The 1883 date is on the south wall.

No. 151 Willow Street, set back from the street and occupying part of the site of a former house, is a nicely restored brick carriage house dating from the 1880s. The stars are the heads of tie rods, used to strengthen a brick bearing wall. (These may be decorative, however.) The adjacent pleasant garden has a brick path leading to a side entrance. Playwright Arthur Miller lived here in the 1950s until he left to marry Marilyn Monroe.

A charming trio of Federal-style houses are **Nos. 155, 157,** and **159** (the latter having lost its dormers to a third-floor addition). All were built before 1829 and retain much of their original appearance. The articulated stone lintels above the windows and doorways are somewhat unusual. The trim buildings are laid in Flemish bond, have handsome entranceways framed by Ionic colonnettes and leaded-glass side lights and transom, and are topped by a peaked, or curb, roof with twin arched dormers set over a simple cornice. Note that the houses are not parallel to the street, as they were built in accordance with an earlier street pattern. (Love Lane [*see* map] formerly extended to Willow Street and emerged adjacent to No. 155.) A tunnel is supposed to lead from No. 159 to a former stable that was located at the site of No. 151. Look for the skylight imbedded in the pavement near the gate of No. 157.

Turn left (east) on Pierrepont Street.

Note: If you are taking only the First Tour, turn *right* on Pierrepont Street, and walk down to the Esplanade for a spectacular view of the Manhattan skyline. A description will be found in the Second Tour. After enjoying the view, follow the itinerary below:

Pierrepont Street, opened in 1832 and named for Hezekiah Beers Pierrepont, whose estate occupied the surrounding area, extends from Cadman Plaza West to the Esplanade. Before the construction of the Brooklyn-Queens Expressway, the western end dipped down to the waterfront. The two oldest houses on the street are Nos. 27 (at the corner of Willow Street) and 58, farther down the block. **No. 27,** one of the oldest Greek Revival houses in Brooklyn Heights, has suffered many alterations, including a dropped entrance and an added mansard roof. **Nos. 24–30** comprise a fine row of ca. 1890 town houses, with uniform L-shaped entrance stairways.

Brooklyn Union Gas Company emergency wagon leaving on a call for assistance, ca. 1900.
(Brooklyn Union Gas Company)

Pierrepont Street is piled high in snowdrifts after a near-record blizzard on February 14,
1899. (Brooklyn Historical Society)

At the southwest corner of Hicks Street, 36 Pierrepont Street, is the **George Hastings House,** an attractive Gothic Revival–style residence. Built ca. 1844, it features the typical hood molds over lancet arches, trefoil and quatrefoil motifs, traceries, a handsome wrought-iron side balcony replete with Gothic designs, and a fence to match.

No. 55, the **former Hotel Pierrepont,** was designed in 1928 by Herman I. Feldman and completed just before ornamentation on commercial buildings became passé. Look up at the griffin gargoyles and lion finials! The hotel ceased operations in 1975 and is now a senior citizens' residence.

Across the street, **No. 58** (previously mentioned) shares with No. 27 the distinction of being the oldest house on Pierrepont Street. Adjacent **No. 60** (ca. 1849) has a Greek Revival–style doorway with "Greek ears." Note the mansard roofs on the whole row. **No. 56** is a neo-Grec renovation.

No. 62 was built in 1911 as **The Woodhull,** a residential apartment house, from plans by George Fred Pelham, in a French Renaissance Eclectic style.

The Herman Behr House, at the southwest corner of Henry Street, is an exquisite Romanesque Revival mansion, designed in 1890 by architect Frank Freeman. This massive style was popularized by Boston architect Henry Hobson Richardson in the early 1880s, and is characterized by heavy masonry walls, usually of rough-faced sandstone; low-relief carvings; a fortresslike design; restrained terra-cotta ornamentation, usually in wide bands or courses; tan-colored upper brickwork; tile or slate roofs with gables and chimneys; arched openings; rounded bays; substantial stone entranceways; and an overall pleasantly asymmetrical composition. This "Richardsonian Romanesque" was applied not only to large residences, but to public buildings as well—banks, offices, city halls, courthouses, and even railroad stations. The style remained popular until the turn of the century. The Behr house was enlarged with a six-story addition in 1919 and became the Hotel Palm. Declining fortunes compromised its former elegance, and according to local legend, "the Behr *House* was no longer a *Home.*" As if to redeem it from its life of sin, the mansion was acquired by nearby St. Francis College as a residence for novitiates. It was sold in 1976 for conversion into apartments.

Diagonally opposite the Behr House, on the northeast corner, is **No. 161 Henry Street,** a delightfully exuberant brick and limestone trim Renaissance Eclectic apartment house. Designed in 1906 by Schneider & Herts, it has a large mansard roof with a huge pediment over the attic windows, plus a monumental Baroque entranceway.

Turn left (north) on Henry Street into Love Lane.

Love Lane was, as its name implies, a favorite path in Colonial times for young swains to promenade with their maidens fair. Earlier, it had been an Indian trail leading from a village to the water's edge. In 1822, the Brooklyn Collegiate Institute for Young Ladies was built on the site between Henry Street and the present **College Place.** The Institute later became a hotel called the *Mansion House,* and the former hotel stables on College Place now serve "horseless carriages." The neo-Federal supermarket at the entrance to Love Lane is a pleasant and appropriate reproduction.

Return to Pierrepont Street and turn left (east).

No. 104 Pierrepont Street, originally the Thomas Clark Residence, is a handsome four-story brownstone row mansion, built ca. 1857. The roof cornice is supported by ornate console brackets, with hoods similarly set on brackets over the windows and doorway. **No. 106** has an attractive bay window and entrance doors, both with art nouveau stained glass, and both surmounted by a decorative frieze.

Nos. 108 and **114** must be compared from across the street. The two were built as an identical pair around 1840 in Greek Revival style for Messrs. P. C. Cornell and George Cornell. Clay Lancaster, in *Old Brooklyn Heights,* calls the pair "the noblest residential building ever to grace Pierrepont Street." Today, only the right-hand half bears any resemblance to the original appearance, as No. 114 was completely remodeled in Romanesque Revival style around 1877 for Alfred C. Barnes. No. 108, the **P. C. Cornell House,** retains just one of its original Greek Revival elements, the pedimented entranceway with anthemion motif as an acroterium. Its former look-alike twin, No. 114, is now sheathed with brownstone, brick, and terra-cotta, with typical Romanesque Revival features, including rounded bays, gables, a turret, and carved reliefs. In 1912, the George Cornell (or Alfred C. Barnes) House became the headquarters of the Brooklyn Women's Club. It was recently converted into co-op apartments.

Across Pierrepont Street is the Unitarian **Church of the Savior,** since the 1950s called the First Unitarian Church (Minard Lafever, 1844). The lovely Gothic Revival–style church is the home of the oldest Unitarian Society in Brooklyn, organized in 1833. The tall pinnacles and high central gable emphasize the verticality of the sandstone edifice, while a broad roof extends beyond the nave over the side aisles, with small skylights illuminating the interior. In 1890 a new set of windows was installed from the studios of Louis Comfort Tiffany. Lafever, a trained carpenter and skilled architect whose buildings were executed almost always in the Greek Revival style, used the *Gothic* Revival exclusively for many churches. (Another of his fine churches will be seen shortly.) The church is on the approximate site of a British fort built here between 1780 and 1781.

On the northwest corner stands the **Appellate Division of the New York State Supreme Court,** designed by Slee & Bryson and built in 1938 in a simple Classic Revival style, and recently cleaned.

Walk up Monroe Place to **No. 46,** on the right side of the street. Set on a paneled pedestal block is a lovely wrought-iron basket urn, once fairly prevalent throughout the Heights, and now reduced to this last survivor. (The matching mate disappeared years ago.) The pineapple (a rare and luxurious fruit in the 19th century) atop the urn was a traditional symbol of hospitality. Both No. 46 and its neighbor No. 44 are Greek Revival–style houses laid in Flemish bond, and like the trio of houses on Willow Place (Nos. 155–159), are built askew from the street line. The houses were originally aligned with Love Lane, which in the early 19th century extended through to Fulton Street.

There is now a skyscraper where the Frank Freeman–designed Brooklyn Savings Bank stood at the northeast corner of Pierrepont and Clinton streets. A delightful Classic Eclectic building erected in 1893, it was taken down in 1962 when the bank built a modern structure around the corner on Montague Street. The site is now occupied by One Pierrepont Plaza. (The Brooklyn Savings Bank)

Monroe Place is the widest street in Brooklyn Heights and, unlike others in the Heights, has the even-numbered houses on the *east* side. It also retains the original house-numbering system, which was abandoned on all other streets in 1871. The street is named for James Monroe, fifth president of the United States, who spent the last years of his retirement in New York City.

Continue east on Pierrepont Street to Clinton Street.

On the southwest corner is the **Brooklyn Historical Society,** formerly the Long Island Historical Society. Built for the Society between 1878 and 1880 from plans by George B. Post (architect of the New York Stock Exchange), it is a pleasing combination of Richardsonian Romanesque and Classical styles. Since its organization in 1863, the Society has amassed one of the finest historical collections in the country. Although now primarily concerned with the history of Brooklyn, it has extensive source material on New York City and New York State. Its Brooklyn Historical Gallery boasts a number of fascinating permanent exhibits: The Brooklyn Dodgers Baseball Hall of Fame, The Brooklyn Bridge, The Brooklyn Navy Yard, Coney Island, Famous Brooklynites, The TV "Honeymooners" Stage Set; plus a regularly changing exhibit. The library contains over 125,000 volumes plus a collection of manuscripts, periodicals, pamphlets, newspapers, maps, paintings, photographs, prints, and other Brooklyn memorabilia. The library is considered one of the three best in the nation in the field of genealogy. Many paintings by famous American artists are displayed in the hall and reference room, and so extensive and valuable are its historical holdings that it was once called "Long Island's strongbox." The building is open Tues. through Sat., 12 noon to 5:00 P.M.; the library closes at 4:45 P.M. (Admission: Adults $2.50, seniors and children $1.00, members free. Admission is free to all on Wednesdays. There is a library use fee of $5.00, which includes admission; free to members.) Take time for a leisurely visit, and browse in the lovely library's reading room. A visit is a "must" (be sure to pick up a membership application!). On exiting, note the high-relief sculptures of the Viking and Indian in the spandrels of the entrance arch, as well as the rich façade with busts of Columbus and Franklin, and the earthy tones of red and brown in the terra-cotta adornments and Philadelphia pressed brick. The Latin inscription on the Clinton Street side is from Cicero, and means "History, the Witness of Time."

On the northwest corner, **St. Ann's Episcopal School** occupies the building of the **former Crescent Club,** one of a number of private athletic clubs that prevailed around the turn of the century. Designed in 1906 by architect Frank Freeman (of the Behr Mansion and the Hotel Margaret), it was the club's second building. Find the little stone crescents set in the upper section of the façade. Across Clinton Street on the northeast corner stood another Frank Freeman building—the Brooklyn Savings Bank—a splendid Classic Eclectic edifice with an extravagant oval interior. Built in 1893, it was lost to the wrecker's ball in 1962, and the bank moved into more modern quarters on Montague Street—the site now of **One Pierrepont Plaza** (Haines, Lundberg & Waehler, 1987). On the southeast corner, and extending to Montague Street, is the old **Brooklyn Trust Company Building,** now a branch of Chemical Bank. Designed in 1915 by the noted architects York & Sawyer, the exterior is said to be patterned after the Palazzo della Gran Guardia in Verona, and the interior possibly after the Tepidarium of the Roman Baths of Caracalla. The impressive granite-and-limestone Renaissance Revival–style *palazzo* was the home office of the Brooklyn Trust Company until 1950, when it was absorbed by the Manufacturers Hanover Trust Company, which in turn was merged with the Chemical Bank. And when you get to Montague Street, don't miss the splendid bronze lamp standards in whose delicately sculptured bases are griffins and turtles.

Turn right on Clinton Street to Montague Street.

Back to back with the Brooklyn Historical Society is the **Diocesan Church of St. Ann and the Holy Trinity, formerly the Holy Trinity Protestant Episcopal Church,** and another fine example of architect Minard Lafever's ecclesiastical work. Completed in 1847 in his customary Gothic Revival style, it is reminiscent, in its dark-red color, of an old English church. Unfortunately, the porous brownstone has weathered very badly. The interior is constructed of cast and painted terra-cotta, a departure from the usual carved stone or plaster. The lovely windows were designed by William Jay Bolton, America's foremost stained-glass artist of the time, and are considered by art historians to be a national treasure. The church's tall spire was dismantled early in the century when blasting for the new Montague Street tunnel of the former BMT subway made it unsafe. St. Ann and the Holy Trinity Church is now headquarters of the Episcopal Diocese of Brooklyn.

Under way for several years is a bold in-house restoration project aimed at returning the magnificent Gothic Revival–style treasure to its original flamboyant glory. In 1988, together with the World Monuments Fund, and supported by state and private grants, the church established the **American Heritage Center for Conservation and Training,** whose purpose is to establish apprenticeship programs in stained glass, sandstone, and wood preservation. The restoration of the glass is under the supervision of the renowned master stained-glass conservator, Mel Greenfield. New techniques for helping to preserve the deteriorating sandstone façade have been developed by the in-house conservation crew, and as each stone section is restored, completed windows are reinstalled, and light again enters the darkened church interior.

On entering the church vestibule, one is greeted by a bust of John Howard Melish, by sculptor William Zorach. The reredos is by Frank Freeman. Above the altar is one of St. Ann's priceless treasures, the **Great Chancel Window.** The 40-foot-tall stained-glass masterpiece is one of Bolton's crowning achievements, its restoration scheduled for completion by 1995.

Cross the intersection of Clinton and Montague streets to the corner diagonally opposite the church.

The block of Montague Street between Clinton and Court streets is considered part of the downtown Brooklyn business section and is known as **"Bank Row."** From left to right across Montague Street are:

The aforementioned Chemical Bank, No. 177, in the building of the old **Brooklyn Trust Company,** erected in 1915. The structure occupies the site of the George Taylor residence, the home of a mid-19th-century congressman. His house was sold to the Brooklyn Trust Company in 1873, and was enlarged and altered through the years until 1914, when it was razed to make way for the present building.

The Citibank branch, No. 181, is in the **former People's Trust Company building,** designed as a reproduction of a Roman temple in 1904, by Mobray & Uffinger. It sports a large and impressive pediment complete with reclining classical figures, and rests on four huge Ionic fluted columns that frame what is known as an engaged tetra-style portico. The effect on the public must have been one of unquestioned security and solvency. An addition was designed in 1929 by Shreve, Lamb & Harmon, whose design for the Empire State Building was being carried out that same year.

The **National Title Guaranty Building,** No. 185, although no longer known by that name, is an imposing 15-story structure in a bold, three-dimensional Art Deco style, and was erected from plans by Helmle, Corbett & Harrison in 1929. The closely spaced stone piers rise dramatically in a group of rhythmic setbacks to create a strong sense of verticality. A mindless alteration in 1970 destroyed the entrance and lobby. The building has seen many banks as tenants through the years, and at present houses the Municipal Credit Union.

Adjacent to the right, and totally unrecognizable in its present "glassy box" disguise, is the nine-story **former Real Estate Exchange,** No. 189–191, erected in 1891. Built originally in a Renaissance Eclectic style, it was remodeled in 1911 by Brooklyn's most famous architect, Frank Freeman. Then in 1916, 1953, and 1957, further modifications were made to the façade and interior; and finally in 1972, the present bronze glass "skin" was attached. The ultimate indignity came with the installation by the building owners of a dark-green tile entrance-way where the EAB (a bank) occupies the ground floor.

The final group of buildings includes the Brooklyn Union Gas Company, the National Westminster Bank USA, and the Brooklyn Savings Bank (now merged with the Crossland Savings Bank), all built between 1959 and 1962. The Gas Company's headquarters occupies the **site of the Mercantile Library** (Peter B. Wright, 1864), a modified High Victorian Gothic–style building which later became the home of the Brooklyn Library, until it merged with the Brooklyn Public Library in 1903. It then became the library system's main office until its central building was erected near Prospect Park in 1941; the building was then reduced to the Montague Street Branch, and was demolished in 1960. Although the name of the Brooklyn Union Gas Company still appears on some of the buildings, the company has moved its headquarters to the new MetroTech Center, a $1 billion commercial and academic complex on a 10-block site that will include eight new and three renovated buildings. Chase Manhattan Bank has also moved in, as have the Internal Revenue Service, the Department of Motor Vehicles, and Polytechnic University.

Cross to the north side of Montague Street.

The tall building halfway down the block on the south side is the **Lawyers Title Insurance Company,** No. 188–190 (Helmle, Huberty & Hudswell, 1904). Adjacent to the east stood another Frank Freeman building, the Title Guaranty & Trust Company, erected in 1905 in neoclassic style, and torn down in 1959. At the far end of the block, at the corner of Court Street, is one of Brooklyn's genuine skyscrapers, the **Montague-Court Building,** (H. Craig Severance, 1927). Rising 35 stories in a series of setbacks (as required by the 1916 zoning resolution), it is an attractive addition to the Brooklyn skyline.

Before the financial institutions came to Montague Street, this block had another distinction. It was **the most important cultural center in all of Brooklyn.** In addition to the library on the north side, the south side was the site of two famous institutions, one of which was the **Brooklyn Art Association.** In 1872, architect J. Cleveland Cady was hired to design an appropriate building for the Association, whose primary purpose was the promotion of the fine arts to Brooklyn residents. The result was an impressive High Victorian Gothic structure with lively use of polychromatic stone and brick whose façade dominated the block. The Art Association merged with the Brooklyn Institute of Arts & Science in 1899 to form one of the nation's greatest cultural institutions, the

Brooklyn Museum. With the completion of the museum's magnificent first building (designed by McKim, Mead & White) on Eastern Parkway near Prospect Park the same year, the Brooklyn Art Association abandoned its Montague Street home, and its name became only a memory. The building, however, survived until 1936, when all but a few interior walls were demolished.

The third cultural institution on the block was the **Brooklyn Academy of Music,** founded in 1859 as an outgrowth of the Brooklyn Philharmonic Society. Architect Leopold Eidlitz designed an enormous brick structure for the BAM, also in High Victorian style, at Nos. 176–190 Montague Street, just to the east of the site that would later be taken by the Brooklyn Art Association. Opening night was January 15, 1861, and Walt Whitman, writing in the *Brooklyn Standard,* described the building as "magnificent...on a scale commensurate with similar buildings, even in some of the largest and most polished capitals of Europe." The Academy remained as the center of all major cultural events in Brooklyn until it was destroyed in a fire in 1903. Five years later, a new Academy building arose a mile to the east [*see* Fort Greene, 14] and soon became one of New York City's major cultural centers. The mid-block Lawyers Title Insurance Company building now occupies the western end of the old Brooklyn Academy site.

Return to the corner of Clinton Street.

Completing the row of banks is the picturesque **Franklin Trust Company Building** on the southwest corner. With the invention of the elevator, the skyscraper came into its own, and this charming Romanesque Revival château, complete with moat, is an outstanding example of the style applied to commercial buildings. Built in 1891 (see date in the pediment) from plans by George L. Morse, the bank presents a striking façade of limestone arches on a granite base, brick and terra-cotta piers, columns topped by arches, and a charming Spanish tile roof with dormer windows.

End of First Tour. To return to Manhattan, the Court Street station of the R line is here at the intersection of Montague and Clinton streets. For the Broadway–Seventh Avenue or Lexington Avenue line, walk one block east on Montague Street to Borough Hall. For the A or E line, take the No. 2 or 3 line to Manhattan and change at Fulton Street.

SECOND TOUR

Continue west on Montague Street.

Montague Street is named for Lady Mary Wortley Montagu, née Pierrepont, the English author of wit and letters who died in 1762. (No one seems to know how Montague Street got its final "e.") It is the principal commercial thoroughfare of Brooklyn Heights and an appropriate place to stop for some refreshment. When the street was opened through to the riverfront around 1850, ferry service was begun to Wall Street in Manhattan.

The "Penny Bridge" over Montague Street, ca. 1922, when the street sloped downhill to the Wall Street Ferry. In the background are the side-by-side Low and White Mansions (Nos. 3 and 2 Pierrepont Place) and the now-demolished Pierrepont Mansion. (Brooklyn Historical Society)

In 1887 a cable car began operating the full length of Montague Street, providing a convenient transportation link for Manhattan commuters who arrived on the brand-new Fulton Street El at the Court Street station and were then whisked down to the Wall Street Ferry. In 1909 the trolley was electrified, remaining in service until 1924 when the BMT's four-year-old Montague Street Tunnel rendered it obsolete.

The street has a variety of shops, boutiques, and ethnic restaurants. Along the south side, cast-iron stoops lead up to raised first-floor retail establishments whose wares are displayed in large triple-bay windows. There is a pleasant, relaxed, continental atmosphere which adds charm to the lively street.

At Henry Street, turn left (south) one block to Remsen Street.

Our Lady of Lebanon Maronite Cathedral, originally the Congregational Church of the Pilgrims, was a radical departure for architect Richard Upjohn, renowned for his Gothic Revival–style churches, particularly Trinity Church in Manhattan; and this early Romanesque Revival church, built in 1846, is thought to be the first building of that style in this country. When the church merged with the Plymouth Church on Orange Street in 1934, the fragment of Plymouth Rock imbedded in the tower was brought along. The new church acquired the building in 1944. It practices the Maronite Rite, serving a large and long-established Lebanese community, some of which is clustered along Atlantic Avenue in "Brooklyn's Middle East" [*see* Cobble Hill walking tour]; however, most of the Lebanese community has moved to Bay Ridge, but many still come back to worship here. The interior of the church is surprisingly delicate, with widely spaced slender columns and semi-circular arches supporting the ceiling. Unfortunately, the steeple deteriorated and was removed. Newly installed windows detract from the overall effect. The west and south portals are made from metal panels rescued from the *Normandie,* which burned and capsized at its Hudson River pier in 1942, during World War II. Only a few of the circular door panels on the west side have religious themes; on the south side there are three medieval castles, and a *steamship!*

Return to Montague Street and turn left (west).

Nos. 111–115 Montague Street are an interesting pair of Queen Anne–style apartment houses, built in 1885, with a particularly engaging common façade. The *Berkeley* and *Grosvenor* display a combination of building materials: red brick, brownstone, and ornamental terra-cotta. The houses were designed by Parfitt Brothers, an important Brooklyn architectural firm of three English-born brothers. Both have been converted to co-ops.

No. 105 Montague Street, by the same architects and from the same period, is another good example of the style. Look up at the sculptured figure in the gable. Built in 1890, The Montague is now a condominium.

The Hotel Bossert, at the corner of Hicks Street, was built for lumber merchant Louis Bossert in 1909–12. Designed by architects Helmle & Huberty, the Bossert was a center of Brooklyn social life for many years; and its Marine Roof, decorated like a yacht, provided an unsurpassed view of the harbor. Alas, the Marine Roof and elegant ballroom are no more. Then cross to the diagonally opposite corner of Montague Street and examine briefly the Beaux Arts lower section of the hotel. On the Hicks Street side are no fewer than twelve tall arches running the full length of the building, each with a carved lion's head in the keystone console. Above the columned main entrance is a balcony with filigree ironwork that includes the hotel's initials as a central design. The Bossert is now another trophy of the ever-expanding Jehovah's Witnesses, and serves as a residence for volunteer workers. While one might take issue with their insatiable quest for more properties, one still must commend them for the restoration and preservation of their historic buildings. When the Witnesses took over the hotel, the few remaining rent-controlled tenants were allowed to stay on. Peek into the spacious lobby with its massive columns and beautifully restored coffered ceiling. They have also done well with the preservation of the exterior. The Witnesses have acquired more than 30 buildings in Brooklyn Heights and seem always ready to gobble up more with plenty of ready cash—a temptation for homeowners and a source of deep concern to the community.

The Heights Casino, 75 Montague Street, an exclusive tennis and squash club, was designed by Boring & Tilton and opened in 1905. In front of the site of the Casino stood the H. B. Pierrepont Mansion, "Four Chimneys," built before the American Revolution and used briefly by General Washington as headquarters before the retreat to Manhattan. The mansion was razed in the mid-19th century when Montague Street was extended to the water's edge. At about the site of No. 63, the street began its descent to the harbor. The street was elevated in the late 1940s when the Esplanade was built. The architects of the Heights Casino also designed the U.S. Immigration Station on Ellis Island.

No. 76 Montague Street, **Sirius House,** a two-and-a-half-story Federal building with a severely modified storefront, was a ship broker's office. The firm had taken its name from the paddle steamer *Sirius,* the first ship of its kind to cross the Atlantic in a westward direction, in 1838. A plaque illustrating the ship, which is named after the navigational star, is imbedded in the sidewalk; a 19th-century British Admiralty–type anchor, secured from a ship-breaker's yard in Staten Island, rests solidly in front. Brooklyn Heights was for many years the home of sea captains and shipping people, and the Sirius Brokers, Inc. found it appropriate to move here from Manhattan in 1981 and restore what was the oldest house on the block (1859) for their offices. (Those making the walking tour in the winter will appreciate that this building and the Brooklyn Union Gas Company's former headquarters are the only two in the Heights to have heated sidewalks, this one by electricity, and the Gas Company's, obviously, by gas.)

Continue west on Montague Street to just opposite **No. 62,** an enormous red-brick apartment house of ca. 1885. Erected in a mixture of Queen Anne and what might be called "Edwardian" styles, it is an early example of the luxury multi-family residence, then called the French flat. The six-story oriel on the Montague Street side is overshadowed by the ten-story round tower that rises majestically, past nine levels of ornate iron fire escapes, to a pyramidal mansard roof.

From this point to the waterfront, Montague Street once dropped steeply to connect with the **Wall Street Ferry** (service discontinued in 1912). At this spot architect Minard Lafever built a charming but short-lived arch in 1855 that spanned Montague Street. And just ahead, where Pierrepont Place and Montague Terrace meet at street level, there was an iron footbridge over the then-depressed Montague Street, known as **The Penny Bridge,** which survived until 1946 when the land was filled in for the Brooklyn-Queens Connecting Highway. Some idea of the depth of the old street can be had by examining the wall and deep cellar of the last house on the left, just at the stop sign at Montague Terrace.

At the end of Montague Street, walk a few steps to the right into Pierrepont Place.

Facing the end of Montague Street are **Nos. 3** and **2 Pierrepont Place,** considered to be the most elegant brownstone dwelling houses in the city. Designed by noted architect Richard Upjohn [*see* page 450] and built in 1856–57, they form a splendid pair of Italianate mansions situated in an ideal location. A third house, No. 1, whose empty plot now serves as a playground, was built for Henry E. Pierrepont, and was demolished in 1946. The twin mini-*palazzi* were built for Abiel Abbott Low, a tea merchant (No. 3), and for Alexander M. White, a fur dealer (No. 2). A. A. Low's son, **Seth Low,** served as mayor of Brooklyn from 1882 to 1886, then as president of Columbia University, and in 1901 was elected mayor of the City of New York. He is remembered for his vigorous campaigns to reform the police, finance, and education departments, and for his donation of the Library to Columbia. No. 2 was later occupied by Alfred Tredway White, a wealthy businessman and philanthropist, and president of the Brooklyn Bureau of Charities. It was White who believed in "philanthropy plus 5%" when he built the Riverside Houses on Columbia Place (to be seen shortly) and the Tower and Home Apartments in the Cobble Hill section [*see* Cobble Hill chapter].

Walk back around the south side of No. 3 to the Esplanade for a rear view of the lavish mansions and a lovely, tall gingko tree that stands in the southwest corner of the private garden. In the popular film *Prizzi's Honor,* No. 3 was the magnificent villa with surrounding gardens that was the home of Don Corrado. Before reaching the Esplanade, read the bronze tablet at the entrance that commemorates the mansion **"Four Chimneys."** The film *No Way to Treat a Lady* was also filmed here some years ago.

The **Brooklyn Heights Promenade,** or "Esplanade," provides one of the most unforgettable harbor panoramas, which can be enjoyed while relaxing on one of the convenient benches. Considered by many to be New York City's most spectacular vantage point, its design is a commendable attempt at separation of vehicular and pedestrian traffic, and a tribute to the planning of our city fathers. Local civic groups such as the Brooklyn Heights Association cooperated with Parks Commissioner Robert Moses in the planning, and the resultant cantilevered Esplanade over the Brooklyn-Queens Connecting Highway, completed in 1950, gave sudden impetus to the redevelopment of Brooklyn Heights. A

The Brooklyn Heights Esplanade provides one of the finest views in the country. This photo was taken in the early 1960s before the construction of the huge boxlike office buildings which now obscure much of the traditional Manhattan skyline. The Singer Tower, demolished in 1968, is visible to the left of the tree. (Brooklyn Union Gas Company)

somewhat better design would have duplicated the almost total separation of roadway from pedestrian mall that was achieved with the East River Drive on the Upper East Side of Manhattan, where traffic noise and fumes were completely eliminated. Spend a few minutes enjoying the magnificent view of the dramatic Lower Manhattan skyline.

Turn right on the Esplanade, and after a few minutes of contemplation, take the next right, exiting just beyond the two mansions. Turn left into Columbia Heights for a brief detour. Walk to No. 210, then turn back.

Nos. 210–220 Columbia Heights, a splendid row of Italianate brownstones (some painted white), were erected between 1857 and 1860. The entrance to No. 210 is flanked by a pair of Corinthian columns, and the doorway is framed by masonry blocks with alternating vermiform ("wormlike") rustication. No. 214's entrance was once as grand as the others. Nos. 216 and 218 are (fortunately) unpainted and show their warm brownstone color. Both had mansard roofs added in the 1870s when the Second Empire style became the rage. Look what was added to the roof of No. 220, giving it an Italian Renaissance *villa* appearance! **No. 222** is a harmonious modern replacement by resident architect Ian Bruce Eichner.

Continue south on Pierrepont Place (the extension of Columbia Heights), past Montague Street, where the street changes its name again to Montague Terrace.

Nos. 1–13 Montague Terrace, built ca. 1886, are a charming English-style "terrace row" in almost pristine condition. Author Thomas Wolfe, while living at No. 5 in 1935, wrote *Of Time and the River*. Wolfe spent a number of years in the Heights and nearby Cobble Hill, and his novels are drawn from personal experiences. **No. 11** is the most authentic, having undergone the fewest alterations, and preserving its broad entrance stairway.

Turn left into Remsen Street.

Named for Henry Remsen, who lived nearby and opened the street in 1825, this shady, quiet thoroughfare is lined with interesting mid- and late-19th-century residences. The houses on the south side to Hicks Street date mostly from the pre–Civil War period, while those on the north were built in the 1880s and '90s.

Turn right (south) into Hicks Street.

Grace Court Alley, a charming little mews running eastward to a dead end, was formerly the stable alley for the patrician residents of Remsen Street. The stables and carriage houses, considered very chic, are luxurious duplexes. Note particularly the solidly built **Nos. 2, 4, 12,** and **14.**

Walk a few yards down **Grace Court** and look through the tall iron fence into the spacious backyards of the houses that face Remsen Street.

Grace (Protestant Episcopal) Church of Brooklyn Heights, another

Richard Upjohn work, was completed in 1848. In style it is typical Gothic Revival, much like an English parish church, but rather low, long, and narrow. The side entrance court offers a delightful spot of repose, tucked under a magnificent 85-foot-high elm. The boldly carved moldings, capitals, and brackets are highlighted against the textured wall surface with its pattern of varied tooled groovings. Inside, open wood-vaulted trusses support the roof, but matching wooden piers were replaced by stone during a 1909 restoration. At that time, the handsome J. Pierpont Morgan Memorial Doorway was installed. In the sanctuary are an alabaster altar and reredos surmounted by an artistic stained-glass window. The church boasts three Tiffany stained-glass windows in the nave and aisles. After years of patchwork repairs, the church now is undergoing a complete stone-by-stone restoration of the exterior.

Turn right (west) into Joralemon Street.

Joralemon Street is named for Teunis Joralemon, who purchased the Philip Livingston estate in 1803. You have doubtless noticed the sudden change in the atmosphere of the neighborhood. While still very attractive, it is apparent that Joralemon Street cannot compare in elegance to the streets just visited. This area was originally a district of small merchants, artisans, and tradesmen. There are no mansions or fancy town houses here, just straightforward Greek Revival–style row houses. The street was opened in the 1840s after the Remsen farm was subdivided. Note, too, the "cobblestoned" street (properly called Belgian blocks) and the old bluestone sidewalks.

Nos. 29–75 Joralemon Street are 24 modified Greek Revival–style houses, built from 1844 to 1848 in neatly descending pairs, each about 30 inches lower than the next, and most still retain their pilastered entranceways and original iron fences. **No. 58** was converted unobtrusively into a **ventilation chamber and emergency exit for the Lexington Avenue line subway tunnel** far below the street.

At the southwest corner of Columbia Place are the remarkable **Riverside Houses,** model tenements built for Alfred Tredway White in 1890 by William Field & Son. These multiple dwellings followed on the heels of his revolutionary Tower and Home Apartments in Cobble Hill [*see* pages 448 and 449], the first such project in America and a rare example (in public housing, anyway) of enlightened self-interest. His motto "Philanthropy plus 5%" actually did bring him a profit. These houses were aptly named, but in the construction of the expressway, the "river side" was demolished, along with a superb view of the harbor. A remnant of the original central garden, which was a major part of the plan to provide as much light and air as possible for the 280 apartments, is still visible between the remaining building and the expressway.

Turn south into Columbia Place.

Across from Riverside Houses is a charming row of four clapboard frame houses, **Nos. 7–13 Columbia Place,** which were once part of the nine-unit "Cottage Row" built in the late 1840s.

Return to Joralemon Street, turn right one block into Willow Place.

Nos. 2–8 Willow Place are a most unusual row of Gothic Revival–style duplex houses, built about 1847. Among their interesting features are the coupled porches with clustered colonnettes, diamond-paned side lights and transoms in the entranceways, Tudor arches with trefoils in the spandrels, recessed panels connecting the second and third floors with wooden "chevron" moldings (forerunners of the spandrels used on tall modern buildings), hood labels over the third-floor windows of No. 8, and an appropriate iron fence and stoop railings. Note the plaque on No. 6.

Farther down the street is the **former Willow Place Chapel** built in 1876 (architect unknown) by the First Unitarian Church, and closed in 1945. The diminutive Victorian Gothic–style building now serves a preschool program for St. Ann's Church, and as a center for productions by the Brooklyn Heights Players.

Buildings **Nos. 38–40, 44,** and **48,** erected in 1966, are an excellent example of the use of modern materials and techniques applied harmoniously in a more traditional environment. Designed by Joseph and Mary Merz, the arrangement of garage space and the use of special 8-by-8-inch cement blocks gives the houses a simple dignity and helps them blend well with their venerable neighbors.

Across the street is the **last surviving "Colonnade Row" in Brooklyn Heights, Nos. 43–49 Willow Place.** Designed ca. 1846 as a middle-class imitation of the elegant multicolumned row houses such as Underhill's Colonnade or the very sumptuous marble Colonnade Row on Manhattan's Lafayette Place, it is reminiscent of an antebellum Southern mansion. The two-story brick houses are revealed behind the twin-story porches whose square wooden columns support the entablature and cornice. Although the continuous portico is only a foot above ground level, the total effect is undiminished—even enhanced by the simple Greek Revival doorways flanked by pilasters. (Across Willow Street, almost hidden by its neighbors and partly obscured by a small but lush garden, its wooden columns overgrown with ivy, is lovely **No. 46,** painted a harmonious shade of green, and looking for all the world like a set from *Gone With the Wind*.) In *Bricks and Brownstone,* author Charles Lockwood refers to the dignified wooden porch of the Willow Place Colonnade Row as "an easily forgivable architectural fraud...[which] holds great appeal today because of its modest scale and the naïveté of its conception and execution."

Turn left (east) on State Street to Hicks Street, then left again.

Nos. 284–276 Hicks Street are a row of five former carriage houses. Note the round and elliptical arches, and the carved woman's head on the dormer of **No. 276,** formerly the studio of sculptor William Zorach. Adjacent is **Engine Company 224,** in a Beaux Arts–style fire house, designed in 1903 by Adams & Warren, and set in perfect scale with its neighbors.

Across the street is the former St. Charles Orthopaedic Clinic (281 Hicks Street). This is the approximate site of the Philip Livingston house, built ca.

1764. It was in the Livingston House that George Washington, on August 29, 1776, planned the strategic withdrawal of his Continental Army to Manhattan, following the Battle of Brooklyn.

Nos. 270–262, built in 1887, add to the variety of the street with their romantic Queen Anne–style grouping of picturesque details.

Turn right (east) on Joralemon Street to Garden Place.

Take a brief detour down **Garden Place,** laid out in 1842 and named for the garden that once graced the Philip Livingston estate. (Livingston was one of the signers of the Declaration of Independence.) Note the Queen Anne style of **No. 26,** and the storybook **converted carriage house** at **No. 21** which, according to the plaque installed by its owners, was built ca. 1846. It was a garage with living quarters above between 1916 and 1936, then a single family residence until the present. Note also the atmosphere created by the addition of the row of London plane trees, which since their planting in the early 1940s have grown to provide a charming umbrella for the street.

Continue east on Joralemon Street to Henry Street, and turn left (north) for a brief detour to Hunts Lane.

Hunts Lane is another former stable alley, whose brick carriage houses were converted to duplexes, and which, like nearby Grace Court Alley, served the affluent homeowners on Remsen Street whose backyards abutted the Lane.

Return to Joralemon Street and continue east.

No. 129 Joralemon Street, the former David Chauncey Mansion, was designed by C. P. H. Gilbert in 1891 in an odd combination of Romanesque Revival and Colonial Revival details. A massive stone and yellow brick mansion, it gives the impression, nonetheless, of being a "bungalow." It is now subdivided into apartments.

No. 135 always astonishes the visitor. Almost hidden between two overpowering neighbors, this delightful gem of a house is reminiscent of No. 24 Middagh Street, its "cousin" seen at the beginning of the tour. Built ca. 1833, and known as the **John Haslet House** (after its first owner, a U.S. Navy surgeon), it is the sole survivor of a row of similar residences that once lined the street, and is an excellent example of Federal-style architecture. The ornate cast-iron porch was added in the mid-19th century and the parlor-floor windows were lowered, but otherwise the house is in virtually pristine condition. Note the Flemish bond brickwork of the basement, the handsome entranceway with Ionic colonnettes, the neat clapboarding, simple cornice, twin dormers, and gambrel roof. The house, which until the early 1980s had been deteriorating badly, was given a complete facelift, but time, weather, and probably lack of funds have prevented the long-time resident-owner from keeping up with the necessary maintenance, and it is again taking on a woefully decrepit air.

Turn right into Sidney Place.

Sidney Place is even more varied than its neighbor Garden Place. It is named after Sir Philip Sidney, or Sydney (1554–1586), an English author, statesman, and soldier who was a distinguished figure in the court of Queen Elizabeth. Most of the houses on the west side date from the 1840s. **No. 2,** the corner house, built about 1848, has a peculiar appendage facing Sidney Place in the form of a wooden two-story-high vestibule, with—lo and behold!—a delicate Federal-style entryway. Twin Ionic colonnettes and wreathed side lights flank the door, with a transom and carved plaque above. It is said that the entranceway originally belonged to a house that was demolished to make way for the construction of the Towers Hotel. **No. 18,** a Greek Revival house of about 1838, has an attractive recessed doorway flanked by Doric columns. Some years later, three additional floors were added, making this doubtless the tallest Greek Revival house in the city.

Beyond Aitken Place, the row of houses on the east side is set back behind lush gardens and iron fences, adding to the charm of the shady street. **Nos. 31–49,** a continuous row of Greek Revival–style houses, were all built about 1845. Most have suffered modifications, but **No. 35** is closest to the original appearance.

Framing the entrance to Aitken Place are the **St. Charles Borromeo (Roman Catholic) Church** (1869), and across the street, the Rectory (1920) and adjacent parish school (1916). The church, designed by that prolific architect of so many Catholic churches in the 19th century, Patrick C. Keely, is a simple modified Gothic Revival–style structure in dark-red painted brick, but in scale with its surrounding neighbors. Inside, the supporting arches and trim are in a delicate "carpenter Gothic" style. The plain, light-colored walls contrast strongly with the dark-brown ceiling. Rev. Ambrose S. Aitken was a former pastor of the congregation, and the adjoining street is named for him.

Follow Aitken Place to Clinton Street.

Clinton Street is named for De Witt Clinton (1769–1828) who served ten annual terms as mayor of New York City and two terms as governor. He was the guiding spirit behind the construction of the Erie Canal, ran unsuccessfully for president, was an amateur naturalist, and for his entire career a dedicated public servant.

At the corner, look to the right (south) down **Clinton Street.** Except for some modifications to the exteriors of the Greek Revival–style row houses, little has changed in the past 100 years. On the southeast corner is a row of four red brick houses, **Nos. 133–139 Clinton Street,** whose appearance is enhanced by the trio of gaslights. The corner house was once the home of the *Excelsiors,* an early Brooklyn baseball team and champions of the world in 1860. Read the plaque on No. 133 and learn who pitched the first curve ball, and how baseball is so closely tied to the history of Brooklyn.

The **former St. Ann's Episcopal Church** was closed in 1966 and merged with the Holy Trinity Church, three blocks north. In a move to cut costs and help maintain their parochial school, the Episcopal Diocese of Brooklyn sold the church to the nearby Packer Collegiate Institute, and moved its headquarters along with its congregation to Holy Trinity. Designed in 1869 by famed architect James Renwick, Jr. (who planned St. Patrick's Cathedral as well as Manhattan's Grace Church), this is the only example in Brooklyn of the Ruskinian or Venetian Gothic style. Where this style differs from the more conventional Gothic Revival is in the use of polychromy in the façade. The arch blocks (voussoirs) are in alternating white and dark brown, while horizontal bands of white stone run across the full width of the exterior. There still has been no decision as to the future of this exceptional edifice, and the protective scaffolding remains year after year while the magnificent façade crumbles.

Nos. 142 and **140,** across the street from the church, are survivors of a row of five similar houses, built ca. 1855. Most unusual are the bracketed gables and the highly ornate black-painted cast-iron lintels set over the windows and entrances. [*See* photo, bottom of page 399.]

Walk north on Clinton Street to Joralemon Street.

The Packer Collegiate Institute, designed in the "Collegiate" Gothic Revival style by Minard Lafever in 1854, was built on the site of the Brooklyn Female Academy destroyed by fire two years earlier. These lovely "halls of ivy" were endowed by Mrs. William S. Packer to honor her late husband's interest in women's education. The delightful exterior was published by Lafever in his *Architectural Instructor* and reflected his belief that churches as well as schools should be constructed in the medieval Gothic tradition. The Gothic-style wing at the east end was added in 1886.

Continue one block to Remsen Street, and turn right (east).

The little Gothic Revival–style brownstone church at the corner is the **former Spencer Memorial Church,** built in 1850–53 (architect unknown) for the First Church (Presbyterian) of Brooklyn. The church was closed in the early 1970s and was later sold to a developer and converted into 11 cooperative apartments. An alley to the left is called "Spencer Mews" and has entrances to some professional apartments. Other tenants enter at what were once the various doorways to the church. On the alley wall is a memorial tablet saved from the interior, honoring the former church's first pastor, Ichabod Spencer.

Just beyond the glass-box main building of **St. Francis College** is the tall Classic Revival–style building that housed the **former headquarters of the Brooklyn Union Gas Company** until their next structure was erected in 1962 on Montague Street. (As described before, the Gas Company is now installed at One MetroTech.) The building was designed in 1914 by Frank Freeman, and has been converted to classroom and office use by St. Francis College. Interesting is the Classic colonnade on the upper stories.

Immediately to the left, in what resembles a Greek temple, is the gem of the block, the **original headquarters of the Brooklyn Gas Light Company,**

Brooklyn's Civic Center at the turn of the century. To the left rear of Brooklyn's City Hall is the Court House (now the site of the Brooklyn Law School). Also gone are the trolley lines and the Brooklyn Rapid Transit Elevated on curving Fulton Street. The statue of Henry Ward Beecher in front of City Hall has been moved several hundred yards farther north. (Author's collection)

erected in 1857. The firm became the Brooklyn Union Gas Company in 1895, and remained in this diminutive white marble building until architect Freeman's plans for its new offices next door were executed twenty years later. Like its neighbor, it too has been incorporated into the St. Francis campus as the McGarry Library. Adjacent **No. 186** (ca. 1885) is a typical Romanesque Revival–style commercial building.

Continue to Court Street, turn right (south) one block to Joralemon Street, and cross to the opposite side of Court Street.

The tall commercial structure on the northwest corner, the **Templar Bar Building** (44 Court Street), was the tallest in Brooklyn when completed in 1901 from plans by George L. Morse. Interesting are the ogee-shaped twin cupolas and the Classic Eclectic details of the façade. Court Street between Livingston and Pierrepont streets was once the major axis of Brooklyn's "Financial District"; however a new commercial renaissance is taking place a half-mile further east in such developments as MetroTech, Livingston Plaza, Renaissance Plaza, and Atlantic Center. Yet this area is still home to several universities, and serves as the civic hub of the borough, with nearby Borough Hall, the Brooklyn Municipal Building, and the various city, state, and federal courthouses, as well as the main Brooklyn post office, the Brooklyn Heights branch of the Brooklyn Public Library, the New York City Transit Authority, and the New York City Board of Education—all within a few blocks' radius.

End of Second Tour. At Borough Hall are the Lexington and Broadway–Seventh Avenue lines, and at Montague Street, the Court Street station of the R line. For the A line, walk past Borough Hall to Fulton Street, then two blocks east to Jay Street.

A BRIEF LOOK AT BROOKLYN'S CIVIC CENTER

The Brooklyn Municipal Building, an immense and functional Indiana limestone structure, was designed in a modified Classic Eclectic style by McKenzie, Voorhees & Gmelin, and completed in 1926. The granite for the base came from Deer Island, Maine, and the interior marble was quarried in Vermont and Tennessee. The building houses most of the offices of borough government, including the files from the demolished Court House and Hall of Records, which stood just to the east.

Directly in front, and facing Cadman Plaza, is **Borough Hall, formerly the Brooklyn City Hall.** Said to be one of the most beautiful public buildings in the entire city, the old City Hall was built in 1836–49 in Greek Revival style, although its cupola is strictly Georgian, and was added in 1898. The Hall was originally planned to be a replica of Manhattan's City Hall, but instead the Greek Revival style was selected. The architect, Gamaliel King, was in fact a grocer and carpenter! An excellent view is from the Plaza where the splendid façade with its broad staircase gracefully ascending to the Ionic colonnade is seen to best advantage. The cupola was added in 1898. Borough Hall houses the offices of the president of the borough of Brooklyn. Borough Hall underwent a major renovation, which was completed in 1989.

From the colonnade of Borough Hall there is a broad perspective of **Cadman Plaza.** Named for Rev. S. Parkes Cadman, an active community leader and America's first radio preacher [*see* Clinton Hill, 8], the Plaza was the result of major urban renewal in the 1950s, including the razing of the Fulton Street El, which came over the Brooklyn Bridge and darkened Fulton Street for miles, the removal of trolley tracks, and the rebuilding of major traffic arteries. Pleasant Columbus Park resulted, which acts as a "buffer zone" between Brooklyn Heights and the rest of the borough.

To the right is the modern **New York State Supreme Court,** designed in 1957 by Shreve, Lamb & Harmon (architects of the Empire State Building). At its south end are **lamp standards from the old Hall of Records**; and to the east, the **Federal Building and Court House,** completed in 1961 from plans by Carson, Lundin & Shaw.

To the north, rising like a medieval château, is the **Brooklyn Central Office of the U.S. Post Office.** Designed in 1885 in Romanesque Revival style by Mifflin E. Bell, the work was later assumed by William A. Freret, supervising architect for the Treasury Department, and completed in 1891. A north section, in harmonious style, was created by James A. Wetmore in 1933. The post office, built of granite while Brooklyn was still an independent city, represents a high standard of government-sponsored architecture, and with the great advances in

Brooklyn's Romanesque Revival–style General Post Office is a designated landmark. Completed in 1891, it represents an unusually high standard of government-sponsored architecture. The tree-lined plot to the right was the site of the Brooklyn Eagle. (Brooklyn Union Gas Company)

Opening day of the Brooklyn Elevated Railroad with its special trainload of city officials, May 13, 1888, from an engraving in Leslie's Illustrated Newspaper of the following week. (Brooklyn Historical Society)

stone-cutting techniques achieved late in the 19th century, it was possible to produce masonry buildings of great beauty. To the south of the post office stood the Brooklyn Eagle Building, built in 1893 and demolished in the late 1950s as part of the civic center redevelopment plan.

Directly in front of Borough Hall is a **Memorial to John Cashmore,** a former Brooklyn borough president under whose administration the Cadman Plaza project was realized. Near the entrance to the Supreme Court is a bronze plaque honoring **Washington Augustus Roebling** and his marvelous Brooklyn Bridge. When completed in 1883, it was the longest suspension bridge in the world. To the west of the plaque, but north of Borough Hall, is a **bust of Senator Robert F. Kennedy,** by Anneta Duveen. Farther to the north is a life-size marble statue of **Christopher Columbus,** by Emma Stebbins which she carved in Rome in 1867.

A half-block farther north is the best piece of sculpture in the plaza, and one of the finest in the city, the extraordinary bronze **statue of Henry Ward Beecher,** by John Quincy Adams Ward, unveiled in 1891, with a black granite pedestal designed by Richard Morris Hunt. When Beecher died on March 8, 1887, Ward received a telegram urgently requesting that he make a death mask within four hours. Complying, he then received the commission for the eight-foot-high statue. In the completed monument an austere Beecher, in a simple knee-length Inverness cape, stands above three intimate figures of youngsters, a young black girl placing a palm frond in gratitude at the abolitionist's feet, and a young boy helping a girl climb the base to lay flowers at Beecher's feet—all three representing his love and devotion to children. The statue originally stood in front of Borough Hall, but was moved to its present site in 1959. The Metropolitan Museum of Art praised the Beecher Monument and called it "public statuary at its best."

End of tour. (The following tour may be made by either walking the short distance indicated below, or by taking the three-minute bus ride.)

     THE FULTON FERRY HISTORIC DISTRICT

Walk down Cadman Plaza to the waterfront (about a third of a mile) or take the B25 or B41 bus to the end of the line at Furman Street. (Cadman Plaza West becomes Old Fulton Street after the Expressway.)

The modern history of Brooklyn began at the waterfront hamlet of Fulton Ferry, which after the introduction of Robert Fulton's steam ferry in 1814 became the gateway not only to Brooklyn but to Long Island as well. (The first record of a ferry to Manhattan was Cornelis Dircksen's regular rowboat crossings in 1642. Crossings were later made with sailboats, and even with boats propelled by horses walking on treadmills.) Other ferries subsequently linked Manhattan and Brooklyn, and in 1872 as many as 1,200 daily crossings were recorded, but the Fulton Ferry was by far the most important. The little village grew rapidly and soon boasted several hotels, a newspaper (the Brooklyn *Daily*

FULTON
FERRY
HISTORIC
DISTRICT

Eagle), a bank, law offices, and a stagecoach terminal. With the opening of the Brooklyn Bridge in 1883, the Fulton Ferry district began a gradual decline, becoming an almost forgotten backwater by the 20th century. The ferry hung on, however, until 1924, for 110 years of service. Plans have been underway for many years to restore many of the old landmarks and to re-create much of the early-19th-century atmosphere of the Village of Fulton Ferry, and the area has been designated a Historic District.

The tour begins on Old Fulton Street in front of the Eagle Warehouse and Storage Company building.

The Eagle Warehouse and Storage Company of Brooklyn engaged architect Frank Freeman to design this massive red brick "fortress" in 1893. Completed a year later, it became a notable example of his Romanesque Revival style. The arched main entrance with the company's bold lettering is particularly impressive. A stylized horse's head is mounted on a gooseneck post at the entry gate, which separates the vehicular entrance from the former office. Very impressive is the symmetrical façade and the heavy iron grilles on the windows. Above is a row of round arches surmounted by corbels that resemble the machicolations of a medieval castle. On the parapet is a clock flanked by the name of the establishment.

The Fulton Ferry terminal, built in 1871 in Victorian style, continued in operation until 1924. This 1891 view shows a steam train of the Brooklyn Elevated Railroad about to leave from the adjacent El station for its run on the Fulton Street line. (Brooklyn Historical Society)

Looking northeast on Fulton Street (now Cadman Plaza) in 1954, toward the old Brooklyn Eagle Building and the still-standing General Post Office Building. (Brooklyn Picture Collection, Brooklyn Public Library)

Once a warehouse for the storage of household furnishings and silverware, the enormous structure was renovated in 1980 and adaptively reused as a cooperative apartment building. In the lobby (if you can persuade the doorman or a tenant to let you peek inside) is an atrium in which "artifacts" from nearby demolished buildings are displayed on the walls. Unfortunately the building's former "birdcage" elevator has been removed and relegated to the roof. The lobby also has a colorful mural of Cadman Plaza West looking toward the river.

Walk around to the rear, on Elizabeth Place, and see if you can discover the old three-story brick building, with segmental-arc window lintels, that has been incorporated into the warehouse. This is the last physical vestige of the *Brooklyn Eagle's* first office, **its old pressroom.** Built in 1882 from a design by George L. Morse, it functioned until 1893 when the newspaper erected its new building next to the Brooklyn post office. The name of the warehouse was appropriated from the newspaper, as two of its directors were executives of the *Eagle.*

Up the hill to the south rise the prominent yellow-painted twin factory buildings that were once the **Squibb Pharmaceutical Company plant.** Connected by a "Bridge of Sighs" over Everit Street (whose name changes to Columbia Heights after one block), the once-busy drug manufacturing facility is now the printing plant of the Watchtower Bible & Tract Society, the Jehovah's Witnesses.

At No. 8 Old Fulton Street, at the corner of Furman Street, is the **former headquarters of the Brooklyn City Railroad Company,** the horsecar enterprise that replaced the stages and built ribbons of track throughout most of the city of Brooklyn. (A track is still visible on the west side, in the rear. It is somewhat hidden, but it can be seen to the right of the entrance to the apartment house on Furman Street.) The structure was designed in Italianate style and is constructed of brick with granite trim. Completed in 1861, it occupies the riverfront site of the former Judge William Furman residence. From 1910 until the mid-1970s, the building housed a toilet-seat factory, and in 1975 it was converted to an apartment house by architect David Morton.

Across Old Fulton Street—which in the early 19th century was called Old Ferry Road—is a **row of commercial structures in Greek Revival style,** built between 1836 and 1839. The corner building once housed the Franklin House, the others comprised a variety of merchandising establishments. Observe the remains of the **old sidewalk canopy in front of No. 15**—a fairly common feature in the 19th century.

Notice the painted names of merchants and their wares fading from the façades of the row of buildings. These four-story houses retain much of their original appearance and are significant as one of the few surviving examples in the city of commercial Greek Revival architecture.

At the end of the commercial row, at the corner of Water Street, the **old Franklin House** was the most important dining saloon and hotel in the district during the 19th century. Its prime location at the Fulton Ferry made it a favored stop for commuters for over sixty years. It is now the Harbor View Restaurant, with rental apartments above.

Ahead, at the river's edge, the small wood-frame building with hipped roof and tower is the **former Marine Fire Boat Station.** Erected in 1930 on the site of the old Victorian-style Ferry Terminal, it served the harbor firefighting patrol until the station became obsolete in the late 1970s. (The tower was used to hang the fire hoses to dry.) The former fireboat pier occupies the site of the old Fulton Ferry slip.

Near the pier is a **plaque** on a boulder marking the spot where Gen. George Washington escaped with his Continental Army to Manhattan on the night of August 29, 1776. [*See* page 439.]

Anchored to the left is **"Bargemusic,"** formerly the Erie-Lackawanna R.R. Coffee Barge 375, which was acquired in 1977 and converted into a floating chamber music concert hall. In this unique ambience, gifted soloists perform year round on Sunday afternoons at 4:00 and Thursday evenings at 7:30 [reservations: (718) 624–4061].

Just to the right and in the shadow of the Brooklyn Bridge is **Fulton Ferry Park.** Built by the city's Department of Ports & Terminals, it is a small patch of green with a nautical motif, and provides a spot for river gazing. The iron railings along the water were salvaged from the "islands" on Manhattan's Park Avenue. In storage for five years, they were installed when the park was opened in 1976. Unfortunately, the private interests who were to maintain the little park seem to have forgotten their promise, and what was once a charming vantage point is now a disaster. The privately owned River Café, set on a barge, offers an unequalled but expensive panorama for dining.

On Water Street, directly under the bridge, is the Art Moderne concrete and brick **New York City Department of General Services Warehouse B-53,** formerly the Department of Purchase Storehouse, built in 1936. Interesting are the horizontal concrete bands that accentuate the wide steel-strip windows.

Follow Water Street to the first street on the left, New Dock Street. The old red brick structure that extends to the next corner was built in the early 1870s as the **Tobacco Inspection Warehouse.** It was used until well after the turn of the century for the storage of tobacco and as a customs inspection center for tobacco imports, since 90 percent of Brooklyn's tobacco trade was carried on here.

Reaching the corner, turn left into *New* Dock Street, and walk to the entrance to **Empire–Fulton Ferry State Park** (*closed in winter*). To the left, an open "cobblestoned" plaza offers dramatic views of the Lower Manhattan skyline and the ships of the South Street Seaport, framed by the towers of the Brooklyn Bridge. A plaque describes the Bridge and its two neighbors to the north, the Manhattan and Williamsburg bridges. In the park itself, follow the boardwalk, relax and watch the passing parade of East River ship traffic, or turn around and enjoy the lush green lawn, designed to be walked on. To the right of the Manhattan Bridge, is the Walentas Building (William Higginson, 1886) with the hipped roof and clocktower. Erected for a corrugated box manufacturer, it was originally called the Gair Building. It and a group of about a dozen similar structures were among the first reinforced-concrete buildings in America, and all were named Gair, but with separate numbers. This one was Gair No. 7. The building was altered in 1986, and is named for the present owner.

The backdrop of the park, and its main feature, is the **Empire Stores,** a monumental row of seven connected brick warehouses with long rows of similar round-arched windows and doors. Erected in two stages, the first group to the west was built in 1870, and the eastern section in 1885, by architect Thomas Stone, they share a unified façade. Loading hoists project from the flat roofs under corbelled roof cornices, and the doors and windows have heavy iron shutters that swing on pintle-type hinges. Metal tie-rod caps in the shape of stars reinforce the walls and add a decorative touch. In front of the Stores and leading to the water's edge were once railroad sidings to accommodate freight cars brought by car floats from the various railroad terminals around the city. The Empire Stores were used originally for the general storage of such raw materials as coffee beans, animal hides, grains, raw sugar and molasses, brought from points all over the world. They were just one of many such warehouses that lined the Brooklyn waterfront for miles, earning the borough the sobriquet "the walled city." No longer in use, they were acquired in 1963 by Con Edison, and later by the city for development by some as yet undecided institution, such as a museum. Return to the park entrance and walk back along New Dock Street to Front Street.

Turn left on Water Street and right on Dock Street to Front Street, then turn right again.

No. 5–7 Front Street is a small Greek Revival structure built in 1834 for the Long Island Insurance Company, and may be the earliest example of an office building which still survives in the entire city. The insurance company lasted until 1867, when the building was sold to the bank that erected its office at the corner to the left. Note the original iron hand-railings, ornamented with scrolls and acorns, which are preserved at the central doorway. The façade above the first floor is in Flemish-bond brickwork, with alternating long bricks (stretchers) and short bricks (headers), typical of better buildings erected during the Federal and Greek Revival periods. Stone windowsills and cap-molded lintels and a brick fascia below the roof cornice are typical of the style. Peek through the window at the rolled sheet-tin walls and ceilings, still in place and in good condition.

At the northwest corner of Old Fulton and Front Streets is a highly ornate cast-iron-front building erected in 1869 for the **Long Island Safe Deposit Company.** Designed by William Mundell at a time when cast iron had come into vogue as a successful building medium, the highly decorative façade is modeled after a Venetian Renaissance palace. The company's safety-deposit vaults were once visible on the first floor of the bank, set in their own granite foundations. The bank closed in 1891 and the building has since served a wide variety of owners. In its latest incarnation it is a disco bar and cabaret-restaurant.

The cast-iron façade is unique in this area, and its delicate detailing is worth a few minutes' examination. The first-floor round-arched windows are protected by iron window guards with fleur-de-lis cresting, and are separated by pilasters with egg-and-dart capitals. The second-story windows are even more ornate and recall the style of the Venetian Renaissance *palazzi.* All details, both of the exterior as well as the interior, were rendered in cast iron, since it was its fireproofing qualities that attracted the original owners. The old bank is on the site of the 19th-century Abraham Remsen home and dry-goods store which had replaced the original stone farmhouse of the Rapelje family.

A BRIEF NOTE ABOUT THE BROOKLYN BRIDGE. Construction began on January 3, 1870, and was completed 13 years later, providing the vital link to Manhattan that ultimately led to the consolidation of Brooklyn into the City of New York in 1898. The monumental bridge represented the largest leap across an open space to that date—1,595.5 feet—and is still considered by many to be the most beautiful span ever built. Engineer John Augustus Roebling had few architectural precedents to draw upon and had to test his designs on the spot. He had built three smaller previous bridges—the Suspension Bridge at Niagara Falls, in 1852, the still-extant Delaware & Hudson Aqueduct Bridge at Lackawaxen, Pennsylvania, and the Ohio River Bridge in Cincinnati. The Delaware bridge originally carried canal boats across the Delaware River and now is used by vehicular traffic. The Cincinnati bridge is also still in service. In planning the bridge, Roebling wisely anticipated the oscillation caused by aerodynamic instability and was a great pioneer in the use of structural steel. He is ranked with Joseph Paxton, who designed London's Crystal Palace Exposition Hall in 1851, and with Alexandre Gustave Eiffel, whose great Tower was erected in Paris in 1889. The Brooklyn Bridge cost in excess of $16 million, some of which ended up in the pockets of "Boss" Tweed and his Ring.

Roebling suffered a fatal accident in the early stages of the bridge's construction. His foot was crushed by a wooden piling as the Fulton ferryboat was docking, and he died of tetanus a few weeks later. His son, Washington Augustus Roebling, carried on the project, and proved himself as capable an engineer as his father. He, too, was struck down by the bridge, suffering a disabling attack of caisson disease (the bends) from a too-rapid ascent from the underwater pressure chambers, and he directed the remaining work from the window of his sickroom, several blocks away. He was assisted by his wife Emily, who taught herself advanced mathematics to be able to better help her husband. Little was known then of nitrogen narcosis, and the dangerous construction job took the lives of many workers. Opening day caused some furor among the Irish population of the city, as the date coincided with Queen Victoria's birthday. Shortly thereafter, a tragedy occurred that took the lives of a number of bridge pedestrians caught in an unexplained panic at the Manhattan end. Newspaper accounts attributed the crush to an organization of pickpockets who spread confusion to facilitate their criminal activities. To date 45 people have leaped from the bridge, of whom only 11 survived, including a Bowery saloonkeeper named Steve Brodie, whose claim of having survived the plunge may have been a publicity stunt. For many years the bridge carried cable cars, then the trains of the Brooklyn Elevated Railway, as well as trolley cars. The trolleys and trains were removed in the early 1940s and replaced by additional traffic lanes. More supporting cables were added later, but the strength and beauty of the bridge remains an enduring monument to the genius and skill of the Roeblings. A few years ago the twin Gothic-style stone piers were sandblasted, and to everyone's surprise, the original color of the granite was revealed to be pink!

The view of the Manhattan skyline at dusk, framed in the dark arches and gossamerlike cables of the great span, is a never-to-be-forgotten experience.

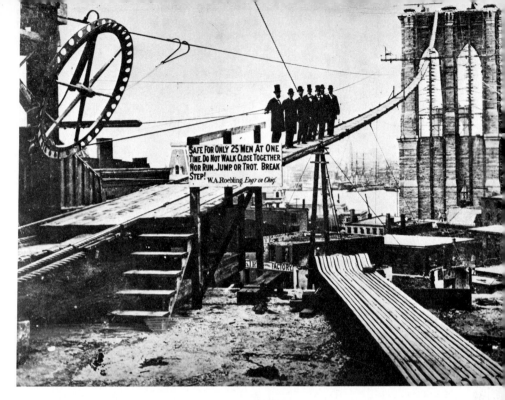

City dignitaries gathered to inspect the cables of the Brooklyn Bridge in 1873. Judging from engineer Roebling's warning sign, the terrifying hike on the Bridge's catwalk across the river must have been fairly commonplace. (Brooklyn Union Gas Company)

The Bridge Promenade has always been a popular attraction. In warm weather hundreds of commuters from Brooklyn Heights still use it daily. (Brooklyn Historical Society)

A two-cent ticket to walk across the Brooklyn Bridge after it was opened to the public in 1883. (Brooklyn Union Gas Company)

Traffic was already heavy on the Brooklyn Bridge in 1905. (Brooklyn Historical Society)

An 1814 newspaper advertisement announcing the commutation fares for Robert Fulton's new steam ferry service to Brooklyn. (Brooklyn Historical Society)

New-York and Brooklyn Ferry.

SUCH persons as are inclined to compound, agreeable to law, in the Steam Ferry-Boat, Barges, or common Horse Boats, will be pleased to apply to the subscribers, who are authorized to settle the same.

GEORGE HICKS, Brooklyn,
JOHN PINTARD, 52 Wall-st

Commutation for a single person not
transferable, for 12 months, $10 00
Do. do. 8 months, 6 67
May 3, 1814. 6m.

The ferry from the tip of lower Manhattan entering its slip at the foot of Atlantic Avenue, Brooklyn, ca. 1830. (South Street Seaport Museum)

Thomas Wolfe, in *Of Time and the River,* extolled the beauty of the bridge "whose wing-like sweep" reached across to the "shining city, far-flung and blazing into tiers of jeweled light."

Walk back along Old Fulton Street to where the Expressway crosses overhead.

To the left is the **Brooklyn Bridge Anchorage,** a vast, cavernous space within the bridge's base where the great anchor chains disappear underground. It was opened to the public during the Brooklyn Bridge Centennial in 1983 and is used for exhibits and performances, usually from late May to early October. In front is a steel sculpture of the creators of the bridge, John, Washington, and Emily Roebling, by Keith Godard.

Continue on Old Fulton Street to Henry Street, and cross carefully! Turn right, and right again into Poplar Street.

The entire block, once a dismal aggregation of decaying factories, warehouses, and residences, was renovated in 1986–87 under supervising architect Richard Ferrara, as a huge condominium complex, called Bridge Harbor Heights. The centerpiece of the development is the **former Brooklyn Children's Aid Society Orphanage,** a Victorian edifice built in 1883 as a home for indigent newsboys.

End of tour. To reach the A or C line, follow Old Fulton Street into Cadman Plaza West. The station entrance is opposite Cranberry Street, adjacent to the Whitman Close town houses, where the first Brooklyn Heights tour began.

COBBLE HILL

Shaded area indicates
boundaries of
Cobble Hill Historic District

STATE ST.

ATLANTIC AVE.

start

PACIFIC ST.

AMITY ST.

CONGRESS ST.

Cobble Hill Park

VERANDAH PL.

WARREN ST.

BALTIC ST.

KANE ST.

DEGRAW ST.

BROOKLYN-QUEENS EXPRESSWAY

WARREN PL.

HICKS ST.

CHEEVER PL.

HENRY ST.

STRONG PL.

CLINTON ST.

TOMPKINS PL.

COURT ST.

To subway⟶

To
Carroll
Gardens

16. Cobble Hill and Carroll Gardens

[Lexington Avenue or Broadway–Seventh Avenue lines to Borough Hall, walk south on Court Street four blocks to Atlantic Avenue; F, G lines to Bergen Street, walk back (north) three blocks to Atlantic Avenue and left (west) two blocks to Court Street]

The history of Cobble Hill began in the mid-17th century when Dutch colonists were granted patents to farm the land between the Gowanus* valley and the East River shore. The hilly terrain was very fertile and the area remained a bucolic suburb for over 200 years.

At the outbreak of the Revolutionary War, Cobble Hill figured in the Battle of Long Island, when the garrison of a small fort built on a promontory known as "Cobbleshill" fired a prearranged two-gun signal to warn General Washington's Continental Army that the British had landed at Gravesend, down the bay. It was from this redoubt—one of several strong points along the heights of Brooklyn—that Washington and his generals on August 27, 1776, observed the massive forces of Lord Howe gradually overwhelm the patriot defenders and force them into a strategic withdrawal across the East River to Manhattan. The British army subsequently destroyed the fort and painstakingly cut away the commanding high ground on which it was built.

During the War of 1812, another fortification was erected nearby, and named Fort Swift; however, no invading forces attacked New York, and the defending cannon remained silent.

In 1834 Cobble Hill was annexed by the newly incorporated City of Brooklyn, joining adjacent Brooklyn Heights, which earlier comprised most of the original Village of Brooklyn. Many of the old Dutch land holdings were broken up into smaller lots for residential development, and with the opening two

---

Gowanus derives from the name of the Indian sachem, Gouwane, who sold the first land to the Dutch in 1636.

years later of the South Ferry connecting District Street (now Atlantic Avenue) with the southern tip of Manhattan, the area grew rapidly. The street pattern of Cobble Hill was laid out from Atlantic Avenue south to what is now Kane Street and Strong Place, and row-house construction began in earnest. By the mid-19th century, the district referred to as "South Brooklyn" had lost all of its rural character and became largely a residential suburb of mostly wealthy merchants and a completely self-contained community with its own shops, churches, school, and bank, and some light manufacturing. The growing population was swelled by an influx of immigrants, particularly from Germany and Italy; and with the opening in 1879 of Alfred T. White's famous "model tenements," other nationality groups—Irish, English, Swedes, and Norwegians—settled in Cobble Hill. After World War I, the neighborhood attracted large numbers of Syrians and Lebanese, and today Atlantic Avenue is known as Brooklyn's Middle East. In more recent times, new immigrants from Latin America and the Orient have joined the proverbial "melting pot"; and young families of all backgrounds, in search of lower-cost housing, have been buying up row houses, carefully restoring them, and putting Cobble Hill into the front ranks of New York's "Brownstone Revolution." What was at the turn of the century merely a "workingman's district" has become a very desirable place to live. Cobble Hill has a unique quality of its own, with 19th-century moderate-income houses, much well-preserved ironwork, a uniform skyline punctuated only by occasional churches—many of them architectural gems—tree-lined streets, and a surprising small-town atmosphere. In 1969 22 blocks were designated by the New York City Landmarks Commission as the **Cobble Hill Historic District.**

The walking tour begins at Atlantic Avenue and Court Street.

In 1836 ferry service was inaugurated between **Atlantic Avenue** (then Atlantic Street) and the southern tip of Manhattan. The same year, the Brooklyn & Jamaica Railroad constructed a right of way along Atlantic Street, connecting the South Ferry with the town of Jamaica and the Long Island Rail Road, and the thoroughfare developed quickly as one of the major commercial arteries of Long Island. The grade up Atlantic Street proved to be too steep for the tiny woodburning locomotives, and in 1844 construction was begun on a half-mile-long tunnel under the street, extending from Columbia Street almost to Boerum Place. Seven months later, New York's first underground railroad began operation, with trains preceded through the tunnel by a man on horseback. It remained in service for only 16 years, as a group of merchants and politicians pushed through legislation banning all steam railroad operations from the City of Brooklyn. The tunnel was closed and the reorganized Brooklyn Central & Jamaica Railroad moved its terminal to Flatbush Avenue, where it was forced to use horsecars as far as the city line. The tunnel is still in existence under Atlantic Avenue and has been the subject of much speculation for many years. In 1911 the Brooklyn *Daily Eagle* reported at length on a fruitless search for an entrance to the tunnel, as rumors were rampant on its use by counterfeiters, smugglers, bootleggers, and white slavers. In 1980 a young engineering student, fascinated by all the stories of the tunnel, came across some old maps, and persuaded the city to let him open a manhole and excavate an entranceway. After much digging by local volunteers, with the help of the Brooklyn Union Gas Company, a passage was opened, and it is now possible to walk almost the full length of the cavernous tunnel whose brick-arch construction is in a remarkable state of preservation. Under the aegis of a group called the Brooklyn Historic Railway Association, visitors may on occasional weekends during the warm months, climb down a ladder at the corner of Atlantic Avenue and Court Street into the old tunnel for a conducted tour of the world's first "subway" for a modest fee.

At the turn of the century, Atlantic Avenue was heavily Swedish and was known locally as "Swedish Broadway." The Avenue is now famous for its variety of Middle Eastern establishments that line the street almost to the river. As you walk along the avenue, notice the restaurants and souvenir stores; but more importantly, the Syrian-Lebanese groceries and specialty food shops, stocked

The Long Island Rail Road tunnel under Atlantic Avenue, from an engraving, ca. 1844. The tunnel was used for only 16 years, before being forced to close by a City of Brooklyn ordinance against steam locomotives. (Brooklyn Historical Society)

with their special flat bread, twisted cheese, halvah, baklava, pistachio nuts, stuffed grape leaves, yoghurt, and a thousand other taste-tempting delicacies. Take a pocketful of goodies with you, as there are few places of refreshment along the way.

The Independence Savings Bank, formerly the South Brooklyn Savings Bank, at the corner of Atlantic Avenue and Court Street, is reminiscent of a Florentine *palazzo.* Typical is the heavily rusticated façade and the highly ornamental door frame with sculpture above (on the Court Street side). The roof cornice is rather unusual with its row of carved stone eagles supporting it. The bank building was completed in 1922 from plans by McKenzie, Voorhees & Gmelin. An addition (No. 136 Court Street) was built in 1936, also in Italian Renaissance style. This was **the site of "Cobbleshill,"** the conical-shaped hill on which the Revolutionary War fort was built. The little promontory was also called "Ponkiesbergh." Nearby, and roughly following the present route of Court Street, was the old Red Hook Lane, laid out in 1760. When the Cobble Hill street grid was laid out, the ancient road was demapped. Read the historical plaque on the Court Street side.

Walk west on the right (north) side of Atlantic Avenue.

No. 180 Atlantic Avenue is a commercial cast-iron-front building, erected in 1873. Except for the storefront, the structure is in pristine condition. Cast iron was a very popular medium of building-front construction during the period 1860–90 [for information on cast-iron building construction, *see* introduction to the SoHo Cast-Iron District walking tour]. The roof cornice has a typical Victorian design. Compare the window enframements of the upper two floors with those of the second story.

Although **Nos. 164–168** would seem to have been built in 1859, according to the date set in the gable, the two houses were each built at a different time, but joined together with a common roof cornice. No. 166–168 was actually erected in 1860, and No. 164 in 1864. The house is somewhat representative of the Italianate style, especially in the bracketed cornice and the stone quoins. Sadly, the ground floor was "modernized" with no understanding of the architectural style of the whole, and mars the elegant appearance of the building.

The building at the southeast corner of Clinton Street was **the original home of the South Brooklyn Savings Bank,** built in 1871. Constructed of Tuckahoe marble and designed by E. L. Roberts, this magnificent Italian Renaissance–style structure recently was refurbished under strict preservation guidelines. The roof balustrade has been removed and the street level has also been "modernized" into incongruity. In its *Cobble Hill Historic District Designation Report,* the Landmarks Commission mentions that "the vault (of the old bank) was constructed of granite blocks mortised out to receive cannon balls between each pair, so that the stones could not be forced out of alignment without demolishing the entire wall." There was once "an imposing central doorway flanked by columns that supported the balcony of a pedimented window which was also enframed by columns."

On the northeast corner of Atlantic Avenue and Clinton Street stood the Atheneum, a public hall built in 1853, which became the home four years later of the Brooklyn Philharmonic Society. The orchestra soon found the space inadequate, and in its search for a "large lyric hall," the idea to erect a grand cultural center for Brooklyn was born. The result was the founding in 1859 of the Brooklyn Academy of Music on Montague Street [*see* page 412]. The Atheneum building survived until 1942.

Beyond Clinton Street is a **group of houses that still show traces of the Greek Revival period.** Most were erected during the years 1848–52. Many still retain their original roof cornices. Note the cap moldings above the second- and third-floor windows on Nos. 152 and 154. Across the avenue, note narrow No. 145 with its wooden cornice, and only two bays wide. Although all were residences, the first-floor stores are original.

No. 132, a much altered Italianate brownstone, was built in the 1850s as Brooklyn's branch office of the City Bank, later the National City Bank, and now the Downstate Headache Center. Observe the typically Italianate pedimented windows and the roof cornice with its dentils ("toothlike" blocks) and supporting brackets, but ignore the altered ground floor.

No. 124–134 was once the most important dry-goods emporium in the neighborhood, **the former Journeay & Burnham Store.** The firm began in 1851, at No. 126, now No. 124, and was so successful that new quarters were built in 1884, adding to an already large annex on Court Street built five years before.

Return to Clinton Street and turn right (south).

Nos. 197 and **199 Clinton Street,** on the east side near the corner of Pacific Street, are the only two surviving Italianate row houses of the group of four that still have any character left. Look for the following typical features: high stoops, round- and segmental-arc entranceways, floor-length parlor windows, and a bracketed roof cornice. The brownstone facing, a type of sandstone, was usually quarried in Connecticut or New Jersey.

The multiple dwelling across the street, **No. 214–220,** was erected in 1892 and reflects the style of multiple-dwelling house construction of the 1890s. Decorated with classical motifs and some Romanesque Revival influence, it is representative of the so-called "transitional period." The sheet-metal bay windows serve two purposes: to admit more light and air, and to add a decorative facet to the broad façade of the building. Note, too, the ornamental doorway with its round arch and carvings, surmounted by a pediment with a carved face in it. The building has another somewhat similar entrance around the corner at 147 Pacific Street.

Turn left (east) into Pacific Street.

The change in atmosphere from bustling Atlantic Avenue to quiet residential **Pacific Street** is immediately evident. The feeling of remoteness and tranquility increases with each block. The architecture of this block is varied, with fine examples of Victorian and Romanesque Revival styles. The diversity is due to the former role of Pacific Street (particularly the north side) as the stable row for the establishments on Atlantic Avenue.

No. 172 Pacific Street, built in an early Romanesque Revival style of the 1850s, was formerly a stable, and has been remodeled as a residence. A rather handsome building with its three arches and gable, it is an interesting counterpart to its neighbor, across the street, **No. 173.** Built about ten years later, it is also an example of the Romanesque Revival–style stable converted to residential use. The center wagon entrance is now the garage door, and the old hayloft above embraces an arched window. Nowadays, a converted stable is often more desirable than an original house.

Old Public School No. 78, remodeled as a condominium apartment building, was built in 1888–89 in the tradition of the small neighborhood public school and designed in early Victorian style. The roof line presents a dramatic profile with its elaborate cornice, gables, and central tower. A truncated slate roof crowns the projecting entrance tower.

A fine example of the Romanesque Revival style is **No. 162,** with its *rundbogenstil,* or round-arch windows and doors on each floor. A divided stoop climbs to a central landing in an eye-catching effect. Notice the elaborate cornice and the blind bull's-eye on the stepped gable, which were added later, and the massiveness of the first floor with its piers and corbeled arches. Typical, too, is the extensive use of red brick. As you return to Clinton Street, observe the second-floor hoist on No. 169.

Return to Clinton Street, and continue west on Pacific Street.

The **south side of Pacific Street** reveals row houses built in groups of two or three, many in the Greek Revival style. Particularly attractive is the wrought ironwork of the stoops' handrailings, with their swirls in Greek motifs. **No. 122 is the oldest house in the neighborhood,** built before 1833. The mansard roof was added later, but the Greek Revival–style doorway with sidelights still remains. The doorways at **Nos. 126–130** and **116–120** are framed by stone pilasters supporting entablatures. Note the yard railings in front of **Nos. 118–120** with anthemion-motif finials.

Three Greek Revival–style houses on the north side of the block near Henry Street (**Nos. 117–119**) are quite simple in design, but the eye is drawn to the very ornate stoop and yard iron railings. The adjacent building, **No. 121–125,** was an extension of the Journeay & Burnham Dry-Goods Store on Atlantic Avenue. It was completed in 1881 and was designed by architect John A. Raymond in neo-Grec style. Note the typical incised floral motifs between the windows. The building is now a condominium.

Turn left (south) on Henry Street.

The **Long Island College Hospital** occupies several blocks, and dates back to 1857, when it was organized by a group of German immigrants who fled persecution in Europe in 1848. None of the original buildings remain. Interestingly, according to hospital records, the original medical staff included a leecher and cupper. Across the street, the main building dates from 1905. At the southeast corner of Pacific and Henry streets stood the Hoagland Laboratory, the first private bacteriological laboratory in the country, built in 1888. The magnificent Flemish Revival building was destroyed by fire some years ago, and the hospital could not afford the exorbitant reconstruction costs. **The Out-Patient Department,** formerly the Nurses' Residence (Beeston & Patterson, 1963) at the northeast corner of Amity Street is a modern addition to the campus. Diagonally across the street is the **Polhemus Clinic** (Marshall L. Emery, 1897), a good example of the Renaissance Eclectic style, representing the transition from the so-called Romantic Era to the more functional and less ornate modern style.

Turn left (east) on Amity Street.

The Dudley Memorial, 110 Amity Street (William C. Hough, 1903), was built in the style of a small French Renaissance château. The roof deck contains a small loggia with Doric columns, and the roof cornice, constructed of sheet metal, is painted to simulate stone and is set on very elaborate brackets. Named for the hospital's first council member, Dr. William H. Dudley, it was originally built as a nurses' residence, but now serves as a developmental disabilities center.

Along the north side of Amity Street are several **rows of Italianate houses,** dating from the period of popularity of the style, 1875–81. Typical are **Nos. 129–133.**

No. 155 is a very late Queen Anne–style building, so late in fact (1903!) that it is almost an anachronism. The treatment of the windows is the interesting element—wooden two-story polygonal bays supported on basket-shaped corbels, with a cartouche design.

Before turning the corner at Clinton Street, step back and admire the magnificent **Degraw Mansion** across the street at the southeast corner (actually **219 Clinton Street**). Built in 1844 and enlarged in 1891, it occupies a beautiful setting on ample grounds with lush plantings. The Landmarks Commission calls it "without a doubt the most imposing property in the Cobble Hill Historic District." The original house, in Greek Revival style, was built for Abraham J. S. Degraw, a Manhattan commission merchant. The major remodeling of the building was planned by the architects D'Oench and Simon for the second owners, Laura and Ralph Cutter. Mr. Cutter was a dry-goods merchant and treasurer of the nearby First Presbyterian Church on Henry Street. The Romanesque touches on the ground floor and the Flemish stepped gable roof stem from the 1891 reconstruction, as well as the lofty tower, which was equipped with the first private passenger elevator in Brooklyn! The sideways-facing brownstone stoop was also added, giving a feeling of elegance and dignity. The house was acquired in 1924 by its third owner, A. N. Saab, who wisely made no exterior changes in this lovely mansion, so that when it was sold to a developer for conversion into a multiple-dwelling house, it was remarkably well preserved. The view of the harbor from the tower is probably reminiscent of the broad panoramas enjoyed by the early landholders whose large houses overlooked the Upper New York Bay in the early 19th century.

(Although not on the itinerary of the tour, No. 197 Amity Street, one block farther, near the corner of Court Street, is the **birthplace of Jennie Jerome** [January 9, 1854], mother of Winston Churchill. The house was built five years earlier in Greek Revival style, but except for some attractive ironwork on the stoop, little remains of the original, the façade having been "modernized" with a fake stone siding. Her father, Leonard Jerome, was a wealthy financier and race-horse fancier who built Jerome Avenue in the Bronx as a direct route to his race track. Jenny grew up to marry Lord Randolph Churchill in 1874. Incidentally, it was commonly believed that Jennie Jerome was born at 426 Henry Street, and a plaque on the house makes the claim; however, it is incorrect—she was indeed born here.)

At the southwest corner of Amity and Clinton streets stood the **Church of St. Mary the Virgin.** Built in 1922, it was planned as a much larger house of worship but was never completed, as the Syrian congregation acquired the former Congregational Church of the Pilgrims in Brooklyn Heights, now renamed Our Lady of Lebanon. The church was demolished in 1982.

Turn right (south) on Clinton Street to Congress Street.

Take a few steps down the block, then turn around and look back again at the Degraw Mansion (219 Clinton Street) and its lofty tower. The need for its elevator is immediately apparent.

The rather large three-story house on the northeast corner (**No. 235**) was built in the 1840s. Originally a Greek Revival house, it was remodeled in the late 19th century with neo-Grec motifs (pedimented lintels); on the Congress Street side, it was given rectangular bay windows of stained glass, but the entrance stairway was removed. It is now the Convent of the Sisters of Charity of nearby St. Paul's Roman Catholic Church, on Court Street.

Turn right (west) on Congress Street, and walk on the park side.

Cobble Hill Park, a pleasant green plot, has become a very attractive open space since its construction in the early 1970s, with many benches for shady sitting and socializing. The original garish light pylons have been replaced with more appropriate older-style lampposts, rescued from the Parks Department's warehouse. The park was not part of a neighborhood plan, but resulted when the Second Unitarian Church was demolished. Built in 1857–58 from plans by J. Wrey Mould, it was fondly referred to as "The Church of the Holy Turtle" because the rather squat building's huge dome-shaped roof resembled the carapace of a Galapagos tortoise. Built by New Englanders, its first pastor was Samuel Longfellow, a brother of the famous poet and an active abolitionist. Until its removal, the Second Unitarian Church was considered an important center of cultural and community activity. When the church was abandoned in the early 1950s, a supermarket was planned for the site; however, local community groups protested so vigorously that the park was substituted by the city.

Congress Street, opposite the park and almost to Henry Street, offers an interesting variety of Anglo-Italianate brownstones. The houses are of various dimensions, but preserve their basic mid-19th century character, having suffered many alterations. Note the ornate door and window lintels on **No. 169. Nos. 159–163** are a trio of Anglo-Italianate houses which share a common double-bracketed cornice, complete with a rope molding and a gablelike pediment in the center.

Look across the street at its little cousin, **Nos. 166–170.** And next door, peek into the entrance of **No. 164,** whose inner doors still retain their etched glass panels. It shares a cast-iron fence with **No. 162,** with huge octagonal newel posts.

Back across the street again, **No. 155** is a *brick* Italianate house, with original entranceway and doors, a fairly elaborate roof cornice and individual window cornices, plus a neat cast-iron fence complete with fancy newels. Observe how the windows diminish in size at each floor, creating the illusion of greater height.

The light brown sheet-metal oriel on the house to the left (which faces Henry Street) is a curiously ornate appendage that was added long after the house was built.

The last house on the north side facing Congress Street, **No. 147,** is also the newest on the block, built around the turn of the century. It is another anachronistic Queen Anne building, but it is nonetheless quite charming. Note how the entry tower, like a medieval *donjon,* culminates in a high pyramidal roof. Note, too, the cast-iron newel posts and the ornate daisies on the handrails. The "brownstone" veneer, however, was added later.

Return to the park, and walk across it to Verandah Place.

Charming **Verandah Place,** which extends for only a block and a half, was probably built as an alley for carriage houses and stables, and dates from the 1840s and 1850s. The owners of the carriages and horses no doubt lived in the large row houses on Clinton, Henry, Congress, and Warren streets. Before the construction of the park, the little mews must have been much less inviting than it is today. **Thomas Wolfe,** who lived for a brief time at little **No. 40,** described his basement apartment in *No Door:*

> *The place is shaped like a Pullman car, except that it is not so long and has only one window at each end. There are bars over the window that your landlady has put there to keep the thugs in that sweet neighborhood from breaking in; in winter the place is cold and dark, and sweats with clammy water, in the summer you do all the sweating yourself.*

The diminutive "railroad flats" have been restored and are now much sought after, and the "sweet neighborhood" is much more peaceful than during Wolfe's Depression-years sojourn. He later moved a mile north to Brooklyn Heights where he finished *Of Time and the River.*

Explore Verandah Place (including the short cul-de-sac that extends on the other side of Clinton Street dating from 1876–78), noting how the new owners have used their imagination to convert their little two-and-a-half and three-story houses into handsome dwellings. The upstairs hayloft doors are now large windows, and some even retain the old iron hoists in the gable. At the Henry Street end, a former 19th-century corner store adds a nostalgic touch, with its ornate sheet-metal cornice and a two-story corner bay window over a doorway which is now a small window.

Turn left (south) on Henry Street.

On the west side of Henry Street is the **Cobble Hill Nursing Home.** The nursing home, rebuilt in 1963, was formerly St. Peter's Hospital, erected in 1888 by William Schickel & Co., and later called the Congress Nursing Home. The original Romanesque Revival building lost all of its distinguishing features in the renovation.

Turn right (west) on Warren Street to Warren Place.

One of the most remarkable housing developments in the city, and probably the earliest, is the **Warren Place Workingmen's Cottages** and adjacent **Tower and Home Apartments.** The "cottages" and apartment houses were built in 1878–79 by businessman Alfred Tredway White, who believed in "Philanthropy plus 5%." White was also president of the Brooklyn Bureau of Charities, and after a visit to the slums of London, he returned convinced that "No European city suffers so much and so unnecessarily from the evils of overcrowding as does New York today." Deciding to help remedy the evil, he engaged the firm of William Field & Son to build the Cottages and Towers, to give the workingmen of the city "the chance to live decently, and to bring up their children to be decent men and women...."

Of the 44 brick cottages, the 26 that face the pedestrian walkway are "triplexes" 24 feet high—precisely the width of the common garden. Only 11 $\frac{1}{2}$ feet wide, they are small by modern standards, but in 1879 they were revolutionary. The flanking cottages at the Warren and Baltic Street ends of the walk are four stories high, neatly framing the garden and its twin row of charming row houses. In White's time, they rented for $18 per month. Each cottage cost $1,100 to build, but at today's prices the purchase price would be at least 80 times that amount (if one ever became available).

Walk around the Tower Apartments to Hicks Street. (For the best view, cross to the west side of the Brooklyn-Queens Expressway.)

Between Warren and Baltic streets are the **Tower Buildings,** and between Baltic and Kane streets, the **Home Buildings.** The architecture of these Victorian-inspired tenement houses is both innovative and attractive. White's aim of supplying each tenant with sunshine and air is admirably accomplished through the use of outside recessed balconies and three open stair towers, providing tenants with separate entrances and cheerful apartments. The buildings are U-shaped to allow for more light and ventilation. (Compare these buildings with the thousands of dismal "dumbbell" tenements built in the following 20 years throughout the city's poor neighborhoods, in which millions lived in squalor and misery.) The bold towers and decorative iron balconies create a dramatic effect. A central courtyard around which the six-story buildings are grouped was designed as a recreational area for the residents of the 226 apartment units. Shortly after opening, a four-room apartment could be rented for $1.93 per week, or $7.00 per month if paid for in advance. Three rooms rented for $1.48 per week, or $6.00 per month. And White still made his 5 percent profit!

Return to the corner of Warren and Hicks streets.

St. Peter's, Our Lady of Pilar Roman Catholic Church (originally St. Peter's) was built in 1859–60 from plans by Patrick Charles Keely. Keely is noted for the number of Catholic churches he designed throughout the country, and the church, an interesting example of early Romanesque Revival style, has some unusual details. Note the crenelated effect of the round-arched window heads, and the little gables above the front side doors. Unfortunately, the tall octagonal spire has disappeared from the steeple. Beneath the louvered belfry are attractive brick corbels extending around the sides of the steeple. Because its congregation has dwindled, most of the church's activities have been moved to St. Paul's R. C. Church on Court Street. Only a Sunday mass is conducted in this building. The ubiquitous architect, Keely, is said to have designed some 700 church buildings in his lifetime. The adjacent **former St. Peter's Academy** (later School) was founded by the church's first pastor, Father Fransioli, in 1866. The architectural style, with its round-arched windows and crenelated doorway, is quite similar to the church. The building is now used by the nursing school of Long Island College Hospital.

Walk south on Hicks Street, past both the Tower and Home Buildings, and turn left (east) on Kane Street.

The street pattern between Kane Street and Degraw Street (one block south) is interrupted by an additional street between each of the major north-south thoroughfares: Cheever Place, Strong Place, and Tompkins Place [*see* map].

On the south side of Kane Street between Hicks Street and Cheever Place are an engaging **group of ca. 1850 town houses** that ascend in pairs to conform to the slope of the street. A corner store at each end enframes the row, but more interesting is the Greek fret design cast into the iron railings on the stoops of each house.

No. 139, across the street, also has attractive ironwork on the stoop and areaway. Star-shaped tie-rod caps strengthen the walls of Nos. 139 and 141. **No. 147** is a fine example of Greek Revival–style architecture, and has survived since its building date of 1845–46 in a relatively good state of preservation. It is believed that the ironwork gate and railing of No. 149 are original.

At the southwest corner of Henry Street, the house (actually No. 424 Henry Street) has a little attic room built in between the chimneys. On the Kane Street side is an **unusual two-story brick garage** (No. 140 Kane Street) which was erected in 1892 by owner-architect Owen McShane as a soda water factory, with space for horse stables. Above, the hayloft doors can still be distinguished under the glass.

Turn right to 426 Henry Street.

Although the plaque proclaims this as the birthplace of Winston Churchill's mother, Jennie Jerome, it is the incorrect location. As previously mentioned, the site is at 197 Amity Street. Before Jennie was born, however, her parents did stay briefly at this address with uncle Addison G. Jerome.

At the northeast corner of Kane and Henry streets is **Public School 29,** built in 1919 in the so-called Collegiate Gothic style of the period. The school blends well with the neighboring brick houses, and is a good example of a modern building complementing its more traditional surroundings.

Continue on Kane Street to Strong Place.

Standing alone at the southeast corner of Strong Place is **No. 176,** an imposing residence built in the late 1840s in largely Italianate style. It is believed that the house once served as the rectory for Christ Church at the corner of Clinton Street.

Christ Church and the Holy Family (Episcopal), formerly Christ Church, was the first religious organization in Cobble Hill, and was designed by architect Richard Upjohn,* and built in 1841–42. Its imposing tower rises 117 feet above the street, adding graceful punctuation to the Cobble Hill skyline. The church is built of varying color sandstone blocks that give the building a venerable and elegant appearance. Typical of the English Gothic style are the pointed windows on the main body of the church, on the chancel, and on the tower; the polygonal turrets above the crenelated tower, and the drip moldings above the windows. The tower itself is divided into several sections: the pointed-arch entrance with drip molding, a triple-pointed window, the clock faces, a belfry with louvered "windows" under pointed arches, and the four turrets. In 1917 the church acquired a number of furnishings designed by Louis Comfort Tiffany (son of the founder of Tiffany & Company, and himself a distinguished artist and noted stained-glass designer), including the altar, altar railings, pulpit, reredos, lectern, and chairs—all damaged in a 1939 fire, but meticulously restored. Upjohn lived

---

*Richard Upjohn designed many beautiful Episcopal churches in New York City: Grace Church in Brooklyn Heights, Christ Church in the Riverdale section of the Bronx, St. Alban's Church in Staten Island, The Church of the Holy Communion and The Church of the Ascension in Manhattan, and many others. His most celebrated is Trinity Church, at Wall Street and Broadway. Upjohn's churches were virtually all built in the Gothic Revival style so popular in the 1840s.

nearby in a house at 296 Clinton Street (near Baltic Street, one block north). Take a moment to visit the attractive interior of the church.

The adjacent **rectory** (No. 326 Clinton Street) is in Greek Revival style. Its most notable feature, and one which is almost unique to the Cobble Hill section, is the splendid ironwork design in the form of a **swirl** at both top and bottom of the hand railings. Notice also the Gothic quatrefoil designs on **No. 328,** and on its twin, **No. 330,** with quatrefoil motifs at the pediments over the parlor windows and doorway, and a very ornate molding on the entrance. The pair of houses was built in the mid-1840s. Note, too, the circular iron coal-chute cover in the sidewalk if, by this writing, it has not been paved over, as so many have.

No. 334, built ca. 1850, has a Queen Anne–style façade, added in 1888. The details in brick, stone, and terra-cotta were designed and assembled with great care, creating the impression of more building width than is there. One of the characteristics of the style is the quaintness caused by asymmetry, very evident in the relative positions of the entrance tower and bay window. The top floor is built into both the mansard roof and the tower, adding to the storybook effect. The remodeling was designed by architect James W. Naughton, who was Superintendent of Buildings of the Brooklyn Board of Education. It is hard to believe that its neighbor, **No. 336,** was an identical twin when built in the mid-19th century. How interesting it would have been to compare its original appearance with the remodeled Queen Anne house, but alas, a "Howard Johnson" doorway and an imitation stone façade deny us the pleasure.

No. 340, built in the early 1860s, is a one-family Victorian-style house. The widest in the Historic District, it has exceptionally high stories and an attic built into the mansard roof.

Cross Clinton Street and walk back toward Kane Street.

Nos. 301–311, reaching to the corner of Kane Street, represent an early example of community planning. The row is part of a group, some of which are immediately around the corner on Kane Street, and some one block farther on Tompkins Place. Built during the period 1849–54, they are interesting for their doorways, which are paired in projecting bays, and for their ironwork with Gothic trefoil motif.

Turn right (east) into Kane Street, and walk on the left (north) side.

Nos. 206–224 Kane Street are a continuation of the development just seen on Clinton Street. The group, built by Gerard W. Morris, a New York lawyer, consists of 18 Italianate row houses on three adjoining blocks. The effect of the paired projecting entranceways with their joined pediments gives an impression of spaciousness and charm, eliminating the monotony sometimes associated with row-house construction. Fortunately, the ironwork with its Gothic trefoil motifs is still intact on most of the houses.

The ironwork on this side is also worthy of mention. Almost all have ornate swirling stoop railings. Note, too, the Italianate ironwork on the balconies of

Nos. 219 and **225**—both with palm-leaf motifs; and the railings on **Nos. 231, 239,** and **241.**

Congregation Baith Israel Anshei Emes, at the corner of Tompkins Place, was organized in 1856, and is **the oldest Jewish congregation in Brooklyn.** The so-called "Mother Synagogue" acquired the building from the Trinity German Lutheran Church in 1905, which in turn had purchased it in 1887 from the original Middle Dutch Reformed Church. The early Romanesque Revival–style church building was erected in 1855. Originally trimmed with brownstone, it is now stuccoed. The main entrance is enframed by round arches supported by clustered columns, between which is a handsome triple doorway. On the Tompkins Place side, pointed buttresses alternate with the windows, and towers of different dimensions rise at the front corners. The interior is lovely, with splendid stained glass windows and clustered columns supporting groined vaulting.

Turn into Tompkins Place.

Nos. 10 and **12** Tompkins Place belong to the same development as Nos. 206–224 Kane Street and 301–311 Clinton Street.

Tompkins Place is a particularly attractive street because of the narrow row-house arrangement as well as its outstanding and varied ironwork. Unusual, too, is the profusion of ornate window and door lintels particularly over the parlor-floor windows.

On the east side of the street are two rows of Greek Revival houses, **Nos. 13–25,** built in the 1840s. The splendid line of stoop railings with their ornamental vertical scrolls and paneled pedestals can best be appreciated by standing alongside the stairway of No. 13 and looking down the row at the diminishing perspective of the line of railings. This angle of view also enhances the three-dimensional effect of the façades, intended by builders of row houses.

Back across the street, a pleasant feature of these houses is the setback arrangement that allows for small gardens and extensive use of yard railings and gates. Note the elaborate curved lintels above the doorways and windows of **No. 42** and **Nos. 48–52,** built in the early 1850s by two owners who wisely decided to share the common design. A passing glance across the street reveals fake Colonial-style façades on Nos. 41–47, although they do have nicely landscaped front gardens. **Nos. 58–62** still retain their original Anglo-Italianate iron-work and low three-step stoops.

The visual effect of **Nos. 53–61** on the east side, in which alternate houses project and are crowned by a pediment, is very striking. Since small houses were very much in demand in this neighborhood, such an architectural procedure compensated for the 15-foot widths of each row house. **No. 61** is probably the best example of the style, with its low stoop and Italianate curved iron-work both on the railings and on the oversize newel posts. **Nos. 53** and **55** in the row have similar ironwork enclosing their front yards. It was not unusual for the builder to live in one of his row houses, and No. 55 was the home of Thomas Sullivan, after Nos. 53–61 were completed in the early 1850s.

A brief detour to the left (east) on Degraw Street reveals three charming houses in the middle of the block. **No. 271** is a Gothic Revival–style house of unusual richness, built in 1850. Notice the characteristic pointed arches of the ironwork designs and the drip moldings over the windows, and don't miss the miniature pointed arches that support the roof cornice. Only 21 ½ feet wide, it has no room for a window in its angular bay. Above the entranceway, a molding ends in ornate impost blocks.

Nos. 273 and **275** display Romanesque Revival touches, particularly in their arcades supporting the dentiled brick roof cornice. Both have a paired entranceway flanked by masonry bays that climb to the full height of the houses, giving an appearance of more than their 42-foot combined width. These lovely forerunners of the Romanesque Revival period were constructed in 1847–48.

Now walk west on Degraw Street.

Degraw Street is named for Abraham J. S. Degraw, who in 1844 built the only remaining freestanding house with spacious grounds in Cobble Hill, at 219 Clinton Street (seen earlier on the tour). The Cobble Hill Historic District extends only to the north side of Degraw Street.

The brick church in the middle of the block, in a late Gothic Revival style (Theobald Engelhardt, 1905), was built for the Trinity German Lutheran Church, which had just sold its building to the synagogue at Kane Street and Tompkins Place. Most of the German population has long since gone, and the building is now the house of worship of the **South Brooklyn Seventh Day Adventist Church.** Worthy of note is the ogee arch over the central doorway, the corniced pointed arches over the windows, and the church's high railing. Unfortunately, most of its stained glass is gone.

Continue on Degraw Street beyond Clinton Street to the church at the corner of Strong Place.

Formerly the Strong Place Baptist Church, this handsome Gothic Revival–style edifice since 1969 has been the **Cabrini Chapel of the Sacred Heart and St. Stephen Roman Catholic Parish.** Erected in 1851–52 from plans by famed architect Minard Lafever,* its massive corner tower dominates the site. At the west aisle, a small turret with lancet windows rises asymmetrically. The main section of the church is designed with a gabled façade and a triple-pointed arched window, while triple-arched belfry openings in the tower are flanked by high stepped buttresses. A solid iron railing with tall gateposts surrounds the church.

Adjoining the church, around the corner on Strong Place, is the Lafever-designed **chapel,** where the church held its first services in 1849. It then became

---

*Minard Lafever designed many churches and a number of private residences in the decade of the 1840s. Among his works are two churches in Brooklyn Heights, the Church of the Saviour and the Holy Trinity Protestant Episcopal Church; and in Manhattan, the Church of the Holy Apostles, St. James Roman Catholic Church, and the Mariners' Temple. He remodeled the Bartow-Pell Mansion in the Bronx, and is believed to be the architect of the Old Merchant's House on East 4th Street in Manhattan's East Village.

the church's Sunday school and is said to have been one of the most popular in Brooklyn. The chapel, now stuccoed, with its adjacent building (No. 56 Strong Place) is now the Strong Place Day Care Center. The Catholic church now caters mostly to the Italian community of Cobble Hill and contiguous Carroll Gardens section.

Return to Clinton Street. End of tour.

Although the Cobble Hill walking tour ends at Clinton and Degraw streets, a short optional walking tour can be made into the Carroll Gardens section, ending conveniently close to subway transportation.

To return directly, walk east on Degraw Street two blocks to Smith Street, where the B25 or B41 bus goes north to Fulton Street near the Borough Hall station of the Lexington and Broadway–Seventh Avenue lines as well as the Jay Street–Borough Hall station of the A and F lines. Or turn south on Smith Street and walk four short blocks to the Carroll Street station of the F and G lines.

A WALK THROUGH CARROLL GARDENS

Continue south on Clinton Street.

No. 363 Clinton Street was formerly a livery stable, where before the advent of the automobile, a horse and carriage could be rented or your own horse boarded. Those who could not afford the luxury of their own stable used such facilities. Before the turn of the century, livery stables were as common as today's public garages. Little evidence remains of its history, as it was gutted and rebuilt as a condominium apartment building, called "Clinton Court"—typical of the variety of conversions taking place throughout the city.

Nos. 382A–386 are a handsome row of ca. 1850 Italianate brownstones, so narrow that they are only two bays wide and occupy only half a lot each. Past Sackett Street, note the enormous cast-iron newel posts and balusters on **No. 392.** Alas, this Italianate brownstone has lost its ornate cornice.

Glance eastward down Union Street at the diminutive Gothic-style garage on the right side, that was once the stable of No. 393 Clinton Street.

No. 396 is the handsome **Carroll Park Branch of the Brooklyn Public Library.** Still an independent library system, the Brooklyn Public Library began lending books in 1897, antedating the New York Public Library by several years. The building, designed in a modified Classic Revival style, was opened in 1905.

Continue south on Clinton Street to Carroll Street.

At the northeast corner of Clinton and Carroll streets is **St. Paul's Episcopal Church of Brooklyn,** another Richard Upjohn church, this one designed together with son Richard W. Upjohn. Built in 1867–84, it is a simple but rather heavy English Gothic Revival–style building. Enter the church and notice the unusual treatment of the interior. The transepts are extremely narrow because of the shape of the lot, and the supporting columns, instead of rising to the clerestory, terminate in capitals under large arches. The arrangement of the pulpit is said to be French in style, set halfway down the nave, together with a *banque* (a row of double pews directly in front of the pulpit to seat clergy and servers who would be too far back in the sanctuary to hear the sermon). The church is constructed of dark-brown sandstone and has no spire. St. Paul's adds "of Brooklyn" to its name to distinguish it from St. Paul's of Flatbush, as the two Episcopal houses of worship were originally in separate towns. The town of Flatbush was not annexed by the City of Brooklyn until 1894. Although it took 17 years to erect the building, the church was never completed. The base of the tower is quite massive, and had the steeple been added, it would have been one of the tallest in the city.

Although **Carroll Gardens** is a veritable "melting pot," the largest group are the Italians. Mainly from southern Italy and Sicily, they began arriving in the late 19th century, and their influence will be clearly visible in the names of many commercial establishments when we come to nearby Court Street.

No. 440 Clinton Street, on the southwest corner, is considered one of the finest masonry Greek Revival town houses in the city. Built ca. 1840 for well-to-do merchant John Rankin, it is in a superb state of preservation in its adaptive

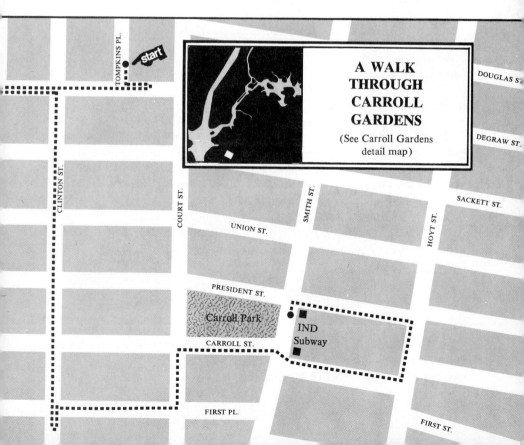

A WALK
THROUGH
CARROLL
GARDENS

(See Carroll Gardens
detail map)

reuse as the Guido Funeral Home. The salmon-colored brick façade is flanked by pilasters that rise to the full height of the house, and are crowned by granite capitals. The stoop, on a slightly projecting central section, is also made of granite, as are the cap-molded window lintels, the sills, newel posts, and basement facings. The Guido family, which lives in the house as well as using it as a funeral parlor, takes pride in maintaining the elegant mansion, and will on special occasions trot out an ornate horse-drawn hearse to re-create a dignified 19th-century funeral. When built, the house was surrounded by farmland and commanded an unobstructed view of the Upper Bay.

One block north, at the corner of Clinton Street and First Place, is the **former Norwegian Seamen's Church,** built ca. 1865 for the Westminster Presbyterian Church. When the last congregation acquired the church in 1929, an imposing Norwegian-style wood pulpit was installed, and an old sailing-ship anchor placed on the lawn. Most of this Scandinavian community has now moved to the Bay Ridge section of Brooklyn, and with their departure the building was sold to a developer and converted into cooperative apartments. Don't try to identify the style of this brownstone church—it is as eclectic as can be, with Gothic, Romanesque, and Renaissance Revival elements.

First Place looking west from Clinton Street, in 1896. Few changes have occurred through the years, giving Carroll Gardens a very special atmosphere not often found in a big city. (Brooklyn Historical Society)

Continue to First Place.

Here we enter the "real" Carroll Gardens (although not yet the Historic District). Look east (left) down **First Place,** then compare the view with the 1896 photograph above…virtually unchanged! The recessed row houses with gardens in front—the hallmark of the neighborhood—are a credit to an unsung hero of a land surveyor, Richard Butts, whose unusual and farsighted urban design of so-called deep blocks was first published in his 1846 survey map.

Turn east into First Place.

No. 70 First Place, although in need of maintenance, is rather well preserved. The stately entrance gates, iron fence, cast-iron balustraded stairway, the consoles framing the doorway, and the enframed windows all add up to a charming and stylistically accurate house.

Turn left (north) on Court Street to Carroll Street, then right, following the park, to Smith Street. Cross Smith Street and continue east on Carroll Street.

The park and street are named for Charles Carroll of Maryland, a signer of the Declaration of Independence. It was a Maryland regiment under Lord Stirling (General William Alexander) that during the Battle of Long Island fought a desperate delaying action at the "Old Stone House at Gowanus"* on August 27, 1776—an act of bravery by a small, outnumbered garrison that permitted General Washington to evacuate the entire Continental Army safely to Manhattan. The park was originally a private garden, but was acquired by the State of New York in 1850 and made into a public park 20 years later.

The Carroll Gardens Historic District [*see* map] is a small, quiet residential district, and very much a separate enclave within the city. Why the Historic District does not encompass the charming streets to the west (First and Second Place, for example) is a source of irritation to many residents who feel that the limited area of designation was the result of local political pressure.

Because of the peculiar street pattern, Carroll and President streets both appear to be dead-end streets, probably a contributory factor to the feeling of separateness of these two blocks. The pleasant appearance of the district is the fortunate result of foresighted 19th-century planning. Immediately evident is the row of set-back front yards, ranging from 25 to 39 feet. The uniform pattern of two- and three-story brick and brownstone houses built in long rows on shady,

---

*The "Old Stone House at Gowanus," known now as the Vechte-Cortelyou House, was reconstructed in 1935 by the Department of Parks with the original stones. The 1699 Dutch farmhouse is located in the James J. Byrne Memorial Playground, at 3rd Street, west of Fifth Avenue, five blocks east and three blocks south. Cross the Gowanus Canal on the Third Street Bridge.

The Vechte-Cortelyou House, known familiarly as the Old Stone House at Gowanus, was built in 1699 and figured importantly in the Battle of Long Island. The house has been reconstructed with the original stones and can be seen in a playground at 3rd Street, west of Fifth Avenue, in Brooklyn. (Brooklyn Historical Society)

tree-lined streets, each with a well-tended garden, creates a sense of open space and architectural harmony. The houses date mostly from the late 1860s to the early 1880s, and represent a spirit of cooperation among the various builders. The row houses, built for middle-class merchants, were designed in two of the popular styles of the late 19th century: late Italianate and French neo-Grec. In spite of some building modifications, most of the neighborhood remains uniquely homogeneous.

Halfway down Carroll Street, approaching Hoyt Street, the houses on the south side become two-story brownstones; later, on President Street, the same pattern appears, but on both sides of the street.

The group of new houses, Nos. 297–299 Carroll Street, erected in 1982, are on **the site of the Church of the South Brooklyn Christian Assembly.** The church began its life as the Carroll Park Methodist Episcopal Church in 1873; with the Scandinavian influx, it became the Norwegian M. E. Church in 1891; and in more recent times, the Christian Assembly. In the late 1970s it fell victim to the arsonist's torch. Built in a flamboyant Victorian Gothic style, it was for years the dominant landmark in the district. Some idea of its ornate polychrome style can be had by examining **No. 295,** the original parsonage of the church, which survived the disastrous fire and is now a residence.

Space does not permit a detailed house-by-house description, but do make a circuit of the District by walking east on Carroll Street, north on Hoyt Street, and west on President Street [*see* map].

Although the tour ends at Smith and President streets, you might want to take a few minutes to walk one block west to Court Street, where on the northwest corner stands the architecturally significant **South Congregational Church.** Erected in 1850 (architect unknown), it has a rather unusual façade with a series of stepped planes rising from the central window, much like a proscenium. Above are verdigris-colored copper finials which contrast well with the red-brick masonry. Walk around to the President Street side for a pleasant surprise. The two adjoining buildings, in different architectural styles, are the **Ladies' Parlor and Sunday School** (F. Carles Merry, 1889) and the **Rectory** (Woodruff Leeming, 1893). Merry worked in the office of Henry Hobson Richardson, and the influence of the master is evident in the riot of terra-cotta adornment and other Richardsonian touches. The rectory, a gem of Gothic Revival style, has typical design elements above, and on the entrance and ground-floor window lintels. The church building was sold to a developer and converted to cooperative apartments, while the congregation worships in the Ladies' Parlor and Sunday School; this deal, negotiated with the developer, included the renovation of the Ladies' Parlor for the religious needs of the congregation. The site for the church was selected personally by the Rev. Henry Ward Beecher.

End of tour. The F line Carroll Street station is at the corner of Smith Street, with another entrance on President Street. For the A line, change at Jay Street–Borough Hall.

start

BERGEN ST.

No. 2, 3 Subway lines

ST. MARK'S AVE.

PROSPECT PL.

PARK PL.

STERLING PL.

ST. JOHN'S PL.

LINCOLN PL.

CARLTON AVE.

VANDERBILT AVE.

BUTLER PL.

UNDERHILL AVE.

FLATBUSH AVE.

No. 2, 3 Subway lines

BERKELEY PL.

UNION ST.

PRESIDENT ST.

CARROLL ST.

GARFIELD PL.

FIRST ST.

SECOND ST.

THIRD ST.

FOURTH ST.

FIFTH ST.

SIXTH ST.

SEVENTH ST.

EIGHTH ST.

NINTH ST.

TENTH ST.

ELEVENTH ST.

TWELFTH ST.

THIRTEENTH ST.

FOURTEENTH ST.

FIFTEENTH ST.

SIXTEENTH ST.

FIFTH AVE.

SIXTH AVE.

POLHEMUS PL.

FISKE PL.

MONTGOMERY PL.

SEVENTH AVE.

EIGHTH AVE.

PROSPECT PARK WEST

WEST DRIVE

GRAND ARMY PLAZA

PLAZA ST.

EASTERN PARKWAY

Brooklyn Museum

Brooklyn Public Library

Botanic Garden

Litchfield Mansion

Prospect P.

← Gowanus Canal

F Line Subway

BARTEL PRITCHARD SQ.

PARK SLOPE

(Shaded Area Indicates Historic District)

17. Park Slope

[Broadway–Seventh Avenue No. 2 or No. 3 line to Bergen Street; Lexington Avenue line to Nevins Street, change for No. 2 or No. 3 to Bergen Street]

The "Slope" rises gradually eastward from the Gowanus Canal to Prospect Park in a several-square-mile sweep; however, the Park Slope neighborhood is usually defined as the area encompassed by Flatbush Avenue and Prospect Park on the east, St. Mark's Place south to Fifteenth Street, and Fifth or Sixth Avenue on the west. The New York City Landmarks Preservation Commission designated a section of Park Slope as a Historic District in 1973 [*see* map]. From Dutch colonial times until the last quarter of the 19th century, the area remained largely rural in character—a hilly terrain of farms, fields, and pastures—bypassed by the developers of the nearby towns of Flatbush and Brooklyn. Flatbush, from the Dutch *Vlacke Bos* (Flat Woods), was not annexed by the City of Brooklyn until 1894.

At the outbreak of the Revolutionary War, the Park Slope area was the scene of the retreat of the Continental Army after the battle of Flatbush Pass. Outnumbered and overwhelmed by the combined British and Hessian forces that had made an amphibious landing on August 26, 1776, at Gravesend, the patriots pulled back along the Port Road, located approximately parallel to the present First Street. A brilliant delaying maneuver was executed by General William Alexander, Lord Stirling, with a small Maryland regiment about a mile west at the "Old Stone House at Gowanus," at the present corner of Fifth Avenue and Third Street [*see* Cobble Hill, pages 457 and 458]. Although his brave defending force was decimated and he himself was captured, Stirling's action permitted General Washington to withdraw safely across the East River to Manhattan.

Development came relatively late to Park Slope, in spite of the proximity of the heavily traveled Flatbush Road (now Avenue) and the opening of Prospect Park in the late 1860s. It was not until the mid-1880s that its potential was really discovered. While it is true that adjacent Prospect Park was a major influence in the growth of Park Slope, the completion in 1883 of the great Brooklyn Bridge was the catalyst. Within a decade, rows of brownstones, like parades of caterpillars, inched their way up the gentle hill. In the blocks closest to the park, wealthy merchants and professionals built lavish town houses and opulent mansions. So many imposing residences were constructed that the section came to be called the "Gold Coast." And so it remained for almost half a century, rivaling Manhattan's

Fifth Avenue in grandeur. The Park Slope neighborhood still retains much of its charm in the tree-lined streets, uniform row houses, attractive churches, tranquil atmosphere, and the exciting variety of architectural styles of its once-rich mansions. It remains a stable family community with a deep sense of civic pride, strongly dedicated to preserving the very special quality of the neighborhood.

The tour begins at the corner of Flatbush Avenue and St. Marks Avenue.

Until late in the 19th century, **Flatbush Avenue** was the main thoroughfare connecting the City of Brooklyn with the towns to the south (Flatbush, Gravesend, New Utrecht, and Flatlands). Stagecoaches gave way to horsecars, then trolleys, and finally buses, while below the street came the subway in 1920—built as the Interborough Rapid Transit and now part of the municipally owned Metropolitan Transit Authority. Even before the mid-19th century, the Long Island Rail Road had its Brooklyn terminal on Flatbush Avenue, one mile north.

The opening in 1909 of the Manhattan Bridge with its direct connection with Flatbush Avenue made it for a time the busiest thoroughfare in the entire city. Until after World War II, it was a bustling and important commercial street, but as population patterns shifted, it declined rapidly, yielding to the effects of urban blight. Yet surprisingly, little of this very contagious decay seems to have seeped across into the Park Slope neighborhood. Looking up Flatbush Avenue, the Brooklyn skyline is dominated by the lofty **Williamsburg Savings Bank Tower** with its 512-foot, gold-domed cupola. Built the same year as Manhattan's Chrysler and Empire State buildings (1929–30), it is Brooklyn's only real skyscraper. [*See* pages 500 and 501.]

Walk south on Flatbush Avenue and turn half-right into Sixth Avenue.

At No. 85 Sixth Avenue, at the little triangle formed by St. Marks Avenue, is the **former Cathedral Club of Brooklyn.** Built in 1890 as the Carlton Club, it was one of several exclusive clubs for the wealthy. It then became the Monroe Club, followed by the Royal Arcanum Club, and in 1907 a Roman Catholic fraternal club organized by a young priest, George Mundelein, who ultimately became Cardinal of Chicago. The Club in recent times was a Haitian Masonic lodge, but in 1986 it was beautifully restored and subdivided into residential units. Notice the gas lamps on the Sixth Avenue side.

Turn left on Prospect Place.

On the left side of the street are three neo-Colonial-style houses completed in 1971, **Nos. 77–85,** called the **"Cinderella of Prospect Place."** They were formerly one-story boarded-up and abandoned stores—an eyesore on the block and a symptom of the growing deterioration of the periphery of Park Slope [*see* photo, next page]. The success of the transformation, using the original strong framework of the stores instead of demolishing them and starting from scratch, was the innovative plan of the Brooklyn Union Gas Company, and a joint endeavor with

Brooklyn Union Gas Company's "Cinderella of Prospect Place" project—a trio of decaying, abandoned stores before their conversion to town houses and the revitalization of the street in 1971. (Brooklyn Union Gas Company)

builders Asen Bros. and Brook. One of a growing number of Brooklyn Union Gas's "Cinderella" projects, they demonstrate the feasibility of restoring decrepit and abandoned buildings, and serve to encourage neighborhood improvement and revitalization. Before this project was undertaken, the row houses across the street were in little better condition than the deteriorated stores in the photograph. Observe the difference and how contagious this revitalization can be.

Return to Sixth Avenue and continue a short distance on Prospect Place.

Nos. 54–64 Prospect Place form an engaging group of Queen Anne–style houses, with an exuberant assemblage of bay windows, ornate gables, stained glass, and L-shaped stoops. The side wall of No. 64 is almost completely covered by English ivy.

Return to Sixth Avenue and turn right.

The rows of brownstones on both sides of **Sixth Avenue** are typical of middle-class row-house architecture of the late 1870s to mid-1880s. Most are built in the earlier Italianate or contemporary neo-Grec styles. Look for these characteristics of the Italianate style: high stoops with cast-iron railings, usually in the

form of a baluster; round-arched doorways with double entrance doors; a pedimented entranceway supported by foliate brackets; segmental-arc lintels over
windows; rusticated basements; and a roof cornice above foliate brackets. The
original brownstone facing may be disguised with ill-conceived coats of paint.
At first glance, the neo-Grec style may appear similar, but observe the curvilinear, incised ornamentation (carved by machine, rather than hand-carved as in the
Italianate); triple vertical grooves on the brackets; door and window lintels with
acroteria ("ears" that protrude at the ends)—all Greek elements introduced at the
Ecole des Beaux Arts in Paris. The neo-Grec houses are also much more angular,
having three-sided, full-height bays up to the roof, and rather massive newel
posts (usually in cast iron, but occasionally in stone) at the tall stoops. It is
apparent that many of the minority groups that have moved into this part of Park
Slope take great pride in the appearance of their new brownstones. Recently the
spirit of preservation has triumphed, and earlier "improvements" of aluminum
siding and garish adornments have now disappeared.

   St. Augustine's Roman Catholic Church, between Sterling and Park
places, is considered one of Brooklyn's finest church buildings. Designed in
1888 by the three English-born Brooklyn architects, Parfitt Brothers, it was completed four years later. Built in Victorian Gothic style of a mottled sandstone, it
rises dramatically above the uniform rows of houses. The interior is almost as
elaborate as the exterior, with excellent stained glass and ornate sculpture work.
The tall tower virtually overwhelms in its mass and detail. Spend a few minutes
inside and examine the well-proportioned and majestic nave. Reflecting the
shifting populations, masses are conducted in English, Spanish, and Creole.
Sterling Place is named for Revolutionary War General William Alexander,
Lord Stirling, mentioned earlier.

   At this point, the walking tour enters the **Park Slope Historic District.**

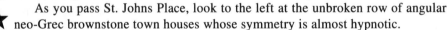

   As you pass St. Johns Place, look to the left at the unbroken row of angular
neo-Grec brownstone town houses whose symmetry is almost hypnotic.

Continue on Sixth Avenue to Lincoln Place.

   The Sixth Avenue Baptist Church was designed in Victorian Gothic style
by Lawrence B. Valk. Built in 1880, this picturesque church unfortunately lost
its steeple in the hurricane of 1938. Unusual is the massive main tower, its
attached polygonal turret, and the cupola over the transept. The horizontal stone
band courses, which contrast with the red brick façade, are typical of the style,
while the buttresses with stepped sandstone shoulders add another interesting
touch. Look, too, at the ornamentation on the arches above the doors and on the
corbels of the main gables.

Turn left on Lincoln Place.

   Named for Abraham Lincoln in 1873, **Lincoln Place** is an extension of
Degraw Street, an important street at the bottom of the "slope," in the Cobble
Hill section.

Lincoln Place between Sixth and Seventh avenues has an interesting and varied collection of row houses. **Nos. 96–110** present an engaging combination of Queen Anne and Romanesque Revival styles, while **Nos. 99–113** show delicately incised neo-Grec detailing on the doors, cornices, and window lintels, including the characteristic "ears" on the lintels. The first two have French Second Empire mansard roofs. All have two-sided bays and the last three are two stories high. The neo-Grec style is personified across the street in **Nos. 114, 116,** and **118.** Note their cast-iron balustrades and lovely newel posts, and the attractive yard railings with maple-leaf motif. Back on the north side is another row of handsome neo-Grec houses, **Nos. 127–135.**

No. 139, originally the John Condon residence, was built in 1881. Observe how the treatment of the bay with its pyramidal slate roof creates the impression of a tower, balanced at the right by a third-story mansard roof. Note, too, the sunflower designs in cut brick below the second-floor windows, and the entrance-door panels—both are typical Queen Anne features. Other little touches are the miniature Ionic capitals on the brackets below the mansard roof. Note the massive cast-iron newels on **No. 143** and many of its neighbors.

No. 153 is a massive Romanesque Revival town house with ample grounds. Now the Lincoln Plaza Hotel, it was built in 1886–87 by the architectural firm of Lamb & Rich as the residence of Frank L. Babbott. Typical of the Romanesque Revival style is the asymmetry of the façade and the varied use of materials. The brick and rough stone front is ornamented with a band of myrtle wreaths and ribbons as well as a Greek fretwork design. A three-sided bay rises from the corner to form a striking peaked turret, emphasizing the sweep of the whole roof. On the east side a lion mask of carved stone is surmounted by a large chimney that rises high over the slate-covered roof gables ornamented with terra-cotta caps. Note, too, the rough-cut lintel blocks above the first-floor windows, tied together below the chimney with rounded lozenge shapes. Money went to money, as they say, for Babbott's wife was the daughter of Charles Pratt (discussed in the Clinton Hill walking tour) who made his fortune in kerosene, later merging with John D. Rockefeller's Standard Oil Company. In 1936, the former Babbott house became a rooming house, like so many in Park Slope. Nine years later it was acquired as a residence for the Presbyterian Home for the Aged, and in 1957 it was converted into a hotel. This once-elegant mansion, now partly burned-out, is a dismal sight indeed. "It may be a hotel," said a neighboring real estate agent, "but no one sleeps there."

Turn left on Seventh Avenue.

The corner mansion, once the William M. Brasher residence and now the **Brooklyn Conservatory of Music,** was erected in 1881 from plans by architect S. F. Evelette. Before becoming a music school in 1944, it had been the Park Slope Masonic Club for twenty years. The attractive Victorian Gothic–style house with some Queen Anne elements, built of brick and trimmed with brownstone and terra-cotta, is in an excellent state of preservation. Notice the decorative cast-iron crestings above the first floor of the projecting corner bay. An

Looking north on Seventh Avenue toward St. John's Place in 1896. To the left rises the spire of Memorial Presbyterian Church, and across the Avenue, Grace Methodist Church. Both were built in 1882 in Gothic Revival style, but Grace Church lost its steeple in the Hurricane of 1944. (Brooklyn Historical Society)

interesting roof line with gable, chimney, and dormer windows tops this fine mansion.

Across Seventh Avenue is the **only complete blockfront of French Second Empire houses** in Park Slope. The row was built in 1871–72.

At the intersection of St. Johns Place are three Gothic Revival churches, **Memorial Presbyterian Church,** on the southwest corner, dominates the site with its octagonal spire rising from a square tower. Considered late Victorian Gothic (1882), it was designed by the firm of Pugin & Walter. The building is constructed entirely of rough Belleville (New Jersey) sandstone, with little of the polychromy so characteristic of most Victorian Gothic structures. Quatrefoils pierce the parapet above, adding a decorative element. The adjacent **Chapel** on St. Johns Place, designed by Marshall & Walter, was added in 1888. A charming decorative feature is the quatrefoil with a carving of three children being comforted by an angel. Only close inspection reveals that the Chapel and Church are separate entities, so well integrated are they architecturally. A number of the stained-glass windows in the chapel and church are from the Tiffany Studios.

Turn left on St. John's Place.

Nos. 176 and **178 St. John's Place** are two charming Queen Anne houses (R. L. Daus, 1888). Built for a pair of physicians, they present a fanciful array of gables, finials, dormer windows, Romanesque and Gothic arches, a conical roof, and even a tower. Although two separate buildings—No. 178 is wider—they blend together as a single unit. Note the caduceus in the ornate gable of No. 178. It was the original residence of one Edward Bunker M.D. Dr. William M. Thallon treated his patients in No. 176. A few minutes must be spent to take in all the delightful details of both houses' façades.

Across the street is the lovely **St. John's Protestant Episcopal Church**— the oldest in Park Slope, built in 1869 from plans by prominent architect Edward T. Potter in the style of an English country parish church. With its setback position on a grassy plot, it presents a harmonious grouping with its adjacent **Rectory** (No. 139), terminating the uniform line of row houses to the left. The church, originally called the Chapel of St. John's Episcopal Church, and rectory are fine examples of the Victorian Gothic style, and are built of rough-faced, random ashlar sandstone. The main gable includes seven narrow lancet windows, stepped over the pointed-arch doorway, and surmounted by a bell cote. The rectory has a Gothic cast-iron porch facing the yard, and an interesting colonnette set in a chamfered recess between paired windows on the southeast corner. St. John's Place, formerly Douglass Street, was renamed in 1870 in honor of the church.

Return to Seventh Avenue.

The third member of the trio of Victorian Gothic churches is **Grace United Methodist Episcopal Church,** on the northeast corner, built from plans by the ubiquitous Parfitt Brothers in 1882. Constructed of a more varicolored stone than its neighbor diagonally across the street, the church presents a very picturesque addition to the cityscape. A rather large window and gable face Seventh Avenue, while a large tower dominates the corner. Its graceful brownstone spire, however, fell victim to the hurricane of 1944. Look for the ornate "diaper" pattern in terra-cotta around the nave's circular windows on the St. Johns Place side, and the foliate capitals on banded columns of the side windows.

To the left of the church, the **Parsonage and Sunday School** are an architectural transition to the row of town houses to the north. Completed five years after the church, also from Parfitt Brothers plans, it is a rough-faced building in a late Romanesque Revival style. Interesting is the two-story bay—curve ended—with transom bars and stone mullions at both levels. Notice the stained glass in the first-floor transoms. In harmony with the turret at the Ward Mansion farther up the block, the parsonage has a third-floor oriel at the south corner, providing visual balance to the blockfront.

The exceptionally fine row of four Romanesque Revival houses from the Parsonage to Sterling Place, **Nos. 21–27 Seventh Avenue,** were built in 1887 from designs by the architect of the Sixth Avenue Baptist Church, Lawrence B. Valk. The row can best be appreciated by viewing it from the southeast corner of Sterling Place. **No. 21** was for a time the residence of opera singer Lillian Ward and, as the first house in the row, is the most handsome. Mounted on a second-floor corbel is an imposing projecting turret with a curvilinear peaked roof. Typical of the Romanesque Revival style are the contrasts in color, details, and materials, and although each house has its own particular details (as in the individual arched porches), the group gives an impression of unity. Note how the brick, brownstone, terra-cotta, and slate were employed, with even some ornate wrought-iron work. Try to find the Victorian "sunburst" motifs on some of the little dormer window gables. The entrance to No. 21 is on Sterling Place. Its handsome arched porch has dwarf columns protecting the original doorway, with wrought-iron work highlighting the transom and sidelights, and a bizarre cast-iron animal figure serves as the newel post for the entrance to the offset stoop. Look up at the Queen Anne–style ornamental band course just below the roof, and the profusion of gables and finials in the steep, hip-shaped slate roof.

Turn left into Sterling Place.

The corner of Seventh Avenue and Sterling Place was the **site of a tragic plane crash,** when on the cold, misty morning of December 16, 1960, two commercial airliners collided over Brooklyn. One of the large planes fell on Staten Island; the other, in a vain attempt to reach the open ground of Prospect Park, careened into Sterling Place, the nose of the broken fuselage coming to rest

A light covering of snow blanketed Grand Army Plaza when this picture was taken in 1898. The triumphal arch by John H. Duncan was still to be adorned by the monumental sculpture groupings by Frederick W. MacMonnies three years later. The Soldiers' and Sailors' Memorial was paid for by the citizens of Brooklyn and dedicated to the defenders of the Union in the Civil War. (Brooklyn Union Gas Company)

against the doorstep of the Ward Mansion. A number of buildings were destroyed by the ensuing fire, including the prophetically named Pillar of Fire Church, which stood on the north side of Sterling Place, just west of Seventh Avenue. None of the passengers survived the crash, but miraculously, no one was even injured on the ground. Among several buildings that sustained damage was No. 116, which recently was razed, and in its place is the condo "100 Sterling Place," completed in 1990.

To the west of the lot which was the site of the burned-out church is a yellow brick building, and adjoining it is the red brick **former Fleetwood Stables** with a pair of two-story carriage houses of ca. 1885 attached. The trio of buildings were converted to co-ops in 1982, in another "Cinderella" project. Formerly a livery stable for the neighborhood, it was also the local "rent-a-horse" agency of the time; horse owners could also board their animals there and rent a suitable carriage, such as a brougham, landau, victoria, or in winter, a cutter. Note the 100-year-old Fleetwood Stables sign that still survives on the west wall.

Return to Seventh Avenue and continue east on Sterling Place.

Just beyond the beautiful Lillian Ward Mansion is charming **No. 146,** a Queen Anne–style house designed by Lawrence B. Valk in 1887, and built at the same time as his handsome Romanesque Revival row around the corner on Seventh Avenue. On the west side are three lovely chimneys; while the main entrance has a pair of unusual wrought-iron hand railings mounted on wing-walls. The distinguishing feature of the house is its asymmetry. Adjoining the arched doorway is a wide-arched parlor-floor window, Romanesque Revival–style in character, divided in three sections. Above is a bay window, sheathed in sheet metal, with a pedimented central arched window. A wide dormer rises on the third story, surmounted by a gable adorned with terra-cotta tiles. A severe detraction are the white-painted mortar lines between the bricks.

The tour departs briefly from the Park Slope Historic District for a visit to Grand Army Plaza.

Continue ahead to Flatbush Avenue, turn right one block, walk through little gaslit Triangle Park, then cross to the mall of Grand Army Plaza.

GRAND ARMY PLAZA

The enormous oval plaza was designed by Frederick Law Olmsted and Calvert Vaux (the landscape architects of Central and Prospect parks) as a grandiose approach to Prospect Park. The plaza was designed in 1862, but the monumental arch and the accompanying groups of sculpture were not added until much later. At the time of the plan, the City of Brooklyn lay almost a mile to the north.

Enter from the north and, passing through a formal circle of sycamores, mount the terrace to see New York's only official **monument to President John**

F. Kennedy. The latest addition to the plaza, the dark-green bronze bust is the work of sculptor Neil Estern. The monument, with its unusually placed bust, was designed by Morris Ketchum, Jr., & Associates, and was installed in 1965. The original plan called for a marble cube with eternal flame, but was rejected as being too similar to the monument in Arlington National Cemetery. [*See* also Neil Estern's new statue of Mayor Fiorello H. LaGuardia on LaGuardia Place, in the Greenwich Village chapter, page 109.]

    The Bailey Fountain, built in 1932 and named for donor Frank Bailey, was designed by architect Edgerton Swarthout with the central sculpture group by Eugene Savage. Male and female figures representing Wisdom and Felicity stand on the prow of a ship, while Neptune and his Tritons, together with a young boy grasping a cornucopia, present a humorous backdrop.

    Ahead is one of the world's most magnificent triumphal arches, **the Soldiers' and Sailors' Memorial Arch,** erected in 1892. Its prizewinning design was done by John Hemingway Duncan (the architect five years later of Grant's Tomb) who planned it as an "armature" for patriotic sculpture dedicated to the Union forces of the Civil War. Several distinguished American sculptors designed the various groups that adorn the 80-foot-high granite arch. Topping the monument is a magnificent **triumphal quadriga** in bronze by Frederick MacMonnies, depicting a female figure carrying a banner and sword, flanked by two winged figures of Victory. The south pedestals display military **groupings representing the Army** (left) **and the Navy** (right)—both by sculptor MacMonnies. (Frederick MacMonnies was a pupil of Augustus Saint-Gaudens and a resident of Brooklyn.) The cornerstone of the arch, incidentally, was laid by General William Tecumseh Sherman in 1889. The **inner bas-reliefs of Lincoln and Grant** were executed by William R. O'Donovan, and their horses by Thomas Eakins (Eakins is best known as one of the great "realist" painters of the late 19th and early 20th centuries). The width of the arch is also 80 feet, and the aperture, 50 feet, with a span of 35 feet. Unfortunately, no sculpture was designed for the north pedestals, so the only view is from the park rather than from the approach. Framing the circular plot is a necklace of stanchions. The Soldiers' and Sailors' Memorial Arch is considered Brooklyn's most splendid monument, and is one of three triumphal arches in New York City. (The other two are the Washington Square Arch and the entrance arch to the Manhattan Bridge.)

    Prospect Park is not within the purview of this walking tour, but should not be missed. At least a day is required for even a superficial visit. With the brief stop at the Litchfield Villa at the end of the tour, more details will be given,* including a suggested walk through the park.

Return to the mall, then cross Grand Army Plaza (carefully!) to Plaza Street, on the west side.

---

*Information on Prospect Park, including a map and list of activities, can be obtained from the organization dedicated to its preservation and protection: the Greensward Foundation, 16 East 8th Street, New York, N.Y. 10003.

An earth mound, or berm, along Plaza Street—part of Olmsted & Vaux's foresighted design for the plaza—shields the residential street from the noise and congestion of traffic. **Nos. 5–11 Plaza Street,** neoclassic-style limestone town houses built in 1901, may be considered the beginning of the **former "Gold Coast."** No. 5 is now a residence for the Sisters of the Good Shepherd. At the turn of the century, elegant mansions lined both sides of the Plaza; however, all but these four residences have been replaced by apartment houses. (The tour has now reentered the Park Slope Historic District.)

Turn right on Lincoln Place to Eighth Avenue.

The spectacular **Montauk Club** is one of Brooklyn's architectural treasures. One of the last of the many private clubs that abounded in Park Slope, the building's elegance is indicative of the affluent and influential membership. Completed in 1891 from plans by Francis H. Kimball,* it was inspired by the Cà d'Oro, a Venetian *palazzo* on the Grand Canal, whose glittering gold-painted façade was symbolic of the glory of the Italian Renaissance. The best view of the building is from the end of Plaza Street at the head of Lincoln Place, where two of the elaborate façades can be studied. A warm golden color is produced through

---

*Architect Kimball also designed the landmark Emmanuel Baptist Church in the Clinton Hill section of Brooklyn, the Trinity and U.S. Realty buildings on lower Broadway in Manhattan, and a number of other office buildings, theaters, and churches.

The house of Guido Plessner, designed by architect Frank Freeman, at the corner of Lincoln Place and Plaza Street ca. 1900. An apartment house now occupies the site. (Brooklyn Historical Society)

the careful blending of yellow and reddish brown bricks, brownstone, and matching terra-cotta. In its *Designation Report* for the Park Slope Historic District, the Landmarks Commission emphasizes "the contrast of solids and voids" in the design for the club. The groupings of traceried windows, the balconies and loggia, and the extravagant use of terra-cotta ornamentation engage the eye almost relentlessly. To the left of the elaborate main entrance is the separate ladies' entrance, as the Montauk Club was restricted exclusively to men. However, it was the first such club to extend the use of its facilities to women. This side entrance leads to the dining room floor, bypassing the main lobby. Above the main entrance is a band of carved Indian heads, while the spandrels between the arches depict American Indian motifs; look, too, for the little animals and birds. Above the second-floor round arch is a frieze representing the founders and builders laying the cornerstone. (The Montauk Club is named for the tribe of Indians that inhabited most of eastern Long Island.) Above the second-floor balcony of the Plaza Street side is a relief panel illustrating the inscription. "Wyandance, Sachame of Pamanack, His Wife and Son Wiankabone Giving a Deed to Lion Gardner of Saybrook, Easthampton, Long Island, July 14, 1659." Most striking, however, is the wide terra-cotta frieze that encircles the three principal façades of the Club, presenting a continuous history of the Montauk Indians.

Spend a few minutes and examine carefully the wide variety of detail in the imaginative façade. Let the eye drift slowly upward from the ornate cast-iron fence to the soaring chimneys above, as this is truly a unique edifice, which in its design successfully combines European tradition with American Indian themes.

Continue south on Eighth Avenue, observing the stately town houses on both sides.

The brownstone town house at **No. 22 Eighth Avenue** was the home of reform mayor William J. Gaynor, who took office in 1910. He regularly *walked* to his office at City Hall, via the Brooklyn Bridge, a distance of nearly four miles! On August 10th of that year, a discharged dock worker shot him, just as he was about to sail from Hoboken on a vacation trip to Europe. After an apparent recovery, he resumed his brisk walks to work; but by 1913 his health began to fail and the walks ended. Nevertheless he remained a staunch reformer, fighting widespread corruption despite ill health. Yet Gaynor sought and won nomination for a second term, and he set off for another trip to Europe. On September 12th, as the liner *Baltic* neared the coast of Ireland, the mayor was found dead in his deck chair. Note the "mayor's lamps" at the entrance.

Turk left on Berkeley Place.

Berkeley Place was renamed in 1881 for George Berkeley, an Episcopal minister and educator. It is said that many of his educational principles were adopted by King's College, later Columbia College. The original name, Sackett Street, is retained west of Fifth Avenue. The street is considered one of the finest in the "Slope."

No. 274–276, an exceptionally fine house, was built in 1890–91 by the architectural firm of Lamb & Rich for George P. Tangeman. The wealthy owner made his fortune through the Royal and Cleveland Baking Powder companies, and his handsome residence has been much admired for its transitional quality between the Romanesque Revival style and the newly awakening neoclassicism. At first glance the house seems to show all the characteristics of Romanesque motifs (massive rough-cut granite wall framing the open front terrace, the Roman-style brick at the second floor, the loggialike window with columns, a large central dormer window, and the tile roof whose windows have small lights in the upper half). The roof treatment is unusual, with a Dutch step-gable effect, meeting high paneled chimneys near the top. However, on closer observation, certain Classic elements can be seen: egg-and-dart molding enframing the entranceway, the Greek anthemion motif in the frieze, Ionic capitals and shell designs in the lintel blocks, and a delicate roof cornice. To the right of the entrance is a recessed, stained-glass window.

Return to Eighth Avenue and turn left (south).

No. 52–54 Eighth Avenue, at the corner of Berkeley Place, is another attractive mansion. Originally two separate town houses, they were built in 1886 and joined together after a fire in 1914. The building is now divided into apartments. Most interesting is the quality and variety of building materials. Euclid stone at the basement and parlor floor, red brick at the upper two stories, red Spanish tile at the roof, and terra-cotta for adornments. Note how the masonry is treated differently at each level. The Euclid stone is laid in rough-faced random ashlar; above the parlor floors, the stone is used to form a checkerboard design; and topping the next floor is a wide brick band of diagonal studding. At the corner of the building, the bay rises the full height of the building to a truncated, cone-shaped roof. On the Eighth Avenue side, the bay rises only two stories. Other noteworthy features are the huge chimney, the semicircular curved window, and the ornate wrought-iron work of the yard railing and the basement windows.

Nos. 64 and **66** are another pair of Parfitt Brothers houses, built in 1889 in a late Romanesque Revival style. Note how the proportions of the two houses mask the fact that No. 64 is four feet narrower than its neighbor. The stonework is excellent, providing an effective backdrop for the elaborate ornamentation. Polished granite columns at the top level support typical Romanesque Revival capitals. Both houses have L-shaped stoops with carved posts and street numbers hidden in the ornament above the doorways. (Since the street was renumbered, the hidden house numbers now are purely ornamental.)

No. 70–72 is a massive Romanesque Revival mansion with some Queen Anne details, which balances the large house at the Berkeley Place end of the block. Built in 1887, it has several charming details: a Jacobean gable on the Union Street side with a brickwork design indicating the chimney flue, and a lovely corner turret with a wide band of studded brick whose design is repeated at the large gable in front of the house above the dormers. Terra-cotta ornamentation appears on the tower in sunflower panels and in the cresting of the roof ridges. Unfortunately, the wide-arched stone entrance has been filled in to accommodate a single entry door. In the early 1930s, the house was used by a bridge club and restaurant.

Make a short detour west on Union Street for a glance at the interesting rows of houses, **Nos. 905–913** and **889–903.** The latter dates from 1889, the former from 1895. Both display a riot of Romanesque Revival and Queen Anne details: oriels, arched windows, bull's-eye windows, crenelations, sheet-metal cornices with ball-topped spikes, dormers, gables, high pediments, and L-shaped stoops. Union Street's name reflects the national patriotic sentiment after the Civil War.

No. 860, across the street, was the carriage house for a mansion that stood at the southwest corner of Eighth Avenue until 1922. Few carriage houses exist in the neighborhood, and this small house, built originally in a Victorian Gothic style, was remodeled into a neo-Tudor residence in 1923. Its attractive leaded four-part window is typical. (*For a "pit-stop," continue to Seventh Avenue where there are several coffee shops.*)

Return to Eighth Avenue and turn right to President Street. Walk down the north side of President Street.

No. 873 President Street is one of the older houses in the neighborhood, completed in 1878. Designed as a "country villa," it has a "stick style" overhang at the front gable together with wooden supporting struts and elongated brackets. Sadly, a wood porch was removed some years ago from the east side. At the apex of the gable of this brick house is an ornate jigsaw grille. Wooden blinds once decorated the small windows under the projecting eaves. Note also the "toothed" brickwork at the parlor floor and second story.

No. 869, before its recent renovation, was a Catholic religious order's residence, and was designed by architect Henry Ogden Avery for Stewart L. Woodford, ambassador to Spain and a prominent member of the Montauk Club. The rather individualistic house was completed in 1885 and is unusually wide (36 feet). Most striking are the twin oriels at the second floor, bracketed out from the masonry wall on struts. Unusual are the three wide arches above the entrance, the wrought-iron grille and glass entrance door with Art Deco–style peacocks, and a wooden roof cornice whose outlookers are carried on brick corbels. The façade is remarkable in its simplicity and is beautifully arranged; and, although somewhat Romanesque in style, its symmetry throughout is quite atypical.

Return to Eighth Avenue.

No. 101 Eighth Avenue, on the southeast corner of President Street, is a handsome neo-Georgian-style mansion built in 1909 for the president of a brewery. The stately building, set behind a wrought-iron fence with granite posts and approached by a low stoop, is a pleasant addition to elegant Eighth Avenue. Take note of the Georgian elements which give such grace to the house: the fluted Doric columns flanking the entranceway, the well detailed roof entablature, the Flemish bond brickwork, the blind limestone arches with carved swags over the windows beside the entrance, and the balustrade above the roof cornice. The building once was the home of the Unity Club, which occupied it for more than 30 years. It was subsequently subdivided into nine apartments.

To its right, **No. 105** is a much more imposing mansion. Built in 1912 of marble in a neoclassic style, it was designed by architect Frank J. Helmle, who also designed the Tennis Pavilion and Boathouse on the Lullwater in Prospect Park, among many other public buildings in the city. A beautiful entablature is supported by four fluted Corinthian columns and is replete with motifs from ancient Greece, while the tall iron fence, main entrance with its bronze and glass doors, fanlight, and imposing central arch radiate elegance. It now houses a Montessori school.

Adjacent **Nos. 109** and **111** are also worthy of note; the former, built in 1887, is in the Queen Anne style, and the latter is a Romanesque Revival house, completed in 1892.

The entire blockfront to Carroll Street remains intact and in pristine condition. The end mansion will be discussed shortly.

Return to President Street and turn right.

Nos. 902–906 are three pleasing Queen Anne houses built in the mid-1880s. The three-sided bays are complemented by triangular pediments in which Tritons' heads and scallop shells provide the embellishment. Unfortunately, No. 4 lost its pediment and stairway. **Nos. 908–934** are a row of 14 town houses with L-shaped stoops, erected in 1899. The angularity of the façades is reflected in the shape of the roof cornices. According to the Landmarks Commission, No. 916 was the residence of novelist Laura Jean Libbey (Mrs. Van Mater Stilwell), author of some 80 books with such romantic titles as *The Price of a Kiss; Lover Then, But Stranger Now;* and *A Fatal Wooing.* Apparently quite popular in her day, her books sold millions of copies. She died in 1924 and is buried in Greenwood Cemetery.

Across the street, look for the unusual **cast-iron balustrades** atop the entrance cornices of **Nos. 923, 925, 931, 933, 935,** and **939.** And on the south side, **Nos. 944** and **946** are another pair of interesting Queen Anne houses, built in 1886. Note the terra-cotta gable shields with the date of construction. Noteworthy are the intricate terra-cotta panels between the parlor floor and the second story and the toothed brickwork. Battered brickwork flanks the parlor-floor windows and their stained glass, and at the left side of No. 946 is an impressive tall chimney. In the 1960s and '70s, the house was the Tollefson School of Music.

Turn right (south) on Prospect Park West.

Typical mansions of the "Gold Coast" are **Nos. 16 and 17 Prospect Park West.** Both were designed by Montrose W. Morris in 1899 and are representative of the "new wave" of Classical Eclecticism that began sweeping the country after its introduction at the 1893 World's Columbian Exposition in Chicago. Architect Morris planned a number of imposing residences in Brooklyn, including Nos. 18, 19, and 22, and the soon-to-be-seen splendid mansion occupied by the Woodward

School. It is said that in the garden of No. 17, Congresswoman Helen Gehegan, whose parents owned the mansion, married actor Melvyn Douglas. A victim of Richard Nixon's "dirty tricks," she coined the term "Tricky Dick."

Prospect Park West was called Ninth Avenue before its "elevation to elegance."

Turn right on Carroll Street.

Carroll Street was named for Charles Carroll of Maryland, a signer of the Declaration of Independence.

The block between Prospect Park West and Eighth Avenue is one of the most interesting architecturally. The north and south sides of the street are quite different in style and arrangement, and it will be necessary to zigzag back and forth to study and compare the rather unusual aggregation of houses designed by some of the best-known architects in New York. (Odd-numbered houses are on the north side, even on the south.)

The house on the northwest corner **(No. 17 Prospect Park West)** has a handsome Ionic loggia on the third floor (Carroll Street side) above arched windows on the first floor. The pair of houses fronting Prospect Park West on the southwest corner (by Montrose W. Morris, 1898) were planned in neo-Italian Renaissance style. The corner residence marks the geographic high point in Park Slope with an appropriate pair of tall chimneys. A charming Palladian window emphasizes the first floor.

No. 863, with a full-height bay and unusual entablature frieze, was built in 1890 from plans by Napoleon LeBrun & Sons, architects of the Metropolitan Life Insurance Company Building and Tower on Manhattan's Madison Square, as well as many of the city's firehouses. Note the windows piercing the frieze and the lovely balustrade at the roof.

Nos. 888–880, built in 1894, are a row of late Romanesque Revival town houses. Look for the variety of window treatments: arched or flat, paired or triple. **No. 886** shows some of the Classic influence of the Columbian Exposition in its swags and dentils in the cornice: **Nos. 888, 882,** and **880** are perhaps the purest in late Romanesque Revival styling.

Adjacent **Nos. 878** and **876** were designed in 1911 by the Brooklyn firm of Chappell & Bosworth. Similar in plan except for their entrance porches and limestone bay on No. 876, they are reminiscent of the neo-Georgian style with their use of red brick and stone and their façade details. Pleasing is the modillioned roof cornice and the horizontal courses of stone at the second- and fourth-story windowsill levels.

Nos. 861–855 are a four-house row with alternate styling of each house. Built in 1892 and designed by Stanley M. Holden, they are basically Romanesque Revival with a proliferation of Italian Renaissance details. Note the polychrome effect achieved by the varying colors of the limestone, rough-cast brick, orange Roman brick, and copper and dark-red tile. The houses have alternating pyramidal and pseudo-hipped roofs, while a loggia effect is created by the columns supporting the lintels above the triple windows at the third floor on the second and fourth houses; but the dominant features are the ornamented copper oriels with tiled hip roofs at the second floor.

No. 853 is a very attractive Romanesque Revival–style house, built in 1888 by Harvey Murdoch, the developer of nearby Montgomery Place (to be discussed later). The massive structure is crowned by a peaked gable and flanked by pseudo-bartizans (small medieval castle-wall overhangs, added for defense).

No. 874, a neo-Georgian-style house built in 1904, has a pleasing Palladian window over the entranceway and a typical baluster over the roof cornice.

The five picturesque Queen Anne houses, **Nos. 864–872,** were designed in 1887 by architect William B. Tubby. Among other Tubby works in Brooklyn are the Charles Millard Pratt Residence and the Library of Pratt Institute [*see* Clinton Hill walking tour], as well as No. 53 Prospect Park West. The rambling quality of the roof line recalls the architectural innovations of English architect Richard Norman Shaw, who is generally credited with the so-called Queen Anne style. The fanciful profile is punctuated with gables, pseudo-hip roofs, and dormers. Note the "eyebrow" window of No. 870 and the Flemish gable of No. 872. A typical Queen Anne feature is the treatment of the windows and bays, in which the upper sash is divided into small lights (panes). A wide selection of building materials is used for contrast: brick, tile, wood, rough-cut brownstone, and sheet metal. Note, too, the "stepping" of the party walls between the individual houses, reminiscent of the Flemish Renaissance.

No. 860 is a satisfying blend of Queen Anne and Romanesque Revival styles, contemporary with its neighbors. The twin arched windows in the tall gable and the charming hooded dormers set in the roof are delightful touches.

Nos. 858 and **856** are a lovely pair of unified town houses that combine the Romanesque Revival with a neo-Colonial style. The rough-cut brownstone basement and stoop contrast in texture and color with the upper façade's smooth, orange-colored Roman brick. Note how the first floors are treated, with paired doors and wide windows unified by their arches. The fan design in the arched lunettes above both doors and windows is typical of the Georgian style. The stained glass, however, is more appropriate to the Romanesque Revival. A garlanded sheet-metal cornice is topped by a slate roof with tall, corbeled chimneys.

No. 848 is a very narrow four-story house, most of whose façade is taken up by the two-story central bay set on fluted columns in front of the entrance. Built in 1905, it reflects the turn-of-the-century popularity of red brick and limestone trim.

Adjacent **No. 846** was completed in 1887 from plans by noted architect Charles P. H. Gilbert.* The house shows a traditional style from the late Romanesque Revival to the neo-Italian Renaissance. The stonework of the first floor—rough-hewn and light in color—and the large, arched doorway are associated with the Romanesque Revival style, as is the general asymmetry of the façade; while the treatment of the upper windows and roof cornice foretells the

---

*Charles P. H. Gilbert is best known for his designs for many of the finest residences in the city (the Warburg Mansion, now the Jewish Museum; the DeLamar Mansion, formerly the National Democratic Club, now the Polish Consulate General; the Burden House, now the Marymount School; plus most of the town houses on neighboring Montgomery Place).

awakening popularity of the Italian Renaissance style. Within a few years, such architectural firms as McKim, Mead & White would raise the style to its zenith. Note the unusual overhang at the roof cornice, with projecting rafters whose brackets end in carved animal heads.

Nos. 842 and **838** are by architect C. P. H. Gilbert, built in 1887. Both are in the late Romanesque Revival style and are particularly fine houses. The latter has an interesting V motif in the arch over the entranceway and a curved bay at the second story. More imposing is No. 838, built for James H. Remington, a president of the United States Law Association and a distinguished member of the Montauk Club. The two houses display the usual Romanesque Revival asymmetry, but the corner tower of 838 with its conical slate roof is its prime attraction. Notice the composition formed by the arched doorway and its adjacent window, surmounted by a three-sided bay, which is in turn topped by four arched windows, the whole being crowned by a triple-window dormer with a highly ornate peaked gable and finials. (There is no No. 840—it was skipped in the street numbering system.)

Across the street, **Nos. 817–831** are an eight-house row in Romanesque Revival–style, built in 1896. Contrast the shallow two-story bays in the middle with the polygonal bays of the pairs at each end. Look, too, for the typical Romanesque Revival ornamentation on the stoops and parlor floors.

No. 803–813 is officially designated 115–119 Eighth Avenue, and is known as the **Thomas Adams, Jr., Residence.** Designed by the ubiquitous C. P. H. Gilbert in 1888, it is considered the **finest example of Romanesque Revival–style residential architecture in the city!** This grand double house was the home for a number of years of the Adams Chewing Gum king, whose huge white factory was a well-known and very visible landmark in Long Island City until its recent abandonment. Most striking is the overall use and variety of the masonry: sandstone, terra-cotta, and salmon-colored brick—the smooth brick contrasting in texture with the rough-cut brownstone base. Dominating the Carroll Street façade is a massive and deep entrance arch with a swirling leaf-pattern carving. Above the arch is a complementary trio of windows, enframed by the same foliate pattern, and supported on columns whose capitals have the Romanesque basket-weave design. Incidentally, note the clustered dwarf columns that support the elaborate entrance arch. The leaf design is again repeated in the peak of the gable. The huge corner tower, which is round at the first level, is polygonal above and rises to a tall, octagonal tile roof. Notice the quite beautiful stained glass in the first-floor transom bars and in the transoms above. Walking around the corner, the Eighth Avenue façade is also dominated by the corner tower, and is balanced by the two-story curved bay to the left, and the entrance arch is duplicated by a window arch to the right. Another member of the Adams family lived in this half of the house; later, relatives of the F. W. Woolworth family occupied the other. However, the day of the single-family mansion is past, a victim of the harsh realities of economics, and the Adams Residence has been subdivided into apartments.

Across Carroll Street, on the southeast corner of Eighth Avenue, **No. 123** is another Montrose W. Morris–designed residence. Built in a restrained neoclassical style, its soft, off-white appearance is extremely handsome. Brick, limestone, and terra-cotta, all of similar color, combine to create this monochromatic effect. The entrance is especially attractive with its arched tympanum above, displaying a variety of Renaissance motifs on composite columns. The anthemion designs on the long frieze below it are repeated around the building to the Carroll Street side. "Ears" can be seen on the corners of the attic story windows, while the roof cornice displays a lovely garland motif on its convex frieze.

Cross Eighth Avenue and continue west on Carroll Street.

In the distance, the 212-foot-high spire of the **Old First Reformed Church** punctuates the skyline. The Reformed Church is the descendant of the old Dutch Reformed Church, the first religious body in America. The church, located at the corner of Seventh Avenue, was designed in 1892 by George L. Morse.

Turn left into Fiske Place.

Charming little **Fiske Place** and its equally diminutive neighbor to the west, Polhemus Place, re-create much of the late 19th-century residential atmosphere of Brooklyn. Ignoring the apartment houses on the east side of the block (whose only merit is the pleasant view for its tenants), the small scale of the row houses across the street is quite appropriate for this short block.

Nos. 12–16 form a symmetrical group of late Romanesque Revival houses that date from the middle of the last decade of the 19th century. The second-floor bays of this trio resemble an exercise in geometry with their squared, semi-circular, and triangular gables; otherwise their composition is basically unified. Back-to-back on Polhemus Place are a complementing trio of houses with identical façades.

Nos. 18–20, a dissimilar pair of town houses, were designed in 1889–90 by Parfitt Brothers. In common they share Romanesque Revival and neo-Italian Renaissance elements, but the differences in detail are clearly evident, and No. 20 is much more Renaissance in style.

The two neo-Grec–style apartment houses, **Nos. 22** and **24,** were built in 1888 and designed as "twins." Note their side-by-side arched doorways, three-sided bays rising full height, heavily bracketed roof cornices, and the still-intact cast-iron railings and newel posts.

Turn left into Garfield Place.

Originally called Macomb Street, the name was changed to honor the 20th president of the United States, James A. Garfield, two years after his assassination in 1881.

Nos. 248–256 Garfield Place are another attractive row of Romanesque Revival houses, each 20 feet wide, with alternating building designs (in a pattern "ABABA"). The "A" houses have full-height polygonal bays, while the "B" houses have only two-story bays, above which is a third-floor balcony

The Charles L. Feltman Mansion stood on the southwest corner of Eighth Avenue and Carroll Street until 1950, when it gave way to an apartment house. Feltman is credited with having invented the "hot dog" at his popular beer garden in Coney Island. (Brooklyn Collection, Brooklyn Public Library)

with Palladian window. Compare the treatment of the doors and windows of the two types.

Across the street, on the north side, are three **eight-family apartment houses,** typical of the kind erected in many sections of the city, including the Park Slope area, during the first decade of the 20th century. Built in 1903 in the then-popular neo–Italian Renaissance style, they bear rather fanciful and enigmatic names: *Serine, Lillian,* and *Ontrinue. (Ontrinue?* Could the builder possibly have meant *Entre Nous?*)

Congregation Beth Elohim ("House of God"), at the northeast corner of Garfield Place and Eighth Avenue, is an impressive eclectic structure with many Classic elements. Built in 1909–10, the synagogue was designed by Simon Eisendrath in association with B. Horwitz. Since the main entrance is at the corner of the building, the plan is pentagonal, possibly representative of the Five Books of Moses. A pair of enormous Ionic columns *in antis* flank the three-sided stairway, and are surmounted by an arched pediment with modillions, while a large dome with lantern on a polygonal drum is set above the entrance. On a pipe railing on both sides of the temple are seven-branched Menorah, or candelabrum, motifs. Across Garfield Place is the congregation's Temple House.

Turn left on Eighth Avenue.

The apartment house numbered **140,** on the west side of Eighth Avenue, has an Art Deco entrance located in a recessed central section. The adjacent building, **No. 130,** occupies the **site of the old Feltman Mansion.** Charles L. Feltman is credited with introducing the "hot dog" to the American scene at his famous beer garden in Coney Island. His opulent Romanesque Revival residence was designed by Montrose W. Morris, and dominated the corner lot until demolished to make way for the apartment house.

Turn right into Montgomery Place.

Montgomery Place, Park Slope's "Block Beautiful," is named for Revolutionary War general Richard Montgomery, who was killed in the abortive Battle of Quebec in 1775. The one-block street was developed as a single real-estate venture by Harvey Murdoch between 1887 and 1892. According to the *AIA Guide to New York City,* Murdoch wished "to create row houses that broke away from the traditional disciplined and repetitive approach." He commissioned C. P. H. Gilbert to design 20 of the 46 houses on the street, and the visitor may judge for himself how eminently successful the master plan was.

The following houses were designed by Gilbert: (north side) 11, 17, 19, 21, and 25; (south side) 14, 16, 18, 36, 38, 40, 42, 44, 46, 48, 50, 54, 56, 58, and 60. Harvey Murdoch himself resided at No. 11, the house with the impressive Dutch stepped gable. By now, the various architectural revival styles popular in Park

The northeast corner of Eighth Avenue and Carroll Street was the site of the J. H. Hannan House, designed ca. 1888 by C. P. H. Gilbert and built shortly before this heliotype was made. Another Gilbert-designed mansion, the Adams House, still stands across the street, while the fourth corner boasts an elegant house by Montrose W. Morris. (Brooklyn Historical Society)

Slope should be fairly familiar. Since space does not permit a building-by-building description, and the amount of time required to read it would render it impractical at this hour of the tour, the visitor should take a leisurely walk down this block, examining and comparing each of the lovely houses, for nowhere else in the neighborhood is there such a picturesque assemblage of residential architecture so rich and so varied in detail and ornamentation. Don't miss a single oriel, arched window, step-gable, bay window, L-shaped stoop, stained-glass transom, triangular pediment, corbel-sill, copper dormer, slate roof, or panel of ornamental brickwork!

Cross to the Prospect Park side of Prospect Park West.

The row of stately mansions along Prospect Park West can best be appreciated from across the street. **No. 22,** just north of the corner, was designed by Montrose W. Morris in neoclassical style in 1899. Built of limestone with a bright-red, steep tile roof, it is an attractive, symmetrical building. **Nos. 24** and **25** also have red tile roofs, but share a façade of yellow Roman brick with limestone trim. Interesting is the frieze at the second-floor cornice of No. 24, with the typical Greek anthemion and palmette design, and the polygonal tower of No. 25, topped by a steep tile roof.

At the southwest corner of Montgomery Place stands a magnificent mansion, **No. 28,** built in 1901 and designed by Charles Brigham of Boston. Rising above

Millionaire industrialist Henry C. Hulbert commissioned this splendid house at 49–50 Prospect Park West by Montrose W. Morris in 1892. When built, it commanded an unobstructed view of the harbor. (Brooklyn Historical Society)

smooth walls is a fanciful roof line with steep gables. Look for the fascinating sculpture work in the Indiana limestone walls: stone relief panels, bizarre human masks, grotesque animals, and finials in the shape of heraldic animals. The central gable is flanked by tall masonry chimneys as well as a pair of Flemish dormers. Note, too, the copper finial on the high dormer window to the left of the gable. Above the recessed doorway is a balcony with ornamental panels and rampant lions.

No. 32, designed in Romanesque Revival style by George W. Chappell in 1888, is approached by an imposing L-shaped stoop leading to a highly ornate entranceway. The color of the Belleville (New Jersey) rough-cut brownstone blends harmoniously with the brickwork on the upper floors. Observe how the coping, with its keystone motif, rises to form a finial, while the steep brick gable with its pair of arched windows and little slot window is highlighted by the upsweep of the stone coping.

Continue south to First Street (the old Port Road to Gowanus).

Montrose W. Morris's Park Slope masterpiece is the **Henry Carlton Hulbert Mansion** at 49–50 Prospect Park West. Built in 1892 for the millionaire industrialist, it is now the Woodward School, and one of the finest examples of residential architecture in the city. Hulbert was a paper-supply magnate and member of the board of a number of large corporations, including the Pullman Palace Car Company of Chicago and the New York Life Insurance & Trust Company. The massive fortresslike edifice is reminiscent of the work of architect Henry Hobson Richardson, one of the greatest exponents of the Romanesque Revival style. In its *Designation Report* for the Park Slope Historic District, the Landmarks Commission states that "one of the most dramatic features of the mansion is its picturesque castellated profile at the skyline created by the penetration of the roof line by bays, towers, gables, dormer windows, and tall chimneys arranged in vertical clusters representing the flues within." The freestanding, light-gray limestone mansion was originally two separate houses, the larger one at the corner the residence of Henry C. Hulbert, and the somewhat smaller one to the south built for his daughter and son-in-law (a practice not uncommon in those days). Although apparently equal in size, they are not quite, as "papa," of course, had to have the more imposing house. The tower on the north house is much more striking because of its polygonal shape on the upper floors. The south tower is designed in just the opposite manner, polygonal below, and round above! Unifying the pair, however, is a splendid entranceway with twin arches over the doors, "so beautifully joined by a single robust column" according to the *Designation Report*, "that they form a point of focus for the front." The houses also share a common entrance staircase and a third-floor loggia. Ornamentation is also used very effectively on the façade, combining Romanesque and Byzantine motifs to provide a pleasing contrast with the rugged walls. Lovely also are the rich carvings on the third-floor loggia enframement. To the rear, a second-floor porch was erected for a panoramic view of the harbor—a vista now totally obliterated by the adjacent houses. (When built, the mansion stood in "splendid isolation" at the crest of the "Slope.") The mansion was acquired in 1927 by the

Brooklyn Ethical Culture School, which kept the building until 1977. After an interlude of ownership by another school, the mansion was taken over by the Woodward School a year later.

The adjacent mansion, **No. 53,** which now serves as **the Meeting House of the Brooklyn Ethical Culture Society,** was designed in 1900 by the noted architect William B. Tubby. The beautiful residence, whose broad entranceway is flanked by heraldic lions, was built for William H. Childs, founder of the Bon-Ami Cleansing Powder Company. The symmetrical red brick street façade is topped by a stepped curved gable. Contrasting with the white limestone bay window enframements and gargoyles are the red tile roof and the bright red Flemish-bond brickwork wall. Pilasters flank the front door and arched window, adding to the symmetry of the house. Above is a wide bay window surmounted by a stone balustrade in front of handsome enframed windows on the third floor. Higher in the gable, these windows are connected to an upper window by a panel, carved medallion and a drip molding. To crown the composition, a finial adorns the tops. Twin tall chimneys and a steep step gable dominate the south façade. A balustraded wing was added by the architect in 1907 to house a sunlit morning room with basement billiard room below. The spacious garden, which lends so much charm to the mansion's setting, is surrounded by an attractive wrought-iron railing set in brick piers. The Childs Mansion is a fine example of the rather scarce neo-Jacobean style in New York City.

No. 61, whose main entrance is on Second Street, was also designed by William B. Tubby. A brick house with a tile roof and striking projecting copper cornice, it presents quite a contrast with Tubby's Childs Mansion across the street. Built for Childs's married daughter, it is separated from "papa" (perhaps intentionally) by Second Street, and is also quite different in design. The architect employed the briefly popular North Italian provincial style, adding many interesting touches, such as the English crossband brick walls, the horizontal stone band courses and panels at the upper level, shallow bay windows, and the cornice brackets.

Between Fourth and Fifth streets, enter Prospect Park on the roadway leading to the Litchfield Villa.

Built almost a decade before the development of Prospect Park, this delightful Tuscan manor house and surrounding estate was the residence of lawyer and railroad magnate Edwin C. Litchfield. Designed in 1857 by Alexander Jackson Davis,* one of the greatest architects of the mid-19th century, it is the oldest mansion in Park Slope, and its survival (relatively) intact is a tribute to the aesthetic sensibilities of the municipal authorities of the old City of Brooklyn.

---

*Alexander Jackson Davis is noted chiefly for his Gothic Revival and Italianate buildings, some remarkable examples of which still survive: the old Custom House, now Federal Hall National Memorial (designed in cooperation with Ithiel Town), and charming Nos. 3 and 4 Gramercy Park—all described in other walking tours. He also designed Jay Gould's palatial Lyndhurst, in Tarrytown—a magnificent mansion with all its furnishings in a charming rural setting, operated by the National Trust for Historic Preservation and open to the public.

Originally called "Ridgewood" and later "Grace Hill Mansion," the richly furnished villa was the center of social life of Brooklyn's high society shortly after
the Civil War. The extensive grounds included virtually all of today's Park
Slope neighborhood, from First to Ninth Streets and all the land in between
down to the Gowanus Canal. Not only did Litchfield make his fortune in
Midwestern railroad development, but his Brooklyn Development Company
undertook the draining of the swampland at the foot of the "Slope" and the construction of the Gowanus Canal. The canal is still one of the city's important
waterways. Litchfield lived in the villa until 1882, having sold part of his estate
to the City of Brooklyn for the development of Prospect Park in 1869. It became
the headquarters of the Brooklyn Parks Department in 1892 and is still the
Brooklyn office of the Department of Parks and Recreation. The Litchfield
Mansion, or Villa, is considered the finest example of Alexander Jackson
Davis's Italianate style. Time and Parks Department use have taken toll of some
of the building's accouterments. Of the rich household furnishings, nothing
whatever remains. Only the double stairway of cast iron, the central rotunda, and
a few carved mantelpieces survive. The original stucco, simulating rough-cut
stone, on the exterior walls has been removed, exposing the bare brickwork
beneath. Unique decorative elements that have survived, however, are the corn
and wheat motifs, instead of the traditional acanthus leaves, on the Corinthian
capitals. The mansion also retains its lovely frieze and cornice, and displays a
delightfully romantic aggregation of towers, turrets, balconies, bay windows,
and porches.

*Brooklyn south of Park Slope in the early 1860s was flat farmland with scarcely a house to
be seen. Ten years later, Olmsted and Vaux's Prospect Park plan completely transformed the
scene. (Brooklyn Union Gas Company)*

The Battle Pass (now in Prospect Park) from a sketch made in 1791, where the Colonial Army failed to halt the advance of English and Hessian troops during the Battle of Long Island. (Brooklyn Historical Society)

To the rear of the villa, and attached by a colonnade, is the handsome **Annex,** designed in an architecturally harmonious style in 1911 by Helmle & Huberty, and completed two years later.

Prospect Park, which rivals Manhattan's Central Park as the city's most beautiful park, contains 562 acres of scenic woodland, broad meadows, picturesque bluffs, exquisite plantings, several ponds, and a lake, together with extensive playing fields and recreational facilities, a zoo, a number of Classic buildings, a Quaker burial ground, and a Dutch Colonial farmhouse. The land for the park was acquired by the City of Brooklyn beginning in 1859, with landscape architects Frederick Law Olmsted and Calvert Vaux selected to draw the plans. (Brooklyn, at the time, was the nation's third largest city.) Much of the credit for the park's creation is due to a 24-year crusade by Parks Commissioner James S. T. Stranahan, whose statue (by sculptor Frederick MacMonnies) can be seen near the Grand Army Plaza entrance. An earlier design, known as the Viele Plan, was rejected by Olmsted and Stranahan to avoid the bisection of the park by Flatbush Avenue; instead, land to the west was acquired for the present layout. Much of the former land to the east was subsequently used for the Brooklyn Botanic Garden, the landmark Brooklyn Museum, and the main branch of the Brooklyn Public Library—all suitable companions to this magnificent natural oasis. With the acceptance of the Olmsted & Vaux *Design for Prospect Park* of 1866–67, the park project gradually took shape, culminating with the monumental approach of the Grand Army Plaza in the 1890s.

End of tour. To return to the subway, walk back along Prospect Park West to Grand Army Plaza, and bear left at the mall. The Grand Army Plaza station is on the left side of Flatbush Avenue. If you wish to return via Prospect Park, walk back on Prospect Park West to the first park entrance (between the panthers) and follow the West Drive to Grand Army Plaza.

MYRTLE AVE.

(Site of Raymond St. Jail)

WILLOUGHBY AVE.

ST. EDWARDS ST.

Monument

Fort Greene Park

Washington Park

⑦

⑥ ⑧

start

① ② ③ ④ DeKALB AVE. ⑤

HUDSON AVE.
ROCKWELL PL.
ASHLAND PL.
ST. FELIX PL.
FORT GREENE PL.
SO. ELLIOTT PL.
SO. PORTLAND AVE.
SO. OXFORD ST.
CUMBERLAND ST.
CARLTON AVE.

FLATBUSH AVENUE EXTENSION

NEVINS ST.

LAFAYETTE AVE.

⑨

⑩ To Clinton Hill

⑪

⑭ FULTON ST.

GREENE AVE.

⑬ HANSON PL. ⑫

LIRR Station

THIRD AVE.

ATLANTIC AVE.

PACIFIC ST.

FORT GREENE

(Shaded Area Indicates Historic District)

FOURTH AVE.
DEAN ST.
FIFTH AVE.
SIXTH AVE.

BERGEN ST.

ST. MARKS PL.

18. Fort Greene

[D, M, N, Q, or R lines to DeKalb Avenue]

The tour begins at DeKalb Avenue and Flatbush Avenue Extension, northeast corner (in Brooklyn).

Flatbush Avenue Extension is a major connecting artery between Canal Street in Manhattan (via the Manhattan Bridge) and the downtown and central part of Brooklyn. Before the construction of the Brooklyn-Battery Tunnel and the network of expressways, Flatbush Avenue Extension was the busiest link between the two boroughs and one of the most heavily traveled streets in the world. Beneath the roadway is the DeKalb Avenue subway station, considered the busiest in the city transit system—particularly at rush hours—as so many lines into Manhattan converge at this station.

1. Long Island University's Main Building, at 385 Flatbush Avenue Extension, was originally the famous **Brooklyn Paramount Theater.** Built in 1928, it was one of the country's grandest movie palaces, and Brooklyn's No. 1 showplace for 34 years. The theater's sign can still be distinguished faintly on the DeKalb Avenue side. When LIU saved it from demolition, the theater and office tower were converted to school use in two major steps. The tower, which housed the offices of many theatrical agents, was redesigned in 1950 for classrooms and administrative offices; and when the theater closed in 1962, the auditorium was rebuilt as a gymnasium and named Founders' Hall. The heavily ornate ceiling, balcony, and statuary are preserved intact, as are several thousand red-plush orchestra seats, which surround the new basketball court. The "mighty Wurlitzer"—second only in size and sound to the Radio City Music Hall organ—is still in use, restored to its original beauty and adding excitement to home basketball games.

When the neighborhood began to decline in the 1950s and '60s and threatened to become a seedy, decaying backwater, the city and local community leaders worked together on a plan for the **Central Brooklyn Urban Renewal Project.** Evidence of its success can be seen in the extensive building boom still in progress. To the southeast of the LIU campus a new commercial district has risen from the urban blight of slums and abandoned factories, in many ways a tribute to the university's confidence in the neighborhood. Phoenix-like, new New York Telephone and Con Edison buildings were erected, the latter on the site of Fabian's Fox Theater, another of the old vaudeville and movie palaces. On the shell of the old Barton's Candy Company factory arose a new structure housing the New York City Department of Human Resources and the New York State Department of Motor Vehicles.

Walk east on DeKalb Avenue one block to Hudson Avenue.

2. During the Revolutionary War this was the site of the *Oblong Redoubt,* one of a series of forts and entrenchments that extended across Brooklyn from Gowanus to nearby Fort Putnam (now Fort Greene Park). The Battle of Brooklyn, which took place in the last week of August 1776, not far from these battlements, was the first major engagement of the war. Outnumbered and outflanked by superior British and Hessian forces, General Washington's Continental Army was forced to withdraw across the East River to Manhattan from Brooklyn Heights, about a mile and a half to the west. Brooklyn was to remain in British hands until the end of the war.

3. On the corner of Rockwell Place is the turn-of-the-century **Goldner Building.** The "stars" on the walls are braces at the end of iron tie-rods, used to reinforce the walls and literally hold the building together. (In the Fulton Fish Market in lower Manhattan, one can even see tie-rod braces in the shape of star*fish*.) The **Benziger Brothers Building** on the diagonally opposite corner is a typical industrial Romanesque Revival–style structure of the 1880s. Until its closing in the mid-1970s the firm manufactured Catholic religious articles.

The Terrace and former Prison Ship Martyrs' Monument in Fort Greene Park before its replacement in 1908 by Stanford White's marble shaft, a year and a half after the architect's death. The landscaping for the park was designed by Olmsted & Vaux, who also planned Central and Prospect parks. (Brooklyn Historical Society)

Typical of the period is the row of corbels below the cornice, imitating the machicolations of medieval castles. It is now a condominium.

Take a short detour down Rockwell Place to the **New York Experimental Glass Workshop** and the **Robert Lehman Gallery** (33–35 Rockwell Place/647 Fulton Street, third floor). Enter this loft building to discover an unexpected delight! The spotless third-floor studios house large kilns for red-hot molten glass. About sixty artists (including Dale Chihuly, Dante Marioni, and others) regularly blow glass, mould glass, and work in neon, but not stained glass, in these not-for-profit studios. Classes and lectures, open to the public, teach these time-honored skills. Visitors are welcome. (Open daily, weekdays 10:00 A.M. to 6:00 P.M., weekends to 4:00 P.M.) Return to DeKalb Avenue, turn right and walk two blocks to St. Felix Street.

At the corner of St. Felix Street, look to the right side of the street and note the former carriage houses at Nos. 8 and 10. No. 8 was refurbished for director Spike Lee's film studio, Forty Acres and a Mule. The entire street is in an advanced state of decay, but despite its seedy appearance, traces of its former elegant rows of Italianate brownstones are still very much in evidence, and new rowhouse versions have begun to fill in the block.

At Ashland Place, Brooklyn's tallest skyscraper, the Williamsburgh Savings Bank Tower (to be seen later) looms in the distance.

4. The Brooklyn Hospital, built in 1920 with additions and alterations in 1967 and again in 1990, occupies the site of Brooklyn's first hospital. The original hospital was established through the efforts of Cyrus Smith, who, as mayor of Brooklyn in 1839, started a vigorous campaign for a public hospital, only to receive a token $200 appropriation from the Board of Aldermen. He then contributed one of his own houses for the project, funding it himself. (Brooklyn was an independent city until 1898.)

5. Brooklyn Technical High School (1931), at the corner of Fort Greene Place, is one of the city's special schools, dedicated to pre-engineering training. Brooklyn Tech has always been considered one of the city's "better" schools. The antenna on the roof broadcasts the signal of the New York City Board of Education's radio station WNYE (95.5 kHz). The antenna is the tallest *structure* in the city, outside Manhattan.

6. Fort Greene Park, with its commanding views of downtown Brooklyn and the Manhattan skyline, was the site of previously mentioned Fort Putnam during the Revolutionary War. When the War of 1812 brought the panic of another British invasion, the hill was fortified again and renamed Fort Greene (after Revolutionary War General Nathanael Greene). In 1847 it was named Washington Park; then in 1868 landscape architects Frederick Law Olmsted and Calvert Vaux combined their talents to convert the 30 acres of hill and old fort into an elegant park, which the City of Brooklyn named City Park. In the early 20th century the name was changed again to Fort Greene Park. (Olmsted & Vaux made their greatest contribution to the beauty of the city with their designs for Manhattan's Central Park and Brooklyn's Prospect Park.)

The Park is the focus of the **Fort Greene Historic District**—an area whose attractive brick and brownstone row houses display all the architectural features

The fortresslike Raymond Street Jail, Brooklyn's own "Tombs," stood alongside Fort Greene Park until it was demolished in the early 1960s. When it neared completion in 1880, it was discovered that an entranceway had not been designed, and a consequent rapid revision of the building plan had to be made. (Brooklyn Historical Society)

popular in the period 1850–70. It is also an integrated neighborhood "on the way up," with much civic pride and sense of history.

Enter the park and follow the path (which appears as an extension of Fort Greene Place) along the western perimeter, into St. Edward's Street, as far as Myrtle Avenue.

At the crest of the hill, the distant twin spires of the Church of St. Michael and St. Edward can be seen among the 38 acres of towers of the Fort Greene Houses, the city's first postwar low-income housing project. Near the base of the hill, immediately to the left of the fence, is the **site of the former Raymond Street Jail,** built in 1880, a dismal gray fortress that was Brooklyn's answer to Manhattan's old "Tombs." (Raymond Street was the former name of Ashland Place.) Some of the *Prison—Keep Clear* signs are still visible on the wall under the fence. A bizarre sidelight to the history of the unlamented prison was the discovery when the building was partly completed in 1880 that there was no front entrance! This rather serious oversight was blamed on both the architect, William A. Mundell, and the Brooklyn Board of Supervisors.

On the site of the old jail, which was demolished in 1964, is the Dr. Edwin Post Maynard, Jr., Staff Residence of Brooklyn Hospital (Walker O. Cain & Associates, 1976), a much more appreciated replacement.

Cross Myrtle Avenue and follow St. Edward's Street to the church.

Rising like some French 17th-century Loire Valley château, the **Church of St. Michael and St. Edward** dominates the surrounding Raymond V. Ingersoll and Walt Whitman Houses. Ornate conical towers frame the angular front façade, which resembles the bow of a huge ship pointing appropriately toward the Brooklyn Navy Yard. Built in 1902 as the Church of St. Edward, it boasts a rather unusual addition, an altar and cross made from parts of the old Myrtle Avenue El and installed in 1972. (The El clattered by the rear of the church until 1969.) By standing in front of the church, one can visualize the demapped Leo Place which formed the other altitude of a triangle with St. Edward's Street whose apex was at this point. Across the street is the diminutive Walt Whitman Branch of the Brooklyn Public Library. (Whitman, in addition to his other literary accomplishments, was editor of the *Brooklyn Eagle* for a time in the mid-19th century.)

Return to Myrtle Avenue, cross to the park side, and enter the park at the first entrance. Follow the path to the stairs, and climb to the top.

 ## THE PRISON SHIP MARTYRS' MONUMENT

7. In 1780, at the height of the Revolutionary War, the British Navy anchored a flotilla of some 12 decrepit ex-men-of-war and hospital ships in Wallabout Bay (near the site of the present Navy Yard), and converted them into floating prisons for captured American seamen. They hoped that the unpleasant conditions aboard the crowded, filthy, and disease-ridden hulks would induce the captives to enlist in His Majesty's Navy. Few did, however, and the tale of

The British prison ship Jersey, *in an old engraving. About 12,000 American prisoners died of disease and maltreatment aboard this and 11 other prison ships anchored in Wallabout Bay. (Brooklyn Historical Society)*

The first Prison Ship Martyrs' Monument, built in 1844 near Hudson Avenue. (Brooklyn Historical Society)

When the first Martyrs' Monument (left, below) fell into decay, its state of collapse was noted by an artist for a contemporary news magazine. In the rather grisly engraving above, coffins containing the heroes' skeletons, and labelled with the names of the 13 original states, are heaped in the neglected tomb. The present, more permanent crypt was built in 1873. (Brooklyn Historical Society)

privation and ultimate death of between 11,500 and 12,500 prisoners—no one will ever know for sure how many—is one of the most sorrowful events in American history. The worst of the prison ships was the H.M.S. *Jersey,* a decommissioned ship of the line, on which 1,100 men were jammed together between decks in unspeakable conditions. About a dozen died each night from a variety of causes—dysentery, typhoid, smallpox, yellow fever, food poisoning, starvation, and flogging. At the end of the war in 1783, there were from the whole prison fleet only 1,400 sick and emaciated survivors.

At the cry each morning of "Rebels, turn out your dead!" the bodies were hauled up on deck, lowered into boats, rowed ashore, and buried in shallow graves. There the bleaching bones remained until 1808 when as much of the remains as could be recovered were unearthed and reburied on the nearby John Jackson estate. The task was performed by the Columbian Order, a patriotic society that was later to become the political Tammany Society. As for the *Jersey,* it wallowed at anchor for several years, slowly rotting away until it disintegrated and slipped beneath the waters of the bay.

Thirty-six years later, a monument to these martyrs was erected; and in 1873, the remains were transferred to a crypt under the stairway of a new monument on the present site. (On June 17, 1973, a brief public ceremony was conducted by the city commemorating the 100th anniversary of this interment.)

EAGLE PHOTO

A heavy snowfall covers Fort Greene Park in this Brooklyn Eagle *photograph taken the morning of December 26, 1926. The new Martyrs' Monument rises solemnly at the top of the hill. (Brooklyn Collection. Brooklyn Public Library)*

On a cold, wet November 18, in 1908, President William Howard Taft dedicated the newest Prison Ship Martyrs' Monument. Designed by noted architect Stanford White, it stands on a 220-foot-square plaza at the top of the stairway, consisting of a simple granite shaft topped by a large brazier, or lantern. Measuring 148 feet 8 inches, it is the tallest Doric column in the world. The bronze brazier was executed by sculptor A. A. Weinman. The base of the fluted column consists of a double platform, or stylobate, with entrances on the north and south sides (now closed). The actual entrance to the crypt (also no longer open to visitors) is located two flights below, at the first landing. The entrance is so unobtrusive that it is usually unnoticed in ascending the stairs. A planned electric elevator for the monument was never installed, although for many years visitors were permitted to climb the interior stairway to the upper platform. In the original plans, a gas flame was to burn perpetually in the lantern. Granite standards at each corner of the plaza have disappeared, and the entire monument suffers from abuse and neglect...a parallel perhaps to the sufferings of the martyrs, but wholly inappropriate to their memory. Significantly, this was one of Stanford White's last commissions. He was shot and killed a year and a half before the monument's dedication [*see* Madison Square, 11].

To the west of the monument is a shady terrace with a large plaque presented by King Juan Carlos of Spain in 1976 for the Bicentennial, commemorating the 126 Spanish volunteers who died in the prison ships.

Just to the east of the monument is a small white marble building designed by McKim, Mead & White as a public comfort station (also closed). The diminutive Doric "temple" has been referred to as "the most elegant outhouse in the world"! It now has a more respectable function as the headquarters of the Fort Greene Park Rangers.

Follow the path to the right of the comfort station down to the exit at Willoughby Avenue and Washington Park.

8. Washington Park was the most fashionable street in the Fort Greene section in the 1870s and '80s, when many of the affluent residents of nearby exclusive Clinton Hill found the newly created Olmsted & Vaux park very attractive. The row of old Italianate brownstone mansions speaks of former opulence, though many have been carved up into apartments, and some into rooming houses. But there is evidence of pride of ownership in sympathetic restoration and repair. Many have become quite attractive again.

Enjoy the variety of architecture from Willoughby to DeKalb avenues, as most of the buildings have been newly refurbished.

Turn right on DeKalb Avenue, past South Oxford Street to South Portland Avenue.

9. The splendid rows of Anglo-Italianate brownstones along shady **South Portland Avenue** are typical of residential construction that became immensely popular throughout the city in the mid-19th century. Brooklyn by the 1870s had become the bastion of the brownstone row house in such neighborhoods as Brooklyn Heights, Cobble Hill, Bedford-Stuyvesant, Park Slope, Clinton Hill, and Fort Greene.

The characteristics of the style are evident in the tall stoop with cast-iron balustrades; elegant entranceway surmounted by a protruding arched pediment supported by consoles decorated with acanthus-leaf motifs; recessed portico with round-arch double entrance doors; stone-enframed windows, usually topped by curved lintels; and an elaborate cornice supported by console brackets with the familiar acanthus-leaf design. The houses were generally four stories high above a raised basement. The front masonry bearing wall was faced with chocolate-colored sandstone, quarried in Connecticut or New Jersey. The windows on the first, or parlor, floor were almost as high as the room itself and, like all the windows, were double-hung (plate glass had become much less expensive by mid-century). Most brownstones were owned by merchants or professionals. One of the early row-house developers was Walt Whitman.

The influence of fashionable London streets can be seen in the names of so many of Fort Greene's thoroughfares: Oxford, Adelphi, Carlton, Cumberland, and Waverly. South Portland Avenue was named for once-elegant Portland

Place. Other nearby avenues honor such Revolutionary War generals as Washington, Greene, DeKalb, Willoughby, Gates, and Lafayette.

With shifting populations in the 1940s and '50s, the Fort Greene neighborhood began to decline, succumbing rapidly to the effects of urban disintegration and decay. All seemed lost until the mid-1960s when a last-minute miracle occurred. A revolution broke out!—a "brownstone revolution"—which was to sweep not only Fort Greene, but virtually all the brownstone neighborhoods in Brooklyn and Manhattan as well. Armies of the middle class, beset by a growing shortage of family living space, began buying up the deteriorating row houses, which were available at bargain prices, and painstakingly renovating and restoring them to their former beauty. These new "brownstoners," banding together in brownstone-revival organizations, pooled their knowledge and experience, and set to work using every spare minute (and dollar) to restore the once-elegant houses. Paradoxically, that rapid deterioration of the neighborhood spared the row houses the effects of gradual "modernization" and great numbers of Fort

The Lafayette Avenue Presbyterian Church, designed in 1860 by J. C. Wells, boasts one of the finest collections of Tiffany stained-glass windows. Pulitzer Prize–winning poet Marianne Moore was one of the church's most celebrated and devoted parishioners. The 200-foot steeple had to be dismantled when the IND subway construction threatened to topple it. (Brooklyn Historical Society)

Greene's brownstones survive in virtually pristine architectural condition. Explore the street, noting the harmonious, uniform cornice lines of the row houses, and the effect of depth created by the block-long repetition of balustrades, entranceways, and windows. The beauty of a brownstone row can best be appreciated when viewed at an angle, rather than *en face*.

Turn left at Lafayette Avenue, and left again at South Oxford Street.

10. Although lacking some of the quality of South Portland Avenue—mostly because of fewer trees—**South Oxford Street** presents a varied panorama of architectural styles used in row-house construction. It was not unusual for an owner to add a French Second Empire mansard roof, providing an extra attic bedroom or two. The sloping mansard roof, with its dormer windows and iron cresting, is not an unpleasant addition to the Anglo-Italianate brownstone.

The Roanoke (No. 69), built ca. 1893, was one of the city of Brooklyn's first luxury apartment houses. A disastrous fire early in 1987 left little but the walls, but it has since risen, phoenix-like, from its ashes and undergone a complete and architecturally accurate restoration, and is now a condominium.

11. The Lafayette Avenue Presbyterian Church was designed in 1860 in a modified Gothic Revival style by Joseph C. Wells (architect Wells was also responsible for the Church of the Pilgrims, in Brooklyn Heights, and the First Presbyterian Church, on Manhattan's Fifth Avenue). The sanctuary of the church boasts a magnificent set of Tiffany art-glass windows. All but one of the upper windows and half of the lower were made in the Tiffany Studios in 1890. In the Underwood Chapel, the large stained-glass window, installed in 1920, was the last to be produced by the firm. A towering 200-foot steeple had to be removed when blasting for the IND subway line under construction beneath Lafayette Avenue threatened to topple it.

One of the church's most celebrated and devoted parishioners in modern times was Pulitzer Prize–winning poet **Marianne Moore** (1887–1972), a long-time resident on nearby Cumberland Street.

At this point there are two alternatives:

(1) The walking tour of Fort Greene may be completed by following the remaining itinerary below, or

(2) the final portion of the Fort Greene tour may be skipped (or returned to later), and a tour made of neighboring **Clinton Hill,** by continuing east on Lafayette Avenue four blocks to the corner of Clermont Avenue [*see* map].

To complete the Fort Greene walking tour, continue south on South Oxford Street to Hanson Place and turn right (west).

Fulton Street is the borough's oldest thoroughfare. During the Colonial and Revolutionary periods it was known as the King's Highway (not to be confused with the present Kings Highway in central Brooklyn), and later as the Old Ferry

A helicopter view of Brooklyn's tallest skyscraper, the Williamsburgh Savings Bank Tower, at 1 Hanson Place. Completed in 1929, the building's observatory commands a spectacular view of downtown Brooklyn and the Manhattan skyline. (Brooklyn Union Gas Company)

Road. Connecting with the first ferry to the island of Manhattan, its name was changed to honor Robert Fulton, whose steam ferry *Nassau* began regular service in 1814, opening the town of Brooklyn to an era of growth and development. The Fulton Street El, which rumbled overhead until it was dismantled in 1940, was built as the Kings County Elevated Railroad in 1887, and contributed to the rapid development of the city. Contrary to expectations, its removal did little to improve the neighborhood.

Turn right into Hanson Place.

12. The Hanson Place Seventh Day Adventist Church (No. 88) was built in 1857–60 as the Hanson Place Baptist Church. An exceptionally interesting combination of Greek Revival and Italianate decorative details, the imposing, gleaming white church building complements the surrounding neighborhood, which despite some urban blight still retains a good deal of its mid-19th-century atmosphere. The dominant features of the church building are the portico with its tall Corinthian columns and pilasters, a large pediment set on a cornice supported by carved modillions, typically Greek twin doorways and surmounting windows, and a similarly typical Italianate row of arcaded windows illuminating the nave. The church was acquired by the Seventh Day Adventists in 1963.

13. Brooklyn's tallest skyscraper, the **former Williamsburgh Savings Bank Tower,** once called "The Tower of Strength," measures 512 feet to the top of its gold dome. Completed in 1929 from plans by Halsey, McCormick & Helmer, this singularly conspicuous Byzantine-style landmark with its four illuminated tower clocks is clearly visible for miles around. The builders hoped in vain that its more central location on Brooklyn's Times Plaza (Brooklyn had its own *Times* for many years) would attract business away from the mile-distant civic center. Apparently the management of the Long Island Rail Road had the same opinion when they built the terminal across the street. A visit to the observatory for sweeping panoramas of Brooklyn and the Manhattan skyline is a "must." The tower may be visited weekdays 9 A.M.–3 P.M., but only by phoning the Building Management Office [(718) 270–4448] in advance. See also the impressive banking room on the ground floor. The institution is now the Manhattan Savings Bank.

The **Long Island Railroad Flatbush Avenue Terminal,** at this writing, is awaiting reconstruction under the new Atlantic Terminal development plan. It is still very much in use by commuters, many of whom recall the former Italianate structure of red brick and limestone that was a neighborhood landmark for almost a century.

Turn right (north) on Ashland Place to Lafayette Avenue, then right again.

14. The Brooklyn Academy of Music, which compares favorably in almost every respect with Carnegie Hall, was constructed in 1908 from plans by Herts & Tallant, and moved to this larger site from its original location on Montague Street in Brooklyn Heights. The BAM is the major cultural institution within the **Brooklyn Academy of Music Historic District**—a neighborhood comprising about three square blocks of residential streets, with row houses dating to the 1850s and '60s, unified by their scale and Italianate features. As Brooklyn's leading cultural center, founded in 1859, the Academy is noted for the variety and high quality of its musical programs, theater productions, lectures, and films. The main auditorium, or Opera House, with a seating capacity of 2,200, was inaugurated on November 14, 1908, with a production of *Faust,* sung by Geraldine Farrar and Enrico Caruso. Caruso opened the gala evening with a spine-tingling rendition of the "Star Spangled Banner."

A 1,400-seat Music Hall and a newly built flexible-seating Lepercq Space offer dance recitals and chamber music concerts. A Chelsea Theater Centre on the fourth floor houses the Academy's resident professional drama company. The Brooklyn Philharmonia, conducted by musical director Dennis Russell Davies, presents a concert series each season, and the resident Pennsylvania Ballet performs a wide spectrum of classical and modern dance. There are also regular series in chamber music, black theater, and films. Visiting groups from out of town and abroad are frequent, with recent performances by the Royal Shakespeare and Young Vic Companies. Some of the notables who have performed or given lectures at the Academy are: Sergei Rachmaninoff, Ignace Jan Paderewski, Ernestine Schumann-Heink, Fritz Kreisler, Jascha Heifetz, Pablo Casals, Carl Sandburg, Edna St. Vincent Millay, Sinclair Lewis, William Jennings Bryan, and Winston Churchill. It is unfortunate that the BAM's elegant cornice and roof balustrade were removed, as the ornate façade now appears "hatless." The nearby Majestic Theater was refurbished by the BAM to house avantgarde productions, but at this writing, severe budget restraints have kept it dark.

Return to the corner in front of the Long Island Rail Road Terminal.

The busy intersection just beyond is **Times Plaza,** the confluence of Flatbush, Atlantic, and Fourth avenues, plus a few side streets. On the center island is the **Atlantic Avenue Control House,** the **former IRT subway kiosk** (Heins and La Farge, 1908), now closed, but its "Atlantic Avenue" sign is still visible, half-hidden by a fast-food establishment. Many years ago, Brooklyn had its own *Times,* one of several dailies, and its publication office (now demolished) faced the plaza. While still a busy spot, the traffic is all motor vehicle. Less than a half-century ago, the streets were lined with trolley tracks whose cars came from all over the borough; the Fifth Avenue Culver Line El clattered overhead, and the streets were crowded with pedestrians streaming to and from the nearby downtown Brooklyn shopping district and such well-known emporiums as Frederick Loeser, Namm's, Oppenheim & Collins, and Abraham & Straus (only the last of which survives).

End of tour. The nearest subway station, Atlantic Avenue, adjacent to the Long Island Rail Road Terminal, is served by the Lexington and Broadway–Seventh Avenue lines, the D and Q lines, and, through a connecting passageway, the B, M, N, and R lines at the Pacific Street Station.

MYRTLE AVE.

WILLOUGHBY AVE.

CLERMONT AVE.

VANDERBILT AVE.

CLINTON AVE.

WAVERLY AVE.

WASHINGTON AVE.

HALL ST.

RYERSON WALK

Pratt Institute

⑮

"T H E

DeKALB AVE.

H I L L"

⑬

⑭

⑫

⑪

⑯

Underwood Park

㉓

㉒

IND

⑳ ⑲

⑦

⑰

start

①

Lafayette ave.

⑱ CLIFTON PL.

⑥ ⑧

⑨

To Fort Greene

⑤

㉑

②

⑩

ST. JAMES PL.

CAMBRIDGE PL.

③

GREENE AVE.

④

GATES AVE.

CLINTON HILL

(Shaded Area Indicates Historic District)

FULTON ST.

19. Clinton Hill

[G line to Clinton–Washington avenues. From lower Manhattan, take the A or C line to Hoyt–Schermerhorn streets and change for the G; from upper Manhattan, take the E or F line to Queens Plaza for the G]

With Brooklyn's rapid growth of population in the mid-19th century, a boom in row-house construction began. Pushing east and west, new neighborhoods developed along the post roads that led to the suburban villages of Bushwick, Jamaica, Flatbush, New Utrecht, and Gravesend. As the Brooklyn Heights section became completely built up, prosperous merchants and professionals found the high ground to the east to be very much to their liking. By the 1840s, the "Hill" [*see* map] became second only to Brooklyn Heights in elegance. The majority of new residents worked in Manhattan, only a 20-minute ride by stagecoach or omnibus to the Fulton Ferry landing, enjoying a quiet suburban life within sight of the city. By the 1880s and '90s, Clinton Avenue became a "Millionaires' Row," lined with the mansions of the wealthy, and it remains in a remarkable state of preservation. Virtually all of Clinton Hill has survived the encroachments of rapid urban growth, and to this day it presents a fascinating collection of architectural styles in its residences, churches, schools, and commercial buildings.

The tour begins at the corner of Clermont and Lafayette avenues.

1. The **Brooklyn Masonic Temple** was built in 1909 from plans by Lord & Hewlett, and it is indeed a temple! The stately Ionic columns and terra-cotta polychrome designs are reminiscent of ancient Greece of the fourth century B.C.

Turn right (south) on Clermont Avenue.

2. Bishop Loughlin High School, built in 1932, marks the **site of the proposed Brooklyn Cathedral,** whose cornerstone was laid in 1868. Planned to be the largest church in the city, construction was suddenly halted when the walls reached a height of 12 feet, and the entire project abandoned, with the money diverted to charitable purposes. The Roman Catholic Diocese of Brooklyn was founded in 1853, with John Loughlin appointed the first bishop.

3. The sole surviving part of the projected cathedral project is the **former Bishop of Brooklyn's Residence,** on the northwest corner of Clermont and Greene avenues, designed by architect Patrick Charles Keeley in 1887. The mansard roof and smoothly grooved granite blocks of this Victorian building give it a somewhat forbidding appearance. The old incomplete cathedral walls were removed in 1931 to make way for the construction of the high school, and the former Episcopal Residence is now used by the school's teachers. Keely is believed to have designed some 700 churches across the country during his lifetime.

4. At 90 Greene Avenue, **The Clinton** was built ca. 1870 as a tenement house. Coinciding with the upgrading of the area at the end of the 19th century, the house was rebuilt in 1890 as a luxury "French flats," or apartment house for the affluent. "Tenement house" in those days did not have quite the negative connotation it does today—it was merely a multiple dwelling for the poorer classes.

Note how the old trolley tracks are again becoming visible through the macadam, at the intersection of Greene and Vanderbilt avenues. Brooklyn's trolley empire was one of the largest in the world by the turn of the century. The last line disappeared in 1955.

Turn left (east) on Greene Avenue to Vanderbilt Avenue.

5. The small residence at **375 Vanderbilt Avenue** was built originally as a stable in the mid-1880s.

6. The charming clapboard house at the southeast corner of Vanderbilt and Lafayette avenues presents something of an architectural mystery. Known officially as the **Joseph Steele House,** and locally as the Skinner House (after the family that has lived in it since 1900), its precise history is unclear. The two-story section that now serves as a wing was built in Federal style, probably in 1812 when the "Hill" area was a remote, rural farmland. In the 1840s the main section was added in Greek Revival style. The house, which was actually located about 150 yards farther east, was moved to the present site around 1853 to make way for the construction of the Clinton Avenue Congregational Church, and further alterations were made—this time in the *Italianate* style! The roof was raised and certain Renaissance features added: the elaborate cornice, a new entranceway, and pedimented lintels over the front windows. It is likely that the wooden cupola dates from this latest modification, but it could be earlier. In spite of the lack of architectural integrity, the Steele (or Skinner) House is a delightful addition to the cityscape.

7. The Catholic Church (and School) of Queen of All Saints, on the northwest corner, was designed by Gustave Steinback in 1911. An impressive edifice, its splendid collection of stained-glass windows suggests the Sainte-Chapelle in Paris, while the 36 excellent sculptures of saints are reminiscent of St. Peter's in Rome. The building of the church was commissioned by George Mundelein, pastor of St. John's parish, who went on to be named Cardinal of Chicago. Oldtimers still refer to it as "Bishop Mundelein's Church." The bishop originally intended this to be the Cathedral Church for the projected Brooklyn Cathedral across the street. The interior, considered a fine example of Gothic-style architecture, has a narrow nave that sets off the magnificent windows, which contain no fewer than 22,882 pieces of stained glass in each complete mosaic window! The windows were manufactured by the Locke Decorative Company, in 1913.

Turn right on Lafayette Avenue to Clinton Avenue.

8. The Cadman Memorial Church is a relative newcomer to Clinton Hill. It was erected in 1923 to replace an earlier Gothic church built in 1853, which had been designed by noted architect James Renwick, Jr. Three beautiful Tiffany art-glass windows were saved from its predecessor, the Clinton Avenue Congregational Church, and incorporated into the design of the new building. In 1943 the congregation was merged with the Central Congregational Church and renamed in memory of the Central Church's former minister, Dr. S. Parkes Cadman. It was the Rev. Cadman who delivered the dedicatory invocation for the Prison Ship Martyrs' Monument in nearby Fort Greene Park [*see* Fort Greene, 7]. He was also the nation's first radio preacher, and was recognized by the City of New York for his activity in community affairs by the naming of downtown Brooklyn's Cadman Plaza.

9. The Clinton Hill Apartments, Section No. 2 of the Clinton Hill Development, were built in 1955 (Harrison & Abramovitz, Irwin Clavan) for families of naval personnel and workers in the nearby New York Naval Shipyard. Each entranceway has a different nautical motif.

10. Tree-lined **Clinton Avenue** still retains its 1880-period charm in the four-block stretch between Gates and Willoughby avenues. Turn right and walk a half-block, and return, observing the variety of styles of architecture.

At the turn of the century, Clinton Avenue was known as the "Fifth Avenue of Brooklyn," and nowhere is this more evident than in the next two blocks north, from Lafayette to DeKalb and Willoughby avenues. Walking on the left side of Clinton Avenue, look at **No. 324,** with a balustrade atop its nicely restored mansard roof, drip mouldings over the windows, and a Classic-style portico. Across the street, **No. 321** is equally eclectic, with both Victorian and Italianate details. **Nos. 315** and **313** are a pair of fanciful Queen Anne–style houses.

Turn right (east) on DeKalb Avenue.

11. Two imposing groups of ca. 1890 town houses bracket DeKalb Avenue near the corner of Waverly Avenue: **Nos. 285–289** with a highly ornate terra-cotta frieze unifying the trio of brick and brownstone buildings, and **Nos. 284–288.** The houses are enormous, and when erected were designed for single-family occupancy. Today they are subdivided into small apartments. Nevertheless the effect is still that of an aristocratic Old English street, with its pleasant mixture of Queen Anne and Romanesque Revival details.

Turn left (north) briefly on Waverly Avenue.

Although it is not within the purview of this guidebook to recommend restaurants, it is not unlikely that hunger has now replaced architecture and history as a primary concern. And inasmuch as there are few places of refreshment in the immediate vicinity, it is fortunate that **Joe's Place** offers good food at modest prices, in a converted carriage house at 264 Waverly Avenue. The simple exterior gives little hint as to the warm and cozy atmosphere inside. The interior garden is particularly pleasant in warm weather. Should Joe's be closed, all is not lost. There are also several modest restaurants along DeKalb Avenue, such as Mike's Coffee Shop, near Pratt Institute, at DeKalb Avenue and St. James Place.

Observe how narrow Waverly Avenue is, compared to Clinton and Washington avenues. Originally the stables and carriage houses of the wealthy residents were located on this street between the two "fashionable" streets.

Return to DeKalb Avenue, and turn right to Clinton Avenue, then right again.

12. No. 275 Clinton Avenue is a well-preserved triple-section luxury apartment building, built ca. 1895.

Across Clinton Avenue, **No. 282** is a stick and shingle-style Victorian house with some Gothic touches, built ca. 1875, and is appropriate in appearance to the bucolic atmosphere of the neighborhood at that time. Adjacent is the wildly

Clinton Avenue between DeKalb and Willoughby avenues ca. 1895, showing three mansions built by petroleum industrialist Charles Pratt for his children. Clinton Avenue justly earned the reputation of being the "Fifth Avenue of Brooklyn." The scene is virtually the same today, only the homeowners are different. (Brooklyn Collection. Brooklyn Public Library)

eclectic **No. 278,** with a corner tower set at a 45-degree angle. **No. 266** is worthy of a passing glance.

13. The block between DeKalb and Willoughby avenues is a living memorial to the **Pratt family,** and unquestionably the most beautiful in Clinton Hill. No less than four family mansions survive, and in pristine condition. Although now in other hands, they are still lovingly preserved.

When Charles Pratt built his huge oil refinery at Kent Avenue and North 12th Street in the Greenpoint section of Brooklyn in 1867, he made his fortune with a successful coal-oil product called "Astral Oil." So widely used was this high-grade kerosene that it was said that "the holy lamps of Tibet are lit with 'Astral Oil.'" The kerosene's advantage and major selling point was its relative safety. It had a higher flash point than competing oils, and would not explode—a virtue that soon made Astral Oil a household term, and helped Pratt make a fortune. In 1874 Pratt became associated with John D. Rockefeller, and the firm was merged with the Standard Oil Company. He settled on Clinton Avenue and subsequently built homes for three of his sons in the same block, presenting each with a lovely mansion as a wedding present. And across the street is the magnificent trio of gifts:

No. 245, now occupied by a department of St. Joseph's College, was built by Pratt for son George DuPont Pratt in 1901. A large, stately mansion, it was designed by the architectural firm of Babb, Cook & Willard in a restrained Georgian style.

No. 241 was built for eldest son Charles Millard Pratt in 1893. Designed by William B. Tubby in Romanesque Revival style, it is probably the most elegant of all his wedding-gift houses. To the south of the building is a conservatory built in semicircular shape; and illuminating the spectacular arched porte-cochère is a decorative spherical bronze lamp (which probably burned "Astral Oil"). The mansion is now the residence of the Roman Catholic Bishop of Brooklyn.

No. 229, now the Caroline Ladd Pratt House, was built for son Frederick B. Pratt in 1898. The gray-and-white Georgian Revival–style house was designed by the same architects as No. 245, and presents a most unusual appearance, attached on its left and freestanding on the right. Atlantean figures and caryatids support a kind of pergola above a colonnaded entranceway.

No. 232, across the street, is the "daddy" of them all—the original Charles Pratt manor house, built ca. 1875. Designed in an Italianate style, the building and picturesque gardens are virtually unchanged—a credit to St. Joseph's College, the present owner. Pratt's fourth son, Harold I., chose instead to live on Manhattan's fashionable Park Avenue, building a mansion of his own in 1920, which still stands at the corner of East 68th Street.

Across the avenue, Nos. 221–225 are an attractive row of town houses, originally designed for single-family occupancy.

Turn right (east) on Willoughby Avenue.

14. Nos. 112–122 Willoughby Avenue are an interesting row of middle-class town houses. Note the swags, or garlands, on the shallow bay windows, and the paired L-shaped entrance stairs.

The Main Building of Pratt Institute on Ryerson Street in 1910, designed in an "industrial Romanesque" style. Charles Pratt founded the institution in 1887 and ran it as his own private project. Adjacent to the right is South Hall, and at the extreme left is the original building of Pratt's Thrift Bank of Brooklyn, demolished in 1915 to make way for Memorial Hall. The school still maintains high standards in its major fields of science and art. (Brooklyn Collection. Brooklyn Public Library)

Continue east on Willoughby Avenue past Hall Street (St. James Place) to the entrance to the Pratt Institute Campus.

15. Pratt Institute was the pet project of Charles Pratt himself. Founded in 1887 and dedicated to science and art, it was directed personally by the industrialist until his death in 1891. The school has an enviable reputation in the fields of art and design, fashion, architecture, engineering and science, and food science and management.

Entering the campus on Ryerson Walk (formerly Ryerson Street, and now demapped), the first building on the left is North Hall, followed by the neo-Byzantine–style **Memorial Hall,** designed in 1927 by John Mead Howells. Adjacent on the right is the original 1887 **Main Building,** designed by Lamb & Rich in an industrial Romanesque Revival style, with its wing, **South Hall.**

Between the Main and South buildings is an iron gate. Enter and walk through the courtyard, past the fountain, to the **East Building,** built at the same time as the Main Building, but designed by John Mead Howells. Originally the Machine Shop

Building, it houses Pratt Institute's unofficial **Industrial Archaeology Museum.** Here on display to the public are the Ames Iron Works steam engines, installed in 1900 and still furnishing 120 volts of direct current to the campus. A number of other 19th-century artifacts are also exhibited: a steam whistle from the DeLavergne Refrigerating Company's ca. 1875 factory in the Bronx, chandeliers from the Singer Tower's board room, and the humorous "No Loafing" sign from the old Jacob Ruppert Brewery in Yorkville, plus other items from our early industrial era.

When Pratt Institute expanded its campus in the 1950s and '60s, a number of streets were closed and several unneeded buildings demolished, resulting in a five-square-block campus area in which the remaining school buildings stand in "splendid isolation."

The **Pratt Institute Library,** across the walk from South Hall, was built by the school's industrialist-benefactor as Brooklyn's first free public library. Completed in 1896 from plans by William B. Tubby (who designed the Charles Millard Pratt House), and altered in 1936 by John Mead Howells, it is a dramatic Romanesque Revival building with some Renaissance details. The heavy brick piers on the west façade (facing Hall Street) give the building a massive and overwhelming aspect. Interesting is the entrance portico with its diminishing arches. Recent extensions to the Pratt Library were made by extending the basement and creating a plaza on top, thus avoiding any alterations to the visible landmark structure. Since 1940 the library has served the needs of the student body only, and is no longer open to the public.

In the small quadrangle beyond the library is a mounted **bronze cannon.** Considered a notable example of bronze foundry work, the highly ornate piece was cast in Spain in 1721 and sent to Havana in 1859. During the Spanish-American War, it was acquired by the board of trustees for the Pratt Art Collection.

To the left of the walk, just before the exit gate, is a Beaux Arts–style red brick and limestone-trim building emblazoned with a beehive and **The Thrift** in the frieze. This was the Thrift Bank of Brooklyn (Shampan & Shampan, 1916), and served depositors until the early 1940s when the bank went out of business, with the building then taken over for Pratt's administrative offices. The Thrift was founded in 1889 by Charles Pratt as one of his investments, and its original building stood on the site of Memorial Hall.

Leave the campus through the DeKalb Avenue gate, and turn right to Hall Street. Then cross DeKalb Avenue and continue south on St. James Place (the extension of Hall Street), past the University Terrace Apartments.

16. An unusual feature of the **University Terrace Apartments** (Kelly & Gruzen, 1963) are the rows of *recessed* balconies, rather than the usual overhanging type.

Continue to the corner of Lafayette Avenue.

17. The enormous pair of brick buildings on the southeast corner, extending to Clifton Place, is **Higgins Hall** (of Pratt Institute). Built in 1887–88 for the for-

mer Adelphi Academy (which has moved to Bay Ridge), the cornerstone was
laid by the outspoken anti-slavery preacher, Henry Ward Beecher. The honors
for the adjacent South Building's cornerstone were performed by Charles Pratt.
The structures are a veritable exercise book in Romanesque Revival motifs, with
their towering piers, corbel tables, and round arches.

Across the street, **Nos. 63–67** form an odd trio of narrow row houses (two bays
wide), of ca. 1875, with large arched doorways and a rather nice mansard roof.

18. Clifton Place, from St. James Place to Grand Avenue, is lined with middle-class row houses dating from the 1870s, set back from the street with pleasant front gardens. Standing at the corner, look down St. James Place at the unre-
lieved rows of brownstones that extend as far as the eye can see, in mute
testimony to Brooklyn's uncontested reputation as the city with the greatest
number of brownstone row houses.

Return to Lafayette Avenue and turn left (west).

19. The Emmanuel Baptist Church was built like a French 13th-century
Gothic cathedral, and its massive square twin towers dominate the entire area.
Architect Francis H. Kimball, who designed it in 1886, employed Ohio sand-
stone, which is by nature somewhat porous, thus creating an effect of aging. The
plan of the interior is in startling contrast, with its radial seating plan spreading
fanlike from the pulpit. The style is similar to that of the First Baptist Church on
Broadway and West 79th Street in Manhattan [*see* West of Central Park, 15].
The church was cited in 1957 for its architectural distinction by the Municipal
Art Society and the Society of Architectural Historians. The adjoining rectory
(to the left) was erected in 1926, but its harmonious design and use of similar
building materials render it almost indistinguishable from the style of the main
structure.

20. The neighboring **Apostolic Faith Mission,** at the northeast corner of
Lafayette and Washington avenues, was built in 1868 as the Orthodox Friends
Meeting House. In restrained Northern Italian, or Lombardian Romanesque
style, it has been "brightened" by coats of white paint with tuscan-red trim.

Turn left (south) on Washington Avenue, for a brief detour.

21. Washington Avenue, between Lafayette and Greene avenues, is a vir-
tual encyclopedia of architectural styles, fads, and fancies. Note the following
houses with their special features: **No. 353,** with added Classic-style porch and
sawtooth ornamentation under the cornice but with its side columns missing,
thus leaving the arches suspended in mid-air! (Hopefully it will soon be
restored.) **Nos. 357** and **359** are a pair of magnificently restored and charming
Greek Revival–style wooden houses with lovely attic windows. **No. 361** is a tall
red brick and brownstone Queen Anne–style house whose oversize bay window
almost hides the delicate entranceway, plus Adam-style swags that ornament a
Classic cornice below a mansard roof. Note, too, its rectangular terra-cotta
plaques and the pair of tiny circular plaques with a griffin or dragon with a beak

in each, and the stained glass in the round-arch windows on the parlor floor. **No. 363** has been remodeled into a neo-Georgian house. Across the street, **No. 364** is an especially engaging house, with its square porch colonnettes supporting a double-bracketed roof, the oriels on the south side, and segmental arc window lintels on the second floor, plus a *rundbogenstil* frieze. (Ignore the ugly protuberance on the roof.)

Walk beyond **No. 374** and look back—a Queen Anne–style house whose clean and largely restored square tower with pyramidal roof and cast-iron finial are best appreciated at a distance. Just beyond the public library, **Nos. 388** and **390** are a fine pair of Italianate brownstones whose red brick side walls rise to a peaked roof and delicately carved cornice. Both houses are balanced with angular protruding bay windows and paired porticos.

No. 379, the Renaissance Eclectic–style **former Hotel Mohawk,** is a good example of how historic district designation, Federal tax subsidies, the city's J-51 Program, and local support (from the Pratt Area Community Council) all combined to facilitate the rehabilitation of this once-dilapidated building. The old hotel had fallen on hard times and became a severe blight on the neighborhood. Unfortunately, project delays and shifts in city housing policies forced the developer to abandon his middle-income rental goal for this 85-unit complex

The former Adelphi Academy at St. James Place and Lafayette Avenue, photographed in 1896. The building is now part of Pratt Institute and was renamed Higgins Hall. The cornerstone was laid in 1887 by Henry Ward Beecher, and is almost a textbook example of the Romanesque Revival style. (Brooklyn Historical Society)

and shift to a much higher market rate condominium, thus threatening gentrification of this stable, integrated, middle-class community.

No. 402, at the southwest corner of Greene Avenue, has an imposing two-story-high oriel that dominates the entire corner. Diagonally across the intersection is a free-standing house, similar to No. 364, but with a Second Empire mansard roof. It is handsomely restored, and although it has been carved up into apartments, it has been refurbished to convey the appearance of a single-family home. Nice!

Return to Lafayette Avenue.

22. Underwood Park, at the corner of Lafayette and Washington avenues, is named for typewriter king John T. Underwood, who donated the plot to the city. His family mansion, which formerly stood on the site, was a red brick and brownstone structure with a glass-enclosed greenhouse, and was demolished, according to his will, to make way for the park.

Turn right (north) on Washington Avenue.

23. One of the oldest structures of its kind in the city is the **former Graham Home for Old Ladies,** at 320 Washington Avenue. Built in 1851 on land

The Graham Home for Old Ladies at the corner of Washington and DeKalb avenues, now a disreputable hotel, was originally named The Brooklyn Society for the Relief of Respectable Aged Indigent Females. Erected in 1851, it is little changed from the outside. (Brooklyn Historical Society)

The dining room of the Brooklyn Society for the Relief of Respectable Aged and Indigent Females in the mid-19th century. The building is now a hotel. (Brooklyn Historical Society)

donated by Underwood, it served for many years as a home for the aged, and was converted into a hotel in the early 1970s. The cornerstone was laid by founder John B. Graham, and the institution named the Brooklyn Society for the Relief of Respectable Aged Indigent Females. According to its charter, it was designed "for the benefit of poor gentlewomen who had been unfitted by previous culture and refinement to accept willingly the public asylum provided by the State for the poor indiscriminately." One wonders what those "respectable poor gentlewomen" might think if they could see the recently changed name of the establishment, Bull Shippers Plaza Motor Inn—an indignity to the neighborhood and an unfortunate (and hopefully temporary) note on which to end the tour.

End of tour. The A and C lines subway station is at the corner of Lafayette and Washington avenues.

20. Historic Flushing

[No. 7 Flushing line to Main Street (travel time about 45 minutes); Long Island Rail Road, Port Washington Branch, from Pennsylvania Station to Flushing–Main Street (travel time 17 minutes)]

Among the earliest settlements in the Dutch colony of New Netherlands was the town of Vlissingen, now known as Flushing. In the charter granted by Governor William Kieft in 1645, six years after he purchased the land from the Matinecock Indians, a sub-tribe of the Algonkian Nation, the original 18 freeholders were assured of their freedom of religious worship. Although the town was named for its Dutch counterpart in Flanders, the settlers were all English. The tiny village on the north shore of Long Island soon figured in one of the great events in the cause of religious freedom in America. With the arrival in 1657 of a group of English Quakers, newly appointed Governor Peter Stuyvesant, ignoring the original charter, issued a proclamation banning all religious observance but the official Dutch Reformed.

In angry response, 30 townspeople signed a document of protest on December 27, 1657, known as the **"Flushing Remonstrance."** Stuyvesant's reaction was swift. A detachment of militia was dispatched to Flushing where all signers were arrested and fined. This did not put an end, however, to meetings by the Religious Society of Friends, as they gathered secretly in the house of a newly arrived Englishman, John Bowne, who invited them to worship in his kitchen. When news of this act of disobedience reached Governor Stuyvesant, he again took punitive action, imprisoning Bowne for a period of several months, then banishing him from the colony. Nevertheless, Bowne ultimately reached Amsterdam, where he successfully pleaded the cause of religious freedom before the Council of the Dutch West India Company. The Council then sent a strong letter to Peter Stuyvesant stating in no uncertain terms that all men could exercise freedom of conscience. The Quakers continued to meet in the Bowne House until a meeting house was built in 1694. Both buildings still remain and will be visited on the tour.

In 1684 the freeholders of Flushing purchased from a group of Matinecocks a broad track of land that extended from Flushing Creek as far east as Hempstead, and south to the Jamaica line. Payment was one axe for each 30 acres, with the Indians reserving the right to cut bulrushes.

Flushing prospered for almost 200 years as one of several independent towns in what is now the borough of Queens, until 1898 when it was consolidated into the City of New York. With the opening of the Queensboro Bridge to Manhattan in 1909 and the Long Island Rail Road tunnel to Pennsylvania Station a year later, Flushing grew rapidly. In 1928 the subway arrived, opening the suburb for even more development. La Guardia Airport was built across Flushing Bay in 1939, the same year the New York World's Fair was inaugurated in nearby Flushing Meadow Park. In 1964–65 a second World's Fair was held at the same site, and with the accompanying construction of several major expressways, Flushing became another extension of the city's urban sprawl.

In recent years Flushing has become one of the most ethnically diverse neighborhoods in the country. The 1960s and early '70s witnessed the arrival of many Puerto Ricans and blacks, but by the end of the '70s and into the decade of the '80s, the area had become a mecca for a large-scale immigration of Asians. So many Koreans, Japanese, Chinese, Indians, and Southeast Asians have arrived that Flushing is often called **"Little Asia."** Add to this a number of Haitians and Latin Americans from many South American countries, plus a goodly number of Russians, and the mix is enormous. The variety of national and racial backgrounds is immediately apparent in the multilingual signs along Main Street and in the faces of the people who throng the thoroughfares; however, the majority of new arrivals are now the Orientals.

Main Street, looking north toward Northern Boulevard from Thirty-seventh Avenue in 1914. Trolleys and horses were the major form of transportation in what still appears to be a typical small town. (Queens Borough Public Library)

A supply of beer has just been delivered by horse and wagon to Edward McCormick's "Klondyke" at 115 Main Street, ca. 1910. (Wiener Collection. Queens Borough Public Library)

Part of the annual Farmers' Parade in front of the Fountain House, at the southeast corner of Main Street and Northern Boulevard, ca. 1898. The Fountain House was a small hotel and saloon, on the "other side of the tracks" from the elegant Flushing Hotel. (Queens Borough Public Library)

St. George's Episcopal Church is the third structure on the site. This view of the second building shows it on Lincoln Street (now Thirty-eighth Avenue) in 1903. It was moved around the corner from Main Street in 1854 to make way for the new church, 33 years after it was built, and was used until 1930. The steeple of the present St. George's is visible at the left. (New-York Historical Society)

John Geddes' Paint Store, at 105 Main Street, ca. 1898. Note the hitching posts and stepping stone. (Wiener Collection, Queens Borough Public Library)

Battery-operated streetcar on Main Street, opposite the stately Flushing Hotel on Broadway (now Northern Boulevard), ca. 1900. The hotel was the center of Flushing social life during the latter 19th and early 20th centuries, and is now the site of the abandoned R.K.O. Keith's movie house. (David G. Oats, Flushing Tribune*)*

So many historic landmarks remain in a relatively small area that local historical societies have designated it as Flushing's "Freedom Mile." (*Note: The best day to visit is Saturday or Sunday when virtually all of the points of interest are open to the public.*)

The tour begins at the intersection of Main Street and Roosevelt Avenue.

Walk north on Main Street, the principal thoroughfare and commercial district of Flushing. The **Chamber of Commerce Building,** No. 39–01 Main Street, at the southeast corner of Thirty-ninth Avenue, is an interesting example of Art Deco style with polychrome tile spandrels and entranceway.

To the west on 39th Avenue is the new multistory **Sheraton LaGuardia East Hotel.** With its entrance flanked by Oriental lions and other Far Eastern motifs, it harmonizes with the neighborhood's ethnic (and mostly Oriental) community. The hotel, owned by Taiwanese interests, is the first to be built in Flushing in almost a century, and boasts an indoor shopping mall, meeting rooms, and a ballroom.

Diagonally across the street is **St. George's Episcopal Church,** occupying the entire block to Thirty-eighth Avenue. An earlier church on the site was built in 1746 and received its charter in 1761 from King George III of England. A

The Prince House, located until the late 1950s at the intersection of Northern Boulevard and Prince Street. William Prince established the first tree nursery in the country in 1737. (David G. Oats, Flushing Tribune)

subsequent house of worship replaced it in 1821, and the present structure dates from 1854. Built in Gothic Revival style from plans by Wills & Dudley, its graceful spire—alas, remodeled with wood shingles—is the tallest landmark in Flushing. Francis Lewis, signer of the Declaration of Independence from New York, served here as churchwarden and vestryman from 1769 to 1790. Peek over the iron fence at the early churchyard which contains the graves of many of the early residents. In keeping with Flushing's changing demographics, St. George's also conducts services in Chinese and Spanish.

Little evidence remains of what Main Street looked like at the turn of the century when it became the main commercial thoroughfare of Flushing; however, a few vestiges can be found, disguised behind numerous remodelings and "modernizations." Directly across the street from St. George's Church, on the northeast corner of Thirty-eighth Avenue, is **No. 38–01,** an aging house with a Second Empire mansard roof and dormers.

On the northeast corner of Main Street and Thirty-seventh Avenue is a branch of the Bank of New York, designed in Art Deco style. Erected for the Flushing National Bank in 1929, its smooth limestone façade with low-relief "modernistic" sculpture and octagon-shaped clock are typical of the period. On the northwest corner of Thirty-seventh Avenue (re-named for the late Queens Congressman Rosenthal) is a red brick house, partially hidden by a furniture store sign, that is typical of those that lined Main Street in the 1870s.

At the head of Main Street, on Northern Boulevard, is the **former RKO Keith's** movie house (Thomas Lamb, 1928). A popular vaudeville theater when it opened, its stage is said to have launched the careers of a number of Hollywood stars. The theater occupies the site of the old Flushing Hotel, a rambling wooden structure whose double tiers of broad porches and well appointed parlors made it the focal point in the 1880s and '90s of Flushing's social life.

After the theater was "triplexed" in 1976, the ornate Spanish Baroque–style interior decor could no longer be seen. At one time the theater boasted machinery that could create the illusion of clouds floating across a sky of twinkling stars—an effect that was even extended to the ceiling of the lavish lobby.

The theater is now closed, and at this writing it is abandoned, its ornate exterior details stripped to the bare gray walls, with a "for sale" sign that is several years old. Efforts to preserve the theater, whose interior was gutted without permission, and is still a designated landmark, have been in vain. The developer claimed that landmark status prevented him from carrying out a viable reconstruction as a shopping mall, but this was hotly contested by local preservationists. At the height of the Save-the-Keith's campaign, former Keith's star Milton Berle, who appeared on its stage six times, was quoted as saying in his comic routines, "This is the only Flushing that never went down the drain"...which remains to be seen.

To the left of the theater, from Prince Street down to Flushing Creek, was the world famous **Prince Nursery.** Established in 1737 by William Prince, it was the first tree nursery in the country. Known later as the Linnaean Botanic Garden, it provided thousands of tree specimens from all over the world. George Washington was a guest at the garden in 1789. Although it is now long since gone, the heritage of William Prince's old nursery lives on in the more than 200 species of trees growing throughout the country.

A scene in the Flushing Town Hall's court room, ca. 1895. Flushing was an independent town until 1898, when it joined the City of New York. The Town Hall then became the Court House. (Wiener Collection, Queens Borough Public Library)

The "island" in the middle of Northern Boulevard marks the center of **Daniel Carter Beard Memorial Square.** "Dan" Beard (1850–1941), a naturalist and illustrator, and a native of Flushing, was one of the founders of the Boy Scouts of America, and the first Scout Commissioner. He was known to generations of boys as "Uncle Dan." Among his noted illustrations were those made for Mark Twain's *A Connecticut Yankee in King Arthur's Court.* He served as National Scout Commissioner until his death. The Square was dedicated in 1943. (Walk right, east, along the center island.)

The flagpole is Flushing's **Spanish-American War Memorial,** erected in 1950. On the east side of the pedestal is a plaque cast from a piece of the battleship *Maine.* To the west of the flagpole are two dogwood trees planted as a Vietnam War Memorial, and to the east are two rows of four cherry trees, which must be seen in the spring! At one time there were five elm trees on the site, but they all fell victim to the Dutch elm disease and to auto pollution. The fifth elm, which had been planted in 1932 and which survived until the mid-1980s, was known as the Washington Elm, as it was planted to recall George Washington's visit to Flushing in 1789.

To the right, opposite Linden Place, is the **Friends Meeting House,** the oldest house of worship in New York City and one of the earliest in the country. Built in 1694, with an addition in 1717, it provided a permanent place for religious observance for those who first met secretly in the home of John Bowne. Except for a period during the Revolutionary War when the occupying British forces used it as a prison, a hospital, and a storage place for hay, the Meeting House has been in continuous use for almost 300 years. The plain, rectangular building with a hip roof faces south—away from the winter winds—toward an interior burial ground. Two doorways on the open front porch originally served as separate entrances for men and women. Devoid of ornamentation, the simple meeting room with its plastered walls and unfinished wood benches reflects the Quaker spirit, which calls for undistracted devotion. Hand-hewn 40-foot oak beams, cut from a single tree, are still in place on the second story, and are as solid as the day they were installed. Timbers from a dismantled sailing ship were used in the 1717 section and ships' "knees" can be seen supporting the ceiling beams. One of two early cast-iron heating stoves dating from 1760, and used until 1956, is on display in the Meeting House, while the original hand-wrought iron door hinges, latches, and locks are still in use. The churchyard, no longer used for interments, contains simple, low stones inscribed with the names of many prominent Long Islanders of the early 19th century. Headstones placed before 1835 bear no inscriptions. The Friends Meeting House, because of its great historical significance is listed in the National Register of Historic Places. Visitors are welcome to visit the Meeting House and grounds, and to attend Sunday-morning worship meetings.

The **Civil War Monument** and surrounding mini-garden were erected in 1866 in memory of the young volunteers of the Flushing Battery who died in the tragic war to preserve the Union. The funds to build the monument were raised through public subscription. Try to decipher the fading inscription on the east side of the pedestal.

Across Northern Boulevard, at the corner of Linden Street, is the **Flushing Town Hall,** recently the Flushing Municipal Court House. Saved at the last minute from the wrecker's ball, it is now well protected as a designated New York City Landmark. Built in 1862 by Cornelius Howard, a local carpenter, in an early Romanesque Revival style, the Flushing Town Hall served the community until 1900 as a center of civic, cultural, and social life. Before the consolidation of Greater New York in 1898, Flushing was one of a number of independent Queens communities with its own seat of government, and its town hall is one of the few such surviving municipal landmarks. In addition to its role as a town meeting house and seat of local government, it hosted a variety of public events. The Hall witnessed celebration balls, political meetings, community gatherings, and even operas and concerts. It was also the headquarters of the local Volunteer Artillery Unit. When it gave up its function as a municipal courthouse in the 1960s, it was slated for demolition. Faced with the loss of their oldest civic structure, concerned citizens and local historical societies raised a storm of protest, which ultimately convinced the city fathers of the need to preserve this picturesque and historic landmark. Note the tall, thin buttresses, the paired arched windows and door with drip moldings, the brick corbels under the cornice, and a charming porch, complete with its "Town Hall" sign.

The Flushing Quaker Meeting House on the south side of Northern Boulevard in the early 1930s. The building faces south, away from winter's north winds. Built in 1694, it is New York's oldest house of worship. (Queens Borough Public Library)

In the Quaker Meeting House, a "ship's knee," removed from an old sailing vessel, helps support a 40-foot beam, hand-hewn in 1717 from a tall oak. (Office of the Borough President of Queens)

After enduring a number of abortive attempts at adaptive reuse, the venerable landmark has finally found a legitimate sponsor, the not-for-profit Flushing Council on Culture & The Arts at Town Hall, a multicultural arts center. Opened to the public in 1993 after a precedent-setting public/private partnership for reconstruction, it boasts a professional art gallery, Jazz Cafe, Visitors' Center, plus performance and rehearsal space and offices, as well as a consortium of smaller cultural organizations.

Also sharing office space is Chief Osceola Townsend of the Matinecock Tribe, and the National Alliance of Native Americans. Although there are other Indian groups in New York City, the Matinecocks are the last remaining tribe in existence within city limits.

Farther down the center mall is the **World War I Memorial Monument,** erected to honor those men of Flushing who lost their lives in the "War to end all Wars." Executed in pink-veined marble by famed sculptor Hermon Atkins MacNeil in 1925, it is best viewed from the north side of the Boulevard. Like the Civil War Monument, it was financed through public subscription.

Reminiscent of a medieval castle is the red brick **New York State National Guard Armory.** With its twin turrets, crenelations, machicolations, tower and ramparts, it resembles a medieval fortress. Built in 1905 in the typical "armory architectural style" popular in the late 19th and early 20th centuries, it still conveys an impression of strength and security. On the site stood the house of Michael Milnor, where in 1657 the Flushing Remonstrance was signed, touching off the first struggle for religious freedom in America. The City of New York is using the Armory temporarily as sleeping quarters for homeless women.

To the left of the Armory, and attached to the rear of the adjacent former Masonic Temple (now the Korean Siloam Reformed Church) is a two-story red brick structure which once served as the **meeting house for a breakaway group of Quakers.** Objecting to the liberal tendencies of preacher Elias Hicks, a

The Samuel Bowne Parsons House stood on the site of Flushing High School's annex, on Broadway (now Northern Boulevard), opposite Bowne Street. Parsons maintained a tree nursery in the mid-19th century and many of his plantings are still to be seen throughout Flushing, particularly the weeping beech and Cedar of Lebanon near the Bowne House. (Queens Borough Public Library)

schism developed, and the more orthodox group separated itself from the "Hicksites," erecting this building in 1827 as their own house of worship. The sect has long since disappeared. If the Armory's parking lot is open, tiptoe in, and examine the rear of the old meeting house, with its ancient brickwork and leaning chimneys.

Flushing High School (C. B. J. Snyder, 1912–15), on the north side of the Boulevard, was built in the then-popular Collegiate Gothic style. The building replaced an earlier structure located a few blocks west, which received its first charter in 1875. Snyder was the superintendent of school buildings and designed many of the city's schools. His campus design is reminiscent of Oxford or Cambridge University in England. Flushing High is the oldest free public high school in the City of New York. The newer east wing was completed in 1954 and is dedicated to those students who gave their lives in World War II. Flushing High School is not only a designated city landmark, but is also listed on the National Register of Historic Places.

Directly opposite Flushing High School, and to the right of the present Y.M.C.A. Building (1925), stood the **old Aspinwall House,** built in 1762. During the Revolutionary War it became the headquarters of the officer corps of the occupying British Army; and in the Civil War it was a station on the Underground Railroad, helping escaping slaves reach freedom. It is said that a

A sketch of the Bowne House at it appeared ca. 1790. The "salt box" was built by John Bowne in 1661 and is considered a shrine to religious freedom in America. (Bowne House Historical Society)

secret tunnel connected the Aspinwall House with the nearby Bowne House, where these runaways were hidden and cared for while awaiting passage on a ship to New England. Unfortunately, the house was razed in the late 1950s.

Turn right at the Y.M.C.A. into Bowne Street.

About 150 yards down the street is a large gray boulder known as the **Fox Oaks Rock.** George Fox, who founded the Religious Society of Friends in England in 1645, came to America to preach in 1672. He intended to hold his meeting in the Bowne House, but the turnout was so great that he was forced to hold it outdoors under some tall oak trees opposite the house. The oaks have disappeared, but the site is marked with the inscription on the rock.

The **Bowne House,** across the street, is a landmark shrine to religious freedom and was built in 1661. Little did John Bowne anticipate when he arrived in Flushing in 1655 that he would be the central figure in a monumental struggle for freedom of religious observance—freedom for a sect to which he did not even belong at the time! That he would defy the law, be arrested, fined, imprisoned, and banished, later to return a hero, never entered his mind.

The Quakers had been holding clandestine worship meetings in nearby woods when Bowne built his home, embraced Quakerism, and invited the Friends to meet in his spacious kitchen. The rest is history. And the well-built house survives intact as a memorial to the accomplishments of this courageous, soft-spoken man. The House is now a museum maintained by the Bowne House Historical Society, which purchased it in 1945, and it is open to the public on Tuesdays, Saturdays, and Sundays, 2:30 to 4:30 P.M. (Adults $2.00; children and seniors $1.00.) The furnishings of the house are all original, with additions provided by each of the successive nine generations of Bowne descendants who lived in it until 1946. A number of periods are represented in the house's fine collection of antiques. Extensions were added to the house in 1680 and 1696— the latter a "salt box" section, with sloping roof. Additional living space was provided in 1830 when the roof on the main house was raised and an extra wing added. The kitchen is the focal point of the house, just as it was when John Bowne entertained George Fox and, later, William Penn.*

---

*It was William Penn, usually thought of only in connection with Pennsylvania, who in 1683 persuaded the Duke of York to grant permission to the towns of Long Island to establish their own Representative Assembly. This body then drafted its historic Charter of Liberties, almost 100 years before the Declaration of Independence!

The Kingsland House, on its former site at 155th Street near Roosevelt Avenue, is the only landmark that had to be relocated before it could be designated. The house was built in 1774 as a middle-class farm house, and has been moved twice. It is now a museum and stands adjacent to Weeping Beech Park. (Office of the Borough President of Queens)

The kitchen has been restored to its original appearance and is the oldest part of the house. Not only was this the center of culinary activities, but it was the center of most of the family's domestic activities. The kitchen even housed overnight guests. Its enormous fireplace could easily roast an ox, and the "beehive" oven extends through the fireplace wall.

The wooden shed in the garden shelters a huge cast-iron cauldron formerly used for washing clothes. In the garden is the **Remonstrance Monument** with a plaque containing the complete text and list of signers of the Flushing Remonstrance. To the rear of the house is a typical herb garden. The original Bowne property extended north for some distance and included much of the land up to where Flushing High School is now located.

After leaving the Bowne House, turn right on Bowne Street and enter the playground. Follow the path through to the cul-de-sac of Thirty-seventh Avenue.

Ahead to the left, the **Kingsland Homestead Museum** is New York City's only building that had to be relocated to maintain its landmark status. Built by

The great weeping beech, a city landmark, in 1926. The house to the left was demolished, and in its place stands the relocated Kingsland House. (Office of the Borough President of Queens)

Charles Doughty ca. 1785 as a typical middle-sized farmhouse, it was situated about one and a half miles east, at what is now the intersection of 155th Street and Northern Boulevard. "Kingsland" was named after Doughty's son-in-law, Joseph King, an English sea captain. In the early 19th century the house was acquired by William King Murray who moved the house to a site at 155th Street and Roosevelt Avenue. The Murray Hill section of Flushing is named for the family which occupied the house until 1932. An earlier relative, Robert Murray, owned a farm in the late 18th century on Manhattan's East River shore, and it is for him that the midtown Murray Hill neighborhood is named.

In 1965 "Kingsland" was scheduled for demolition to make way for a shopping center. The Kingsland Preservation Committee was organized to save the house, and after four years of painstaking effort and negotiation, the 200-year-old house was moved on a flat-bed trailer to its present site in Weeping Beech Park. The operation required the cooperation of nine city departments, plus the New York Telephone Company and Con Edison. Six hundred feet of telephone and utility wires had to be removed from the city streets before the 38-foot-high house could make the journey.

The two-story house represents both Dutch and English Colonial architectural styles, particularly in the gambrel roof, central chimney, and round-headed and quadrant window in the gables. It is the second-oldest house in Flushing and the only surviving house from the 18th century. "Kingsland" is owned by the Queens Historical Society and the land by New York City's Department of Parks and Recreation, and serves as a research center, social history museum, and an architectural structure representative of the post-Colonial era. It is the headquarters of the Queens Historical Society, and the house is listed on the National Register of Historic Places. Exhibits are presented throughout the year. (Open Tues., Sat., Sun., 2:30–4:30 P.M.; adults $2.00, children and seniors $1.00.)

At the rear of "Kingsland," in diminutive **Weeping Beech Park,** is one of the most extraordinary trees in the world. The weeping beech's enormous canopy of lush foliage presents an incredible vista of long, spreading branches reaching skyward, then arching gracefully to the ground, to create a charming, enclosed bower. The tree was planted by Samuel Parsons in 1847 from a small shoot brought by his son from Belgium. Parsons, who married into the Bowne family, established his nursery in 1838 on land obtained from his in-laws. Much of the nursery was located where the playground is today. Like the earlier Prince Nursery, Parsons grew many species of trees and specialized in exotic varieties that could adapt to the local environment. The lovely beech is one of his enduring successes. In the late 19th century the nurseries were moved to the Kissena Park district; however, a number of beautiful trees scattered throughout Flushing are reminders of the extensive horticultural industry. Flushing's involvement with trees is seen in the names of so many of its streets: Ash, Quince, Hawthorn, Laburnum, Maple, etc. The weeping beech is the "mother" of all weeping beeches in America. There are eight offspring in the park; wherever the beech's main root surfaces, a new tree develops. In the spring "mother beech" sprouts her leaves first, then the offspring sprout theirs. It is quite a sight to behold! It is the oldest tree of its kind in the country, and one of two official landmark trees

The Cedar of Lebanon tree in mid-19th century stood alone in this uncultivated field. Today the tree, a little the worse for wear, is almost lost in the center of a playground on Bowne Street, surrounded by other trees and apartment houses. (Queens Borough Public Library)

in New York City (the other is a magnolia grandiflora, in Brooklyn, at 679 Lafayette Avenue).

Another example of the legacy of the Parsons Nursery is the **Golden Larch** on the lawn of the Kingsland House, facing Thirty-seventh Avenue, considered a very rare species by the Queens Botanical Garden. In the fall, its pinelike needles turn golden yellow and drop off.

On returning to Bowne Street by the path alongside the playground, stop for a moment at the **Margaret I. Carmen Memorial Green,** just beyond the end of the Thirty-seventh Avenue dead end. Named for the educator and historian who dedicated her retirement years to the preservation of Flushing history, she was the president of the Bowne House Historical Society and is credited with having such historic structures as the Bowne House, Flushing Town Hall, and Friends Meeting House designated as landmarks. A few yards farther is the unusual **Cedar of Lebanon** in the middle of the playground; and at curbside on Bowne Street, a mighty **Swamp Oak.** These trees are living evidence of Samuel Parsons's horticultural skill; his name is also immortalized by Parsons Boulevard, the next major thoroughfare to the east. The local community is very protective of these unusual trees and is quick to alert the Queens Historical

Society whenever harm threatens. Not long ago the Golden Larch was struck by lightning and the top caught fire. A prompt call to the fire department by concerned citizens brought immediate rescue to the tree.

Turn left (south) on Bowne Street, past the Bowne House to the corner of Roosevelt Avenue.

On the northeast corner of Bowne Street and Roosevelt Avenue is the **Bowne Street Community Church.** Built in 1892 as the Protestant Reformed Church of Flushing, it is a descendant of the oldest denomination in New York, dating from 1628 when the Dutch Reformed Church was established in Nieuw Amsterdam. The church merged with the First Congregational Church of Flushing after the latter's 114-year-old building on Bowne Street and Thirty-eighth Avenue was destroyed by fire at Christmas 1970. Four years later the Church was incorporated as the Bowne Street Community Church, preserving the tradition of religious freedom established by John Bowne. The Church is also associated with the United Church of Christ. The massive red brick structure is Romanesque Revival in style, but its huge free-standing bell tower, somewhat Bohemian in style, dominates the corner. Note the elaborate detailing above the round-arched windows on the Roosevelt Avenue side.

On the northwest corner is the **site of "Dan" Beard's home.**

A half-block to the south is the "cut" used by the Long Island Railroad Port Washington Branch. The ancestor of this line was the Flushing North Side Railroad, which reached Flushing in 1854.

Daniel Carter Beard's home at the northwest corner of Roosevelt Avenue and Bowne Street in a 1941 sketch. The site is now a supermarket. (Queens Borough Public Library)

Turn right (west) on Roosevelt Avenue to Main Street (the No. 7 line and Long Island Rail Road stations), and the end of the "Freedom Mile" tour.

A most interesting side trip can be made to the Hindu Temple of North America, located eight and a half blocks south, at 45–47 Bowne Street, beyond the railroad overpass. Walking south on Bowne Street after Forty-first Avenue, the cross streets begin their *alphabetica botanica* with Ash, Beech, and Cherry avenues, etc. (If you have the strength, take a brief detour left on Ash Avenue for one block as far as Parsons Boulevard, and enjoy the variety of residential architecture on this shady street, from Classic and Moorish to Stick-and-Shingle styles.)

As you continue along Bowne Street, notice how the scale of the houses is more suggestive of a small town. Were it not for the armies of aluminum-siding and Permastone salesmen that invaded the neighborhood after World War II, the effect would be even more pronounced. After Cherry Street there is a small Hindu temple on the right; however, the big surprise will appear on the left just after Forty-fifth Avenue, almost to Holly Avenue.

The Hindu Temple of North America was erected over a period of several years in the late 1970s by artisans brought from India specifically for the task. The building is divided into three pavilions covered with intricate carvings of deities and other religious symbols, and surmounted by pyramidal roofs with gilt finials. Enter at the right-hand doorway, remove your shoes, and walk upstairs. (Visitors are welcome, but be respectful and unobtrusive.) The effect upon entering is so overwhelming that some time must be allowed to absorb it all. At the four corners of the marble-floor sanctuary are shrines to major deities, and dominating the center is the black Shrine of Lord Ganesha, the god with the elephant's trunk. On the walls are highly ornate sculptures of Vishnu, Siva, and many other deities of the Hindu pantheon; and scattered about the temple at different shrines are groups of monks and congregants chanting prayers, while in the background, bells are chimed and the air is perfumed with the aroma of exotic incense. (A small contribution would be appreciated.)

You can return quickly to the starting point of the tour by walking ahead to Holly Avenue, where the Q27 bus takes five minutes to reach Main Street and Roosevelt Avenue. (Turn right at the corner to the first yellow-painted curb for the bus stop.) Or, if you wish to walk back, retrace your steps on Bowne Street to Cherry Street, turn left to Kissena Boulevard, then right. At Sanford Avenue, note the neoclassic-style **Free Synagogue of Flushing,** built in 1926 from plans by Maurice Courland, a noted synagogue architect, and situated diagonally on its corner plot. For more than 60 years this Reform congregation has been a significant, if unofficial, landmark in Flushing. Just beyond on Sanford Avenue is a large Greek Revival–style "bungalow" built ca. 1905. It once stood on the corner of Kissena Boulevard, and served from 1917 to 1925 as the house of worship and community house of the Free Synagogue, when it was moved to its present site to make room for the new building. The house is now rented to the Windsor School.

Continue down Sanford Avenue to the northeast corner of Main Street. **The Flushing Branch of the U.S. Post Office** is an impressive Georgian-style building, erected in 1932, and designed by William W. Knowles and Dwight James Baum, with James A. Wetmore. Its imposing neo-Classic details, marble columns, limestone trim, and dark-red brick are a pleasant reminder of the days when government buildings combined function with aesthetics. Go inside and examine the murals executed by Vincent Aderente in 1933–34 that depict early scenes in the towns of Flushing, Corona, Douglaston, Forest Hills, Bayside, etc. Turn right (north) on Main Street, which joins Kissena Boulevard one block ahead at the Flushing Public Library.

The Long Island Rail Road Station is just beyond the viaduct; turn left on Fortieth Avenue. The Main Street station of the No. 7 line is one block farther at the corner of Roosevelt Avenue.

Recommended Reading: New York City Architecture and History

ALBION, ROBERT GREENHALGH. *The Rise of New York Port (1815–1860).* New York: Charles Scribner's Sons, 1967.

ANDREWS, WAYNE. *Architecture in New York.* New York: Atheneum, 1969. Reprint, New York: Harper & Row Icon Books, 1973.

———. *Architecture, Ambition and Americans.* New York: The Free Press, 1964.

ASBURY, HERBERT. *All Around the Town.* New York: Knopf, 1929.

———. *The Gangs of New York.* Garden City, N.Y.: Garden City Publishing Co., 1927.

BALDWIN, CHARLES C. *Stanford White.* New York, 1931. Reprint with introduction by Paul Goldberger. New York: DaCapo Press, 1976.

BARAL, ROBERT. *Turn West on 23rd.* New York: Fleet Press, 1965.

BARLOW, ELIZABETH. *Frederick Law Olmsted's New York.* With an illustrative portfolio by William Alex. In association with the Whitney Museum of American Art. New York: Praeger, 1972.

———, with Vernon Gray, Roger Pasquier, and Lewis Sharp. *The Central Park Book.* New York: The Central Park Task Force, 1977.

BATTERBERRY, MICHAEL and ARIANE BATTERBERRY. *On the Town in New York, from 1776 to the Present.* New York: Charles Scribner's Sons, 1973.

BERGER, MEYER. *Meyer Berger's New York.* New York: Random House, 1960.

BETTMAN, OTTO L. *The Good Old Days—They Were Terrible!* New York: Random House, 1974.

BIXBY, WILLIAM. *South Street, New York's Seaport Museum.* New York: David McKay, 1972.

BLACK, MARY, ed. *Old New York in Early Photographs.* From the collection of the New-York Historical Society. New York: Dover, 1973.

BLIVEN, BRUCE, JR. *The Battle for Manhattan.* Baltimore: Penguin Books, 1965.

———. *Under the Guns—New York: 1775–1776.* New York: Harper & Row, 1972.

BOTKIN, B. A., ed. *New York City Folklore.* New York: Random House, 1956.

BOYER, M. CHRISTINE. *Manhattan Manners, Architecture and Style, 1850–1900.* New York: Rizzoli, 1985.

Brown, Henry Collins, ed. *Valentine's Manual of the City of New York, 1916–1928* (New Series) 12 vols. published annually. New York: The Valentine Co., 1916–1928.

Brown, Joshua and David Ment. *Factories, Foundries, and Refineries.* "A History of Five Brooklyn Industries." Brooklyn: Brooklyn Rediscovery, Brooklyn Educational & Cultural Alliance, 1980.

Burnham, Alan, ed. *New York Landmarks.* Middletown, Conn.: Wesleyan University Press, 1963.

Buttenwieser, Ann L. *Manhattan Water-Bound.* New York: New York University Press, 1987.

Cable, Mary. *The Blizzard of '88.* New York: Atheneum, 1988.

Cantor, Mindy, ed. *Around the Square, 1830–1890.* New York: New York University, 1982.

Caplovich, Judd. *Blizzard! The Great Storm of '88.* Vernon, CT: VeRo Publishing Co., 1987.

Chase, W. Parker. *New York 1932: The Wonder City* (facsimile edition). Introduction by Paul Goldberger. New York: New York Bound, 1983.

Christman, Henry M., ed. *Walt Whitman's New York.* New York: Macmillan, 1963.

Cohen, Barbara, Seymour Chwast, and Steven Heller, eds. *New York Observed. Artists and Writers Look at the City.* New York: Harry N. Abrams, 1987.

Condit, Carl W. *American Building.* Chicago: University of Chicago Press, 1968.

———. *The Port of New York,* Vol. 1: *A History of the Rail and Terminal System from the Beginnings to Pennsylvania Station,* Vol. 2: *A History of the Rail and Terminal System from the Grand Central Electrification to the Present.* Chicago: University of Chicago Press, 1980, 1981.

Condon, Thomas J. *New York Beginnings: The Commercial Origins of New Netherland.* New York: New York University Press, 1968.

Cromley, Elizabeth Collins. *Alone Together: A History of New York's Early Apartments.* Ithaca: Cornell University Press, 1990.

Cudahy, Brian. *Under the Sidewalks of New York: The Story of the Greatest Subway System in the World.* Brattleboro, Vt.: The Stephen Greene Press, 1979.

Delaney, Edmund T. *New York's Greenwich Village.* Barre, Mass.: Barre Publishers, 1965.

———. *New York's Turtle Bay—Old and New.* Barre, Mass.: Barre Publishers, 1965.

Diamonstein, Barbaralee. *The Landmarks of New York.* New York: Harry N. Abrams, 1988.

Dickens, Charles. *American Notes.* Philadelphia: Lippincott, 1885.

Dolkart, Andrew S., comp. *Guide to New York City Landmarks.* National Trust for Historic Preservation. Washington, D.C.: The Preservation Press, 1992.

Dunlap, David. *On Broadway: A Journey Uptown over Time.* New York: Rizzoli, 1990.

Dunshee, Kenneth Holcomb. *As You Pass By: Old Manhattan Through the Fire Laddies' Eyes.* New York: Hastings House, 1962.

Edmiston, Susan and Linda D. Cirino. *Literary New York—A History and Guide.* Boston: Houghton Mifflin, 1991.

Ellis, Edward Robb. *The Epic of New York City.* New York: Coward-McCann, 1966.

Fabos, Julius Gy, Gordon T. Milde, and V. Michael Weinmayr. *Frederick Law Olmsted, Sr.* Amherst, Mass.: University of Massachusetts Press, 1968.

Finney, Jack. *Time and Again.* New York: Simon & Schuster, 1970, 1978.

Fischler, Stan. *Uptown, Downtown: A Trip Through Time on New York's Subway.* New York: Hawthorn Books, 1976.

Fleming, John, Hugh Honour, and Nikolaus Pevsner, eds. *The Penguin Dictionary of Architecture.* Baltimore: Penguin Books, 1966.

Fried, Frederick and Edmund V. Gillon, photographer. *New York Civic Sculpture—A Pictorial Guide.* New York: Dover, 1976.

Friedman, Joe and Richard Berenholts, photographer. *Inside New York: Discovering New York's Classic Interiors.* New York: Harper Collins, 1992.

Garmey, Stephen. *Gramercy Park.* Foreword by Paul Goldberger. New York: Balsam Press Rutledge Books, 1984.

Gayle, Margot, ed. and Edmund V. Gillon, Jr., photographer. *Cast-Iron Architecture in New York.* New York: Dover, 1974.

————, and MICHELE COHEN. *A Guide to Manhattan's Outdoor Sculpture.* The Art Commission and the Municipal Art Society. New York: Prentice Hall, 1988.

GILL, BRENDAN. *Flatiron: A Photographic History of the World's First Steel Frame Skyscraper.* Washington: AIA Press, 1990.

GINTER, VAL. *Manhattan Trivia: The Ultimate Challenge.* Boston: Quinlan Press, 1985.

GLUECK, GRACE and PAUL GARDNER. *Brooklyn: People and Places, Past and Present.* New York: Harry N. Abrams, 1991.

GOLD, JOYCE. *From Trout Stream to Bohemia.* New York: Old Warren Road Press.

————. *From Windmills to the World Trade Center.* New York: Old Warren Road Press.

GOLDBERGER, PAUL. *The City Observed: New York. A Guide to the Architecture of Manhattan.* New York: Vintage Books, 1979.

————. *On the Rise: Architecture and Design in a Postmodern Age.* New York: Times Books, 1983.

————. *The Skyscraper.* New York: Knopf, 1981.

GOLDSTONE, HARMON and MARTHA DALRYMPLE. *History Preserved: A Guide to New York City Landmarks and Historic Districts.* New York: Simon & Schuster, 1974.

GREENTHAL, KATHRYN. *Augustus Saint-Gaudens, Master Sculptor.* New York: Metropolitan Museum of Art, 1985.

HAAS, RICHARD. *An Architecture of Illusion.* New York: Rizzoli, 1981.

HAMLIN, TALBOT. *Greek Revival Architecture in America.* New York: Oxford University Press, 1944. Reprint, New York: Dover, 1964.

HEADLEY, JOEL TYLER. *The Great Riots of New York, 1712–1873.* A facsimile of the 1873 edition. New York: Dover, 1971.

HENDRICKSON, ROBERT. *The Grand Emporiums: The Illustrated History of America's Great Department Stores.* New York: Stein & Day, 1979.

HUXTABLE, ADA LOUISE. *Architecture, Anyone?* New York: Random House, 1986.

————. *Classic New York: Georgian Gentility to Greek Elegance.* Garden City, N.Y.: Doubleday Anchor Books, 1964.

IRVING, WASHINGTON. *Knickerbocker's History of New York.* New York, 1809.

JOHNSON, HARRY and FREDERICK S. LIGHTFOOT. *Maritime New York in Nineteenth-Century Photographs.* New York: Dover, 1980.

KAHN, ALAN PAUL. *The Tracks of New York, 1907: The Metropolitan Street Railway.* New York: Electric Railroaders' Association, 1973.

KAUFMANN, EDGAR, JR., ed. *The Rise of an American Architecture.* Henry-Russell Hitchcock, Albert Fein, Winston Weisman, Vincent Scully, contributors. In association with The Metropolitan Museum of Art. New York: Praeger, 1970.

KIDNEY, WALTER C. *The Architecture of Choice: Eclecticism in America, 1880–1930.* New York: George Braziller, 1974.

KING, MOSES, ed. *King's Handbook of New York City.* A facsimile of the 1896 edition. New York: Arno Press, 1974.

————. *King's Views of New York 1896–1915, and Brooklyn 1905.* A facsimile of editions published between 1896 and 1915. Introduction by A. E. Santaniello. New York: Benjamin Blom, 1974.

KLOTZ, HEINRICH. *New York Architecture, 1970–1990.* New York: Rizzoli, 1989.

KOUWENHOVEN, JOHN A. *The Columbia Historical Portrait of New York.* New York: Doubleday, 1953. Reprint, New York: Harper & Row Icon Books, 1972.

KREITLER, PETER GWILLIM. *Flatiron.* Washington: AIA Press, 1992.

LAAS, WILLIAM. *Crossroads of the World—The Story of Times Square.* New York: Popular Library, 1963.

LAMB, MRS. MARTHA J. *History of the City of New York.* 2 vols. New York: A. S. Barnes, 1877.

LANCASTER, CLAY. *Old Brooklyn Heights.* Rutland, Vt.: Charles E. Tuttle, 1961. Reprint, New York: Dover, 1979.

LEDERER, JOSEPH and ARLEY BONDARIN, photographer. *All Around the Town: A Walking Guide to Outdoor Sculpture in New York City.* New York: Charles Scribner's Sons, 1975.

LOCKWOOD, CHARLES. *Bricks and Brownstones: The Row House, 1783–1929: An Architectural and Social History.* New York: McGraw-Hill, 1972.

———. *Manhattan Moves Uptown: An Illustrated History.* Boston: Houghton Mifflin, 1976.

LOPEZ, MANUEL D., ed. *New York: A Guide to Information and Reference Sources.* Metuchen, N.J.: Scarecrow Press, 1980.

LOWE, DAVID GARRARD. *Stanford White's New York.* New York: Doubleday, 1992.

LYMAN, SUSAN. *The Story of New York: An Informal History of the City from the First Settlement to the Present Day.* New York: Crown Publishers, 1975.

——— and ANDREAS FEININGER, photographer. *The Face of New York: The City as It Was and as It Is.* New York: Crown Publishers, 1954.

MARCUSE, MAXWELL F. *This Was New York! A Nostalgic Picture of Gotham in the Gaslit Era.* New York: LIM Press, 1969.

Master Builders: A Guide to Famous American Architects. Washington: The Preservation Press of the National Trust for Historic Preservation, 1985.

MAYER, GRACE M. *Once Upon a City.* New York: Macmillan, 1958.

McCABE, JAMES D., JR. *Lights and Shadows of New York Life, or The Sights and Sensations of the Great City.* A facsimile of the 1872 edition. New York: Farrar, Straus & Giroux, 1970.

———. *New York by Gaslight.* Introduction by Gerard R. Wolfe. A facsimile of the 1882 edition. New York: Crown Publishers, 1984.

McCAUSLAND, ELIZABETH, ed. *New York in the Thirties as Photographed by Berenice Abbott.* Formerly titled *Changing New York,* New York, 1939. New York: Dover, 1963.

McCULLOUGH, DAVID. *The Great Bridge, The Epic Story of the Building of the Brooklyn Bridge.* New York: Simon & Schuster, 1972. Reprint, New York: Avon, 1976.

MENT, DAVID with ANTHONY ROBINS and DAVID FRAMBERGER. *Building Blocks of Brooklyn,* "A Study of Urban Growth." Brooklyn: Brooklyn Rediscovery, Brooklyn Educational & Cultural Alliance, 1979.

MILLER, TERRY. *Greenwich Village and How It Got That Way.* New York: Crown Publishers, 1990.

A Monograph of the Works of McKim, Mead & White, 1879–1915. Introduction by Leland Roth. First published in 1915. New York: Benjamin Blom, 1973. Reprint, New York: Arno Press, 1977. Student's Edition, with introduction by Allan Greenberg and Michael George, New York: Architectural Publishing Co., 1981.

MOORE, MARGARET and TRUMAN MOORE, photographer. *End of the Road for Ladies' Mile?* Foreword by David Garrard Lowe. New York: The Drive to Protect the Ladies' Mile District, 1986.

MORRIS, LLOYD. *Incredible New York.* New York: Random House, 1951.

MOSCOW, HENRY. *The Book of New York Firsts.* New York: Collier Books, 1982.

———. *The Street Book: An Encyclopedia of Manhattan's Street Names and Their Origins.* New York: Hagstrom, 1978.

NEVINS, ALLAN, ed. *The Diary of George Templeton Strong, 1835–1875.* New York: Macmillan, 1952.

———, ed. *The Diary of Philip Hone, 1828–1851.* 2 vols. New York: Dodd, Mead, 1936.

New York City Guide. Guilds' Committee for Federal Writers' Publications, Works Progress Administration. New York: Random House, 1939.

PATTERSON, JERRY E. *The City of New York: A History Illustrated from the Collections of the Museum of the City of New York:* New York: Harry N. Abrams, 1978.

PLOTCH, BATIA, ed. with John Morse, with various contributors. *New Yorkwalks.* New York: Henry Holt, 1992.

POPPELIERS, JOHN, S. ALLEN CHAMBERS, and NANCY B. SCHWARTZ. *What Style Is It?* Washington: The Preservation Press of the National Trust for Historic Preservation, 1983.

——— and SOPHIA DUCKWORTH. *Central Park. A History and Guide.* New York: Clarkson N. Potter, 1972.

REED, HENRY HOPE. *The Golden City.* New York: W. W. Norton, 1971.

———. *The New York Public Library: Its Architecture and Decoration.* New York: W. W. Norton, 1986.

———, and EDMUND V. GILLON, JR., photographer. *Beaux-Arts Architecture in New York: A Photographic Guide.* New York: Dover, 1988.

RIFKIND, CAROLE. *A Field Guide to American Architecture: The Periods, the Styles, the Form and Function of Historical Buildings from Colonial Times to Today.* New York: New American Library Plume Books, 1980.

RIIS, JACOB. *How the Other Half Lives—Studies Among the Tenements of New York.* New York: Charles Scribner's Sons, 1890. Reprint, New York: Dover, 1971.

ROBERTO, JOSEPH J. and BAYRD STILL, eds. *Greenwich Village: A Brief Architectural and Pictorial Guide.* New York: New York University, 1981.

ROBINSON, CERVIN and ROSEMARY HAAG BLETTER. *Skyscraper Style: Art Deco New York.* New York: Oxford University Press, 1975.

ROSEN, LAURA. *The Top of the City: New York's Hidden Rooftop World.* New York: Thames & Hudson, 1982.

RUTTENBAUM, STEVEN. *Mansions in the Clouds: The Skyscraper Palazzi of Emery Roth.* New York: Balsam Press, 1986.

SALWEN, PETER. *Upper West Side Story.* New York: Abbeville Press, 1989.

SANDERS, RONALD. *The Downtown Jews—Portraits of an Immigrant Generation.* New York: Harper & Row, 1969.

——— and EDMUND V. GILLON, JR., photographer. *The Lower East Side—A Guide to Its Jewish Past in 99 New Photographs.* New York: Dover, 1979.

SHANOR, REBECCA READ. *The City That Never Was.* New York: Viking, 1988.

SHARP, LEWIS I. *John Quincy Adams Ward, Dean of American Sculpture.* Newark, Del.: University of Delaware Press, 1985.

——— and DAVID W. KIEHL, eds., *New York Public Sculpture by 19th Century American Artists.* New York: Metropolitan Museum of Art, 1974.

SHEPARD, RICHARD F. *Broadway, from the Battery to the Bronx.* New York: Harry N. Abrams, 1987.

SHOPSIN, WILLIAM C. and MOSETTE BRODERICK. *The Villard Houses: Life Story of a Landmark.* Foreword by Henry-Russell Hitchcock, introduction by Brendan Gill, prologue by Sarah Bradford Landau. In cooperation with the Municipal Art Society of New York. New York: Viking Press, 1980.

SILVER, NATHAN. *Lost New York.* Boston: Houghton Mifflin, 1967. Reprint, New York: Schocken, 1971.

SMALL, VERNA. *Nineteenth Century Dwelling Houses of Greenwich Village.* New York: Landmarks Committee. Association of Village Homeowners, 1968.

SMITH, THOMAS E. V. *The City of New York in the Year of Washington's Inauguration, 1789.* A reprint of the 1889 Trow's edition. Introduction by Joseph Veach Noble. In cooperation with the U.S. Department of the Interior, National Park Service. Riverside, Conn.: Chatham Press, 1972.

STEIN, LEON. *The Triangle Fire.* Philadelphia: Lippincott, 1962.

STEIN, SUSAN R., ed. *The Architecture of Richard Morris Hunt.* Chicago: University of Chicago Press, 1986.

STERN, ROBERT A. M., GREGORY GILMARTIN and JOHN MASSENGALE. *New York: 1900.* New York: Rizzoli, 1983.

———, and THOMAS MELLINS. *New York: 1930.* New York: Rizzoli, 1987.

STILES, HENRY R., ed. *History of the County of Kings and the City of Brooklyn, N.Y., 1684–1884.* 3 vols. Brooklyn, 1884.

STILL, BAYRD. *Mirror for Gotham.* New York: New York University Press, 1956.

STOKES, ISAAC NEWTON PHELPS. *The Iconography of Manhattan Island, 1498–1909.* 6 vols. New York: Robert H. Dodd, 1915. Reprint, New York: Arno Press, 1971.

STURGES, WALTER KNIGHT, ed. *Origins of Cast Iron Architecture in America.* Daniel D. Badger's

"Illustrations of Iron Architecture" (1865), and James Bogardus's "Cast Iron Buildings, Their Construction and Advantages" (1856). A facsimile edition. New York: DaCapo Press, 1970.

STURM, JAMES L. and JAMES CHOTAS, photographer. *Stained Glass from Medieval Times to the Present: Treasures to Be Seen in New York.* New York: E. P. Dutton, 1982.

TAURANAC, JOHN. *Essential New York: A Guide to the History and Architecture of Manhattan's Important Buildings, Parks, and Bridges.* New York: Holt, Rinehart, Winston, 1979.

———— and CHRISTOPHER LITTLE. *Elegant New York: The Builders and the Buildings, 1885–1915.* New York: Abbeville Press, 1985.

TRAGER, JAMES. *Park Avenue: Street of Dreams.* New York: Atheneum, 1990.

TRENT, GEORGE D., ed. *The Gentle Art of Walking.* A compilation from *The New York Times.* New York: Arno Press/Random House, 1971.

TUNICK, SUSAN. *Apartment Building Architecture: An Illustrated Overview Providing a Simple Way to Identify Building Parts, Styles and Materials.* New York: Friends of Terra Cotta/New York, 1986.

VLACK, DON. *Art Deco Architecture in New York, 1920–1940.* New York: Harper & Row, 1974.

WAITE, JOHN G., ed. *Iron Architecture in New York City.* The Edgar Laing Stores and the Cooper Union. Albany: New York State Historic Trust in conjunction with the Society for Industrial Archeology, 1972.

WHARTON, EDITH. *The Age of Innocence.* New York: D. Appleton & Co., 1921.

WHIFFEN, MARCUS. *American Architecture Since 1870: A Guide to the Styles.* Cambridge: M.I.T. Press, 1969.

WHITE, NORVAL and ELLIOT WILLENSKY. *The AIA Guide to New York City.* Orlando, Fla.: Harcourt Brace Jovanovich, 1988.

WILLENSKY, ELLIOT. *When Brooklyn Was the World, 1920–1957.* New York: Harmony Books, 1986.

WHITEHOUSE, ROGER. *New York Sunshine and Shadow: A Photographic Record of the City and Its People from 1850–1915.* New York: Harper & Row, 1974.

WOLFE, GERARD R. *The House of Appleton: The History of a Publishing House and Its Relationship to the Cultural, Social, and Political Events that Helped Shape the Destiny of New York City.* Metuchen, N.J.: Scarecrow Press, 1981.

————. *42nd Street: River-to-River Guide.* New York: 42nd Street E.T.C., Inc., 1991.

———— and JO RENÉE FINE, photographer. *The Synagogues of New York's Lower East Side.* New York: New York University Press, 1978.

Index

German Dispensary (former), 134
German Exchange Bank, 122
Germania Building, 5
Germania Life Insurance Building, 68
Gershon, Irving E., 11
Gertel's pastry, 164
Gibson, Robert W., 242, 379
Gift of the Magi, The (O. Henry), 248, 249
Gilbert, Cass, 20, 78, 79, 85, 96, 258, 259
Gilbert, Cass, Jr., 96
Gilbert, Charles P. H., 288, 420, 477, 478, 481
Giles, James, 236
Gilman, Arthur D., 39
Gilsey House, 256
Ginnever, Charles, 33
Gleckman, William, 349
Globe and Commercial Advertiser Building, 77
Godard, Keith, 436
Goelet Building, 235
Goethe, Johann Wolfgang von (statue), 313
"Gold Coast," 461, 471
Golden Hill, Battle of, 69
Golden Larch (Kingsland House, Flushing), 532, 533
Goldner Building, 490
Goldwater Memorial Hospital, 364
Goldwyn Starrett, 319
Gordon, James Riely, 247
Gorham Company, 236, 384
Gori, Ottavino, 85
Gottesman Exhibition Hall (Central Research Library), 315
Gould, Jay, 280–281
Grace, W. R. & Company Building, 310
    former, 51
Grace Church (Manhattan), 213–214
Grace Church Houses and School, 135
Grace (Protestant Episcopal) Church of Brooklyn Heights, 417–418
Grace Court Alley, 417
Grace Memorial House, 135
Grace United Methodist Episcopal Church, 467
Gracie, Archibald, 353
Gracie Mansion, 111, 353
Graduate Center of the City University of New York, 310
Graham, Ernest R., 14
Graham Home for Old Ladies, 514–515
Gramercy, the, 247
Gramercy Park, 241–252
Gramercy Park Building, 242
Grand Army Plaza (Brooklyn), 109, 469–470
Grand Central Terminal, 323–325
Grand Hotel, 256
Grand Hyatt Hotel, 325, 327–328
Grand Opera House, 280–281
Grand Union Hotel (site), 327
Grant, W. T. Company Building, 303
Graves & DuBoy, 376
Graybar Building, 328
Great Fire of 1835, 63–65
Great Hall (Cooper Union), 131
"Great White Way," 304
Greeley, Horace, 74, 75, 340
    statue, 74
Greene, Gen. Nathanael, 179
Greene, George Sears, Jr., 22
Greenhut, Joseph B., 228
Greenwich House, 114
Greenwich Village Historic District, 99–117
Greenwich Village Outdoor Art Show, 102
Griffen, Percy, 350
Grinnell, William G., 39
Gropius, Walter, 325
Grosvenor Apartment House, 414
Grosvenor Building, 206
Group of Four Trees (sculpture), 67
Grove Court, 113

Gruzen & Partners, 11, 40, 90, 327, 338, 382
Gruzen Samton Steinglass, 12, 362
Guaranty Trust Company, 14, 318
Guardian Angel Roman Catholic Church, 285–286
Guggenheim Museum SoHo, 196–197
Guido Funeral Home, 455–456
Gunther Building, 185
Guss' Pickles (*see* Essex Street Pickles)

Haas, Richard, 42, 191
Hafner, Charles Andrew, 353
Hagop Kevorkian Center for Near Eastern Studies (N.Y.U.), 109, 110
Haight, Charles Coolidge, 288, 374, 382
Haines, Lundberg & Waehler, 92, 409
Hale, Nathan, 341
    (statue), 102
Hall of Records (former), 89
Halsey, McCormack & Helmer, 60, 501
Hamilton, Alexander, 15, 60–61, 67, 77, 114
Hamlin, Talbot, 314
Hammerstein, Oscar, 221, 277, 299
Hanging Elm, 101
Hanna/Olin, Ltd., 312
Hanover Square, 50–51, 64
    No. 7, 51
Hanson Place Baptist Church (former), 501
Hanson Place Seventh Day Adventist Church, 501
Harak, Rudolph de, 41, 51, 52
Harde & Short, 350, 384
Hardenbergh, Henry Janeway, 124, 234, 250, 371, 373
Harding & Gooch, 256
Hardy Holzman Pfeifer, 312
Harnden, William F., 16
Harney, George E., 121, 128
Harper, J. & J. publishing house, 245
Harper, Mayor James, 245
Harris Theater, 296
Harrison & Abramovitz, 329, 330, 347–348, 507
Harrison, Abramovitz & Harris, 337, 338, 339
Harrison, Wallace K., 337
Harry's restaurant, 51
Harsenville, 375–376
Harte, Bret, 112
Hartley, Jonathan Scott, 22, 265
Harvard Club, 318–319
Hasidim, 166–167
Hastings, Thomas, 18, 271, 313
    statue, 315
Hatch, Stephen D., 121, 256
Hatfield, August, 398
Haughwout Building, 178, 194, 201–202
Hayden Planetarium, 385
Hearn, George, 217, 237
Hearn, James A., 217, 237
Hearst, William Randolph, 76
Hebrew Actor's Union, 133
Hebrew Immigrant Aid & Sheltering Society (HIAS), 127
Hebrew National *Wurstfabrik* (site), 143
Hebrew Publishing Company, 159–160
Hecla Iron Works, 271, 372
Heere Graft (Broad Street), 56
Heights Casino, 414–415
Heins & LaFarge, 36, 135, 375, 502
Hejduk, John, 131
Helen Hayes Theater (former), 306
Hell Gate Bridge, 348, 351–352
Hellmuth, Obata & Kassabaum, 348, 353
Helmle, Corbett & Harrison, 410, 411
Helmle, Frank J., 475
Helmle & Corbett, 308–309
Helmle & Huberty, 414, 486
Helmsley, Harry, 329
Helmsley Building, 325
Henderson, John C., 354
Henderson Place Historic District, 353–355

About the Author

Gerard R. Wolfe, Ph.D., currently director of the Arts & Liberal Studies Program at the University of Wisconsin–Milwaukee, is a native New Yorker who is widely regarded as a leading authority on the history and architecture of New York City. The author of several books on New York, including *The Synagogues of New York's Lower East Side, The House of Appleton,* and *42nd Street: River-to-River Guide.* He is a graduate of City College of New York and holds a master's degree from New York University and a doctorate from the Union Graduate School in Cincinnati. Dr. Wolfe writes and lectures extensively on New York and still conducts walking tours.